THE CAMBRIDGE
ANCIENT HISTORY

VOLUME III
PART 3

THE CAMBRIDGE
ANCIENT HISTORY

SECOND EDITION

VOLUME III
PART 3

The Expansion of the Greek World,
Eighth to Sixth Centuries B.C.

Edited by

JOHN BOARDMAN F.B.A.

*Lincoln Professor of Classical Archaeology and Art
in the University of Oxford*

N. G. L. HAMMOND F.B.A.

*Professor Emeritus of Greek
University of Bristol*

CAMBRIDGE
UNIVERSITY PRESS

Published by the Press Syndicate of the University of Cambridge
The Pitt Building, Trumpington Street, Cambridge CB2 1RP
40 West 20th Street, New York, NY 10011–4211, USA
10 Stamford Road, Oakleigh, Melbourne 3166, Australia

© Cambridge University Press 1982

First published 1925
Second edition 1982
Reprinted 1990, 1992, 1997

Printed in Great Britain at the University Press, Cambridge

British Library cataloguing in publication data

The Cambridge ancient histoty. – 2nd ed.
Vol. 3: Part 3: The expansion of the Greek world, eighth
to sixth centuries B.C.
1. History, Ancient
I. Boardman, John II. Hammond, N. G. L.
930 D57 75-85719

ISBN 0 521 23447 6

CONTENTS

MAPS

TEXT-FIGURES

xii TEXT-FIGURES

PREFACE

Volume III.1 described the emergence of Greece from Dark Ages of depopulation and relative poverty to the acme of its Geometric civilization. The new prosperity and growth of the young city-states led them to look for new frontiers to conquer or settle, to eye each other's prosperity with cupidity, and their rulers and people to give thought to safeguarding their own wealth and status in the new societies of Archaic Greece. Volume III.3 explores this growth, its causes and course, the dissensions and the faltering steps along the path to political stability.

The first chapter deals with that intercourse with the older civilizations of the east and Egypt which opened Greek eyes to materials, techniques and trading profits denied to them since the collapse of their Bronze Age civilization. This is a story which begins in the ninth and eighth centuries; but in the eighth and seventh the Greeks begin to turn to other Mediterranean areas, and we witness that spread of the Greek city-state to the coasts and islands of the Mediterranean sea, to the sea of Marmara and the Black Sea, which opened a new epoch in the history of western man.

The effects of this expansion, unprecedented in geographical scope, were manifold. The Greeks of the founding states gained greatly in prosperity, because the volume of seaborne trade increased by leaps and bounds and they were still the main exporters of manpower, weapons and finished goods. This was particularly true of the states near the Isthmus, to which ship-captains, making use of the coastal winds in the summer months, came both from the west via south Italy and Corcyra and from the east either via Chalcidice and Euboea or from island to island across the Aegean Sea. The founded states were not colonies in the Roman or British sense of the word but independent city-states, and the citizen of the new state shed the citizenship of his homeland from the day he set sail. This cutting of the political cord at birth had many advantages. The new state had to face and solve its own problems in its new setting from the outset, and it was not subject to the intervention of a homeland government which knew little of the local conditions.

The system proved highly successful not only in the growth of the new states themselves but in their ability to found other independent states.

The new states were at first so small that the arrival of Greeks on offshore islands or peninsulas did not cause the native peoples to see any threat to their own independence. Indeed the first waves of Greeks were often helped by the natives and sometimes joined with them in the initial stages of establishing a settlement. But once established the Greeks became exclusive both racially and culturally. Thus, unlike other colonizing peoples, they did not become an imperial elite among vastly more numerous native peoples but maintained the same forms of social, political and cultural life as the states of old Greece. One of these was slavery. In the new states the slaves were natives captured in war or bought from slave-dealers. This led to bitter animosities, for instance in Sicily, but the native peoples were divided among themselves by similar problems. The interaction of Greek states and native peoples was most beneficial in the exchange of goods and ideas, and it was the Greek side which contributed most towards the development of what was ultimately to be a Hellenized civilization.

East Greece and the Aegean islands led the way in exploration overseas and in the planting of new states. They depended upon the sea for different reasons: the East Greek states, set along the coast of Turkey like a string of widely-spaced beads, trafficked with one another by sea, and most of the islands could support a rising population only by importing foodstuffs and raw materials. The states which gained most lay on the coasting routes on either side of the Aegean, Miletus and Samos in the east and Chalcis and Eretria in the west. But even the small island states were engaged in the carrying trade and joined in the exploration and settlement, especially on the north coast of the Aegean basin. Of the founding states in East Greece Miletus was by far the most important and she held the leading position in the exploration of the Black Sea. During the sixth century when the states of East Greece had greater facilities for trade with the interior of Asia and with Egypt, they reached a very high level of prosperity and built the largest naval force in Greek waters. Crete held a key position on the trading routes from the Greek mainland to the southern Mediterranean and from Rhodes in the east to Cythera and Corcyra in the west, and her numerous city-states enjoyed a prosperous period in the seventh century. Their idiosyncratic laws and the structure of their society are subjects of great interest.

The Greek mainland was fortunate in its geographic situation, since it formed the bridge between the western and the eastern areas of the Greek expansion. There was an ever-expanding market not only for Greek goods but also for Greek settlers, adventurers and mercenaries overseas. The social and political effects of the economic revolution became apparent first in those states of old Greece which lay closest to the Isthmus and were subject to the impact of new forms of wealth. The long-established rule of landed aristocracies of birth collapsed through divisions within the upper echelons of society, and the Greek genius for political experimentation and for political strife was given free rein in the sixth century. But in other parts of the mainland the traditional way of life persisted and modifications came slowly. In the north the tribal states were brought into contact with the world of city-states, because they were able to supply timber, wood, minerals and foodstuffs. But they retained their age-old institutions and held the European frontier of the Greek-speaking lands against the similar tribal states of the Illyrian and Thracian peoples.

Expansion and prosperity did not bring peace to the mainland states. Ambition and acquisitiveness led to wars between neighbours, not least in the Isthmus area between Megara and Corinth and between Megara and Athens. The rivalry of Argos and Sparta resulted in war after war, and in order to strengthen her own position Sparta created the first large-scale military coalition of city-states. Athens did not become a leading state until the latter part of the sixth century, when the social and economic reforms of Solon were implemented in many respects by the gifted tyrant Pisistratus. It was rather Corinth which pioneered the way in the organization of naval power in her home waters and in the north-western area where she planted many vigorous new states.

The last chapter reflects upon the social, economic and material history of Greece in these years, the first in Greek history in which texts have as much to tell us as the spade. Problems of the ownership of land, slavery, industrialization in a mainly agricultural community, the impact of the invention of coinage, all lie behind the conventional historical narrative of wars, colonies and constitutions. The history of Greek thought, religion and literature is not, as such, studied here, but there will be occasion to reflect on it in the new edition of Volume IV. Nor is any summary of the art history of the period offered here; instead, there is an account of the material evidence for the world in which the events described in other chapters were conducted, since the fuller picture we can now win of the quality of life in Greece lends an immediacy and vividness to our understanding of the history of the times. This is a subject which is dealt with also, in pictures and commentary, in the Plates Volume which will accompany this new edition of Volume III.

The editors have again to thank David Cox of Cox Cartographic Ltd for the maps; and Marion Cox for preparing many of the illustrations to chapters 36–9, 41, 45b.

The index was compiled by Jenny Morris.

J.B.
N.G.L.H.

NOTE ON FOOTNOTE REFERENCES

Works cited in the various sections of the Bibliography are referred to in footnotes by the appropriate section letter followed by the number assigned to the work in the sectional bibliography, followed by volume number, page references etc. Thus A 50, II 1 is a reference to p. 1 of vol. II of H. W. Parke's and D. E. W. Wormell's *The Delphic Oracle* – no. 50 of Bibliography A: General.

CHAPTER 36a

THE GREEKS IN THE NEAR EAST

T. F. R. G. BRAUN

I. NAMES AND PLACES

The Hellenes, ever since their great movement of renewed expansion
that began in the ninth century B.C., have had different names in east
and west. Westerners came to know them as Graeci, Greeks. Easterners
call them Ionians. Even today, a Greek is an Ionian – a Yūnāni – in
Arabic, Turkish and Persian. For the people of the Levant and
Mesopotamia to name the Greeks after the Ionians was natural, for it
was the Ionians who had come to be the chief inhabitants of the eastern
parts of the Greek homeland: the Aegean Islands and the coastline of
western Asia Minor. The peculiar form of the name 'Ionians' that the
ancient Near East adopted is just what we should expect to have resulted
from ninth- and eighth-century contacts. From the archaic Greek
Iāones < *Iāwones* is derived the *Yawan* of the Bible. The Mesopotamians
probably pronounced it the same, though the convention of their
syllabary resulted in the spelling *Yaman*.[1] The name could only have
come into use after the Ionians occupied their East Greek territories
in the post-Mycenaean period. Homer looked back to an age in which
there was as yet no such Ionian settlement. The '*Iāones* with trailing
tunics' only appear once in the *Iliad*, named together with mainland
Greeks in an anachronistic-looking passage (XIII.685).[2] The *Iliad* here
uses the archaic form, as does the Homeric Hymn describing the
Ionians' festival on the island of Delos (III.147, 152), and it was still
in use in Solon's time, *c.* 600 B.C.[3] Later, in the fifth century, the normal
usage among Greeks was *Iōnes, Iōnia*.[4] Orientals, however, had learned
the older form and stuck to it. When Aeschylus and Aristophanes bring
orientals on to the Athenian stage, they are made to speak of Greeks,
and address them, as *Iāones*.[5]

---

[1] B 67, 6–7, §21d, §31a.
[2] Two or three mentions of *I-ja-wo-ne* in Cnossus tablets may refer to these mainland Ionians:
A 65, 547.
[3] Solon 4a.2 West; oracle *ap.* Plut. *Solon* 10.
[4] Hecataeus, *FGrH* 1 F 228–41; Aesch. *Pers.* 771; Hdt. 1. 6 etc.
[5] Aesch. *Pers.* 178, 563, 899; *Supp.* 69; Ar. *Ach.* 104.

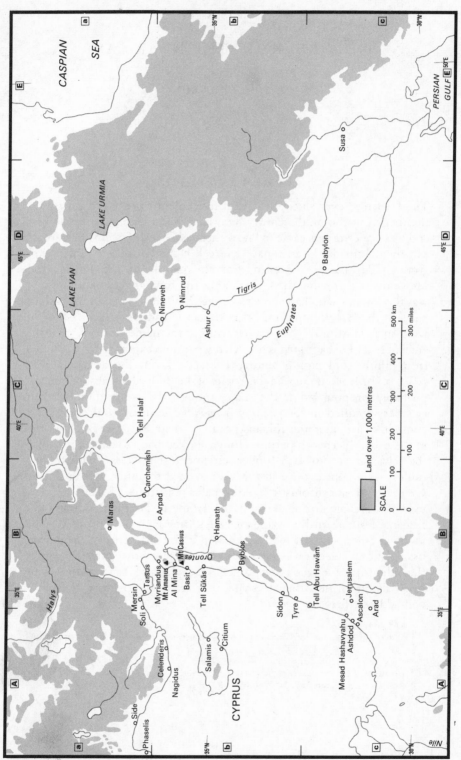

Map 1. The Near East.

Occasional references to *Yawan/Yaman* in oriental sources help to piece together the story of Greek contacts with the Near East. There is evidence to clinch the identification of this name with Greeks. In Darius I's multi-lingual inscriptions listing his subject lands, the old Persian lists give *Yauna* among the western nations and immediately after *Sparda* (Sardis) – the right context for Ionia.[6] The Accadian equivalent is given as *Yaman*.[7] In Hellenistic times, the Septuagint translation of the Bible into Greek took *Yawan* to mean Hellas, Hellenes.[8] The Egyptians, unlike their Asian neighbours, had an old indigenous name, unrelated to Ionians: *Ḥȝw-nbw*, which from the seventh century on was applied to Greeks. Here, too, there is no doubt about the identification, for the Hellenistic bilingual Rosetta and Canopus inscriptions translate *Ḥȝw-nbw* as Hellenes.[9]

The sixth-century world genealogy in Genesis names four sons of *Yawan*: Elisha (Alashiya = Cyprus), Tarshish (Tartessus), Kittim (Kition/Citium) and Rodanim (Rhodes).[10] The Jews, no sailors themselves but with some knowledge of what came into Levantine ports from over the sea, found it natural to associate 'the distant islands' with Yawan (cf. also Isaiah 66: 19): it made no difference that Citium was a Phoenician city.[11] In the 670s Esarhaddon claimed that 'the kings in the midst of the sea, all of them from the land of Yadnana (Cyprus), the land of Yaman, to the land of Tarsisi (Tartessus) threw themselves at my feet' (below, p. 20). With these far-flung associations, we should not expect orientals to distinguish sharply between different kinds of Greek. Yawan/Yaman might do for them all. And the Anatolian neighbours of the Greeks could sometimes count as Greeks too. When Greek soldiers came to Egypt in Saïte times, they came with Carians, of different race and speech but armed and organized in the same way (see ch. 36*b*). Both Greeks and Carians could be called *Ḥȝw-nbw*. Lydians, too, dressed like Greeks (cf. Hdt. 1.94). It is not surprising that among Nebuchadrezzar's prisoners in sixth-century Babylon there should have been *Yamani* men with non-Greek, presumably Anatolian names (below, p. 23).

The evidence for Greeks in surviving Near Eastern records is in any event fragmentary. Some Greek traders, we believe, had settled in Al Mina as early as about 825 B.C., but the first written oriental reference to Greeks in the Levant dates to the 730s, and thereafter they are only spasmodically mentioned. Why is the record not earlier and fuller?

[6] B 38, 117 (DB I 15), 136 (DPe 12–13), 137 (DNa 28), 141 (DSe 27–8). Identifications discussed in B 75, 27–50.   [7] B 78, 10–11.

[8] Gen. 10: 2, 4; I Chron. 1: 5, 7; Isa. 66: 19; Ezek. 27: 13; Dan. 8: 21; 10: 20; 11: 2; Joel 3: 6; Zech. 9: 13.   [9] B 128.

[10] Gen. 10: 2.4; cf. I Chron. 1: 5.7.

[11] Gen. 10: 4; Numbers 24: 24; Isa. 23: 1; Jer. 2: 10; Ezek. 27: 6; Jer. 2: 10; cf. B 1.

Partly because the Greeks made no massive impact, as they did when they began to immigrate into Egypt. But another reason is that we have to wait for Assyrian documentation. In the half-century between Adad-Nirari III's last intervention in 796 and Tiglath-Pileser III's great victories of 743–740, the Assyrian kings paid only intermittent attention to Syria and the Levant. The independent North Syrian states, with whom the Greeks had at first to deal, have left comparatively few and brief inscriptions. After 743–740, Assyrian royal inscriptions include Levantine campaigns in their boastful record. Greeks do from now on get an occasional mention, but it required exceptional circumstances for them to come to the royal chroniclers' notice. Administrative correspondence will have had more frequent occasion to mention them. One such reference, recently discovered, will be discussed. But it happens that only a few letters dealing with the western dominions of Assyria have so far come to light. The huge letter archive discovered in the last century at Nineveh[12] is concerned with other parts of the empire, and for this reason has no single allusion to Greeks.

Greek literary evidence for relations between Greeks and the Near East is fragmentary for different reasons. No Greek state kept historical records; nor was there any publication of a prose geographical or historical work before Hecataeus, *c.* 500 B.C. From the eighth century on there was a great output of poetry, epic, elegiac and lyric; from the seventh, laws and treaties began to be inscribed. But what survives of all this writing only rarely happens to touch on the Near East. Herodotus' great history, published shortly after 430,[13] has the relations between Greeks and non-Greeks as its principal theme (1. 1); but its main narrative begins with the accession of Croesus, *c.* 560 (1. 6). And though he provides a long digression on Egypt, where there had been large-scale Greek settlement, Herodotus says comparatively little about Mesopotamia and less about the Levant. His account of Mesopotamia and Babylon includes no consecutive Assyrian or Babylonian history. At two points he promises a further Assyrian account (1. 106, 184), but in the book as we now have it the promise remains unfulfilled. There is an intriguing citation by Aristotle of a lost Herodotean *disquisition on the siege of Nineveh* (*HA* VIII. 18, 601b3), but no other trace of it survives. The classical Greeks did tell stories about Ashurbanipal, whom they remembered as Sardanapalus (below, p. 21); but they seem to have had no recollection at all of the name of Nebuchadrezzar, so menacing and powerful in the biblical record. It was not until after Alexander's conquest that the Babylonian priest Berossus published this name with

---

[12] B 30; B 76.   [13] Cf. VII. 137, the last datable allusion.

those of other kings in his Greek version of Babylonian historical chronicles, dedicated to the Seleucid king Antiochus I Soter.[14]

It is characteristic that the earliest datable oriental references to Greeks, such as they are, come from royal records. The eastern kings, great or small, dominated their world. When Greeks entered it, they did so mostly by royal favour, as traders or mercenaries. The alternative was to attack the coast in raiding parties or infiltrate individually as adventurers. There could be no question at this stage of Greek political supremacy. In the west, the great Greek settlement colonies, from the eighth century on, were often established at the expense of the natives. Archias settled Syracuse in 733, Thucydides says, 'having first driven the Sicels from the island where the inner city...stands today' (Thuc. VI. 3.2). But in the East Greeks could not drive out the natives and assert their full independence; they settled only if they were allowed to settle. Nor, at this early stage, was there any doubt about oriental cultural superiority. In Etruria, the Greeks found a people eager for Greek artefacts, who bought the finest Greek vases and imitated Greek art themselves. In the East there was a scattering of Greek painted ware over a wide area, but its presence in any quantity is taken to show not importation by orientals, but the presence of Greeks who were using it themselves.[15] The orient was not yet much interested in Greek art for its own sake, though we shall note a few instances where orientals do seem to have found Greek ware useful or decorative (below, p. 9). When eventually, at the outset of the Persian period, we have evidence of Greek craftsmen working for orientals in the building of Persian palaces, we find they were made to serve essentially non-Greek concepts of design.[16] The Greeks themselves knew their place. Not until after the establishment of the Persian empire do we find them first referring to non-Greeks as 'barbarians' (Heraclitus, B. 107 D–K), as they regularly did in Classical times, sometimes though not always with a pejorative overtone. The reference in the *Iliad* to the Carians as βαρβαρόφωνοι, barbarian-speaking, is isolated (II. 867). In Egypt, the Greeks in the sixth century called *themselves* ἀλλόγλωσσοι – people of alien speech – in contrast to the people of the land.[17]

II. PHOENICIANS IN GREECE

Homer describes Phoenicians trading in Greek waters as well as with Egypt and Libya. They buy the goodwill of the king of Lemnos with a marvellous silver bowl (*Il.* XXIII. 740–5; cf. VII. 468). They have trade

[14] *FGrH* 680 F 7–9.
[15] G 10, 122.
[16] B 53, 144–9.
[17] M–L no. 7 (a) 4; Hdt. II. 154.4.

goods to tempt humbler people, too: we see 'Phoenicians, famous as seamen, tricksters, bringing tens of thousands of trinkets in their black ship' to a Greek island, 'rich in cattle and sheep, wine and corn'. The ship stays for a whole year, doing business until it is full. Meanwhile one of the seamen has seduced a servant-girl from the palace, herself a kidnapped Sidonian who wants to go home. Together they hatch a plot. A Phoenician engages the attention of the queen and her maidservants with a gold necklace strung with amber beads, and tips the wink to the Sidonian girl. Slipping under her dress three gold cups which the king has left on the dinner table after taking his guests off to a council meeting, she hurries down to the harbour with the king's little boy Eumaeus innocently trotting behind her, the ship makes off under cover of darkness, and in due course the Phoenicians sell Eumaeus for a good price in Ithaca (*Od.* xv. 403–84).

This story, with its many recognizable features, rings true. The Phoenician trade-goods that appear in Greece from the ninth century on must have been brought at least partly by Phoenicians, not only by returning Greeks. Accounts of Phoenician settlement and colonization in Greece are less convincing. They are given by Greek historians from the fifth century onwards. Thucydides (I. 8.1) states that the Aegean islanders included Phoenician pirates before Minos policed the sea. Rhodian historians told how, after Danaus from Egypt had founded the temple of Athena at Lindus, Cadmus had next come from Phoenicia, and had dedicated a bronze cauldron at Lindus inscribed in Phoenician letters. He founded the temple of Poseidon at Ialysus and left Phoenician overseers there.[18] The Phoenicians fortified Ialysus and held Rhodes until besieged by Greek invaders; then they buried their treasure and left the island.[19] Melos was similarly supposed to have been a Phoenician colony, named Byblis, before it became Greek.[20]

These accounts of Phoenician settlement enlarge on Herodotus. For him east–west conflict had begun with the rape of Io from Argos by Phoenician sailors, after which Greeks came to Tyre and carried off Europa, King Agenor's daughter (I. 1–2). He tells these introductory stories with some humour, but frequently returns to the search for Europa which he takes seriously enough. The European continent takes its name from her (IV. 45). She is the sister of Cadmus who left Phoenicia to look for her all over Greece. Cadmus put in at Thera, where his Phoenicians colonized the island for eight generations (IV. 147). He founded the temple of Heracles at Thasos (II. 44–6). The Thasian mines,

---

[18] Anagraphe of Lindus, *FGrH* 532 (3) quoting Polyzelos of Rhodes, *FGrH* 521 F 1; Zenon of Rhodes, *FGrH* 523 F 1 (Diod. v. 58).

[19] Ergias of Rhodes, *FGrH* 513 F 1; Polyzelos of Rhodes, *FGrH* 521 F 6 (Ath. 260D–361B).

[20] Steph. Byz. *s.v.* 'Melos'; cf. Festus *s.v.* 'Melos' p. 124 Müller.

too, were discovered by Phoenicians (VI. 47). He settled Phoenicians in
Boeotia (II. 49, V. 57). They included the Cadmeians of Thebes, who
after their expulsion joined the colonizers of Ionia (I. 146). He introduced
Dionysus worship (II. 49) and the Phoenician alphabet (v. 58)[21] to
Greece. 'Phoenicians from Palestinian Syria', furthermore, founded the
temple of Aphrodite at Cythera (I. 105).

Archaeologists have found little substance for any of this. French
excavation of the temple of Heracles at Thasos has produced no
evidence for Phoenician foundation.[22] There is none at Thebes except
for a hoard of Near Eastern cylinder seals in the Mycenaean Cadmeia.[23]
Recent attempts to prove early Semitic influences on Greece by
providing etymologies for place names, and through interpretations of
Linear A tablets, are mostly speculative.[24] We shall find that the link
between Cadmus and Phoenicia is a literary invention contrived after
Homer and Hesiod, and as such it will be considered in section VI.
Cadmus was dated to the dawn of Greek history, over a thousand years
before Herodotus' time (II. 145). The alleged colonization by
Phoenicians, if it were historical, would thus in any case long antedate
such evidence as we have of infiltration by Phoenicians into Greece
between the ninth and the sixth centuries B.C.[25]

III. GREEK TRADE AND SETTLEMENT IN THE LEVANT

It has been shown elsewhere that Cyprus was continuously inhabited
by Greeks from late Mycenaean times on (*CAH* II.2[3], ch. 22*b*), and that
the Pamphylian dialect gives good grounds for thinking that there was
some continuity of Greek settlement along the coast of southern
Anatolia (below, pp. 92–4). This is not true of the east Mediterranean
coast. There is a hiatus of some 150 years between the last Mycenaean
imports into the Levant and the ninth century B.C. when pottery from
Greece reappears. Fragments of Geometric ware have been found over
an area from the mouth of the Orontes southwards as far as Ascalon, and
eastwards as far as Nineveh. They are distributed sporadically: only a
dozen find-spots are so far known (fig. 1). The earliest items may be
Euboean (or Cycladic) cups from Tell Abu Hawām, near the foot of
Mt Carmel. A piece at Tabbāt al Hammām, not far from Aradus Island,
was found with Phoenician/Cypriot ware in a ninth-century settlement
built with an ashlar breakwater, clearly with a view to sea trade.[26] Inland,
at Hamath on the Orontes, the capital of an Aramaic kingdom, a number

---

[21] Cf. Arist. fr. 501 Rose; Ephorus, *FGrH* 70 F 105 (Diod. III. 67). Below, pp. 29f.
[22] C 200, 123–5; C 201, I 20, 117–18.
[23] B 74; *BCH* 88 (1964) 775–9.
[24] e.g. B 3.
[25] A 7, 35–8 and 54–84 *passim*; D 78, 360–3.
[26] B 63, 152.

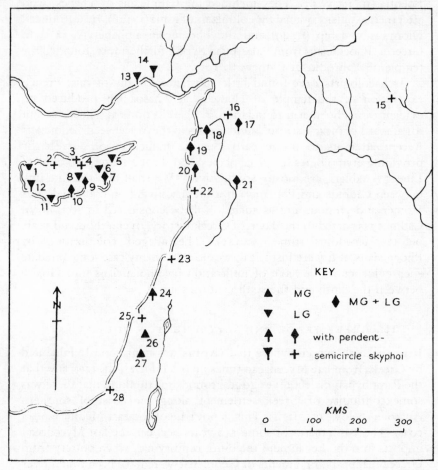

KEY

▲ MG   ◆ MG + LG

▼ LG

⬆ ⬇ with pendent-

⬇ ＋ semicircle skyphoi

KMS

0   100   200   300

1. Finds of Greek Middle and Late Geometric pottery in the east. (Prepared with the kind help of Professor J. N. Coldstream; cf. H 25, 422–4; H 27, 94, fig. 29.)

Sites:

1 Marium	10 Amathus	20 Tell Sūkās
2 Soli	11 Curium	21 Hamath
3 Kazaphani	12 Paphus	22 Tabbāt al Hammām
4 Palekythro	13 Mersin	23 Khaldeh
5 A. Theodoros	14 Tarsus	24 Tyre
6 Stylli	15 Tell Halaf	25 Tell Abu Hawām
7 Salamis	16 Tell Tayinat	26 Megiddo
8 Idalium	17 Tell Judaidah	27 Samaria
9 Citium	18 Al Mina	28 Ascalon
	19 Basit	

of Euboean/Cycladic pendent-semicircle cups were found in a native cremation cemetery. That shows that they could be preferred by orientals to the local, more friable earthenware cups; the presence of Greek cups does not therefore necessarily argue the presence of Greek owners, for all that Greeks liked to carry their personal cups with them.[27] A big Attic krater, probably of the late ninth century, was evidently judged a worthy votive offering in a Syrian shrine here.[28] Hamath was destroyed by the Assyrians in 720 B.C. (*CAH* III. 1², ch. 9), a definite *terminus ante quem*. Samaria, destroyed in 722 (*ibid.* 275), provides a similar *terminus* for one sherd with which others, from disturbed levels, are clearly related. Here again was a big ninth-century krater, from the Cyclades.[29]

Only in two known coastal settlements is the quantity of Greek Geometric ware so great that we may conclude that Greeks lived there. In each case we find not a colony but an ἐνοικισμός, a settlement of Greeks among natives, comparable to the sixth-century Greek quarter at Gravisca, in the port of an Etruscan city. The most important of these two eastern settlements is Al Mina, at the mouth of the Orontes in what is today the Turkish territory of Hatay.[30] Here, between 1936 and 1939, Woolley excavated a mound which proved to have ten levels of occupation between *c.* 825 and 301 B.C. It was a trading depot, with a Greek element from the beginning. The levels of between *c.* 825 and *c.* 700 were of huts built on pebble foundations over virgin sand. But the combined effects of silting and erosion caused the settlement to shift throughout its history, and it is possible, as Woolley thought, that there was occupation before *c.* 825 on a part of the site that the river has washed away. Most of the earliest pots are of a type that could be local, or derive from Cyprus, or both. But among these are Greek sherds, a handful at first but growing more numerous throughout the eighth century. This Greek ware is from the Aegean islands. Improved knowledge of Euboea and Euboean colonies in the west since Woolley's time has shown that there is a distinctive Euboean element at Al Mina, lightly reinforced by East Greek in the last quarter of the eighth century. Euboean pendent-semicircle cups are extremely scarce in the west: evidently the Euboeans' interest in Al Mina preceded their mid-eighth century colony at Pithecusa/Ischia. But in the second half of the eighth century a later variety of cup, decorated with concentric circles, is found in both places.[31] The levels at Al Mina are not always sharply to be distinguished, but there is a minor break *c.* 720 and a decisive one *c.* 700, perhaps in connexion with the Cilician revolt that we shall discuss. Al

---

[27] H 27, 95. [28] B 63, 153–4. [29] B 63, 146–7.
[30] B 83 with map pl. 1 opp. p. 2; B 84; B 85; B 86, 165–81; A 7, 38–54.
[31] D 18, 7–8; cf. B 12, 12–13 and n. 27; *AR* 1966–7, 13; B 72.

Mina was presumably destroyed. It was rebuilt with a stronger Greek element than before. Alongside Cypriot pottery, which becomes less plentiful, we find Rhodian bird bowls and East Greek Wild Goat ware; there is a good deal of Corinthian. Euboean disappears. It looks as if the Euboeans were discouraged or lost interest. The Corinthian ware may well signal the arrival of Aeginetans, the great carriers of the seventh and sixth centuries, who made no pottery themselves but traded in that of their neighbours: Corinth, and in the sixth century Athens. In the later seventh century there was rebuilding after a period of some decay; in the first half of the sixth century there seems to be a hiatus of many years, perhaps only because the action of the river has made our knowledge of the site incomplete, but possibly because the Babylonian conquest had had unfavourable consequences. From c. 520, under the Persians, the site was laid out again in new blocks. Imports from Greece, especially Athens, now increased further in volume and variety. The depot seems to have prospered, regardless of the wars between Greeks and Persians, until Al Mina was replaced by Seleucia, the port of Antioch, in 301.

From c. 700 B.C. the site was of warehouses, best observed in their later form: single-storied, rectangular buildings, each of them with a range of store-rooms round a central courtyard with a smaller room that could have been the tally-clerk's office, surrounded by thick mud-brick, mud-plastered walls whose stone foundations were continued above floor level to serve as a damp course, and presumably roofed with reeds, timber and clay, since no roof-tiles are found. Between the warehouses ran gravel lanes, intersecting at right angles, often with a central drain covered with stone slabs. Small, disconnected rooms along the street front seem to have been retail shops or workshops. There were no dwelling-houses in this dreary place, and until the latest levels no burials. Woolley thought that the merchants who came down to work here might have lived on Sabouni hill about 5 km inland. There are no Greek graffiti or inscriptions either, before or after 700 B.C. Nor is the place mentioned in Greek literature. Woolley sought to identify it with the city of Posideum, mentioned by Herodotus in his list of Darius I's provinces as 'founded by Amphilochus the son of Amphiaraus on the boundary of the Cilicians and the Syrians' (Hdt. III. 91). But Posideum is commonly a Greek name for a cape; and Strabo's geographical work specifically located this Posideum south of the Orontes mouth, on the other side of Mount Casius (Musa Dağ) (Strabo XVI. 2.8.751). Here, some 24 km from Al Mina, is Cape Basit, whose name can hardly fail to derive from Posideum. Its ancient ruins were conspicuous in the early nineteenth century, and recent French excavations have shown that it has a history of Greek imports nearly as long as that of Al Mina. Its merits as a trading site are not immediately obvious, but it does give access to a route through the hills, directly to the Orontes valley.[32] The ancient Greek name of Al Mina itself therefore remains unknown.

Tell Sūkās, some 72 km to the south of Al Mina, is another Syro-Phoenician Iron Age coastal settlement, smaller than Al Mina and built over a Bronze Age mound. The excavators distinguish a level which they have dated from *c.* 850 to a destruction in *c.* 675, with similar Greek sherds to those at Al Mina, principally Euboean and Cycladic. The next level, which they date to between *c.* 675 and *c.* 498, interrupted by destruction *c.* 588 and worse destruction still in *c.* 552, was strongly marked by Greek influence. There was a sanctuary of Greek design, quite unlike those of the Syro-Phoenicians, and a Greek woman in *c.* 600 B.C. left proof of Greek habitation by putting her name on her loom-weight.[33]

Greek commerce with the Levant is natural. What is surprising is not that it was resumed in the ninth century, but that it had ever been interrupted. There is occasional literary evidence for it from now on. In the sixth century Ezekiel speaks of Yawan bringing trade to Tyre;[34] by the fifth there was a shrine of the Thasian Heracles in Tyre itself, probably the result of Thasian commerce.[35] At Myriandus, some 80 km north of Al Mina in the gulf of Alexandretta, Xenophon's Ten Thousand saw many merchant ships at anchor in 401 (Xen. *Anab.* I. 4.6). In 396, during one of the Graeco-Persian wars, it was a Syracusan sea-captain returning from Phoenicia who brought to Sparta the news of the building of the latest Persian armada (Xen. *Hell.* III. 4.1). In the context of this Levantine trade, the lower Orontes valley has an especial attraction. It is at the Mediterranean end of the shortest caravan route from Mesopotamia, by way of the north Syrian towns. Whoever controls it also bestrides the chief route by which land traffic passes between Anatolia and the countries to the south.[36] In the late ninth and eighth centuries, it had a further attraction. The north Syrian states were still independent and, despite warfare between themselves and intermittent raids from Assyria, flourishing. Al Mina belonged to the neo-Hittite kingdom of Pa(t)tin, alternatively known to the Assyrians as Unqi, Aramaic 'Amq. (The Lower Orontes valley is still called in Arabic El-'Amuq, Turkish Amik: *CAH* III.1², ch. 9, 375.) With its capital at Kunulua, the biblical Calneh, perhaps to be identified with Tell Ta'yinat, the kingdom of Unqi played its part in local wars: it joined the coalition which unsuccessfully attacked Zakur of Hamath *c.* 796 (*ibid.* 403). Possibly Tell Sūkās, though less well placed for inland

---

[32] B 63, 137–9 and fig. 45.   [33] B 63, 126–30, 158 and fig. d, p. 157.
[34] Ezek. 27: 13. See below, p. 14.   [35] Hdt. II. 44; B 110 *ad loc.*
[36] B 18, 15.

communication, was outside Unqi's borders and so provided alternative access to Hamath. In 738 Tutamu, the last independent ruler of Unqi, was deposed and the region constituted an Assyrian province (*ibid.* 411). The loot taken on this occasion is comparable to that from any other substantial Phoenician or North Syrian state: 300 talents of silver, a no longer identifiable number of talents of gold, 100 talents of copper, linen and dyed woollen garments, all kinds of herbs, prisoners, and horses and mules.[37] On other occasions, the Assyrian kings single out for praise the vegetation of the adjoining Mt Amanus, whose shrubs, fruit trees and fine timber, notably cedarwood, had no equal in their eyes.[38]

This prosperous kingdom enjoyed, at the time of the first Greek settlement, easy access to Urartu, a kingdom richer still. Urartu in the first half of the eighth century was extending its power west of the Taurus over Melid, Tabal and Kummukh (*CAH* III.1², ch. 9, 405–6). Its political control never reached quite as far as the Mediterranean coast; but in 743 it mustered an anti-Assyrian alliance which included Gurgum with its capital Marqasi (Maraş) and Arpad north of Aleppo (*ibid.* 409). It was Tiglath-Pileser III's defeat of this alliance that inaugurated a new era of Assyrian domination of the Levant, marked by the installation of permanent Assyrian governors in place of native rulers and by wholesale deportations (*ibid.* 410). When in 714 Sargon II struck at Urartu and plundered its temple of Khaldi, the catalogue of loot, comprising 61 different varieties and 333,500 objects in all, reveals wealth to make one gasp and stretch one's eyes.[39] There were precious stones, unworked metal – 3,600 talents of bronze ingots (109 tons) – besides many objects made of silver and gold, and large bronze vessels for sacrificial use. These had not all been made locally, for the Assyrian records refer to workmanship of Urartu, Assyria and Tabal – whose eponym Tubal-Cain is the archetypal bronzeworker in the Bible (Genesis 4: 22).

Among these goods, worked and unworked metal must have been especially attractive to the first Greek traders at Al Mina. Euboean Chalcis, 'the brazen', had been an early home of bronzeworking in Greece; the Euboeans' experience with both bronze and iron, and their need for importing these metals once their own supplies had run out, has been discussed elsewhere (*CAH* III.1², chs. 18*b*, 19). Iron workings on Pithecusa show that when the Euboeans got there they used ore from Elba.[40] In the east, copper for bronze was principally imported from Cyprus, from which (through Latin *Cyprium*) our own word *copper* derives: the copper ingot was the island's symbol. The *Odyssey* speaks of a Taphian sea-captain taking his ship 'to Temesē for bronze, and I

[37] B 43, I §769.
[38] B 55, 145 *s.v.* Hamānu.
[39] B 29, II §172–4.
[40] C 98; A 7, 168.

carry gleaming iron' (I. 184). Temesē is presumably Cypriot Tamassus, which must have had a port at its disposal. Now, it was a short distance from Cyprus to the Levantine coast: Mt Casius can be seen from Cyprus on a clear day. Together with Cypriots, as we may conclude from the pottery, Euboean traders must have gone on from Cyprus to Al Mina to extend their trade to the metal brought down to the coast from the rich sources inland. Sidon was known for 'much bronze' (*Od.* xv. 495). It must have been through Levantine ports that bronze cauldrons with cast siren or animal-head attachments, made in Urartu, Tabal, Assyria or northern Syria, were imported into many parts of the Greek world throughout the seventh century B.C., and perhaps as early as the eighth.[41]

The dyed cloth of Unqi will have been another object of Al Mina's trade. The art of making sea-purple dye had long since spread to other parts of the Mediterranean; but that of Phoenicia was always considered the best.[42] It is highly probable that the Greek name *Phoinīkes* for the Phoenicians, already found in Homer, derives from the Greek *phoinós*, crimson, and was given to them because of the dye.[43] We now know that the native name 'Canaanite' has the same meaning (*CAH* II.2³, 520). In the *Iliad* Hecuba's store of fine embroidered robes was brought for her by Paris from Sidon (*Il.* VI. 288–92). The cloth trade has left no archaeological trace. For the Greek fondness for jewellery from the east we have tangible evidence. Oriental trinkets are found in Euboea as early as the ninth century,[44] and in the eighth Cilician seals and Egyptian scarabs buried on Pithecusa testify to the links established by the Euboeans between their trading posts in east and west.[45] Above all, the Greeks were fascinated by gold and silver plate. In Patroclus' funeral games Achilles is made to offer the prize of a Sidonian bowl, the finest on earth, which had been worked by Sidonian craftsmen and brought to Greece by Phoenician merchants (*Il.* XXIII. 740–5). Menelaus, in the *Odyssey*, had travelled to Phoenicia and Egypt himself and brought home magnificent gifts in precious metal. The best was a silver bowl with gilded rim from the king of the Sidonians (*Od.* IV. 612–19). Helen's work-basket of silver with gilded rims, set on wheels, was given her in Egypt (*Od.* IV. 125–7) but corresponds closely to a surviving item of Phoenician work in bronze.[46] It cost the poet nothing to sing of these splendid vessels. Finds of plate in Archaic Greece are rare; Greek princely houses cannot have afforded very much of it. But Homer's dreams of wealth from the orient are based on fact.

[41] Cf. A 7, 65–7. [42] B 65; B 61.
[43] A 23A, 1032–4, *s.vv.* 1. φοίνικες, 5; φοῖνιξ; φοινός.
[44] H 27, 41–2, 64–5. [45] H 27, 228–30.
[46] A 7, 37, fig. 8.

One commodity that Greeks could provide in return was slaves, got by kidnapping or raiding. There was thus a close link between trade and piracy. Piracy as a way-of life was taken for granted in the *Odyssey* (III. 71–4; IX. 252–5) and the Homeric *Hymn to Apollo* (452–3). Thucydides later deduced that the Archaic Greeks

used to fall on communities that were unwalled and living in villages, plunder them, and make most of their living that way. This profession was not shameful as yet, and indeed was held in some esteem. Among some mainlanders even now it is a distinction to succeed in doing this; and the old poets testify to the practice, showing the regular question asked of those who arrive by sea to be: 'Are you pirates?' – on the assumption that the questioned would not deny the fact, and that those who were interested to know would not reproach them with it. (Thuc. I. 5)

In the *Odyssey* the Phoenicians of Sidon, a sneaking lot, are the most successful in combining trade with kidnapping (XV. 403–84; XIV. 287–98; above p. 6). But Greeks do not hesitate to try their hand. The Taphians, the race of Greeks, evidently from the north-west, who have been mentioned as traders in metals (above, pp. 12–13), reappear as the kidnappers of a Sidonian girl whom they carried off from her own country when she had been coming in from the fields one day, and then sold to the king of a Greek island for a good price (*Od.* XIV. 425–9). Odysseus tells a plausible story of how he had taken his ships to raid the Egyptian coast, 'killing the men and carrying off the women and little children' (*Od.* XIV. 257–65, XVII. 425–34). Oriental evidence bears out Greek. In the sixth century Ezekiel (27: 13) associates Greek merchants at Tyre with trade in slaves, as well as with the bronze cauldrons mentioned above: 'Yawan, Tubal (Tabal) and Meshech (Accadian Mushki, Greek Phrygia) were thy merchants: they traded the persons of men and vessels of bronze in thy market.'

IV. ASSYRIAN KINGS AND THE GREEKS

Eastern rulers might have welcomed trade in slaves, as long as these had been got from outside their dominions. But it will have been in their interest to regulate the movements and residence of Greek traders so as to prevent casual kidnapping. This must be remembered when we come to consider the special privileges accorded to the Greek settlement of Naucratis in Egypt. Worse still was the danger of organized raids from the sea. In the story of Odysseus' raid the local ruler was alerted by the Greeks' recklessness and brought armed force swiftly to the rescue (*Od.* XIV. 266–84; XVII. 435–44). It is interesting that the first known Assyrian reference to Greeks, published in 1963[47]

[47] B 64, 76–8.

but so far unnoticed by Hellenists, tells of just such a raid on the south Phoenician coast, and of the timely reaction of the Assyrian governor of Tyre and Sidon. It is a fragmentary report to Tiglath-Pileser III written soon after 738 B.C.:

To the king my lord, your servant Qurdi-Asshur-Lamur. The Ionians (KURIa-u-na-a-a) have come. They have made an attack on the city of Samsimuruna, on the city of Harisū, and on the city of...As for the...-officer, he went to the city of...[and told me?] The people of the zakku-class I took with me and went. They have not taken anyone. As far as...[I pursued them?] in his ships...in the midst of the sea...[48]

The pattern is a familiar one. Even so might the Persian satrap Oroites, governor of the province of Sardis, have reported back in the 520s B.C. on how Polycrates of Samos with his hundred penteconters was 'plundering and looting without distinction', and taking places on the mainland as well as islands (Hdt. III. 39).

Where did the Greek raiders of the 730s come from? Cyprus is the most obvious possibility. But the southern Anatolian coast is another. Cilicia Tracheia in particular offers splendid hide-outs for pirates, and was for centuries much like the Barbary Coast before the French conquest of Algeria. The Greek arrival at Al Mina presupposes knowledge of the south Anatolian coast, and Greek pirates will have used it from then on, whether or not there were organized Greek towns along it. There probably were. Elsewhere the likelihood of some continuity of settlement from Mycenaean times, to be inferred from the peculiarities of the Pamphylian dialect, is discussed along with the admittedly scrappy evidence for resettlement in Archaic times of Phaselis from Rhodes, Side from Cyme, Nagidus and Celenderis in Cilicia Tracheia from Samos, and Soli on the edge of Cilicia Pedias from Rhodes (below, pp. 92–4). A possible indication that Soli had already been settled by the end of the eighth century is at Tarsus, where some Greek sherds older than c. 700 B.C. have the same provenances as those at contemporary Al Mina, and have even been thought to testify to the presence of a small Greek minority in this inland town. There are East Greek 'Ionian cups' here but not at Al Mina. They could have come from Rhodes through Soli.[49]

Greeks may have had something to do with the revolt in Cilicia Pedias, known to the Assyrians as Que, which Mita (Midas) of Mushki (Phrygia) supported and which Sargon II put down in 715 B.C. The sea is mentioned in this context, and it is tempting to insert Ionians into a gap in Sargon's Annals for that year:

[48] Improved translation kindly supplied by Dr Nadav Na'aman. Samsimuruna, in Sidonian territory, is attested elsewhere (B 55, s.v.).   [49] B 12, discussing B 27.

[? The Ionians who dwell in (or beside?)] the sea, who from distant days the [men of] Que had slaughtered, and... heard the advance of my expedition... To the sea I came down upon them, and both small and great with my weapons I fought down. The cities Khurrua, Ushnanis and (?)Qumasi of the land of Que, which Mita, king of the land of Mushki, had taken, I conquered...[50]

The supplement is attractive because, if correct, it would explain why, in the inscriptions summarizing the great deeds of his reign, Sargon II boasts of being 'he who caught the Ionians ([KUR] Ya-am-na-aya) out of the midst of the sea, like a fish',[51] and again says 'I caught, like fishes, the Ionians who live amid the Sea of the Setting Sun.'[52]

In the eleventh year of Sargon II's annals, 711, comes a story of which there are three other extant versions. Put together, they tell how Sargon deposed Azuri, king of Ashdod, for plotting against him and sending messages to neighbouring kings, and enthroned Azuri's brother in his stead. 'But the Khatti, planning treachery, hated his rule, and Yamani ([LÚ] Ya-am-na-aya), who was not entitled to the throne, but was just like them and had no respect for the lordship, they elevated above themselves.' The fullest available text adds that Yamani was a soldier, or set up by soldiers. Sargon goes on to say how he reacted by marching in person. He besieged and captured Ashdod and its confederate cities, despoiled it and settled it with prisoners deported from elsewhere under his own governor.

Yamani of Ashdod feared my weapons, left his wife, sons and daughters, fled to the border of Egypt which is on the frontier of Ethiopia, and lived there like a thief... As for the king of Ethiopia, the fear of the splendour of Ashur, my lord, overwhelmed him, and he cast Yamani into fetters, (binding) his hands and feet, and brought him into Assyria into my presence...[53]

Could Yamani have been a Greek mercenary of Azuri's bodyguard? The name surely means 'Greek': attempts to derive it from nearby Palestinian place-names are unconvincing. But the name could be bestowed on a non-Greek. It proves no more than that Greeks were by now familiar to the Levant.[54] Accadian names, like those of modern times, are sometimes ethnic (compare A-mu-ru-u, Amorite);[55] but these may easily have originated as nicknames. Their owners were lucky by comparison with those named 'Drunkard', 'Stinking Oil' or

---

[50] B 42, 20–1, line 118; supplement, B 54, 266, following B 81, 365.

[51] Bull inscription, Khorsabad, B 45, 14, no. 2.25; translated, B 44, II §92.

[52] Pavement inscription, B 80, 148, 34, translated B 44, II §99; cf. B 45, 4, no. 1.21 (cylinder seal); B 23, 199, 19 (inscribed prism from Nimrud).

[53] Annals: B 42, 39–41, translated B 44, II §30; B 59, 286. Inscription of Room XIV, Khorsabad (fullest text), B 79, 178, 15, translated B 44, II §79–80; B 59, 285; B 73, 61–2. Display inscription: B 80, 114. 95.101, translated B 44, II §62–3. British Museum Prism A from Nineveh, translated B 44, II §194 5; B 73, 61.   [54] B 70, 80, n. 217.

[55] B 68, 268–71.

'Disobedient-to-the-Gods'.[56] We find the name Yamani again in later Assyrian documents. A Yamani turns up in a seventh-century census of the Harran district, but since he had two brothers with the Syrian names Dui and Ilu it is hard to believe he was a pure-bred Greek himself.[57] Similarly, the worthy Aigyptios whom the *Odyssey* names as a speaker in the assembly at Ithaca was surely a Greek, not a naturalized Egyptian (*Od.* II. 15f).

Sargon proved some of his claims by setting up steles in conquered territory. A basalt stele in Ashdod is unfortunately too battered to yield any more information about Yamani's revolt.[58] But it is impressive that Sargon's annals for 709, claiming that tribute was sent to him by 'seven kings of Ya (Ya-aʻ), a district of Yadnana whose distant abodes are situated a seven-days' journey in the sea of the setting sun',[59] is confirmed by a stele set up at Citium in Cyprus 'at the base of a mountain ravine...of Yadnana'.[60] So Yadnana is Cyprus, and since Cyprus had ten kings in all in the 670s, it follows that, unless the seven kings of unidentified Ya were sub-kings, Sargon's suzerainty must have extended well beyond Citium into Greek territory (below, p. 57). Sargon's foothold in Citium itself is explained by his control of Tyre and Sidon. Citium is identical with Qartikhadast ('New City', the 'Carthage' of Cyprus) whose governor, 'servant of Hiram king of the Sidonians', dedicated two of those familiar bronze vessels (sold in Limassol in 1877).[61] This Hiram was the king of Tyre who submitted to Assyria in 738. According to a Hellenistic edition of Tyrian chronicles, Hiram's successor Lulī (Eululaios) sailed from Tyre to put down a revolt in Citium.[62] Sennacherib boasts that in 701, when he moved to suppress Lulī's rebellion, 'the terrifying splendour of my lordship overcame him and from Tyre he fled to Yadnana in the midst of the sea...'.[63] Sennacherib replaced him in Phoenicia by Tu'balu (Ethba'al) but did not follow him to Cyprus. 'There', he elsewhere says, 'Lulī sought a refuge. In that land, in terror of the weapons of Ashur my lord, he died.'[64] Eventually it may have become too embarrassing to admit that Cyprus was now beyond Assyria's reach: it is stated more vaguely that Lulī 'fled far away, into the midst of the sea, and died'.[65]

Sennacherib did, however, reassert his power over a rebellion in Cilicia in two campaigns in 696 and 695, waged in the king's absence by his generals. They have been noticed in the chapter on the Neo-Hittite

---

[56] B 68, 268. [57] B 35, no. 7, II 4, cf. p. 61. [58] B 71.

[59] Sargon's annals: B 42, 69, lines 457–60, translated B 44, II §44.

[60] Larnaca stele: B 80, 174–85, esp. col. II (IV) 52–3 = *Vorderasiatische Schriftdenkmäler* (Leipzig, 1907) I no. 71; translated, B 44, II §180–9.

[61] B 17, no. 31; from B 62; *CIS* i 5.

[62] Menander of Ephesus, *FGrH* 783 F 4; from Josephus, *AJ* IX. 283.

[63] B 43, 68–9. [64] B 43, 77. [65] B 43, 29; B 31, 131.

states in Syria and Anatolia (*CAH* III.1², 426–7); but they deserve further consideration here because Greeks participated in the revolt. The brief royal record of 694 does not, it is true, mention them. There we are only told that Kirua, ruler of Illubru, had stirred up the Khilakku (the Cilicians of the Taurus mountains) and the cities Ingira (Anchiale) and Tarzu (Tarsus) in the Plain. Illubru was besieged and stormed, Kirua captured and flayed, and Illubru was then rebuilt and Sennacherib's stele set up in it. This account squares with what was reported by the Babylonian Berossus in Hellenistic times, when he published what was evidently a Greek version of the master-copy from which our various surviving Babylonian historical chronicles are also derived. This has not come down to us direct. What we have are two accounts of the same events in the Armenian version of Eusebius' *Chronika*, which Eusebius had taken from an historian of the second century A.D., Abydenus, who drew on Berossus through an intermediary, Alexander Polyhistor:

(1) When the report came to him (Sennacherib) that Greeks had entered the land of the Cilicians to make war, he hastened against them. He set up front against front. After many of his own troops had been cut down by the enemy, he won in battle. As a memorial of victory he left his image erected on the spot, and commanded that his valour and heroism should be engraved for the remembrance of future ages. And the town Tarson, so he reports, he built after the model of Babylon, and gave it the name of Tharsin...So far Polyhistor.[66]

(2) Abydenus on Sinecherim...Sennacherib...on the seacoast of the Cilician land defeated the warships of the Ionians and drove them to flight. And he also built the temple of the Athenians [sic], erected bronze pillars, and in inscriptions indeed, so he says, he had engraved his great deeds. He also rebuilt Tarson according to the plan and pattern of Babylon, so that the river Cydnus might flow through Tarson as the Euphrates flows through Babylon...[67]

Despite their involved pedigree, not much seems to have gone wrong in the transmission of these two passages, apart from the incidental nonsense about the 'temple of the Athenians'. Sennacherib's victory has, understandably, been attributed to him personally and not to his generals. A simple hypothesis will resolve the remaining inconsistencies. Illubru must be Greek Olymbrus, named in a geographical genealogy as a brother of Adanus, the eponym of Adana,[68] but never reappearing as a place-name. Let us take it that Olymbrus lay immediately to the east of Gözlü Kule, identified as Archaic Tarsus by its excavators.[69] Olymbrus contained the governor's residence, and here Sennacherib's main rebuilding must have taken place; it will have then developed into Classical Tarsus and lost its old name. The Cydnus will have run

[66] Berossus, *FGrH* 680 F 7 (31) from Euseb. *Arm. Chron.* 13–15 Karst.
[67] Abydenus, *FGrH* 685 F 5 (6) from Euseb. *Arm. Chron.* 17–18 Karst.
[68] Steph. Byz. *s.v.* Ἄδανα.   [69] Above, n. 49.

between Archaic and Classical Tarsus until diverted to the east by Justinian after a disastrous flood (Procop. *Aed.* v. 14–20). The excavators found that Archaic Tarsus was destroyed *c.* 696 and unimpressively rebuilt, to be abandoned completely in the sixth century by which time Classical Tarsus must have engrossed attention.[70] It was presumably Sennacherib who had his royal statue set up at Anchiale, to be identified as belonging to Sardanapalus by Alexander's generals in 333 B.C.[71]

A naval victory against Greeks in Cilicia in 696–5 will explain why, in 694, Sennacherib embarked on a programme of building warships at home for use in other campaigns, and how he came to have Greek as well as Phoenician prisoners to do the work for him: 'Khatti people, plunder of my bow, I settled in Nineveh. Mighty ships after the workmanship of their land, they built dexterously. Tyrian, Sidonian and Ionian sailors, captives of my hand, I ordered (to descend) the Tigris with them...' These ships were dragged overland and then brought through canals into the Euphrates, and down the Euphrates to the head of the Persian Gulf, to be used in war against the Elamite coast.[72]

It may be significant that Al Mina was at this time destroyed, to be reoccupied by different sorts of Greeks using more Corinthian pottery and no Euboean.[73] In Unqi Sennacherib could take what measures he pleased. But his boast of reprisals against the Khilakku in the Taurus sounds hollow: one settlement destroyed, but no plunder mentioned, no tribute imposed, no governor installed (*CAH* III.1[2], 427). The Khilakku remained unsubdued until Ashurbanipal's time (*ibid.* 432). Any Greek allies of the Khilakku nesting in Cilicia Tracheia must have remained similarly independent, despite Assyria's reconquest of the Plain. It is noteworthy, in this connexion, that an Assyrian geographical list dating from the reign of Ashurbanipal and Shamash-shum-ukin names the land of Khilakku and the land of Yamana conjointly, and, it would seem, independently of Cyprus.[74]

Esarhaddon (681–669) re-established suzerainty over Cyprus. Two prisms from Nineveh give a text describing the magnificent rebuilding of his palace there. Among the tributary kings who provided timber and building materials are ten kings of Yadnana. Their names and cities are given. They cover the whole island, and are listed in full below, pp. 57–9. It is of interest here to note that, whereas plausible Greek equivalents have been proposed for the names of the other kings, there are two cases where no guesswork is needed: Pilagura of Kitrus (Chytri) and Ituandar of Pappa (Paphus), unmistakably Pylagoras and Eteander. The identical list of kings is given as supporting Ashurbanipal

---

[70] B 12, 11–12.
[71] Callisthenes, *FGrH* 124 F 34; Aristobulus, *FGrH* 139 F 9; B 81.
[72] B 43, 73, 60.   [73] Above, p. 10.   [74] B 21, 53.

against Taharqa in 667, after so short an interval that it is perhaps unjust
to harbour suspicion that the list has merely been copied so as to transfer
the glories of Esarhaddon's reign to Ashurbanipal (below, p. 59).

Reference has already been made to the alabaster tablet from Ashur
in which Esarhaddon asserts:

the kings of the midst of the sea, all of them, from Yadnana,
Yaman, as far as Tarsisi, submitted at my feet. Rich tribute I received.

This vast and vague claim defies close analysis: are Yadnana and
Yaman identical? Is one a part of the other? Or are they different
regions? An important reference to the west can be seen in Tarsisi, the
reading of the best modern edition which emends the scribal error
Nusisi.[75] Tarsisi must be identical with biblical Tarshish, linked closely,
as we have seen, with Yawan in the genealogy of Genesis (cf. CAH
II.2³, 768–9). Esarhaddon's text and the biblical passages alike imply
that it is far distant: Jonah's voyage on a ship from Joppa bound for
Tarshish was meant to be over-long, and he deserved to be swallowed
by a sea-monster (Jonah 1: 3–2: 1). Although the Septuagint translators
did not spot the identification, Tarshish must be the Greek Tartess(us).
(It is strange that efforts are still made to identify it with Tars(us), Hittite
Tarsa, Accadian Tarzu.)[76] The evocative name of Tarshish, it seems,
had originally been applied to a distant coast not clearly localized, much
as the Ethiopians and the River Phasis figured in Greek imagination
as remote fairy-tale lands before they came to be applied to Kush and
to a Black Sea river respectively. In King Solomon's time 'ships of
Tarshish' had set out on distant voyages from Eilath through the Red
Sea (I Kings 9: 26–7, 10: 22). By the seventh century Tarshish is set
in the western Mediterranean. It is named in an early Phoenician
dedication at Nora in Sardinia.[77] By c. 638 there can be no doubt that
Tarshish/Tartessus is a kingdom of the Guadalquivir Valley, centred
on Seville and Cádiz. It was then that the first Greek reached it, Colaeus
of Samos, who had been blown off course from an Egyptian voyage
and made his fortune by bringing back silver from an untapped market
(Hdt. IV. 152). The Spanish mines remained the richest source of silver
for centuries; Tartessus was an entrepôt for tin and lead from Galicia,
Brittany and the Scillies.[78] In the sixth century the Ionian Phocaeans
traded with Tartessus, finding favour with its king Arganthonius and
bringing silver back in warships. Tartessus caught the fancy of the poets
Stesichorus (184.2 Page) and Anacreon (361.4 Page). In the same century
Ezekiel writes of the 'silver, iron, tin and lead' that came from Tarshish

[75] B 14, §57 As.Bb.E = Assur 3916 (Istanbul no. 6262) line 10f, following Weidner's
emendation.   [76] E.g. B 25; cf. B 4, 87, n. 4.
[77] B 16; B 56.   [78] C 171; B 47.

to Tyre (Ezekiel 27: 12), and Jeremiah of the 'silver, beaten into plates, that is brought from Tarshish' (Jeremiah 10: 9).

From Ashurbanipal's accession until the fall of Nineveh in 612 there are, to our knowledge, no more explicit references to Greeks in the royal records, though the account of Gyges' embassy of 669/4, and of Gyges' subsequent help to Egypt, are of value to Greek history as well as to that of Lydia (*CAH* III.2², ch. 34a) and Egypt (below, p. 36). We come across another man named Yamani: he sold a slave woman to an officer at Nineveh *c*. 661, and is presumably identical with the Yamani who was Captain of Fifty and witnessed a similar sale in 659, and the Yamani who was again a witness in 654.[79] Was he a Greek?

Ashurbanipal is the one Assyrian king who, under the name of Sardanapalus, made an impact on the Greeks and was alive in popular memory in the fifth century. Hellanicus wrote of *two* Sardanapali (*FGrH* 4 F 63) – a sign that there were several stories about him which seemed to require rationalization. Herodotus names him as a king of Nineveh whose great treasure was plundered by thieves who dug an underground tunnel to it (Hdt. II. 150.3). The Greek doctor Ctesias, who returned from service at the Persian Court in 397 and wrote voluminously on the east, on the basis of pretended research into ancient manuscripts, composed a brilliant, if fictitious, account of how Sardanapalus, the richest and most effeminate of kings, immolated himself, his concubines and immense treasure on a huge pyre when faced with rebellion led by a Mede general (*FGrH* 688 F 1). This romance embodied a truth which was known to the Greeks before Ctesias: that the Assyrian empire paid the price of its greed and recklessness. Phocylides of Miletus, dated by the Suda to *c*. 540 (Suda *s.v.*), wrote the telling epigram:

> This too, is by Phocylides: a city settled upon a rock,
> in good order and small, is stronger than Nineveh in its folly.[80]

V. THE NEO-BABYLONIAN EMPIRE AND THE GREEKS

Chapter 36b tells how Psammetichus I and Necho II used their Greek mercenaries against the new Babylonian power between 616 and 605. Recent discoveries in Palestine must be seen in the context of these campaigns. In the fort Mesad Hashavyahu, between Jaffa and Ashdod, there is a site with Greek pottery of the last third of the seventh century and a workshop for making iron implements. Greek mercenaries must have been stationed here.[81] Since a Hebrew letter implies that the place had a Jewish governor,[82] they may have been in the service of the king

---

[79] B 39, nos. 510.4; 208.29, 32; 654.11. [80] Fr. 5 Diehl, from Dio Prus. XXXVI. 11.
[81] B 52. [82] B 50–1; B 59, 568.

of Judah, and forced to abandon the outpost because of the Egyptian invasion of 609.

At the fortress of Tell Arad, shortly before its destruction by the Babylonians in 598/7, were found Hebrew ostraca addressed to one Eliashib, with instructions to supply provisions of wine, bread and oil 'to the Kittim' (*lktym*), who are evidently in transit. These too may be Greek mercenaries serving Judah. We have seen how Jews associate Kittim (Citium) with Yawan despite the fact that Cypriot Citium was Phoenician (above, p. 3). Tell Arad has no Greek pottery, but the men would have left none if only passing through.[83]

We find at least one instance of Babylon's employing Greek mercenaries also, either following the Egyptian example or perhaps because pockets of Greek mercenaries had been left behind after the Egyptian collapse and retreat of 605 B.C. Alcaeus of Mytilene had a brother, Antimenidas, who fought for the Babylonians and whom he welcomed back in a poem: 'From the ends of the earth you are come, with your sword-hilt of ivory bound with gold... You accomplished a great feat, and delivered (the Babylonians) from distress, for you a slew a warrior of five royal cubits less a span.'[84]

Exactly the same height, some $2\frac{1}{2}$ m, is attributed to a Persian who died supervising the building of the Athos canal for Xerxes (Hdt. VII. 117): it was evidently the standard size for a gigantic warrior.

A papyrus containing the ends of the lines of another of Alcaeus' poems gives a clue to the campaign in which Antimenidas fought: 'the sea...takes alive...of sacred Babylon...Ascalon...stirred up cruel war...utterly [destroyed]...to the abode of Death...decorations for us...' (Alcaeus B 16).

Ascalon, as we now know from a Babylonian chronicle, was taken in 604, the year after the battle of Carchemish, by Nebuchadrezzar. It was plundered and turned into a heap of ruins.[85] So it was to join in the destruction of Ascalon that Antimenidas crossed the sea, and here that he won glory by killing and capturing the enemies of Babylon.

The Ascalon campaign was typical of the early decades of Nebuchadrezzar's reign. The massive deportations he visited upon Jerusalem in 597, 586 and 582 were paralleled in other Levantine cities. Ration tablets of the years 595 to 570 in Babylon give some indication of the variety of nationalities captive there. Distinguished prisoners include two sons of the king of Ascalon, and the young king of Judah, Jehoiachin, besides other Philistines and Jews, Phoenicians, Elamites, Medes, Persians and Egyptians. There are Lydians and Ionians too. The Ionians are said to be craftsmen. They could have been deported from

[83] B 1; B 59, 568–9.   [84] Alcaeus, z 27 Page, from Strabo 617.
[85] B 82, 69; B 29, 100.

any of the courts of the minor states that had emerged from Assyrian domination to fall under Babylon, like the craftsmen and smiths who were all carried off from Jerusalem. But the names that survive, Ku-un-zu-um-pi-ja, Lab(?)bunu, Azijak and Pa-ta-am (?), look very un-Greek.[86] Κο(ν)ζαπεας and Κουανζαπεας are known as Lycian names,[87] so these 'Ionian' prisoners may be Anatolians.

At the same time as Nebuchadrezzar was carrying through his Levantine conquests, Babylonian influence came closer to the Greek homelands than ever before by virtue of the act of mediation between Alyattes of Lydia and Cyaxares of Media after the battle of the eclipse, 28 May 585, which Greeks present on the Lydian side had witnessed. It must have been Nebuchadrezzar, not as Herodotus says, Labynetus of Babylon, who as one of the mediators arranged peace and a marriage-alliance between the parties (1. 73). Nabonidus (Labynetus) was in fact the last king of Babylon (556–539) who 'had not had the honour of being a somebody' before his usurpation,[88] and would never have been sent as Nebuchadrezzar's representative. Herodotus mistakenly thought that the last King Labynetus was the son of a king of the same name (1. 188).

Greek trade with the Levant continued during the Babylonian period; but, as has been seen, the history of the trading settlements at Al Mina and Tell Sūkās seems to have been chequered, and the hiatus at Al Mina in the sixth century (above, p. 10), and the two destructions of Tell Sūkās c. 588 and c. 552 (above, p. 11) may be the consequence of Babylonian policy.

War was continually expected to recur between Babylonia and Egypt, and Jeremiah in Egypt (Jer. 43: 9–13, cf. 46) and Ezekiel (Ezekiel 29: 13, cf. 30–2) were convinced that Babylonia would win. Nothing came of this threat, though a fragmentary chronicle for 568/7 reports a confrontation between Nebuchadrezzar and Amasis. It seems to show Babylonian awareness of Egypt's use of Greek mercenaries:

In his 37th year Nebuchadrezzar king of Babylon marched against Egypt to deliver a battle. Ama?-su of Egypt called up his army...ku from the town of Putu-Yaman, distant regions which are (situated on islands) amidst the sea...may...which are in Egypt...carrying weapons, horses and chariots...he called to assist him and...did...in front of him...he put his trust...[89]

In the reign of Nabonidus (Nabuna'id) the new power of Persia suddenly emerged, with Cyrus revolting from Astyages in 553 and seizing Ecbatana in 550. Herodotus tells us that Babylon now made a

[86] B 77, 932–3.   [87] B 88, 238–9, §647.4, 5, 6.
[88] *Pace* Mellink in *CAH* III. 2², ch. 34a; cf. B 24, 56–7.
[89] B 41, 206, no. 48; translated B 59, 308.

fourth in the alliance against Persia which was formed by the kings of
Lydia and Egypt together with the most formidable military power in
mainland Greece, Sparta (I. 77). That the alliance was really made is
proved by the passage of diplomatic gifts, intercepted and still on view
a century later, from Egypt to Sparta and from Sparta to Lydia (I. 70,
III. 47). But no gifts from or to Nabonidus are mentioned, and if he
joined the alliance his heart was not in it. His own records say nothing
of it; instead they welcome Cyrus' overthrow of the Medes because this
enabled Nabonidus to rebuild the Harran temples where his aged
mother was priestess.[90] For ten years, from before 549 to after 545,
Nabonidus was far from Babylon, in the oasis of Tema.[91] He gave no
help to Croesus, and when Cyrus attacked Babylon it was isolated. Later
Greeks told stories to account for Babylon's falling to Cyrus without
a blow (Hdt. I. 190-1), and remembered with mild surprise that Babylon
was so vast that it took three whole days for the news to spread to all
its inhabitants (Arist. *Pol.* III. 3.5, 1276a).

VI. NEAR EASTERN INFLUENCES ON THE GREEKS

The inspiration and influence of imported eastern goods, and most
probably of immigrant eastern artists as well, transformed the artistic
culture of the Greek homeland. Geometric styles rapidly gave way to
'orientalizing' art. Archaeologists and art historians have tried to
explain the transition and trace its sources. Readers will find the subject
discussed in ch. 19 in *CAH* III.1[2] and in ch. 45*b* below.

Of even greater importance is the Greek importation of the Phoenician
alphabet in the eighth century B.C. It is considered at length in ch. 20
of *CAH* III.1[2]. But it cannot be excluded from the discussions that now
follow of the influence of eastern loan words upon the Greek language,
and the infiltration of eastern names into Greek mythology.

1. *Loan-words*

Loan-words are an excellent guide to cultural influence. Semitic words
that have found their way into Greek are few enough to be listed,[92]
unlike the pre-Greek roots which form a major component of the Greek
language and are generally inseparable from Anatolian borrowings.

I here give the list in chronological order, with each word assigned
to the period of its first attested use. But it is always possible that a
loan-word was imported long before it appears in a literary text or an

---

[90] B 41, Nabonid no. 1 i. 8 – ii. 46; B 24.
[91] B 24, ins. H 2a and b; Nabonidus chronicle, B 29, 58-9.
[92] B 48; cf. A 23A; B 34; B 2; *The Assyrian Dictionary* (Chicago 1956).

inscription. This is illustrated by the Greek names of the letters of the alphabet. Most of them are not attested before the fourth century B.C. But they were originally words with Semitic meanings. ἄλφα comes from Phoenician '*lp*, cf. Hebrew *alep*, bull or ox; βῆτα from Phoenician *byt*, cf. Hebrew *bēt*, house. The Greeks learned these names by rote without understanding them, and must have imported the names along with the letters in the eighth century B.C.

Names of letters are omitted from our list, as are many words whose etymology is uncertain, and proposed etymologies of proper names, which, however intriguing and plausible, are not susceptible to satisfactory controls. The list is given in simplified form. Most variants and derivatives are ignored, and only a limited selection of the known parallels in Semitic languages is provided.

Mycenaean

ki-to, χιτών, Ionic κιθών, tunic. Phoenician *ktn*.

ku-ru-so, χρυσός, gold. Phoenician *ḥrs*.

e-re-pa, ἐλέφας, ivory. Cf. Hittite *laḫpa*, possibly derived from Phoenician '*lp*, bull, though there is no known case of this word being used for a bull-elephant.

re-wo, λέων, lion. Possibly related to Ugaritic *lbᵘ*, Hebrew *labî*, Accadian *labbu*.

ku-mi-no, κύμῑνον, cummin. Cf. Hebrew *kammōn*.

sa-sa-ma, σήσαμον, sesame. Phoenician *ššmn*.

Epic

λῖς, lion. Cf. Hebrew *layiš*.

γαυλός, bowl, bucket. Cf. Ugaritic *gl*, Hebrew *gullāh*. Hence in the fifth century γαῦλος, a round Phoenician merchant vessel.

κανέον, basket, and κανών, shield-grip, derive from κάννα, reed. Cf. Ugaritic *qn*, Punic and Royal Aramaic *qn'*, Hebrew *qāneh*.

κρόκος, saffron. Cf. Hebrew *karkōm*, Accadian *kurkānû*.

βύβλινος, from βύβλος, papyrus plant. Connected with *Gbl*, Hebrew *Geēbāl*, Greek *Byblos*, the entrepôt for papyrus in Phoenicia. But the derivation *Bbl* from *Gbl* is not easy.

ὀθόνη, fine tissue. Cf. Hebrew *etûn*, fine linen, Egyptian *idmj*, red linen.

7th–6th centuries B.C.

μνᾶ, mina, one-sixtieth of a talent (normally of silver). Cf. Hebrew *māneh*, Royal Aramaic *mnh*, biblical Aramaic *mnē'*, from Accadian *manû*.

σάκκος, rough goatskin, hence sack. Cf. Hebrew *śaq*, Accadian *saqqu*.

κασία, cassia. Cf. Accadian *kasû*, Neo-Babylonian *kesīa*, Hebrew *qeṣîah*.

λίβανος, λιβανωτός, frankincense. Cf. Punic *lbnt*, Royal Aramaic *lbwnh*.

μύρρα, myrrh. Cf. Canaanite gloss (Amarna letters) *mu-ur-ra*, Ugaritic *mr*, Hebrew *mōr*, Royal Aramaic *mwr*, Accadian *murru*, all derived from the Semitic root *mrr*, to be bitter.

κάδος, wine-jar. Cf. Ugaritic *kd*, Punic *kd*, Royal Aramic *kd*, Hebrew *kad*.

βῖκος, big pot with handles. Possibly related to royal Aramaic *bq*, potsherd.

5th–4th centuries B.C.

δέλτος, writing-tablet. Cf. Phoenician *dlt*, Hebrew *deleṭ*.

βύσσος, fine linen. Phoenician *bṣ*, Punic *bwṣ*, Hebrew *bûṣ*.

σινδών, fine linen. Cf. Accadian *saddinu*, Hebrew *saḏin*.

κασᾶς, horse-cloth. Cf. Ugaritic *kst*, Punic *kst*, Royal Aramaic *kst*.

ἀρραβών, pledge. Cf. Phoenician *'rb*, guarantor; Ugaritic *'rbn*, Royal Aramaic *'rbn*, Hebrew *'erabôn*, pledge.

σίγλος, Achaemenid silver coin. Cf. Punic *šql*, Royal Aramaic *šql*, Hebrew *šeqel*.

ἴασπις, jasper. Cf. Hebrew *yašpeh*, Accadian *yaš(u)pû*.

κάμηλος, camel. Cf. Hebrew *gāmāl*, Royal Aramaic *gml*.

κάκκαβος, cooking-pot. Cf. Accadian *kukkubu*, libation-jar, drinking-flask.

σιπύη, bread-bin. Phoenician *sp*, Hebrew *sap*.

κύπρος, henna. Cf. Hebrew *koper*.

νάρδος, nard. Cf. Sanskrit *nálada, narada*, Hebrew *nardᵉ*.

σοῦσον, lily. Egyptian *sššn* > *ššn*, Hebrew *šûšan*.

νάβλας, a ten- or twelve-stringed harp. Cf. Egyptian *nfr*, Punic *nbl*.

σαμβύκη, a Syrian harp of four to seven strings. Cf. Accadian *šebītu*, biblical Aramaic *šabbᵉkā'*.

σής, moth. Cf. Accadian *sāsu*, Royal Aramaic *ss*, Hebrew *sās*.

χαλβάνη, galbanum. Cf. Hebrew *ḥelbᵉnāh* from *ḥālāb*, milk.

κιννάμωμον, cinnamon. Cf. Hebrew *qinnāmôn*.

Before the Persian conquests, it looks as if all Semitic loan-words in Greek were taken from Phoenician. The Phoenicians themselves derived the words for certain articles of trade from the Accadian of Mesopotamia, or even from further east. The words are often not available to us in the original Phoenician, because of the scantiness of surviving inscriptions. But the related Aramaic or Hebrew, and Punic which is descended from Phoenician, provide satisfactory analogies.

The establishment of Persian power throughout the Near East brought with it Royal Aramaic as the chancery language and *lingua franca*. From now on, Semitic loan-words in Greek are more likely to have come through Aramaic than Phoenician. We cannot, however, draw a clear line between these two classes of loan-word, because of the possible time-lag between the importation of a word into Greek and its first known attestation. For this reason, our list includes fourth-century citations. An instructive case is the mina, first mentioned in known literature by Hipponax of Ephesus (fr. 36.3 West) who flourished at the time of Cyrus' capture of Sardis.[93] We might have taken it for a Persian introduction, were it not for a silver plaque under the foundations of the Ephesian temple financed by Croesus, which records gold and silver contributions already in minas.[94]

It will be seen at once that nearly all the borrowings are of the kind that are made when 'a district or a people is in possession of some special thing or product wanted by some other nation and not produced in that country. Here quite naturally the name used by the natives is taken over along with the thing.'[95] The analogy is with our *tea* from Chinese and *coffee* from Arabic. Thus we get the early words for gold (imported into Greece before the Thasos and Pangaeum mines were opened up) and for ivory, later for jasper. There are numerous words for cloth and clothing, beginning with the tunic – a household word because every male Greek normally wore one. Massive importation of textiles from the East may account for the oddity that the Greek word for clothes-moth is identical with that in west Semitic languages. The large number of plant-names also derives from commerce. Cane was used for basketwork, and papyrus, the first time it is mentioned, for ropes. A continually growing number of loan-words in this class describes spices, perfumes, gums and colorants, that either derive from the Levant or came by way of the Levant from countries beyond. This trade continued to flourish in Roman times.[96] It is no doubt partly because of their imported contents that the Semitic names of various kinds of vessels and containers became familiar to the Greeks. These words then came to be applied to Greek-made articles.

Words that are used to describe things that are known to exist in a foreign country, but are not usually imported, testify to knowledge of that country. Thus, the Greeks knew of the camel because some of them had seen it, and they later spoke of the shekels with which Persian commanders paid their mercenaries. More interesting is the class of loan-words which 'bear witness to the cultural superiority of some nation in some one specified sphere of activity'.[95] But here again we are back to commerce. The Greek word for *pledge*, and their adoption of the mina as a weight and unit of currency, are analogous to our loan-words *bank*, *bankrupt*, *florin*. The words for musical instruments should probably be referred to the fourth century, when a jaded musical appetite was developing a taste for the exotic, to the annoyance of purists (Plato, *Resp.* 399c, d). Loan-words for instruments, analogous to our *piccolo*, are not matched by any foreign musical terms in Greek

[93] Marmor Parium, *FGrH* 239 A 42.
[94] B 36, 339, no. 53, 414 (text), pl. 66.
[95] Otto Jespersen, *Language, its nature, development and origin* (London, 1922) 209.
[96] J. Innes Miller, *The spice trade of the Roman empire* (Oxford, 1969).

analogous to *soprano* or *andante*. The Levantines did not teach the Greeks how to play.

The lesson is not palatable to all modern scholars, but it is inescapable. The Greeks were influenced by what they bought from Semitic peoples, but they did not import from them any abstract, political, philosophical or even artistic notions that made a direct impact on the Greek language. Most Semitic loan-words in Greek attest trading contacts only.

We must pause, however, at the word *deltos*. Herodotus writes of a δελτίον δίπτυχον (VIII. 239) – two wooden tablets, coated with wax for writing on, which were joined into a folding diptych. This was a Semitic invention, described by Ezekiel (37: 16–17). Such tablets were in use throughout the Graeco-Roman world for a millennium. The importation into Greece of writing-tablets goes together with the Greek adoption and adaptation of the Phoenician alphabet.

The adaptation by the Greeks of the letters of the Phoenician alphabet to express vowels as well as consonants is one of the most important events in world history. It is baffling to reflect that we do not know exactly where or how the adaptation took place, or even whether the creation of the vowel-system was by accident or design. But the Greek tradition that the alphabet came from Phoenicia is confirmed by the name φοινικήια, almost certainly meaning 'Phoenician letters',[97] which we find given to the alphabet in Crete,[98] in Ionian Teos (M–L no. 30, 37–8) and in Aeolian Mytilene[99] as well as by Herodotus (III. 67.1; v. 74.1). The Phoenician letters were supplemented and developed in different ways in different parts of Greece. These divergent local scripts can be grouped into three major families: (1) that of the Doric islands of Crete, Thera and Melos, which is closest to the original Phoenician, (2) that of the East Greeks including Rhodes, Attica, Aegina, Corinth and Euboea, which colonists brought to Italy and Sicily, and (3) that of much of mainland Greece. The families differ principally in their supplementary letters; they have much in common, including the universal use of *alep* as A, *hê* as E, and *'ayin* as O. They must therefore have been diffused from a single adaptation. The earliest alphabetic inscriptions in Greek, from Attica and Euboean Pithecusa, date to the middle of the eighth century; they cannot be very much later than this original adaptation.[100]

Where it was effected remains an open question. Al Mina would have greater attraction if there were any traces of writing among its early remains. Otherwise we must look to Rhodes and Crete, in each of which islands Phoenician jewellers may have settled. Though Rhodes sent

---

[97] Cf. B 20.   [98] D 128.

[99] *IG* XII.2, 96–7; A 36, 5 n. 2.   [100] A 36, 12–21.

colonists eastwards and the *Rodanim* were known to the Jews, its alphabet is further removed than the Cretan from the Phoenician prototype. On the other hand, though a bronze bowl with a Phoenician inscription of *c.* 900 B.C. has been found near Cnossus,[101] so far no Cretan inscription is known earlier than the seventh century B.C. Further than setting out these alternatives we cannot, for the present, go.

The Greeks liked to posit an 'inventor' for most things, and an extensive literature grew up among them about the origin of the Greek alphabet,[102] of which a lengthy summary survives.[103] Not everyone drew the obvious connexion from the old term 'Phoenician letters'. It did not escape Herodotus, who attributed the introduction of the alphabet into Greece from Phoenicia to Cadmus (v. 58), a view later endorsed by Ephorus (*FGrH* 70 F 105) and Aristotle (fr. 501 Rose). But others attributed the alphabet to Prometheus (Stesichorus fr. 36 Page, Aeschylus, *PV* 460), Palamedes (Euripides fr. 578 Nauck), or the god Hermes (Mnaseas, *FHG* III, p. 156, no. 44). Herodotus' great predecessor Hecataeus had decided for Danaus, supposed to have come from Egypt to Greece before Cadmus' arrival from Phoenicia: knowledge of the high antiquity of Egyptian civilization had already confused the issue (*FGrH* 1 F 20). From the range of these intelligent guesses about who introduced the alphabet we draw a simple conclusion: the Greeks did not know.

2. *Oriental names in Greek genealogies*

The deployment of the mythical Danaus and Cadmus is in itself of interest. Such knowledge as the Greeks acquired of foreign peoples was woven into genealogical mythology by the epic bards and writers of lyric poetry. By the end of the sixth century, when the first prose genealogical compilations were made, there were a good number of eponyms of foreign peoples to be incorporated. Eponyms, like inventors, were always presupposed. It did not occur to Greeks that they could do without them. When a Greek heard of a foreign people, he would ask: 'After whom are they named? and from whom was the eponym descended?' Among the eponyms towards the end of Hesiod's *Theogony* (1001) we note a son of Medea, *Medeio*, no doubt supposed to have given his name to the Medes. In the fragments of the Hesiodic *Eoiai* we find, already associated with colourful stories, a genealogy embracing *Danaus* (eponym of the Homeric Danaans) believed to have come from Egypt to Greece with his fifty daughters to escape marrying them to the fifty sons of *Aegyptus*, who followed (frs. 127–8 Merkelbach–

---

[101] B 69.   [102] H 46A.
[103] Bekker, *Anecd.* 781–6 = Sch. Dion. Thrax, *Gramm. Graeci* I iii 182 Hilgard = *FGrH* 1 F 20.

West). *Phoenix* is the husband of *Arabus'* daughter, and the father of *Cilix* and Europa, herself the mother of the Cretan Minos. To these perspicuous names, after whom the Greeks imagined the Egyptians, Phoenicians, Arabs and Cilicians to be called, must be added *Bēlus* the grandfather of Arabus, a name drawn from Greek contacts with the Levant, where Ba'al-shamayn, the Lord of Heaven, was the chief god. *Mopsus*, otherwise known as *Moxos*, figured in the Hesiodic *Melampodia* (frs. 278–9 Merkelbach–West). He was supposed to have taken over from Amphilochus the leadership of the survivors from the Trojan War, led them through Asia Minor and settled them on the south coast.[104] Pamphylian cities later honoured him as their founder.[105] He is identical with Mukshas, Phoenician *Mpš*, known from the eighth-century Hittite–Phoenician bilingual texts of Azitawataya (Karatepe) in Cilicia to have been revered as the ancestor of the *Dnnym*, the people of Adana (*CAH* III.1^2, 430). This looks like a parallel case to Bêl: Greeks arriving in the Levant will have learned of this native name and incorporated it into their own mythology.

These stories grew to have an overwhelming importance in Greek minds. We have observed how Cadmus' Phoenicians, entering Greece to chase after Europa, dominate the scene for Herodotus.[106] Cadmus, the eponym of the Cadmeans who had been the first inhabitants of Thebes, does not seem to have been connected with the orient according to Hesiodic poetry. It may have been Eumelus of Corinth who first linked Cadmus with Europa, and thus with Phoenicia, if it is correct that Eumelus (frs. 10–12 Kinkel) wrote a poem *Europeia* which touched on Thebes. Certainly in the sixth century Stesichorus' *Europeia* (fr. 195 Page) incorporated the legend of the dragon's teeth sown by Cadmus at Thebes. By the end of the sixth century Europa had herself been turned into an eponym. Hecataeus drew a map dividing the world into Europe, Asia and Libya (Africa), three continents of equal size separated by rivers flowing from the Ocean into the Black Sea and Mediterranean.[107] Herodotus (IV. 45.2) knew the work of Hecataeus well, but could not say who had given names to the three continents. It may have been Hecataeus' predecessor and fellow-Milesian Anaximander, the first Greek to draw a world map.[108] These artificial divisions loomed large for the fifth-century Greeks,[109] and, despite our knowledge that Europe and Asia are a single land-mass, are more influential than ever today.

---

[104] B 5; B 40.
[105] B 32, 56–8.
[106] Above, pp. 6–7. Cf. B 28.
[107] *FGrH* T 12a, from Agathemerus i 1; F 18a; Hdt. IV. 36.2.
[108] Anaximander A 1 D–K, from Diog. Laert. II. 1–2; A 6 D–K (= *FGrH* T 12a).
[109] E.g. in Hippocrates, *Aër.*

The elaboration of etymologies forced a surprising conclusion upon the Greeks. All Greek states invoked the protection of the heroes of mythology; their noblest families claimed descent from them. The barbarian eponyms who had been worked into Greek heroic genealogy were consequently found to be related to the guardian spirits of Greek cities and to living Greeks. One could go a step further. A nation was not necessarily descended from its eponym: Athena had given her name to Athens but was a virgin goddess with no progeny. But in most cases it was natural to think that those who bore a hero's name were also his descendants. Thus, at the very time when Greeks were beginning to sense a closer kinship among themselves, and to distinguish between Greeks and barbarians, the work of the poets and compilers invited a belief in the relationship of Greek cities and families with one or other barbarian people. Hence Herodotus' view that Heracles, the hero who meant most of all to the Greeks, was an Egyptian by descent (II. 43), and that Phoenician ancestry could be traced for Thales of Miletus, the first of the wise men (I. 170.3), and for Harmodius and Aristogeiton, the tyrannicides revered at Athens (V. 57.1). It could be claimed that Athens, where Medeios or Medus, the son of Medea, was supposed once to have reigned, had a special relationship with the Medes (Diod. x. 27). Perseus had ruled in the Argolid; from the time that Cyrus had first brought the Persians to Greek notice, Perseus had naturally been reckoned as their eponym; it evidently followed that Argives and Persians were kinsmen (Hdt. VII. 150, cf. VII. 61.3, Hellanicus, *FGrH* 4 F 60). These notions were exploited with some success by the agents of Darius and Xerxes in the great wars between Persia and mainland Greece in 490 and 480–479 B.C.

CHAPTER 36b

THE GREEKS IN EGYPT

T. F. R. G. BRAUN

I. GREEK-EGYPTIAN RELATIONS BEFORE PSAMMETICHUS I

Greeks arrived to settle in Egypt in the reign of Psammetichus I (664–610 B.C.). For the period that follows, Herodotus found that Egyptian and non-Egyptian information could be combined (II. 147). Thanks to Greek settlers mingling with the Egyptians, knowledge was now accurate (II. 154). Significantly, no Greek pottery datable to the period between Mycenaean times and 664 B.C. has so far been found in Egypt. Egyptian trinkets, on the other hand, were reaching the Greek world in the eighth century,[1] and a bronze Egyptian jug at Lefkandi in Euboea would seem to date back as far as the ninth.[2] These could have arrived by way of Phoenicia or Cyprus.

Some contact then, even if indirect, there must have been in the disturbed century before Psammetichus I. The Greeks retained some recollection of the Egyptian history of this time. We have seen how the king of Ethiopia and Egypt, who must have been Shabako (c. 716–c. 702 B.C.) in 711 surrendered Yamani of Ashdod, possibly a Greek (above, p. 16). This 'Sabakōs' is an historical figure for Herodotus (II. 137, 139) who in the fifth century could get a fair amount of information about the 25th (Nubian or Kushite) dynasty. Shabako's enemy was the delta king Bakenrenef son of Tefnakhte (c. 720–715?), whom he eventually captured and burnt alive.[3] Bakenrenef, as Bocchoris, was to figure in Greek imagination, though Herodotus does not mention him. He is celebrated as a sagacious lawgiver in the Egyptian account of Diodorus (I. 45, 65, 79, 94) which derives from earlier Greek writing – probably in large measure from Hecataeus of Abdera, c. 300 B.C.[4] Bakenrenef's survival here and elsewhere in Greek literature[5] is the more remarkable because his reign left little physical trace in Egypt. The few known occurrences of his cartouche include two in a Greek context: on a scarab in a late eighth-century grave at Pithecusa,[6] and a Phoenician

[1] A 7, 112, fig. 131.
[2] H 27, 65.
[3] Manetho, *FGrH* 609 F 2 (p. 48).
[4] P–W *s.v.* 'Diodorus' 670–2.
[5] P–W *s.v.* 'Bokchoris' 666–8.
[6] *AR* 1957, 41.

faience flask, showing Bakenrenef flanked by deities over bound Nubian prisoners, among early seventh-century Greek pottery in a grave in Etruscan Tarquinia.[7]

The Homeric epics give some clues to the earliest Greek contacts with Egypt. In the *Iliad*, Achilles rejects Agamemnon's gifts in these terms:

> Not if he offered me ten and twenty times as much
> as now he does – not even if more came from elsewhere –
> as much as comes in to Orchomenus, or to Thebes –
> Egyptian Thebes, where the most treasures lie in the houses
> and which has a hundred gates, with two hundred men
> sallying through each with their horses and chariots –
> not even if he gave me as much as the sand and the dust –
> not even then could Agamemnon change my mood. (IX. 379–86)

Orchomenus should normally go with Boeotian Thebes: the surprise switch to Egyptian Thebes provides the only mention of Egypt in the *Iliad*. But this is no inorganic interpolation, for without it the rhetorical crescendo of the whole passage would be spoilt.[8] The poet had learned of the great city far up the Nile, endowed by the Greeks with a Greek name from their first acquaintance. Does his reference enshrine a recollection of the remote age when Thebes was the capital of the New Kingdom, and when Cretans carrying Kamares vases were depicted on its tomb-paintings? Not necessarily. Thebes was still splendid – and its splendours liable to exaggeration at a distance – in the troubled eighth century: Shabako did much to restore it.[9] In the seventh, its sack by the Assyrians, described with terrible eloquence by the prophet Nahum (3 : 8–10), could have drawn attention to how rich it had been. But *Iliad* IX can hardly be later than the *Odyssey*, which is pre-Saïte, for its Egypt is a land of kinglets with no dominant pharaoh.

The poet of the *Odyssey* knows that Egypt is reached by way of Crete, and is the land of the Egypt River (IV. 447, 581; XIV. 246–58) – not yet called Nile: that name is first used by Hesiod (*Theog.* 338). Here, Menelaus made his fortune out of collecting gifts. From Thebes he got two silver baths, a pair of three-legged cauldrons, and ten talents of gold; Helen was given a golden distaff and a silver work-basket on wheels that we can identify as Phoenician (*Od.* IV. 125–32). Like Thebes itself, Menelaus' benefactors are given Greek names (IV. 126, 228). An exception is the Egyptian-sounding Thōn whose wife gave Helen a magic drug.[10] Egypt, the poet explains, produces the most medicinal herbs and its people are skilled physicians (IV. 227–31). Here is some

---

[7] B 96, 106–8; *Mon. Ant.* 8 (1898) pls. 2–4.
[8] B 93A, esp. 9–10.
[9] B 93A, 16, n. 32.
[10] Cf. Hdt. II. 113–16; Hellanicus, *FGrH* 4 F 153; Strabo 800, Thonis.

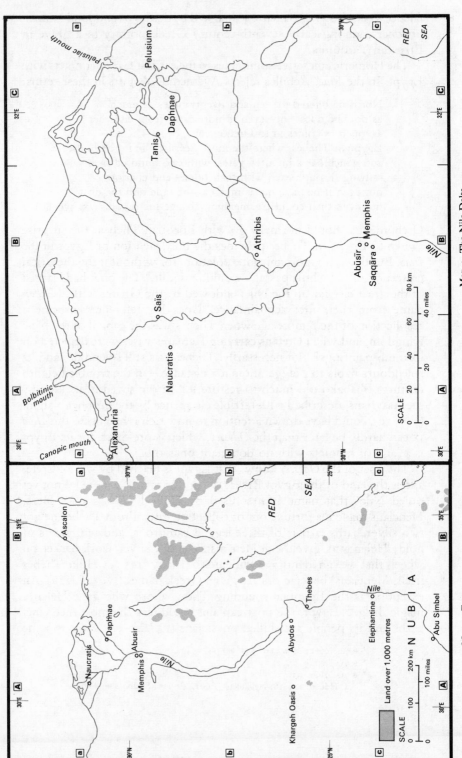

Map 3. The Nile Delta.

Map 2. Egypt.

genuine local colour, for Egyptian use of sedative and anodyne drugs is well attested and the repute of Egyptian practitioners continued.[11]

Later in the narrative, Odysseus tells a plausible story of a raid on Egypt. He pretends to be a Cretan who had taken his nine pirate ships on the five days' journey to anchor in the Egypt River. His men, sent to spy out the land, rashly disobeyed his orders and took prematurely to plundering the fields, killing the Egyptians and carrying off their wives and children. So the nearby king came swiftly from his city with horse and foot and scattered the raiders. Some he took alive for forced labour, but the leader on surrendering was spared, and stayed seven years in the country, making a fortune out of the good-natured Egyptians. In the end he left with a Phoenician sea-captain who promised to take him to Sidon, but would have sold him on the African coast had he not been shipwrecked (XIV. 246–316). In another version the Egyptians hand him over as a gift to a Greek Cypriot king (XVII. 424–44).

Everything in this story rings true in an eighth- or early seventh-century context: the shameless Greek piracy, with a special view to kidnapping slaves (these are the men of Yawan who, Ezekiel was to say (27: 13) 'traded the persons of men' in the harbour of Tyre); the Phoenician trafficking in the direction of Carthage; the vulnerability of Egypt; the Delta kinglet. One feature of both the Menelaus and the Odysseus stories remains true: the good nature of the Egyptians. Unless prevented by the government of the day, foreigners usually find it easy to make money out of them. In the Saïte period, many Greeks were to try.

II. PSAMMETICHUS I AND THE FIRST SETTLEMENT OF GREEKS AND CARIANS

Herodotus tells how Psammetichus I (664–610 B.C.) was the son of Necho I, who had been killed by Shabako. He fled, but was brought back after the Nubian withdrawal, and became one of twelve Delta kings. Having escaped from the enmity of his fellow-kings into the northern marshes, he was told by the oracle of Buto that 'vengeance would come from the sea when bronze men appeared'. Subsequently Ionian and Carian pirates in bronze armour arrived in Egypt and ravaged the plains. Psammetichus recognized the fulfilment of the oracle, persuaded them to join him by great promises, and with their help overcame the other kings and mastered Egypt (II. 147–52).

A variant oracle story told by Polyaenus (VII. 3) must derive from the fourth-century Aristagoras of Miletus (cf. *FGrH* 608 F 9), who wrote two or more books of *Aigyptiaka*. This time it is the oracle of Zeus

[11] B 112 on Hdt. II. 84; B 105; B 108; B 106.

Ammon that is said to have warned 'Tementhes king of Egypt' to
'beware of the cocks'. Psammetichus discovered this, and from Pigres
the Carian who was with him he learned that the Carians had been the
first to fit crests to their helmets; he thus caught the meaning of the
oracle, brought Carian mercenaries to Memphis, and with their help
won a battle 'round the temple of Isis five stades from the palace'. 'From
these Carians a part of Memphis was called Karomemphitai.'

In both stories riddling oracles foreshadow hoplite armour, new to
the Egyptians. This sort of oracular ambiguity is Greek, not Egyptian.
The stories must be Greek inventions. But they have authentic features.
'Tementhes' must be Tantamani, who as late as 656 was still in some
degree recognized as king in Thebes. Pigres is a good Carian name, and
the circumstantial detail about Memphis carries conviction.

Neither author realizes what we know from Assyrian sources: that
Necho I had been set up as king by Esarhaddon, had been shackled and
brought to Nineveh for treating with Tantamani's father Taharqa, and
then forgiven and sent back to Saïs. Psammetichus I began his reign
as an Assyrian nominee in Athribis under the alien name of
Nabashezibanni.[12] Egyptian pride seems to have suppressed the fact of
Assyrian domination and Saïte vassalage. Herodotus' only information
about Assyrian intervention in Egypt is his version of the expedition
of Sennacherib in 701, when the Assyrian came down like a wolf on
the fold but withdrew without fighting (II. 141).

Assyrian records provide another fact of importance. At some time
between his accession and 639, the date of the Rassam Cylinder, Gyges
of Lydia stopped sending his messenger to Nineveh to do homage to
Ashurbanipal. Instead 'he sent his forces to the aid of Tushamilki king
of Egypt, who had thrown off the yoke of my sovereignty'.[13] (Tushamilki
must be a mistaken rendering of Pishamitki, Accadian for Psamtik,
Psammetichus.[14] A better shot at the name was made by the scribe who
listed among Nebuchadrezzar's Egyptian prisoners a Pusamiski, keeper
of the royal monkeys.[15]) Ashurbanipal's curses on Gyges were rewarded:
the Cimmerians invaded Lydia, Gyges died, and his son reaffirmed his
loyalty. But cursing has its limitations. Ashurbanipal never won Egypt
back.

The forces sent by Gyges must surely have been Greek and Carian
soldiers. Gyges had recruited a Carian prince, Arselis of Mylae, to help
overthrow his predecessor Candaules.[16] Later, King Alyattes of Lydia

---

[12] Editions E and B: B 57, 12–15, 31–41. Great Egyptian tablets: B 68A, II 159–65; B 44, II §900–5.
Rassam cylinder: B 68A, II 6–15; B 44, II §772–5.
[13] Rassam cylinder: B 68A, II 20–3; B 44, II §784–5.
[14] B 68A, II 22, n. 6.   [15] B 77, 923–4.
[16] Plut. *Quaest. Graec.* 45 = *Mor.* 302 A.

used Colophonian cavalrymen and outwitted them when they went on strike (Polyaenus VII. 2.2). While still crown prince, Croesus collected mercenaries on the west coast of Asia Minor to help in a campaign of his father's;[17] as king, he had a mercenary army which he unwisely sent home – presumably to the Ionian and Carian towns – in the winter when Cyrus attacked him (Hdt. 1. 77).

It does not follow, however, that the first 'bronze men from the sea' were sent by Gyges. It is quite possible that Psammetichus began by recruiting casually arrived pirates, then, as Diodorus says (1. 66.12) 'sent for mercenaries from Caria and Ionia', and after having promoted himself from King of Saïs – the title the Assyrians had given his father Necho – to the 'King of Egypt' of the Rassam Cylinder, took the final step of throwing over Assyrian suzerainty with the help of still more Greek and Carian troops from Gyges. Though official dating puts Psammetichus I's first year in 664, it may have taken him many years to consolidate his power. For the first nine years there is no dated monument of his with a known provenance. In 656 the 'Adoption stele' celebrates Psammetichus I's great diplomatic coup of having his daughter, Nitocris, adopted by the God's Wife of Amun at Thebes, Shepenupet II, herself the aunt of Tantamani.[18] But even after this, he may still have had to combat rivals or rebels in the Delta. As the example of Amyrtaeus in the fifth century shows, it is possible to hold out in the marshes for a long time. Psammetichus I's final assertion of independence against Assyria could have been as late as the 640s.

III. NAUCRATIS

This activity of the Greeks in Egypt must be kept in mind when we consider Strabo's account (XVII. 801–2) of the origin of the Greek settlement of Naucratis. The Milesians came with thirty ships, he says, and founded 'the Milesian fort' at the Bolbitinic mouth of the Nile in the reign of Psammetichus I. In due course, they moved upstream, defeated Inarōs in a sea-battle and founded Naucratis. There is a suggestion of Egyptian resistance, if not of fighting, in a further fragment from Aristagoras of Miletus (FGrH 608 F 8): one of three possible explanations of the name Gynaikospolis, 'Woman's city', given by the Greeks to the Egyptian town opposite Naucratis on the west side of the river, was that this was the only town so womanly as not to prevent the first Greek settlers landing when they sailed upstream.

We have no other satisfactory evidence about this Inarōs, but as a name associated with Libya it fits well with the extreme western Delta,[19]

---

[17] Nicolaus of Damascus, FGrH 90 F 65.
[18] Adoption stele: B 93, §942–58; B 94; B 127; B 107, 48–54.   [19] B 110, 25, n. 1.

and Strabo's story is consistent with the evidence we have. The 'Milesian fort' has not yet been found. The first Corinthian pottery at Naucratis dates from *c.* 630–620; the East Greek pottery there is less easy to date and may be earlier.[20] The literary and archaeological evidence is thus compatible with a wide range of dating, between Psammetichus I's accession and *c.* 620, for the foundation of Naucratis.

Herodotus says that it was Amasis who 'gave Naucratis to the Greeks as a city to live in' (II. 178). Presumably this refers to a new charter for the Naucratites under Amasis; if Herodotus thought that Amasis founded Naucratis, he was wrong. Later Greeks had access to better information than he on the subject, for Naucratis continued as an important city into Roman times, and local traditions were collected and published. The learned Apollonius of Rhodes wrote a poem, *The foundation of Naucratis* (Ath. 283D). A Naucratite, Polycharmus, wrote a book *On Aphrodite* incorporating local history; he writes of a Naucratite merchant who landed at Cyprian Paphus and bought a statuette of Aphrodite, which he held to have saved his ship on the homeward journey and dedicated in the temple of Aphrodite at Naucratis (*FGrH* 640 F 1). It is worth noting that this incident was given a date, though it has come down to us in a corrupt form as the twenty-third Olympiad (688/5), which is impossibly early. Charon (*FGrH* 612) and Philistos (*FGrH* 615) are names of Naucratite historians. We may take it that Strabo's foundation story derives from local tradition. It is echoed in a Milesian inscription of A.D. 195 which glories in Miletus' having been 'the mother-city of great cities in the Pontus and in Egypt' (*CIG* 2878 lines 1–7): Naucratis is surely meant.

What seems to have begun as a Milesian military fort became, from at least *c.* 620 onwards, a great Greek trading city adjoining an Egyptian quarter. Greek merchants of all races, Aeolians, Ionians and Dorians, here lived side by side. There was nothing like it in the Greek world until the Panhellenic foundations, Thurii and Amphipolis, of Periclean Athens; but whereas these did not maintain a balance between different kinds of Greek and soon turned against their mother city, Naucratis continued without serious conflict for centuries. There is an analogy between Naucratis and Shanghai while it was still a treaty port, run by the representatives of various European states. Naucratis' development as a trading city came at a significant time. The most important Milesian foundations in the Black Sea area are synchronous with it. The first Greek pottery at Olbia also dates from *c.* 620. Olbia opened the Ukraine to Greek commerce; from now on it was possible for Aeginetan merchantmen to bring corn through the Hellespont to the Peloponnese, as they were doing when Xerxes arrived at the Hellespont in 481. Cyrene

[20] A 7, 121.

had been settled in the 630s, at the same time as the first Greek trader reached the silver of Tartessus (blown off course from an Egyptian trade-voyage; Hdt. IV. 152). Massalia, the key to trade with Gaul and the overland tin route from Britain, was founded by Phocaea *c*. 600. The last third of the seventh century brought about a prodigious acceleration of Greek trade. New wealth accrued to the East Greek entrepreneurs, to the Aeginetan carriers, to the Megarians who as founders of Byzantium were in a key position to benefit from the Black Sea trade, and to the great entrepôt of Corinth. This new wealth distorted the pattern of Greek social life and increased political tension in many Greek states. In Attica, it meant that the rich could find a richer market in neighbouring states to sell debt-slaves and agricultural produce, while at home the poor were expropriated. Hence the Athenian crisis which led, in 594, to the legislation of Solon.

The Greeks must have bought corn from Egypt. Bacchylides, writing in the first half of the fifth century, describes how

> corn-carrying ships over the gleaming sea
> bear from Egypt the greatest wealth. (Fr. 20B 14–16 Snell)

Papyrus and linen will also have been carried. Originally, papyrus must have come to Greece by way of Phoenicia. The Phoenician port Gubla, Greek Byblos, was the entrepôt. The Greek word for the papyrus plant, βύβλος (whence Bible) was in use by the time of the *Odyssey* (XXI. 391).[21] Linen is one of the staples that Ezekiel says came to Tyre from Egypt (27: 7). We should expect papyrus and linen to be sent directly from Egypt to Greece after Naucratis had been established. The seagoing Greeks could make good use of papyrus for ships' ropes as well as writing material, and linen for sails as well as clothing. In 396 B.C. the pharaoh of newly-independent Egypt gave the Spartans for their war effort against Persia equipment for a hundred triremes, and five hundred thousand measures of corn (Diod. XIV. 79.4). Alum was another staple (Hdt. II. 180). Greece imported many more Egyptian trinkets in the seventh century than previously; during the sixth a faience factory was operating at Naucratis. But better Egyptian artifacts also began to come direct into Greece, especially to Crete and the Samian Heraeum: carved ivory and fine bronzes.[22]

In return, the Greeks exported wine to Egypt. The Egyptians did produce some wine, but Greek wine was far superior, and Herodotus was at fault in remarking that there were no vines in Egypt (Hdt. II. 77).[23] Around the turn of the seventh and sixth centuries, Sappho's brother Charaxus was a merchant who carried Lesbian wine to Egypt

---

[21] Cf. B 48, 101–7. Above, p. 25. [22] A 7, 125–9, 141–2.
[23] B 112 *ad loc.*

(Strabo 808). It may be because of him that the name Sappho appears at Naucratis. Wine-jars and wine-jar handles at Naucratis testify to the trade. Herodotus tells us that the empty jars were filled with water in his time and put out for the use of travellers along the desert route from Egypt to Palestine (Hdt. III. 6), and indeed many Greek wine-jars have been found east of Pelusium, though not in fact all along the route. Olive oil, much superior to Egyptian castor oil (cf. Hdt. II. 94), is another possible Greek export. There is a story that Plato defrayed the cost of his journey to Egypt by selling oil there (Plut. *Solon* 2.8). But above all, Greeks could profit by exporting silver to Egypt. The Egyptians had no supplies of their own, but had esteemed the metal from earliest times, and the purchasing power of silver was greater in Egypt than elsewhere. Coined Greek silver is found in Egyptian hoards from the later sixth century on. Much of it came from Thrace and Macedonia which were rich in mines. There was probably a three-cornered trade: Aeginetans and East Greeks could ship woollens and other goods to the Thracian and Macedonian coast, sell them for silver and take the silver to Egypt.[24] East Greek interest in this coast was strong. Aenus had been settled there from Lesbos and Cyme (Strabo VII Fr. 51), Abdera from Clazomenae (Hdt. I. 168). Colophonians expelled by Lydia worked the mines near the mouth of the Strymon with other Ionians;[25] silver mines were among the attractions that led Histiaeus of Miletus to settle a colony here towards the end of the sixth century (Hdt. V. 23). The silver coins brought by Greeks to Egypt were kept for their bullion value, as the presence of uncoined silver and of gashed and drilled coins shows. At Mīt-Rahīna there were only twenty-three coins in a hoard of silver ingots weighing 75 kg.[26] Unminted silver must have been an article of Greek trade with Egypt from the beginning.

After speaking of Amasis' privileges to Naucratis, Herodotus goes on to say:

Naucratis was anciently the only trading post, and there was no other in Egypt. If anyone came to any of the other mouths of the Nile, he had to swear that he had not come there on purpose, and after swearing, sail in the same ship to the Canopic mouth; but if the ship was unable to sail because of contrary winds, he had to carry the cargo in barges around the Delta until he arrived in Naucratis. Such was the privilege accorded to Naucratis. (II. 179)

In the context, 'anciently' should refer to Amasis' reign. But the contrast is between the privileged status of Naucratis and its curtailed rights under the Persians. The old privilege had implied no restriction

---

[24] H 73A, nos. 1634-40, 1642; G 33A, 143-4.   [25] Suda *s.v.* Χρυσὸς Κολοφώνιος.
[26] H 73A, no. 1636; H 47A, 44.

of Greek settlement elsewhere in Egypt. Greeks could live in other places, and trade with goods as long as these, if they were imports, had passed through Naucratis. What it had done was to prevent any other Delta town from competing with Naucratis; and any Phoenician or other non-Greek ship was forced to put in to this one Greek port in Egypt. Thus Naucratis was privileged indeed. It was in the interest of the Saïte pharaohs to treat it well. Their capital, Saïs, was not on the Nile; Naucratis, only ten miles away, served as its port. The Egyptians had never taken the initiative over Mediterranean trade: no pharaoh had ever thought of developing the site of Alexandria, where they merely set a garrison to ward off pirates (Strabo 792). But it was worth their while to give trading privileges to Naucratis, as long as these were paid for. Members of a chartered city could hardly practice kidnapping and piracy, as the first Milesian invaders must have done. In the fourth century, if not earlier, the pharaoh could insist on a 10 per cent tax on imports into Naucratis and the goods produced there. A stele of Nectanebes I (378–360) makes this clear, and incidentally speaks of imports of wood which could have been brought into Naucratis from Phoenicia or Cyprus:

And His Majesty said: 'Let there be given (*a*) the tithe of the gold and of the silver, of the timber and of the worked wood, and of everything which comes from the Greek Sea, and of all goods (?) which are reckoned to the King's Domain in the city called Henwe; and (*b*) the tithe of the gold and of the silver and of all things which are produced in Pi-emrōye, called [Nau]kratis, on the bank of the 'Anu, and which are reckoned to the King's Domain, to be a temple-endowment of my mother Neith for all time, in excess of what has existed formerly. And let them be converted into one portion of an ox, one fat *ro*-goose and five measures (*mnw*) of wine, as a continual daily offering, the delivery of them to be at the treasury of my mother Neith, for she is the mistress of the ocean, and it is she who bestows its bounty...' And His Majesty ordered that this should be recorded upon this stela, which should be placed in Naukratis on the bank of the 'Anu; thus would his goodness be remembered to the end of eternity. (Trans. Gunn)[27]

Petrie's incomplete and non-stratigraphical excavation of Naucratis in 1884–5,[28] supplemented by Hogarth's in 1899 and 1903,[29] unearthed numerous temples, identified by means of the painted or inscribed votive texts found on pottery in their sites (fig. 2). The temple of Apollo, which Herodotus says was built by the Milesians (II. 178), was surrounded by an enclosure wall; it goes back to the early days of the colony. Next to it is the sanctuary and temple of Hera which Herodotus

[27] B 110, 28 and n. 108, quoting B 97; B 101; B 119.   [28] B 116; B 100.
[29] B 102; B 103; B 120; cf. A 7, 118–33.

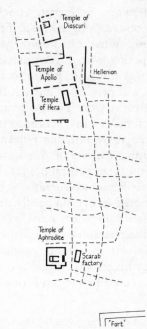

2. Sketch plan of the site at Naucratis.
(After A 7, 119, fig. 137.)

says was built by the Samians. Here, far from home, the buildings of
two perennial enemies stood side by side, just as in Tehran the great
enclosures of the Russian and British embassies stand opposite one
another. Further north was the temple of the Dioscuri, and some way
to the south that of Aphrodite, mentioned by Polycharmus (above,
p. 38) though not named by Herodotus. The Aeginetans, says Herodotus, built a temple of Zeus; this has not been found. To the east of
the temple of Apollo was the Hellenium, evidently dating from the time
of Amasis. Votive inscriptions found on the site include some to 'the
gods of the Greeks'. There was nothing like this temple elsewhere in
the Greek world, even at the great international sanctuaries. It was
erected at the common charge of four East Greek Ionian cities, Chios,
Teos, Phocaea and Clazomenae, of Aeolian Mytilene, and of four East
Greek Dorian cities, Rhodes, Cnidus, Halicarnassus and Phaselis, and
belonged to these cities jointly. Herodotus adds that they sent προστάται
τοῦ ἐμπορίου to Naucratis, and that the other cities who shared in this
had no business to do so: there is a hint here of an unsuccessful attempt
by a group of Greek states to resist the influence of the founding city
Miletus and of the major trading cities Samos and Aegina.

There were also magistrates called τιμοῦχοι (*timouchoi*) who supervised the solemn feasting in the πρυτανεῖον (*prytaneion*, town hall), on ceremonial occasions, so characteristic of the ancient Greek world (Ath. 149D). *Timouchoi* appear in aristocratically ruled Ionian cities elsewhere in the Greek world from *c.* 600 B.C. on (cf. Teos, M–L no. 30, 29); in the third century B.C. we find *timouchoi* connected with another Hellenium, at Memphis.[30] It looks, then, as if Naucratis was a city run partly by representatives of the founding cities and partly by magistrates who were chosen locally. In Hadrian's time the laws of Naucratis forbade its citizens ἐπιγαμία, intermarriage with Egyptians. This prohibition may go back to earlier times, but whatever its date it must be self-imposed, not dictated by any Egyptian government and not applicable to Greeks in Egypt who were not Naucratites.[31]

'Somehow', says Herodotus, 'attractive courtesans tend to flourish at Naucratis.' The most famous was Rhodopis, a Thracian girl, who made a fortune by her person in the reign of Amasis, and dedicated a tithe of it in the form of iron spits at Delphi which could still be seen in Herodotus' time (II. 134), piled up behind the great altar. Part of an inscription at Delphi with Rhodopis' dedication has been found; its lettering points to *c.* 550–525.[32] Second to her in fame, according to Herodotus, was Archedike (II. 135), who dedicated a vase that has been discovered at Naucratis.[33] Yet another was Doricha, whom Sappho's brother, the wine merchant Charaxus, bought and freed. We have a papyrus of a poem by Sappho, hostile to Doricha's influence on Charaxus (fr. 15 (8) Lobel–Page). Herodotus thought it was Rhodopis at whom Sappho 'gibed in a poem', but he appears to have confused the two courtesans, as Athenaeus, himself a Naucratite and prodigiously learned, pointed out (569B–D). The date of Rhodopis, who could afford to retire early, is much too late for Sappho who flourished in 612/609 (Suda) or 600/599 (Jerome). The temple of Aphrodite must have had especial importance for courtesans. A certain Doris, presumably a member of the same profession, dedicated a love charm there.[34]

IV. OTHER GREEK AND CARIAN SETTLEMENTS IN EGYPT

Psammetichus I, says Herodotus, gave the Ionians and Carians who had helped him to power lands opposite each other, with the Nile flowing between them: to these were given the name of Stratopeda, camps. They were in the eastern Delta on the Pelusiac branch of the Nile, only a short way from the sea (II. 154). So far, they have not been identified. Petrie

---

[30] B 129, no. 30.
[31] B 125, no. 506; cf. B 89, 28; B 110, 17–20.
[32] A 36, 102.
[33] B 102, pl. 6. 108.
[34] B 100, 66, no. 798.

unearthed some burials at Nebesha[35] which he later believed to have been of Carian mercenaries from the Stratopeda, because of the type of spear-heads found with them.[36] But the total absence here of Carian inscriptions, which elsewhere in Egypt are numerous, makes this identification doubtful. Amasis later removed the Ionians and Carians from the Stratopeda to make them his bodyguard at Memphis; but the ruins of their buildings, and the slipways for their ships, could still be seen in Herodotus' time.

Besides the Stratopeda, Herodotus tells us that Psammetichus concentrated garrisons in three places: at Elephantine (the island opposite Aswan) on the Nubian border; at Marea, west of what is now Alexandria, against the Libyans; and at Daphnae in the east (II. 30). They were manned with Egyptians, of whom a great number deserted to settle in Nubia. But although Herodotus does not expressly say so, Greek soldiers were posted in them too. Marea remains unexcavated and there is still some controversy about its exact site.[37] Elephantine, as we shall see, served as the base from which Greeks and non-Greeks set out on the Nubian expedition of 591 B.C. (below, p. 50). Daphnae cannot fail to be identical with Tell Defenneh, excavated in 1886.[38] Here there were fragments of Greek painted pottery from the late seventh century, found in two rooms of a massive square building, either a fort or a store-house, dating from the reign of Psammetichus I. In the sixth century non-Egyptians made their homes there. Jeremiah fled to Daphnae – Hebrew Tahpanhes – with a Jewish contingent to escape the Babylonian captivity in 582. Here he proclaimed (43: 6–7; cf. 46) to his fellow-refugees the coming Babylonian conquest of Egypt – a prophecy that remained happily unfulfilled. The great majority of Greek pottery fragments at Daphnae date from between 570 and the Persian conquest of Egypt in 525. Fragments of iron weapons and scale armour confirm that Amasis had a Greek garrison here. Some 20 km from Daphnae, south of Pelusium, is another fort which is much greater, covering some 4 ha. Here recent Israeli excavations have brought to light Greeks cremation burials and many sixth-century Greek amphorae.[39] It may be Jeremiah's Migdol.[40]

We have seen (p. 36) how the *Karomemphitai* originated from the battle for Memphis won by Psammetichus I's Carian mercenaries. Strictly speaking the *Karomemphitai* were the descendants of the Carians who now settled in Memphis and married Egyptian women. The quarter they inhabited was the *Karikon*. They buried their dead in a western cemetery in the region of Saqqāra which was evidently broken

35 B 115, 7, 17–18 ('Cypriote').   36 B 118, 64.
37 B 112 on Hdt. II. 18.   38 B 115, 47–8; D 32, 40–4, 57–60.
39 A 7, 134–5, fig. 156.   40 Jeremiah 44: 1, 46: 14; Ezekiel 29: 10.

3. Grave stele from Abusir. The laying-out (*prothesis*) is shown in the Greek manner; the setting, technique and winged disk are Egyptian; the inscription Carian. About 500 B.C. Height 27 cm. (Berlin (East) Staatliche Museen 19553; cf. B 113A, 64–5, pl. 30.)

up during the last phase of Egyptian independence in the fourth century. Many reused gravestones have been discovered, most recently during excavations in 1968–75 of the catacomb for mummified sacred baboons. A good number of these are limestone stelai in the form of a 'false door' with inscriptions only in Carian letters, similar to Greek but not entirely decipherable and so far untranslatable.[41] Others show conventional Egyptian funeral representations, evidently carved by Egyptian craftsmen, but with Carian as well as hieroglyphic inscriptions. The hieroglyphic inscriptions sometimes give an Egyptian name for the deceased, but sometimes a name which might be Anatolian.[42] The base of a statue of Neith from Saïs gives the genealogy of a certain Pedineith who was evidently the son of a Carian man, KRR, and of an Egyptian woman, Neithemhat.[43] Though this is not a Karomemphite inscription,

[41] B 113A, 29–43, nos. 12–38, 47–48d; B 113B, 1–6 (A, B).
[42] B 113A, nos. 1, 2, 7 (pp. 20–2, 25–6, 58–61, 86–7; pls. 1.1, 2.1, 6, 31.1, 2, 35.1); B 113B, E (pp. 17–20, pl. 1), F (pp. 20–7, pl. 2; cf. B 113A, 92), G (pp. 28–31, pl. 3), H (pp. 31–5, pl. 4a).
[43] B 113B, M (pp. 55–64, pl. 8a).

it surely illustrates what had been happening at Memphis as well as elsewhere in Egypt. There cannot have been enough Carian and Greek women in Egypt for the immigrant mercenaries to marry, and we must take it that Egyptian repugnance to the ritually unclean cow-eating foreigners (Hdt. II. 41) could sometimes be overcome. Several grave-stones from Saqqāra and Abūsīr, deriving from the Karomemphite cemetery, also show conventional Egyptian funerary imagery, but are from the workshop of one or more East Greeks or Carians. Here Egyptian prototypes have been copied but not wholly understood. Scenes in which offerings are brought to Osiris, with Isis standing behind him, and to the statue of Apis, are fairly successful Egyptianizing work, but contain several solecisms which no Egyptian artist would have committed. Of especial interest are adjoining representations of the *prothesis* or laying-out of the corpse in the manner of Greek funerals, surrounded by mourners (fig. 3).[44] One gravestone has a touching, un-Egyptian carving of a man and woman taking their last affectionate farewell.[45] These scenes show a curious adaptation of Greek dress to Egyptian conditions. A man seems to have worn a thin, almost transparent linen *chiton* reaching to the calves, with sleeves almost to the elbows, and a short *chlamys* on the shoulders. A full hair-style, ending abruptly at the nape, is suggestive of an Egyptian wig. Women's dress was a distinctive trailing *chiton*, hitched up over the girdle in front to fall in a deep fold.

There were *Hellenomemphitai*[46] whose name must be explained in the same way as the *Karomemphitai*. Corinthian and East Greek pottery at Memphis dates back as far as does that at Naucratis; at Saqqāra a bronze griffin cauldron-attachment dates to the mid-seventh century.[47] Greek settlement at Memphis in Psammetichus I's time is confirmed by the name of the father of the Greek who purchased Rhodopis for a time: he was called Hephaestopolis ('city of Ptah', i.e. Memphis: Hdt. II. 134.3) and must have been born in the seventh century. East Greek pottery was imported into Memphis throughout the sixth century, and from this period comes the bronze sheath of the base of an Egyptian statuette, with a dedication to 'Zeus of Egyptian Thebes' in Ionic lettering by one Melanthius (fig. 4),[48] and a dedication in Ionic Greek by one Pythermus on an Egyptian statuette.[49]

At Abydos we find more Greek mercenary graffiti, of the sixth and fifth centuries, on the funerary temple of Seti I, which the Greeks took for the temple of Memnon, son of Eos, the handsome dusky warrior

---

[44] B 113A, nos. 3–6 (pp. 22–5, 70–86, pls. 4.1, 2, 5.1, 33.1–34.2). Abūsīr stele: B 113A, 91; A 7, 135, fig. 159.   [45] B 113A, no. 3 (pp. 22, 61–70, pls. 2.2, 3, 32); A 7, fig. 158.
[46] Aristagoras of Miletus, *FGrH* 608 F 9.   [47] A 7, 135.
[48] A 36, 355, 358, no. 49, pl. 70.   [49] A 36, 355, no. 50, pl. 70.

4. Egyptian bronze base for a statuette from Memphis, with Greek dedicatory inscription. 'Melanthios dedicated me, a statue (*agalma*) to Zeus of Thebes.' Third quarter of the sixth century B.C. 91 × 43 × 30 cm. (Private Collection; after F. Ll. Griffith, *CR* 5 (1891) 77–9; cf. A 36, 355, pl. 70, no. 49.)

who fought for Priam at Troy. At the temples of Thebes, farther yet up the Nile, dedications of Greek pottery are found from early in the sixth century. They include a range of fine East Greek vases, including one showing an Ionian festival in which the ship of Dionysus is carried, which must have been deliberately chosen or even painted for the way its theme echoed the important local ceremony of carrying the bark of the Sun god. There are scraps too of a superb Athenian volute crater, of the same hand and quality as the famous François Vase.[50]

The Greek population in Egypt became numerous. Herodotus says that Apries had 30,000 Greek and Carian mercenaries. Outside the garrison towns and Naucratis there were other Greek settlements. Hecataeus named islands in the Nile called Ephesus, Chios, Lesbos, Cyprus and Samos (*FGrH* 1 F 310). These may be only Greek names for native places, like Abydos and Thebes which were not Abydene or Theban settlements. But the Nile islands bear the names of Greek cities and islands known to have engaged in Egyptian commerce, so they could be Greek trading-posts. A 'New City' (Nea Polis) in Upper Egypt may well be a Greek settlement too. Herodotus observed that at neighbouring Chemmis (Akhmīm) there were gymnastic contests for prizes in the Greek manner (II. 91): racial admixture seems the only way of accounting for this. (See B 108A.)

In Herodotus' day Greeks were scattered all over Egypt. There is a vivid example of how self-evident their presence was. Among Egyptian taboos was one against eating the head of a sacrificial animal. The Egyptians curse it, and 'where there is a market and resident Greek

[50] A 36, 314; A 7, 137–8; fragments in Moscow (H 8, 77.2) and Basel.

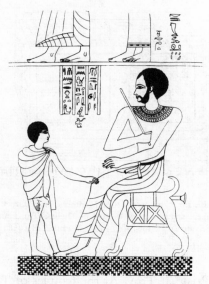

5. Tomb painting at Siwa Oasis, from the tomb of Siamun. Fifth century B.C. (After A. Fakhry, *Annales du Service* 40 (1940) 795, fig. 87 = B 99, 86; cf. A 7, 159.)

traders, they take it to the market and sell it; where there are no Greeks they throw it into the river' (Hdt. II. 39). By the fifth century, there were even Greeks living in the oases of the western desert. Herodotus speaks of the 'Samians of the Aeschrionian tribe' living in the 'isles of the blest', evidently the great oasis of Khargeh, seven days' journey from Thebes (III. 26). In the oasis of Siwa stood the temple of the oracle of Ammon, controlled by a local Libyan dynasty recognizing the suzerainty of the pharaoh: the cartouche of Amasis has been found here, and he is shown sacrificing to the right of the temple entrance, opposite the local ruler Sutekhirdis similarly employed on the left.[51] Among the Greeks this oracle, reached by a desert track from Cyrene, gained surprising prestige, possibly as early as Amasis' reign and certainly from the beginning of the Persian period.[52] At Siwa a tomb-painting, dating from some time between the 26th and 30th Dynasties, shows Siamun, a man with Greek hairstyle but Egyptian dress, with his Egyptian wife and his white-skinned son wearing a Greek chlamys – a striking instance of intermarriage (fig. 5).[53]

[51] B 98, 90–1, pl. 19.   [52] A 49, 194–291.
[53] B 98, 132–59; B 99, 85–95; B 114, 66, n. 108.

V. GREEK FORCES IN CAMPAIGNS OF THE SAÏTE DYNASTY

In 616 and again in 610, we find Psammetichus I sending armies into northern Syria to support the Assyrians against the insurgent power of the Neo-Babylonian kingdom. Necho II (610–594) continued his father's policy. In 609 he marched into the Levant in an attempt to help Ashuruballit, the last king of Assyria. Josiah, the king of Judah, met his death trying to stop Necho's advance at Megiddo in Palestine (II Kings 23: 29). Herodotus speaks of Necho's victory at Magdolos, possibly confusing Megiddo with one of the places named Migdol, *Magdolos*. Necho, he adds, consecrated the clothes he wore during this battle by sending them to Branchidae (Didyma) of the Milesians (II. 159). This is the first official Egyptian dedication known to have been sent to a shrine in the Greek homeland; the choice of Miletus is appropriate. Herodotus does not mention the major battle of Carchemish in 605 when Necho was defeated by Nebuchadrezzar and abandoned the Egyptian intervention in Syria. A Greek greave, and a Greek bronze shield of the later seventh century – this last found in an arrow-riddled building together with Egyptian objects, some of them with Necho's cartouche – make it certain that Greek soldiers fought in this battle.[54]

Necho II devoted great effort to the building of a canal to link the Nile with the Gulf of Suez, a project finally completed by Darius I. When the canal proved abortive, Herodotus tells us that 'he turned to military matters, and triremes were built, some for the northern sea (the Mediterranean), some in the Arabian gulf (the Red Sea) looking to the Erythraean Sea (the Indian Ocean), whose slipways can be seen. And he used these ships as he had need' (II. 158–9). Necho had excellent cause to build warships once the failure at Carchemish had brought Phoenicia under Babylonian rule, so much more aggressive than the Assyrian had been in its declining years. Phoenician ramming warships could make short work of traditional Egyptian craft. The earliest history of triremes is obscure, but they were known to Hipponax (fr. 28.2 West) who wrote at the time of the fall of Sardis in the 540s (Marmor Parium, *FGrH* 244 A 42). It may be that Herodotus is using this specialized term carelessly, but what was possible in the 540s could well have been anticipated in the 590s. Herodotus does not say who built Necho's ships for him, and recent controversy has pitted the claims of Greek shipbuilders against Phoenician.[55] But it would be strange if Necho did not employ both, as Sennacherib had done in 694 B.C. (above, p. 19). Phoenician refugees must have been available, for we are told Necho used them to circumnavigate Africa (IV. 142). So were Greeks; and we are expressly told that the Stratopeda where Necho's father had

[54] A 7, 51, 115.　　　　[55] B 90; B 109; B 111; B 91; B 113.

6. Graffito by a Greek mercenary on the leg of a colossal statue at Abu Simbel (see text for translation). 591 B.C. The letters are 4 to 9 cm high. (M–L no. 7.)

installed Greek troops had slipways for ships (II. 154). There was no possibility of recruiting sailors on a large scale from Babylonian-occupied Phoenicia, and in the reign of Psammetichus II (595–589) we find the Saïte navy manned by Greeks, as is shown by the titles of his admiral Hor: 'chief of the fighting ships in the Great Green (the Mediterranean) and commander of the Greeks (*Hȝw-nbw*)'.[56]

To the third year of Psammetichus II, 591, as we know from a stele erected at Tanis which complements a text from Karnak,[57] must be dated the campaign into Nubia which provides the most interesting documentation of Greek mercenaries. Scratched on the legs of the colossi of Rameses II before the great temple of Abu Simbel in Nubia – colossi that had been carved over six centuries earlier – are the most celebrated and interesting of the graffiti left by the mercenaries:

When King Psammetichus came to Elephantine, those who sailed with Psamatichos son of Theocles wrote this; and they came above Kerkis as far as the river allowed; and Potasimto had command of those of foreign speech and Amasis of the Egyptians; and Archon the son of Amoibichos wrote us and Peleqos son of Eudamos (fig. 6).

Names are added: 'Helesibios the Teian'; 'Telephos the Ialysian wrote me'; 'Python son of Amoibichos'; '...and Krithis wrote me'; 'Pabis the Colophonian with Psammatas'; 'Anaxanor the Ialysian ...when the King first brought his army...Psamatichos'.[58]

East Greek Doric and Ionian dialect and letter forms are mixed in these graffiti. Possibly some of the names without ethnics are those of second- or third-generation settlers; Psamatichos son of Theocles must have been born in Egypt.

Potasimto's sarcophagus survives, as does a libation-bowl of his and an *ushabti*-figure. The sarcophagus confirms that he had been commander

[56] B 117, 18, pls. 15, 20.   [57] B 124.
[58] M–L no. 7.

of 'those of foreign speech', as the Greeks in Egypt called themselves, for he is given the title of 'commander of the Greeks'. A statuette of an Amasis 'who fulfils what His Majesty desires in Nubia' also survives and appropriately has the title 'commander of the Egyptians'.[59] The Nubian expedition is recounted by Herodotus. From the 'Letter of Aristeas' (III. 13 Pelletier), an account written in Hellenistic times of the Ptolemaic translation of the Bible from Hebrew into Greek, we learn that Jews, too, took part in this same expedition. From these the Jewish mercenaries of fifth-century Elephantine, known from their Aramaic letters, must be descended. By the time Jeremiah was prophesying in Egypt (40: 1), after 582, there were numerous Jewish communities scattered through Egypt.

Apries (589–570) agreed to help the Libyan king Adikran against the encroaching Greek settlers of Cyrene, and sent an Egyptian army against the Cyrenaeans, presumably because he could not trust his Greek mercenaries to fight other Greeks. He met with complete defeat, which unleashed an Egyptian revolt against him at home. Another general Amasis put himself at the head of this revolt. Apries, Herodotus tells us, sent his thirty thousand Carian and Ionian mercenaries against the insurgents, but they were outnumbered and beaten at the battle of Momemphis, and Apries was captured and dethroned (570: Hdt. II. 161–9). A fragmentary text from a stele at Elephantine tells of a bid by Apries to reassert himself in 570/69, with the help of 'Greeks without number in the northland'.[60] Amasis' final victory over Apries must have meant a check to Greek influence for a time.

However, Amasis (570–526) turned out to be a strong philhellene, continued to make use of Greek troops and, as we have seen (pp. 40–1), gave signal privileges to Naucratis. The withdrawal of the Greeks and Carians from the Stratopeda to Memphis (Hdt. II. 154) was not necessarily to their disadvantage. Reversing Apries' policy, Amasis contracted a friendship and an alliance with the Cyreneans, and married a Greek heiress from Cyrene, Ladice, who dedicated a statue at Cyrene which could still be seen in Herodotus' time (Hdt. II. 181–2). Amasis dedicated a gilded statue of Athena at Cyrene, and his own portrait. Cyprus, by contrast, he made tributary (II. 182; below, p. 65). In the years before Cyrus' conquest of Lydia in the 540s, Amasis was a key figure in the quadruple alliance of Egypt, Babylon, Lydia and Sparta against the Persian threat (Hdt. I. 70). Diplomatic gifts to cement this alliance survived into the fifth century to confirm that it really existed and was meant seriously. One of these was a gift from Amasis to Sparta which was intercepted by the pirate state of Samos: a marvellous linen corselet, embroidered with many figures of animals whose fine gold

[59] B 123; B 130; B 121.
[60] B 93, §1000–7. For the date, cf. G. Posener, Rev. Phil. 73 (1947) 129 and n. 2.

threads each contained three hundred and sixty distinct strands (Hdt.
III. 47). Xenophon's *Cyropaedia* says that Croesus had Egyptian troops
who fought well in his battle against Cyrus. Cyrus then settled them
in Lydian territory (VII. 32–45). Larisa near Cyme was known in the
fourth century as 'Egyptian Larisa' (Xen. *Hell.* III. 1.7), so this is not
historical romancing.

Even after the collapse of Lydia and then of Babylonia, Amasis did
not give up hope of finding allies against the Persians; and in the early
520s we find him formally linked with Polycrates, tyrant of Samos,
whose independent pirate navy was a thorn in the flesh of the Persian
empire (Hdt. III. 39). To this period must date the images of Amasis
in wood which Herodotus saw as dedications in the temple of Hera at
Samos (II. 182). Some time after the burning of the temple of Apollo
at Delphi in 548 Amasis contributed a thousand talents of alum to the
restoration fund, putting to shame the Greeks in Egypt who only gave
twenty minas between them (II. 180). Amasis' dedications at the temple
of Athena in Rhodian Lindus could have been at any time during his
reign. Here he dedicated two stone statues and a corselet like the one
meant for the Spartans. Eight Greek writers besides Herodotus (II. 182;
III. 47) mentioned them, as we learn from the Lindus Temple Chronicle
of 99 B.C. One of them noted that one of the two statues had a
hieroglyphic inscription, while the other had a Greek hexameter line:

> Gift of Amasis, the far-famed king of Egypt.

Lindus also had ten phialai dedicated by Amasis. (*FGrH* 532 F 1 (29))

According to Herodotus, it was Amasis who first renounced Polycrates' friendship. At any rate, when the news of the preparation of the
Phoenician fleet reached Polycrates, he decided it was more prudent to
throw in his lot with Cambyses, and sent forty ships to help the Persians.
These did not carry out their mission (III. 43–5). But Cambyses had
other Greek help. Phanes of Halicarnassus, one of Amasis' mercenaries
who had escaped by sea, gave Cambyses the information he needed to
cross the desert, if not Egypt (III. 4). He may be the Phanes son of
Glaukos who dedicated a large and costly bowl at Naucratis.[61] Before
the battle of Pelusium of 525 the Greek and Carian mercenaries
performed a frightful ceremony: they cut the throats of Phanes' sons,
whom he had left in Egypt, over a mixing-bowl, poured wine and water
into the bowl and all drank of it (Hdt. III. 11). They then fought
ferociously; but Cambyses won and Egypt was lost.

[61] B 116, 55.

VI. THE GREEK DEBT TO EGYPT

There is little evidence of Greek hostility to the Egyptians. One story got into circulation which was to their discredit: that a king Busiris, the eponym of the Delta town of Busiris, with his priests used to sacrifice strangers until Heracles arrived and killed the lot of them.[62] Heracles' deed and the ludicrous discomfiture of the priests is illustrated on the Busiris hydria from Caere (c. 520 B.C.),[63] and the story was first narrated by Pherecydes (*FGrH* 3 F 17), an early fifth-century Athenian logographer. Herodotus' cousin Panyassis told the story as part of his epic poem on Heracles (fr. 26 K), though Herodotus himself (II. 45) emphatically and rightly refutes the suggestion that any Egyptian had ever practised human sacrifice. Euripides wrote a satyr-play on Busiris (Nauck, *TGF* pp. 452–3), and Isocrates an encomium (XI) just to show it could be done. But normally the Greeks were eager to be impressed by Egypt. Homer's favourable account has been mentioned. Not for nothing is a kindly and wise old senator in Odyssus' Ithaca named Aigyptios (II. 15f). Once it was realized that Egyptian civilization was much older than Greek, Greeks were swift to assume, mostly because of superficial similarities, that much of the Greek heritage was Egyptian in origin. Herodotus insisted that the Egyptians had transmitted to the Greeks the names of the gods (II. 50), their festivals and processions (II. 58), religious mysteries (II. 49, 51, 81, 171), belief in metempsychosis (II. 109) and geometry (II. 109).[64] Later writers followed this fashion. 'You Greeks are always children', Plato has a wise Egyptian priest say to Solon. 'There is no such thing as an old Greek' (*Timaeus* 22b). Hence a readiness to believe that Greek poets, philosophers and artists must have travelled to Egypt to learn Egyptian wisdom. The Egyptians, especially in Ptolemaic times, were not averse to encouraging the belief. 'The priests of Egypt', says Diodorus,

recount from the records of their sacred books that they were visited in early times by Orpheus, Musaeus, Melampus, and Daedalus, also by the poet Homer and Lycurgus of Sparta, later by Solon of Athens and the philosopher Plato, and that there also came Pythagoras of Samos and the mathematician Eudoxus, as well as Democritus of Abdera and Oenopides of Chios. (I. 96)

Much of this tradition need not be taken seriously. But Greeks did travel out of curiosity, and links between Greece and Egypt were so close in the sixth century, and commerce so regular, that some visits cannot be denied.

[62] A 41, 126–7.
[63] A 7, 150, fig. 186. *Ibid.* 141–53 on Egyptian influence in Greece; and see the Plates Volume.
[64] B 110, 147–9: 'post hoc ergo propter hoc'; B 104.

Solon's visit to Egypt under Amasis (i.e. after 570) is mentioned by Herodotus (II. 177). That an item of Solon's legislation for Athens (594) should have been borrowed from Amasis is chronologically impossible, but the visit itself is likely. Solon's verses referred to the Canopic mouth of the Nile (fr. 26 West) through which you sailed to Naucratis. His visit to Cyprus is confirmed by his surviving elegiac farewell to King Philocyprus of Soli (fr. 19 West), who could hardly have been ruling before 570 since his son revolted against Persia in 498 (Hdt. v. 113). Solon lived to an active old age (cf. fr. 20 West). His travels must have been in the last years of his life, not (as an implausible tradition has it) immediately after his legislation of 594 so as to shake off requests to change it (Hdt. I. 29, Plut. *Solon* 25). He could have visited Lydia, too, after Croesus' accession in 560 or previously (Hdt I. 29–34) when he had been a territorial ruler under his father (*FGrH* 90 F 5).)

Again, the notion that Pythagoras got the theory of rebirth from Egypt (cf. Hdt. II. 123) does not square with what we now know of Egyptian religion; but since Pythagoras left Samos during the rule of Polycrates (Apollodorus, *FGrH* 244 F 338(d), 339), there may well be truth in the persistent Greek belief that this mysterious sage visited Egypt. Links between Samos and Egypt were particularly close, and never more so than during Polycrates' alliance with Amasis. Similarly, it is difficult to discount entirely the late tradition, not in Herodotus or Diodorus, that Thales visited Egypt and measured the pyramids there from the shadow they cast.[65] For a sixth-century citizen of Miletus a visit to Naucratis and Egypt was easy, and it could have tempted a practical man who, as we know from Herodotus (I. 74–5, 170), was adviser to the Ionian Greeks and accompanied Croesus on campaign. But it is much less probable that the part played by water in some Egyptian mythological accounts gave any stimulus to Thales' cosmological theories, themselves quite different in character.[66] Hecataeus of Miletus, the adviser of the Ionians in the 490s, definitely visited Egypt (Hdt. II. 143).

On the whole, the advance of modern knowledge has found the ancient belief in Egyptian cultural influence on Greece to be mistaken. Apparent resemblances between Egyptian and Greek religion and thought prove superficial on closer study: comparison emphasizes the differences. Despite what we know of racial fusion and bilingual inscriptions, and for all their curiosity, most Greeks were ill-equipped to learn from the Egyptians. The immigrants who named Egyptian cities after Greek, gave the jocular names 'pyramid' (cheese-cake) and 'obelisk' (skewer) to Egyptian monuments, and called themselves

---

[65] Hieronymus fr. 21 Hiller, ap. Diog. Laert. I. 27 = Thales, DK 11 A 1.
[66] B 110, 52–5.

'those of alien speech' clearly made little effort to learn Egyptian. Herodotus could not understand or speak the language. The 'interpreters', supposedly descended from those taught by the first Greek and Carian mercenaries (II. 154) and forming one of the seven classes in Egypt (II. 164) were all Egyptians. They were not priests or scribes and did not transmit Egyptian lore. If they had done so, it is hard to believe that Greek speculative thought would have gained. The knowledge that they were a young people, faced with a land whose civilization went back thousands of years, gave the Greeks a sense of proportion. Egyptian wisdom had nothing better to give.

But in the visual arts, which can be appreciated regardless of the barrier of language, Egyptian influence on Greece was immediate and profound. This is especially true of sculpture. Greeks in the Levant must already have seen monumental Neo-Hittite and Assyrian statues, but except for what seems to be a reference in the *Iliad* (VI. 92) to a seated statue of Athena, it does not look as if before *c.* 650 B.C. the Greeks made much attempt at truly monumental sculpture. The Greeks who came in numbers to Egypt in the mid-seventh century were much impressed by Egyptian life-size statues. These obviously inspired the *kouroi* that appear from now on in the Greek homelands, carved out of island marble. The resemblances are striking: a similar stance, clenched hands at the sides instead of the outstretched ones of the figurines. The differences are in dress: Egyptians wore wigs and aprons, the Greek *kouroi* are naked.

Here a story given by Diodorus has especial relevance. Theodorus of Samos, the most celebrated architect and statue-maker of the sixth century, with his brother (or more probably father) Telecles, learned a technique from Egypt which enabled them each to make a vertical half of the same statue independently, the one in Samos and the other at Ephesus. When brought together the two halves fitted perfectly (I. 98). This squares with what is known of Saïte and earlier Egyptian methods. Egyptian statues were plotted out in advance on a grid of squares, with the key points determined before cutting began. But the Greek sculptors did not follow the Saïte procedure as a matter of course; if they had, the anecdote about Theodorus would have been unremarkable. Characteristically, they preferred to a fixed grid principles of relative proportion, perfected in due course to conform to an ideal canon but always allowing for individual variation.

The other great influence was in architecture.[67] Mesopotamian cities, and Levantine towns as far as can be judged from Assyrian reliefs, were impressive, with walls and towers, multi-storey buildings and roof gardens; but they were mostly built of brick or rubble. In Egypt the

[67] A 7, 143; H 33, 32–5, 137.

Greeks encountered excellent building with stone blocks, columns, mouldings and capitals. It is highly probable that it was the sight of Egyptian buildings that gave the stimulus for the first monumental Greek architecture: early Doric colonnades in Greece are similar in proportion and general appearance to certain Egyptian ones. But the details differ. The Doric order of mainland Greece must have been an adaptation from local wooden buildings, and has associations with Mycenaean work. The eastern Greeks, in evolving the Ionic style, followed oriental patterns for their capitals and bases, drawing no doubt on what they had learned from Levantine textiles and furniture as well as architecture. Palm capitals, however, were borrowed from Egypt: a seventh-century example in Crete was followed by others in western Asia Minor in the sixth century, and the style was revived by Pergamene architects in Hellenistic times.

CYPRUS

V. KARAGEORGHIS

I. ASSYRIAN DOMINATION AND A CENTURY OF INDEPENDENCE

The middle of the eighth century B.C. marks the initial stage of the Cypro-Archaic I period. This was previously put at the very end of the century, about 700 B.C., but recent research, based especially on the Greek ceramic material found in Cyprus, has rightly raised the date.[1] Part of this period has been discussed already in *CAH* III.1[2], ch. 12, down to the year 709, when Sargon II conquered Cyprus, this event appearing as an appropriate landmark for the end of that chapter.

In this chapter we shall cover a period of about two centuries and the basic evidence will again be archaeological; but for the latest part of the period, from the Egyptian domination onwards (about 560 B.C.), we have information from Herodotus, mainly with regard to the period of Persian rule in Cyprus. We also possess some Assyrian records which throw light on the names of the various kingdoms of Cyprus. In Volume III.1[2], 533, reference was made to the inscription on the stele of Sargon II, where the names of the seven kings of Yadnana (Cyprus) who accepted his sovereignty are mentioned. The conquest of Cyprus by Sargon (724–705 B.C.) is mentioned also in his 'Display inscription' at Khorsabad, which reads as follows: 'I cut down all my foes from Yadnana which is in the sea of the setting sun.'[2]

Assyrian rule continued firm, and some thirty years after the occupation of Cyprus by Sargon Assyrian domination is mentioned again in the prism-inscription of Esarhaddon, which was written in 673/2 B.C. to commemorate the rebuilding of the Royal Palace of Nineveh.[3] The inscription reads as follows:

I summoned the kings of the Hittite land and those across the river... Ekishtura, king of Ediil, Pilāgura, king of Kitrus, Kīsu, king of Sillūa, Itūandar, king of Pappa, Erēsu, king of Sillu, Damasu, king of Kurī, Atmesu, king of Tamesu, Damūsi, king of Qartikhadast, Unasagusu, king of Lidir, Bususu, king of

---

[1] H 25, 318–20. [2] B 137, I 104.
[3] B 137, 105; B 134, 449–50; B 44, II §690.

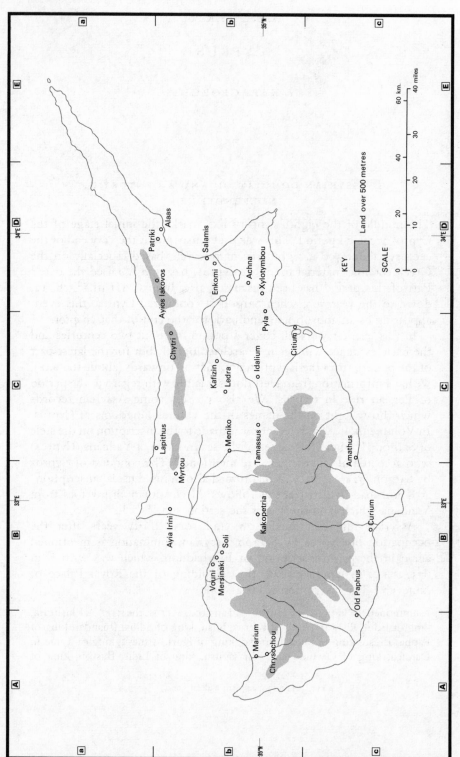

KEY

Land over 500 metres

SCALE

Map 4. Cyprus.

Nuria – ten kings of the land of Yadnana, in the midst of the sea . . . I gave them their orders and great beams.

Thus, at the beginning of the Cypro-Archaic period we have ten kingdoms in Cyprus, nine of which may be identified as the kingdoms of Idalium, Chytri, Salamis, Paphus, Soli, Curium, Tamassus, Citium (Qartikhadast), Ledra. The only kingdom which cannot be identified with certainty is Nuria, which may be Amathus. There has been a suggestion that Qartikhadast should also be identified with Amathus, but this is unlikely.[4] Some of the names of the kings who are mentioned may recall Greek names, e.g. Eteander, Damasus, Pylagoras, but the name of the king of Citium is Phoenician. We may assume that the Phoenicians preserved their kingdom at Citium even after the separation from Tyre. In fact life at Citium continues without any interruption throughout the eighth and seventh centuries B.C. and the Phoenician temples in the northern part of the city function as Phoenician institutions without the slightest deviation from their previous charac-ter. The only conceivable change which may have occurred is in the name of the city, which must have been named Citium (Kition) while Qartikhadast remained the name of the Carthaginian town. This makes sense after the separation of Citium from Tyre and the independence which the Cypriot cities enjoyed as long as they paid their tribute to the Assyrians.

A text identical with that of the Esarhaddon prism-inscription is given in a list which mentions all those who helped Ashurbanipal in 667 B.C., in his campaign against the Nubian king Taharqa.[5] Those who helped him are twenty-two kings from Syria, Palestine and Cyprus. The Cypriot kings are exactly those who are mentioned on the prism of Esarhaddon. It has been suggested that since it is unlikely that none of these kings changed from the time of Esarhaddon to the time of Ashurbanipal, the list of Ashurbanipal may be a copy of the earlier one and not a true record. In other words, the kings of Cyprus did not help Ashurbanipal. It is further suggested that already in the first years of Ashurbanipal's reign Cyprus had gained an independence which lasted for about one hundred years.[6] This period is rather obscure and the only mention of Cyprus which we have is that the Egyptian king Apries attacked Cyprus and defeated the Cypriot and Phoenician fleets, but did not conquer the island.[7]

Assyrian domination was lenient and was confined to political matters and to the payment of tribute by the Cypriot kings, who were ·

[4] B 134, 450; see, however, B 147, 62 and B 135, 233–41.
[5] B 134, 450–1; B 44, II §876.   [6] B 134, 450–1.
[7] B 137, I 109.

left free to exercise their own rule over their kingdoms and develop their own cultural life. The 'royal' tombs of Salamis, which continue on the same grand scale as in the last years of the eighth century B.C., illustrate very eloquently the position of the king as a superhuman being, who was accompanied to his tomb by pomp and wealth which only the Assyrian kings could possibly rival. Richly decorated hearses, war chariots, 'Phoenician' bronzes, large quantities of pottery and other gifts were offered to the dead kings or nobles, in the same way as they had been before Assyrian domination.[8] This is yet another indication that there was cultural continuity from the Cypro-Geometric to the Cypro-Archaic period, based on the solid foundations which were laid during the Cypro-Geometric period. In the 'royal' built tombs and the ordinary rock-cut tombs of the Salamis necropolis imported Greek pottery, mainly Euboean, is to be found, but Attic (or Euboean) 'SOS amphorae' also make their appearance both at Salamis[9] and at Citium.[10] These may have contained olive oil which was being exported from Central Greece throughout the Mediterranean. The relatively large number of these (though fragmentary) which have been found in the sacred area of Citium, may suggest a brisk trade between Athens and Citium, even if the latter was ruled by a Phoenician king; in commerce national antagonisms are often ignored.

It has been remarked already that the Phoenicians may have been obliged to renounce their allegiance to Tyre at the beginning of Assyrian domination, but their king continued to reign and there is no indication that their political control over the city had diminished in any way. Three temples existed side by side at Citium (Area II), of which the largest was the Temple of Astarte. Rich gifts were found on the floors of these temples, including Phoenician pottery, objects of faience, statuettes of bronze and one anthropomorphic flask of faience of the kind which was used by the Phoenicians to carry 'rejuvenating' water from the Nile to many places in the Mediterranean.[11]

The temples of Aphrodite at Paphus, of Zeus at Salamis and of Apollo at Curium, continued to function, to judge from the rich deposits of votive objects which have been found in *favissae* near two of them (Paphus and Curium); of the temple of Zeus only Hellenistic and Roman remains have so far been uncovered. Sacred architecture outside the main centres lacks monumentality and follows the tradition of small rural sanctuaries. In most cases there is a *temenos* in the open air, with a boundary wall and an altar. At Ayia Irini, on the north-west coast, there were sacred trees near the altar, within enclosures, recalling the

---

[8] B 138.   [9] B 138, II 23, pl. 66.
[10] They are all fragmentary and have been found in *favissae* of the eighth and seventh centuries.
F 18, 113–14.   [11] B 132, 183–289.

Late Bronze Age gardens in the sacred quarter of Citium. There was also an inner Holy of Holies. About two thousand terracotta votive figures were found in the *temenos*, including 'minotaurs', warriors, chariot models, bulls etc. The divinity which was worshipped in this sanctuary bore the burden of about fifteen centuries of religious conservatism and tradition. The idea of fertility, which is symbolized by the bull in the Early Bronze Age, persists throughout, but the rural divinity of Ayia Irini acquired in the meantime other qualities as well, to suit the needs of the worshippers: the fertility of the fields and cattle is now taken care of by a god who also protects the population in time of war, hence the numerous terracotta figures of armed men and war chariots.[12] Sanctuaries of the same type existed also at Achna and Tamassus.[13] The sanctuary of Ayios Iakovos which was built in the Cypro-Geometric I period as a cult chapel without any adjoining *temenos*, is now enlarged. On the Acropolis of Citium a sanctuary was built in honour of the Phoenician god Melkart, the protector of the city, about the middle of the seventh century. It combined a *temenos* with a chapel and was filled with numerous statues in limestone. The goddess Anat-Athena had been worshipped on the western Acropolis of Idalium since the Cypro-Geometric III period. Her sanctuary was enclosed by the fortifications of the city, a phenomenon which stresses her warlike qualities, remembered down to the Classical period, when she is worshipped in Vouni Palace, at Kakopetria and at Mersinaki.[14] The sanctuary of Anat-Athena lasted until the very end of the Cypro-Archaic period. Two other divinities were worshipped at Idalium during this time, Aphrodite and Apollo. Their sanctuaries consisted of courtyards and a temple cella. It is significant to note that the gods of the Greek pantheon began to be worshipped in Cyprus, and that even in the case of Phoenician temples divinities had been chosen who had counterparts in Greek religion: Anat–Athena, Astarte–Aphrodite, Melkart–Heracles.

Tomb architecture, which began in a monumental style at the end of the eighth century (as we saw in the necropolis of Salamis) continued during the seventh century in the same style. The kings and nobles are buried in monumental built chamber-tombs with large *dromoi*. Though the fashion of these built tombs started earlier and may even have been a revival of Late Bronze Age architecture, there are indications that at least during the end of the Cypro-Archaic I period itinerant builders from Anatolia may have influenced the tomb architecture of Cyprus.[15] The occurrence of a tumulus above Tomb 3 at Salamis, the architectural scheme and stone carving of the chamber, and above all the features of wooden architecture which are apparent in the construction of the

[12] B 148.   [13] B 134, 9ff.
[14] B 141.   [15] B 144.

'royal' tombs of Tamassus, leave no doubt that architects from Anatolia, already experts in tomb architecture in wood or in stone, may have taught the Cypriots how to build their own tombs. Apart from Salamis and Tamassus built tombs of the Archaic period have been found also at Amathus, Xylotymbou and Patriki. In their *dromoi* horses and occasionally slaves were sacrificed and among the tomb-gifts there are weapons, large quantities of pottery and also spits and firedogs. The fact that we find similar spits and firedogs in tombs of warriors at Argos and in Crete (Kavousi), may not be accidental. It is very probable that such funerary customs may have travelled from the Aegean to Cyprus at a time when commercial and cultural relations between the two regions were intense.

Inhumation continued to be the only general practice of burial, but in some rare cases, as in Salamis Tombs 1, 19 and 31, the dead person was cremated.[16] The tombs of ordinary folk were rock-cut chamber-tombs, separate from the 'royal' built tombs, as at Salamis. In some of the rich rock-cut tombs, however, at the site 'Cellarka' where the common citizens of Salamis were buried, horse sacrifices and slave sacrifices were practised, according to the wealth of the deceased.[17] But the highest honours were reserved for kings and nobles, who continued to have absolute power, almost divine, when living and were accompanied by pomp and wealth to their final resting place.

Cypro-Archaic I vase-painting, with its stylized pictorial motifs, has high artistic merits and may be considered as one of the most successful among its contemporaries in the other lands of the Near East and the Mediterranean region.[18] The vase-painter is often inspired by other arts, tapestries or engraving on metal, ivory or wood. Influence from the arts and crafts of the Near East is very strong and is particularly clear in the iconography of the pictorial compositions. This, of course, is understandable at a time when Phoenician merchants must have flooded the Cypriot market with luxury goods from the whole of the Near Eastern region. Particularly worthy of mention are the richly decorated metal bowls, of silver or bronze, some of them gilded, which are known as Cypro-Phoenician.[19] They are decorated with engraved or *repoussé* narrative representations, often inspired by the Near East and Egypt. They are found mainly in Cyprus but also in other parts of the Mediterranean and were probably made by Phoenician artists working in Phoenicia or in Cyprus. Bronze vessels like the cauldron from Salamis Tomb 79,[20] which is decorated with griffin protomes and sirens and stands on an iron tripod, or horse-gear from the same tomb, richly

[16] B 138, I 119.

[17] B 138, II.

[18] B 145.

[19] B 133; B 138, I 19–20.

[20] B 138, III 97ff.

7. Decoration from a Bichrome IV jug from Karpass. A ship with furled sail carrying two large storage jars. A man at the prow raises the hoop anchor; another squats on one of the two steering oars to feed the fishes. Seventh century B.C. (London, British Museum 1926.6–28.9; after B 145, 122, XI. 1.)

decorated in *repoussé*, may have been made in Cyprus by foreign or Cypriot craftsmen, in a style which constituted a *koine* in the eastern Mediterranean during the last part of the eighth or the beginning of the seventh centuries, with a strong Phoenician element. Cyprus, where copper was plentiful and where the courts of the various kings provided an excellent patronage, must have been a centre of production of such exotic goods in bronze. Some of the bronze incense-burners and vessels which have recently been found on the Atlantic coast of Spain, at Huelva, in tombs where chariot burials were found, may also have been made in Cyprus.[21]

The island may also have been a place where luxury furniture was made. Assyrian texts mention furniture of Cypriot workmanship, of maple wood and box-wood, offered as tribute to the Assyrian king on the part of the Cypriot kings.[22] Such furniture, but decorated with ivory plaques of Phoenician style, was found in the 'royal' tombs of Salamis.[23] Ship building must have been one of the most important industries of Cyprus, where wood was plentiful. Several ancient authors mention the ability of the Cypriots in this craft and it is said (Pliny, *HN* VII. 56(57).208) that the light ship *kerkouros* was invented in the naval workshops of Cyprus.[24] Ships are often represented in Cypriot vase-painting of the seventh century B.C. (fig. 7) and terracotta models of ships are often found in tombs. In the well known lament over Tyre, Ezekiel (27: 6) mentions that the Tyrians used wood for ships from the isles of Kittim.

Immediately after the Assyrian domination a purely Cypriot style appeared in limestone and terracotta sculpture, which is known as the Proto-Cypriot. It is full of vigour, with Syro-Anatolian connexions,

[21] C 43, pls. 148–53.   [22] B 134, 460; B 44, II 36, 103.
[23] B 138, III 87ff.   [24] B 134, 459–60.

some Egyptian as well, but the result is genuinely Cypriot, though the idea of monumental sculpture may have derived from Egypt. The expressive portrait-like faces declare the confidence which the Cypriots had acquired during their period of independence, after Assyrian domination. Their outlook, however, as seen in their dress and ornaments, is oriental.[25]

The oriental repertory dominated in the art of vase-painting, but Aegean influences are not completely lacking. Often the Cypriot vase-painter imitated motifs and compositions from East Greek vase-painting, particularly the 'Wild Goat style' of the end of the seventh century B.C.[26] He also imitated various shapes of Greek or East Greek pottery.

Commercial relations between Cyprus and her neighbours were intensified. It is not known whether this commerce was in the hands of the Phoenicians, but even if it were, the Cypriots themselves must have played an important role. Through the harbours of Tyre and Sidon and through the mouth of the Orontes Cypriot goods found their way to the Near East and to Egypt. There were also trading factories in several places in Syria and Cilicia, for instance at Tell Sheikh Yusuf and Tarsus.[27] Recent excavations at Tell Keisan in Palestine have brought to light large quantities of Cypriot storage jars, proof that Cypriot liquid commodities were exported on a large scale to the Near East.[28]

Trade with the west was also brisk, particularly with Rhodes, but some Cypriot goods found their way also to Crete, the Cyclades and Athens.[29] Though the number of Cypriot goods in the Greek colonies of south Italy and even in Spain is increasing this may have been due to the activities of the Phoenicians. In any case, Rhodes must have been a clearing station for westward trade. Cypriot pottery and other works of art were very much appreciated in the Aegean. In Rhodes we have local vases which imitate Cypriot prototypes and there may also have been Cypriot potters working in Rhodes. Finally, the role of Cyprus in the transfer of oriental elements to the orientalizing arts of Greece should not be overlooked.

II. EGYPTIAN DOMINATION

The history of Cyprus during the first half of the first millennium B.C. is characterized by a series of foreign dominations, which follow the pattern of political developments in the eastern Mediterranean. The

[25] B 134, 457–8.
[26] A striking example has been excavated recently in a tomb at Goudhi near Marium, *Ann. Rept. Director Dept. Ant., Cyprus* 1976, fig. 40.   [27] B 134, 462–3.
[28] *Rev. Bibl.* 83 (1976) 90.   [29] B 134, 464–5.

Assyrian empire collapsed in 612 B.C. and a new power, the Egyptian, appeared on the scene. The strategic position of Cyprus and her wealth in copper and timber were not overlooked by the Egyptians and in about 560 B.C. Amasis occupied Cyprus and put an end to Assyrian rule. At the same time, however, the relative independence which was enjoyed by the Cypriot kingdoms came to an end. The occupation of Cyprus by Amasis is recorded by Herodotus (II. 182), who writes that he was the first person to subdue Cyprus and make it tributary. From now on historical events relating to Cyprus are recorded by Herodotus, but archaeology and the study of the material culture in general continue to help in the reconstruction of the history of the island and particularly of her commercial and cultural relations with her neighbours.

The Egyptians no doubt preserved the old political structure in the kingdoms of Cyprus as long as the Cypriot kings were prepared to pay their tribute to them. In the cultural field the Egyptians exercised considerable influence. This is manifested in Cypriot sculpture. We have remarked already that in the seventh century the idea of monumental sculpture was introduced from Egypt; now the Cypriots imitate Egyptian styles in stone sculpture and a Cypro-Egyptian style is created where even Egyptian dress is represented. At the same time, however, the Neo-Cypriot style appears in sculpture, a natural development of the Proto-Cypriot style (see below). In tomb architecture we may observe similar influences. The vaulted chamber of a built tomb at Salamis, dated to about the middle of the sixth century B.C., is decorated inside with multi-coloured painted papyrus flowers and lotus buds on the side walls and with star-like motifs on the ceiling, in a style which recalls the painted interior of Egyptian sarcophagi.[30] In other arts and crafts we witness the appearance of Egyptian motifs, such as the Hathor head; it is common in the decoration of a class of pottery produced in an atelier centred in Amathus of the so-called 'Amathus style'. The same style, however, also borrowed elements from Greek vase-painting, such as the black-figure technique, using incised lines to render details.[31]

Through the Phoenicians a large number of Egyptian goods were imported to Cyprus, such as objects of faience (flasks, amulets, scarabs) which are found usually as offerings in tombs and temples. The Phoenician temples at Citium have produced large quantities of these.[32] It was not only goods that travelled as a result of trade in the whole region of the eastern Mediterranean, but also artistic ideas and styles. Cypriot trading factories were established in places like the Greek settlement of Naucratis in Egypt and at Amrit in Syria,[33] both receiving influences from these regions and at the same time introducing to them

[30] B 138, III 126–7.   [31] B 145, II 91–3.
[32] B 132.   [33] B 134, 469–70.

fashions of Cypriot art. Cypriot sculptures in terracotta and limestone have been found in large quantities in the Heraeum of Samos, in Rhodes and other East Greek centres along the Ionian coast.[34] We know the name of Sikon,[35] a Cypriot sculptor who worked in Naucratis. Characteristic of the popularity of Cypriot sculpture at Naucratis is the story narrated by Athenaeus (675 F; 676 A–C) about a citizen of Naucratis named Herostrates, who found himself in Paphus on one of his voyages, where he bought a statuette of Aphrodite. On his homeward journey his ship was caught in a storm and the passengers prayed in front of the statue to save them. They survived, reached Naucratis in safety and dedicated the statuette of Aphrodite to her local temple. In fact a large number of Cypriot statuettes were found in this temple.

The harbours of Cyprus may have been used as intermediary ports for trade between the Near East and the Aegean. All the trade routes passed through Cyprus and this obviously had a most beneficial effect on the economic and cultural development of the island, contributing to the cosmopolitan character of its culture. This, indeed, is a pattern which characterizes the whole history of Cyprus. In the field of culture we mention as an example of this phenomenon the development of Cypriot sculpture during the second half of the sixth century and the creation, side by side with the Cypro-Egyptian style, of the so-called Neo-Cypriot sculpture, which, in the western part of the island, was influenced by the sculpture of Ionia, and exercised a reciprocal influence at the same time; but in the eastern part the Syrian and Egyptian elements are stronger.[36]

This summary shows that the sixth century followed more or less the same pattern of foreign relations and cultural tendencies in Cyprus which were apparent already at the end of the eighth century. These started with the installation of Greek trading posts in the east on the one hand and with the foundation of a Phoenician colony at Citium, and were intensified during the seventh century, the period of Cypriot independence. The sixth century, however, brought Cyprus closer to the Greek world. The Greek presence at Tarsus and Al Mina and Greek trading posts in Syria brought many Greeks through Cyprus. It is also known that there were several Cypriots in the Greek settlements and trading towns. This renewal of contact must have contributed to the awakening of national feelings in Cyprus, where a conservative spirit preserved many Mycenaean Greek elements in art, in religion and even in the language. The successive occupations by foreign powers (the Assyrians, the Egyptians) and the traditional antagonism between the

---

[34] B 146; D 85.   [35] B 134, 470; B 102, 32.
[36] B 134, 468.

Greeks and the Phoenicians may also have encouraged the creation of a strong Hellenic consciousness in a large portion of the Cypriot population, particularly those who lived in traditionally Greek areas. This is the time (first half of the sixth century B.C.) when the Greek philosopher Solon visited Cyprus (Hdt. v. 113) at the invitation of King Philocyprus of Aepeia (a city usually located in the area of the Palace of Vouni). According to a worthless story in Diogenes Laertius (I. 51.62) Solon advised his host to transfer his town to a more suitable area in the same district, and he chose the site in the plain, near the sea, where he built a new town, naming it Soli after his distinguished guest. It was also said (Plut. *Solon* 26.2–4; Solon Fr. 19 West) that Solon dedicated a short elegy to Philocyprus. This story is unlikely to be entirely true, especially on chronological grounds, but also because Soli existed under this name a century before the visit of Solon (it is mentioned as Sillu in the prism-inscription of Esarhaddon); recent archaeological discoveries have also demonstrated the existence of a settlement here as early as the Late Bronze Age (*CAH* III.1², 517). Nevertheless the importance of this story should not be decried: it underlines the strong ties which existed between Cyprus and the Greek world, and which became yet closer towards the end of the sixth and the beginning of the fifth century. We may mention other characteristic examples of these relations: a Cypriot called Hermaeus dedicated in the seventh century a tripod at the temple of Apollo at Delphi and inscribed it in the Cypriot syllabary. A fragment of this tripod with its inscription has recently been found.[37] We know of two famous textile-makers from Salamis who lived in the sixth century. The latter dedicated a renowned *peplos* in the sanctuary of the temple of Apollo at Delphi. According to Athenaeus (48b) an inscription on the *peplos* mentioned that this was the work of Helicon of Salamis, son of Acesas, and that he derived his inspiration from the goddess Athena.

Hellenic culture and artistic fashions developed in the major towns which preserved the basic elements of the old Mycenaean Greek tradition. But in the rural districts the old Eteo-Cypriot cultural traditions lingered on, occasionally blended with Greek or Phoenician elements.

The rural sanctuary of Meniko (fig. 8), near the northern slopes of the Troödos mountain range, not far from the copper mines of Mitsero, has produced material which is characteristic of the cultural and religious tendencies which persisted in the Cypriot countryside. The sanctuary, dedicated to the Phoenician god Baal Hamman,[38] may be dated to the middle of the sixth century B.C. The terracotta image of the god, seated on a throne, is accompanied by numerous incense-

---

[37] B 156.   [38] B 142, 17–66.

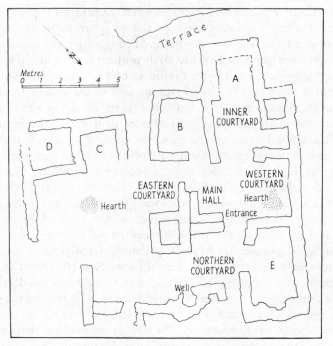

8. Plan of the site at Meniko Litharkes.

burners, since he is the 'god of fire', but he is also associated with cattle, since a number of ram and bull terracotta figurines have been found among the votive offerings; there was also a clay model of a war chariot; all these recall the votive offerings of the sanctuary of Ayia Irini where also a god with many qualities was worshipped. An East Greek skyphos illustrates the penetration of Greek imported goods to this remote part of the country, which the Phoenicians also reached, no doubt in order to control the production of the copper mines of the district.

The end of Egyptian domination in Cyprus finds the island at the peak of her cultural development. The Eteo-Cypriot culture, blended with influences from the east and the Aegean, flourished in an atmosphere of wealth and intensive international interchange. Old traditions, mainly in religion, were preserved, but a lively new spirit is to be found in artistic production, a result of the multiple interconnexions.

III. THE FIRST YEARS OF PERSIAN DOMINATION

Egyptian rule over Cyprus lasted for only twenty-five years, and the Cypriots submitted to the Persian king Cyrus in about 545 B.C., as soon as they saw that Egyptian power was dwindling (Hdt. III. 19).[39] The Persians did not at the beginning interfere with the political power of the local kings, and followed a policy very much like that of the Assyrians. The Cypriot kings were considered and treated like allies of the Persians; the latter were satisfied as long as the Cypriots were prepared to pay their tribute and help the Great King in his military expeditions. Thus we see the Cypriot kings helping the Persians in the Carian war (545 B.C.), in the conquest of Babylonia (539 B.C.; Xen. *Cyr.* VIII. 6.8) and in the Persian attack against Egypt (525 B.C.). In this last expedition we know from Herodotus (III. 19.44) that there were also Phoenicians, Ionians and Samians.

Salamis must have been the principal kingdom of the island and its king Euelthon had serious political ambitions. He was the first to strike his own coinage,[40] perhaps in the 520s B.C., using the Persian standard. On the obverse of his coins there is a ram, which is an oriental symbol; on the reverse we see the Egyptian symbol *ankh*, and in some cases, within the circle of the *ankh*, there is the sign *ku* of the Cypriot syllabary, denoting $Κυ(πρίων)$ = of the Cypriots (fig. 9). This implies that King Euelthon had the ambition to be regarded as king of the whole of Cyprus. This supremacy was recognized by Queen Pheretima of Cyrene who, as we know from Herodotus (IV. 162), went to Cyprus in 530 B.C. and asked Euelthon for military assistance against her son Arcesilas III. This could never have happened had the Persian rule over Cyprus been oppressive. Euelthon was apparently at liberty to carry out a free foreign policy as an independent king. There is no doubt that the Persians allowed this state of affairs because they were certain that Euelthon was loyal to them and in their turn they assisted him in his political ambitions over the whole island. Euelthon, however, did not forget his Greek connexions; thus, we learn from Herodotus (*ibid.*) that he dedicated to the temple of Apollo at Delphi an incense-burner which was 'worth seeing'.

We have seen the strong influence of Egypt on the development of Cypriot art during the period of Egyptian domination. This influence disappeared after the end of Egyptian rule. The Persians exercised a very modest influence on the cultural life of Cyprus. Ionian influence, on the other hand, was strong and widespread, and it is apparent mainly in sculpture, where we have the appearance of the Cypro-Greek style, with all the characteristics of Archaic Greek sculpture.[41] Greek moulds for

---

[39] B 134, 471–2.   [40] H 48, 301.   [41] B 134, 473–4.

9. Silver coin naming
Euelthon.

terracottas are also imported from Greece or are made locally under
strong Greek influence. Greek vases, mainly East Greek but also Attic,[42]
find their way to Cyprus as luxury goods and influence the development
of Cypriot vase-painting, which, however, starts to lose its originality.
Though we do not yet possess monumental architecture, there are
indications, from architectural members found at Curium, Citium and
elsewhere, that there were temples of the Greek style in the main centres
of the island.

Towards the end of the sixth century Greek influence became
predominant in all aspects of Cypriot life and culture. In the main cities
the political atmosphere was divided, with strong pro-Greek and
pro-Persian political parties. The pro-Greek population accepted Greek
culture, as a means of defence against Persian rule, but this meant the
weakening and the gradual eclipse of the native Cypriot cultural
tradition, which had persisted for so many centuries.

When Darius (521–485 B.C.) organized the structure of the Persian
empire, placed Cyprus within the fifth satrapy and fixed the annual
tribute of the Cypriots, it became evident that the initial 'alliance' and
independence which the Cypriot kings enjoyed under Cyrus belonged
to the past.[43] Anti-Persian feeling was growing in the towns and Persian
propaganda was at the same time trying to strengthen the pro-Persian
parties, no doubt assisted by the Phoenician population. Thus, the first
seeds of antagonism and strife among the Cypriot kingdoms were sown
and this formed the prelude to a long period of struggles in the island,
either against the Persians for freedom or among the Cypriot kings for
mutual extermination. The Greek army was involved in these struggles
and Cyprus thus found herself in the turmoil of antagonism between
Greece and Persia.

[42] B 136.   [43] B 134, 475.

THE CYPRIOT SYLLABARY

T. B. MITFORD and OLIVIER MASSON

Cyprus possesses in the Classical Syllabary a unique system of writing. Except for the Phoenician alphabet used by the Semitic element in the island's population,[1] and for the Greek alphabet on certain coins and in the rare epitaphs of foreigners, the syllabary was in almost exclusive use throughout the Archaic and Classical periods. With two early exceptions (Marium, Golgi), only in the Hellenistic period do 'digraphic' inscriptions (with the same or a similar text in both alphabet and syllabary) occur, notably at Paphus and Soli, whose kings were among the earliest Cypriot allies of Ptolemy Soter. The syllabary, in the main or 'Common' variant and in the South-Western or 'Paphian' repertory, was the vehicle of the Cypriot dialect, the eastern branch of the Arcado-Cypriot group; in some parts of the island, especially at Amathus, the syllabary was also used for the still undeciphered 'Eteo-Cypriot' language. The Cypriot dialect[2] and the syllabary are complementary, and (save for Eteo-Cypriot) they are not to be found the one without the other.

Decipherment, based on the Phoenician bilingual of Idalium (*ICS* no. 220) was ingeniously initiated in 1871 by George Smith, later assisted by S. Birch, and rapidly advanced by Brandis, M. Schmidt, Deecke and Siegismund.[3] By 1876, the Bronze Tablet of Idalium (*ICS* no. 217; see Plates Volume), complete and very legible, with more than 1,000 signs, had received an established alphabetic text and full commentary, and it remains to this day without a rival as a source of knowledge alike of the dialect and of syllabic usage. In 1961, O. Masson could assemble in *ICS* about 380 inscriptions on stone, metal, coins and pots from Cyprus itself, and from Egypt about 80 graffiti, for the most part the signatures of Cypriot mercenaries in the service of the pharaoh.[4] To this total some 40 have since been added, the most significant of them without doubt from Curium.[5] To be published shortly are 66 ceramic

---

[1] B 147; B 131.
[2] For the dialect see A 34, 104ff, 127ff; A 4, 397–454; A 64, 141–74; A 57, 87–94.
[3] See summary in B 154 (cited in the text here as *ICS* for inscription numbers), 48–51.
[4] For Abydos, *ICS* nos. 374–419; for Karnak, *ICS* nos. 421–53; to be completed in B 160.
[5] B 163.

inscriptions from the Nymphaeum of Kafizin, in Idalian territory;[6] they are in general repetitive, but four are of very considerable length, their value enhanced by the confirmation they receive from their context and in some cases by the parallels that can be drawn with alphabetic versions. Further, there are more than 200 dedications – mainly very brief and fragmentary – from the Siege-Mound of Old Paphus, where excavations give the Ionian Revolt as their *terminus ante quem*;[7] also more than 100 from the contemporary rustic sanctuary of Rantidi about 5 kilometres to the south-east of Paphus.[8] All these Archaic Paphian texts, with the exception of a fine royal dedication (*ICS* no. 15), are very short, being restricted in general to the names of votaries. In all, therefore, nearly 1,000 syllabic inscriptions are now known.[9] These vary greatly, however, both in length and credibility – even where it is certain that their language is Greek; and in this connexion it is instructive to consider the fortunes of the six documents which in the number of their signs come nearest to the Tablet of Idalium.

It is not necessary to stress here the immense value of the Tablet (*ICS* no. 217) as a complete and well understood Greek document of the period 480–470 B.C.: there are no gaps or restitutions, and the meaning is always clear; only a few features in the morphology and vocabulary are still under discussion. The text is an agreement made by the king Stasicyprus and the city of Idalium with the physician Onasilus and his brothers for their unpaid care of the warriors wounded during the siege of the city by the Medes (Persians) and the inhabitants of Citium. Instead of a fee, the physicians are to receive certain plots of land, equivalent to money. The agreement is put under the protection of the goddess Athena, in her sanctuary.

The smaller text of the Idalian bilingual already noticed (*ICS* no. 220), was firmly established since the early years of the decipherment, with the help of the Phoenician version. In contrast to this, the inscribed votive relief of Golgi (*ICS* no. 264), with 78 signs clearly cut, making four dactylic hexameters (the only metrical text of the syllabary), is still relatively difficult, and the many versions suggested differ in a number of details. The Salamis Ostrakon (*ICS* no. 318, about 600 B.C.), bears 216 signs (little better than graffiti) painted in red on both sides of the sherd forming, it would seem, several disconnected texts. Its meaning is in great part obscure: only face B provides some Greek words or locutions.[10] The clay tablet called the 'Bulwer Tablet' (*ICS* no. 327; fig. 10) preserves some 163 signs, representing from two thirds to three quarters of the original total. Since 1910, this text, although clearly cut

---

[6] B 165.　　　　　　　[7] B 162; B 167.　　　　　　　[8] B 162; B 166.

[9] B 157, with supplements for the years 1961–75.

[10] The *ICS* commentary is revised and completed in B 138, I 133–42, and B 155.

```
                                        KE . ro . to . a

                                        5
                                        i . ka . tu . i

                                        10
                                        SE . ri . ka . lo . se . e

                                20              15
                                ra . va . zo  ne . to . pa . la

                                        25
                                TA . lo . pi  o . te . la . ka . mi    5

                                35              30
                                RE . ke . vo . zo  ne . vo . ra . za . a

                                45              40
                                lo . se . e  jo . si . ti . ro . po . a

                                55              50
                                lo . pi . i . ve . ti  o . si . nu . vo . ti

                                65              60
                                A se . to . si . ri . a  ne . o . vi . ti

                                75              70
                                SE . ta . si . ri . a . jo . vi . ve . ro . ko    10

                                85              80
                                MA . ti . ku  JO . ri . ti . su . u . ve . ku . a

                                95              90
                                se . lo . mi . ti  jo . ri . te  se . ke . u . MO


                                        105             100
                                        ne . mi . ko . ra . a  ne . jo . mi . ri . va

                                        115             110
                                        VA . to . si . ri . a  jo . si . ki . va . ta

                                        125             120
                                        NU . ta  ne . ti . ka  se . ka . te . i  xe   15

                                        135             130
                                        PO te . e  e . se . re . ve  ma . to

                                        145             140
                                        ma . a . to  ne . ko . la  te . i

                                        150
                                        mi . to  te . e  se . re . po

                                        155
                                        te . i  se . i . ta . mi

                                        160
                                        i . se . i . pe    20
```

10. The 'Bulwer Tablet', clay. Text (two sides) and transcription following Mitford's reading and transliteration. 16 × 10 × 2 cm. (London, British Museum 1950. 5–25.1; *ICS* no. 327.)

and written in a language not open to question, has given rise to three rather diverging interpretations,[11] but here the incompleteness of the tablet is mainly responsible. Two other complete documents remain full of difficulties, the 'Tsepis Stele' (ICS no. 306, Pyla) and the 'Pierides Bowl' (ICS no. 352, source unknown).

To this group of 'long' inscriptions (all already in ICS), we can now add two recently discovered objects. First, a small vase with two inscribed faces (unknown source; beginning of fifth century),[12] giving two lists of personal names with very interesting Greek formations. Secondly, a marble fragment in Paphian script (Old Paphus, about 325–309 B.C.),[13] unfortunately broken, which is a fragment of an oath, several times mentioning King Nicocles, the last king of Paphus, already known from inscriptions (ICS nos. 1, 6, 7, etc.); the text contains some important words and locutions.

Thus, the picture offered today by Cypriot epigraphy is not as melancholy as some scholars, such as Bechtel and Schwyzer,[14] thought at the beginning of the century. They knew only the Idalium Tablet and some short texts from Paphus, Marium and Soli, with the bilinguals of Tamassus. From the middle of this century the discovery and publication of many new texts has put us in a stronger position, and given reasonable hope of further discoveries.

Returning to the problems caused by the syllabary, we must admit that it is ill suited to the writing of a Greek dialect. The first Greeks who settled in the island probably found it in some ancestral form then in use to express a language which was not Hellenic. That language was not necessarily Eteo-Cypriot (whose early stages are unknown), but all speculation about that particular question is premature.

After Evans' discoveries and Ventris' decipherment, it is natural that we should look to Linear B Script and its manifest relationship to Minoan Linear A. Any attempt, however, to establish a direct line of descent to the younger from the older of the two main syllabaries, the Cypriot and the Mycenaean, must be approached with great caution. Syllabaries were well known in Cyprus and elsewhere before the emergence of Linear B, and the earliest of these are therefore to be derived ex hypothesi from Linear A (or another related Linear script).

We now know that literacy was already important in Cyprus during the Late Bronze Age. At the present state of our knowledge, we may distinguish three main varieties[15] of the script which Evans called 'Cypro-Minoan': 'C.M.1', the local script, scattered over all the island;

---

[11] Commentary in ICS 324–8 with criticism of the first edition by R. Meister (1910), and 402–3 with summary of the new edition in B 162, 38–45. Latest study, B 168.

[12] Published by J. Karageorghis, Biblioteca di antichità cipriote 3 (1976) 59–68.

[13] B 159.   [14] A 4, 399ff; A 58, 327–34.   [15] B 150–1.

'C.M.2', restricted to a few (but lengthy) clay tablets from Enkomi; 'C.M.3', only in use at Ras Shamra–Ugarit. The evidence is too complicated and too scanty to admit as yet a precise history of the immediate prototype (or prototypes) of what emerged after the Geometric period as the Archaic and Classical Syllabaries. But two facts have now to be considered. First, certain analogies, both in the sign shapes and in the structure of some inscriptions, could point to a closer relationship between 'C.M.1' and the oldest forms of writing in the south-west or Paphian area.[16] Secondly, a surprising confirmation of the importance of the Paphian region was afforded by the recent discovery (early 1979), in a Geometric tomb near Old Paphus (Skales, tomb 49; end of eleventh century) of a bronze spit with a very clear incised inscription of five signs:[17] they are no longer Cypro-Minoan, but already Cypriot, with a mixture of 'Paphian' and 'Common' shapes, which it is tempting to call 'Proto-Paphian'; even more surprising is that we are able to read the whole text (dextroverse) as *o-pe-le-ta-u* and to recognize even at this very early stage a Greek name with an Arcado-Cypriot genitive, namely *Opheltau*. The name Opheltas or -tes, an heroic one, is not mentioned by Homer, but had already been supposed in Mycenaean (Cnossus KN B 799). To sum up: it seems clear that in a tomb near Old Paphus people were buried who already spoke in Greek, and more precisely in a form of Cypriot dialect (as expected). They also wrote in a script which is very near to the Archaic Syllabary, and now appears as the oldest form of syllabary known to us, since it is much earlier than the small vase-inscription dated to the eighth century (*ICS* no. 174, also from the Old Paphus area, not from Marium as first alleged).[18]

Thus, the old problem of the supposed existence of a 'Dark Age' characterized by centuries of illiteracy, is now satisfactorily solved. We may infer that the syllabary already existed at the end of the eleventh century: the absence of texts until the eighth century could result from a general diminution of literacy in these times, also perhaps from a greater use of perishable material, such as wood or leather. But the main point is that the syllabary is now shown to be the continuation of some kind of Late Bronze Age script, exactly as had been supposed: the strength of the local tradition thus prevailed against the possible innovations, either the adoption of the old Phoenician letters, or the introduction, as in Greece, of a newly-fashioned alphabet.

If we again compare the syllabary with Linear B, as typical of this kind of writing, we have to observe some differences. First, the dis-

[16] B 153.
[17] Preliminary notice in B 149, with comments by E. and O. Masson.
[18] For revision and origin see B 155; attempt at Greek interpretation in B 169, 169–73.

	A	E	I	O	U
K					
T					
P					
L					
R					
M					
N					
Y					
V					
S					
Z					
X					

11. The Common Syllabary (Idalium, fifth century B.C.).

appearance of ideograms, which were very frequent and important (as in Linear A) for the countless palatial inventories. It is unlikely that ideograms are to be expected in the Bronze Age scripts of Cyprus, as distinct from potter's or mason's marks, although no inventories have yet been recognized. Secondly, while Linear B is exclusively dextroverse, like the Cypro-Minoan scripts, the Cypriot syllabary is predominantly sinistroverse, with important exceptions in the South-Western signaries.

To the 55 signs already identified in the early years of decipherment,[19] one only has since been added, the syllable *yo* recognized by R. Meister in 1910 on the 'Bulwer Tablet' (*ICS* no. 327), in use equally in the 'Common' and the 'Paphian' repertories. Theoretically, as many as 65 signs can have existed, but it is improbable that more will now emerge. With the exception of *yo*, fig. 11 tabulates the signary current in central Cyprus at the outset of Cypro-Classical times. It is at once evident that in comparison with the 87 signs of Linear B,[20] it is a tidy signary, both simpler and more systematic. The seven homophones and the fifteen unidentified signs have vanished, and so too the complex signs *dwe*, *nwa*, *pte*, etc., to be represented in our syllabary only by *xe* = '*kse*'. For the rest, both syllabaries recognize, always without distinction of length, the five basic vowels *a*, *e*, *i*, *o*, *u* (but the isolated *au* diphthong of the Linear script has disappeared); both form groups of signs by prefixing to the vowels each consonant in turn, as *ka*, *ke*, *ki*, *ko*, *ku*, etc., *la*, *le*, *li*, etc. However, they are not in complete agreement in the consonants they recognize. The labio-velars of the Mycenaean dialect have indeed become extinct and cannot therefore be considered here. But, whereas Linear B combines the liquids (*l* and *r*), separating two series for the dentals (*d* and *t*), the Cypriot distinguishes the former and conflates the latter. While Linear B still has a possibility of noting aspiration, with a_2 = '*ha*', Cypriot completely ignores aspiration. Both preserve the sound later represented by *digamma*, with *wa*, *we*, *wi*, *wo*, and both, more notably, have certain signs for the glide or semi-vowel, in Cypriot for *ya*, *ye*, *yo*.

In considering the relationship of these scripts, we must give full weight to a fact long known – that eight signs of simple form manifestly have kept their shapes without significant alteration: the decipherment of Linear B has now shown that from the fifteenth to the third centuries before our era these have retained their values also. They are: *da* and *ta*, *ti*, *to*, *pa*, *po*, *ro* and *lo*, *na*, *se*. Such are the similarities: it is perhaps left to future discoveries to explain the divergencies, but the principle of kinship cannot be denied.

[19] *ICS* 48–57.
[20] See the table in *CAH* II.1³, 600, fig. 17.

Some words are necessary about the spelling rules of the syllabary.[21] For vowels and diphthongs, there are no problems: e.g. *a-ro-u-ra-i* = ἄρουραι. In the rendering of consonants, some series are not ambiguous: those beginning with *r* and *l*, *m* and *n*, *s*, and also *w*. But, in the labial, dental and guttural series, ambiguity was unavoidable. For instance, the sign transliterated with *pa* is employed for βα, πα or φα; the *ta* for δα, τα or θα; *ke* for γε, κε or χε, and we have *pa-si-le-u-se* = βασιλεύς, *pa-si-te-mi-se* = Πασίθεμις, *pa-u-o-se* = Φαῦος, and so forth. Double consonants are not rendered, *wa-na-sa-se* = Ϝανάσ(σ)ας. A nasal before a consonant is not expressed, *pa-ta* = πά(ν)τα, etc., but a nasal at the end of a word is noted, with a few exceptions. More precisely, the problem of the final consonants is elegantly solved (with a great improvement on Linear B) by the regular use of syllables ending in *e*, where the vowel is not meant to be pronounced: *po-to-li-se* = πτόλις, *ke-re-o-ne* = Κρέων, *te-a-no-re* = Θεάνωρ. In the case of consonantal clusters, several rules are in use, based on the principle that the first consonant is rendered by the sign containing the vowel of the syllable to which this consonant belongs: *pa-ti-ri* = πατρί, etc.

To exemplify these rules and the general aspect of the transliterated syllabary, we reproduce here the beginning of the Idalium Tablet (*ICS* no. 217), which also shows the frequent inconsistencies in punctuation (a feature which is by no means compulsory):

o-te ' ta-po-to-li-ne-e-ta-li-o-ne ' ka-te-wo-ro-ko-ne-ma-to-i ' ka-se-ke-ti-e-we-se ' i-to-i ' pi-lo-ku-po-ro-ne-we-te-i-to-o-na-sa-ko-ra-u ' ...

Ὅτε τὰ(ν) πτόλιν Ἐδάλιον κατέϜοργον Μᾶδοι κὰς Κετιῆϝες ἰ(ν) τῶι Φιλοκύπρων Ϝέτει τῶ Ὀνασαγόραυ...

Another interesting question is that of syllabic palaeography. The table of the Cypriot signary published by Deecke in 1883[22] was chiefly arranged on a geographic, not chronological basis, and is of course completely superseded. Later evidence has established the existence not merely of local variants like that of Marium, but of a real dichotomy in south-western Cyprus, so that the syllabary must be subdivided, as already noted, into the 'Common' and the South-Western or 'Paphian' signaries. A detailed syllabic palaeography still remains out of reach. Syllabaries have an inherent conservatism which can readily deceive, and for each locality a sequence of dated or datable texts is required. Thus Marium can boast nearly 100 inscriptions from its tombs, all intelligible, Golgi some 45 from its sanctuaries, many difficult or incomprehensible – but neither site has yet yielded a single date. Many of these inscriptions, moreover, with the exception of a few pieces

---

[21] *ICS* 68–78.　　　　[22] A 15, I.

12. The Old Paphian Syllabary (Archaic Paphian, sixth century B.C.).

recently found, were acquired in circumstances which do not allow more than an approximate archaeological date.

The Paphian area is somewhat more fortunate.[23] A multitude of brief inscriptions, in particular from an Archaic sanctuary (destroyed by Persians besieging Paphus), but also from the rustic shrine of Rantidi, are assigned archaeologically to the sixth and seventh centuries. The Old Paphian signary is tabulated here (fig. 12, Archaic Paphian), and appears to be predominantly rectilinear. It shows 20 sign-forms which are foreign to the Common Cypriot of comparable date, notably *to*, *le*, *li*, *ri*, *wa*, *so*, etc.; it has a singular fluctuation in direction whereby 73 per cent of the Old Paphian texts, 70 per cent of those from Rantidi are dextroverse; and, finally, an intimate kinship has recently been established with the Archaic signary of Curium,[24] which is, however, ordinarily sinistroverse. Both Paphus and Curium had enjoyed an opulent Mycenaean civilization. They were related but independent cities, isolated by a mountainous hinterland, to the east by the Eteo-Cypriot Amathus, and farther off by the Phoenician Citium. This isolation was broken by the Persian response to Cypriot participation in the Ionian Revolt: Curium joined the Persian cause, Paphus resisted and was sacked. The Curium signary thereafter became merged in the Common Cypriot. Paphus, after the defeat, developed a theocratic regime, and if we may transpose this ideology in terms of writing, we observe that the city emphasizes here uniqueness not merely by the retention but by the exaggeration of her peculiar signary into the form preserved in the well-dated inscriptions of Nicocles, her last priest-king. This Late Paphian signary in fact retains a majority of Archaic forms, but they are now in general curvilinear and exclusively dextroverse (like the few texts known for Classical Paphus). In its final years it retains, as in the writing of its king, a surprising vigour.

If Idalium can be considered typical of the Common Cypriot – as may well prove to be the case, although far too little is yet known of the syllabaries of the important kingdoms of Salamis and Soli – a sequence can be established through Idalium for the Common Syllabary. The signary of the Bronze Tablet is given here (fig. 11) as representative of the close of the Cypro-Archaic period. Astonishingly, this script is still in use later, in the territory of Idalium, at the Nymphaeum of Kafizin.[25] The ceramic inscriptions from this hillock, assigned with certainty by over 100 dated pots to the years 225–218 B.C., place the last occurrence of the Cypriot syllabary in the year 220/219. It is certain that by then both the Syllabic script and the local dialect were on the defensive, under heavy pressure from the alphabet and the *koine*; and neither at Kafizin

[23] B 162; B 166; B 167.   [24] B 162; B 163.
[25] B 161; B 165.

13. The Signaries of Kafizin (225–218 B.C.).

nor elsewhere is there any suggestion of survival even to the close of
the century. But the erratic forms of certain signs (fig. 13), in particular
for the syllables *e*, *o*, and *pi*, do not seem attributable to degeneration,
but rather to a plurality of hands using the local scripts, because the
potters who wrote at Kafizin were recruited widely, from much of
central Cyprus. We may note, at this late period, the occurrence of
unique forms for *a*, *nu*, and *so*, interesting variants for *ko*, *pa*, *ra*, *ro*, *mi*,
and the adoption of Paphian *to*. Thus, one of the numerous revelations
given by the surprising documents of Kafizin is the demonstration that
the syllabary was capable of innovation even in this, the final chapter
of its very long history.

CHAPTER 37

THE COLONIAL EXPANSION OF GREECE

A. J. GRAHAM

I. INTRODUCTION

Greek colonies of the Archaic period are found on or off the coasts of modern Spain, France, Italy, Sicily, Albania, Greece, Turkey in Europe, Bulgaria, Romania, Russia, Turkey in Asia, Egypt and Libya. Hence this is often regarded as the 'age of colonization' or period of Greek colonization *par excellence*. In fact colonization was practised in all periods of Greek history. What distinguishes the colonization of the Archaic period is, firstly, its scale and extent, only rivalled by the very different colonization of Alexander and the Hellenistic period, and, secondly, its character, as a product of the world of the independent city-state, the *polis*. Later colonization of the Classical, and, even more clearly, of the Hellenistic, periods reveals in many ways that it emanated from a world dominated by larger political units. It is more difficult to distinguish Archaic colonization from its predecessor in the migratory period, when the Greeks settled the islands of the Aegean and west coast of Asia Minor. Indeed, the ancients themselves made no such distinction. However, it seems doubtful if the dominating political units of those days could properly be called *poleis*. In any case, a distinction is required by the great difference in the quality of our knowledge of the colonization of the migratory period as compared with that of Archaic times. With some over-simplification one might say that the literary sources for the Archaic period present real historical evidence, even though they are partly contaminated by legendary elements, whereas those for the migratory period are all legend, even if a kernel of truth is concealed somewhere within them. As for archaeological evidence, even though the material is constantly being enriched for both periods, it remains incomparably more abundant for the Archaic colonizing movement.

This argument brings us to the sources for Greek colonization in the Archaic period, which we may divide for the purpose of discussion into literary and archaeological.

The extant literary sources are extremely widely spread, and informa-

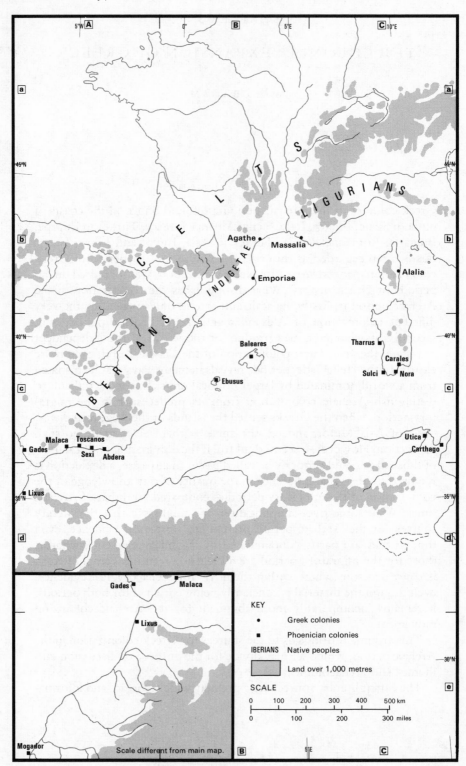

Map 5. The western Mediterranean.

tion on Greek colonies comes from virtually the whole range of Greek and Latin authors. From Homer we have not only much indirectly informative material, on geography, for instance, or trade, or life in the *polis*, but also a clear description of an ideal colonial site (*Od.* IX. 116–41). This occurs in the Cyclops episode, which is generally enlightening on many aspects of Greek colonization. The activities of a city-founder are also briefly described (*Od.* VI. 7–11).[1] Hesiod too, although he never mentions colonization directly, provides valuable information on contemporary economic, social and political conditions (e.g. his famous advice to have no more than one son), as well as his (possibly idiosyncratic) hostile attitude to seafaring (*Op.* 376–7, 618–94). Of later poets Archilochus stands out, above all because of his connexion with Thasos. His value for facts is lessened by the fragmentary and allusive character of his extant poetry (and the later accounts of his life partly preserved in inscriptions on Paros are similarly incomplete and enigmatic),[2] but, as a contemporary witness, he is uniquely valuable for his spirit and attitude to colonization.

Even though a very large number of extant Greek and Roman authors provide some piece of information directly or indirectly relevant to the history of Greek colonization, a few are of overriding importance. In any fully documented treatment of Greek colonization in the Archaic period (as, for instance, that of Jean Bérard,[3] or, of the older ones, the very thorough chapters of Busolt)[4] the names that occur most frequently in the footnotes are those of Herodotus, Thucydides, Strabo, Ps.-Scymnus and Eusebius; in other words, historians, geographers and a chronographer.

Neither Herodotus nor Thucydides was primarily concerned with writing a history of colonization. Their importance lies, firstly, in their relatively early date; although they belong to the period after the Archaic colonizing movement, they are nearer to it than our other substantial extant sources, and they both knew at firsthand about colonization in the Classical period. Secondly, they are both manifestly interested in colonies and colonizing activity. From Herodotus we have invaluable passages on the Phocaeans in the west (I. 163–7), Greeks in Egypt (II. 154, 178–9), the Greek cities in the Black Sea (II. 33; IV. 17–18, 24, 51–4, 78–9), the history of Cyrene (IV. 150–67), and the attempts at colonization in Africa and Sicily by Dorieus (V. 42–6) – to mention only the most important. Thucydides is best known to historians of colonization for his fundamental, if very succinct, history of Greek colonization in Sicily (VI. 3–5), but there are many other vital pieces

---

[1] Cf. C 13.
[2] *IG* XII Suppl. pp. 212–14; Diehl, *Anth. Lyr. Graec.*[3] fr. 51; *SEG* XV. 517; D 93, 52–62, 152–4; D 87, 18*f, T4, T5.   [3] C 1.   [4] A 13.

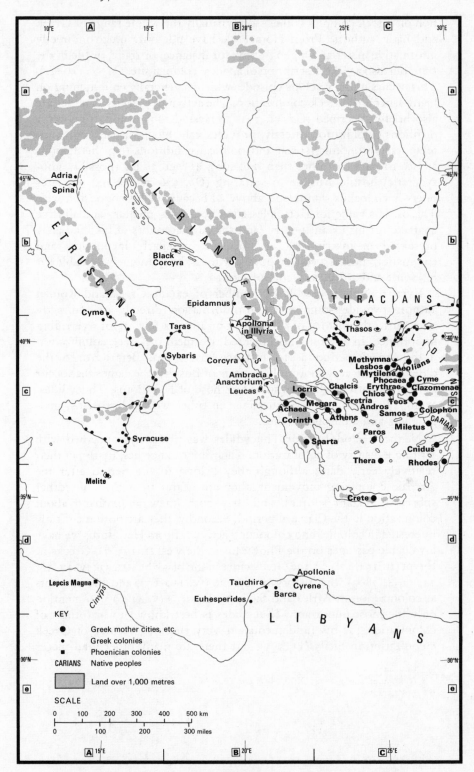

Map 6. The central Mediterranean.

of information scattered about his work, and, in particular, he is richly revealing on institutions and relationships in the colonial field (e.g. I. 24ff). Between them Herodotus and Thucydides determine our picture of Greek colonization.

However, it is the ancient geographers who provide the nearest thing we have to a systematic account of Greek colonization, because their methods and aims led them to list great numbers of Greek colonies, and often to furnish such further information as the mother city (or cities), the date of foundation, and the *oikistes* or *oikistai*. Strabo is the doyen of such sources. A contemporary of Augustus, he was familiar with the learned literature produced down to his day and has the virtue of frequently indicating his authorities.

Less great Greek geographers are also often helpful. Of these we may single out the author of a poem in iambic trimeters, long referred to as Ps.-Scymnus.[5] The aim of his work (lines 65–8) was to describe briefly the whole accessible world and, in particular, the colonies and foundation of cities. His description of Europe is complete, but that of Asia is lost except for the Asiatic coast of the Pontus. This skilful compression of much basic geographical and historical knowledge is frequently valuable to the modern historian, especially in areas for which earlier or better literary sources are not abundant, as, for instance, in the northern Aegean, Propontis and Pontus. The poem was written within the years 138 to 75/4 B.C. (to give the widest termini).[6] The old attribution to Scymnus of Chios was entirely unjustifiable, for Scymnus of Chios wrote in prose and lived about a century earlier. Diller has therefore most reasonably suggested that we should give up the term Ps.-Scymnus and call the author (from his dedication) 'Auctor ad Nicomedem regem', abbreviated 'Nic.', but it is difficult to oust an appellation sanctified by long usage.[7]

It is clear that by the time of Herodotus the foundations of colonies had become a theme for history – and for legend. His account of the colonization of Cyrene bears all the marks of the genre *ktisis*,[8] with its forged Delphic oracles, folk-tale motifs and concentration on individuals. The ancestor of the genre can be seen in Homer's description (*Il.* II. 653–70) of the settlement of Rhodes, and the colonization of Colophon was described by Mimnermus (fr. 9 West). The first lengthy treatment of an Archaic colonial foundation known to us was that of Elea by Xenophanes (Diog. Laert. IX. 20), and from the fifth century onwards *ktiseis* were written in large numbers. Polybius (IX. 1.4) regarded the history of foundations as a separate branch of history,

[5] *GGM* I. 197–237; A 16, 165–76.
[6] Cf. lines 2, 45–50. Müller, *GGM* I. LXXIV–LXXX; A 17.
[7] A 16, 20f; A 17.　　　　[8] C 14.

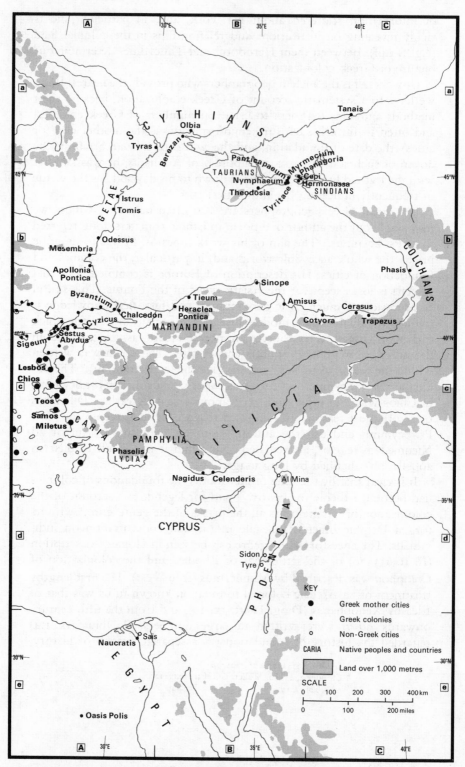

Map 7. The eastern Mediterranean and the Black Sea.

which appealed especially to the curious and the lover of the recondite, of whom he cites Ephorus as a characteristic example. So a great lost literature lies behind the meagre and skeletal information preserved for us in the extant historians and geographers.

One feature of this literature was undoubtedly the attempt to fix the foundations of colonies chronologically. The most abundant testimony to that chronographical work that we possess now is the *Chronica* of Eusebius, which is preserved in an Armenian version, in the slightly later chronological tables of St Jerome (Hieronymus), a work often called Eusebius Hieronymi, and in other subsequent chronographies.[9] A relatively large number of exact colonial dates figure in these tables,[10] dates which doubtless derive from the work of scholars of the Classical and Hellenistic periods. We can see from the careful indications of chronology in Thucydides' account of the colonization of Sicily that foundation dates were already present in the history of Greek colonies at the end of the fifth century. It was at that same period that Greek historians were fashioning chronological frameworks for the whole of Greek history. When they were dealing with early periods for which no actual dates were available, their method (though not clear in all details) was to take existing lists of names, such as kings, magistrates, athletic victors or priestesses, and then compute generations. Many scholars believe that this method was also used in order to achieve the precise foundation dates of Greek colonies, and therefore consider these dates to be strictly artificial, and liable to the inaccuracies inherent in the method of calculation, as, for instance, an arbitrary number of years to a generation, such as thirty or thirty-five.

It is obviously of great importance to decide whether these foundation dates are true dates or the product of calculation. Thucydides' dates for the Sicilian colonies (VI. 3–5), being the earliest attested and transmitted by a historian of such authority, inevitably constitute the test case. In his most valuable and convenient analysis of these dates Dunbabin argued strongly against the notion that they were calculated by reckoning generations,[11] but since he wrote there has been more than one attempt to show that a definite genealogical schema can be recognized in the dates and intervals of time given by Thucydides. Of these the most impressive and subtly argued is that of van Compernolle,[12] who maintained that the whole edifice of the Sicilian colonial dates was a construction created out of genealogies, especially those of the Deinomenids of Gela and the Emmenids of Acragas, on the basis of thirty-five years to a generation. This result could only be achieved by his choosing different base dates as starting points for the various

[9] A 56; A 33.   [10] D 29, 77; C 116.
[11] C 65, 435–71.   [12] C 61.

calculations, and the choice of those dates was inevitably arbitrary. No argument containing such a flaw could be convincing, but it has, in any case, since also been shown that the ancestors of Gelon, one of the major elements in van Compernolle's scheme, cannot be listed with the assurance he supposed.[13] So the best attempt to show that Thucydides' Sicilian dates are a product of calculation must be adjudged a failure, and we may conclude that all such attempts must inevitably rest on arbitrary and unjustifiable assumptions.

In default of satisfactory proof that these dates are calculated, what case can be made for believing that the citizens of the Sicilian colonies in the fifth century actually knew when their cities had been founded? Since their foundation occurred two centuries and more before the Greeks began to write history, it is necessary to postulate some procedure by which the era of the colony was recorded or could be worked out. It has been pointed out[14] that in a colonial city the annual ceremonies in honour of the *oikistes* might provide a specially favourable framework for an accurate count of years, but it must be admitted that, while the annual ceremonies are well attested,[15] we have no evidence that they gave birth to chronological records. Another point concerns Thucydides. In view of his very demanding chronological principles (cf. I. 97.2; V. 20, 2–3), it could be argued that, if he knew that the Sicilian colonial dates were not true dates, but had been calculated in ways such as those suggested above, he would not have transmitted them.[16] We can hardly believe that he would have been deceived. Whether he took his chronology of the Sicilian colonies from the *Sikelika* of Antiochus of Syracuse,[17] or, as seems more likely, pursued his own researches and used a variety of sources, both literary and oral,[18] the force of this argument is unaltered. As our knowledge stands, it seems better to make the assumption, bold though it may be, that the true foundation dates of the colonies had been recorded in some way, than to embrace the unattractive premises required by any other hypothesis.

Since we cannot be certain about the origin and authority of these dates, it is not surprising that some modern historians have treated them very cavalierly. In his stimulating chapter Beloch[19] was characteristically wilful in setting aside the traditional dates in favour of *a priori* ideas of his own, but he also had the insight to perceive that the chronology would be settled by thorough investigation of colonial cemeteries. And what the archaeological investigation of numerous colonial cemeteries

---

[13] C 97.   [14] C 1, 83.

[15] Cf. Hdt. VI. 38.1; Thuc. V. 11.1; Ath. 149D (with A 20, V. 348); Callim. *Aetia* fr. 43, 54–65, 72–83 (with C 151).   [16] C 178; C 130.

[17] *FGrH* 555; cf. C 61, 437–500; A 24, IV 199–210.

[18] Cf. *FGrH* 577, commentary 610f.

[19] A 5, I. 1, 229–64.

since he wrote has shown is that he was entirely unjustified in his low opinion of the literary foundation dates.

Apart from the early poets, none of the literary evidence for Greek colonization in the Archaic period is contemporary. Ultimately we cannot make good this lacuna, because there is no substitute for the precise and detailed information of contemporary literary sources, but archaeological evidence has the great advantage that it is primary and contemporary, and not affected by later ideas or selection.

Archaeological evidence has been most valuable in establishing colonial chronology. Greek painted pottery is now well dated independently of the literary foundation dates for the colonies,[20] and, as a result, when sufficient material is available to ensure a representative sample, the archaeological date for the foundation of a colony can be confidently determined. The nature of pottery evidence does not allow such dating to be closer than to the nearest quarter century, but, even so, the historian has for numerous Greek colonies an archaeological date, which can in many cases be set beside a literary date, much to the advantage of his interpretation. Archaeological evidence has thus to some extent compensated for the uncertainties which inevitably attach to the literary foundation dates. But it has also, by showing how reliable in general the literary tradition is, increased our confidence in the authority of the literary sources for Archaic Greek colonization.

There are many other fields in which the material evidence can either verify the literary evidence or add something totally new. One thinks of topography, town plans, sizes of cities, defences, public and private buildings; of achievements in all the arts expressed in durable materials; of evidence for standards of material life, for exports and imports. For all these subjects archaeological evidence is entirely appropriate, so no great problems are presented by the fact that the great bulk of our evidence is due to the spade.

It is when we turn to the life and practices of the community, and to relationships between different groups, that the archaeological evidence may become very difficult to interpret. Take, for instance, the relations between the Greeks and the indigenous population. This is undoubtedly a subject in which archaeological evidence has vastly extended the material available for discussion, just as it is certainly the topic which is currently most enthusiastically pursued in the whole field of Greek colonization. But, if we often cannot tell who the people are whose remains have been discovered (whether Greeks, Hellenized natives, natives who merely liked Greek objects, or a mixture), the first, fundamental, question, on which all interpretation must depend, cannot be answered. On the basis of archaeological evidence alone it will always

[20] H 28; B 12; H 25, 316f, 322–7; C 6.

be difficult to draw a clear picture of Hellenization, intermarriage, mixed communities, exploitation of natives by Greeks, and so forth. Yet these are the very topics on which archaeological evidence is continually asked to throw light, and for which the great bulk of the evidence – and all the new evidence likely to accrue – is archaeological. In such circumstances the only safe procedure is to use first the literary sources, however exiguous, simply because they are explicit, and to interpret the much more abundant, but inarticulate, material evidence under their guidance.

In the arrangement of this chapter the order is imposed by the nature of the subject: first, the history of the foundations by area; secondly, discussion of topics. For much of the factual detail belonging to the first part the reader is referred to the table at the end and to the maps. As a general principle, little attempt is made to treat the history of colonies after their foundation. The chronological limits of this chapter are 800–500 B.C.. Within that period, apart from a few specially favoured cities, such as Cyrene, there are few colonies of which anything approaching history can be written. In the discussion of topics we cannot exclude all material subsequent to 500. Contemporary literary or epigraphic evidence on many of the most important questions about Greek colonization is virtually absent before the fifth century. Furthermore, some of the ideas and practices described then are expressly termed traditional. There is thus sufficient justification, so long as we do it with our eyes open, for using this material to illuminate a picture of Greek colonization in Archaic times, which would otherwise be obscure indeed.

HISTORY OF THE FOUNDATIONS

II. THE SOUTH COAST OF ASIA MINOR AND NORTH SYRIA

The Greeks on the coasts of Lycia, Pamphylia, Cilicia and north Syria are discussed elsewhere in this volume. In the Archaic colonizing movement this is a very minor area. Those who see it otherwise have either failed to distinguish between legendary, possibly Bronze Age, foundations and those of the Archaic period, or have misinterpreted archaeological evidence. It is hardly surprising that there were very few Greek colonies planted here in Archaic times, since the geographical conditions were largely uninviting and the area was inhabited by long-established peoples whose political and military organization was not inferior to that of the Greeks.

Three cities on the south coast of Asia Minor appear to have a good claim to be Archaic Greek settlements, Phaselis, Nagidus and Celenderis. The last two are said to be Samian foundations.[21] They were small sea-ports on the rocky coast of Cilicia Tracheia. Phaselis is firmly attested as a Dorian city by the sixth century, because we know from Herodotus (II. 178.2) that it was one of the participating cities in the Hellenium at Naucratis. The detailed tradition of its foundation is most confused and unsatisfactory.[22] Nothing firm can be deduced about chronology, though we may probably accept Rhodian origin. A small point of interest is the story that the colonists gave a local shepherd a gift of salt fish in payment for the land. Although obviously aetiological this is the only instance in our record of Greek colonization where land is said to have been bought from native inhabitants.

All the other cities in Pamphylia and Cilicia which have been regarded as historical Greek foundations on the basis of late and conflicting literary evidence seem unlikely to have been so.[23] There is to date no archaeological evidence which throws light on these questions. On the north coast of Syria, however, historical Greek colonization has been postulated solely on the basis of archaeological evidence. It is necessary to state here that in the opinion of this author there is nothing at Al Mina[24] or Tell Sūkās[25] which shows that they were Greek colonies. At Al Mina in the early period we have no Greek graves, no Greek writing, no Greek cults and no Greek architecture. Nor can the identification with the presumed Greek town of Posideum be maintained in the face of ancient topographical evidence and the much more convincing localization at Ras-el-Basit.[26] Greek settlement has been assumed solely on the basis of the Greek pottery, which is very abundant (though equalled in quantity by the non-Greek in the early period). Pottery alone cannot tell us who the inhabitants were, especially as the old belief that Greek pottery was not acceptable to orientals,[27] a belief based on conditions in Egypt, has long since been shown to be false by discoveries of Greek pottery at many eastern sites, such as Tyre for instance,[28] where Greek settlers are most improbable (not to mention the Phoenician sites in the western Mediterranean). A better argument is by analogy from Tell Sūkās, where an inscribed loom-weight which has been tentatively dated c. 600 shows that at least one Greek woman was among the inhabitants at that time.[29]

[21] Pomp. Mela I. 77; Scymnus apud Herodian, μον. λέξ., II. 2. p. 925 7L.
[22] Aristaenetus, FGrH 771 F 1; cf. Philostephanus, FHG III p. 28; Heropythus, FGrH 448 F 1 (with Jacoby's commentary ad loc.).   [23] B 37; B 11; B 9; B 46, 1132f, n. 3.
[24] B 84; B 86, 153–67; cf. A 19, 25–8; D 18; A 7, 43f.
[25] B 63; B 58, 90–9; B 13; B 15.   [26] B 63, 137f; B 19, 418f; B 60.
[27] B 63, 129; G 10, 122.
[28] B 8. [For a variant view, observing the different relative quantities of Greek pottery on the sites – considerable at Al Mina, negligible at Tyre – see above, pp. 9–11. Ed.]
[29] B 58, no. 424 (p. 90).

The character of these settlements on the north Syrian coast, as revealed by the finds, puts them firmly in the common Cypro-Levantine culture of the Early Iron Age.[30] Even if they were not Greek colonies, however, they have a significance for the history of the Archaic colonizing movement because they reveal the commercial contacts between Greeks and Phoenicians in the ninth and eighth centuries. The importance of these relations is most clearly illustrated by the Greek adoption of the Phoenician alphabet, but it is not improbable that they also influenced the course of Greek colonization, as may be seen in an area where both Greeks and Phoenicians were active colonizers, the western Mediterranean.

III. SICILY AND SOUTHERN ITALY

The relative abundance of information about the Greek colonization of Sicily and southern Italy, which is better known than that of any other large area, makes it necessary to confine ourselves in this section solely to the early colonies. Colonization later than 700 is treated in the next chapter.

The southern Italian climate of hot, dry summers and (at the coasts) mild winters, and the characteristic landscape of mountain and sea, offered the Greeks fundamentally familiar geographical conditions, in which they could transplant their way of life, and especially their agriculture, virtually unchanged. Only the scale was different. Sicily was the largest island then known and the extent of continental Italy was impressive. Presumably that was the basic reason for calling southern Italy 'Great Greece' (ἡ Μεγάλη 'Ελλάς, Magna Graecia), though a fully satisfactory, detailed, explanation of this title, which is not attested till Polybius (II. 39.1), has evaded a long and inconclusive debate.[31]

At the time of the arrival of the Greek colonists the peoples of Sicily and southern Italy were organized in stable communities, which had in some cases existed for centuries, and some of their settlements were large enough to be called towns, as, for example, Pantalica near Syracuse, or Francavilla Marittima near Sybaris.[32] They possessed the technical skills of advanced Iron Age culture, practising agriculture, metalwork and ceramics. Since their chosen sites were in strong positions on hills and generally away from the sea, we may presume that, like the Cyclopes in the Homeric passage, 'they had no red-cheeked ships' (Od. IX. 116ff). They were grouped in tribes and ruled by kings, one of whom we know by name, the Sicel Hyblon (Thuc. VI. 4.1).

[30] B 72; Birmingham, AJA 67 (1963) 15–42; B 63, 159.
[31] C 54. The passage Strabo VI. 253, which appears to state that Sicily was also part of Magna Graecia, is corrupt; see C 56A; C 80.
[32] C 65, 95f; C 37, 149ff; C 21, 70ff; C 183; C 184; C 75; C 76.

There would have been one category of inhabitants who were not afraid of the sea, if we could believe Thucydides' statement (VI. 2.6) that, before the Greeks came, the Phoenicians had settled the headlands and offshore islands all round Sicily for the sake of trade with the Sicels. However, no evidence has been found anywhere in Sicily for Phoenician settlements which antedate the arrival of the Greeks. Since Sicily is far from unexplored archaeologically, the *argumentum ex silentio* is strong, and few will be happy to accept Thucydides' information until it has been confirmed on the ground.

In the Late Bronze Age there had been close contacts between the Aegean world and Sicily and southern Italy, and settlements of Mycenaean merchants have been postulated at Scoglio del Tonno (Taranto), Lipari and Thapsus, near Syracuse.[33] Between *c.* 1100 and *c.* 800 the general lack of Aegean products in the west shows that most contact ceased. However, a little Greek Protogeometric (tenth-century) pottery has been recognized in the Tarentine region,[34] and, more important, some of the painted pottery made in Sicily and southern Italy during these centuries seems to imply Greek inspiration.[35] So there were probably rare, sporadic, contacts, which is what we should expect, given the physical proximity of the two areas.[36]

From the early eighth century products of the Aegean and the east start to appear at western sites, showing that by that date some trade was beginning again. At Francavilla Marittima a splendid Phoenician bronze cup (fig. 14) was found in a grave dated by its pottery to the second quarter of the eighth century,[37] and the same site shows other eastern objects, such as scarabs and glass, in the period before Sybaris was founded near by.[38] Greek cups of the Middle Geometric II period (*c.* 800–*c.* 750) have been found in Etruria (Veii), Campania (pre-Greek Cyme, Capua, Pontecagnano),[39] at Incoronata near Metapontum,[40] at Scoglio del Tonno,[41] and in Sicily at Villasmundo between Leontini and Megara Hyblaea.[42] In the absence of the right kind of evidence, for example a good wreck, we cannot tell who carried these goods, but we may guess either Phoenicians or Greeks, or (perhaps most probably) both.

None of the Greek colonies has yet produced earlier material than Late Geometric I (*c.* 750–*c.* 725), so the idea of pre-colonization trade has again found favour.[43] The original 'pre-colonization' theory, associated especially with the name of Blakeway,[44] suffered an eclipse

[33] C 38; C 181, 20–4; C 70, 67; *CAH.* II.2³, 165–87.
[34] C 108, 251; C 21, 59.   [35] C 140, 159.
[36] C 76, 238f.   [37] C 21, 51.
[38] C 158, 45.   [39] C 21, 16f; C 148.
[40] C 70, 56.   [41] C 21, 59.
[42] C 70, 66f.   [43] C 147.   [44] C 42.

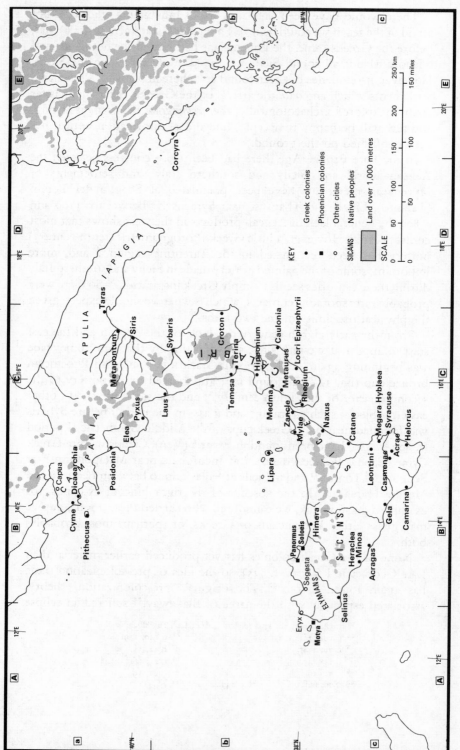

Map 8. Sicily and Magna Graecia.

14. Phoenician bronze bowl, from Francavilla. Eighth century B.C. Diameter 19·5 cm. (Reggio, Museo Civico; after P. Zancani, *ASMG* 11/12 (1970/1) 9–33.)

when the dating of the pottery types on which he depended was changed.[45] This new theory is itself vulnerable, partly because there is room for doubt about the length of life of some of the pottery types in question, notably the chevron skyphoi and skyphoi with pendent concentric semicricles,[46] but most of all because of the uncertainty of the dates of the first Greek colonies in the west, Pithecusa and Cyme (see below). With this *caveat* we may nevertheless accept on present evidence that Greek goods were traded along the coasts of southern Italy and eastern Sicily before Greek colonies were founded there.

Pithecusa and Cyme

In the eighth century Euboean colonists settled two sites in the Campanian region, Pithecusa and Cyme. Pithecusa (modern Ischia) is the largest of the islands off Naples, has an area of about forty-six square

[45] D 29, 80f; cf. C 161, 43f.
[46] H 25, plates 18, 32; C 21, 16f; C 148.

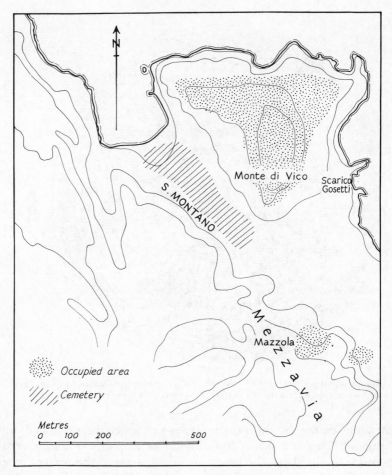

15. Plan of Pithecusa. (After c 50, 86, pl. 1.)

kilometres and is some eleven kilometres from the mainland at its
nearest point, Cape Misenum. The Greek colony (fig. 15) was at Monte
di Vico at the north-west extremity of the island, where a flattish-topped
headland with steep slopes has sheltered harbours at its foot on both
its east and west sides. Cyme (Latin Cumae) lies on the coast north of
the Bay of Naples. Its splendid acropolis hill stands out from the long,
flat shore, dominating the surrounding country and coastal sea traffic.
The oft-repeated statement that Cyme had no harbour is misconceived.
A plausible identification of a good harbour to the south of the acropolis
(and now on land) has been made,[47] but, if the sea then washed the foot
of the acropolis, as is probable, there were adequate beaching bays both
north and south of the headland, and the position becomes strongly

[47] C 129.

reminiscent of Monte di Vico. The acropolis of Cyme is some 14 km from the Greek city of Pithecusa and the two hills are in easy sight of one another. For both these colonies our literary evidence is slender and unsatisfactory, but the archaeological testimony is rich and revealing. Most of the material from Cyme was obtained long ago,[48] but excavations have been conducted at the site of Pithecusa since 1952 by G. Buchner.[49] Of these it can be said without exaggeration that no excavation of recent times has made a more important contribution to our knowledge of the Greeks in the west and of Greek colonization as a whole.

The excavations have taken place in three main areas: the so-called Scarico Gosetti, a great unstratified dump on the east slope of the Monte di Vico, the cemetery, and at Mazzola, one of the outlying, discontinuous, settlements in the Mezzavia area, some 200 to 400 metres south of the foot of Monte di Vico. This work has shown that in the Late Geometric II period (c. 725–c. 700) the city and its outlying settlements extended over some three to four square kilometres.

No Early Iron Age material has appeared in the excavated parts of Pithecusa, so it may be that the site of the city was uninhabited when the Greeks came. However, at Castiglione, on the north coast some four kilometres east of Monte di Vico, there was an Early Iron Age village,[50] and the colonists obviously chose their headland site with defence in mind. The presence of natives is also presupposed in Buchner's hypothesis that most of the women of the colony were indigenous,[51] which will be considered when we discuss intermarriage below.

Although we have no public buildings or shrines, the character of life in the eighth century can be partly grasped from the grave and settlement evidence. Widespread use of writing is shown by the many graffiti, of which the most famous is on 'the cup of Nestor', a Late Geometric bird kotyle, found in a grave dated to c. 720–c. 710 by Protocorinthian aryballoi (fig. 16): 'Nestor's cup was fine to drink from. But whoever drinks from this cup will immediately be seized by the desire of fair-crowned Aphrodite.' We note the handling of metres and reference to Homeric material.[52] Pithecusa has also produced the first potter's signature known – on a vase of local make.[53] In the cemetery the graves, which are arranged in family plots, include some convincingly identified as slave burials. Since these are found with relatively humble families, slave ownership went well down society's ladder of wealth.[54]

Eighth-century Pithecusa imported goods on a large scale and from

[48] C 71.

[49] C 47; C 48; C 49; C 50; C 98.

[50] C 45; C 50, 64.

[51] C 50, 79.

[52] C 53; A 27, 226f; H 25, 227f, 358 n. 4; M–L no. 1.

[53] C 98, 38f; C 50, 69.

[54] C 50, 69–73.

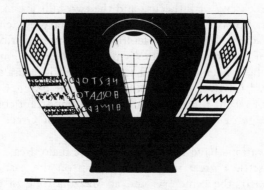

16. 'Nestor's cup', from Pithecusa, East Greek. For the inscription see text and n. 52. Late eighth century B.C. Height 10·3 cm. (Ischia Museum.)

17. 'Lyre-Player' group seal, probably of Cilician origin, from Pithecusa. Lion and bird. Second half of eighth century B.C. Length 1·55 cm. (Ischia Museum; C 52, no. 14.)

a wide variety of regions: scaraboid seals of the so-called 'Lyre-player' group, probably from the north Syrian/Cilician area (fig. 17);[55] scarabs and Egyptian (or Egyptianizing) amulets, presumably from Phoenicia; Greek fine pottery, Phoenician amphorae and small vessels, impasto from south Etruria, Apulian Geometric, and the so-called 'SOS' amphorae, which occur very frequently.[56] These last were made in Attica and Euboea and are found at numerous western sites in the eighth and seventh centuries, even as far afield as Toscanos in southern Spain and Mogador off the west coast of Morocco.[57] They are thought to have contained oil.[58] There was also much local industry, including iron-working, fine metalwork and pottery, some of the products of which were exported to the Italian mainland.[59]

At this large importing, exporting and industrial settlement there is evidence that there were Phoenicians living beside the Greeks, of which the most striking is a graffito on an amphora reused for a child's burial in the Late Geometric II period (c. 725–c. 700). This has been interpreted as showing that Phoenicians could bury their dead in the same cemetery among the Greeks.[60] We are reminded of the close contacts between Greeks and Phoenicians in the Levant.

We do not know for certain when either Cyme or Pithecusa was founded. The Eusebian date for Cyme (1050) is obviously an error, presumably the result of early confusion with Aeolian Cyme; and Strabo's statement that Cyme was the oldest Greek settlement in the west[61] is in conflict with Livy (VIII. 22. 5–6), who says that the Chalcidians first settled Pithecusa and then transferred to Cyme on the mainland.[62] Nor is Strabo confirmed by archaeological discoveries, since the earliest material from Cyme is of the Late Geometric II (= Early Protocorinthian) period, c. 725–c. 700,[63] i.e. later than that from not only Pithecusa, but also several colonies in Sicily. The most definite evidence that Cyme was founded earlier than the first archaeological material now known is the information from Thucydides (VI. 4.5) that Zancle was settled from Cyme, for Zancle, though itself not precisely dated, was probably founded within the third quarter of the eighth century. At Pithecusa we have no literary foundation date but an abundance of Late Geometric I material, including plenty regarded by experts as ushering in that period. So on current evidence we may date Pithecusa's foundation to c. 750, but the size and character

[55] C 52. [56] C 50, 68.
[57] F 18; C 154, 233–6; C 93, 61ff; C 244, 6–8.
[58] C 163; but contrast C 22, 52 n. 264.
[59] C 98; C 48, 67; C 49, 364–72; C 50, 68–86.
[60] C 51; C 72. [61] Strabo v. 247.
[62] Cf. C 161, 51f.
[63] C 96, 102; H 25, 326.

of the city in the Late Geometric period, as Buchner has convincingly argued, suggest rather that it was founded earlier still.[64]

The archaeological material of the early period at Cyme is closely comparable to that at Pithecusa, but the early burials include seven of the 'princely' type, containing the ashes of men and women of a noble, warrior class, who prided themselves on their splendid weapons and wealth in fine and precious metal goods. One of these tombs is clearly dated within the eighth century by an 'SOS' amphora of the earliest type.[65] These burials are now precisely paralleled by those found at the west gate of Eretria, where the rite is identical. It has been plausibly suggested that their ceremonial reveals the influence of Homeric ideas.[66]

The Euboean cities, Chalcis and Eretria, both of which we may regard, in spite of some confusion in the literary evidence, as the founders of Pithecusa and Cyme, were in the eighth century perhaps the greatest cities of Greece, famous in war and credited with a Cycladic empire (Strabo x. 446–9). Their maritime experience is attested by a *koine* recognizable from the tenth century in the pottery of an area stretching from coastal Thessaly to Naxos, with Euboea as its centre,[67] and by close relations with the eastern Mediterranean.[68] We now know that already in the eighth century the Eretrians had laid out their own city on a grand scale, and were building ambitiously, at a site with a small bay for harbour and a powerful acropolis.[69] We are not surprised, therefore, that these warriors, seamen and builders of cities, were able to achieve far-flung colonization in the west.

The purpose and character of that colonization has long been a subject for speculation, and no doubt always will be in default of explicit literary evidence. But one thing is clear: Pithecusa and Cyme were linked. Livy states this explicitly and archaeology seems to support him. From *c.* 700 there is a marked decline at Pithecusa,[70] for which the simplest explanation is that Cyme's superior attractions drew the population away. If Pithecusa and Cyme were linked, there is no doubt that we are dealing with true colonization or settlement.

In view of this it seems vain to deny that one attraction for the colonists will have been the extremely fertile land to be found in the vicinity of Cyme and on the island of Pithecusa.[71] But that cannot be the sole explanation why the earliest Greek colonies in the west are also the most distant, since there were plenty of fertile sites nearer Greece, sites which were shortly afterwards colonized in rapid succession.

[64] C 48, 67; C 49, 373; C 50, 66f.

[65] C 25; C 50, 74ff.   [66] D 13, 13–32; H 26.

[67] C 3.   [68] A 7, 39ff; C 147.

[69] D 5.   [70] C 50, 65.

[71] C 50, 80; C 147, 12; cf. C 62; C 161, 57 n. 3; C 101, 112.

Of other suggestions one is that this colonization is to be explained by the search for metals.[72] This was regarded as triumphantly vindicated when abundant evidence for metalworking was found at Pithecusa, and one piece of mineral iron from the Scarico Gosetti proved to have come from Elba.[73] In its simplest form this explanation cannot be right. Greeks in Euboea did not need to found colonies in Campania in order to obtain iron or copper.[74] However, the availability of metals would be an added attraction to colonists seeking a good site.

Another theory is that Pithecusa was an *emporion* through which goods brought by Euboeans from the Aegean and the East were distributed to Italian cities.[75] This depends partly on the idea (which seems false to this writer) that Al Mina was a Euboean colony, and requires the assumption, for which we have no evidence, that this trade was in Euboean hands, but the general proposition that there was plenty of commercial activity at Pithecusa and Cyme is undeniable.

The advantages that the region offered – land, raw materials for industry and opportunities for trade – all depended on satisfactory relations with local people. Our evidence is not such as to make clear those relations, but the old theory that it was particularly the Etruscans who drew the Greeks so far north seems to be strengthened by our recently-acquired knowledge that there were Etruscan settlements in Campania and further south from early in the eighth century.[76] The greatest of these was at Capua, a mere forty kilometres from Cyme. Unless the colonists had some understanding with Capua it is difficult to understand the foundation of Cyme.[77] It is also interesting that the Etruscan aristocracy adopted the same burial practices as the Euboean warrior élite, which we know from Cyme and Eretria.[78] Perhaps one of the keys to the Euboean colonization in the Campanian region may have been their relations with the Etruscans, who were themselves already aware of the possibility of settlement in that favoured area.

Sicily

The first Greek colony in Sicily was Naxus, founded by Chalcidians from Euboea under the leadership of Theocles in 734, according to Thucydides (VI. 3.1). Theocles also established the altar of Apollo Archegetes (the founder), which stood outside the city of Thucydides' day. On this altar all Sicilian envoys to the gods of Greece sacrificed first before their departure. Eighth-century remains uncovered at Naxus

[72] C 65, 3, 7f.

[73] C 49, 378; C 50, 68f.

[74] C 6, 43–5.

[75] C 49, 374; C 147.

[76] C 21, 11ff.

[77] C 164, 132.

[78] C 22; C 23.

include some houses, which were apparently not built close together, and pottery both imported and locally produced. Some of this belongs to the Late Geometric I period (c. 750–c. 725).[79] So the archaeological finds suit the Thucydidean foundation date well, and we need no longer contemplate the higher dating proposed by Vallet and Villard in an article on Sicilian colonial dates, which once won widespread accept-ance[80] but was based on assumptions about archaeological evidence now known to be incorrect.

The site of Naxus, a low peninsula on the coast north of Etna (modern Punta di Schisò), was not outstanding and offered little scope for growth, so it is not surprising that, five years later, in 729, Theocles founded a second colony at Leontini (Thuc. VI. 3.3).

Leontini lies inland in the hills at the southern edge of the plain of Catania, the largest stretch of fertile plain in eastern Sicily. The upland pastures near by were so rich that the feeding time of the sheep had to be restricted (Arist. HA III. 17). It is a hill site with excellent water supply which had been inhabited since very early times.[81] Although Thucydides says that the Chalcidians drove out the Sicels by war, there is a more complex story in the Strategemata collected by Polyaenus (V. 5.1) for the emperor Lucius Verus in the second century A.D. The Chalcidians made an agreement on oath to live in peace side by side with the Sicels of Leontini, but then admitted the Megarian colonists, who later settled at Megara Hyblaea, on condition that they expelled the Sicels by force, since they were not bound by oath. Archaeological evidence has shown that the site of the Greek colony was occupied by Sicels before the Greeks came and there were Sicels living within sight and sound of the Greeks after the colony was established.[82] For daily life to be possible relations must then have been formalized in some way. The choice of an inland site occupied by Sicels and the continued presence of Sicels in the immediate neighbourhood both seem to imply an agreement of some sort, whatever credence we give to Polyaenus. On the other hand, the first Greek city was on a strong hill, Monte S. Mauro, and was surrounded by a powerful wall, which may be dated to the early seventh century.[83]

The earliest colonial material from Leontini is of Late Geometric I date (c. 750–c. 725),[84] so here too Thucydides' date is confirmed. We have no such archaeological evidence to throw light on the period of foundation at the third eighth-century Chalcidian colony in eastern Sicily, Catane, which was founded on the coast under Mt Etna, where the volcanic soil was exceptionally fertile (Strabo VI. 269). This was part

[79] C 131; C 135.
[80] C 166; C 153, 17f.
[81] C 150.
[82] C 150, 25f; C 37, 171f.
[83] H 79, 128f; C 149.
[84] C 150, 22f and plate VI.

of the same colonizing activity, but here the *oikistes* was Euarchus (Thuc. VI. 3.3). We cannot explain the pluralism of Theocles, *oikistes* of both Naxus and Leontini, which is unique in our record, nor why it was limited to two. With Catane's foundation the Chalcidians had colonies on both the north and south edges of the plain of Catania, and some have concluded that they intended from the first to control the whole plain.[85] Whether or not that is right, it is clear that for these three Chalcidian colonies, founded in rapid succession, agricultural land was the first consideration.

Syracuse had in the meantime been colonized in 733 by Corinthians under the leadership of Archias, one of the Bacchiad family, who ruled at Corinth and traced their ancestry to Heracles (Thuc. VI. 3.2).[86] According to Strabo, Chersicrates, also a Bacchiad, left on the same expedition with Archias, and founded the Corinthian colony at Corcyra (Strabo VI. 269). This seems plausible, because Corcyra was a most important port of call for Greeks sailing to the west (cf. Thuc. I. 44.3), but the synchronism is suspect. Eusebius' date for the Corinthian colonization of Corcyra is 706, which seems to indicate a different tradition, and, in the same passage, Strabo relates a patently false synchronism of Croton and Syracuse. The earliest pottery found at Corcyra is of the last two decades of the eighth century and cannot settle the question.[87]

The site of Syracuse was outstanding (fig. 18). Ortygia, the offshore island, is so placed in relation to the main island that it makes two excellent harbours, of which the southern, the Great Harbour, is of magnificent dimensions. Ortygia itself is large enough at forty hectares for a fair-sized town, and possesses a freshwater spring, Arethusa, famous for its quality and abundance. On the adjacent main island the plain of the Anapus offered agricultural wealth.

According to Thucydides, the colonists expelled the Sicels from Ortygia, and the earliest Greek houses have duly been found built directly on top of the remains of the Sicel village.[89] The Corinthians expanded on to the main island with very little delay. Eighth-century settlement has been found a kilometre from the narrow strait (which was later bridged) between Ortygia and the main island,[90] and the first cemetery at Fusco is about a kilometre and a half from there. They also controlled a much wider surrounding territory. The great Sicel site at Pantalica, some twenty-four kilometres west of Syracuse, was apparently abandoned at about the time of the Corinthian colonization,[91] and by

[85] C 65, 10.
[86] Cf. C 5, 220.
[87] C 95, 150f.
[88] C 64A, 11ff.
[89] C 127; C 134, 143.
[90] C 138, 23f.
[91] C 164, 110f.

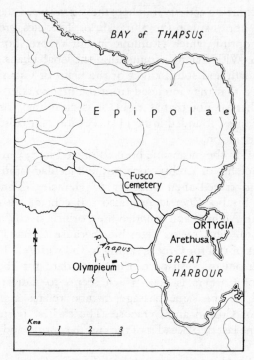

18. Plan of Syracuse. (After c 64A, 94, fig. 19.)

c. 700 the colonists had occupied Helorus, a strong position on the coast some thirty kilometres to the south.[92]

The earliest houses of the colonists were rectangular, single-roomed, about four metres square and closely built.[93] The general impression of the first graves from Fusco is also not rich.[94] Presumably the famous wealth of Syracuse did not spring up in the first generation (unless there was inequality and the rich have so far eluded us).

Megara Hyblaea was settled by Megarian colonists in 728, according to Thucydides (VI. 4.1), after many vicissitudes. Their first attempt was at Trotilum, which is probably to be identified with a site above the small bay of La Bruca at the south end of the Gulf of Catania.[95] Abandoning that they shared briefly in Leontini, but were expelled by the Chalcidians. Then they tried the small peninsula of Thapsus, almost an offshore island in the Gulf of Augusta, less than sixteen kilometres north of Syracuse. Here their *oikistes* Lamis died. Among the numerous Bronze Age burials on Thapsus Orsi found a single later grave at a

[92] C 137, 117f.   [93] C 137, 73; cf. C 170, 269 n. 2.

[94] H 54, 341; C 86.   [95] C 34, 112.

higher level, which contained two skeletons, two Corinthian Late
Geometric cups and a pair of tweezers.[96] Being of the right date, this
has regularly been recognized as Lamis' grave,[97] but the sparse grave
goods tell no precise story and the two skeletons (? man and wife)[98]
do not help the interpretation. Finally, the wanderers were given land
to settle on the coast some eight kilometres to the north by the local
Sicel king, Hyblon, whose name may be commemorated in that of the
colony.

The site where they finally settled is quite defenceless and could only
have been occupied by permission of the local people. However, it was
well watered, had small beaching harbours and formed part of a coastal
plain some fifteen kilometres long by six to seven deep. Because urban
occupation ceased in 213 B.C.,[99] this site offers great opportunities to
archaeologists, which have been seized above all in recent years by
Vallet, Villard and their colleagues.

On the basis of trials and surface exploration, it seems likely that the
whole of the north part of the low plateau, on which the city stood,
as far as the later wall on the landward side was settled in the eighth
century.[100] This is a relatively large area, some thirty-six hectares or
ninety acres, but the small number of eighth-century houses that have
been unearthed in the excavated portion are not set close together, and
a low density of occupation may be assumed, even if, regrettably, no
estimate of population can be hazarded.[101]

The excavation of the agora and its environs has shown that this area
was laid out in the second half of the seventh century, after which its
form remained basically unchanged.[102] Furthermore, the eighth-century
houses, although they rarely face on to a street, are invariably aligned
with the main streets in their section, and no road, much less the agora
itself, destroyed an earlier house.[103] The excavators' conclusion seems
inescapable: the street plan and public centre were established at the
beginning and Megara Hyblaea was a planned city of the eighth century
(fig. 19). There are many regular elements in this plan, but also some
surprising irregularities, of which the most striking is the trapezoidal
shape of the agora, which creates two networks of streets and blocks
with different orientations. This shows that the planners were not
interested in orthogonality, the very hallmark of later planned cities,
which we find as early as the seventh century in western colonies.[104]

The earliest houses were simple, rectangular, single-roomed struc-

[96] C 126, 103f, plate IV no. 16; C 166, 337.
[97] C 65, 19.
[98] H 51, 194; cf. C 57, 34.
[99] C 170, 8.
[100] C 165, 91f.
[101] C 170, 263–70, plan XI; cf. 411f.
[102] C 165, 87; C 170, 388–90.
[103] C 165, 89f, 92; C 170, 270.
[104] C 164, 76, 112; C 56; H 77, 22–4; C 31.

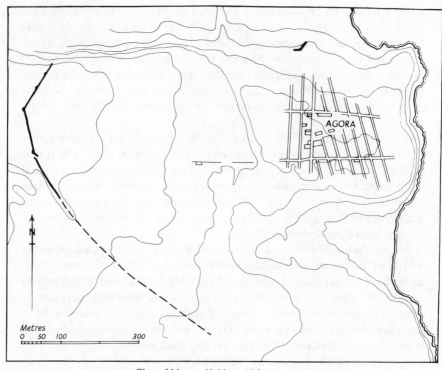

19. Plan of Megara Hyblaea. (After C 170, plan 1.)

tures, about five metres square and built of stone. Some had storage pits
for grain nearby.[105] There is abundant pottery, of which the earliest is
of the Late Geometric I period (*c.* 750–*c.* 725),[106] and thus confirms
Thucydides' foundation date. Since much of this pottery was made
locally, we have evidence of local industry, and since the colonists were
able to import fine pottery and the contents, wine or oil, of pottery
containers, they clearly achieved a certain prosperity.[107]

Zancle (later Messana, modern Messina) took its name (the indigenous
word for a sickle) from the long, narrow, curved spit of land which
made the harbour and created a fine seafarers' site on the west side of
the dramatic narrows that divide Sicily from Italy. According to
Thucydides (VI. 4.5), it was settled first by pirates from Italian Cyme;
then numerous settlers from Chalcis and the rest of Euboea joined in
the settlement, the *oikistai* being Perieres from Cyme and Crataemenes
from Chalcis. Thucydides gives no date, but the few finds include a sherd
of the Late Geometric I period, *c.* 750–*c.* 725.[108] Zancle made up for

[105] C 170, 263–70.   [106] C 167; H 25, 323–5, 427.
[107] C 170, 411.   [108] H 25, 323, 325; C 161, plate VII.

its almost total lack of territory by founding a dependent colony at
Mylae, on the isthmus of a long and narrow peninsula which points
north to the Lipari islands.[109] There is cultivable land on the peninsula north of the isthmus and a useful coastal plain in the vicinity.
Archaeological evidence shows that Mylae was previously inhabited and
that the Greek settlement occurred in the last quarter of the eighth
century.[110] A Eusebian entry under 717 may refer to Mylae, in which
case that would be the firm *terminus ante quem* for the colonization of
Zancle.

South Italy

On the Italian side of the Straits of Messina the Chalcidians founded
another colony, Rhegium (modern Reggio). The literary evidence for
its foundation is confused and full of obviously fictional material, so
it is tempting to reject everything except Antiochus' short and sober
statement (*FGrH* 555 F 9) that the people of Zancle sent for the
colonists from Chalcis and appointed the *oikistes*, Antimnestus. However, he may have been rationalizing from the close connexion of the
two cities in historical times, and the participation of Messenians, which
is a strong element in the tradition, is hard to explain away.[111] These
Messenians provide our only chronological indication in the literary
sources, as they are said to be refugees from the first Messenian War,
which is traditionally dated 743–720. If we could rely on a single
oenochoe, which is Late Geometric and presumably from a grave, the
foundation date would be before *c.* 720.[112] The evidence is not good,
but Rhegium may be the first Greek colony in the far south of Italy.

    There is very little good agricultural land close to the city, and
Rhegium's *raison d'être* must always have been the sea and its strategic
position. Throughout its history its close relations were with the Greek
cities of Sicily. We move to a different world and different Greeks in
the Gulf of Taranto, where the remaining eighth-century colonization
took place.

    Sybaris lay on the coast of Calabria at the southern end of the
'instep' of Italy, where the land between the Gulf of Taranto and the
Tyrrhenian sea is narrowest. The Achaean origin is clear from our
sources and from testimonials of writing found in recent excavations,[113]
but Aristotle tells us (*Pol.* v, 1303a) that colonists from Troezen also
participated. Interesting though this is, the complete absence of further
evidence on the topic makes interpretation difficult.

    The discovery of the site of Sybaris has been one of the heroic stories

[109] C 65, 211; C 34, 97f; C 161, 81.
[110] C 39, 83, 116f; C 161, 84; H 25, 104, 323.
[111] C 161, 66–80; C 5, 17–19.   [112] H 25, 372.   [113] C 83, 303.

of modern archaeology.[114] We now know definitely that the ancient city lay beneath its successors, Thurii and Copia, north of the old course of the river Crati, some three kilometres inland from the modern coastline. The city seems to have been laid out parallel to the coast and was bounded on the north and south by the rivers Sybaris (modern Coscile) and Crathis (modern Crati) (Strabo VI. 263). Since the conjectured ancient courses of these rivers at the city site are some six kilometres apart, we should apparently envisage a very large, flat, low-lying site on sand-dunes by the shore.[115]

The date of foundation, 720, is reached by combining the statements that it was destroyed in 510 and existed for 210 years (Diod. XI. 90.3; Ps.-Scymnus 357–60).[116] Although the latter figure has been suspected as a calculation of generations (e.g. 6 × 35), the date of destruction seems to be well confirmed by the finds and part of a 'Thapsus' style cup has been found, which is datable to the third quarter of the eighth century.[117]

The large and magnificently fertile alluvial plain of Sybaris is enclosed by mountains which contained numerous Iron Age settlements.[118] Some of these have been investigated, and show that the Achaean colonists were strong enough to end the existence of settlements which had previously dominated the plain. Torre Mordillo, for example, a strong position on the right bank of the river Coscile, some ten kilometres inland from Sybaris, was apparently violently destroyed at the time of Sybaris' foundation, and the two flourishing native settlements at Francavilla Marittima (about fourteen kilometres north-west of Sybaris) and Amendolara (about thirty kilometres north of Sybaris) came to an end at the same time. At Amendolara the successors of the previous Iron Age town betook themselves to S. Nicola, some three kilometres to the east. At Francavilla Marittima the Greeks had established a sanctuary of Athena by 700, though a small successor settlement of the previous population appears to have existed near by.[119]

Another Achaean colony, Croton, was founded under the leadership of Myscellus of Rhype[120] on the east coast of Calabria, just inside the Gulf of Taranto at its western end. Here a strong headland with harbours on both sides offered the best protection for ships on the whole coast after Taranto. Eusebius dates the foundation of both Croton and Sybaris to 709. The synchronism is doubtless false, the product of a desire to connect the great historical rivals from the beginning, but the date seems appropriate for Croton, where the excavations at the Post

[114] C 145; C 68.   [115] C 56.
[116] Cf. C 115.   [117] C 83, 292f, fig. 5.
[118] C 144; C 76, plate XIII.   [119] C 75, 625f; C 76, 244; C 77.
[120] Hdt. VIII. 47; Strabo VI. 262; Hippys of Rhegium, FGrH 544 F 1.

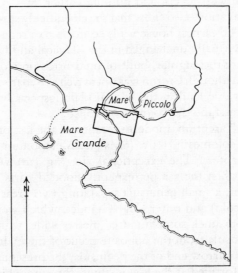

20. Plan of the Taras area. (After C 109, pl. 55.)

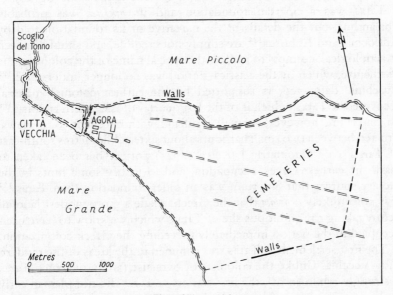

21. Plan of Taras. (After C 152.)

Office site have revealed abundant Early Protocorinthian (*c.* 725–*c.* 700) pottery in the lowest levels, and nothing earlier.[121]

The new excavations also show that the city quickly spread far beyond the headland. The earliest house walls conform to a regular street plan, which persists virtually unchanged in the Classical and Hellenistic city. These houses are rectangular, built of mud-brick on stone socles, and not closely set. Although Croton was not as rich as Sybaris agriculturally, there was cultivable land in the coastal plain, especially to the south, which we may assume the colony controlled.

Taras (Latin Tarentum, modern Taranto) is the last of the definitely eighth-century colonies in Italy. (Siris and Metapontum are discussed in the next chapter.) The exceptional site (fig. 20) was created by 'submersion', when the sea permanently flooded parts of the coastal plain.[122] This left a small peninsula separating two great harbours, the inner (Mar Piccolo) and outer (Mar Grande), which were joined only by the narrow channel, some hundred metres wide, which divides the end of the peninsula from the opposite point of the mainland, Scoglio del Tonno. The narrow end of the peninsula, the present Città Vecchia, could easily be fortified at the low isthmus, through which the present canal was dug in A.D. 1480. The colonists then had a virtual island site, some 900 metres long by 250 wide at the widest point (about 16 hectares or forty acres), with fairly steep sides on the long dimensions (fig. 21).[123]

Taras was a Spartan foundation and its *oikistes* was probably Phalanthus, but the details of the narrative of its foundation told by Antiochus and Ephorus[124] are simply not credible, and should be seen as aetiological attempts to explain the special name of the colonists, the Partheniae, which by the classical period was no longer understood.[125] Eusebius' date, 706, is supported by the earliest colonial material recovered at Taras, which is of the last quarter of the eighth century.[126] At Satyrium, however, a small headland with excellent long views, situated between two small harbours about sixteen kilometres south-east of Taras, Late Geometric I (*c.* 750–*c.* 725) pottery has been taken to mark the earliest Greek occupation, and to justify some hints in the literary sources that Satyrium was an older foundation than Taras.[127] It is not unlikely *a priori* that the Greeks made a more modest landfall before taking the ambitious site of Taras, which we know to have been occupied in the period immediately preceding the Greek colonization.

The first settlement at Taras was confined to the areas of the modern Città Vecchia. Unlike the colonists of Syracuse (a city of which Taras is strongly reminiscent), the first settlers at Taras did not plan an early

[121] C 70, 61f.   [122] C 152, 32–6.   [123] C 109.
[124] Strabo VI. 278–80; FGrH 555 F 13; FGrH 70 F 216.
[125] C 182, 40f.   [126] C 109, 358; H 25, 104, 323.   [127] C 105; C 106.

extension of their living space beyond the isthmus to the south-east, because that is where they buried their dead, on ground that was to be in the middle of the Classical and Hellenistic city.[128] Perhaps they feared the native inhabitants. Apulia and Iapygia were in general not Greek colonial territory, in spite of their attractions and proximity to Greece. Presumably the inhabitants both wished and were able to exclude Greek colonists – except at Taras. We have two conflicting accounts of the reception of the Greek colonists, but both are contaminated by references to legendary times (Strabo VI. 279–80). On general grounds it seems likely that this was an act of forcible colonization.

Thus, in a short space of time, Greeks had established themselves in Campania, eastern Sicily, the Straits of Messina and the Gulf of Taranto. Even though most of the mother cities responsible are known to have been strong, the speed and scale of the movement, once the region was opened to Greek colonization, are striking. It has been suggested that the Phoenicians taught the Greeks to colonize.[129] Although the arguments for this contention – that the Greeks were preceded in Sicily by the Phoenicians, and that Greek colonial sites are like those of the Phoenicians – are easily refuted,[130] it remains an interesting speculation that it was through their contacts with the Phoenicians that the Greeks were introduced to the opportunities for colonization in the west.

IV. THE NORTH COAST OF THE AEGEAN

Plutarch (*Quaest. Graec.* XI) tells us that the Eretrian colonists, who were expelled from Corcyra by Corinthians under Charicrates (*sic*), sought to return to their mother city, but were driven off. They then sailed to 'Thrace', where they settled at Methone.[131] Methone lies on the west shore of the Gulf of Therme,[132] the western end of the colonial region under discussion; the eastern boundary may be placed at the Thracian Chersonese. In between, the whole coast of Thrace was dotted with Greek colonies, but the Chalcidice peninsula offered special opportunities to a seafaring people, because its three southward prongs of Pallene, Sithonia and Acte create a very long coastline. The area also includes the offshore islands of Thasos and Samothrace.

Geographically this region is close enough to be, if not part of Greece, then certainly part of the Aegean world. Its climate is less purely Mediterranean than that of southern Greece; it has more summer rainfall, more severe winters, and large rivers of European type, which flow permanently. These create valuable plains at their mouths. Rich

---

[128] C 109, 357f, 380. [129] A 38, 47f. [130] C 64, 46, 55f.
[131] Cf. C 84; A 29, 63–5; C 55; C 6, 46; E 34, 425f. [132] E 34, 129.

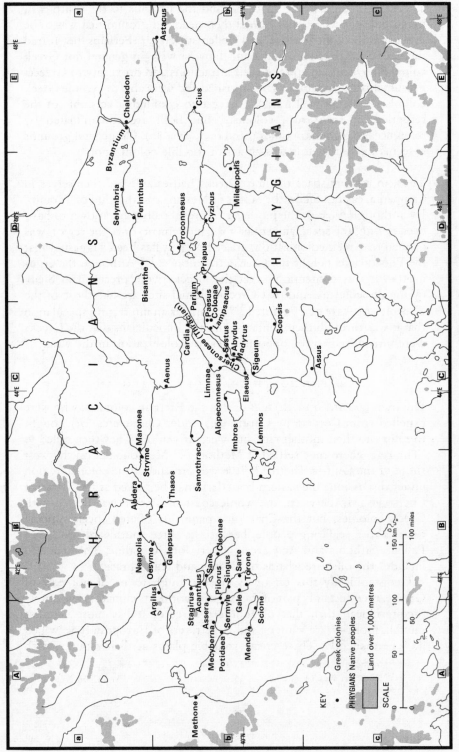

Map 9. The north Aegean and the Propontis.

THRACIANS

PHRYGIANS

Astacus
Chalcedon
Byzantium
Cius
Selymbria
Perinthus
Proconnesus
Cyzicus
Miletopolis
Bisanthe
Priapus
Parium
Paesus
Colonae
Lampsacus
Cardia
Chersonese (Thracian)
Sestus
Abydus
Madytus
Sigeum
Aenus
Limnae
Elaeus
Scepsis
Maronea
Alopeconnesus
Assus
Stryme
Samothrace
Imbros
Lemnos
Abdera
Thasos
Neapolis
Oesyme
Galepsus
Argilus
Stagirus
Sane
Acanthus
Cleonae
Assera
Pilorus
Singus
Sarte
Mecyberna
Sermyle
Gale
Torone
Potidaea
Scione
Mende
Methone

KEY

● Greek colonies

PHRYGIANS Native peoples

Land over 1,000 metres

SCALE

0   50   100   150 km
0   50   100 miles

supplies of timber and valuable mineral resources, especially precious metals, add to the attractions of the area.[133]

In the colonizing epoch this whole region was thought of as Thrace and occupied, with few exceptions, by tribes whom the Greeks called (perhaps loosely in some cases) Thracians.[134] The most notable exception appear to be the enigmatic Pelasgians, the name given by Greeks to the non-Greek inhabitants of Acte and Samothrace (not to mention a very large number of other places outside the region under discussion). On Lemnos these people used a language akin to Etruscan, while in Samothrace they are thought to be in origin Thracian. We must at least conclude that by the historical period they were clearly distinguishable from the Thracians, and, to judge by the little evidence we have, it seems that the Greeks found them easier neighbours too. At the western end of the area the Macedonians were clearly not yet sufficiently strong or united to prevent Greek colonization in the Gulf of Therme or Chalcidice. So the native peoples with whom the Greeks had to reckon were mainly different tribes of Thracians.

The ancient evidence for the Greek colonization of the north Aegean is so poor that there is much room for theorizing, and it has even been suggested that the name Chalcidice and such terms as Chalcidians in Thrace had nothing to do with Euboean Chalcis.[135] This rather perverse hypothesis has been adequately rebutted by Bradeen in a most useful study of the Chalcidian colonization in Thrace,[136] which reconstructed the most complete list of these Chalcidian settlements that we are likely to achieve.

Apart from some Andrian colonization in the north-east, Achaean Scione and Corinthian Potidaea, Chalcidice was colonized by Chalcis and Eretria. Eretrian settlements were planted on Pallene and the Gulf of Therme, Chalcis colonized Sithone and, according to Thucydides (IV. 109.3–4), also parts of Acte, though there the non-Greek population remained strong. The chronology of this colonization is open to dispute. However, some eighth-century settlement is implied by a small amount of literary evidence,[137] and this should be given more weight than the indirect and *a priori* arguments that have been advanced against such early dating.[138] The complete absence of archaeological evidence precludes certainty, but for the moment we should consider Chalcidice an important area of Greek colonization in the eighth century.

East of Chalcidice, the offshore island of Thasos was to become the greatest Greek colony of the north Aegean region. It is almost circular

---

E 16.   [134] E 34, 418.

[135] C 195.   [136] C 187.

[137] Arist. *Erotikos* fr. 3 (OCT); Plut. *Quaest. Graec.* XI; Strabo 447. Cf. C 6, 46f.

[138] E.g. D 29, 71; E 34, 432 n. 2, 440.

in shape, measuring 25·5 kilometres north to south and 23·5 east to west, with an area of *c.* 398 square kilometres. The channel separating the island from the Thracian coast measures a mere six kilometres. Although the terrain is mountainous, there are a number of fertile valleys and abundant water. Furthermore, there were in antiquity important mineral resources, including gold.[139]

Before the arrival of the Greeks Thasos was occupied by Thracians. One of their settlements has been discovered in a mountainous region in the south of the island on a peak called Kastri, between the modern villages of Theologos and Potos. Another was on the site of the later Greek city, a magnificent position on the north coast, looking towards the mainland, where a large harbour surrounded by hills recalls the shape of an ancient theatre. These Thracians had commercial relations with overseas traders and permitted Phoenicians to work the gold mines.[140] It may well be that the Phoenicians established the cult of Melkart at Thasos, which the Greeks later maintained as a cult of Heracles.[141]

The date of the colonization of Thasos by the Cycladic island of Paros has long been a matter of uncertainty, but it is now clear that both the best literary indications and the material evidence point to *c.* 650.[142] Archilochus experienced the beginnings, or at least the early days, of Greek Thasos, and referred to some of those experiences in his poetry. He described the physical appearance of the island and compared it unfavourably with Siris in southern Italy: 'This land stands like the backbone of an ass covered with wild woods. It is not a fine land, nor lovely and desirable, like that by the streams of Siris' (frs. 21, 22 West). To this place he complained that the 'misery of all Greece had congregated' (fr. 102), which seems to imply that the Parians had not restricted participation in the colony to their own citizens, but had invited settlers very widely. Archilochus (fr. 20) wept for the 'woes of the Thasians' rather than those of Magnesia (which had been destroyed by the Cimmerians), and he called Thasos 'thrice-wretched' (fr. 228). These imprecise but obviously unfavourable references may be explained by the fighting with the Thracians, which is mentioned more than once and which probably took place on Thasos as well as on the mainland. In addition to war, there were other dealings with the Thracians, in which the Greeks behaved in a way the poet thought shameful.[143] It may not be too bold to deduce from Archilochus' fragments that the Greek colonization was achieved by force and fraud.

---

[139] C 196; C 188.   [140] C 194.

[141] C 35.   [142] C 194.

[143] Frr. 5, 101 West; *IG* XII Suppl. pp. 212ff, A.I. 40–52; Callim. *Aetia* fr. 104 (with commentary, A 52). Cf. C 194, 85.

The Parian colonists quickly controlled the whole island. Aliki, a site in the south-east corner of the island, was already occupied in the seventh century,[144] and the Thracian settlement at Kastri came to an end at about the time of the Greek colonization.[145] Nor was this all. We now know that several of the Thasian settlements on the Thracian coast opposite were established within a generation of the colonization of Thasos itself. Greek pottery of the third quarter of the seventh century has been found at Neapolis (modern Kavalla), Oesyme and Galepsus.[146] So the coast opposite was turned into the Thasian *peraea* as part of the same colonizing enterprise that established Parian Thasos. As for the extent of the *peraea*, the furthest west of the Thasian colonies on the mainland was Galepsus, while to the east we know that the Thasians were disputing the control of Stryme with Maronea during Archilochus' lifetime.[147]

It is interesting to note that at both the western and the eastern ends of the Thasian *peraea* other Greek colonization was also achieved or attempted around the middle of the seventh century. In north-east Chalcidice there were four colonies of Andros, three of which are dated by literary sources to 655.[148] To the east of the Thasian *peraea* the Chian colony of Maronea was already founded by the time of Archilochus, and the city itself had existed since much earlier,[149] but the first attempt to settle Abdera by Timesias of Clazomenae (which failed owing to Thracian opposition: Hdt. I. 168) is dated 654 in our tradition.

From these dates it seems reasonable to conclude that this part of the Thracian coast, together with Thasos itself, became open to Greek colonization about the middle of the seventh century. The Parian colonists won the lion's share of an area with outstanding natural advantages. In the Classical period we know that Thasos kept political control over its dependent colonies on the adjacent mainland, and won great economic advantages therefrom.[150] We have no reason to doubt that those conditions obtained from the beginning.

The steep and rocky island of Samothrace, famous in antiquity for the sanctuary of the Great Gods, was colonized, according to the ruling modern view, in c. 700 by Aeolian Greeks.[151] However, the bases of this belief are shaky, and it seems better to follow our earliest and best authority, Antiphon, who attributes the colonization to Samos and dates it, by implication, to the sixth century, probably the second half.[152] He is in general supported by a passage of Herodotus (VIII. 90.2–3), by what

[144] C 189, 84–8.   [145] C 194, 72.   [146] C 194, 95.
[147] Philochorus, *FGrH* 328 F 43. Cf. C 185, 91–7.
[148] Eusebius (Acanthus and Stagira); Plut. *Quaest. Graec.* XXX (Sane).
[149] Philochorus, *FGrH* 328 F 43; Homer, *Od.* IX. 197f (cf. P–W *s.v.* 'Ismaros' (3)).
[150] C 5, 81–90.   [151] C 199, 15.
[152] Fr. 50 (49) Teubner = *FGrH* 548 F 5a (with Jacoby's commentary, p. 474). Cf. C 194, 68f.

we know of the Samothracian calendar,[153] by the little evidence we
have from the cemeteries of the ancient city,[154] and by the date of the
appearance of the Greek language in dedications from the sanctuary.[155]
There are also inscriptions in a non-Greek language (though written
in Greek letters) which has been interpreted, on the basis of very meagre
comparative material, as Thracian.[156] These dedications show that both
Greeks and non-Greeks were using the sanctuary from the second half
of the sixth century, so we have an early and interesting example of
mixed settlement, which may be compared to those on Acte.

The evident attractions of the north Aegean area were always counter-
balanced by the difficulties of achieving settlements in the face of the
hostility of the existing population, some of whom maintained their
place among the Greek colonies down to the Classical period. Probably
for this reason successful colonization was achieved almost exclusively
by near-by mother cities, Chalcis, Eretria, Paros and Andros. The
establishment of Potidaea in a powerful position on the isthmus of
Pallene in western Chalcidice by Corinth during the reign of Periander
$(625-585)$[157] is an obvious exception, but confirms the rule. Potidaea
was a dependent colony of a very powerful mother city, and its
foundation is to be understood in relation to Corinth's similar imperial
colonization in north-western Greece (see below).

V. HELLESPONT, PROPONTIS, BOSPORUS

The Propontis (Sea of Marmara), which separates the Pontus (Black Sea)
from the Aegean, is virtually a sea lake, with the two narrow straits of
the Bosporus and Hellespont (Dardanelles) like rivers at its eastern and
western ends. Although the current in both straits sets generally from
the Black Sea to the Aegean, and this current can be strong, especially
in the Bosporus, the notion that it presented an impassable barrier to
Greek entry into the Pontus (and *a fortiori* into the Propontis) at any
time within our period has been shown to be false.[158] The climate and
other geographical characteristics of the Propontis make it, given its
proximity to Greece, in theory ideal colonial territory. Its colonization
was in fact somewhat slow and hesitant, a good example of the principle
that it was not geography but politics that determined the course of the
Greek colonizing movement.

At the western end of the region Aeolians of Lesbos and elsewhere
established themselves in the Troad and on the coasts of the Thracian

[153] C 202, 224f.

[155] C 198, 21.

[157] Thuc. I. 56.2; Nic. Dam. *FGrH* 90 F 59.

[154] C 197, 64f; C 190; C 191; C 192.

[156] C 198, 8–19; C 186.

[158] C 217; C 222.

Chersonese.[159] Unfortunately, just as for other Aeolian colonies, we have no dates for these settlements. The only chronological indication seems to be the beginning of Greek Troy (Troy Settlement VIII), which should be put, on archaeological grounds, in the eighth century.[160] This may give an approximate dating for Aeolian expansion in the Troad, but it would be too hazardous to draw from it any conclusions about the chronology of Aeolian colonization north of the Hellespont. To judge from the securely dated colonies, Greek settlements on the north shore of the Propontis were sparse and relatively late, which is most easily explained by the hostility and strength of the existing Thracian inhabitants.

The majority of the remaining colonies in the Propontid region were established by two mother cities, Miletus and Megara. Milesian Cyzicus would be the oldest, if we could trust the first of Eusebius' two foundation dates, 756 and 679. When we have more than one foundation date in the chronographers, it is often right, as at Cyrene, to reject the earlier date or dates. However, it is possible that Cyzicus, having been founded first in the middle of the eighth century, was destroyed by the Cimmerians, whose destructions in Asia Minor in the first half of the seventh century included Gordium, the capital of the Phrygian empire,[161] at the edge of which Cyzicus was situated. Thus 679 could be regarded as the date of refoundation. This was the pattern of events at Sinope in the Pontus, according to one of our sources, where we also have (by implication) two foundation dates in our record.[162] There is possibly indirect support for this reconstruction in the discovery at Hisartepe, some thirty-two kilometres inland from Cyzicus, of a thoroughly Greek city, which yielded pottery as early as the first half of the seventh century.[163] For it seems likely that Greeks would have been settled for some time on the coast before they would venture to establish themselves inland. Perhaps one day these rather unsatisfactory theoretical assumptions will be rendered unnecessary by good archaeological evidence from Cyzicus itself.

Apart from Parium, which was probably founded jointly by Paros, Erythrae and Miletus in 709 (Strabo XIII. 588), the remaining early foundation dates in the Propontis relate to the Megarian colonies at the further end of the region, Astacus, Chalcedon, Selymbria and Byzantium. The Eusebian date for Astacus is 711, but this seems to be in conflict with our earliest and best authority, Charon of Lampsacus (FGrH 262 F 6), who says that Astacus was founded from Chalcedon, which was

[159] Ps.-Scymnus 709f, 706.   [160] H 25, 376; D 27, 101.
[161] Strabo I. 61; Eusebius ad 696; cf. B 87, 351.
[162] Ps.-Scymnus 986–97 (Diller); cf. Hdt. IV. 12.2 and C 217, 33f.
[163] C 204; H 25, 377; A 7, 242, 246.

itself established in 685, again according to Eusebius. So we should probaby regard the Eusebian date for Astacus as suspect, and take Chalcedon for the first Megarian colony in the Propontis.

Late observers found it hard to understand how the Megarian settlers could have chosen the mediocre site of Chalcedon in preference to the magnificent position opposite, on the European side of the Bosporus, which Byzantium was to occupy. So they followed the Persian Megabazus and called Chalcedon 'the city of the blind'.[164] A more rational explanation would be that the first Megarian colonists were not strong enough to venture a settlement on the dangerous European side, but needed to establish themselves on the easier Asiatic shore and build up their strength before colonizing Byzantium. No Greek colonists could have ignored the advantages of its position. Herodotus says that seventeen years elapsed between the foundation of Chalcedon and that of Byzantium (iv. 144.2).

Greek Byzantium lay on the eastern point of the headland, the area occupied in later times by the sultans' palace (Old Serail). To the north was the superb natural harbour of the Golden Horn, while the south side is protected by the waters of the Propontis. Only the third, western, side of the triangular site needed land defences. By its position and because of the flow of the Bosporus current, Byzantium is fated to control the dramatically narrow entry to the Black Sea (cf. Polyb. iv. 38, 43–4). On a more mundane level, it has excellent fishing and there is good land in the immediate vicinity. Our sources give a rather confused account of the origin of the colony.[165] However, detailed analysis of cults, institutions and personal names has provided confirmation that Megara was the founder while also suggesting that there were substantial quantities of settlers from other regions too.[166] Perhaps the Megarians needed to invite settlers widely to make a success of their ambitious act of colonization.

Before establishing Byzantium, Megarians had also settled Selymbria further west on the north shore (Ps.-Scymnus 715–16). They thus had four colonies fairly close together, which controlled not only the Bosporus itself, but also the eastern end of the Propontis. That they regarded the area as their sphere of interest emerges from Plutarch's story (*Quaest. Graec.* LVII) that they tried to prevent the Samians from establishing a colony at Perinthus. They were unsuccessful, however, for Perinthus was founded in 602, and, at unrecorded dates, the Samians planted other settlements on the same north shore.

---

[164] Hdt. iv. 144.1–2; Strabo vii. 320; Tacitus, *Ann.* xii. 63.

[165] Ps.-Scymnus 717; Strabo vii. 320; Vell. Pat. ii. 7.7; Dion. Byz. (Ed. A 28, 7 line 3; 15 line 7; 17 line 5 etc.).

[166] E 218, 123ff; C 216A.

On the south side, west of Megarian Astacus, we have the impression that Miletus virtually monopolized colonization. A clue to such domination may be seen in Strabo's information that Abydus, which lay on the Asiatic side of the Hellespont, was founded by Miletus with the permission of Gyges, king of Lydia.[167] That not only gives an approximate foundation date – Gyges ruled from c. 680 to 652 – but also shows that at that time the Lydians already aspired to control this part of Asia Minor. At a later date, under Alyattes and Croesus, the Milesians had specially close relations with Lydia. If such relations were already foreshadowed under Gyges, it is an attractive surmise that Miletus was given the privilege of colonizing on the coasts of territory under Lydian control.[168]

In the second half of the sixth century the growing power of Athens and Athens' interest in imported corn affected the colonial situation in the Propontid region.

The first colony planted by the Athenians was at Sigeum, on the south side of the entry to the Hellespont. Although the tradition is not unambiguously clear, the Athenians appear to have settled here at the end of the seventh century, under the leadership of Phrynon, an Olympic victor.[169] This colonization involved a long struggle with the Mytileneans, who regarded the place as theirs, and Sigeum did not become an Athenian colony beyond any question until Pisistratus sent his son, Hegesistratus, to seize it. The date of that event has been calculated as c. 530 by reference to the presumed age of Hegesistratus, but that creates a severe difficulty, since the coast was then part of the Persian empire. So there is much attraction in the suggestion that Pisistratus sent his son to seize Sigeum in c. 546, at the precise moment of uncertainty between the end of Lydian rule and the establishment of Persian domination, when Pisistratus himself had just recovered the tyranny at Athens.[170]

Before that time Miltiades the Elder had acceded to the request of the Thracian Dolonci that he should bring an Athenian colony to the Thracian Chersonese and help to defend the inhabitants against local enemies (Hdt. VI. 34ff). Miltiades' expedition took place when Pisistratus was tyrant at Athens, almost certainly before the second exile, i.e. between 561 and 556.[171] Miltiades was opposed by Lampsacus (Hdt. VI. 37.1, 38.2), which perhaps suggests that his colonization was seen as a threat to the Hellespont. In any case, once the tyrants had taken control of Sigeum, we may legitimately think that it was Athenian policy

---

[167] Strabo XIII. 590; cf. C 6, 41f. [168] D 48, 508.

[169] Hdt. v. 94f; Strabo XIII. 599. Cf. C 5, 32–4.

[170] This suggestion was made in lectures at Athens by the late Mary White. I owe this important information to Cynthia Harrison. [171] C 5, 32.

to dominate that route. The sons of Pisistratus later sent Miltiades the Younger to take over his family's hereditary rule of the Chersonese (between 523 and 513),[172] and a further important step in controlling the sea route was taken about 500 by Miltiades himself, when he expelled the Pelasgian inhabitants of Lemnos (and presumably also Imbros) and settled Athenians on the two islands (Hdt. VI. 140).[173]

Until we have more archaeological evidence the history of Greek colonization in the Propontid region will remain obscure and hypothetical. However, the domination of Miletus and Megara seems clear. Miletus was a powerful commercial and seagoing city, which, according to a persuasive interpretation,[174] was forced by Lydian control of the interior to turn to colonization and overseas trade. Megara also had small agricultural resources and was denied the possibility of expanding at home by powerful neighbours. Her attempt to colonize in the west came near to failure, but in the Propontis she was in the van and grasped the opportunity to settle the key sites which controlled the Bosporus, thus ensuring these colonies a rich and splendid future.

VI. PONTUS

The climate of the Black Sea is generally wetter and colder than that of Greece and the Aegean, and in the northern parts the winter cold is more extreme than in any other area of Greek colonization. On the south coast conditions were more familiar, but there the mountains come down close to the sea, and harbours which provide shelter from the north wind, as at Sinope, are extremely rare. Even more markedly, in the east the Caucasus mountains fashion a coast which is almost totally inhospitable. The great majority of good sites in terms of position and resources are on the western and northern coasts, especially in the enclosed estuaries (*limans*) of the great rivers, which offered protected harbours, abundant fish and salt to preserve them. In addition these rivers provided routes into the interior, which we know were used for commerce from a time as early as the first foundations.

The Greek colonists faced difficulties from the native inhabitants of the Pontus. Besides the Scythians, who, according to some Greeks, 'practised human sacrifice on strangers, ate human flesh and used skulls as drinking vessels' (Strabo VII. 298), the Thracians in the west, Taurians in the Tauric Chersonese (Crimea), and Colchians in the Caucasus were all feared by Greeks, and caused them to avoid some areas entirely (e.g. the south-east coast of the Tauric Chersonese).

[172] The closer date, *c.* 516–515, depends on a hazardous interpretation of a corrupt passage in Hdt. VI. 40.1. F 91, 216f.   [173] C 5, 32, 175.   [174] C 10.

However, here as elsewhere, a *modus vivendi* with the existing population was an essential element in the success of Greek colonization.

The chief colony on the south coast was Sinope, founded by Miletus on a classic isthmus/peninsula site which provided much the best haven on the whole southern shore.[175] The date of Sinope's foundation lies at the centre of one of the main controversial questions in the history of Greek colonization: did the Greek colonization of the Pontus begin in the eighth century?[176]

Eusebius dates Sinope's foundation in 631, but our fullest source for its colonization puts the first Milesian settlement before the Cimmerian invasion, which implies an eighth-century date.[177] Furthermore, Eusebius himself dates Trapezus to 756 and Trapezus was a colony of Sinope (Xen. *An.* IV. 8.22). We can easily reconcile this rather slight literary evidence by applying Eusebius' date of 631 to the post-Cimmerian refoundation of Sinope by Coos and Cretines, but many would argue that the excavations at Sinope, from which the earliest material is of the last third of the seventh century,[178] have shown that there was no foundation before 631. Since Greek material does not appear in quantity in the Pontus before the second half of the seventh century, that is the time when many would put the beginning of all Greek colonization in the Black Sea. Greek literature shows that Greeks had penetrated the Pontus by the eighth century,[179] and Greek objects much earlier than the second half of the seventh century have been found at Black Sea sites, viz.: from Istrus, part of a Late Geometric cup (*c.* 720),[180] and from Berezan, a Middle Geometric jug (second half of the eighth century).[181] However, contacts do not necessarily imply colonization, so, though it is bad method to prefer an archaeological *argumentum e silentio* to statements in literary sources, until there has been thorough archaeological exploration at either Sinope or Trapezus, the question is not likely to be regarded as settled.

The best known of the colonies on the south coast is Heraclea Pontica (modern Eregli), which was founded by Megarians with a substantial admixture of Boeotians in *c.* 560,[182] under the leadership of Gnesiolochus,[183] in a position 217 kilometres sail east of the Bosporus, where a headland creates a protected harbour and the farmland and sea-fishing are good. Here the city stood on a theatre-shaped site of *c.* 0·42 square kilometres, which has been calculated as sufficient for a

---

[175] Polyb. IV. 56.5; C 217, 32.

[176] A 7, 240ff; C 214; C 217.

[177] Ps.-Scymnus 986–97 (Diller).

[178] C 204; A 7, 242; C 219.

[179] C 223, 437; C 211, 14; C 217.

[180] H 25, 377 n. 8; cf. 191, 421. There is no doubt about the provenance (AJG).

[181] H 25, 377 n. 7; cf. 421; C 215, 227 fig. 27.

[182] C 211, 12–22; E 218, 128f.

[183] Schol. Ap. Rhod. II. 351; cf. Ephorus, *FGrH* 70 F 44; Plut. *De Pyth. orac.* 27 (*Mor.* 408).

maximum of 10,000 inhabitants.[184] The colonists made the surrounding native people, the Maryandini, their serfs, but they were bound by a rule that none of the Maryandini could be sold outside their own country.[185] Heraclea is exceptional in that we are told the initial constitution of the colony, a democracy, and have a rare glimpse of early colonial politics. Very soon after the foundation notables (γνώριμοι) were driven into exile by demagogues. The exiles banded together, overthrew the democracy and set up a narrow oligarchy.[186]

Although mistaken, Strabo's statement that Heraclea was a Milesian foundation is not surprising.[187] Milesian domination of the colonization of the Pontus is an undoubted fact. The only quite clearly non-Milesian colonies before c. 500 are Heraclea, Phanagoria, founded by Teian refugees from the Persians in c. 545,[188] and Mesembria, founded by Megara in c. 510.[189] Before about 560 all colonies in the Pontus were Milesian. After that time there is no definitely Milesian foundation dated either in literary sources or by archaeological evidence. Two historical conclusions seem inescapable: (1) before the middle of the sixth century Miletus successfully operated some kind of *mare clausum* policy in the Pontus (presumably by agreement with the Megarian colonies at the Bosporus); (2) after that date colonization by other Greek cities became possible and Miletus herself apparently ceased to colonize.

The Milesian colonizing effort of the seventh and sixth centuries was concentrated on the west and north coasts, though the little settlement on the eastern shore was also theirs. Archaeological investigations have been conducted in these regions as long as in any Greek colonial area except Italy.[190] The evidence recovered, when combined with our literary sources, provides us with clear chronology and a fair quantity of detail about social and economic history. The best-explored sites of our period are Istrus (Istria, Histria), Olbia and Panticapaeum (modern Kerch), of which we select Olbia for attention here, because it exemplifies the character of this Milesian colonization and shows how the possibilities of a *liman* site were exploited.

The estuaries of the Dnepr (ancient Borysthenes) and Bug (ancient Hypanis) combine to create the greatest of the Black Sea *limans*. Here the Milesians founded Olbia on the right bank of the Bug, about seven kilometres above the point where the *limans* of Bug and Dnepr join, a nodal point in the centre of the three navigable routes in the region,

---

[184] C 220, 20ff; B 33, 37.
[185] Posidonius, *FGrH* 87 F 8.
[186] Arist. *Pol.* v. 1304b31ff; C 206A, 28–31.
[187] Strabo XII. 542. Cf. C 211, 13–15; C 206A, 12–17.
[188] Ps.-Scymnus 885f (Diller); Eustathius 549 (*GGM* II. 324f).
[189] Hdt. VI. 33.2; Strabo VII. 319; Ps.-Scymnus 741f.
[190] C 228, 1–14; C 207, 22ff.

22. Plan of the Olbia area. (After C 207, 19, fig. 3.)

thirty-eight kilometres from the open sea to the west, thirty-four
kilometres from the beginning of the Bug *liman* to the north, and
thirty-five kilometres from the beginning of the Dnepr *liman* to the east
(fig. 22).[191] In addition the Milesians settled on the island of Berezan
at the outlet of the Bug–Dnepr *liman*. Berezan controls the route from
the open sea to the *liman*. With both sites under their control the
colonists were in a fine position to profit from the natural resources of
land and sea and from the routes of communication far into the interior
provided by the great rivers.

The Greek name for Berezan is not known,[192] and some false ideas
exist about its relationship with Olbia, as, for instance, that the colonists
settled Berezan first and then transferred to Olbia, or that there was
synoecism between Berezan and Olbia. One reason for such theories
has been the mistaken belief that the settlement on Berezan is significantly
earlier than that at Olbia. Eusebius dates the foundation of Borysthenes
to 647, and (apart from the Middle Geometric jug mentioned above)

---

[191] C 230, 41–4.   [192] Cf. Strabo VII. 306; C 209, 170ff.

the earliest pottery found at both Olbia and Berezan is of the second half of the seventh century.[193] There is a much greater quantity of early material from Berezan, but since there has been very little exploration of early levels at Olbia, this comparison is without significance. In general the material remains at both sites are closely similar, except that those at Olbia are richer.

In addition to Berezan there were numerous other contemporary settlements on the shores of the Bug–Dnepr *liman*.[194] We should not doubt that they all, including Berezan, formed part of a single state which came to be called Olbia from the name of the *polis* proper. Although the men of Olbia were calling themselves *Olbiopolitai* by the time of Herodotus, he reveals that in his day the name Olbia was not used by Greeks generally (IV. 18.1; cf. Strabo VII. 306). Herodotus calls the people of Olbia 'men of Borysthenes' (Βορυσθενεῖται) and their city the town (ἄστυ), city (πόλις) or trading city (ἐμπόριον) of the Βορυσθενεῖται (IV. 78.3, 79.2, 17.1). The state was originally named after its great river, in the same way that Istrus, Tyras, Tanais and Phasis were named. Such a name was entirely appropriate for communities, such as Olbia, where the *liman* constituted the *chora* of the colony.[195]

Olbia consisted of an upper town on a plateau about forty metres above sea level, and a lower town on the shore of the Bug *liman* (fig. 23).[196] Because the sea level has risen since antiquity, some 300–500 metres of the lower town is now under water.[197] Hence there has been little investigation of the lower town. In the upper town the public areas of agora, *temenos* and sacred grove, which have been identified roughly in the centre, are thought to have been laid out in the second half of the sixth century.[198] Herodotus' story of Scyles (IV. 78–80) shows that Olbia was walled at that time (presumably sixth or early fifth centuries), and his mention of a suburb chimes in with the discovery of Archaic occupation beyond the western boundary of the city ('Hare's Ravine').[199] North of the agora there were houses, workshops and storage pits in the sixth century,[200] but for living quarters in the early period Berezan is more informative. The houses there are single-roomed structures, usually rectangular but sometimes circular, and from two by three to three by four metres in size. They are regularly set low in the ground, i.e. semi-pit dwellings, no doubt for protection in winter, and they all have fireplaces. Roofs were thatched and pits for storage or rubbish are frequent.[201]

[193] C 219; cf. C 216, pl. 1.   [194] C 230, 58ff.
[195] C 230, 63.   [196] C 224, 110.
[197] C 230, 41–4.   [198] C 230, 46.
[199] Cf. C 230, 45.   [200] C 230, 49f.
[201] C 230, 32f.

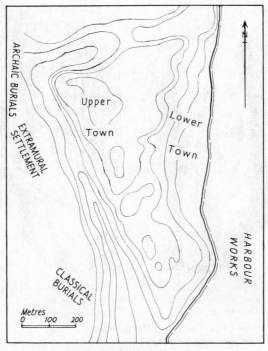

23. Plan of Olbia. (After C 219.)

Scyles was a Scythian king, who had been taught by his Greek mother, a woman from Istrus, to know and like Greek religion and the Greek way of life generally. He had a house and a Greek wife in Olbia, and regularly stayed there (leaving his army outside), in order to indulge his philhellene tastes, until his actions were discovered and led to his death. Apart from its general interest for Graeco-Scythian relations, this story has been taken to imply that Olbia existed by Scythian permission and under Scythian protection.[202] Certainly Olbia itself is not a strong site, and would hardly have been tenable if the Scythians had been unwilling to accept the Greek colony.

Close relations with Scythians are also revealed by other evidence. In Herodotus' time there were people, the Callipidae, whom he describes as 'Helleno-Scythians' (IV. 17.1: Ἕλληνες Σκύθαι), and others, the Geloni, who were originally Greeks from the trading cities (*emporia*) and spoke partly Scythian, partly Greek (IV. 108.2). At a later date people in the area can be described as 'mixed Greeks' (Μιξέλληνες).[203] Native hand-made pottery and contracted (crouched)

[202] C 228, 64f.
[203] Ditt. *Syll.*³ 495.

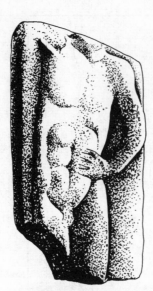

24. Leoxos' stele, marble gravestone from Olbia. A two-sided relief showing a naked athlete and a bowman in Scythian archer's dress. Inscribed on the side:

[Μνῆμ]ά εἰ[μι Λεώξου τοῦ Μολπαγόρ]εω.
...ἔστ]ηκα, λέγω δ'ὅτι τῆλε πόλε[ώς που]
[ἐν Σκυθίηι? κεῖτα]ι Λέωξος ὁ Μολπαγόρε[ω].

'I am the memorial for Leoxos, son of Molpagoras...and I tell that Leoxos, son of Molpagoras lies far from his home city [in Scythia?].' About 490 B.C. Height 66 cm. (Cherson Museum; H 24, pl. 5.)

burials occur in the surrounding settlements of the Olbian *liman*.[204] Similar evidence in the area round the Cimmerian Bosporus is there made explicit by the gravestone of Tychon the Taurian at Panticapaeum. This was put up in the fifth century, to judge by the letter forms, over a burial of native type. The race of the deceased is clearly stated in a Greek elegiac couplet.[205] So we should not try to explain away the presence of natives in the settlements round Olbia. From the city itself there is much less native pottery in proportion to the Greek,[206] and onomastic evidence shows that Olbia was a thoroughly Greek city in the Archaic and Classical periods.[207] Even so, Scythians were doubtless a common sight in the city. In view of all this evidence the famous and beautiful 'amphiglyph' gravestone of Leoxos (fig. 24), son of Molpagoras, which has on one side a nude 'athlete' and on the other

[204] C 230, 34f.
[205] C 223, 626 and App. 25; *SEG* III. 608; A 36, 368 no. 67.
[206] C 221.   [207] C 5, 106f.

an archer in Scythian dress, and is dated by sculptural style to the early
fifth century, seems, whether or not both figures represent Leoxos,
happily symbolic of the role of Olbia.[208]

From Olbia Greek goods penetrated far up the river valleys into the
interior, including fine pottery, weapons, luxurious metal objects and
plenty of Greek wine.[209] In later times we know from literary evidence
that the main exports from the Pontus were corn, salt fish, hides and
slaves.[210] For our period archaeological evidence alone is available. At
Shirokaja Balka, not two kilometres south of Olbia, there were in the
sixth century twelve large storage pits for corn and an oven, the purpose
of which, it has been suggested, was for drying corn.[211] More directly
informative are the stones from the Aegean that have been found at
Berezan and Jagorlik.[212] These came as ships' ballast and show that the
return cargoes were the heavier. Since the goods from the Aegean
included wine and oil, we may infer that corn was an early export from
the Pontus.

The dramatic evidence for trading activity and Herodotus' frequent
use of the word *emporion* (trading city) when referring to these Greek
colonies in the north Pontus (IV. 17.1, 20.1, 24, 108.2) show that
commerce was a major economic function. Archaeological evidence
(grain pits, animal bones, fish bones etc.) proves that many of the
colonists were also engaged in agriculture and fishing. Others made a
living from the manufacture of metal and other goods for home
consumption and for export. Since all these activities may be postulated
from the seventh century onwards, the rapid growth of Olbia and the
peripheral settlements attested by archaeology is not hard to understand.

The Tauric Chersonese with its mountainous terrain and dreaded
inhabitants saw very little Greek settlement in the Archaic period, but
the country round the Cimmerian Bosporus offered attractive possibilities on both the European and Asiatic sides. This area also controlled
important communication routes up the Kuban river (ancient Hypanis)
to the east, and across the Sea of Azov (Palus Maeotis) to the mouth
of the Don (ancient Tanais).

Of the many Greek colonies which clustered round this Bosporus,
Panticapaeum was the most important. It was founded by Miletus in
about 600, according to the archaeological evidence, on an ideal site with
a strong acropolis.[213] When the whole area of the Cimmerian Bosporus
was organized into a kingdom under the rulers of Panticapaeum (about
480 at the earliest, it seems; Diod. XII. 31.1), it contained native peoples

[208] H 24, 31–3; H 7, 39, 46–50; H 58.　　[209] C 227; C 206.
[210] Polyb. IV. 38; Strabo XI. 493. Cf. C 10, 124–30.
[211] C 225.　　　[212] C 219; C 210.　　　[213] C 226; C 219.

as well as the Greek settlements. There was strong Hellenization of the local people, and we know that this phenomenon occurred far beyond the Bosporus itself. Up the Kuban valley the Sindians were by the fifth century issuing coins of Greek style inscribed with Greek legends. It is likely that commerce provided the first steps in this process. In a native burial at Temir Gora near Panticapaeum a famous oenochoe was discovered which is dated *c*. 640–*c*. 620,[214] and (more sensationally because of the distances) parts of two oenochoae of similar date were found in the Don valley, one at Krivorožija about 200 kilometres from the mouth of the Don, and the other on the banks of the river Tsuskan, some 300 kilometres inland.[215] This commerce was presumably associated with the most remote of Greek colonies in the Pontus region, Tanais, at the mouth of the Don. The Archaic settlement was not on the same site as the great multiracial emporium vividly described by Strabo (XI. 493, cf. VII. 310), but it now seems possible that it was at Taganrog, where a site which is now under water has yielded Greek pottery from the seventh century and later.[216]

VII. NORTH-WEST GREECE AND THE ADRIATIC

The first Greeks to sail far up the Adriatic were, according to Herodotus (I. 163.1), Phocaeans.[217] That was presumably in the seventh century, if we may apply the analogy of the Phocaean voyages further west, which Herodotus mentions in the same sentence, but no known colonization resulted. Off the Dalmatian coast the island of Black Corcyra (modern Korčula) was colonized by Cnidians,[218] and the hypothesis has received wide acceptance that this occurred at the time when Cnidians helped Corcyra against Periander (since that might explain why a Cnidian colony was called Black Corcyra).[219] The date would then fall in Periander's reign, *c*. 625–*c*. 585, and the little archaeological evidence[220] does not conflict, but the whole reconstruction remains speculative. Similarly, it is possible that there were other minor early settlements on and off the Dalmatian coast.[221] On the Italian side the only definite settlements of the Archaic period were Adria and Spina on the north and south sides of the Po delta. These were apparently mixed settlements of traders, both Greeks and Etruscans, which had a short but prosperous existence, beginning in the last quarter of the sixth century and ending with the decline of Etruscan

[214] C 229, 27, fig. 7; cf. H 29, plate 30A.
[215] A 7, 243f; C 206, 65.
[216] C 208; cf. C 223, 567.
[217] C 44, 63ff; C 119, 857f.
[218] C 44, 104ff; C 5, 43.
[219] C 33, 173ff.
[220] A 7, 227.
[221] C 33, 184ff.

power in the fourth.[222] We do not know the origin of the Greek inhabitants.[223]

Thus the upper Adriatic seems to have been only marginally Greek colonial territory. It can be argued that this impression is due to the failings of our sources, but as the evidence now stands the only substantial early Greek colonization in the Adriatic was that of Corinth and Corcyra on the coasts of north-western Greece (Acarnania and Epirus) and Illyria. However, the first colonization in the area was achieved by Eretrians from Euboea, who settled at Corcyra (Corfu) until they were expelled by the Corinthians under Chersicrates.[224] As we have seen, our sources are at variance about the date of Chersicrates' venture, but, at the latest, Corinthian occupation was established before the end of the eighth century. Corfu is a large island, famous for its beneficent climate, with rich land to cultivate, but we need not doubt that it was especially valued as the important port of call on the route from Greece to southern Italy which it has always been.

Corcyra was sufficiently strong to defeat her mother city in the first naval battle known to Thucydides (I. 13.4), which took place in c. 664. This has often been interpreted as part of a war of independence, but there is no reason to assume that Corcyra was established as a dependent colony, any more than Syracuse was.[225] Apart from a short period when Corcyra was under the control of Periander, tyrant of Corinth,[226] the relations of colony and metropolis were those of two closely related but independent states, and varied from peaceable cooperation to outright hostility.[227]

The remaining Corinthian and Corcyrean colonization in this area took place during the reigns of the Corinthian tyrants Cypselus and Periander (c. 655–c. 585), and shows signs of cooperation between the two mother cities. It was under Cypselus that the Corinthians established control of the Gulf of Ambracia (modern Arta) by placing colonies on the island of Leucas, at Anactorium and at Ambracia itself.[228] The oikistai of all these colonies were sons of Cypselus, and the dates of foundation lie within the limits of his reign, c. 655–c. 625. Only at Anactorium has there been useful archaeological exploration, and there the earliest graves investigated yielded pottery of the last quarter of the seventh century.[229]

This colonization was unusual in that the colonies were from the beginning in a dependent relationship vis-à-vis their mother city,

[222] C 44, 135ff.; A 7, 228f.   [223] C 5, 6.
[224] Strabo VI. 269; Plut. Quaest. Graec. XI.   [225] C 5, 146.
[226] Hdt. III. 52f; Nic. Dam. FGrH 90 F 59. Cf. C 5, 30f.
[227] C 5, 146–9.
[228] Strabo X. 452; Ps.-Scymnus 453ff; Nic. Dam. FGrH 90 F 57.7.
[229] C 63.

Corinth, just as Corcyra was dependent when Periander's son was ruling there. We know from later evidence that this dependent relationship did not cease with the fall of the tyrants.[230] It was also unusual in that the pre-colonial population probably consisted of people who spoke a form of Greek.[231] However, they were sufficiently unlike Greeks for Thucydides (II. 68.6, 9) to call them *barbaroi* at the time of the Peloponnesian War, and they were so far behind the Corinthians in political and military development that the colonists were able to establish city-states in regions where such strong and advanced political organizations did not exist. We do not know definitely that this was forcible colonization, but there is a proud Homeric-style epitaph at Corcyra of one Arniadas, who died 'as he fought by the ships at the streams of Arachthus, displaying the highest valour amid the groans and shouts of war'.[232] It is hard to envisage any occasion *after* the Corinthians had established their control of the Ambraciot Gulf, when a Corcyrean would have been fighting by the river on which Ambracia lies,[233] so it is a tempting speculation that the engagement was connected with the actual colonization of Ambracia.

If that bold conjecture is right, there were Corcyreans who helped in the foundation of Ambracia. There is actual evidence to suggest that they participated in the colonization of Leucas and Anactorium, and kept some rights in those colonies, even though our sources unanimously describe them as Corinthian foundations.[234] Epidamnus, on the other hand, was definitely a colony of Corcyra, even though the Corcyreans summoned the *oikistes* from Corinth in accordance with the traditional practice, and invited Corinthian settlers (as well as some other Dorians) (Thuc. I. 24.1). This colonization was also in the time of Cypselus, for the Eusebian foundation date is 627, and there is archaeological evidence which provides general chronological confirmation.[235] Epidamnus was in Illyrian territory, and as Dyrrhachium (modern Durazzo) it formed the western end of the great Roman road, the Via Egnatia, which crossed the north of the Greek peninsula on the way to the Bosporus. But it was also an attractive site in itself, set on an isthmus and possessing a good harbour and cultivable land.

On the basis of late literary evidence and inscriptions of long after our period, it has been suggested that the colonists made a mixed settlement with the local Taulantians.[236] However, better evidence rather suggests that the distinction between colonists and neighbouring natives was strictly observed at Epidamnus. This is the natural

[230] C 5, 118–53.
[232] A 23, no. 25; A 36, 233, 234 no. 11.
[234] C 5, 128–30.
[236] Appian, *BC* II. 39. C 28.

[231] E 33, 419–23.
[233] *Contra* E 33, 443.
[235] E 33, 426.

deduction from Thucydides' brief narrative of the events of 437 (e.g. I. 24), as also, even more clearly, from Plutarch's interesting information (*Quaest. Graec.* xxix) that the Epidamnians chose annually an official called 'the seller' (πωλήτης), who organized and supervised a market where all commercial transactions between the Greeks and neighbouring Illyrians took place. Plutarch's source was presumably the Aristotelian *politeia* of Epidamnus,[237] so we may place this institution in Classical or Archaic times.

Thucydides' description of the quarrel between Corinth and Corcyra over Epidamnus reveals that in the 430s Corcyra regarded the colony as within her sphere of influence, at the least, and Epidamnus' coinage suggests some dependence on Corcyra at an earlier date, so it is reasonable to assume that the relationship was similar to that between Corinth and Ambracia, Leucas or Anactorium.[238] The first coins of Apollonia in Illyria, which was founded in about 600,[239] suggest a similar relationship to Corcyra, so the sources which call it a joint foundation of Corinth and Corcyra are perhaps to be preferred to those which name Corinth alone.[240]

Since Corinth's colonization under the tyrants was imperial in character, it is natural to look for a major Corinthian interest which the colonies were to subserve. No ancient writer suggests anything outside the normally stated motives for Greek colonization – in this instance the standard desire of tyrants to remove undesirable elements in the city's population[241] – but the favourite modern theory is that Corinth intended to control the route to the silver of the Illyrian area.[242] There are some good theoretical and indirect arguments in favour of this hypothesis. Furthermore, the great treasures of Trebenište near Lake Ochrid, including the famous bronze vases of the sixth century which may be of Corinthian workmanship,[243] show that the peoples of the interior of Illyria wanted Greek goods at the time in question and had something valuable to offer in return. By establishing dependent colonies on the Adriatic coast and at Potidaea in Chalcidice Corinth was possibly ensuring her access to the region from both west and east.[244] Without explicit evidence we cannot say definitely that these suggestions are right, but such motives are not impossible or even improbable, since Corinth was a rich city with strong commercial and industrial interests, a naval power, and under the strong rule of tyrants.

---

[237] A 29, 137–9.
[238] C 5, 149–51.
[239] C 60; E 33, 426.
[240] C 5, 130f.
[241] Nic. Dam. *FGrH* 90 F 57.7.
[242] C 33, 181–4; E 52 viii f, 2f.
[243] E 33, 437ff; A 7, 237.
[244] Cf. H 43, 203f.

VIII. NORTH AFRICA

Greek colonization in North Africa was confined to Egypt and Libya (Cyrenaica). While Cyrene and the neighbouring colonies in Libya conform to the normal Greek type, in that the colonists lived in independent city-states among a more backward native population, Egypt presented an immemorially ancient civilization in most respects more developed than the Greek, and a land long since fully occupied and organized politically. The forms that Greek colonization took in Egypt were thus inevitably shaped by the requirements of the advanced host population. The Greeks in Egypt are discussed elsewhere in this volume, but they have a place, even if an unusual or unique place, in the Archaic Greek colonizing movement.

The Saïte pharaohs wanted Greeks of two distinct categories, mercenaries and merchants. The large, permanent, settlements of mercenary soldiers, though not at all like Greek colonies in their organization, nevertheless bear witness to the need of numerous Greeks to settle abroad, and to their ability to find a livelihood by suiting their skills to the foreign environment.[245] Herodotus' surprising information that there was a colony of Samians at one of the oases of the Libyan desert (Ὄασις πόλις) at the time of Cambyses' conquest of Egypt, c. 525, is perhaps best understood in the context of these mercenary settlements (Hdt. III. 26).[246]

Naucratis might seem much more like other Greek colonies. But if we follow Herodotus (II. 178–9) and reject the later sources,[247] we see a trading port (emporion) without a definite mother city, organized under strict Egyptian control, which probably had no independent citizenship as late as the last years of the fifth century.[248] The government of the emporion was in the hands of the participating Greek states, those whom Herodotus lists as sharing in the Hellenium: Chios, Teos, Phocaea, Clazomenae, Rhodes, Cnidus, Halicarnassus, Phaselis and Mytilene. To these we may probably add the three states with separate sanctuaries, Aegina, Samos and Miletus. This was the sole port in Egypt to which Greek merchants were allowed to sail. These unique arrangements presumably offered mutual benefits to Greeks and Egyptians. The participating Greek states, all East Greeks with the sole exception of Aegina, had access to the Egyptian market, to which they brought Greek wine, oil and silver. In return, we may confidently assume, they took chiefly Egyptian corn. This commerce was under the strict control of the pharaoh. The population of the flourishing emporion consisted of

---

[245] B 89, 15–22.   [246] C 235, 63–6.
[247] Especially Strabo XVII. 801–2; cf. B 89, 22f.
[248] D 16, no. 16; cf. B 89, 66.

temporary visiting merchants and permanent residents,[249] the latter of whom eventually formed the basis for the development of a normal Greek *polis*. When and how this happened is not known, but it seems to have been long after our period. (See also above, ch. 36*b*.)

Cyrenaica is a massive promontory on the north coast of Africa, lying between the Greater Syrtis on the west and the Gulf of Bomba to the east. It is isolated by deserts from the other habitable parts of North Africa, and closer to the Greek world by sea than to Egypt, being about 300 kilometres from Crete compared with 900 from Naucratis. The land divides by contour into three clearly distinguished regions: a narrow coastal plain, an intermediate plateau 200 to 300 metres above sea level, and the interior plateau (the Jebel) some 300 metres higher still. This big land-barrier relieves the prevailing north and north-west winds of their great charge of moisture collected from the sea, and the resulting abundant rainfall made for exceptionally favourable agricultural conditions.[250]

Before the arrival of the Greeks the country was inhabited by a mixed population dominated by the light-skinned Berbers, which was divided into tribes and ruled by kings. Although some Egyptian influence may be perceived in their religion (Hdt. IV. 186), there was no political control. Each tribe occupied a defined territory, but since their economy was chiefly pastoral, there do not seem to have been any large agglomerations of population.[251]

Chiefly because of Herodotus the history of Cyrene is the best known of all Greek colonies of the Archaic period. In addition we have separate information from Pindar (*Pyth.* IV. 4–8, 59–63; V. 85–95), much archaeological evidence,[252] and a document which purports to be the original foundation decree of the colony.[253] This is preserved in an inscription, which may be roughly dated to the fourth century B.C., as an appendix to a Cyrenaean decree of that date. It is a matter of uncertainty whether, or to what extent, the document faithfully represents a Theraean public act of the seventh century. Some of the wording of our text is very unlikely to be that of a seventh-century decree. However, arguments for taking the whole document and its contents as a later fabrication can be shown to be unconvincing, so it is preferable to regard it as a basically authentic record of the arrangements for despatching the colony.[254]

From these sources we can draw up the following historical reconstruction. The island of Thera suffered drought and consequent famine. On the advice of Apollo's oracle at Delphi, they decided to relieve their

---

[249] B 89, 29–31.
[250] C 235, 11–17.
[251] C 235, 66f, 227–9.
[252] C 243; C 240; C 241; C 245; C 231.
[253] M–L no. 5.
[254] C 238; *contra* C 236.

population by sending out a colony to North Africa. The picturesque details of their search for a site with the help of the Cretan fisher for purple-dye, Corobius, and the timely assistance of Samian merchants, are not incredible *per se*. The first attempt at colonization was on a small island off the Libyan coast called Platea, which must be one of the islets in the Gulf of Bomba.[255] For this they conscripted settlers on pain of death (probably one son from every family with more than one), and in addition made provision for volunteers. They then despatched two penteconters to Platea. These would require some 200 men,[256] so they presumably expected to reinforce the initial party once a settlement was established.

The colonists were not happy about their prospects and tried to return to their mother city. It is a sign of the desperate circumstances at home that this was not allowed, even though provision is made in the foundation decree for return to citizen rights if the expedition failed to establish itself. So they went back to Platea where they stayed for two years. The next attempt was at a more promising site on the Libyan coast itself, a place called Aziris, which Herodotus describes as having a favoured situation, and which has been identified with the modern Wadi el Chalig, some twenty-eight kilometres east of Derna. Here there are remains of ancient settlement and surface finds are consistent with a shortlived occupation in the 630s.[257] The colonists stayed at Aziris for six years, but in 632 (if we may attribute Eusebius' foundation date to this event), the local Libyans offered to show them a better position and led them to Cyrene (about 100 kilometres to the west), where, they said, 'there was a hole in the sky', i.e. there was exceptional rainfall.

Cyrene is about ten kilometres inland, at the north edge of the high plateau. It is very well watered and surrounded by rich agricultural land. Ravines made the original city-site defensible in case of need, but it seems very improbable that Greeks would have settled inland unless their relations with the indigenous people were good. Cyrene and Leontini are the only important Greek colonies of the Archaic period away from the coast, and in both cases the sites imply the sort of relations with native peoples that Herodotus actually specifies for Cyrene. (These relations are also thought to have included large-scale intermarriage, but this subject is discussed below.)

At Cyrene, as at Thera, the constitution was a monarchy, and the *oikistes* Battus became the first king and established a dynasty that lasted for eight generations. Under the third of the Battiad kings, Battus II, in *c*. 580, Cyrene invited new settlers from Greece on a grand scale. This involved dispossessing the local Libyans of their land and major

[255] C 231, 149f.   [256] H 59, 46f, 68.
[257] C 231, 150–2; C 234.

hostility followed. The Egyptian pharaoh, Apries, came to the assistance of the Libyans, but was defeated in battle at Irasa in *c.* 570 (Hdt. IV. 159). It has been plausibly suggested that it was at that time that the neighbouring Libyans became subjects of Cyrene, as they certainly were in the time of the next king, Arcesilas II, the Cruel.[258] He quarrelled so bitterly with his brothers that they withdrew about 100 kilometres to the west and founded Barca, while at the same time inciting the Libyans to revolt from Cyrene. In the ensuing battle the king was defeated and 7,000 Cyrenaean hoplites fell (Hdt. IV. 160).

This evidence of serious civil strife and native hostility is supported by our information that the next king, Battus III, the Lame, invited a famous wise man, Demonax of Mantinea, to arbitrate the disputes at Cyrene. Demonax' solution was to reduce the prerogatives of the king and divide the people into three new tribes: the Theraeans, the Peloponnesians and Cretans, and the remaining islanders (Hdt. IV. 161). From this we learn, apart from political history, the main origins of the colonists at Cyrene after the big subsidiary immigration. The presence of 'islanders' offers a way to understand the puzzling passage of the Lindian Chronicle which says that some Lindians went with Battus to found Cyrene. Although the Hellenistic historian was clearly thinking of the original foundation and the first Battus, the modern interpretation that these Lindians came in the big subsidiary immigration under Battus II is clearly preferable.[259]

The civil and dynastic strife at Cyrene was not ended by Demonax, but pursued the Battiad monarchy intermittently to the end of its days, when it was replaced by a democracy (*c.* 440). However, political disturbances did not hinder the growth of Cyrene's prosperity. In Archaic and Classical times it was already one of the richest Greek cities. This wealth came primarily from agriculture, and Cyrene's riches in corn, sheep and horses were proverbial. In addition to these a unique source of wealth was provided by the silphium plant, which even became one of the city's symbols on its coinage (fig. 25). This wild plant died out in the early years of our era, and its botanical identity has eluded the experts, but it once grew abundantly in the dry steppe-like areas of Cyrenaica and yielded an extract which was highly regarded in the Greek world generally as a cure for all ills. The plant was in Libyan territory and was harvested by Libyans, but it is clear that this harvest came to Cyrene in some way or other, possibly, it has been suggested, as tribute.[260] Cyrene therefore monopolized the very profitable export of silphium, and in the time of the monarchy this monopoly belonged

[258] C 235, 136.
[259] D 16, no. 2B.XVII; cf. 44; *FGrH* 240 F 10; C 235, 124f.
[260] C 235, 249.

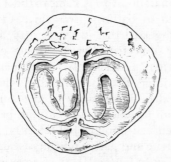
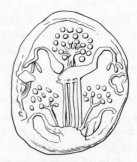

25. Silphium fruit and plant on two silver tetradrachms of Cyrene. Late sixth century B.C. (Paris, Bibliothèque Nationale; after C. M. Kraay and H. Hirmer, *Greek Coins* (1966) pl. 213, nos. 783–4.)

to the king.[261] In a unique visual depiction of the life of an Archaic Greek colony on the Arcesilas cup, we see Arcesilas II, seated on his stool, shaded by an awning, ornately clad and holding his kingly sceptre, supervising the weighing and storage of his silphium, at a date which will be a little before the middle of the sixth century.[262]

During the period of the Battiad dynasty a number of subsidiary colonies in the same general region were founded by Cyrene. Barca was established, as we have seen, *c.* 560–550, at an inland site which contained very fertile territory. In Herodotus' day it is clear that Cyrene and Barca were the two chief cities of Cyrenaica.[263] On the coast, Euhesperides (modern Benghazi) is shown by archaeological finds to have been settled by *c.* 600–575, and Tauchira (modern Tocra) was established as early as Cyrene itself, *c.* 630.[264] Apollonia, on the other hand, which became the port of Cyrene and is described as a Theraean foundation by Strabo (XVII. 837), has so far yielded no material earlier than *c.* 600.[265]

Thus the area of Cyrenaica came to be dominated by Greek colonies. The Greeks occupied all the land with abundant rainfall and confined the native Libyans to the arid remainder.[266] Outside this part of the North African coast, however, the Greeks were not able to colonize.[267] There are attractive sites along the coast to the west, but the Phoenicians had a sufficiently firm grip on the whole shore of the Gulf of Syrtis to make Greek settlement impossible. This is shown by the failure of the attempted colonization at the river Cinyps under the leadership of the Spartan Dorieus in *c.* 514–512 (Hdt v. 42).[268]

[261] Ar. *Plutus* 925 and Schol. (= Aristotle fr. 528, Teubner).
[262] H 68, 59–61, plate xv; C 235, 258–63.   [263] C 235, 225.
[264] C 231–3; C 243, 41.   [265] C 231.   [266] C 235, 229, plate xxv.
[267] *Contra* C 242; B 49, 117–20.   [268] Cf. C 235, 162.

IX. THE FAR WEST

If we confine ourselves to what is historically established, Greek colonization on the coasts of modern France and Spain was the work of the Phocaeans. There is a persistent tradition of Rhodian colonization, but it seems probable that the local place-names, Rhode, Rhodanus, Rhodanusia, gave rise to the notion of Rhodian origin. Certainly there is no evidence to date, in regions that are well explored archaeologically, for any Greek colonization earlier than the chief Phocaean foundations, Massalia and Emporiae. Here the excavation of Rhode (modern Rosas) is naturally of great importance; so far nothing at all of Archaic date has been discovered.[269]

It is natural to associate this Phocaean colonization with Herodotus' famous statements about Phocaean sea-going and trade (I. 163.1–3):

These Phocaeans were the first of the Greeks to undertake long voyages, and the Adriatic and Tyrrhenian seas, Iberia and Tartessus, were discovered by them. They did not sail in merchant ships but in fifty-oared warships. Arriving at Tartessus, they became friendly with the king of the Tartessians, whose name was Arganthonius. He was king of Tartessus for eighty years and lived in all for one hundred and twenty. The Phocaeans became so friendly with this man that he first urged them to leave Ionia and settle in his land, wherever they wished. Afterwards, when he could not persuade them, and learnt that they were threatened by the growing power of Persia, he gave them money to build a wall round their city.

This passage shows that one of the most important areas for Phocaean trade was Spanish Tartessus, which had been reached by Greeks for the first time in *c.* 640, when the Samian Colaeus was blown beyond the Pillars of Hercules (Straits of Gibraltar) (Hdt. IV. 152). Although the exact location of Tartessus is a notorious problem, it was presumably in the south-west of the Spanish peninsula and thus far away from the well-attested Phocaean colonies in southern France and north-eastern Spain. Phocaean colonies nearer to Tartessus are regularly seen in Hemeroscopeum, which was presumably near the southern cape of the Gulf of Valencia, and Maenace, on the south coast to the east of Malaga. These foundations are not dated in our literary sources,[270] and the only reason for placing them early was the strange scholarly phantasy that the *Ora Maritima* of Avienus is based on a sixth-century Massaliot 'sailing manual', which is now known to be baseless.[271] Nor is there any archaeological evidence for Archaic Greek settlement in these regions, in spite of intensive and systematic investigations.[272] It seems

[269] C 119, 868.
[271] C 88.
[270] Strabo III. 156, 159; Ps.-Scymnus 146–9.
[272] C 119, 885–92.

probable, therefore, that Archaic Phocaean colonization was confined to the north-eastern region of Spain.

Even so, it is not wrong to see Phocaean colonization in the west as determined by commercial considerations. Aristotle expressly linked the foundation of Massalia to Phocaean trade,[273] and it has been well pointed out that just as Phocaea itself, so all her colonies in the west had effectively little or no surrounding territory (*chora*).[274] The Phocaeans were well known for establishing trading ports (*emporia*). When they fled their city rather than submit to the Persians, the Chiots would not sell them the Oenussae Islands because they were afraid that the Phocaeans would create an *emporion* which would shut out Chios itself (Hdt. 1. 165.1).

Massalia was founded at the eastern edge of the Rhône delta, on a hill to the north of a deep inlet which offered an excellent protected harbour (the Lacydon, modern Vieux Port). In the sixth and fifth centuries the city's *chora* was confined to the small plain neighbouring the city,[275] the rocky soil of which was better for vines and olives than for corn, as Strabo says (IV. 179), when he points out that the site was chosen because of its natural advantages for seafaring. There were two divergent traditions about the date of foundation, one putting it *c.* 600 and the other *c.* 545, after the capture of Phocaea by the Persians. Archaeological work has now provided sufficient material to show that the high tradition is certainly correct.[276] Perhaps we should explain the divergent, low, dating by the assumption that in *c.* 545 some refugees from Phocaea were received in the existing colony of Massalia.

The Phocaean colonization was not preceded by a period of pre-colonization trade. Investigation of sites on the west of the Rhône delta has shown that in the last third of the seventh century these people were importing Etruscan fine pottery and wine (or oil) on a large scale, while Greek finds are few and sporadic.[277] That the Etruscan goods were carried by Etruscans seems to be proved by the discovery of an Etruscan wreck off the Cap d'Antibes, which has been dated *c.* 570–*c.* 560.[278] However, from the time of Massalia's foundation Greek material becomes much more abundant, and by the middle of the sixth century most imported pottery at Gallic sites is Greek, much of it actually manufactured at Massalia.[279]

More distant trade with the interior in the sixth century is attested by finds in the settlements and graves of 'Late Hallstatt culture' in west central Europe (approximately eastern France, south-west Germany and

[273] Fr. 549 (Teubner).
[275] C 179.
[277] C 119, 870f; C 24.
[279] C 119, 882; C 171, 132.

[274] C 164; 136–40; C 119, 856f.
[276] C 171, 73ff; C 119, 866.
[278] C 142; C 24.

north-west Switzerland),[280] of which the most sensational are those discovered at Vix, the cemetery of the *oppidum* at Mt Lassois, including the justly famous bronze crater of enormous size. However, at this and other contemporary sites in the same general area there is also plenty of ordinary pottery and wine amphorae from Massalia.[281] The outstanding works of art are usually interpreted as splendid gifts to win the favour of local rulers, but the more mundane objects bear witness to an active import of Greek goods, especially wine and drinking vessels. We do not know what the Greeks received in return. Quite a good theoretical case has been made for tin from Cornwall, which the Phocaeans are thought to have already learnt to exploit at Tartessus,[282] but this is vulnerable to the objection that it does not readily explain the presence of Greek imports at all the sites of the widespread region in question.[283] Whatever the truth of this matter, the mutually beneficial relationship between Massalia and the Hallstatt rulers is certain. In these *oppida* the evidence of luxury and of contacts with the Mediterranean world ceases abruptly in *c.* 500, while at Massalia in the fifth century there is so much less evidence for trading activity that some have assumed that the city was in economic decline during that period.[284]

Massalia's important relations with native people both near and far should be distinguished from Hellenization proper. The famous Hellenization of Gaul by Massalia (Justin XLIII. 4.1–2) was a product of later times, the fourth century and Hellenistic period.[285] It is probable that Massalia's own subsidiary colonization of sites along the southern French coast also belongs largely to that later period. In this well-explored region the only sixth-century Greek settlement discovered is one near Agathe (Agde).[286]

Emporiae (Greek Emporion, modern Ampurias) was a Phocaean/Massaliot foundation in the Gulf of Rosas, at the eastern end of the Pyrenean range.[287] The functional name Emporion, meaning the trading port, must signify the nature of the place, and may possibly have displaced an earlier name derived from the most notable local geographical feature, if Herodotus' 'Pyrene polis' was Emporiae (II. 33.3).[288] Although we have no literary evidence for the date of foundation, Emporiae has been much explored archaeologically, and it is clear that the colony's life began in *c.* 600 or very shortly afterwards.[289] The first settlement was on a small island just off the coast, but the

---

[280] C 176; C 177.   [281] C 171, 141.
[282] C 171, 143–61.   [283] C 177.
[284] C 171, 138f; C 119, 873; C 177.
[285] C 171, 108f; C 164, 136–9.
[286] C 119, 866f, 877.
[287] Strabo III. 159f; Ps.-Scymnus 204; Livy XXXIV. 9.
[288] C 88.   [289] A 7, 218; C 119, 866f.

colonists soon also established themselves on the adjacent mainland, on a headland at the opposite (south) end of the small harbour protected by the offshore island.[290]

Strabo and Livy provide interesting information about the relations between the colonists and the local population. The neighbouring Indigetae maintained an independent state, but wished to have a common wall-circuit with the Greeks for the sake of security. So Emporiae was two cities in one, divided by a cross-wall. Later it developed into a single state, with a mixture of Greek and non-Greek institutions. Both Strabo and Livy are here ultimately dependent on the Elder Cato's account of his consulship in 195 B.C.,[291] and the situation described cannot be closely dated, but it is one of the clearest examples of the very close relations with the local population which were necessary for a successful trading settlement.

The Phocaeans had thus established two important trading colonies on the Gulf of Lion. Their route to this area was up the west coast of Italy, and in c. 565 they founded a colony on the east coast of Corsica at Alalia (modern Aleria) (Hdt. I. 165.1). Alalia lies close to and opposite the coast of Etruria, then an area of very active overseas commerce. Greeks were certainly not excluded from that coast, as the important discoveries at Gravisca have shown.[292] Gravisca was the port of Etruscan Tarquinii, yet it contained a Greek sanctuary of Hera, established in the first part of the sixth century, which provided a centre for the community of Greek traders who used the port. Alalia, founded in the same general area and at the same period, was presumably intended to be a port of call which could exploit local opportunities for trade.

The arrival of large numbers of refugees from Phocaea under the leadership of Creontiades in c. 545 (Hdt. I. 166.1) gave the colony great strength but also the need to find immediately substantial new sources of livelihood. They yielded to temptation and turned to plundering their neighbours, but this quickly produced the strong coalition of Etruscans and Carthaginians, who, though nominally defeated at the naval battle of Alalia in c. 540, had done such damage to the ships of the Phocaeans that they had to abandon Corsica. They took refuge first in Rhegium, but then established themselves in a new colony at Elea (Hyele in Herodotus, Latin Velia) on the west coast of Italy, some fifty kilometres south of Posidonia (Paestum) (Hdt. I. 166–7).

A man of Posidonia helped the Phocaeans to re-interpret their oracle, and we may infer that Posidonia helped them to choose for their colony a dramatically high and steep hill overlooking the sea, which had

[290] C 27, 52ff.   [291] C 157.
[292] C 119, 862f; C 156.

virtually no adjacent territory (if, as is possible, the present narrow coastal plain did not then exist).[293] Here they laid out a regular and skilfully built city, using refined 'Lesbian' polygonal masonry closely similar to some discovered at Phocaea itself.[294] If, as we must assume, they lived from the sea, they quickly prospered. Elea was soon the home of a famous school of philosophy, and, as Aristotle remarked (*Metaph.* A, 982b23ff), men turn to philosophy when their material needs are satisfied.

The aims and character of the Phocaean colonization in the far west are unusually clear. By this date such Greek cities were skilful colonizers, who could use colonization for specific ends – commerce or the evacuation of the mother city – as need required. However, the story of Alalia shows that there were always limits which had to be observed if colonization was to be successful.

TOPICS

X. FOUNDATION

In turning from the history of the foundations to the treatment of topics, we may begin with those which can be subsumed under the general heading of the process of foundation.

The decision to send out a colony was sometimes taken by an individual or a group as a private venture, as Miltiades the Elder's expedition to the Chersonese or Dorieus' to North Africa. Or colonies could be founded as a result of civil strife, by the defeated party or exiles, as for instance Sinope (Ps.-Scymnus 994–7 Diller) or Barca. But the majority of Greek colonies were established as public ventures, duly decided upon by an act of state in the founding (mother) city.

Inscriptions have preserved for us a small number of such foundation decrees, four of which are preserved complete or to a substantial extent. They concern the colonization of Cyrene by Thera (M–L no. 5), of Naupactus by the Eastern Locrians (M–L no. 20), of Brea by Athens (M–L no. 49), and of Black Corcyra by Issa.[295] We have already seen that the foundation decree of Cyrene is preserved in an inscription of the fourth century B.C., so only the Naupactus decree, which has been tentatively dated c. 500–c. 475, strictly belongs, and then only just, to our period. (Brea was founded at an uncertain date in the 440s to 430s, while the decree about Black Corcyra may be roughly dated to the fourth century.) However, we can say that when the Greeks came to record

---

[293] C 120.
[294] C 120, figs. 2, 3; D 2, 8, plates II, IVA; C 119, 855.
[295] Ditt. *Syll.*³ 141; H 55, no. 57.

such decisions permanently, their foundation decrees might comprise any of the following subjects: (1) the decision to found a colony; (2) practical arrangements for the colonization, of which the most important were the choice of the *oikistes* and the recruitment of colonists as conscripts or volunteers; and (3) legal provisions concerning status and relationships.[296]

One formal act which took place on occasions was a solemn oath. In the document about Cyrene we have a description of the oath taken by all those who went to the colony and all those who stayed behind in Thera, which was accompanied by a ceremony of primitive magic and curses against transgressors. We may compare the solemn oath taken by all the Phocaeans when they were leaving their city in order to found a colony in the west (Hdt. I. 165.2–3), and Herodotus' statement (III. 19.2) that the Phoenicians would not sail against their colonists in Carthage because they were bound by great oaths and they would commit sacrilege by doing so.

The choice of the *oikistes*, or founder, was the essential preliminary to all active steps, since he became the leader with complete responsibility.[297] Apart from Thucydides' statement that, when a colony itself founded a colony, according to ancient custom they summoned an *oikistes* from their own mother city (Thuc. I. 24.2; cf. VI. 4.2), we have no evidence that the *oikistes* had to come from any particular group or class. However, in many cases we know that they were nobles, as, for instance, Archias of Syracuse or Chersicrates of Corcyra – both Heraclids from Corinth's ruling house, the Bacchiads[298] – and we may confidently assume that they were always men of distinction, who would possess the necessary talents and tradition of leadership.

Probably the first task, and certainly an essential one, for the *oikistes* was to obtain the approval of the gods for his venture. By the Classical period Apollo was pre-eminently the colonists' god, who was himself regarded as the founder of many Greek colonies,[299] and it was his oracle at Delphi that the *oikistes* was expected to consult. As a result every foundation story had to have its oracle (or oracles), and the god at Delphi is depicted as directing Greek colonizaton in the most detailed way, offering numerous enigmatic or ridiculous oracles, most of which are patently later forgeries.[300] This material must be largely swept away before we can attain any true picture of Delphi's role in colonization.

Herodotus (V. 42.2) shows us that consultation of the Delphic oracle was an obligatory preliminary to colonization by his day, and Thucydides (III. 92.5) shows us one instance of such consultation, writing

---

[296] C 5, 40–68.   [297] C 5, 29–39.
[298] Thuc. VI. 3.2; Strabo VI. 269; cf. C 5, 220.
[299] C 8, 8–20.   [300] E 130, I. 49–81.

as a contemporary witness. Not surprisingly, in view of the extremely dubious evidence about Delphi's role in earlier times, some have suggested that it was in fact a relatively late development, and the oracle played no part in, for example, the colonization of the eighth and seventh centuries. The general argument that Delphi only became an international religious centre at a late date has been shown to be unconvincing, and the importance of Apollo, at least, in the earliest colonization of Sicily is clearly attested by the altar of Apollo Archegetes at Naxus. So it seems better to accept that the Delphic oracle was important from the beginning of the Archaic colonizing movement, even if none of the consultations attested for that period is securely historical.[301]

Why did Greek colonists consult the Delphic oracle? Herodotus says (v. 42.2) that 'Dorieus did not ask the oracle at Delphi which land he should go to colonize, nor did he perform any of the customary practices'. On the other hand, when Dorieus does turn to the oracle, he asks 'if he will take the land to which he is setting forth', and the god replies 'that he will take it' (v. 43). In Thucydides' account (III. 92.5) of the colonization of Heraclea in Trachis in 426 the Spartans have taken all the decisions about the colony before they consult the oracle, and merely ask the god to approve. On general grounds it seems likely that this was the most common form of a question about colonization, as about any other state act. The god's sanction or approval is asked for a policy already formulated. However, what Herodotus says about Dorieus' shortcomings shows that the tradition that the oracle gave geographical directions to colonists was established by his day, and it may have some basis in historical fact.

The sanction of the god was required for any major act of state, but it was especially necessary for colonization. In founding a new Greek city the colonists were creating a new home for Greek gods as well as human beings, an act full of religious significance and traditionally performed by gods themselves on many occasions. Such a venture was also inherently hazardous and the confidence of the participants was essential to success. Such confidence demanded the belief that their actions were approved by the gods, in particular because their main action – taking other people's land – might otherwise seem to be a crime. This aspect is well illustrated by the Greek desire to possess some title to the land that they settled, for which they frequently made use of mythical stories, showing, for instance, that the land had belonged in the past to some Greek hero.[302] But if Apollo approved they had a general moral justification. *Per contra*, when an expedition failed, it was necessary to show either that no oracle had been obtained, as by

Dorieus in North Africa, or that the oracle given had been misinterpreted, as by the Phocaeans in Corsica.

To find a suitable site reconnaissance might be necessary, as at Cyrene, but often the reports of traders must have made the knowledge of possible sites widespread. Pre-colonization trade has been an overworked term in modern discussions of Greek colonization, especially when it implies that colonization was just an intensification of commercial activity, but it cannot be denied that the knowledge necessary for colonization must in most cases have resulted from trade.

In later periods, when we have good evidence, there seems to have been no difficulty in recruitment of settlers. In the fifth century it was possible to assemble 10,000 colonists from volunteers on more than one occasion,[303] and when Corinth announced a supplementary settlement at Epidamnus, there were many ready to go immediately and many others willing to secure their admission later by payment of a deposit in money (Thuc. I. 27.1). It is legitimate to assume that similar conditions obtained earlier, in the Archaic period, but our only good evidence about recruitment at that time relates to Cyrene (Hdt. IV. 153; M–L no. 5.27–30), where conscription on pain of death was employed in order to man the colony (even if there was also provision for volunteers). Otherwise our evidence at that time concerns expeditions which were irregular, general evacuations, as of Phocaea, where the whole population, men, women and children, were originally intended to find a new home (Hdt. I. 164.3), or private ventures, as that of Miltiades the Elder, who took those Athenians who wished to come (Hdt. VI. 36.1).

The evidence is also very defective on the question of numbers. The only actual figures attested for colonies of the Archaic period are 1,000 at Leucas,[304] 200 at Apollonia in Illyria[305] and the two penteconters, i.e. 200 men at the maximum, at Cyrene. (At Thasos it has also been thought that there was an expedition of 1,000 settlers on the basis of a fragment of Archilochus, but the context is too uncertain for this conclusion to be secure.)[306] There is very glaring contrast between these low numbers and the rapid growth to large size at some colonial cities which have been well explored archaeologically, as, for instance, Pithecusa or Syracuse. The answer to the question how population built up so rapidly is not to be found in such improbable hypotheses as that natives were admitted on a substantial scale, but rather in the relatively well attested practice of bringing in further settlers from the mother

[303] C 5, 37f.
[304] Ps.-Scylax 34 (GGM I. 36).
[305] Steph. Byz. s.v. 'Apollonia'.
[306] IG XII. Suppl. 212–14, AIV 22; cf. C 1, 93.

city, or more widely from Greece generally, once the colony had established itself.[307]

Numbers and population raise the questions of women and intermarriage.[308] Greeks did not object to intermarriage and Greek colonies could have arrangements permitting intermarriage with a non-Greek community, as Selinus had with Segesta (Thuc. VI. 6.2). Where Greeks shared a city with non-Greeks, as briefly at Leontini, intermarriage was presumably permitted. However, intermarriage on a much more substantial scale is widely held to have been practised by Greeks as the rule in their colonization. It is thought that in Greek colonizing expeditions only men went, who then took native women as their wives. This is what Herodotus tells us happened in the Ionian colonization of Miletus (I. 146.2–3):

...these men did not take women to the colony, but married Carian women, whose fathers they killed. Because of this killing the women themselves made a law and imposed an oath on themselves (which they handed down to their daughters), never to eat together with their husbands, nor to call their own husband by his name...

This passage relates to a foundation of the migratory period, and is presumably aetiological rather than historical; nor is it at all clear whether Herodotus regarded it as normal or exceptional; nevertheless it is widely used as the 'model' by which we should reconstruct the practices of Greek colonization in the Archaic period.

Something similar is thought to have happened at Cyrene,[309] because Herodotus only mentions men as participants in the expedition, and there is a fair quantity of evidence to show that there was intermarriage between Greek men and Libyan women,[310] and the women of Cyrene and Barca observed food taboos which were like those observed by some Libyans, under Egyptian influence (Hdt. IV. 186). It is frequently stated that the same thing happened at Thasos, but the case is bad, since it rests on a fragmentary and quite uncertain passage of Archilochus, some misinterpreted onomastic evidence, and the false notion that Thasos reveals non-Greek institutions in the Archaic and Classical periods.[311] As for the wider attempt to argue that women of the Italian colonies were of native origin, because they did not drink wine, it was long since shown to be unconvincing by Dunbabin.[312] On similar lines Buchner has suggested that the reason why fibulae of Italian type were used by the Greeks of the west was that at least the majority of the colonists' wives were not Greek, but native women who preferred to

[307] C 5, 64–7; C 13, 87.   [308] C 11.
[309] C 235, 129; A 7, 153–5; C 11.
[310] Hdt. IV. 153; Pindar, *Pyth.* IX. 103–25; Callim. *Hymns* II. 86; *SEG* IX. 1.1–3.
[311] C 194, 92f.   [312] C 65, 185f.

keep their familiar ornaments.[313] But the appearance of such fibulae in large numbers in the princely tombs of Greek nobles at Cyme,[314] and their use as an occasional substitute for the straight pins to fasten the Doric *peplos* in early graves at Syracuse,[315] both seem hard to understand on Buchner's racial interpretation.

There is no instance where the evidence shows certainly that Greek colonists of the Archaic period behaved in a way similar to Herodotus' colonists at Miletus. And there are general objections to the belief that such behaviour was normal practice. Where we have evidence about women in Greek colonies, their names for instance, or their graves, we find them just as clearly Greek as the men. Some of these graves date to very early days in the colony's history, as those in the Fusco cemetery at Syracuse just mentioned. So if the colonists all married native women, they immediately transformed them into Greeks. Secondly, we do hear of Greek women who went on colonial expeditions, as, for instance, the priestesses at Thasos and Massalia (Paus. x. 28.3; Strabo IV. 179). Presumably Greek women were needed to fulfil such important roles in all colonies. It has been argued that these are exceptions,[316] but it seems better to recognize that there were many tasks performed by women which were essential to the economy of an Archaic Greek community, tasks needing skills which women from other societies might not possess. We can understand that women would not normally accompany the initial colonizing expedition, which was virtually a military undertaking. The obvious time for them to come was when the colony was established. However, as long as our only instance of women participating in an Archaic colonizing expedition is the general evacuation of Phocaea (Hdt. 1. 164.3), Herodotus' tale about Miletus will continue to be cited and the question will remain debatable.

We may assume that before departure the *oikistes* would sacrifice to obtain good omens, though our evidence does not antedate the fifth century (M–L no. 49.3–6). Another important ritual act was to take fire from the sacred hearth, the goddess Hestia, of the mother city in order to kindle therewith the sacred hearth of the colony.[317] This is only attested in late sources, but Herodotus' reference to the Ionian colonists who set out from the prytaneum at Athens (1. 146) presumably implies the practice.[318] The interpretation of this act is not necessarily self-evident, and many ideas may have been comprehended in it. The extremely conservative Spartans took with them on campaigns sacred fire from the altar on which the king had made a well-omened sacrifice

---

[313] C 50, 79.   [314] C 25; C 50, 74ff.
[315] H 54, 338.   [316] C 11, 312.
[317] *Etym. Magn. s.v.* πρυτανεῖα (p. 694.28); Schol. Aristides III p. 48.8 (Dindorf).
[318] H 81, 166–77.

before setting out (Xen. *Lac.* 13.1–3). On that analogy the colonists were trying to ensure their success by taking with them part of the physical sign of the god's approval. Fire is also simply a symbol of continuing life, so that idea may also have been present.[319] But since the fire on Hestia's altar symbolized above all the life of that particular community,[320] the act seems especially to mirror the idea that the colony was a continuation of the life of the mother city. In addition, it is possible that it also reflects the creation of a new *polis*, if Theseus' synoecism of Attica, as described by Thucydides (II. 15.2), involved the destruction of the prytanea of all the various communities of Attica other than Athens, and hence the extinction of their sacred hearths.

The voyage took place, in the only two instances where we are informed (Cyrene and the evacuation of Phocaea), in warships (pente-conters) (Hdt. IV. 153; I. 164.3), which reflects the military nature of the undertaking. The first task of the *oikistes* after the journey was completed would be to pick the site of the new city. There is too much variety among the sites of Greek colonies for us to speak of a typical Greek colonial site, but certain configurations of land (and sea) were so well suited to the needs of Greek colonists that they were chosen again and again, for instance, offshore islands, peninsulas, headlands, and coastal sites lying between two rivers.[321] Water supply was an essential determinant, and its lack has been used to explain the neglect of apparently attractive sites, such as Augusta in Sicily.[322]

In the Classical period the *oikistes* named the new city, and it seems likely that this was the ancient practice (Thuc. IV. 102.3). The way in which it was planned and built is not described for us in any historical source for the Archaic period, but must be pieced together from scattered literary and archaeological information. Homer says that Nausithous, when founding the new city of the Phaeacians, surrounded the city with a wall, built houses, made temples of the gods and divided the land (*Od.* VI. 7–11). The practical tasks of an *oikistes* included all of these. One of the most interesting discoveries of recent years is that the orthogonal planning, which has been long associated with Hippodamus, in fact occurs much earlier. Archaeology and air photography have revealed that several colonial sites of the west were regularly planned with a rectangular layout as early as the seventh century.[323] Even earlier, before the orthogonal pattern became the ideal, eighth-century Megara Hyblaea was a planned city in which many elements were regular from the beginning. Although we do not possess the evidence for surveying and planning which is available for Roman colonization,[324] it is clear

[319] A 22.
[321] H 79, 12–29.
[323] C 56; H 77, 22–4; C 31; C 164, 76.
[320] A 20, V. 353f.
[322] C 65, 19.
[324] C 12.

that from the eighth century onwards the Greeks must have been using systems and methods which are comparable.

The provision of a wall of defence may not have been necessary for all colonial cities, as at Megara Hyblaea,[325] but for most a partial or complete circuit was probably required from the first. The theory, which has been put forward and won some acceptance,[326] that such walls are a late development in Greek cities and colonies, is certainly false. We know of very early colonial walls at Siris and Leontini,[327] for example, and one need only recall the large and skilfully built wall at Old Smyrna, which dates from the beginning of Middle Geometric (i.e. *c.* 850),[328] to understand that the Greeks knew the advantages of such defences, and how to build them, before the inception of the Archaic colonizing movement.

At one colony of the Classical period, Brea, we know that the precincts of the gods were laid out before the colonizing expedition proper and the general division of the land (M–L no. 49.9–11), and we need not doubt that the *oikistes* would set aside land for sanctuaries and for their support as one of his first acts in laying out city and territory. Pindar (*Pyth.* v. 89) drew special attention to the splendid sanctuaries for the gods established by Battus at Cyrene, and Theocles erected the altar of Apollo Archegetes at Naxus.

The first houses of the colonists have now been discovered at a number of sites, and they vary little. Apart from one apsidal and one oval example at Pithecusa,[329] and some that are circular at Berezan, they are normally rectangular, small, single-roomed and single-storeyed structures of stone or mud-brick, with thatched roofs and earth floors. The modest domestic requirements of the colonists would be a great advantage, since such simple houses would not require much time or labour to build. Such evidence as we have suggests that their siting was planned and controlled, and we may assume that the plots for houses were allotted in the initial division of the land.[330] At several sites we know that the first houses were not closely set in typical ancient urban fashion, so it appears that, when land was plentiful, the Greeks aspired to a garden city.

Although we do not know how it was arranged, provision was also made for the dead. Where a site had been occupied before, as at Mylae in Sicily, the colonists continued to use the cemetery of their predecessors.[331] At Istrus the great Greek necropolis seems to have grown up round some prominent native tumuli of the sixth century,

[325] C 165, 91.
[326] C 230, 45.
[327] C 85, 429–43; H 79, 128.
[328] D 73, 122, 82ff.
[329] C 98, 36.
[330] Cf. Ditt. *Syll.*[3] 141, 4f, 9f.
[331] C 39, 61, 83, 116f; C 161, 84.

in which there is a curious mixture of strikingly barbarous ritual and Greek grave goods.[332] In some cases, where new cemeteries were created, they were sited at a distance from the original settlement. This might have been to allow for the anticipated growth of the city, or, perhaps more probably, because the land close by was desired for cultivation.

Apart from a few obvious exceptions, such as Naucratis, land division was an essential part, one might even say the most important part, of the act of colonization. In Classical times Athens employed special 'land-distributors' ($\gamma\epsilon\omega\nu\acute{o}\mu\omega$) to carry out this delicate task (M–L no. 49.6–8), but it seems likely that it was performed by the *oikistes* himself in earlier periods, as in Homer. The distribution was made by lot, and hence a colonist's parcel of land was called an allotment (*kleros*). Although the land-divisions of the territory of more than one Greek colony have now been recognized,[333] none of these can be securely attributed to the original division of land in a settlement of Archaic times. Furthermore all our literary and epigraphic evidence on the subject belongs to the Classical period. So it must be conceded that we cannot certainly know how the land was distributed in Archaic Greek colonies, and we can do no more than pose questions on the basis of later analogies and probability.

The major problem concerns equality. It is quite certain that in the Classical period all colonists went on equal terms, which implies above all equal allotments of land.[334] The only clear example of inequality in an Archaic colony are the special privileges of the kings at Cyrene (Hdt. IV. 161), which are manifestly exceptional, if not unique. Furthermore, at one eighth-century colony which is well known archaeologically, Megara Hyblaea, the finds suggested to the excavators that the earliest settlers were on terms of equality. Equal shares in general are also a concept familiar in Homer, and Solon speaks of equal shares in the land.[335] On the other hand, the princely tombs at Cyme show us an unmistakable nobility, established in an eighth-century colony, who certainly did not belong to an equal society. It is unfortunately not possible to say how long Cyme had then existed, but it can hardly be more than two generations and may well have been less. At Pithecusa too the graves show definite economic differences, even if we exclude the slaves, again probably within a generation or two of the foundation. In any case it might well be argued that the highly oligarchic societies of Greece cannot conceivably have founded colonies in which the citizens were equal.[336] We have seen that the *oikistes* will have belonged

[332] C 205; C 212, 410ff.

[334] G 4, 13–16; C 5, 58f.

[336] Cf. Strabo x. 447.

[333] C 16; G 24.

[335] G 4, 13; Solon fr. 23, 21.

to the nobility. Pentathlus and Dorieus took fellow-nobles as companions (Hdt. v. 46.1; Diod. v. 9). Without such participants, would the *oikistes* have been confident of the military potential of his new community, at a time when nobles had a monopoly of military skill? Thus the position seems to be that the theory and practice of the Classical world and some other evidence points to equal rights and equal allotments, but some archaeological evidence and strong arguments from probability make it doubtful if such principles were observed in the colonization of at least the early Archaic period.

It seems to have been the practice on some occasions for land to be left undistributed in order to provide for later settlers.[337] Similarly the large house plots within the city allowed for the expansion of the population by 'infilling'.

The death of the *oikistes* may be called the end of the foundation procedure. It is true that in the Classical period, when the *oikistes* did not necessarily stay in the colony that he had founded,[338] the procedure of foundation could be called complete during his lifetime, but we may deduce from the way in which the founder's cult grew up around his tomb[339] that, in the Archaic period, an *oikistes* would normally live in the colony that he had established. Apart from Battus, who became king of Cyrene, we have no evidence which bears on the question how the great powers of the *oikistes* lapsed and a constitutional government assumed control. Perhaps such an act was barely conceivable while an *oikistes* was alive and present in his new colony. Whatever the answer to such questions, we reach greater certainty at his death, when the *oikistes* became a hero, who was worshipped with ritual and offerings in the belief that he was immortal and would, if propitiated, care for the welfare of his foundation.[340] Battus is the first founder of whom this worship is attested clearly and early, but we have archaeological evidence for the worship of Antiphemus, the *oikistes* of Gela, a colony founded in 688.[341] This is a great rarity, since archaeological evidence for the cult of the *oikistes* barely exists and no completely convincing identification of the tomb of an *oikistes* has yet been made.[342]

Since it is possible to follow the development of so few Archaic Greek colonies, we may confine our attention here to the two relationships which could have an important influence on that development, viz. relations with the mother city and relations with the native population.

---

[337] G 4, 10, 15; C 5, 64f.   [338] C 5, 34–9.
[339] Pindar, *Pyth.* v. 93–5; Hdt. vi. 38.1; cf. Thuc. v. 11.1.
[340] Hdt. vi. 38.1; Thuc. v. 11.1; Callim. *Aetia* (A 52) fr. 43, 54–65, 72–83; cf. C 151.
[341] C 5, 21f.   [342] Contrast C 239, 4ff and C 237 with C 240, 109ff.

XI. RELATIONS WITH THE MOTHER CITY

The institutions of a colony, as we should expect, normally reproduced faithfully those of the mother city, and where our evidence allows we find the same cults, calendar, dialect, script, state offices and citizen divisions in colonies and mother cities. This need not imply any active continuing relationship, and we know instances where a colony preserved institutions which were changed in the mother city.[343] However, Greek colonies also shared in the general developments of Greek culture, which shows that they remained in close contact with the wider Greek world, and such contacts would often be pre-eminently with their mother cities. Corcyra was dominated by Corinth in such fields as the arts, even if their political relationship was frequently unhappy. The consciousness that the graves of their ancestors were at the mother city provided a powerful sentimental link at the personal level (Thuc. 1. 26.3), which existed in all colonies. It also seems probable that the traditional and religious connexions for which we have scattered evidence were a regular feature of the relationship.

We have already seen one such traditional practice in the choice of the *oikistes* when a colony itself colonized, which Thucydides called an ancient custom. Thucydides (1. 25.4) also tells us that it was normal at sacrifices in the colony for a citizen from the metropolis to receive the first portion, and for colonies to make offerings at the common festivals at the metropolis.[344] We have evidence of other privileges enjoyed by citizens of the mother city in the religious ceremonies and on public occasions in the colonies, but this all comes from the Classical period or later.[345] Since we are dealing with practices which are particularly ruled by tradition, however, it is a reasonable assumption that they have their roots in earlier times. Evidence for offerings from the colonies to gods of the metropolis is also only abundant from Classical times (when we find such offerings imposed as a duty on her colonies by Athens), but some Archaic instances are attested.[346] An interesting sixth-century inscription from Samos records the dedications to Hera by two Perinthians and states the total cost in money.[347] In the wording the kinship of colony and mother city is stressed, and it has been suggested that the emphasis on the exact sum paid shows that the offerings were a regular obligation on the part of the colony.[348]

It is clear, on the other hand, that there was great variety in the active political relationships between Greek colonies and mother cities. It was normal for the colony to be from the first a separate state with a separate

citizenship. This is well reflected in the wording of the foundation decree
for Naupactus, which says more than once 'when (the colonist) becomes
a Naupactian'.[349] As a result political relationships did not depend on
any defined and generally recognized status but on the extent to which
colony or mother city chose to exploit the tie of relationship. That
tie was a sufficient reason for either state to give the other political
support, especially support in war. They were considered natural allies
and, conversely, wars fought between colonies and mother cities were
regarded as shameful.[350]

The degree to which the status of mother city conferred hegemony
was disputed by the Greeks themselves. In debate at Athens in 433 the
Corinthians asserted that as a mother city they should be leaders and
receive reasonable respect, while the Corcyreans replied that they were
sent out to be not the slaves but the equals of those who stayed behind
(Thuc. I. 43.1, 38.2). If the circumstances were favourable, mother cities
could and did establish dependent colonies. This happened especially
when the colonies were at a short distance from the mother city, as for
instance those of Thasos on the adjacent mainland, or the near-by cities
established by Syracuse, but a seapower such as Corinth (or, later,
Athens) would found colonies far away which remained in a position
of dependence.[351] So while it may be right to state that as a rule a Greek
colony was independent of its mother city, imperial colonization could
occur and was justified by the tie of the relationship. In such colonization
we find signs of dependence such as officials in the colonies sent from
the mother city, legislation by the mother city affecting colonies,
decisions about foreign policy and war taken by mother cities which
involved colonies, and financial obligations due from colony to
metropolis.

Another category of relationships, which may have nothing to do
with hegemony, were those involving mutual citizenship and the
movement of people from one community to the other. Isopolity,
the right of exercising citizenship in both communities, is not unambiguously attested for the Archaic period, though it can be argued
that the complete isopolity between Miletus and Olbia provided for in
a decree of c. 330 originated much earlier,[352] and the career of Aceratus,
who was archon at both Paros and Thasos in the later sixth century,
has been taken to imply something like isopolity.[353] Perhaps, however,
we should not deduce general rules from this obviously exceptional
individual. Since it was necessary to make special provision for colonists
to return to citizen rights at home, we may infer that there was no
universal right for colonists to take up citizenship in the metropolis.

---

[349] M–L no. 20.1f, 22f.   [350] C 5, 10, 73f, 84–7, 132, 136, 140f, 143ff.
[351] C 5, 71–97, 118–53.   [352] C 5, 99–103.   [353] C 5, 74–6.

On the other hand, the conditions for return could be very easy, as at Naupactus, where the rules about inheritance show that frequent interchange of people between the two communities was envisaged.[354] We have already seen that mother cities frequently sent in further settlers to colonies, and scattered evidence suggests that movement of domicile by individuals between colonies and mother cities was frequent. There are also plenty of examples of the reception of fugitives from colonies and mother cities by the other community.[355] All of this suggests that, at the least, there was much greater readiness to open citizenship to members of the related community than there was to aliens generally.

In sum, the relationship between colony and mother city was fundamentally based on shared cults, ancestors, dialect and institutions. As such it was especially expressed in religion. It would be quite wrong to conclude from this that it was purely formal. Far from it, in a period when political relations grew out of shared religious centres and shared worship (as shown by the early Greek leagues) it is not surprising that the relationship between colony and metropolis was often important, practical and effective.

XII. RELATIONS WITH THE NATIVE POPULATION

We have seen examples of many of these relationships at the time of foundation and of some subsequent to it. More will be found in the next chapter, since our evidence is especially abundant in Sicily and southern Italy. Here too there is in general great variety. Some colonies were established after the native population had been expelled, as Syracuse and (probably) Thasos, others by invitation of a local ruler, as Megara Hyblaea and perhaps Massalia. The Greeks were opportunistic and ready to use friendship, force or fraud to gain the main end, a place to settle.

To the natives a small Greek establishment which provided desirable goods and help in local struggles might well seem welcome. In the early days, or even for a long period, it might present no threat, especially in relatively thinly populated country, as we may imagine, for example, on the shores of the Pontus. In such circumstances a *modus vivendi* might easily persist for long periods. On the other hand, we saw at Cyrene how pressure on the land could increase with the growth of a Greek colony, leading to hostile relations. The sites usually chosen show that few Greek colonies had such confidence in good relations with their native neighbours that they took no thought for defence. Rightly, since

---

[354] C 5, 52–8, 100f.   [355] C 5, 104, 111–15.

it was possible for a Greek colony which had existed for centuries to succumb to the attack of neighbouring natives, as Cyme was taken by the Campanians at the end of the fifth century.[356]

Long-term relations between a colony and the local native population were, however, almost bound by definition to reach some kind of stability. At one end of the spectrum we know of examples where the natives were turned into serfs by the Greek colonists. This happened at Syracuse, where the Cyllyrii were native serfs, and at Heraclea Pontica, where the Maryandini were in the same situation.[357] We have seen that some of the Libyans were subject to Cyrene, but their precise status is not attested. It has been suggested of many Greek colonies that their rapid growth and great wealth imply a similar exploitation of native labour, but definite evidence is lacking.

The converse, where the Greek colonists were politically subordinate to the non-Greek local power is most obvious at Naucratis, but there are some indications that the colonies in Scythian territory on the north coast of the Pontus were in a somewhat similar position.

While the relationship of political power might vary so greatly, the Greeks exercised cultural domination almost throughout their colonial region. (Only Egypt appears to have been immune to the attractions of Greek culture.) This is interestingly revealed precisely in Scythia, where the Greeks, even if in some cases inferior politically, were certainly dominant culturally. In Scythian art Greek styles and techniques become universal, and a Scythian king such as Scyles had a Greek mother, a Greek wife, and an ultimately fatal passion for Greek religion, dress and way of life. As a general rule Hellenization was to a greater or lesser degree a concomitant of Greek colonization. Barbarization of the Greek communities, on the other hand, was not a feature of the Archaic or Classical periods.

We have seen that one of the most difficult questions in Greek colonization is the extent to which it produced mixed settlements. Strabo said (III. 160), writing of Emporiae, that such settlements were very common, but that statement doubtless refers to a longer span of time than the Archaic period. Herodotus attests mixed populations in the Pontus and Thucydides in Chalcidice, while many settlements discovered by excavation have been regarded as mixed. Given the freedom of intermarriage such mixture is not surprising. On the other hand, when we are dealing with actual cities in the Archaic period the evidence tends to show that they remained thoroughly Greek. If there were mixed or shared settlements, as perhaps at Leontini, they were shortlived. Possibly the general pattern was for the cities to remain

---

[356] Diod. XII. 76.4; Dion. Hal. *Ant. Rom.* XV. 6.4; Strabo V. 243.
[357] Hdt. VII. 155.2 (with A 35, commentary *ad loc.*); Strabo XII. 542.

entirely Greek and maintain exclusive ideas about citizenship, but for mixed populations to appear in peripheral areas. This is how Dunbabin read the evidence in the west.[358]

XIII. CAUSATION

The question of the cause or causes of the great colonizing movement of the Archaic period is endlessly debated. We need to distinguish first between active and passive causes. Certainly the Greeks could not colonize without favourable passive causes, i.e. the opportunities to found colonies, which were dependent on geography, the attitudes, power and development of other peoples, and their own possession of the necessary knowledge and techniques. But the active causes must be sought solely in the states of Greece. Without their desire and need to colonize, whatever the opportunities, there would have been no colonization.

We may take it as axiomatic that no one leaves home and embarks on colonization for fun. This means that by definition there was overpopulation in the colonizing states, since overpopulation is a relative concept and there were certainly large numbers of people for whom conditions at home were so unsatisfactory that they preferred to join colonizing expeditions. On this argument, even if all participants went voluntarily, there was overpopulation, but in fact we know that sometimes colonists were conscripted, because the community decided that it could not support the existing population. This is most clearly attested in Thera's colonization of Cyrene, but the stories of the dedication of one tenth of the population to Apollo at Delphi, who then sent them to found a colony, though mythical and influenced by the Italian practice of *ver sacrum*, presumably reflect actual instances of forced colonization.[359]

Simple theoretical considerations show, therefore, that the basic active cause of the colonizing movement was overpopulation. But we are not confined to theory. When the ancient Greeks themselves discussed colonization, they describe it as a cure for overpopulation and compare it to the swarming of bees (Plato, *Leg.* 740e, 708b; Thuc. 1. 15.1). In addition we have the persuasive argument from archaeology that, at the very time when the Archaic colonizing movement began, in the second half of the eighth century, there was a marked increase in population in Greece.[360]

It has been argued that, since those who would want to join a colonizing expedition would be the poor, and since the poor had no

[358] C 65, 187ff.   [359] C 87, 27–31.
[360] H 25, 360ff.

political power, overpopulation cannot have been the cause, which must have been something that affected the ruling class.[361] But this fails to see that the ruling class clearly benefited from the removal of people for whom there was no livelihood at home. Such people, even if they had no political power (though that is itself uncertain), could make their discontent a political factor, especially in relatively small communities. The ancient Greeks were well aware of this, as is shown by the classical role of the poor and discontented in the rise of tyrants. We should also remember the ancient view that when tyrants – who represented a ruling class of one – colonized, they did it to get rid of undesirable surplus population.

If the colonists were people without livelihood in their old home, what means of support were they going to find in their new one? According to Aristotle (*Pol.* 1, 1256a35ff), the five primary ways of making a living were pastoral farming, arable farming, piracy, fishing and hunting. (Trade, which involves exchange and sale, is not seen as a primary way of provision.) The most numerous part of mankind, he states, lives from agriculture. Whatever one may think of his distinctions, there is no doubt that his picture reflects the economic realities of the ancient world. It follows that most Greek colonies and most Greek colonists lived mainly by agriculture, and the motive of the majority in joining colonial expeditions was to obtain land to cultivate which was not available at home. The conclusion that most Greek colonization was predominantly agricultural in character seems, therefore, to be inescapable, and was argued convincingly long ago by Gwynn in a justly famous paper.[362]

Of Aristotle's means of provision we have seen that piracy was practised by some colonies, and fishing is clearly attested in many (cf. Arist. *Pol.* IV, 1291b23). Hunting may readily be assumed in addition to pastoral and arable farming. The great area of dispute concerns trade, and the degree to which commercial motives were a cause of colonization.[363] We need not be distracted here by false analogies with primitive peoples, whose methods of exchange cannot properly be called trade, since they are sufficiently refuted by Homer's many references to what is clearly commerce, not to mention Hesiod. As for Hasebroek's exaggerated thesis that Greek states had no commercial policies,[364] salutary though this was in sweeping away false and anachronistic modern analogies, it cannot alter the actual fact that Greek colonies were active in trade. However, to show that a colony was founded for trade one needs clear evidence, either of pre-colonization trade, or that the colony lived by trade from the first, or, preferably,

---

[361] C 89.
[363] Cf. C 104.
[362] C 7.
[364] G 19.

both. Such evidence is rare, partly no doubt because many trade objects are not preserved for the archaeologist, but partly also because of chronological or other uncertainties. So more or less plausible conjectures are normally the most that one can achieve. This is especially so, when we try to determine whether a colony was established in order that the mother city should acquire some important trade goods, such as corn or metals. Although such motives have often been postulated, proof that they were the *raison d'être* of colonization can rarely or never be attained. In spite of these uncertainties, however, since literary and archaeological evidence show quite clearly that Greeks were fully aware of the possibilities of trade from the beginning of the Archaic colonizing movement, it is hard to believe that these possibilities were never in the minds of founders, and we only find ourselves in difficulty if we demand unitary explanations. The correct conclusion would appear to be that Greek colonists sought their livelihood in various ways, the majority certainly from agriculture. But it was a rare colony in which trade was entirely negligible, and there were many where it was important, and a few where it was all-important.

XIV. CONCLUSION

In conclusion we may consider the reasons for the success of the Greeks in establishing their numerous colonies so widely in the Archaic period. Clearly they possessed the various practical skills necessary for the task, and they were normally superior in seamanship and soldiering to the people among whom they settled. But it was probably more important that they brought with them a highly effective social and political organization, the *polis*, which proved easily transplantable and adaptable to very varied conditions, and was as a rule more cohesive and stronger than the political organizations of their native neighbours. Above all this, however, the secret of their success should be seen in their possession of a strong 'culture pattern'. Believing in their gods and hence in themselves they had the morale required to create permanent new communities far from home.

List of Greek colonies founded between 800 and 500

Colony	Mother city or cities	Literary foundation date	Earliest archaeological material	Map reference
Abdera	(1) Clazomenae; (2) Teos	(1) 654; (2) c. 545	c. 600	9 Ba
Abydus	Miletus	c. 680–652		9 Cb
Acanthus	Andros	655		9 Bb
Acrae	Syracuse	663	c. 640–625	8 Cc
Acragas	Gela	580	c. 600–575	8 Bc
Adria			c. 525–500	6 Ab
Aenus	Alopeconnesus, Mytilene, Cyme			9 Cb
Agathe	Massalia		c. 600–500	5 Bb
Alalia	Phocaea	c. 565	c. 575–550	5 Cb
Alopeconnesus	Aeolians			9 Cb
Ambracia	Corinth	c. 655–625		6 Bc
Amisus	Miletus and Phocaea	c. 564	c. 600–575	7 Bb
Anactorium	Corinth and Corcyra	c. 655–625	c. 625–600	6 Bc
Apollonia Pontica	Miletus	c. 610	c. 600–575	7 Ab
Apollonia in Illyria	Corinth and Corcyra	c. 600	c. 600	6 Bc
Apollonia in Libya	Thera		c. 600	6 Bd
Argilus	Andros			9 Bb
Assera	Chalcis			9 Bb
Assus	Methymna		c. 600–500	9 Cc
Astacus	Megara or Chalcedon	?711		9 Eb
Barca	Cyrene	c. 560–550		6 Bd
Berezan	Miletus	647	c. 650–600	7 Ba
Bisanthe	Samos			9 Da
Black Corcyra	Cnidus	?c. 625–585	c. 600–575	6 Bb
Byzantium	Megara	659 or 668	c. 625–600	9 Ea
Camarina	Syracuse	598	c. 600–570	8 Bc
Cardia	Miletus and Clazomenae			9 Cb
Casmenae	Syracuse	643	c. 600	8 Bc
Catane	Chalcis	729		8 Cc
Caulonia	Achaea (Croton)		c. 650	8 Cb
Celenderis	Samos			7 Bd
Cepi	Miletus		c. 575–550	7 Bb
Cerasus	Sinope			7 Cb
Chalcedon	Megara	676 or 685		9 Ea
Chersonese (Thracian)	Athens	561–556		9 Cb
Cius	Miletus	627		9 Eb
Cleonae	Chalcis			9 Bb
Colonae	Miletus			9 Cb
Corcyra	(1) Eretria; (2) Corinth	(2) 706 or 733	c. 720–700	6 Bc
Cotyora	Sinope			7 Cc
Croton	Achaea	709	c. 725–700	8 Cb
Cyme (Italy)	Chalcis and Eretria		c. 725–700	8 Ba
Cyrene	Thera	632	c. 625–600	6 Bd
Cyzicus	Miletus	(1) 756; (2) 679		9 Db

Colony	Mother city or cities	Literary foundation date	Earliest archaeological material	Map reference
Dicaearchia	Samos	531		8 Ba
Elaeus	Teos		c. 600	9 Cb
Elea	Phocaea	c. 540	c. 540	8 Ca
Emporiae	Massalia/Phocaea		c. 600–575	5 Bb
Epidamnus	Corcyra	627		6 Bb
Euhesperides	Cyrene	before c. 515	c. 600–575	6 Bd
Gale	Chalcis			9 Bb
Galepsus	Thasos		c. 650–625	9 Bb
Gela	Rhodes and Crete	688	c. 725–690	8 Bc
Helorus	Syracuse		c. 700	8 Cc
Heraclea Minoa	Selinus	before c. 510	c. 550	8 Bc
Heraclea Pontica	Megara	c. 560		7 Bb
Hermonassa	?Miletus		c. 600–575	7 Bb
Himera	Zancle	c. 648	c. 625–600	8 Bc
Hipponium	Locri Epizephyrii		c. 650	8 Cb
Imbros	Athens	c. 500		9 Cb
Istrus	Miletus	657	c. 630–600	7 Ab
Lampsacus	Phocaea	654		9 Cb
Laus	Sybaris			8 Cb
Lemnos	Athens	c. 500	c. 500	9 Cb
Leontini	Chalcis	729	c. 750–725	8 Cc
Leucas	Corinth	c. 655–625		6 Bc
Limnae	Miletus			9 Cb
Lipara	Cnidus	c. 580	c. 575–50	8 Cb
Locri Epizephyrii	Locris	679	c. 690–650	8 Cb
Madytus	Lesbos			9 Cb
Maronea	Chios	before c. 650		9 Ca
Massalia	Phocaea	c. 600	c. 600	5 Bb
Mecyberna	Chalcis			9 Ab
Medma	Locri Epizephyrii		c. 625–600	8 Cb
Megara Hyblaea	Megara	728	c. 750–725	8 Cc
Mende	Eretria			9 Ab
Mesembria	Megara, Byzantium, Chalcedon	c. 510	c. 500	7 Ab
Metapontum	Achaea	773	c. 650	8 Ca
Metaurus	(1) Zancle; (2) Locri Epizephyrii		(1) c. 650; (2) c. 550	8 Cb
Methone	Eretria	c. 706 or c. 733		9 Ab
Miletopolis	Miletus			9 Db
Mylae	Zancle	?716	c. 725–700	8 Cb
Myrmecium	Miletus or Panticapaeum		c. 600–575	7 Bb
Nagidus	Samos			7 Bd
Naucratis			c. 610	7 Ae
Naxus (Sicily)	Chalcis	734	c. 750–725	8 Cc
Neapolis (Kavalla)	Thasos		c. 650–625	9 Ba
Nymphaeum	?Miletus		c. 600	7 Bb
Oasis Polis	Samos	before c. 525		7 Ae
Odessus	Miletus		c. 600–575	7 Ab
Oesyme	Thasos		c. 650–625	9 Bb
Olbia	Miletus	647	c. 640–610	7 Ba
Paesus	Miletus			9 Cb
Panticapaeum	Miletus		c. 600	7 Bb

Colony	Mother city or cities	Literary foundation date	Earliest archaeological material	Map reference
Parium	Paros, Miletus, Erythrae	709		9 Db
Perinthus	Samos	602		9 Da
Phanagoria	Teos	c. 545	c. 550–500	7 Bb
Phaselis	Rhodes	?688		7 Ac
Phasis	Miletus			7 Cb
Pilorus	Chalcis			9 Bb
Pithecusa	Chalcis and Eretria		c. 750–725	8 Ba
Posidonia	Sybaris		c. 625–600	8 Ca
Potidaea	Corinth	c. 625–585		9 Ab
Priapus	Miletus			9 Db
Proconnesus	Miletus	before c. 690		9 Db
Pyxus	Sybaris			8 Ca
Rhegium	Chalcis		c. 730–720	8 Cb
Samothrace	Samos	c. 600–500	c. 550–500	9 Cb
Sane	Andros	655		9 Bb
Sarte	Chalcis			9 Bb
Scepsis	Miletus			9 Cb
Scione	Achaea			9 Ab
Selinus	Megara Hyblaea	628	c. 630–620	8 Bc
Selymbria	Megara	before 668		9 Da
Sermyle	Chalcis			9 Ab
Sestus	Lesbos			9 Cb
Sigeum	Athens	c. 600		9 Cb
Singus	Chalcis			9 Bb
Sinope	Miletus	(1) before 756; (2) 631	c. 640–600	7 Bb
Siris	Colophon	c. 680–652	c. 700	8 Ca
Spina			c. 525–500	6 Ab
Stagirus	Andros	655		9 Bb
Stryme	Thasos	c. 650		9 Ba
Sybaris	Achaea	c. 720	c. 700	8 Cb
Syracuse	Corinth	733	c. 750–725	8 Cc
Tanais	?Miletus		c. 625–600	7 Ca
Taras	Sparta	706	c. 725–700	8 Ca
Tauchira	Cyrene		c. 630	6 Bd
Temesa	?Croton		c. 500	8 Cb
Terina	Croton		c. 500	8 Cb
Thasos	Paros	c. 650	c. 650	9 Bb
Theodosia	Miletus		c. 575–500	7 Bb
Tieum	Miletus			7 Bb
Tomis	Miletus		c. 500–475	7 Ab
Torone	Chalcis	before c. 650		9 Bb
Trapezus	Sinope	756		7 Cc
Tyras	Miletus		? c. 600–500	7 Aa
Tyritace	?Panticapaeum		c. 550	7 Bb
Zancle	Chalcis		c. 730–720	8 Cb

CHAPTER 38

THE WESTERN GREEKS

A. J. GRAHAM

The history of the Greeks in Sicily and southern Italy down to 500 B.C. is hardly at any point a connected story. We have, on the one hand, a number of isolated events, or, at best, episodes, preserved in very varied literary sources from Herodotus to Athenaeus, and, on the other, a constantly growing body of archaeological material, which is richly informative on a restricted range of topics, and which presents the historian with many difficulties in interpretation. T. J. Dunbabin attempted a historical synthesis on the basis of the literary sources and the archaeological evidence then available in his book *The Western Greeks* (1948), to which the title of this chapter pays tribute. More is known archaeologically today, but in many respects his historical interpretation still dominates scholars in the field.

In the period under discussion the largest quantity of solid historical material about the western Greeks relates to colonization,[1] and so much of this chapter is inevitably about colonization. We have discussed the major foundations in Sicily and southern Italy before 700 in the previous chapter, so our first section concerns the major foundations between 700 and 500. The next discusses the expansion of the Greek colonies, which includes further colonization in addition to the relations with the non-Greek peoples. Then we shall look at the relations between Greeks and Phoenicians in Sicily, which also involve the last major attempts at colonization by the Greeks in the period under review. Finally we shall consider the internal developments of the Greek city-states, and their relations.

I. MAJOR FOUNDATIONS AFTER 700

In this section we shall take Sicily first, and follow an order determined by geographical as well as chronological factors.

Gela was the first Greek colony in the island to be established away from the east coast (apart from Mylae on the north). Here (fig. 26) a long, narrow hill with steep sides lies along the coast between the river

---

[1] C 34.

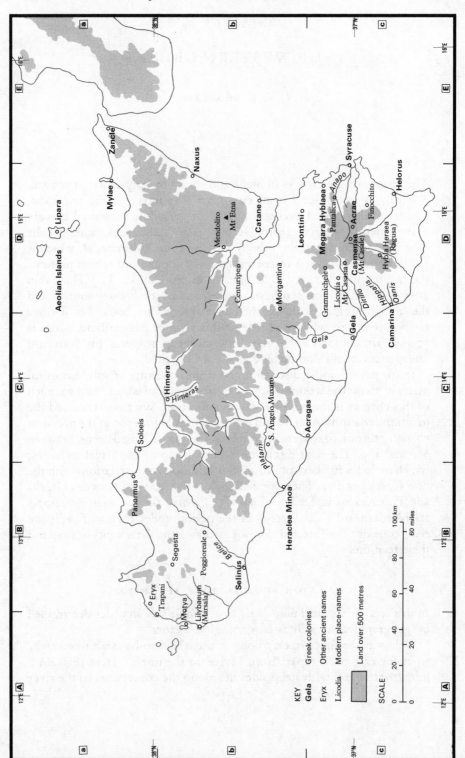

Map 10. Sicily.

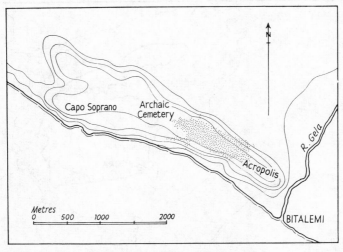

26. Plan of Gela. (After C 123, fig. 2.)

Gela, at its eastern end, and a smaller stream to the west. The flat top of the hill extends for a good three kilometres east to west, though the width is often 500 metres or less, especially at the eastern end, where the Archaic city stood, with its acropolis at the tip overlooking the river mouth.[2] There is no outstanding harbour, though the long beach and the river mouth offered adequate facilities for ancient shipping. The surrounding plain, on the other hand, is large and fertile, and made the hill on the coast a fine colonial site.

The colony was founded by Rhodians and Cretans under the leadership of Antiphemus from Rhodes and Entimus from Crete (Thuc. VI. 4.3). Although some of our sources, including Herodotus (VII. 153.1), speak of foundation by Rhodes alone, the Cretan participation is firmly supported by some material evidence,[3] and by the statement of Pausanias (VIII. 46.2) that Antiphemus carried off a statue made by Daedalus after sacking a town called Omphace, since Daedalus points clearly to Crete. This story also implies that the colonization was achieved by force. The colonists needed to wrest control of the rich farmland from the natives who lived in the surrounding hills, and archaeological evidence seems to show that their settlements fell under Greek domination from the time of Gela's foundation (see below).

The Thucydidean date of foundation, c. 688, has been thought to conflict with a small amount of fine pottery which is normally dated before 700, but the calibration of our pottery chronology is not sufficiently close and definite to measure such small intervals, and there

[2] C 123, 176, fig. 3.   [3] A 7, 178.

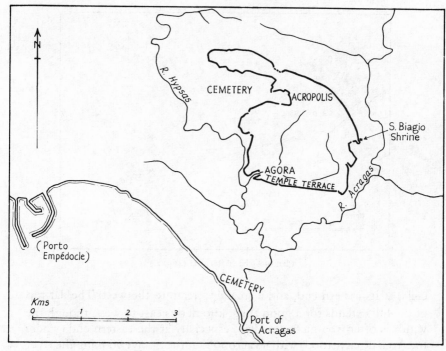

27. Plan of Acragas. (After c 175, 282, fig. 4.)

is no need to envisage a 'pre-colonization phase', nor to doubt the literary date.[4]

Acragas lies some sixty kilometres to the west of Gela. It has often been stated that there was some Geloan occupation of the site before the colony was founded, but minute examination of the pottery evidence has shown that there is no reason to assume any Greek settlement before 580.[5] Even so, it is widely believed that the Geloans had spread their power westward along the coast to such an extent that the site of Acragas was essentially under their control well before that date.[6] However, actual evidence for Geloan control of the area before 580 is not available, and the belief arises especially from the assumption that the colonists of Selinus, which was founded in 628, would not have 'passed by' such a position as Acragas if it had been 'free'. There are many unknowns here, but the Selinuntians went so far to the west that they 'passed by' many apparently suitable sites, and their behaviour tells us nothing about the site of Acragas at that time.

Acragas offered its colonists a splendid hill site some three kilometres

[4] C 125, 405–7; H 25, 326.   [5] C 175, 90–6.
[6] C 117.

inland (fig. 27).[7] As planned and built it became one of the greatest and richest Greek cities, but the site could only be exploited by a large expedition confident enough in their strength to move away from the sea. We also know that there was a powerful native site at S. Angelo Muxaro about twenty-five kilometres to the north (see below), so the land may have been strongly held.

Thucydides (VI. 4.4) attributes the foundation to Gela alone (though he gives two *oikistai*), but other sources state that some colonists came directly from Rhodes, and Polybius even calls Acragas a Rhodian colony.[8] We may follow Dunbabin in seeing it as settled by both Gela and Rhodes, with one *oikistes* from each.[9] The foundation date, 580, is established by Thucydides (*ibid.*), Pindar (*Ol.* II. 166) and the Pindaric scholia (*ad loc.*).

Selinus had been founded considerably earlier, in 628, near the western end of the south coast of the island, by colonists from Megara Hyblaea under the leadership of Pamillus, who was summoned from the original mother city, Megara in Greece (Thuc. VI. 4.2).[10] The first settlement was made on a low hill by the sea enclosed by rivers on both sides, the later acropolis (fig. 28). Although a characteristic Greek colonial site it was not outstandingly defensible, and the harbours offered by the mouths of the rivers were also not exceptional.

The reasons why the colonists went so far west only to choose a mediocre site for their city have been long debated, and, given our evidence, are bound to remain a matter of conjecture. The city is surrounded by good corn-growing land, which has seemed a sufficient motive to some,[11] but good land existed further east. Trade with the Phoenicians, who were present in the west of the island and would appear to offer a good market, has been canvassed, but is not supported by the evidence we possess.[12] This rather shows that Selinus' early commercial relations seem to have been with the Elymians at Segesta to the north, who were importing fine pottery from Selinus virtually as soon as the colony was founded.[13] We also have striking evidence of Selinuntian penetration inland to the north up the valley of the river Belice in a very early inscription found near Poggioreale, where Early Corinthian pottery as early as any at Selinus has been discovered.[14] This inscription attests the presence of Greeks from Selinus, who had established a cult place of Heracles not later than the first half of the sixth century.[15]

[7] C 65, 312–13.
[8] Schol. Pind. *Ol.* II. 15–16 = Timaeus, *FGrH* 566 F 92; Polyb. IX. 27.7–8.
[9] C 65, 310.   [10] On the date see above, p. 104.
[11] C 65, 301.   [12] de la Genière, *CRAI* 1977, 255–6.
[13] C 78, 38–40.   [14] C 160, 406.
[15] C 141; C 81C, 272–5.

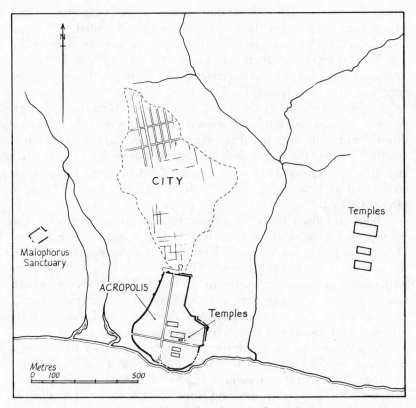

28. Plan of Selinus. (After c 65, 302; cf. c 152.)

Recent excavations on the plateau of Manuzza (which became part
of the city to the north-west of the acropolis) have discovered a native
site, which preceded the Greek colonization and seems to have
continued in existence, taking in Greek goods, in the first generation
of the life of the colony.[16] If that is so, the first colonists who established
themselves on the virgin site of the acropolis were living next to a native
settlement, and the good relations already suggested by the evidence
from Segesta and Poggioreale are even more strikingly illustrated.
These good relations seem likely to have drawn the founders so far west,
where they could seek prosperity by agriculture and commerce,
occupying a site which, like their mother city's, was not strong but could
be left undefended.[17]

Himera was only the second Greek colony of Archaic times on the
north coast of Sicily (Mylae being the first), and its isolated postion

[16] c 113, 53.
[17] On the date of the walls of the acropolis see c 78, 35–6.

far to the west has aroused questions similar to those about Selinus. Thucydides tells us that it was settled by a mixture of Chalcidians from Zancle and an exiled Syracusan clan, the Myletidae. The dialect was a mixture of Dorian and Chalcidian, but laws and customs were Chalcidian (Thuc. VI. 5.1). Strabo's different statement, that it was founded by Zanclaeans from Mylae, has been reconciled with Thucydides by the assumption that the Myletidae took their name from Mylae because they settled for some time there before taking part in the colonization of Himera (Strabo VI. 272),[18] which seems a possible explanation. The literary evidence for the foundation date, 648, is solely from Diodorus, who says that the city had existed for 240 years when it was destroyed by the Carthaginians in 409/8 (Diod. XIII. 62.5, cf. 54.1). So far the earliest pottery found in the excavations dates from the end of the third quarter of the seventh century.

The site is much more fully understood after the extensive excavations of recent times.[19] On the west side of the river Himeras, near its mouth, there was a high city on the edge of the hills overlooking the river and the sea, which was then about a kilometre distant. A lower city lay beneath by the mouth of the river, and, no doubt, the ancient harbour. The high city could be made a strong site by the use of defensive walls in the necessary places.[20]

The surrounding land, both coastal plain and above, on the plateau, offers plenty of scope for agriculture, while the river valley makes for good communications with the interior, but much further-flung connexions have been advanced for the choice of site. Himera has been seen as well placed for trade with Spain, or as a port of call on the trade route between Etruria and Carthage. Dunbabin suggested that it was placed as near as possible to the Phoenician settlements in Sicily in order to claim the whole island to the east for the Greeks.[21] But there is no evidence to support any of these conjectures, and the last seems to be in danger of using the exciting events of the fifth century in order to explain the different world of the seventh. It is safer to admit our ignorance; the colonists may have been influenced by so many factors of which we know nothing.

In southern Italy there are three major post-700 foundations to be discussed, Locri Epizephyrii, Siris and Metapontum (Posidonia belongs with the expansion of Sybaris, and Elea has been considered above). Locri lay on the east coast of modern Calabria (Italy's 'toe'), where the hills of the interior leave a narrow coastal plain. The ancient city of Classical and Hellenistic times covered a vast area of about 230 hectares

---

[18] C 34, 240–3.   [19] C 20; C 26.
[20] C 20, 7–9 and Planimetria e Sezioni Tav. 1–3.
[21] C 65, 300.

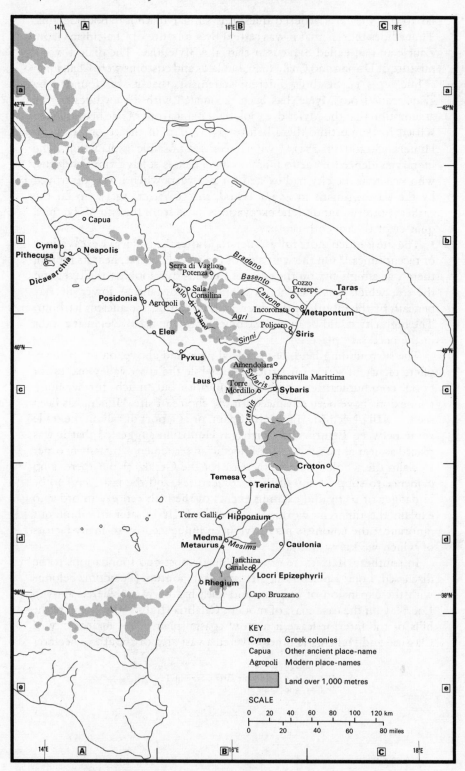

Map 11. South Italy.

and was defended by walls about seven and a half kilometres long, stretching from the three-peaked acropolis area in the foothills all the way across the coastal plain to the sea. The earliest city has not been discovered and the absence of dominating natural features makes it hard to place, but the theory that it was originally in the hills which later became the acropolis seems most probable. In that case we may assume that a harbour town quickly grew up on the coast, where sporadic seventh-century pottery is found.[22]

Although our literary sources present a conflicting story,[23] they are agreed that Epizephyrian Locri was founded by the Locrians from central Greece, and the name of the *oikistes*, Euanthes, is recorded (Strabo VI. 259). The foundation date in Eusebius varies slightly according to version, 679 or 673, but is broadly confirmed by the earliest pottery found in Greek graves, which is Middle Protocorinthian (*c.* 690–*c.* 650).[24] We need not pursue the main dispute in our sources, as to which branch of the Locrians was responsible for the foundation. We cannot settle it now, though the claim of the Eastern Locrians seems the stronger.[25] There was also contention about the social status of the colonists, whom some authorities described as the dregs of society (Arist. *ap.* Polyb. XII. 5.4ff), but since some members of the Locrian aristocracy, the so-called Hundred Houses, took part (Polyb. XII. 5.6–8),[26] we may assume that the colony was a normal settlement.

Strabo's statement (VI. 259) that the colonists' first place of abode was at the Zephyrian promontory, modern Capo Bruzzano, some twenty kilometres to the south-west, is commonly accepted, though the view that the story arose from a simple misunderstanding of the name 'Epizephyrian' (which means western) could be right.[27] In any event the site of Locri was inhabited before the colonists' arrival, and they may even have chosen to settle there because it was inhabited. Our sources call the pre-colonial population Sicels,[28] and their cemeteries (at Canale and Janchina) show by their burial practices that the inhabitants were indeed a people similar to those in eastern Sicily, who were open to overseas commerce and used and copied Greek pottery.[29]

Polybius and Polyaenus tell the story that the Locrian colonists swore on oath that they would keep peace with the native inhabitants and possess the land in common 'as long as they trod on this earth and bore their heads on their shoulders'. Before taking the oath they put earth in their shoes and concealed heads of garlic inside their clothing on their

[22] C 64, 59–61.
[23] C 34, 199–209.
[24] C 76, 245.
[25] C 34, 199–209.
[26] C 34, 202ff.
[27] C 64, 59.
[28] Polyb. XII. 6.2–5; Polyaenus, *Strat.* VI. 22; cf. Thuc. VI. 2.4.
[29] C 34, 208; C 74; H 25, 372.

shoulders. After they had sworn they emptied their shoes and threw away the heads of garlic, and then expelled the indigenous people.[30] The story sounds apocryphal, but it is certainly interesting that the native cemeteries die out at about the time the colony was founded. It is possible that the natives withdrew some twenty kilometres to the north, for graves at S. Stefano di Grotteria have yielded pottery and metal objects of the same style as those at Canale, but of a more advanced stage.[31]

Between Sybaris and Taras, on the coast of the 'instep' of Italy, two Greek colonies were founded, Siris and Metapontum. The region that they exploited is a rich coastal plain ideal for cereal cultivation, watered by the many rivers which flow down from the fine hill country of eastern Lucania.

According to Strabo, Siris was originally a Trojan foundation, which was occupied by people called Chones when it was taken and settled by Ionians in flight from Lydia (Strabo VI. 264). Athenaeus, citing Timaeus and Aristotle, amplifies this with the information that the Ionians were from Colophon.[32] Archilochus, we recall, compared Thasos unfavourably with Siris.[33] On the basis of these passages the foundation has generally been placed in the reign of Gyges (c. 680–652), who attacked the Greek cities of Asia Minor, including Colophon (Hdt. I. 14.4).

Antiochus of Syracuse (FGrH 555 F 12) is, however, apparently out of harmony with our other sources, when he says that the Achaeans of Sybaris advised the colonization of Metapontum rather than Siris, since that would give the whole region, including Siris, to the Achaeans, and deny it to neighbouring Taras. Impressed by the authority and antiquity of Antiochus some modern scholars have taken Siris for an Achaean foundation, but this line has been conclusively refuted by the archaeological evidence for the presence of Ionians in the area, and in particular by the Archaic loom-weight of Isodice, inscribed in the Ionic dialect and letters.[34] Possibly Antiochus was misled by the situation of Siris after it was overcome by its Achaean neighbours in the sixth century (Justin XX. 2.3–4).

The archaeological evidence, which has helped to clarify the literary tradition in one respect, has in other ways created problems rather than solutions. Firstly there is the question of geographical position. In our most detailed literary statement Strabo (VI. 264) says that Siris was on

---

[30] Polyb. XII. 6.2–5; Polyaenus, Strat. VI. 22.
[31] C 34, 208; C 74.
[32] XII. 523C FGrH 566 F 51; Aristotle fr. 584 [Teubner].
[33] Archilochus fr. 22 West; above, p. 116.
[34] A 36, 286, 288 no. 1, pl. 54; cf. C 34, 196.

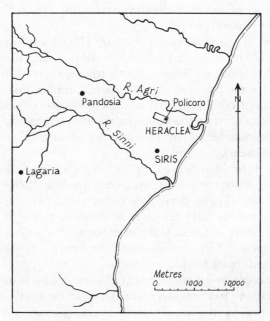

29. Plan of the Siris area, showing the relationship between
Siris and Heraclea according to Strabo. (After C 143, 225,
figs. 405–6.)

the river of the same name (modern Sinni) and twenty-four stades
distant from Heraclea, which was on the river Aciris (modern Agri) (fig.
29). Heraclea was jointly founded by Thurii and Taras as a successor
to Siris in 433 B.C., and Strabo says that Siris was its harbour town.[35]
Archaeological investigations have conclusively proved that Heraclea
was situated at the modern Policoro, where a steep-sided, flat-topped
hill, now crowned at its eastern end by the splendid Castello del Barone,
lies parallel with the river.[36] This hill, which was in antiquity on the
coast,[37] is far the strongest position in the whole region, and we now
know that it was inhabited by Greeks long before the time of Heraclea.
Pottery from the settlement and graves goes back to the late eighth
century, and the place was defended by a massive wall of mud-brick,
dated to shortly after 700, which was at least 2·60 metres thick and
enclosed an area c. 400 by c. 150 metres. Since this wall has a close
parallel at seventh-century Smyrna, and since there is much East Greek
pottery, it is not surprising that some have decided that this very
considerable settlement was Siris.[38] They have the negative support

[35] *Ibid.* (= Antiochus *FGrH* 555 F 12); Diod. XII. 36.4.
[36] C 122; C 85; C 17, 93ff.   [37] C 143.   [38] C 85, 429–43, 491–2.

that no evidence of ancient settlement has been found on the river Siris, where Strabo placed the city.

If Siris was at the same site as the later Heraclea, Pliny, who states this briefly (*HN* III. 97), is, paradoxically, more correct than the precise and detailed account of Strabo. Furthermore, there seems to be no explanation for the name Siris, which surely implies that the city was situated on that river. But if Siris was not at Policoro, the colonists did not choose for their city the strongest position in the area, which was a mere four kilometres distant (though they did use it for a substantial separate settlement).

The second problem raised by the archaeological discoveries is chronological, since the Ionian settlement found at Policoro seems to be too early for Gyges. Strabo says that the Ionians took over an existing city, and an early cemetery at Policoro seems to show quite definitely a mixture of Greek and native burials,[39] so material for many hypotheses exists. For the moment, however, we should admit uncertainty and await further evidence.

Along the coast to the north-east lay Metapontum, situated between the rivers Bradano to the north and Basento to the south, on a flat site which was then by the sea. In their ancient courses the two rivers approached to within 600 metres of each other, and thus offered a suitable and defensible site for a big city, similar in its general character to that of Sybaris.

The Achaean origin of Metapontum is clearly attested in our sources, and has been confirmed by Archaic inscriptions,[40] but the detailed story from Antiochus (reported by Strabo), that the site was settled on the advice of Sybaris in order to deny it to Taras, has already been seen to be suspect in what it implies about Siris and cannot be trusted. Antiochus clearly thought that the Greek settlement of Metapontum preceded that of Siris, and modern scholars have used Siris' presumed foundation date as a *terminus ante quem* for that of Metapontum,[41] but recent archaeological discoveries seem to show that the priority belongs with Siris.

We have a Eusebian date for Metapontum, 773, which is so improbably high that it has generally been rejected. If we abandon that literary indication we have to rely entirely on the material evidence. Archaeological work at Metapontum has yielded very important results about the extent and plan of the town, and about the central sacred area,[42] but neither the first settlement nor the first graves have been

---

[39] C 17, 111–13.
[40] Strabo VI. 264–5 (Antiochus, *FGrH* 555 F 12); Ps.-Scymnus 326–9; Bacchylides X(XI). 114, 126. A 36, 254f; C 17, 26–32.   [41] C 34, 177.
[42] C 107; C 17, 16–65.

discovered. The earliest pottery found in excavations within the city site belongs to the second half of the seventh century, and for the time being that is our best indication of the date of Greek colonization.

Although the site of the city itself was apparently not previously occupied,[43] the hills which overlook the Metapontine plain, higher up the river valleys, were densely inhabited well before the Achaean colonists arrived by people who enjoyed a homogeneous Early Iron Age culture.[44] They were not unfamiliar with Greeks, and at one site, Incoronata, Greek pottery is so abundant that a Greek settlement has been postulated.[45] This is a strong hill site on the right bank of the river Basento some seven kilometres distant from Metapontum. The Greek pottery is similar to that found at Policoro, and so it has been suggested that Incoronata was a forward post of the Ionian colonists at Siris, established for purposes of trade with the natives. The presumed Greek settlement began in the last quarter of the eighth century and died out in the third quarter of the seventh, at the very time when the Achaeans are thought to have founded Metapontum. So it is suggested that they brought about its end.[46] This picture of Ionian domination challenged by the Achaean colonization of Metapontum is clearly a possible interpretation, especially in view of the later Achaean attack on Siris, but since it is entirely based on limited archaeological evidence it must be adjudged hypothetical.

II. THE EXPANSION OF THE GREEK COLONIES

In Sicily, we may begin with the expansion of Syracuse, since the combination of literary and archaeological evidence makes it the best known. As we saw above, the great inland Sicel sites up the river valleys to the west, Pantalica and Finocchito, come to an end at approximately the time of Syracuse's foundation, and the colonists had won control of the adjacent coastal plain to the west, and to the south as far as Helorus, before the end of the eighth century. There are no settlements of the Archaic period on the plain, as far as our knowledge goes, though several villages and farms are known in the poorer hill country, even quite near the city. This pattern has been attractively interpreted as showing that the rich plain land became the property of the first settlers and their descendants, who lived in the city, including no doubt the ruling aristocracy, significantly called *Gamoroi*, landowners (cf. Hdt. VII. 155.2), while later settlers and other less privileged people found their homes and living in the peripheral hill country.[47]

---

[43] Though a little pre-colonial pottery is known; C 107, 149.
[44] C 18; C 17, 66ff; C 110.   [45] C 18, 36ff; C 17, 67ff.
[46] C 17, 76.   [47] C 164, 100–1.

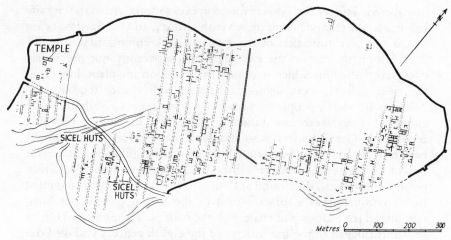

30. Plan of Casmenae. (After c 133, pl. 69.)

Thucydides (VI. 5.2) tells us that Syracuse founded colonies at Acrae
and Casmenae in 663 and 643. The site of Acrae is well known, close
to the modern town of Palazzolo Acreide. Nothing earlier than
Transitional Corinthian (*c.* 640–625) has been found there, but the
excavations have not been so comprehensive that we need depart from
the literary date.[48] It is now very generally agreed that Casmenae was
at Monte Casale some twelve kilometres further west. These sites are
both in the mountainous country high up the valley of the Anapo, to
the west of Syracuse. Acrae has a very strong position on a flat-topped,
steep-sided hill with commanding views, and Casmenae is even higher.
Both are in areas where there was plentiful Sicel habitation, and both
were chosen for their strength. Casmenae in particular seems to have true
military character, with its unattractive situation, extreme climate and
early orthogonal layout (fig. 30), and it is symbolic, if not significant,
that a great deposit of weapons was found there in the precinct of the
temple.[49]

Thucydides names no *oikistai* for these colonies, which are to be seen
as subordinate foundations completely dependent on Syracuse.[50] Their
function was, no doubt, partly to defend Syracusan territory, which
now extends over the whole Anapo valley to a distance of about fifty
kilometres from the city as the crow flies. But we must remember that
the Syracusans turned some of the Sicels into serfs, and, in the fifth
century at least, others were tribute-paying dependants.[51] These sub-

[48] c 36, 17–18; c 137, 127–8.
[49] c 172, 186–96; c 164, 111–12; c 137, 129ff.
[50] c 5, 92–4.   [51] Thuc. III. 103.1; VI. 20.4; 88.5; Diod. XII. 30.1.

ordinate colonies were well suited to keep watch over a subject population.

The third of Syracuse's colonies, Camarina, was established on the south coast of the island, about 112 kilometres south-west of Syracuse as the crow flies, on low hills between the rivers Hipparis and Oanis, an attractive site not apparently previously inhabited,[52] which lies amid rich surrounding countryside. Thucydides' foundation date, 598, is confirmed by other literary sources,[53] and the earliest graves in the Archaic cemetery of Rifriscolaro north-east of the city are dated by pottery of the end of the seventh century and first quarter of the sixth.[54]

There were two *oikistai* and Camarina is normally regarded, in contrast to Acrae and Casmenae, as a separate *polis*. Even so, we know that it was politically dependent on Syracuse, because it fought a war of revolt about fifty years after its foundation.[55] It might seem natural to assume from Camarina's geographical position and dependent status that Syracuse intended to control the whole south-east corner of Sicily. If so, the intention was apparently frustrated for a time not only by Camarina's independent spirit, but also by her friendly relations with the Sicels, who lived in large numbers in the intervening hill country. At their largest settlement, the modern Ragusa, which is plausibly identified with Hybla Heraea, the evidence of graves and grave goods suggests that there were Greek inhabitants living side by side with the Sicels from *c.* 570.[56] The Camarinaeans had Sicel allies in their war of independence (if it is right to attribute a fragment of Philistus to that war),[57] so it looks as if Syracusan pressure led her own colonists to make common cause with the natives against her. The Syracusans defeated their colony and expelled the inhabitants, but they must soon have resettled it, for archaeological evidence shows that it was inhabited after *c.* 550, and it was a Syracusan possession at the beginning of the fifth century, when it was ceded to Hippocrates of Gela.[58]

Thus Syracuse acquired a large territory, calculated by Dunbabin at about 4,000 square kilometres,[59] by colonization and by imposing subjection on at least some of the native population. The Chalcidian colonies of eastern Sicily seem to have maintained very different relations with the Sicels.

We have almost no literary evidence for the expansion of these Chalcidian colonies. We know the names, but no more, of two subsidiary foundations, Euboea and Callipolis, established respectively

[52] C 133, 355.   [53] C 34, 133–5.   [54] C 138, 30.
[55] Thuc. VI. 5.2. For the date Schol. Pind. *Ol.* v. 16.
[56] C 173, 354–5; C 164, 113–15.
[57] *FGrH* 556 F 5; cf. C 65, 105–6; C 34, 135.
[58] Hdt. VII. 154.3; C 65, 106–7.
[59] C 65, 107.

by Leontini and Naxus.[60] On the other hand, there is abundant archaeological evidence for the areas accessible from Leontini and Catane, namely the Heraean hills west of Leontini, east central Sicily and the country west of Mt Etna.[61] The interpretation of this purely archaeological evidence is somewhat hazardous, as always in such cases. The main difficulties arise in the recognition and historical reconstruction of mixed settlements. The presence of Greeks in a site known only archaeologically can only be firmly established by a combination of indications: Greek religion, Greek writing, Greek architecture, as well as Greek graves. This ideal combination is rarely present; often the argument rests entirely on grave evidence, which may be ambiguous. Apart from burials of Greek or native type with appropriate grave goods, we often find burials of native type with a mixture of Greek and native goods, or even a preponderance of Greek material, burials of Greek type which contain some native pottery, and even some where the rite is apparently mixed. Archaeologists have come to different conclusions about the race of the dead in such instances, and we should be chary of postulating mixed settlements on such evidence alone. Even when we certainly have a mixed settlement, it is often impossible to reconstruct the political and social relations of the two races.

With these provisos we can nevertheless accept the widely held view that the relations of Greeks and Sicels in the Chalcidian region were friendly, and Greek penetration, where it occurred, was peaceable.[62] In the first place we see that Sicel sites, occupied from times before Greek colonization, remain undisturbed, continuing their independent way of life. In the Heraean hills Licodia is one such, a very big Sicel settlement on important land routes between the east and south coasts, which imports Greek goods from the seventh century and in great quantities from the second half of the sixth.[63] There is no sure evidence for Greek settlers, but the abundance of Greek goods and the progressive Hellenization show very close relations. In the same area of the headwaters of the Dirillo, a short distance to the south, Monte Casasia is a more recently explored native site, which kept its independent existence in the seventh and sixth centuries. This is a very high and strong position, which was presumably just beyond Syracusan control – for Casmenae (Monte Casale) is some twenty kilometres to the east. Here too Greek imports appear in the seventh century and became abundant in the sixth. The inhabitants were writing their language in the Greek alphabet by the middle of the sixth century.[64]

[60] Strabo VI. 272; cf. Hdt. VII. 154.2.
[61] C 162; C 164, 131–4.
[62] C 65, 121ff; C 162; C 164, 131–4.
[63] C 162, 34–5.   [64] C 138, 35–6.

In the Heraean hills we also know sites where Greeks and Sicels lived side by side. At Grammichele there was a native settlement before the Greek colonies were founded, which continued in existence in the seventh and sixth centuries. Greek inhabitants are clearly attested from the middle of the sixth century or earlier by Greek sanctuaries and graves with a purely Greek rite. These graves contain some native pots and are in the same cemetery with contemporary Sicel burials. Apart from fine imported Greek products, the site has yielded terracottas and sculpture of Greek style which were produced locally, some of them by natives.[65] This is an unmistakable instance of peaceful coexistence.

At Morgantina there was a native settlement with a long history. Down to the middle of the sixth century the natives lived in a hut-village and imported very little Greek material. At that date the place was transformed into an urban settlement of Archaic Greek type, with temples and Greek terracottas. However, the Sicel occupation continued, and their huts stood beside the Greek buildings. The mixture of burial rites in one tomb was interpreted as showing real cultural intermingling, perhaps as a result of intermarriage.[66]

With Greeks to the east, south and west, it is not surprising that the Sicels of the Heraean hills were open to such powerful Greek influences and penetration. Further north there were strong Sicel centres that maintained their independence down into the fifth century, such as Centuripe and Mendolito, to the west of Catane. At these sites too, however, Greek imports begin in the seventh century, and thorough Hellenization is observable by the end of the sixth. From both places we have Sicel inscriptions, written in Greek letters and dated to the sixth century.[67]

The contrasting ways in which the Syracusans and the Chalcidian colonies dealt with the Sicels suit the picture we have of later times. Naxus had Sicel allies in the fifth century (Thuc. IV. 25.6–7), and Thucydides' narrative of events in Sicily in the Peloponnesian War shows the Syracusans with Sicel subjects, whose loyalty is doubtful, while the Athenians, who were allied to Catane, expect, and generally gain, the help of the independent Sicels (cf. VI. 88.5–6; VII. 57.10).

The expansion of Gela has been traced on the basis of some slight literary evidence of poor quality and much archaeological exploration.[68] A completely clear historical picture is not attainable, but the indications we have, when combined with the lack of signs of peaceful coexistence, suggest that by the sixth century the Geloans controlled and occupied an area that spread far beyond their plain into the hill country to the

[65] C 162, 35–9.   [66] C 153, 28–35.
[67] C 162, 40–3; C 132, 245–52.
[68] C 15, 158–70; C 164, 119–21; C 153, 39–43.

north. They were also establishing settlements along the coast to the west by the end of the seventh century.[69]

At Acragas too we have some poor literary evidence, which attests violent relations with the native people early in the colony's history.[70] But there is very little solid or clear evidence for Acragantine expansion within our period, and such reconstructions as have been attempted are inevitably fragile.[71] It seems clear that the colonists cannot have established early control along the coast to the west for any distance, because Selinus was able to found the colony of Minoa at the mouth of the river Platani in about the middle of the sixth century (Hdt. v. 46.1).[72]

At Selinus itself, as we have seen, there is evidence of peaceful, commercial relations with native neighbours, especially the Elymians at Segesta, and of the penetration of Selinuntine settlers inland to the north. On the other hand, the probable involvement of Selinus in Pentathlus' attempt to found a Greek colony at Lilybaeum in c. 580 (see below) seems to imply a more aggressive, expansionist policy at the expense of the Elymians and Phoenicians, and the foundation of Minoa, about which, unfortunately, we know virtually nothing, could also be interpreted as a sign of ambitious expansion. Perhaps we should separate foreign policy from trading and individual relationships. As their place in Greek legend shows, the Elymians were particularly well suited for close relationships with Greeks.[73] The Hellenization of Segesta seems to have been more complete than that of any other non-Greek community in this early period.[74] So it is not surprising that in the fifth century Selinus had an arrangement for intermarriage with Segesta (Thuc. VI. 6.2). On the other hand, interests of close neighbours can clash, as they did apparently at the time of Pentathlus' expedition, and no doubt on other occasions.

Just as in Sicily, where we know nothing about Himera, for example, and Naxus and Zancle effectively do not expand, so also in southern Italy the Greek colonies vary greatly in the extent of their expansion and in our knowledge of it. Rhegium, Taras and Elea did not expand in the Archaic period beyond their immediately surrounding territory.[75] Of Cyme's expansion in the same period we know virtually nothing certain, but the settlement that preceded Neapolis (Naples), whatever it was called, was established by the middle of the seventh century.[76] Dicaearchia, the Roman Puteoli, is said by some authors to have been

[69] C 117, 128–35.
[70] Polyaenus, *Strat.* V. 1.3–4; Frontinus, *Strat.* III. 4.6; *Lindian Chronicle* XXVII (D 16, 171); cf. C 65, 316f.
[71] C 117.
[72] C 117, 144–6.
[73] C 59.
[74] C 78.
[75] C 164, 132–6.
[76] C 82; C 64, 41; cf. C 164, 132.

founded by Samians in 531, but the place is also called a port of Cyme, so perhaps it was a Cymean possession at which refugees from the Samian tyranny were allowed to settle.[77]

A colony which probably did expand much more, but for which good evidence is lacking, is Croton. Northward expansion up the coast may be assumed, but evidence and chronology are both very dubious.[78] On the Tyrrhenian shore Terina and Temesa lay close together to the north of the Hipponiate Gulf. The former is attested as a colony of Croton and was issuing coins by early in the fifth century, while Temesa was apparently under Croton's influence by c. 500, to judge by its coins of that time.[79] On the Calabrian coast to the south-west the only solid fact is the colonization of Caulonia at the modern Punta di Stilo. Here a number of lowish hills between two rivers offered a possible place to settle. There is no real harbour (though there is a good flat beach), but the surrounding land is rolling plain country.[80] From Strabo (VI. 261) and Pausanias (VI. 3.12) we learn that the colony was founded by Achaeans under the leadership of Typhon of Aegium. Other sources attribute the colony to Croton,[81] but there is no real conflict, since Croton could have summoned the *oikistes* and invited settlers from the mother country (as at the foundation of Epidamnus by Corcyra). There is no literary foundation date, but excavations have shown that Caulonia was settled early in the second half of the seventh century.[82] If Caulonia was a dependent colony, as some have taken it, its proximity to Locri would suggest that Croton was ambitiously laying claim to a long stretch of the coast of Calabria. But the dependence is not certain, for Caulonia issued its own coins in the sixth century. So it would be rash, on our present evidence, to draw the south-western boundary of Crotoniate territory in the seventh century on the far side of Caulonia.

Whether or not Croton controlled that territory at an early date, Locri's expansion was all on the opposite (Tyrrhenian) coast of the Calabrian promontory.[83] Hipponium was founded as early as the middle of the seventh century on a dominating site north of the modern Vibo Valentia. Here long views command the land routes across the Calabrian mountains and a great expanse of sea.[84] This is rich agricultural territory, and the site chosen, which is five hundred metres above the level of the sea and some distance from it, shows clearly that the settlers looked primarily to the land. Medma was also well inland, occupying a hill site on the south bank of the river Mesma (modern Mesima), a big river which flows along the northern edge of a rich and extensive

[77] C 34, 54–5.
[79] Ps.-Scymnus 306f; H 48, 167f, 179.
[81] Ps.-Scymnus 318–19; Steph. Byz. *s.v.* Αὐλών.
[83] Thuc. V. 5.3; Ps.-Scymnus 307–8; Strabo VI. 256.

[78] C 65, 159–62.
[80] H 79, 95, fig. 71.
[82] C 155.
[84] C 64, 61; C 67, 348.

plain. The archaeological finds suggest that it was already settled in the
seventh century.[85] The material remains from both these sites are
virtually indistinguishable from those of Locri itself, and we also know
that they were allied with Locri in a war against Croton in Late Archaic
times.[86] They seem to have been separate *poleis* but very closely linked
with their near-by mother city.[87] In the fifth century Thucydides
describes them as colonies and neighbours of Locri, which has been
taken to show that Locri's territory marched with theirs.[88] If that is
right, as it may be, the solid block of Locrian territory stretching across
the Calabrian promontory was presumably established in Archaic times.

A smaller Greek settlement has been recognized at Torre Galli, a high
site on the promontory formed by the coast between Hipponium and
Medma. The finds date from *c.* 600 to *c.* 550.[89] A short distance to the
south of Medma, at the southern edge of the same plain, Metaurus stood
on the right bank of the river of the same name. Although the literary
evidence is very poor,[90] it seems probable that this was originally a
Chalcidian settlement from Zancle, as stated by a late Latin author
(Solinus II. 11), since the earliest burials, dating from the mid seventh
to the mid sixth centuries, are like those of Zancle's colony at Mylae.
The tradition that Stesichorus, the lyric poet of Himera, was born at
Metaurus, also points to Zancle. However, other sources call Metaurus
a colony of Locri, and it has been suggested that burials of a different
type, dating from the mid sixth to the early fifth centuries, attest Locrian
occupation.[91]

The combination of literary and archaeological evidence allows us
to reconstruct the history of Locrian expansion with some confidence.
Sybarite expansion, even though it was presumably much greater, is
much more difficult to grasp. We have the fundamental statement of
Strabo (VI. 263) that Sybaris controlled four tribes (ἔθνη) and twenty-five
cities (πόλεις). On the basis of this, with the help of the names of inland
cities known from Hecataeus and of coins which were clearly struck
on the model of those of Sybaris, attempts have been made to trace the
limits of the Sybarite 'empire',[92] but they are all largely hypothetical,
since we lack solid and clear evidence for the necessary topographical
identifications.

Archaeological investigations have shown, as we have seen, that the
Achaean colonists controlled, from the moment of foundation, both the
plain of Sybaris and the surrounding hills. Their temple at the important
earlier native site of Francavilla Marittima, in the hills to the north-west,

[85] C 29.
[87] C 5, 94.
[89] C 74.
[91] C 69.

[86] E 235, 77–9 and plates 24–5.
[88] C 112.
[90] C 34, 211–12; C 65, 165–6.
[92] C 65, 153–9; C 34, 145–6.

was established before 700. In the sixth century this site was occupied by a big Greek settlement, with possibly also some native inhabitants. It was so closely linked to Sybaris that we can regard it as part of the same political entity, and it shared Sybaris' fall at the end of the sixth century.[93] Further north, Amendolara's history and character in the sixth century seems to have been identical.[94] These may have been two of Strabo's 'cities'.

Sybaris established colonies at Laus and Scidrus, the first certainly, the second probably, on the Tyrrhenian coast, but we know virtually nothing of them except that they received refugees from Sybaris on its fall (Hdt. VI. 21.1; Strabo VI. 253). Laus is at the opposite end of the 'isthmus' from Sybaris to the Tyrrhenian sea. Further north, Pyxus is generally assumed on the evidence of its coinage to have been subordinate to Sybaris.[95]

The greatest colony of Sybaris, Posidonia (Latin Paestum), was situated further up the west coast of Italy in the modern Bay of Salerno. The standing remains show us a big city in the plain, separated from the sea by a distance of about 750 metres. The presence of ancient material between the present coastline and the city disproves the theory that in ancient times the city was on the sea.[96] Strabo's statement (v. 252) that the Sybarites first established a fort by the sea, but the colonists moved further inland, has led to much rather fruitless debate. We cannot be sure where the fort was, though the very Greek-looking and strong site of Agropoli, with its significant name, is an attractive speculation. It is no more than six kilometres to the south of Paestum.[97]

Our sources unanimously state that Posidonia was a colony of Sybaris, but they give us no foundation date. Later constructions cover the ground and we have no traces of the first settlement or graves, but the earliest pottery from the site is Early Corinthian, c. 625–c. 600, and this seems likely to be the approximate date of foundation.[98]

The choice of a site without natural defences, after the presumably brief stay at the coastal fort, shows that the colonists had no fears of the neighbouring natives. Was this confidence due to Sybaris' good relations with these people, or control over them? It is unfortunate that we cannot answer such questions. The old idea that Sybaris' prosperity partly arose from the exploitation of the so-called 'isthmus route' from the Tyrrhenian to the Ionian sea has fallen into disfavour recently, because it does not seem well supported by detailed archaeological investigations, but it is still a possible hypothesis that Sybaris was friendly with, or dominated, the tribes of the interior from sea to sea.

[93] C 183, 170–8; C 184, 219–26.
[94] C 79; C 77.
[95] H 48, 166.
[96] C 174.
[97] C 81.
[98] C 121.

It has been interestingly observed that the large native settlement at Sala Consilina, in the upland Vallo di Diano, seems to have much closer relations with the Greeks at the very time that Sybarite refugees are assumed to have arrived in Posidonia.[99]

If we may judge by its earliest coins, Posidonia itself was not closely dependent on Sybaris. However, even though we have no literary evidence, there are good reasons for thinking that, when Sybaris fell, a large number of refugees were received into Posidonia. The coin evidence even suggests that they were numerous enough to create a kind of synoecism, or joint state of Sybaris/Posidonia, as seems also to have happened at Laus.[100] During one of the shortlived attempts to refound Sybaris in the fifth century Posidonia acts as a guarantor of an alliance made by the new Sybaris.[101] Thus Sybaris and Posidonia maintained close and good relations, whatever the exact political status of Posidonia.

It is clear that historical reconstruction of Sybaris' expansion must depend greatly on hypothesis. No boundary of Sybarite territory is certainly known, though Amendolara gives us a minimum distance to the north. The size and wealth of the city and Strabo's statement about its empire have encouraged historians to think in large terms, probably correctly, and many have said that Sybaris must have turned the natives into serfs, in order to acquire the necessary manpower, but here, as elsewhere, certainty is denied us by lack of evidence.

Our knowledge of the expansion of Siris and Metapontum is entirely derived from rich archaeological evidence, most of which has accrued in recent years. The colonists at Siris are shown to have been friendly with the natives by the mixed cemetery of the early seventh century at Policoro and by their presumed settlement at Incoronata, a site which also seems to prove early expansion northwards. Inland, up the Agri valley, Greek goods are found at many sites from the seventh century, so we may at least assume that there was vigorous commerce from Siris.[102]

The territory of Metapontum and its organization have been brilliantly explored by means of air photography and other archaeological investigation.[103] To the west of the city, between the rivers Bradano and Basento, and again to the south, between the Basento and the Cavone – a total area of about 14 × 8 kilometres – the ground was seen to be covered with long, straight, parallel lines, c. 220 metres apart. These lines have been shown to have been ditches or canals in antiquity, and, as they are roughly perpendicular to the line of the coast, some

[99] C 73; C 164, 127.

[101] M–L no. 10; see C 114.

[103] C 16; C 17, 78–88.

[100] H 48, 169f, 173; C 5, 91f, 114; C 73.

[102] C 110, 234–40; C 18, 42–3; C 17, 125.

experts have considered that their primary purpose was drainage.[104] However, since large numbers of farms have also been discovered, the siting of which is clearly related to the parallel ditches, it seems likely that these were also intended as land divisions. The earliest farms date from about the middle of the sixth century, so this great work of land organization and division has been placed at that time. It is not, therefore, the original division of the land, since Metapontum is thought to have been founded a hundred years earlier. Since the land divided seems to include territory of Siris, it may be that a new division was carried out after the defeat of Siris some time in the sixth century, but this is mere speculation.

There is no trace of transverse divisions, though they must surely have existed. Without them we cannot estimate the size of allotments, but some clear facts about the land settlement are provided by the very numerous individual farms. These begin at a distance of about three kilometres from the city, so we may presume that those who had land close to the city lived within it. The most distant farm found is some ten kilometres away. In the Archaic period the occupants buried their dead around their farms. They also had extramural sanctuaries. That of Zeus Aglaios at S. Biagio is six and a half kilometres from the city.[105]

This is the best-known example of the organization of its territory by an Archaic Greek colony, a colony famous for its agricultural wealth, which dedicated a golden harvest at Delphi (Strabo vi. 264) and chose an ear of barley as the city's symbol on its coinage.

Beyond the immediate territory of Metapontum Greek influences penetrated freely inland along the easy communications provided by the river valleys. Numerous native sites have been shown to be imitating Greek pottery from the seventh century.[106] Evidence of actual Greek expansion is more sparse, but Cozzo Presepe, which is a strong position dominating the plain of Metapontum at a distance of about fifteen kilometres from the city, seems from the finds to be a Greek fort from the sixth century,[107] and, much further away, at Serra di Vaglio near Potenza, which is about one hundred kilometres from Metapontum, a big native site of the seventh century received Greek settlers early in the sixth. Their architectural terracottas attest Greek architecture and a regular Greek street plan has been recognized. Close analogies for the works of art exist at Metapontum.[108]

In both Sicily and southern Italy the general picture is that the Greek colonies established close control of an immediate territory that they

[104] C 144, 210.
[105] C 17, 55–65.
[106] C 110; C 18.
[107] C 17, 77ff.
[108] C 19; C 17, 144–58.

farmed, beyond which, usually in higher country, lived native populations under growing Greek influence and subject to Greek penetration.
It is widely accepted that the Dorian colonies tended to subjugate the
natives by force, while the Ionians maintained pacific, commercial
relations.[109] The formula fits some of our evidence (especially if we
bring in the Phocaean colonization in the western Mediterranean), but
cannot be universally applied. The Dorians of Megara Hyblaea and
Selinus did not forcefully subjugate the native people, and some of the
Chalcidian colonies expelled native people at the beginning of their
history.[110]

III. GREEKS AND PHOENICIANS

From the sixth century to the third the relations between Greeks and
Phoenicians in Sicily present a sorry tale of repeated wars and
destruction, but at the beginning they may have been different. We have
seen that Thucydides' famous statement (VI. 2.6) about the first
Phoenician settlements in Sicily raises difficulties (above, p. 95). He
states further that, when the Greeks came in large numbers, the
Phoenicians withdrew to the western end of the island, where they
joined forces to make three settlements, at Motya, Soloeis and Panormus,
partly because they trusted in their alliance with the Elymians, but also
because from there the voyage from Sicily to Carthage was shortest.
It might be objected that this reflects more recent conditions than those
of the eighth century, but in some respects archaeological investigations
have borne Thucydides out.

Motya is a small, low-lying island, two and a half kilometres in
circumference, situated in a shallow lagoon just off the west coast of
Sicily, a little north of the site of the later Lilybaeum (modern Marsala).
To judge by the Greek pottery found, it was first settled late in the eighth
century.[111] It was a typical Phoenician trading colony, like the
contemporary Toscanos and others recently unearthed in southern
Spain, a small settlement without territorial ambitions, whose livelihood
depended on good relations with the neighbouring native people, the
Elymians. The settlers were not nervous about their security; the town
was unwalled in its early days.[112] Greek pottery is plentiful, as at other
contemporary Phoenician sites, and we should remember that at this
time there is abundant evidence for peaceful intercourse between Greeks
and Phoenicians, in the Levant, for example, on Rhodes and at
Pithecusa.[113] The curious and significant fact that the Phoenician

[109] C 65, 95–145; C 153; C 164, 107–42.
[110] Diod. XIV. 88.1; Dion. Hal. *Ant. Rom. Exc.* XIX. 2.1.
[111] C 91, 580–2; C 92, 83.   [112] C 180, 208; C 41, 79–81.
[113] D 34A; see above, p. 101.

settlement at Panormus (modern Palermo) had a Greek name, used officially on coins from the fifth century, suggests that relations were close in Sicily from an early date.

The foundations of Himera, traditionally in 648, and Selinus, in 628, were not necessarily overt challenges to the Phoenicians or the Elymians, but they brought permanent Greek populations much closer. If it is right that the story of Heracles' adventures in western Sicily was first worked out by Stesichorus, the great lyric poet of Himera, whose *floruit* falls at the turn of the seventh and sixth centuries, some Greeks were by that date seeking to establish a claim to the area. The adventures occur during the western journey in the tenth labour, the winning of the arms of Geryon (Diod. IV. 23–24.6), a subject treated by Stesichorus in his famous *Geryoneïs*.[114] Although no extant fragment of Stesichorus relates to Sicily, we know that the Sicilian episodes were current by the end of the sixth century, when Hecataeus was writing and Dorieus was trying to found a colony on the west coast of Sicily.[115] In the same poem Stesichorus showed an interest in Spanish silver,[116] and the hypothesis has been advanced that the Greeks of Sicily desired to control the west of the island for the sake of the trade with Spain, which we know was exploited from c. 640.[117] Too much is missing for this interpretation to be more than speculation, but it is a historical fact that by the late seventh century or early sixth the Greeks represented a threat to the Phoenicians of western Sicily.

The first defensive wall at Motya, which involved cutting through the original cemetery, was built at this time.[118] This reflects the changed situation, whether or not we should bring it into direct relation with Pentathlus' attempt in c. 580 to establish a colony of Cnidians and Rhodians at Lilybaeum on the immediately adjacent mainland. This colony plainly threatened Motya's existence as a port and the symbiotic relationship of Phoenicians and Elymians in western Sicily.

We have two main literary sources for this attempt, a fairly full account by Diodorus, which is almost certainly derived from Timaeus,[119] and a much briefer statement by Pausanias, who actually cites Antiochus of Syracuse.[120] According to Pausanias, Pentathlus founded a city at Lilybaeum, but was driven out by Phoenicians and Elymians. This could have been an isolated venture. Diodorus (Timaeus) reports that the colonists found the Selinuntines at war with Segesta and helped them, only to be defeated and lose their leader. The combination with Selinus

[114] C 128.
[115] Hecataeus, *FGrH* 1 frs. 76, 77; Hdt. v. 43.
[116] Fr. 7 Page.
[117] C 65, 329–30.
[118] C 180, 208; C 41, 79–81.
[119] v. 9 (Timaeus, *FGrH* 566 F 164; cf. Jacoby's commentary).
[120] x. 11.3 (Antiochus, *FGrH* 555 F 1).

seems to imply a general Hellenic enterprise. In this source too Pentathlus' descent from Heracles is emphasized. It is tempting to reject the details of Diodorus' account on the grounds that they look like embroidery based on knowledge of later history, but none of the actual facts is incredible *per se*, and the circumstantial naming of Pentathlus' kinsmen who accompanied him inspires confidence. Nor do we know how much of Antiochus Pausanias reproduced. So we cannot decide between the two sources on *a priori* arguments, and should be content with the basic fact that a Greek attempt at colonization within the Phoenician/Elymian area was forcibly defeated.

The defeated Cnidians and Rhodians sailed back along the north coast of Sicily and established themselves in the Aeolian (Lipari) Islands. For this colonization we are chiefly dependent on the same two sources, to which we can add a brief excursus by Thucydides, which is commonly regarded as derived, like the passage of Pausanias, from Antiochus, though that is not certain.[121] The most important difference between our sources concerns the inhabitants of the islands found by the Greek colonists. Pausanias (Antiochus) does not know if the islands were uninhabited or the people dispossessed. Diodorus (Timaeus) has a romantic story that a remnant of five hundred descendants of the colonists established by Aeolus were glad to welcome the newcomers. The desire to connect Greek colonization in the west with the heroic period, found so often in Timaeus, is patent, and one is tempted to follow Jacoby, who thought that Antiochus consciously rejected such ideas. Although traces have been found of many periods of prehistoric habitation of the islands, there is, as yet, no evidence of settlers who immediately precede the Greeks.[122]

Of the scattered group of volcanic islands Lipara is the largest, and the colonists settled there, at a strong hill site by the sea, with a harbour at each end, an ideal position for warlike seamen. They crossed over by boat to farm the other islands. Their original regime, whereby some devoted themselves to fighting and others to farming, while the land was owned in common, probably owed more to military necessities than ideals of communism. It was presumably when they became more secure that they divided the land, firstly of Lipara, and later on the other islands too (Diod. v. 9.4–5). The suggestion that this interesting social organization can be seen in the archaeological evidence from graves[123] is over-audacious. On the other hand, this evidence provides approximate confirmation of a foundation date in *c.* 580–576,[124] and Eusebius' alternative, 628, should be rejected.

---

[121] III. 88.1–3; cf. Jacoby's commentary to *FGrH* 555 F 1.
[122] C 37, 137–47.   [123] C 164, 101–2.
[124] C 40, 197–8; cf. C 65, 328.

The next clear and certain stage in the story of Graeco-Phoenician relations in Sicily was Dorieus' attempt to colonize Drepanon (modern Trapani) close to the Elymians' second city at Eryx (Hdt. v. 43–6). Having failed in Libya, Dorieus decided to recover some of the inheritance of Heracles in western Sicily, and sailed with four fellow-founders (συγκτίσται). On the way, according to the Sybarite tradition, Dorieus helped Croton against Sybaris. Although Herodotus could not determine the truth of this matter, it does apparently fix the date of Dorieus' expedition at *c.* 510. In Herodotus' account Dorieus was defeated and killed by Phoenicians and Segestans; according to Diodorus (IV. 23.3), he established the city of Heraclea, which was destroyed by the Carthaginians because they were envious and feared that 'it might deprive the Phoenicians of their hegemony'. Although some historians believe the implication of Diodorus that the city had some years of existence, we need not hesitate in preferring Herodotus, since Dorieus' threat to the Phoenicians and Elymians would call for an immediate response.

After the death of Dorieus, the sole surviving leader, Euryleon, with the remnants of the colonists, first seized Selinus' colony of Minoa (which was possibly then renamed Heraclea Minoa). From there he won control of Selinus by liberating it from a tyrant, became himself tyrant in turn and was assassinated (Hdt. v. 46). These actions have been interpreted as revenge against Selinus for its pro-Phoenician, anti-Hellenic stance, on the assumption that it was already in alliance with the Phoenicians,[125] but they could have been simple opportunism.

IV. THE INTERNAL DEVELOPMENTS OF THE GREEK STATES AND THEIR RELATIONS

These topics were deemed 'most obscure' by Dunbabin, and will always so remain, given the defective literary sources, however much we may enlarge the archaeological evidence.

In political history we have tantalizing episodes. Civil strife at Gela led to the withdrawal of one party to a place called Mactorium. One Telines, an ancestor of the later tyrant, Gelon, succeeded in bringing them back to Gela simply by his possession of the sacred objects of the chthonian deities (Hdt. VII. 153). Herodotus could not tell how he came to possess them, but from then on the priesthood was a hereditary possession of the family. We cannot date these events, and Mactorium cannot be certainly identified, yet this is our sole information about internal politics at Gela between the foundation and the rise of the tyrants at the end of the sixth century.

[125] C 65, 352–4.

At Syracuse, because of the history of the foundation of Himera, we know that there was civil strife at some time before *c.* 648, which led to the expulsion of a group called the Myletidae, who were sufficiently numerous to influence the dialect spoken at Himera (Thuc. VI. 5.1). It is probable on general grounds that these were powerful people, possibly a clan and its retainers defeated in a struggle within the ruling oligarchy, but we have no certain knowledge. Apart from this episode, all the attempts to reconstruct the political history of early Syracuse are built on an incomplete story related by Aristotle (*Pol.* v, 1303b20ff) and Plutarch (*Praec. reipubl. ger.* 825C), which cannot be dated, and a fragment of Diodorus (VIII. 11), which is also undated and need not refer to Syracuse at all.[126]

We know as little or less about the internal political history of all western Greek states in this period. However, some generalizations can be made about the constitutions of the colonies. Aristotle (*Pol.* v, 1316a35ff) says that tyrants in Sicily mostly arose in oligarchies, and all the western constitutions known in this period were some kind of oligarchy. A landowning oligarchy held power at Syracuse;[127] Rhegium's constitution was 'aristocratic' and a body of one thousand, chosen by wealth, governed everything;[128] at Locri there was an aristocracy, the so-called Hundred Houses, and a body of one thousand again had sovereign power (Polyb. XII. 15.6–7; 16.10); and Taras seems to have enjoyed a constitution closely modelled on that of Sparta, with kings and ephors.[129] This evidence is not so rich that we can confidently assume oligarchy to have been universal. The first western tyrant known to us, Panaetius of Leontini, dated by Eusebius to 608, owed his rise to demagogy,[130] and it is *a priori* likely that some at least of the many other tyrants recorded in the west found their support outside the ranks of the oligarchs. But we have no good evidence for a democratic constitution in our period, and the general picture seems to have been oligarchy interrupted by tyranny. The best-known tyrant in this period is Phalaris of Acragas, who ruled, according to Eusebius, for sixteen years, beginning in 571, within a decade of the colony's foundation. Aristotle says that he rose to power from some public office, and the tradition of his monstrous cruelty was established by the time of Pindar.[131]

Distinguished lawgivers appeared among the western Greeks: Zaleucus of Locri Epizephyrii, Charondas of Catane and Androdamas

---

126 Cf. c 90, 52.
127 Hdt. VII. 155.2; *Marmor Parium* (*IG* XII. 5, 444) XXXVI.
128 Heracl. Pont. fr. 25 (*FHG* II. 219).   129 c 65, 93.
130 Arist. *Pol.* v, 1310b29ff; cf. Polyaen. *Strat.* V. 47.
131 Arist. *Pol.* v, 1310b28; Pind. *Pyth.* I. 95–6.

of Rhegium, who made laws for the Chalcidians in Thrace.[132] Our information about Zaleucus and Charondas is very restricted, once we have cleared away the tendentious inventions of later times, and what remains is patently anecdotal,[133] but there is no reason to doubt their early date. Zaleucus flourished in 663, according to Eusebius, and is the earliest historical Greek lawgiver whose date seems trustworthy. Thus he was writing a law code for Epizephyrian Locri in the first generation of its existence. Of the content and character of this code we know only that penalties for crimes were fixed and very severe, and that changes in the laws were powerfully discouraged.[134] If the Locrian law forbidding the sale of land except in desperate circumstances was his (Arist. *Pol.* II, 1266b18ff), as is possible, he was determined to maintain the status quo and to keep up the number of settlers. Whether or not he passed laws about the constitution, his apparent aim of creating a strongly disciplined society ruled by unchanging laws seems well suited to the oligarchic constitution that we know at Locri.

Charondas of Catane's laws were used in the Chalcidian colonies of Sicily and Italy. We have no trustworthy statement about his date and know no more about his laws than those of Zaleucus. His only special contribution to Greek lawmaking, according to Aristotle (*Pol.* II, 1274b6ff), concerned the law of evidence, which shows that he made provisions about procedure. The tendency of his laws is probably revealed by his imposition of large penalties on the rich for nonattendance at the courts of justice, and small penalties on the poor (Arist. *Pol.* IV, 1297a20ff), with the result (which Aristotle presumed was intentional) that the rich dominated the judicial process.

Using the analogy of other Greek lawgivers we may assume that both Zaleucus and Charondas provided comprehensive, written, codes of law, which ranged over most, if not all, aspects of the life of the community. In old Greece the introduction of such codes was sometimes the result of serious disagreements or strife in society, so it is commonly assumed that they reflect the same circumstances in western Greek cities. Although we can only speculate, we should also admit the possibility that newly-founded communities felt the need for a settled framework provided by a written code of laws.

When we leave political history and consider, firstly, economic matters, we find that the most striking aspect of these western colonies was their prosperity. The luxury of Sybaris became proverbial and the tradition was established by the time of Herodotus. At the wooing of Agariste, that quintessential picture of Archaic Greece, there were two

[132] Arist. *Pol.* II, 1274a22ff; 1274b23ff.
[133] E.g. Dem. *Against Timocrates* 139–41.
[134] Ephorus, *FGrH* 70 F 139; Dem. *ibid.*

suitors from the west, Damasus, son of Amyris (the Wise) of Siris and Smindyrides, son of Hippocrates, from Sybaris (Hdt. VI. 127.1). Herodotus wrote that the latter had achieved the greatest degree of luxury of which one man was capable. The wealth of these western colonies was primarily agricultural, as is stated by ancient authors (Diod. XII. 9; cf. Thuc. VI. 20.4) and attested by the symbols on western coins, notably Metapontum's ear of barley and the bull of Sybaris. On the other hand, there is no doubt that all the industries required by a developed Greek community were practised in these cities, and they participated in vigorous and widespread overseas commerce. The famous mourning at Miletus for the fate of Sybaris (Hdt. VI. 21.1) was presumably stimulated by the loss of mutually profitable trading relations, for Sybaris was a great market for the luxurious Milesian textiles.[135]

This rapid economic growth is a phenomenon commonly met in colonial history of all periods, resulting from the exploitation of new land and other new sources of wealth. When we look at the way the surplus was spent, we can see something of the nature of society in these western Greek colonies in the Archaic period.

Apart from navies, the most ambitious expenditure undertaken by Archaic Greek states was on public buildings, especially temples. The western Greeks were most enthusiastic builders of temples. In the seventh century these were small structures, partly built of mud-brick with terracotta facings, such as the recently-discovered Temple A at Himera, but from early in the sixth century ambitious stone temples began to be erected. Some were 'pre-Doric', all of stone but without peristyle, as Temple B at Himera, which was built about the middle of the century, but before that date Doric temples had appeared at Syracuse and Selinus, and from then on they become very numerous.[136]

This temple-building may legitimately be used as an index of prosperity, but it also reveals the main emphasis of social life. In their material remains these communities show us that throughout the period under discussion they were dominated by religion. In addition to the splendid stone temples we may point to the curious early dedications to Apollo of unmarked stone (ἄργοι λίθοι) in the central sanctuary at Metapontum, which perfectly exemplify Pausanias' description (VII. 22.4–5) of similar early dedications at Pharae in Achaea;[137] to the small, extramural shrines dedicated to the worship of Demeter and Persephone, as, for instance, at Bitalemi, by Gela, or at Helorus, where vast numbers of modest offerings reveal the popular nature of the worship;[138] or to the more splendid and more distant extramural

[135] Timaeus, *FGrH* 566 F 50.
[136] C 20, 12–14, 65–71; H 12; C 100.
[137] C 17, 28–32.   [138] C 124; C 137, 117.

sanctuaries, placed at important points on the coast, which were presumably closely linked with navigation,[139] such as that of Hera at the mouth of the Sele, founded at roughly the same time as the nearby Posidonia, or that of Hera Lacinia near Croton.

Religion was served by the arts of architecture, sculpture and work in terracotta (ranging from splendid architectural attachments to tiny figurines).[140] In all these fields work of respectable, and sometimes high, standard was achieved, but it is clear that the western Greeks followed the lead of artists in Greece. Only in town-planning is it possible, on our present evidence, that they were innovators. Not only did they create magnificent, spacious cities, such as Acragas, but, in particular, the earliest orthogonal layouts known in Greek cities are in the west. From the seventh century on such systems may be presumed to have been the rule, whenever a new city was planned or an existing one re-planned. However, the claim to priority of invention rests on the shaky foundation of our lack of similar evidence in the same period for most other parts of the Greek world, and orthogonality as such is a principle of town-planning at much earlier dates in non-Greek cultures.[141]

The relations between the Greek cities of the west seem to have been reasonably good in the eighth and seventh centuries, but to have deteriorated badly in the sixth. This picture may, of course, owe less to historical truth than to the character of our sources – bad in the sixth century, but worse for earlier times – and a border war between Leontini and Megara in c. 609 is attested by Polyaenus (though in a generally suspect passage: *Strat.* v. 47). However, it seems plausible on general grounds to imagine that, while the Greek cities had plenty of room to expand, they did not war against each other, but when their territories were limited by those of other Greeks, wars followed.

The Chalcidian cities of Sicily and the Straits were closely linked from the beginning, a unity which only reflects the remarkable solidarity of Chalcidian colonists generally.[142] Less good relations elsewhere in Sicily are revealed by Camarina's war of revolt against Syracuse in c. 550, when the Syracusan side included Megara and Camarina tried unsuccessfully to enlist the aid of Gela.[143] More warfare between Greek states is known from Magna Graecia, but the low quality of our evidence denies us a clear picture.

Epizephyrian Locri defeated Croton in a great battle on the Sagra river, but the story we are told is so markedly romantic and fictional

[139] C 164, 91–4.   [140] C 102.
[141] H 77, 22–4; H 23; C 31.   [142] A 40, 61–2.
[143] *FGrH* 556 F 5; cf. C 65, 105–6.

that it cannot be rationalized into history.[144] The probable kernel of fact
is that Locri, with the help of Rhegium, defeated Croton so unexpectedly
that the gods were credited with the victory. Since the date may lie
anywhere between the late seventh and the fifth centuries, we cannot
relate this war to other events with any assurance, nor can it be
confidently identified with the war against Croton in which Locri had
Hipponium and Medma as allies.[145]

We know too that the Achaean cities of Magna Graecia united to
overthrow Ionian Siris (Justin xx. 2.3–8), probably in the first half of
the sixth century. Literary evidence shows that Siris continued to exist
into the fifth century, if not later, and we have an inscription relating
to Siris in the Doric dialect and Achaean alphabet. So it seems most
likely that the Ionian inhabitants were expelled and an Achaean
population took their place. The notoriously enigmatic coins of
Sybarite type, which bear the double legend $\Sigma IPINO\Sigma$ and $\Pi Y\Xi OE\Sigma$,
probably show that this new, Achaean, Siris was a dependant of
Sybaris.[146]

The union of Achaean cities in Magna Graecia seems to be reflected
in the famous and beautiful 'incuse' coins of Sybaris, Croton, Metapontum and Caulonia, which are on the same standard and share a
distinctive and difficult minting technique. These coins were produced
in abundance before Sybaris' destruction in c. 510, so their beginning
is placed at approximately the middle of the sixth century.[147]

The good relations that they attest were cruelly shattered by the bitter
quarrel which led to the destruction of Sybaris. Our tradition is again
very poor. It was so vitiated by the desire to find moral justification
for Sybaris' fall and by Pythagorean hagiology that, a mere seventy years
later, Herodotus could not decide the truth about the relatively simple
question of Dorieus' participation. The clear facts seem to be that a
tyrant, Telys, established himself at Sybaris with the help of the *demos*
and expelled the leading men. Their cause was espoused by Croton,
where they took refuge, and war followed, which ended with the defeat
of Sybaris and its complete destruction, effected partly by the diversion
of the river Crathis.[148] So a typically Greek quarrel between people and
oligarchs was exploited by the Crotoniates, who may perhaps have
genuinely sympathized with the oligarchs, and may even have listened
to Pythagoras' moral and political exhortation, but who were presumably chiefly influenced by the opportunity of destroying a powerful
neighbour.

[144] Strabo VI. 261; Justin xx. 2.10–3.9; Diod. VIII. 32; Paus. III. 19.11–12. Cf. C 41A.
[145] E 235, 77–9.   [146] C 41B; C 81A, B; A 35A, 32–3.   [147] H 48, 163.
[148] Hdt. v. 44–5; Heracl. Pont. (Wehrli, *Schule des Aristoteles* VII) fr. 49; Phylarchus, *FGrH* 81
F 45; Diod. XII. 9–10.

In the period that we have considered the western Greeks successfully
mastered their colonial environment. They were not yet seriously
threatened by outside powers, nor by the native population, and only
towards the end by their fellow Greeks. Their achievements went
beyond material success. Greeks from the west won many victories at
Olympia, and towards the end of our period great schools of western
philosophy were growing up as a result of the arrival of refugees from
East Greece. Altogether they ranked among the leading cities of the
Greek world. The richest, if not the greatest, of these cities was Sybaris,
where the citizens pitied anyone who had to go abroad and 'prided
themselves on growing old on the bridges of their rivers'.[149] The
destruction of such a city may truly be called the end of an epoch.

[149] Timaeus, *FGrH* 566 F 50.

THE EASTERN GREEKS

J. M. COOK

The period dealt with here extends from about 700 B.C. to the time of Polycrates' rule in the 530s and 520s. In the wider historical perspective it saw the rise of the Mermnad dynasty in Lydia, the aggression of Gyges and his successors against the cities of the Ionian coast and their subjection by Croesus, and finally the conquest of Croesus' realm by Cyrus and the establishment of Persian rule over the eastern Greeks of the Asiatic mainland. It does not reach so far as the organization and extension of Persian rule by Darius. As regards our sources of information, archaeology gives occasional glimpses of habitations and sanctuaries and casts light on trade movements; and the works of art that have been discovered testify to a taste and sense of form that is peculiarly East Greek. Inscriptions have little to offer; contemporary ones that are relevant from a historical point of view can be counted on the fingers of one hand. Among the literary sources Herodotus is pre-eminent. But his aim was to present the sequences of events that preceded and led up to the conquests of the kingdoms of Asia and Egypt by Cyrus and his successors and to the Persian Wars; and as far as Asia Minor is concerned the rulers of Lydia and the Medes were more central to his theme than the history of the East Greek cities, of which he tells us many things but offers no continuous narrative. Later writers provide scraps of information which can not be entirely neglected. But their reliability is more questionable; and even if we gave credence to them all, the difficulty of fitting them into their proper positions is often insuperable.

I. THE LITERARY EVIDENCE

A great change occurred on the landward horizon of the eastern Greeks about the beginning of the seventh century. The incursions of the Cimmerians had been felt at the eastern end of Anatolia as early as 714 B.C., and a decade or two later the Phrygian realm of Midas was overthrown when they captured its capital at Gordium (see *CAH* III.2², chs. 33*a*, 34*a*). To the West of this, in Lydia, the throne at Sardis was usurped by Gyges, who founded a dynasty (the Mermnads) that was to be the dominant power in peninsular Asia Minor until the Persian conquest.[1] Scholars now seem almost agreed in rejecting Herodotus' dates for Gyges' reign (716–678 B.C.) and bringing his accession down to about 680, at a time when the collapse of Midas' kingdom had left a power vacuum in Anatolia; his negotiations with Assyria (as early as 663) and subsequent alliance with Egypt show that he took determined action to fill the vacuum and build up a powerful kingdom; and the Greeks of the eastern Aegean thus found themselves confronted by a major power much closer at hand than the Phrygian had been and commanding a number of different routes to the coast so that the Greek cities could not plan a common defence.

Gyges was an aggressive neighbour. It is true that he is said to have made offerings of silver and gold at Delphi and permitted the Milesians to plant a colony at Abydus on the Dardanelles (above, p. 121); so it may be that he was conciliatory towards the Greeks at times when he had other warlike commitments on hand (as those against the Cimmerians). But in Herodotus (I. 14) we read that he attacked Smyrna and Miletus and captured the town of Colophon. Another Cimmerian onslaught proved fatal to Gyges – indeed the Greek cities too were rocked by these and perhaps other intermittent incursions; and Gyges' successors Ardys and Sadyattes in the second half of the seventh century seem to have confined their Greek campaigns to southern Ionia, where they captured Priene and raided Milesian territory. Alyattes inherited Sadyattes' war against Miletus, which after five years he terminated with a lasting treaty (according to Herodotus, I. 21, he was tricked by the tyrant Thrasybulus into believing that food supplies were plentiful in the city); and he destroyed Smyrna, which he seems to have captured (probably about 600 B.C. by means of a siege mound that enabled him to surmount the massive city wall).[2] But when he advanced against Clazomenae he is said to have suffered a serious reverse, presumably at the hands of the Colophonian cavalry; and after that he seems to have allowed the Greek cities to live in peace until his son Croesus resumed the offensive against them. Before this, the Lydian attacks were not aimed at gaining permanent possession of the Ionian sea-board, though they effectively blocked any further Greek penetration of the interior. But Croesus was a conqueror at heart, and Herodotus (I. 28) tells us that he reduced to subjection practically all the peoples of Asia as far as the River Halys, including of course the Carians, Dorians, Ionians, and Aeolians of the coast lands. Sardis became increasingly the metropolis of the Greek East, with Croesus acting not only as a conqueror but as patron of the Greeks of Asia and (in moralizing

[1] For the history of the Lydian kings see Hdt. I. 6ff.
[2] D 24, 23–7; D 73, 88–91, 128–34.

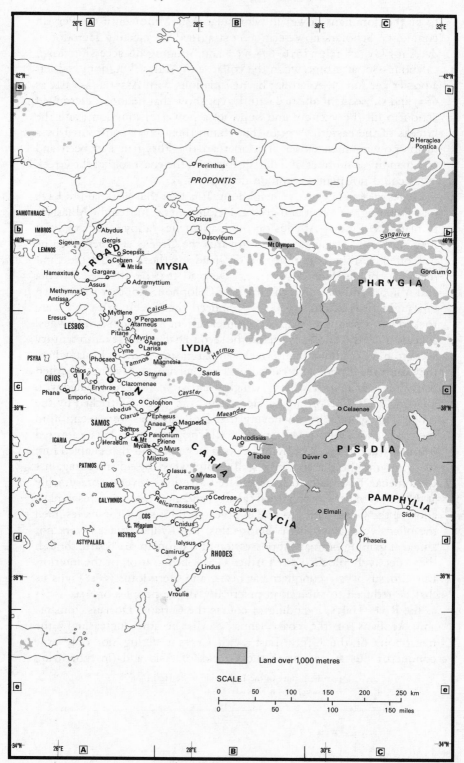

Map 12. East Greece.

anecdotes retailed by Herodotus, I. 27–33; VI. 125) graciously giving
interviews to Greek statesmen such as Bias or Pittacus, Solon, and
Alcmaeon. There was evidently intermarriage between Lydians and
eastern Greeks in the higher social stratum. The material culture of
Sardis in the sixth-century levels shows much that is Greek in
character – the more so because, unlike Phrygia, Lydia had not had a
distinctive civilization of its own; and much of its art has a very Greek
appearance. As against this, the Ionians received new ideas and modes
in religion (e.g. the cults of Cybele and Bacchus), music, and perhaps
the organization and exploitation of wealth; in the sixth century Sappho
and the Colophonian thinker Xenophanes looked to Sardis as the source
of luxuries – the one nostalgically and the other with disapproval.

Croesus came to the throne some time about 560 B.C. and had reigned
only fourteen years when he and his kingdom fell to Cyrus the Persian,
who asserted his claim to the whole of Croesus' realm by right of
conquest. The peoples of Ionia, Caria, and Lycia resisted. But after
fighting which was especially stubborn in the south the cities were taken
by Cyrus' Median general Harpagus; and though a large part of the
population of Phocaea sailed away to join their kinsmen in the western
Mediterranean and a body from Teos went to settle at Abdera in Thrace,
the Greeks of Asia had fallen under Persian rule by about 540 B.C. (Hdt.
I. 164–9). On the mainland Miletus alone preserved the treaty rights that
its inaccessible situation had conferred on it. But the offshore islands
were not threatened at this time (the attribution of destruction of this
date on Samos to the Persians being quite conjectural); and since Cyrus
had no fleet the only constraint on the islanders before Darius' time was
their possession of agricultural land on the mainland opposite. This may
have prompted them to a nominal submission (Herodotus seems to
contradict himself in the matter of their independence). But it seems
clear that with Miletus, Samos, Chios, Lesbos, and Rhodes effectively
free the eastern Greeks still enjoyed a fair degree of initiative. Sardis
of course had become the Persian administrative centre in the west, and
may perhaps not have continued to offer the same opportunities for
commercial and cultural enrichment as it had done under Croesus.

The ancient sources agree in postulating the existence of kingship in
the Ionian cities at the time of the migrations. But it seems to have been
mostly short-lived, and the odd mentions of it surviving, as in Chios
and Aeolic Cyme, hardly bring us down beyond the end of the Dark
Age. The most significant reminder is the family name Basilidae which
survived in places like Ephesus and Erythrae and carried much prestige
and some power as late as the seventh century; in Lesbos the founder's
family (the Penthilidae) seems likewise to have wielded power in the
seventh century. In Samos political power seems to have been in the

hands of landowners (the *Geomoroi*) at the end of the seventh century
after the murder of a tyrant; a coup was effected on the return of an
expedition to Perinthus (the new Samian colony in the Propontis); but
it is not clear whether this was a struggle between classes or between
factions among the landowners, nor whether the landowners were at
this time so few as to constitute an oligarchy. For Miletus we have
stories indicating civil strife and atrocities, and the names given to the
political groups by later writers are suggestive on the one hand of
wealth, and on the other of artisanry or manual labour (and possibly
a suppressed native population), while the Parian arbitration that
followed in due course is said to have conferred the government on the
owners of well-kept land-holdings (thus setting up a moderate oligarchy
which will hardly have corresponded to the main aggregation of
wealth). We do not know when these troubles occurred; and if class
warfare is implied we do not know its alignments: whether for instance
a wealthy mercantile class was already in being and at variance with the
landowners, or whether a large body of urban poor was coming into
existence. And here again the troubles seem to have followed a tyranny
(that of Thoas and Damasenor).[3]

There are two things that emerge from the literary (and in a lesser
degree epigraphical) evidence. One is that 'tyrants' were common in
East Greece from the later seventh century on, and that (as Aristotle
implies) they arose because of the great power vested for long periods
in the principal magistrate of a city. They need not be regarded as a
stage in a normal development from the rule of the few to some form
of democracy; in a time of rapid social and economic change the demand
for a strong executive could have been irresistible. The second point
concerns the tribes. The four old Ionic tribes, whatever their names may
have signified at the outset (*Geleontes* = radiant ones?, *Aigikoreis* =
herdsmen?, *Argadeis* = handworkers or farmers?, *Hopletes* = warriors or
the younger?), seem to have no connotation of status, and so far as our
limited knowledge carries they seem to be attested in early times in
southern and central Ionia at least (Miletus, Samos, Ephesus, Teos, but
not (it would seem) Phocaea, in whose colony of Lampsacus other
names were current); to these were added two additional names which
presumably represent accretions to the citizen bodies (*Boreis* and
Oinopes). For Samos the evidence is derived from Perinthus which was
settled about 600 B.C.; but on the island itself the tribe names found
in later sources are quite different, and at Ephesus the old Ionian tribes
were down-graded to subdivisions of a single tribe *Ephesioi* and new
ones were created (partly at least with territorial names). At Ephesus
the reorganization occurred long before the time of Ephorus in the
fourth century, in Samos evidently after 600 B.C. On the assumption

---

[3] The troubles at Samos and Miletus: D 49, 7f.

that at Ephesus they date to the period of independence before the Lydian and Persian conquest, scholars have recently attributed the changes to the tyrants in the first half of the sixth century; and in that case we may see in them a great extension of citizenship to incorporate Greek metics and immigrants, not to mention non-Greek natives, in the body politic on a partly territorial basis.[4] It is at this time also that a reform in Chios, attested by the well-known 'constitution' stele, established a new council containing fifty members from each tribe, thus greatly increasing the power of the *demos*.[5] At Miletus there seems to have been no corresponding reorganization of the old tribes (the old names continued), and political strife seems to have been endemic there through the sixth century. But at Ephesus at least, and perhaps elsewhere in Ionia, the reforms may well have resulted in a broadening of the basis of citizenship and spreading of political power at a time when the great expansion of trade and manufacture had altered the whole structure of an originally land-based society. The developing social groups may have looked to tyrants as catalysts; and the changes did not eliminate the need for tyrants because we hear the names of more than half a dozen such who managed Ephesus in succession through the greater part of the sixth century. The earlier ones at least had to excise opposition, to judge by stories that have come down through later writers; and Herodotus (v. 92) lends some support to this when he relates the Milesian tyrant Thrasybulus' advice to Periander – to chop down any ear of corn that stood clear above its fellows; later tyrants of Ephesus are said to have banished their citizen Hipponax whose satirical verses give us our best indication of the polyglot society that had come into being there after the middle of the sixth century.

The interest aroused among later Greek writers by the poems of Alcaeus permits some insight into the troubles that beset Mytilene in the first half of the sixth century. After the overthrow of the Penthilidae violence and intrigue were prevalent. A tyrant named Melanchrus did not last long against a combination of leading families. But his successor Myrsilus had the support of moderates like Pittacus, though not of Alcaeus and his friends who plotted unsuccessfully to unseat him. Myrsilus died, and Alcaeus was exultant – but not for long, for Pittacus, who had won fame by killing the Athenian leader Phrynon in the war for the possession of Sigeum at the entry to the Hellespont, was entrusted with supreme power by the people of Mytilene and Alcaeus was once again in exile plotting a return. Pittacus ruled with restraint, revising the laws rather than the constitution, and treating his opponents with clemency when he had them in his power. He resigned his office after ten years, leaving Mytilene on an even keel at last.[6]

---

[4] D 84; D 82.   [5] D 56; D 74.
[6] D 75.

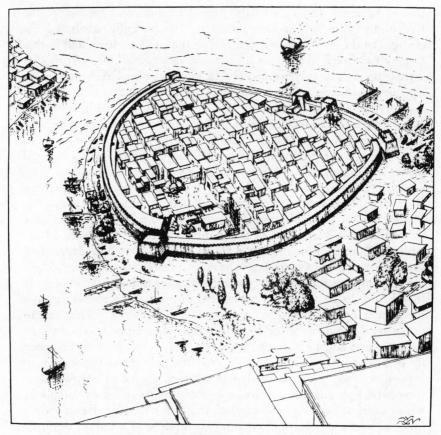

31. Reconstruction of the city of Smyrna at the end of the seventh century B.C., by R. V. Nicholls. See also pp. 446ff, figs. 54, 56. (After D 24, 15.)

II. THE MATERIAL EVIDENCE

The eighth century no doubt saw a great increase in population in the Greek world generally, and on the Ionian migration sites, where space in the city area was restricted, housing must have begun to constitute a problem. Smyrna was remodelled in the seventh century (fig. 31), apparently with parallel streets on a north–south axis flanked by regularly built spacious houses inside the massive curtain of the wall-circuit on the peninsula, and also with a part of the population living outside it.[7] This incidentally is of interest as showing some form of public authority which could override property rights. Smyrna is not likely to have been the only instance of such remodelling. At Miletus,

[7] D 24

where the peninsula was much more capacious, the Archaic settlement is now known to have extended far to the north and south of the Athena temple before the destruction of 494 B.C.; and here again there seem to have been parallel streets with well-built houses in the sixth century at least, though on the hill of Kalabaktepe half a mile to the south the settlement, which goes back to the eighth century, was altogether more irregular.[8] At Ephesus the claim that there was a habitational grid fitting with the Archaic Artemisium seems as yet to be only a conjecture; and on other city sites, such as Iasus on the coast of Caria, it is easier to establish the existence of Archaic settlement than to determine its layout. The evidence for city layouts is in fact slight, except at Smyrna; but we are probably justified in supposing that the seventh century saw a major advance in urbanization in Ionia. A couple of minor sites command attention. At Emporio in the south of Chios the houses brought to light were simple in form and scattered to fit the contours of the hillside; this of course was not a city, and its date is early (it was abandoned by the end of the seventh century).[9] More surprising is the settlement at Vroulia in the south of the island of Rhodes.[10] Here the seaward edge of the promontory was fenced off by a defensive wall about 300 metres long against which for the greater part of its length rectangular houses were built, with a shorter row inside and a tower-like building overlooking a sanctuary and open area on the crest. Occupation seems to have started before the middle of the seventh century and lasted a hundred years or so. Presumably this was an outpost and at least semi-military.

If there is little that we can say with assurance about the development of housing in Archaic East Greece, still less can be said about developments in domestic life. Bath tubs seem to have come into use in seventh-century Ionian houses; with the growth of trade fine pottery and a range of wines were imported; and where solidly constructed two-storeyed houses were built life was no doubt more commodious. In the later Archaic period the manufacture of terracotta sarcophagi (of which the painted ones known as 'Clazomenian' are spectacular) attests a desire to make handsome provision for the accommodation of the dead.[11]

Apart from the long narrow temple at the Samian Heraeum, we know almost nothing of shrines in East Greece before the seventh century, and even at a quite advanced date in that century prestige buildings such as the 60 m-long stoa at the Heraeum (fig. 32) were of quite simple unadorned construction.[12] The first temples with stone columns in a

[8] D 61.

[10] D 60; *CAH* III.1[2], 784, fig. 87.

[12] D 95, 50, 47ff; D 32, 21–3, 27, 280.

[9] D 22; *CAH* III.1[2] 753, fig. 76.

[11] D 32; D 33.

32. Reconstruction of the South Stoa at the Heraeum, Samos. Late seventh century B.C. (After
G. Gruben, *Athenische Mitteilungen* 72 (1957) pl. 7; cf. H 32, 280.)

tentative architectural order seem to make their appearance in the Ionian
cities only towards the end of the century, and we might think of the
Ionians as having been self-indulgent enough to provide for their own
comfort before that of their gods; but the balance was redressed by the
building of the gigantic temples in the middle ranges of the sixth
century.

The Ionic order was slower in taking shape than the Doric of
mainland Greece, and it was only in these huge stone temples of Ionia
that it formed recognizable conventions. It seems to have been the
original Samian dipteron, laid down perhaps shortly before 560 B.C.,
that set the pace; and this great building not only excited the rivalry
of the Ephesians but set the pattern for architectural forms on Chios
also.[13] It was 105 m in length and half that in width; with a double
colonnade on the exterior, a deep columned porch, and inner colonnades,
it formed a veritable forest of columns. It was destroyed by fire and
replaced later in the sixth century by an even larger temple intended
to outdo the one that was being built at Ephesus, but this second Samian
dipteron was never completed.[14] One of the problems confronted was
that of marshy ground by the river Imbrasus, whose course had to be
diverted; this seems to have been the work of the Samian engineer
Theodorus, who was also called in as consultant at Ephesus. The
Artemisium at Ephesus was designed to be slightly larger than the first
Samian dipteron, with a lavish use of marble carving and sculpture,
regular Ionic volute capitals, and columns that bore the dedication of
Croesus, the king of Lydia. Another great temple, that at the oracular
sanctuary of the Milesians at Didyma,[15] nearly approached the two giant

[13] D 20.   [14] H II, 236–43.
[15] D 42; D 37.

ones in scale and rivalled Ephesus in sophistication; and there were of course other temples, like that at Phana in Chios, which by ordinary standards were substantial.[16] The construction of the great stone and marble temples demanded high skill in organization and engineering.[17] Huge stone blocks had to be transported, hoisted, and fitted (at Ephesus the architrave blocks weighed up to forty tons), and Theodorus must have used to advantage the square, the level, and the lathe (which was employed on the Heraeum column drums), for he was later said to have invented them. In these buildings techniques and carved ornamentation were evolved which were applied in the new architecture of the Persian capitals a decade or two later.

Places that have yielded works of Archaic East Greek art and craftsmanship in some quantity are the Samian Heraeum, Miletus, Ephesus and Didyma (most productive of sculpture), and the cemeteries of Rhodes; Old Smyrna and graves at Clazomenae and Pitane have yielded painted pottery including terracotta sarcophagi; the Larisa site by the Hermus and the island of Nisyros have produced local wares in somewhat wayward styles; Sardis yields finds which come within the ambit of East Greek art, though sometimes with a distinctive idiom; and East Greek pottery has been found in overseas settlements such as Naucratis and Tell Defenneh in Egypt, Tocra (Taucheira) and Cyrene in North Africa, and the Black Sea area. The view that Ionia (or East Greece) was artistically in the lead in comparison with mainland Greece originated a hundred years ago; but a strong reaction set in a generation ago, and in particular it has become clear that Near Eastern impulses were transmitted to Greece direct and not through Ionia.[18]

In pottery Geometric decorative motifs and bird cups show something of a common style spread over the East Greek area from before 700 B.C., and after that we find bird bowls and rosette bowls made to more or less standard types in most parts of East Greece. From the mid seventh century on a very distinctive style of vase-painting established itself throughout East Greece – what is known as the Wild Goat Style (fig. 33).[19] It has its characteristic vase shapes (broad wine-jugs, plates with tondo decoration, and stemmed dishes); and in addition to freehand floral ornaments it has a limited repertory of animals in more or less schematic poses (principally lion, sphinx, griffin, bull, boar, deer, dog and hare, duck, and above all the wild goats whose files often form zones around a jug), all painted in silhouette and outline technique on a white-slipped ground with some use of applied colour. The motifs and arrangement quickly became canonical so that different schools can not very easily be recognized in the East Greek area; but there was some

[16] D 20, 171–87.   [17] H 30.
[18] D 29; D 46; F 13.   [19] H 29, 115–41; D 57.

33. Wild Goat style oenochoe from Vroulia, Rhodes. About 600 B.C.
Height 30 cm. (Rhodes Museum; after D 60, pl. 16.1.)

general development, and broadly speaking the use of incision on animal
forms seems to have been adopted sooner in north Ionia than in the
south, while Chian workshops evolved a delicate genre of their own
with the fine chalice as the distinctive shape. In contrast to Attic and
Corinthian, the Wild Goat style was content to serve a decorative
purpose during the two and a half or three generations in which it
dominated the fine pottery of East Greece; and there was little advance
in the arrangement and forms, with human beings hardly introduced
at all and no concern with narrative scenes. The forms, however, were
attractive in themselves and well adapted to the adornment of the vases.
The Wild Goat style was for a long time best known to scholars from
finds in the island of Rhodes and therefore commonly called 'Rhodian';
but we can now see it as an almost universal East Greek style, and the
output of Rhodes appears perhaps rather conventional in comparison
with some Ionian centres.

In the second quarter of the sixth century the domination of the Wild Goat style came to an end. Chios continued to produce its distinctive fine ware without intermission.[20] But north Ionia and the south diverged at this time. In the south, from Samos to Rhodes, a curious experimental style asserted itself – that known as Fikellura.[21] The most characteristic shape is the dumpy amphora; and the decoration is broadly conceived, often with a main motif isolated in an empty field. Men are now shown in vigorous motion, the figures being done in dark silhouette with the inner detail not incised but reserved. Here again, though a locality in the island of Rhodes gave its name to this class of pottery, the Rhodian output is not the finest. In the vase-painting of northern Ionia the influence from Attica was stronger, and the style that came to prevail there was a colourful black-figure one. Finds show it at home in Clazomenae and Old Smyrna, but a body of material of this class was found at the Iono-Carian military cantonment at Tell Defenneh which seems to have come to an end with Cambyses' conquest of Egypt in 525 B.C.[22] Sphinxes and human-headed birds often dominate the files of these vases. But dancers and bacchants are not infrequent; occasionally motifs are derived from the Greek mythology, but no iconographical tradition comparable to that of Athens was formed. A small but distinctive part of the East Greek ware found in Egypt may perhaps have been produced there for the resident Greeks by immigrant craftsmen from East Greece;[23] and it is also possible that emigrants from north Ionia after the Persian conquest set up workshops for painted pottery in Etruria.[24] But the belief in a massive Ionian contribution to the formation of Etruscan art belonged to the time when Ionia was thought to be in the lead artistically, and is now less widely held.

Painted terracotta sarcophagi gave the East Greek artists an ampler field for their figure style on the broadened upper rim flange of the vessel.[25] They seem to have made their appearance in north Ionia about 530 B.C. and been manufactured for a couple of generations; scattered examples have been found on Lesbos and beyond in the north and Rhodes in the south, but the main production seems to have centred on the Gulf of Smyrna, and the name 'Clazomenian' has with some justice been applied to the class. Much of the decoration (including animals) harks back to the Wild Goat style, which had continued in use among vase-painters of the lower Hermus region; but a black-figure style (and occasionally red-figure) took possession of the broader head end of the rim, and here scenes of human activity (chariots and battles)

[20] D 22, 156–71; C 232, 57–63; D 233, 24–8; D 99, 67–73.
[21] D 28; D 99 passim.   [22] D 31; D 32; D 26.
[23] D 17; D 19; A 7, 123, 137–9.   [24] D 34; A 7, 203–5.
[25] See n. 11.

were dominant. Some acquaintance with contemporary Attic art is evident; and though lacking in originality these vessels show the painters handling designs on a larger scale than vases would permit.

Eastern Greeks who visited Egypt must have been astonished at the wealth of sculpture which they saw there. But they do not seem at first to have been prompted to emulation; and it was only after the white marble of Naxos had been brought into use and a sculptural tradition established in the Cyclades that they turned seriously to the making of full-scale statuary. What especially captured their interest was the representation of drapery with its emphasis on slanting and radiating folds; with the skirt pulled tight over the legs it formed an attractive theme not only for marble statues but for plastic terracotta vases manufactured in southern Ionia and Rhodes. Chios had a famous sculptural school, to judge by the literary sources, a family of sculptors being named (Mikkiades, Archermus, and Boupalos and Athenis) whose activity must have spanned the greater part of the sixth century and covered the Central Aegean and Athens. The indications seem to be that this was a fashionable school in the main stream of Aegean development. The sculptural style of Samos and Miletus, as revealed by finds of the two middle quarters of the sixth century there and at Didyma, was more distinctive; and this seems to have been the characteristic East Greek style. The anatomy of the athletic male figure and the underlying bone structure did not have the compulsive appeal here that it had on the other side of the Aegean; in fact in their statues East Greek men were commonly shown as well nourished, amply draped, and not infrequently seated, and they do not appear less dignified for being so. This East Greek sculpture is superficial in the sense that what lies beneath the surface has not been explored. Simple forms of sphere and cylinder (or cube in the case of seated figures) lend coherence to the design, as heads and skirts most clearly show; and the effect of the curving planes is heightened by the variation between deceptively simple unadorned surfaces and piquant facial features or fine repetitive patterns. The impression created is ample, sometimes voluptuous, and on occasion exotic.[26]

In other arts the East Greeks were no less original in their treatment of forms and techniques learned from their neighbours or customers. Several of the finer seventh-century ivories found in Greece carry clear suggestions of East Greek or Lydian origin – a head at Perachora, the 'Apollo' with a lion at Delphi – and at home the sanctuary sites have offered both imports from the East and Egypt, and the products of distinctive local schools: best known the ivories of the Ephesus foundation deposit and lyre-fittings like the kneeling youth from

[26] D 39; D 94; H 19, 68–72, 87–8, 160–1; H 66, 70–86.

Samos.[27] Some time before the middle of the sixth century East Greek artists learned eastern techniques of cutting hardstone gem intaglios and inaugurated an art which was to be taken up later by other areas of Greece.[28] In metalwork there was a studio for the production of orientalizing griffin-head cauldrons in Samos,[29] matching the workshops in the Peloponnese, and a limited vogue for the production of Phrygian-style belts in bronze for the women of Ionia.[30] The skills in metal-working of Glaucus of Chios were legendary, while Samos was the pioneer in hollow bronze casting and Theodorus – architect, sculptor, *toreutes* and gem-engraver – appears to foreshadow Renaissance man in versatility.[31]

In examining East Greek art we can not fail to be conscious that despite local variants and occasional divergences there is a recognizable homogeneity in both forms and development. So far as we can tell, the Wild Goat Style arrived more or less simultaneously in the different parts of East Greece, and it is remarkably uniform. In the sixth century Chios and north Ionia diverged to some extent, or adopted an intermediate position in contact with new movements on the other side of the Aegean. But there still remained a system of forms and an ethos that can be characterized as East Greek, and in general we seem justified in recognizing an artistic '*koine*'. To the eastern Greeks art was something more decorative and less intellectually exacting than it was in Athens. It was not a medium of story-telling and transmission of the legends rivalling the literary genres; nor did it involve a rigorous exploration of the structure of the human form in all its details or perseverance in a progressing tradition from generation to generation. The East Greek vase-painters were concerned to produce a harmonious relationship between vase form and decoration rather than major paintings in miniature. At the same time the Eastern Greeks were not petty in the scale of their creations, as is shown by the enormous cauldron that Colaeus is said to have dedicated at the Samian Heraeum from the profits of his voyage to Tartessus (Hdt. IV. 152), the fragments of colossal statues found there and the sculptural group of a whole family carved by Geneleus,[32] and of course the huge temples of the mid sixth century. What is historically most interesting, however, is the conscious adherence of the eastern Greeks to a common tradition in their art which not only united them but distinguished them from other Greeks. In the Archaic Greek world there was no other artistic *koine* with a comparable territorial spread; and it was not simply Ionian, because Rhodes and to some extent the Aeolis participated in it. Rhodes,

27 D 38; D 41.
28 H 15; H 16 ch. 4.
29 H 44; H 45.
30 D 22, 214–21; A 7, 90–1.
31 H 60, nos. 261–93.
32 D 39.

which by the chance of archaeological discoveries seemed at one time to be altogether the most productive centre in vase-painting at least, does not show signs of any great originating power, and Chios tended to be on a fringe of its own. If we had to select an Ionian city as the leader in the creation of this artistic *koine*, it would not be easy to choose between Miletus and Samos, for not nearly enough relevant material is to hand. But it may be that we should not look for one single leader; Samos and Miletus, together with Ephesus, formed the cultural heart of Ionia, and they could have been capable, in collaboration and competition, of promoting artistic movements which would find favour with their East Greek neighbours and so encouraging the formation of a common style. That the Rhodians so readily embraced this style implies that their cultural links were with the Ionian cities by the time that they became associated with them in commerce with the Levant and Egypt.

East Greek craftsmen seem also to have worked at inland centres in the sixth century, to judge by the court art of Sardis, fragments of wall-paintings excavated at Gordium, and perhaps East Greek influence on the carving of Phrygian tomb monuments. Of especial interest is the recent discovery of painted terracotta gutter plaques with designs of a griffin and an Iranian rider at Düver in the southern Phrygian region.[33] These date about the third quarter of the sixth century and belong to a class of terracotta revetments which was widespread in the East Greek area and with painted relief designs of banquets, chariot scenes, and predatory animals, formed an East Greek artistic genre at this time.[34] In this region of the south-west Anatolian plateau south of the Phrygian heart-land a few sherds from imported East Greek pots of Archaic date have been picked up,[35] and there are other possible Greek connexions such as the name Celaenae by which a settlement here (at Dinar) appears to have been known when Xerxes passed this way (Hdt. VII. 26). In addition, a variety of forms and motifs in the pottery of this region show resemblances with East Greek. So it is at first sight tempting to think in terms of Ionian penetration to the top of the Maeander valley in the seventh and sixth centuries. There seems, however, to have been a strong native tradition of painted pottery in Iron Age southern Anatolia, into which the motifs may be fitted without any great discrepancy; and connexions with Lydia and inner Anatolian ceramics may be postulated. It would be premature to claim that the south-west of Anatolia was penetrated in depth by Ionians before the Persian conquest; and on the other hand the evidence hardly permits us to speak

[33] D 1; D 88.   [34] D 3.
[35] B 10; D 67; D 70.

of a western Anatolian artistic style in which the eastern Greeks were participants.[36]

With their Iranian rider the Düver plaques seem to show East Greek art being brought into use for the benefit of the new masters; and in recent years evidence has been mounting up in the form of sculptured reliefs and even of wall-paintings (Gordium and northern Lycia), in both of which East Greek artistic forms govern the iconography but are converted to suit the life-style of local potentates or Persian grandees. With these, however, we are descending below the limits of the present volume.

III. THE OVERSEAS EXPANSION OF THE EASTERN GREEKS

In the centuries that followed their establishment on the coast of Asia Minor the East Greek cities there seem to have steadily consolidated their frontier on the inland side so that in places their territory extended for a couple of days' walk from the sea; and the gaps between the individual cities were filled up. Miletus affords an example. Herodotus (I. 18 and VI. 20) speaks of three distinct lots of Milesian territory: their own land (the peninsula on which Miletus and Didyma stood), the *Hyperakria* (the hill country to the east of this), and the Maeander plain across the gulf. But we also know of Milesian possession of Thebe on Mt Mycale and in the region of Panionium; and at some early date, contrary to the normal trend, the islands facing the Milesian coast were annexed by the mainland city. Miletus appears to have turned her attention to the Hellespontine region in the first half of the seventh century, and it is an easy surmise that the Ionian colonization in the north-east resulted from the blocking of her landward frontier by the new Lydian power under Gyges. But it is probably no more than a half truth. Before the end of the eighth century Mytilene was expanding on to the mainland south of the Dardanelles, and not long after that Mytilene and Chios seem to have been planting settlements on the Thracian coasts; so Lydian aggression is not the sole cause of the East Greek expansion, and in the case of Chios there are grounds for thinking that the aim may have been economic.

The eastern Greeks were late-comers in the history of Greek colonization; and they were not in the forefront of trade with the Near East (see above, ch. 36a). At Tarsus and Al Mina excavations have shown that Greek traders were active in the eighth century before the Assyrian conquest, but they seem to have been mainly Euboeans. It was only in the seventh century, to judge by the pottery found there, that

[36] D 68.

eastern Greeks came to dominate the Greek element that helped to make these places (and in a lesser degree Mersin and Tell Sūkās) important ports (above, pp. 7–11). The wealth of Cypriot objects found by excavators in Samos and Rhodes suggests that in the seventh century Cyprus was involved in the trade with eastern Greece[37] (and no doubt supplying metal); and in the absence of firm archaeological evidence on the spot we must tentatively assign to this period the foundations in Pamphylia and Cilicia on the south coast of Asia Minor that are recorded as East Greek colonies and would have provided shelter to ships passing between the Aegean and Cyprus or the Levant: Nagidus and Celenderis (founded from Samos), Side (alleged to be from Aeolic Cyme), Phaselis and Soli (from Rhodes, with the Phaselites soon participating in the Hellenium at Naucratis in their own right), and Holmi (of uncertain origin). Archaeological evidence for their Hellenism is slight, but Classical coins and literary sources attest consciousness of the Greek heritage on this coast.

Egypt was more distant and at first less accessible. Whether as raiders on their own account or on the instigation of Gyges, Ionian and Carian bronze-clad mercenaries arrived in the Delta about 660 B.C. and were taken into the employment of Psammetichus I, who in due course settled a large body of them in encampments on the banks of the Pelusiac arm of the Nile; Herodotus (II. 154) tells us that they were the first aliens to be given settlements in Egypt, and recent excavations of sites on the eastern edge of the Delta there show eastern Greeks resident in the sixth century at least. The Iono-Carian guard itself was transferred by Amasis to Memphis; but the Ionic presence in the Delta was augmented by the establishment of a self-regulating community at Naucratis on the Canopic arm of the Nile. Herodotus (II. 178) speaks of the place as having been granted to Greek settlers and traders by Amasis (so after 570 B.C.); but Strabo (XVII. 801) tells us that Naucratis was founded by Milesians who had established a fort in the Delta in the time of Psammetichus, and in fact the finds at Naucratis show that Greek occupation dates back to the last quarter of the seventh century (see above, p. 37ff). Clearly this was a settlement whose *raison d'être* was trade. Grain must have been the principal commodity sought, though manufactured products such as linen and papyrus were also required by the Greeks at home; against this, silver is assumed to have been the most important import, with perhaps a limited market for Aegean specialities such as wine and olive oil. Herodotus speaks of the Hellenium at Naucratis as being a joint venture of nine cities of East Greece (of the Ionians Chios, Teos, Phocaea, and Clazomenae, of the Dorians Rhodes, Cnidus, Halicarnassus, and Phaselis, and of the

[37] B 146; D 85.

Aeolians Mytilene); but he adds that the Milesians and Samians, as also the Aeginetans, set up shrines there. Finds on the site (including ethnics on votive inscriptions) and coin hoards accord with his enumeration of the participating cities. It is clear that the eastern Greeks played the largest part in the Greek trade with Egypt before the Persian conquest (525 B.C.) and that northern Ionia had a substantial share in it. The mention of participation by several south Dorian cities is of special interest. The corporate action of the eastern Greeks from their different cities will presumably have resulted more from cooperation on the spot than by agreement between the cities themselves, though Herodotus' mention of Rhodes as though it were a single city is suggestive. But it shows a sense of unity and common purpose among the eastern Greeks which corresponds to the artistic *koine* that has been remarked above. The consciousness of belonging together seems to have affected the eastern Greeks as a whole, and their readiness to cooperate may not be unconnected with the previous East Greek ventures in the Levant. This background of collaboration in the development of markets may have influenced the course of Ionian colonization.

There are signs of Ionian interest in the North African coasts of Libya and Numidia. But the two main Ionian colonial fields were the north-east and the European far west; and in either case it was a single city that provided the leadership (see above, ch. 37). In the north-east Miletus set the pace, as possibly she may have done initially at Naucratis. She is said by Latin writers to have been the mother city of 75 or even 90 colonies; this is no doubt an exaggeration, but we can give names to two dozen places between the Hellespont and the far coasts of the Black Sea for which a Milesian foundation was claimed. In the second half of the seventh century Greek footholds were established on the shores of the Black Sea, which came in time to be studded with settlements of predominantly Milesian origin. Ultimately the more prosperous ones provided a livelihood for a substantial population; it may be supposed that many men from other East Greek cities joined in under Milesian leadership, and in due course viticulture and manufactures were developed (especially in the Crimea). These shores were not such as the Greeks would choose to inhabit by preference; and there is some ground for the belief that on the northern shores of the Black Sea at least regular colonization was preceded by trading stations or fishing factories which were frequented seasonally and only gradually developed into city communities. In the sixth century these Pontic settlements must have added a new dimension to the commerce of East Greece. Grain, preserved fish, and hides no doubt formed a large part of the output, with Cappadocian red ochre, Chalybian steel, and hardwood for furniture exported from the southern coast. In this respect the Pontic colonies differed from the older ones in Sicily and south Italy, that they complemented rather than duplicated the products of the Greek lands and were able to furnish essential commodities in bulk. This could not but affect the economic balance of the East Greek cities themselves.

In the far west the dominant force was the north Ionian city of Phocaea, whose situation on the end of a promontory made maritime activity a necessity if it was to prosper. The Phocaeans may not have been the first Greeks in the far west – Herodotus tells us (IV. 152) that Colaeus the Samian accidentally made a pioneering voyage which disclosed the rich market for metals (silver, and no doubt bronze) at Tartessus beyond the Straits of Gibraltar, apparently about 638 B.C.; and there is a possible hint of Rhodian activity on the north-east Spanish coast and around the Rhône mouths. But it was the Phocaeans who gained the confidence of Arganthonius the king of Tartessus and for many years had a monopoly of the metal trade there. They were not averse to planting agriculturally self-sufficient colonies in suitable spots. Their foundation of about 600 B.C. at Massalia (Marseille) became one of the great cities, and we can name over a dozen settlements that were said to have been planted by the Phocaeans or Massaliots on the coasts between Hyele (Elea) in south Italy and Maenace near the Straits of Gibraltar. On the other hand Emporiae (Ampurias) on the north-eastern Spanish coast proclaims by its name a deliberate function as a trading station across the gulf from Massalia. The Phocaeans traded in fifty-oared war galleys in these waters, which may imply that the state was deeply implicated in the commercial enterprise of its people in the west (Thucydides speaks of the Phocaeans as having a fleet with which they defeated the Carthaginians there). In his account of the Phocaeans' activity (I. 163–7) Herodotus stresses the long-distance character of their voyaging in the different seas; and after refugees from Phocaea itself had come to reinforce their settlement at Alalia in Corsica shortly before 540 B.C. (above, p. 199), the seas west of the Straits of Messina seem to have been infested by Phocaeans for five years until their losses in the 'Cadmean' victory over superior Etruscan and Carthaginian forces off Alalia put a check to their aggressiveness. But if the Phocaeans ceased to exist as a power, their colonies remained; and Massalia and its satellites brought the essentials of the Greek way of life, including vines, olives, and agriculture, to the natives of southern Gaul and promoted trade up the Rhône valley until it perhaps even tapped a tin route up the Seine.

Here again we may surmise that though one single Ionian city provided the leadership, citizens of others joined in manning the settlements; in fact the principal Greek deity of this stretch of coast was Artemis of Ephesus. Carians may also have participated with the eastern Greeks in ventures in the Black Sea and the west; for Carian place-names have been claimed there, and recent archaeological discoveries show that the Carians at home were more receptive of Greek culture in early times than has hitherto been supposed. But at the same time, if we may judge by the finds, the far west did not attract so wide a range of East Greek traders as Naucratis and the Pontic colonies did; with the Carthaginian competition conditions must have been less favourable for general trade, and the Phocaeans seem to have been unusually tough and uncompromising people.

It is striking that these East Greek ventures in Egypt, the Pontic region, and the far west all seem to have flowered at about the same time, in the years towards the close of the seventh century (at Tell Sūkās, the port serving Hama in Syria, the volume of East Greek imports is also stepped up at this time, but at Al Mina the reverse seems to be the case, so this may be a reflexion of the vicissitudes of Near Eastern history).[38] This sudden burst of enterprise is not likely to have been prompted to any large degree by the menace from Lydia but seems in the main to have sprung from a realization in Eastern Greece of the possibilities of mercantile expansion. The sixth century was bound to be very different from the seventh.

IV. THE EAST GREEK ACME

The decisive stage in the overseas expansion seems to have set in towards the end of the seventh century. Before that time there is hardly likely to have been the sort of trading community in the cities which could fund overseas ventures, and coinage had barely come into use to facilitate payment for services or commercial transactions. Presumably the expansion of trade must have depended initially on men of standing who were also men of vision. But the inevitable result must have been the growth of a professional trading class in those East Greek cities which took part in the enterprises. The import of metals in quantity will have promoted the growth of industry; the seafaring population will have increased greatly in numbers, and the need for export goods must have involved many people in manufacture at what by this time was a high level of technical skills and in specialized agriculture. This is the background of economic pressure on the social system against which the political turmoil and changes referred to above have to be envisaged. Sardis was becoming an important centre for the eastern Greeks (not to mention a source of funds for political exiles who wished, like the poet Alcaeus, to regain power at home). It was also the source of electrum and increasingly of gold; and we may think of it almost as a focal point in an East Greek 'common market'.

After planting a settlement, perhaps in the early seventh century, at

[38] Above, pp. 10–11, 23; A 7, 51–4.

34. Chian wine amphora
from Smyrna. About 600
B.C. (After D 24, 16, fig. 4.)

Maronea on the Thracian coast the people of Chios played no overt part
in the main Ionian colonizing movement. But discoveries at Naucratis
and in the Black Sea colonies show Chios as having a substantial share
in the trade that resulted from it. Her fine pottery and standard wine
jars (fig. 34) are easily recognizable, and the profusion of the latter are
an index to her trade.[39] From Thrace she could obtain silver (for
purchase of grain in Egypt) and slaves, as also timber and further
supplies of wine. She was a major slave-owning state (more so,
according to Thucydides, VIII. 40, than any other Greek state save
Sparta); and she came to have a very large population, for at the
beginning of the fifth century she manned a hundred ships (the largest
single contingent) in the Ionian fleet at Lade. But her production of
grain (even allowing for the small plain she had acquired at Atarneus
on the mainland opposite and retained by a bargain with the Persians)
must have been quite inadequate for her home needs; and here we seem
to have a case of deliberate organization of economic resources.
Self-sufficiency was abandoned. Intensive production of wine, combined
with the acquiring of silver, enabled the Chians to exploit the markets
that were opened up by the eastern Greeks and import what was
required to support their growing population. In the Aegean generally,
but perhaps most of all in Ionia, this may be thought of as a time of
increasing specialization in production and the use of resources. Not
only Chios but Mytilene (and in due course the south Dorian cities) were

[39] D 30.

producing wine in quantity. Teos and Miletus became famous for their wool, and the tyrant Polycrates imported select livestock including Milesian sheep to improve the Samian strains. Chians dealt not only in slaves but in supplying eunuchs to Ephesus and the Persians. We learn of numerous specializations in East Greece, though not necessarily all of so early a date: sponges from Rhodes, honey from Caria and figs from Caunus, silks and raisins from Cos, resin from Colophon, textiles and mastic gum from Chios, saffron from Aegae, and the fisheries of Myus and furniture manufacture of Miletus.[40]

Herodotus (I. 142–3) insists that the twelve cities that formed the Ionian dodecapolis not only claimed for themselves the name of Ionians but established a common sanctuary of their own at Panionium (*CAH* II.2³, 782 and 802f); and he twice refers to councils held there in times of crisis (after the fall of Croesus, when Bias of Priene urged a mass emigration to Sardinia, and in the throes of the Ionian Revolt). The impression is thus created that the twelve cities had formed themselves into a league. But he also speaks in similar terms of the Dorian cities of the south-east Aegean, and there we hear nothing of any federal activity in the political sphere. The recent excavations at Panionium have yielded no trace of buildings of Archaic date (cf. *CAH* III.1², 749f.), and it seems unlikely that there was any provision there for regular meetings; and from Herodotus himself (I. 170) we learn that when Thales urged the cities of Ionia to form a federal union, the centre that he indicated was not Panionium but Teos. The notion of a Panionian league now begins to appear less rapidly apprehensible than the artistic and commercial *koine* of the wider East Greek bloc. This of course does not mean that all the cities were in amity with one another. It was normal for Miletus to be at enmity with Samos, whose situation upwind enabled her to interfere with her rival's shipping; and Chios, on the other side of Samos, tended to be friendly to Miletus and on bad terms with Erythrae on the mainland opposite. But a change of government might at any time reverse the trends; and it is doubtful whether there were any permanent commercial and political alignments between the cities of Ionia and those of Old Greece.

Attempts to give figures for the population of East Greek cities can be based on the capacity of a very few explored sites, on the number of triremes they could man in the full muster of the Ionians at Lade, and at Ephesus on the assumed number of 'thousands' (*chiliastyes*) which formed subdivisions of the reorganized tribes. On the first method fairly low populations would seem to result for the small peninsular cities (which would hardly have had any subordinate villages), and one might think that few cities would have had a population running to five figures.

[40] B 106; G 29, 136. C 10 for early Ionian trade generally.

The second gives some higher figures for the maritime states (not only 80,000, 56,000, and 48,000 for the islands of Chios, Lesbos, and Samos, but 64,000 for Miletus), while the third (if the basis is correct) would yield nearly 40,000 for Ephesus.[41] What we can believe is that from the late seventh century on the eastern Greeks were progressing rapidly in power and prosperity. Herodotus, who greatly admired the splendour of Polycrates' Samos and use of sea power, speaks of the Ionians (using the name in the broad sense) as having in earlier times been much the weakest of the ethnic divisions of the Greek people; and Thucydides implies that the Ionians had only recently advanced to greatness when Cyrus the Persian subjected Ionia, and elsewhere remarks that their command of the sea was a new thing in Cyrus' time (I. 13).

To Herodotus and Thucydides the high point came with the tyranny of Polycrates. For Samos itself archaeological evidence combines with the literary to give an impression of increasing grandeur. At the site of a prehistoric settlement by the river Imbrasus a goddess whom the Greeks identified with Hera was worshipped with a ritual bath and an altar by her sacred tree. In the eighth century a temple no less than 30 m long was built; in the second half of the seventh century it was rebuilt more monumentally and other substantial buildings were being put up, so that the sanctuary outside the city became a show-place. The dedications included pottery not only from the East Greek cities but from Corinth, Sparta, and Etruria, numerous terracotta and limestone statuettes from Cyprus, Egyptian and Near Eastern objects in ivory, stone, faience, and shell, and bronzes from Phrygia, Syria, Egypt, Assyria, and Iran and the northern nomads. The desire for grandeur, already seen in massive dedications in the sanctuary, was fulfilled when the great temple over 100 metres long (the first dipteron) was built in the second quarter of the sixth century. At the same time, occupying the key position as the eastern pivot of the least hazardous crossing of the Aegean, Samos seems to have become dominant at sea.

Polycrates had a fleet of a hundred penteconters (fifty-oared galleys), but evidently turned to the construction of the more modern and powerful triremes; in order to keep his ships secure he constructed a mole a couple of furlongs long in twenty fathoms of water, and the first ship-sheds to be mentioned in the Greek world were his. For military needs he maintained a force of a thousand archers. He dominated the islands, not refraining from indiscriminate piracy, and established a festival on Delos. Of his piracy Herodotus (III. 39) reports his dictum that he gained greater goodwill by returning to his friends what he had robbed them of than by not robbing them in the first place. He fought the Milesians and captured an expedition sent to their aid by the

---

[41] D 81, 10–12; G 29, 21–3; D 84, 229.

Mytilenaeans; he then used the prisoners to excavate a ditch outside the circuit wall of Samos. He also repelled a contingent that the Spartans sent to succour his political opponents (I. 46f, 54ff). Herodotus says that everything he turned his hand to prospered. The city of Samos was a worthy capital, with a well-sited, strong circuit wall enclosing an area about three quarters of a mile square and with an aqueduct tunnelled for a distance of 1,000 metres under the mountain crest to bring water into the city. Herodotus speaks of the engineering feats as the greatest works in existence among the Greeks. On grounds of date we can not, as he would seem to do, assign the building of the original dipteron to Polycrates (though he may have been concerned with its even larger successor), and doubts have been cast on the attribution to him of the other works and the building up of Samian sea power. It could be that, although he had to seize power by a coup, Polycrates had had a predecessor in the tyranny whose policies he was able to continue and implement.[42] But as he appears in Herodotus (and to a lesser extent Thucydides) Polycrates was a uniquely active and forceful personality; and Herodotus is believed to have resided in Samos in his youth, so he should have had good sources of information.[43]

In the generation that ended with Polycrates' death (522/21 B.C.) the stable world that the Greeks were familiar with in nearer Asia was shattered by the rising power of Cyrus the Persian. The kingdom of the Medes, pacific under the ageing Astyages, had fallen into his hands; Croesus' kingdom of Lydia was overthrown; Babylon fell in 539 B.C., and the position of Egypt began to look precarious. Herodotus (I. 122) speaks of Polycrates as conceiving the hope of ruling Ionia and the islands; and in an epoch when a ruler needed to think ahead of the march of events he no doubt calculated that by the exertion of overwhelming sea power he could build up an empire that might avail to sway the balance of power in the Aegean and beyond. His alliances, with Egypt, and then with Persia, show the scope of his ambition, which finally betrayed him into the hands of a similarly ambitious Persian governor on the Ionian mainland. Polycrates appears also as a patron of the arts and sciences, with Anacreon of Teos and Ibycus of Rhegium to provide musical entertainment at his court and a skilled doctor (Democedes of Croton) and engineer (Eupalinus of Megara) in his employ. Life had certainly become more gracious and to some extent more luxurious; but the vigorous activity of Samians and Phocaeans and the emergence of capable men of affairs such as appear in Herodotus' anecdotes should restrain us from charging the eastern Greeks with undue effeminacy at this stage.

[42] If that were the case we might assume that the predecessor was his father Aeaces.
[43] D 100; D 9; D 72; D 91.

The spirit of Odysseus lived on in Ionia; and their expansion gave the eastern Greeks an acquaintance with the cities and ways of thought of many peoples. In the north-east they came to know the customs and way of life of Scythians and other tribes and learned of the peoples of the east European forests and central Asian steppes; they had reached the Atlantic coasts and Nubia, and Babylon must have been known to some who, like Alcaeus' brother, enlisted in the service of Nebuchad-rezzar (above, p. 22). In Egypt above all they had become conscious of monumental creations on a colossal scale and of a very old and sophisticated civilization which harked back to ancient models and precedents. The stability and traditionalism of Egypt and the Near East at this time were not only impressive to the observer and intimations of the smallness and newness of the Greeks' world at home, but they will have facilitated the acquisition of oriental lore by Greek residents and travellers. That the Greeks were not content to be mere recipients of knowledge is a commonplace. But we may believe that men like Thales would not have developed their powers of observation and reasoning to the full if they had not been stimulated by the wisdom of an older world.[44] It was in the period of the East Greek expansion that the Aegean world became fully intercommunicating. Thinkers became public figures, even celebrities; though he does not appear to have written anything, posterity was well informed about Thales' thought and attainments. He was evidently versatile – otherwise he would hardly have been ranked high among the 'Seven Sages' along with men of affairs like Bias of Priene and Pittacus. But he and his disciple Anaximander set the pattern of Ionian rationalism with their endeavours to explain the world they inhabited in the light of observation and reasoned theories rather than inherited assumptions. While the Samians seem to have excelled in practical applications of scientific and technological advance, the Milesians above all took the lead in the investigation of nature in all her aspects; and study extended to beaches and clay deposits, winds, phenomena such as evaporation and condensation, magnetism, and phosphorescence, and the range of technical processes in everyday life.

Eastern Greece was the home of epic poetry, and the tradition continued long, especially in Colophon and Smyrna. In Mimnermus' elegiacs a new, more personal feeling appears in a framework of the old skills and diction. In Lesbos the habit of singing to the lyre was strong. Terpander and Arion were famed for their musical settings; and Alcaeus and Sappho introduced a lyrical genre, using the vernacular tongue and expressing their individual temperaments, the latter intimate and passionate, the former graphic and addicted to political intrigue and

[44] A 70.

35. Hecataeus' map of the world. (After *Grosser historischer Weltatlas* I
(ed. H. Bengston, et al., 1972) 12c.)

conviviality. The eastern Greeks, then, were far from lacking distinction
in poetry in the age of their expansion. But perhaps the most significant
contribution of the Ionian enlightenment was the realization of the need
to transmit the knowledge that they assembled. Though the Milesian
thinkers had a special interest in what we may call speculative physics,
the range of learned enquiry (*historiē*) came to embrace mythology and
genealogy, history, and systematic geography; and maps of the known
world were constructed, first by Anaximander, and then towards the
end of the century by Hecataeus (fig. 35). The natural vehicle for such
information was prose, and prose is not memorable unless it is written
down. It is not absolutely clear when prose writing made its first
appearance in Archaic Greece. But it has been well remarked that the
appearance of cursive forms in the script of Ionic inscriptions in the
first half of the sixth century presupposes the existence of a 'book hand'
there;[45] and when we learn that in the middle years of the century
Anaximander committed his thoughts to writing and the architects both
of the Samian dipteron and of the Ephesian Artemisium wrote books
on the subject we are entitled to speak for the first time of the emergence
of a literate culture.

[45] A 36, 57, 327.

CHAPTER 39*b*

CRETE

JOHN BOARDMAN

The burgeoning prosperity of Crete in the Geometric period continues through the seventh century. The record is clear from the archaeological evidence of its many sites and this is a record which must be respected, for there is no other. The reticence of ancient authors about this period in Cretan history stands in marked contrast with their readiness to discuss Crete's laws and society: the latter is due to Crete's distinctive practices and their alleged similarities to those of Sparta, the former to the island's comparative unimportance economically and militarily in the Classical period. Crete's society and laws will be discussed in the following section: here we deal with her archaeology and the history of her material culture.

Crete of the hundred – or ninety – cities (*Il.* II. 649; *Od.* XIX. 174) was not the only part of Greece to enjoy a wholly distinctive orientalizing culture, nourished by continued contact with Cyprus, Egypt and the Near East. But in Crete the culture is idiosyncratic and it is mainly inbred. It is expressed in a great diversity of products – painted and relief vases, jewellery, sculpture, bronzework and especially armour – and from city to city there seems to have been no less diversity in ways of life, and death.

In the later Geometric period (the second half of the eighth century and a little later) and the rest of the seventh century close on one hundred sites are known in the island.[1] The Late Geometric is the period of maximum activity, it seems, though the fact that nearly two fifths of the sites seem not to survive far into the seventh century could well be illusory since the later material is not always easily identified or it has yet to be found. Equally, the fact that more than one in five of the Archaic sites seems a new foundation may mean little: many of them had been occupied in the Bronze Age and their Geometric cemeteries may yet be located. The more important sites whose archaeological record spans our period are Cnossus, Prinias, Arkades, Gortyn, Drerus, Kavousi and Praesus. The new sites of the seventh century, or those which seem to have taken on a new lease of life, are Axus, Lyttus, Lato,

[1] H 25, 415–17; D 148, 316–44; A 54.

Kato Syme. The cave sanctuaries on Ida and Dicte (Psychro) are still visited and it is notable that several of the seventh-century sites have been detected from their sanctuaries rather than their cemeteries. The practice of constructing more substantial sanctuary buildings and of depositing a greater variety of votive objects has drawn attention to these sites more readily than to houses, walls, or tombs.

For most of the sites mentioned or known the archaeological evidence peters out by the end of the seventh century or in the early sixth. The change is dramatic and not readily explicable, but this was the turning point in Crete's fortunes and it determines the need to discuss here first the island's orientalizing heyday, and separately its decline.

Crete's prosperity lay only partly in her material wealth, in land, metals and men. In common with other areas of Archaic Greece her good fortune was to no small degree determined by her associations with the rest of the Greek world, and especially with lands outside Greece, to the east and with Egypt. The crossing to North Africa was an easy one, and from the east the route via the coastline of southern Anatolia, past Rhodes and the Dodecanese, led as readily to Crete as through the Cyclades islands and to central Greece. It is hard to say how much of the trade with Crete was conducted in Cretan ships, or indeed how much could at this date be dignified by the title 'trade'. The Cretan who knows nothing of the sea was an old paradox (Alcman fr. 164 Page), though no longer so paradoxical by the time of Ephorus (Strabo 481). The Cretan sailors of the Hymn to Pythian Apollo (lines 392–9) sailed to sandy Pylus for business and profit (ἐπὶ πρῆξιν καὶ χρήματα), and the arch-wanderer Odysseus readily pretends to Crete as his home when he arrives on Ithaca (*Od.* XIX. 173ff). Crete was nearly as populous as Homer describes it in the poet's day as it must have been in Odysseus', and the 'Cretan' Odysseus waxes eloquent about the fine living, love of the sea and fighting, piracy and raids on Egypt (*Od.* XIX. 199ff). Far later, under Rome, it was to be a haven for pirates, and the disguised Demeter of the Homeric Hymn (line 122) claims that pirates brought her from Crete.[2] If the Eusebian thalassocracy list is in any way historical we might have expected a place for Crete.

Within the Greek world there is little enough to demonstrate close involvement between Crete and other states. The island stood culturally and geographically closest to the Dorian islands of Melos, Thera and Rhodes, and this shows in pottery styles. Cretans led by Entimus joined Rhodians in the foundation of Gela in Sicily in 688 B.C. (Thuc. VI. 4.3) and the pottery of Cretan style at Gela seems to hail from the south-central

[2] A 21. The Eusebian date for the 'Carians', who cause trouble in justificatory accounts of the list, would in fact suit orientalizing Crete. But see A 37, 252–3.

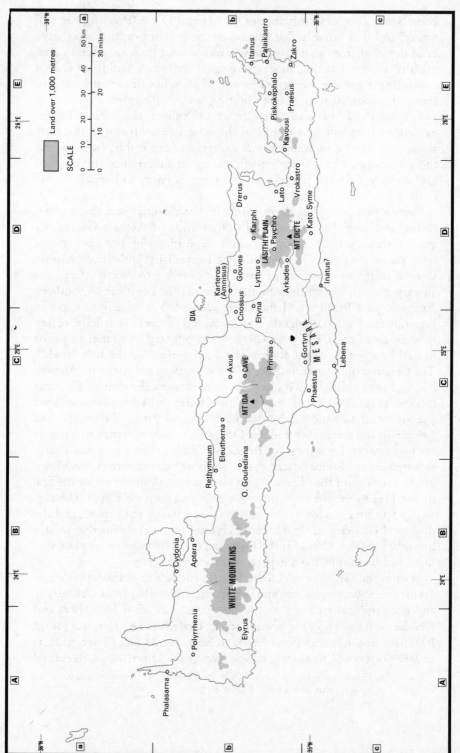

Map 13. Crete.

areas of the island.[3] And it was a Cretan purple-fisher, Corobius of Itanus (Hdt. IV. 151–3), who led the Therans south to settle on the shores of Cyrenaica in about 639 B.C. The story which introduces a Cretan princess of Axus as mother of Battus, first Theran king of Cyrene, might indicate Cretan involvement in the colonizing, for which we shall observe further evidence. The same story involves a Theran merchant, Themison, living in Axus. The special relationship between Crete and Delphi has been mentioned in an earlier volume (III. 1², 778) and is further explored in this (pp. 305ff). Delphi remains one of the few Greek sites of the seventh century to receive Cretan goods.

A rather specialist market for orientalizing metalwork and armour from Crete need not, however, indicate any especially close trading or other links with the receiving areas. Shields of the type made for the Idaean Cave[4] reached the Greek sanctuaries of Delphi and Dodona and, surprisingly, Miletus. More practical pieces of armour are found in Delphi and Olympia, but some of the bronzes of central Italy, notably the stand from the Bernardini tomb at Praeneste, closely match both work found in Olympia and the tympanum which was made, it seems, especially for dedication in the Idaean Cave in Crete.[5] The island has been suspected of being an important link in the routes from the east to Italy and an earlier generation of scholars saw Cretan vases in several Greek colonies in the west, but most of these identifications are now discredited.[6]

Other orientalizing studios in Crete may offer evidence for more far-reaching cultural influence in the Greek world. The Cnossian 'guild' is identified at the end of the ninth century but probably does not long survive the eighth century.[7] The workshop for the Idaean Cave shields seems to have continued in production until around the mid seventh century. A more unusual phenomenon is the appearance of imitations of eastern goods in clay in central and south Crete of the middle of the seventh century (fig. 36). Some burials at Arkades resemble nothing so much as contemporary burials on the Euphrates, and this is the time, this the area, in which Greeks for the first time adopt the eastern practice of writing down their law codes.[8] All this suggests influence borne not by trade or even by travelling craftsmen but by immigrant families.[9]

During the first quarter of the seventh century the 'Daedalic' style of minor relief sculpture, expressed mainly in mould-made terracottas, appears in Greece for the first time and it seems probable that its origin was Near Eastern (Syria) and that the place in which it was first adopted,

[3] H 25, 257, n. 4.   [4] D 133; D 104A, 138–40; A 7, 58–60.
[5] D 111, 17; E 233, 179–80.   [6] C 42; H 25, 194–5, cf. 370; C 46, 268–9.
[7] CAH III.1², 776. Pace D 135, 172–4. A 7, 56–7.
[8] A 36, 309–16.   [9] D 111, 18–23; A 7, 60; D 124; H 51, 173–4.

36. Clay vessel (the bowl partly reconstructed). Mid seventh century B.C.
Width 15·7 cm. (Heidelberg University 59/1; after D 124, pl. 7.)

certainly the place in which it was most vigorously later developed, was Crete. It was rendered mainly in clay, for plaques or on relief clay vases (pithoi) in the production of which Crete had enjoyed a long tradition, but also in gold jewellery, reviving techniques long forgotten in Greece, in ivory, and in stone works which bid to represent Greece's first major sculptural style.[10] All this is best displayed in the island, and at Karteros (Amnisus), Gortyn and Prinias we find the stone sculpture applied decoratively to buildings, in a manner which anticipates the monumental architectural statuary of the later Archaic period. These works, and examples of seated or standing figures in the round, are found in Crete to the very end of the century. By that time the new, truly monumental styles of life-size and larger statuary, executed in hard white marble rather than the soft limestone used in Crete, had appeared in the Cyclades. The new style is that ascribed by ancient writers to the Cretan Daedalus[11] (if we distinguish him from his Bronze Age namesake and wizard, as they did not) but Crete had not the material for the new fashion, though we may well believe that Crete's strong tradition in statuary and in creating the tools of the craft helped determine the work and styles of the new studios in the marble islands, Naxos and Paros.

The Idaean Cave shields were impractical, highly decorated objects, intended for dedication. Other Cretan studios, working in a more purely Greek style from soon after the middle of the seventh century to the early sixth, produced equally decorative pieces of real armour[12] – hoplite helmets whose origins may be traced back to the eighth century in the island and which offered rather less protection for the front of the face than the Corinthian; two-piece bell corselets; and the miscalled *mitrai*, semicircular plaques which appear to have been suspended from a belt (but not the corselet) to protect the belly. This is distinctive armour, more elaborately decorated than any from other parts of Greece, and

[10] H 19, 13–15; H 47; D 112; D 111; H 67; D 101.
[11] H 60, nos. 74–142; D 111, 5–13; D 104A, 158–9; D 106.
[12] D 126.

some of it was taken to the mainland and imitated there. Its production argues an interest in martial arts which Cretans must have practised mainly on each other. That their society and legislation had been designed to promote military efficiency had been observed in antiquity (Plato, *Leg.* 626b). Cretan mercenaries were archers, not hoplites, and these served Sparta in the Messenian Wars, Lyttus (a Spartan 'colony') and Aptera being named as two of the sources (Paus. IV. 8.3; 19.4; 20.8). Mid-seventh-century dedications of miniature bronze armour at Bassae, near Mt Hira, which was the setting for a long siege during the Second Messenian War, are matched in Crete (at Gortyn) and may attest Cretan mercenary participation.[13] This was a continuing role for them in the Classical period and they may be credited with the development of a particularly effective type of composite bow and the popularizing of the heavy barbed and tanged arrowhead which figures on later Cretan coins and rings.[14]

An important find of armour,[15] dedicated in a shrine at Arkades and datable by style to the later seventh century, may be evidence for a military event of some importance. It includes five helmets, eight corselets and sixteen *mitrai*. Several carry dedicatory inscriptions naming the donor who took or seized ($\mathring{\eta}\lambda\epsilon = \epsilon\mathring{\imath}\lambda\epsilon$) the piece in battle. This suggests local warfare with the dedication of booty by the victors, presumably the men of Arkades, though an epigraphical peculiarity (double circle for omega) is otherwise attested so far only at nearby Lyttus. Decorated Cretan armour of this type has also been found at Axus, Drerus, Palaikastro and Onythe Goulediana (and perhaps Rethymnum) and was carried to Delphi and Olympia.

The rich patchwork of the archaeological record of Archaic Crete gives an impression of vigorous independence for the main centres but no intense or damaging rivalries until, perhaps, the later seventh century. The variety is expressed chiefly in artefacts and manners of burial. We still know little of the cities in the west, though Cydonia will figure later in a historical episode. The site at Onythe Goulediana, possibly the ancient Phallanna, has been more productive of Archaic finds, notably in the elaborate (for this period) architecture of a house of around 600 B.C. (fig. 37), its store rooms packed with relief pithoi and other vessels.[16] The cities around Mt Ida are of more moment – Eleutherna and Axus to the north of the massif both yield important sculpture and the latter a sanctuary of Aphrodite with a remarkable range of Daedalic terracottas which conflate eastern and Greek views of the goddess, as well as bronze armour.[17]

[13] D 154.   [14] H 69, 142–8; H 16, 227, fig. 233.
[15] D 126.   [16] D 150.
[17] D 112, 37; D 142; D 153A.

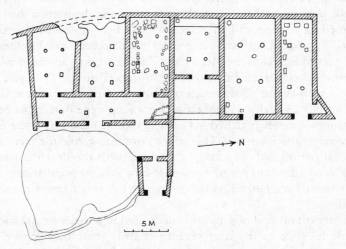

37. Houses at Goulediana. Seventh century B.C. (After D 150, 1956, 227, fig. 1.)

38. Stele from Prinias. Second half of seventh century B.C. Height 48·5 cm. (Heraklion Museum 396; after D 139A, B 11; cf. H 19, fig. 252.2.)

South-east of Ida Prinias and Gortyn are the best known sites: Prinias for its temple and incised stelai (fig. 38),[18] Gortyn for its acropolis temple of a goddess assimilated to Athena, and the altar and votives found lower on the east slope.[19] Gortyn may have dominated the rich Mesara plain much as Phaestus did in the Bronze Age. Its port was at Lebena and a late sixth-century inscription records a treaty between the towns. It was also the home of the seventh-century poet and lawgiver Thaletas.[20]

Archaic Cnossus is a city of the dead, and we know its Archaic history as we know its Geometric, from the rich cemeteries in the neighbourhood of the city.[21] Most are composed of reused Bronze Age graves and if there was any new tomb digging subsequently it may have been confined to the Protogeometric period. The cremations and grave goods are packed into fine pithoi which display the distinctive Cnossian orientalizing styles, notably the polychrome which are unique in appearance in the Greek world.[22] Some note is taken of the new styles of Central Greece, including the black-figure technique of Corinthian vase-painters, but the most distinguished work of the seventh century is in a purely local tradition.[23] Since very close dating is not possible the relative frequency of burials in different periods is hard to gauge accurately, but maximum use of the cemeteries appears to centre on the late eighth and early seventh centuries, then to decline with hardly any burials or other finds assignable to the last quarter of the century. Karteros (Amnisus), port of Cnossus, is also a source of Archaic architectural sculpture,[24] and there are seventh-century tombs at Gouves, a little farther east, inland.[25]

Between the main north–south route in the island and Lasithi, to the east, Lyttus is the major city, impressive as a site, but the finds have yet to match its apparent importance in later sources.[26] To the south Arkades (Afrati) is the source of the armour already discussed and its cemetery presents a variety of burial types difficult to match in any other Greek town of this date: circular tholoi for cremations, rectangular built tombs for inhumations, an 'urn field' with some burials covered with upturned vessels, mainly above ground, in what may be an eastern manner, and well defined cremation platforms.[27]

Kato Syme lies to the east, site of a sanctuary of Hermes Dendrites and Aphrodite, source of remarkable orientalizing and Archaic bronzes,[28] and on the coast at Tsoutsouros, probably the ancient Inatus, is an important cave sanctuary of Eileithyia.[29]

[18] D 147; D 139A; H 19, 14, 165. [19] D 143; D 153. [20] *Ins. Cret.* Gortyn no. 63.
[21] D 126A, 16–22. [22] D 108. [23] D 105; D 104; D 110.
[24] D 145; D 20, 211–12. [25] D 136. [26] D 137; A 54.
[27] D 141; H 51, 171–3. [28] D 138. [29] D 102.

Around the Lasithi plain the towns seem to have declined, and with them the attention paid to the cave at Psychro. To the east Drerus, inveterate enemy of Lyttus and therefore friend of Cnossus, is flourishing[30] and Lato becomes important, although the buildings and plan of its agora, once dated to the Archaic period, have now been shown to be later.[31] Scattered Archaic finds[32] suggest that settlement may have been well distributed in minor villages though not populous. Farther east the Eteo-Cretans are the only island community whose substantial continuing prosperity into the sixth century can be demonstrated, as we shall see.

The archaeological record of virtually all the sites named barely outlasts the seventh century.[33] On many the finds appear to dry up well before 600 and there is no major site which offers a continuous record through the sixth century and into the fifth. In an island so carefully explored and heavily excavated this observation cannot be dismissed as an accident of survival or discovery, but we are at a loss to explain the massive depopulation and possible abandonment of sites which it seems to imply. The find of armour at Arkades (see above) may indicate internal discord and it has been suggested that record of a war between Cnossus and Sparta, possibly in aid of Sparta's colony Lyttus, is of this period or soon after.[34] But it is generally placed much later, when Spartan intervention would be more plausible. At any rate, these military fracas cannot provide the whole explanation and a hypothetical deterioration in trade could not have reduced such a naturally rich island to this pass. While the rest of the Greek world, and even centres like Naxos, Samos and Rhodes, wax rich and occupy the historical and archaeological records, Crete falls into a silence which we can only attribute to some unknown natural disaster, climatic or physiological. Instead of the many towns with teeming cemeteries and well-visited shrines we have isolated indications of life, not by any means impoverished, but extremely scant.

Thus, at Cnossus, in the sanctuary of Demeter there is a sharp falling off in the number of votives, which does not pick up again until the construction of the late fifth-century temples,[35] and there are few finds from occupation and tombs though these include Athenian pottery and a fine bronze vessel (fig. 39).[36] South central Crete seems to have been an area last affected, to judge from the architectural sculpture at Prinias,

[30] *Ins. Cret.* Dreros no. 1 (3rd century A.D.); D 130; A 54; D 115–17; D 156; D 146 (251–3 for a stone gorgoneion decorating the temple in the sixth century).
[31] D 119; D 120; D 130; D 156, 90–3; A 54.	[32] D 114.
[33] On the decline see Dunbabin, 195–7 on D 113. D 132, 153. And for sixth-century finds in the island, D 148, 327–44; D 129; D 103; D 105.
[34] Paus. II. 21.3; E 162, 67; D 126A.
[35] D 109, 182.	[36] D 105.

39. Bronze '*kothon*' from near Cnossus. Late sixth century B.C. Diameter
21·6 cm (Heraklion Museum 2460; after D 105, 28–9.)

40. Bronze plaque showing Hermes Dendrites, from the sanctuary at Kato Syme.
Late seventh century B.C. (After D 138, 1974,
pl. 167a; *Arch. Rep.* 1974–5, 28, fig. 53.)

the armour at Arkades and the attractive bronze appliqués from Kato
Syme (fig. 40), which run into the sixth century. But the final generation
of major artists in Archaic Crete sought work elsewhere – the sculptors
Dipoinos and Scyllis, 'sons of Daedalus', in the Peloponnese;[37]
Chersiphron of Cnossus and his son Metagenes, at Ephesus;[38] all these
in the second quarter of the sixth century.

In the west Phalasarna only begins to offer finds with the sixth century
but they are slight;[39] yet it is in the west that we can find historical record
for an event, the character of which may typify the troubled state of
the island. In about 524 some Samians, expelled after an abortive revolt
against Polycrates in which they were helped by Sparta, moved off to
terrorize Siphnos and then, according to Herodotus (III. 57–9), turned
to Crete whence they intended to expel the Zacynthians but instead
settled in Cydonia. There they stayed five years, building temples,
including that of Dictynna (of which a little of the early sixth century
has been found[40]); but were defeated at sea by Aeginetans with the help
of Cretans and reduced to slavery. The story of intervention in Crete
by men from a western Greek island (Zacynthos), Ionia and Aegina,[41]
may be commentary enough on the island's condition in the sixth
century.

It is in the east of the island only that some measure of continuing
prosperity can be observed. This is the home of the Eteo-Cretans,
Minoan stock, no doubt, retaining their non-Greek language but totally
Hellenized in culture and, apparently, religion. Early stories of the birth
and nurture of Zeus in Crete had centred on Lyttus (Hes. *Theog.* 477)
and it is likely that the so-called Dictaean Cave at Psychro had been
associated with the story,[42] as was the Idaean Cave to the west. Both
cave sanctuaries were still visited in the Archaic period, notably the
Idaean where the orientalizing bronze shields and the tympanum recall
stories of the Kouretes clashing their arms to drown the cries of the
infant god. By the sixth century, however, the finds in the caves
diminish and it is in the east, at Palaikastro, in Eteo-Cretan territory,
that a temple of Dictaean Zeus is built, and decorated with elaborate
terracotta revetments in the later sixth century.[43] It is here that the
famous later Hymn to Dictaean Zeus was found.[44] The area of
Palaikastro is rather bleak and hilly but this is not true of all east Crete,
and Praesus, the main Eteo-Cretan city, is set in rolling fertile hills and
valleys. Praesus too has yielded a number of sixth-century finds, some
of high merit, including major architectural terracotta sculpture.[45] The

[37] H 60, nos. 321–7.   [38] Pliny, *NH* 7.125; Vitruvius 10.2.12.
[39] D 157.   [40] D 159.   [41] Also Strabo 376; Plato, *Leg.* 707e.
[42] D 104A, ch. 1; A 71.   [43] D 127, 41–2.   [44] D 123; D 160.
[45] D 107; D 122; D 127, 41–2, 56–9 (bronzes); D 149.

port at Itanus, a site with alleged Phoenician connexions and home of Corobius who led the Therans to Africa, has something to offer in the seventh century.[46]

For other sixth-century activity we look south. The island's part in the colonizing of Cyrenaica has been remarked and a Cretan sherd was found at Aziris, the first, short-lived settlement on the African mainland.[47] At Taucheira, a colony founded soon after Cyrene, near modern Benghazi, Cretan pottery is found in a level of about 590–565 B.C., which is remarkable since it is rare enough on the island itself and not otherwise exported, so it indicates a continuing interest.[48] In mid-sixth-century Cyrene the reformer Demonax composed one of his three new tribes of Peloponnesians (no doubt Spartan) and Cretans (Hdt. IV. 161). And in the 470s *stasis* in Cnossus prompted Ergoteles, an Olympic victor hymned by Pindar (*Ol.* XII), to flee to Himera in Sicily. Emigration may be another factor or symptom in the decline of Archaic Crete.

At the very end of the Archaic period there are signs of more sophisticated life and art with the relief grave stelai found at Eleutherna, Eltyna and Rethymnum.[49] Aeginetan coins appear in the island but Crete does not strike its own coinage until the fifth century, and in the Archaic period tripods, cauldrons and spits (or corresponding weights of metal) are its currency.[50] Slowly the island creeps back into the light of recorded history, but never again to dominate and influence the Aegean world as it had in the Bronze Age and in the seventh century B.C. Its history had been long and brilliant. It is easy to understand why Cretan scholars bridle still at Herodotus' account of the Cretans' alleged absence from the Greek battle line at Salamis, and his explanation for it, that the Delphic oracle had reminded them how they had suffered at Minos' hands for helping Menelaus (VII. 168–71).[51]

---

[46] D 118.
[47] C 231, 151.
[48] C 232, 14, 78–9; D 233, 36–7, 73.
[49] D 139; D 103.
[50] A 36, 313; D 140, 167–8; H 48, 79.
[51] D 155.

CHAPTER 39c

CRETAN LAWS AND SOCIETY

R. F. WILLETTS

The distinctive achievements of Cretan civilization in the colonization period, based within a framework of early urbanization and of alphabetic literacy, owed much to the legacies of a famous past. Though it is not possible to present these influences in detail, our ancient sources illustrate their prevalence and their stimulus towards a remarkable renaissance, which once more allowed the island to make abiding contributions to Greek and European cultural history.

Opinion differed in antiquity as to whether Homer taught others the art of framing lies in the right way. However, the considerable evidence now available to us from archaeological exploration and epigraphic sources, confirms the correctness of Homeric descriptions of Crete as an island of many cities. Similarly, the discovery of pre-alphabetic Bronze Age scripts has brought a fresh significance to the familiar passage of the *Odyssey* (XIX. 172–9) describing Crete as thickly populated, with ninety cities including Cnossus, with a mixture of languages, and naming Achaeans, Eteocretans, Cydonians, Pelasgians and also Dorians with their three tribes. The possibility that this description may really apply to prehistoric times is supported by an ancient tradition of a Dorian incursion into Crete which preceded the so-called 'Dorian invasion' of the mainland.[1] If there is a genuine substance in this tradition it could be that some Dorians had indeed followed Achaean settlers into Crete in the later Bronze Age. For it seems to be the case that Dorians normally possessed themselves of mainland areas and islands already settled by Greek speakers. They were not, as compared with earlier arrivals, in the habit of taking over places which had been occupied by older indigenous peoples.[2]

Despite the internecine struggles between the city-states of Crete which increasingly dominated the history of the island in Classical and Hellenistic times, there is an emphasis in the writings of philosophers and historians, and especially by Aristotle in the *Politics*, of a common

[1] *CAH* II.2³, 675–7, 689; D 162, 131–7. The possibility is controversial. Cf. A 12, 99 and 524, n. 12.

[2] A 47, 239.

unity, indeed of a specific Cretan constitution which could properly be compared and contrasted with the Spartan. It is clear from the history of the Cretan *Koinon* that this abiding concept of unity and solidarity contrasted with the separatist conflicts even of Hellenistic times; and equally clear that this concept was based upon strong internal traditions which could have originated at a time earlier than the establishment of a common Dorian heritage.[3] In Aristotle's opinion, although the Cretan form of constitution approximated to the Spartan and was, in a few particulars, not inferior, it was for the most part less polished. The Spartan constitution seemed, and was said, to have been copied in most respects from the Cretan: it was generally true that the old was less perfected than the new. He then goes on to report the tradition that Spartan institutions were not Dorian but pre-Dorian, established in Crete originally by Minos, received from the previous inhabitants by the Spartan colony of Lyttus and thence passed to Lycurgus when he visited Crete. This also was the reason why the laws of Minos were still in force among the subject-population of Crete (Arist. *Pol.* 1271b20–33; cf. Hdt. 1. 65).

Oral tradition certainly played a part in the sphere of law, in the sense that Spartan, Cretan, perhaps also Athenian youths learnt their laws by heart. The writing down of early Greek law has analogies with the writing down of epic poetry, because both respond to the same kind of climate of cultural history.[4] Legal codification has a prehistory antedating public records on stone. It is relevant in this context to remind ourselves that it was verse rather than prose that was still being cultivated in the educational system of Crete when historians, orators and pamphleteers had already fashioned a prose medium in Ionia and Attica.[5] As J. W. Headlam properly observed, in Greece alone of all European races the highest political and literary achievements came at a time when the introduction of writing was so recent that law had not had time completely to supersede primitive custom. Greek cities in their highest prosperity still retained many of the usages peculiar to the tribal communities from which they had sprung.[6]

Certain factors operated in favour of a peculiarly Cretan conservatism. There was a general trend toward the codification of law in the Greek world in the course of the seventh century B.C. This remarkable inno-

---

[3] D 165, 143–8.

[4] Cf. A 51, Introduction and especially the caution expressed at lxi, n. 1, containing the remark relevant to the point made above that 'they [i.e. the *Iliad* and *Odyssey*] owe to their use of writing both their large-scale coherence and their subtlety, qualities in which no known oral poem has begun to equal them'. On the novel phenomenon of Greeks using the recently acquired alphabet for serious purposes related to intellectual influences from the east into Crete in the seventh century see D 111, 23.   [5] D 161, 5–6; Strabo 482; cf. Heraclid. fr. 15.

[6] D 125.

vation[7] began, not on the mainland, but in the Greek colonies, in the western colonies first of all, which were both more distant and less accessible than the eastern. One cause of the development might have been prompted by the need to provide a single code of law for colonists who originated from different cities with different systems of customary law. Hence the appearance of a whole series of famed lawgivers including Zaleucus in Achaean Locris, Charondas in Ionian Catana, Diocles in Dorian Syracuse. The laws of Zaleucus and Charondas were commonly considered to be the oldest written Greek laws and they were probably issued in the first half of the seventh century B.C. Some western codes found their way into eastern Greece, such for instance as that of Charondas in the island of Cos. In certain cities of Asia Minor and the islands there were native lawgivers like Pittacus of Mytilene. Others, such as Lycurgus of Sparta, Dracon of Athens and Philolaus of Corinth produced codes (unwritten, of course, in Sparta) for mainland cities.[8]

The lawgivers were traditionally reputed to have travelled in search of information about customary and written law. Thus, Zaleucus and Lycurgus were supposed to have visited Crete and other places. These awesome early lawgivers were looked upon as inspired, their laws as sacrosanct if not divine. In fact, a reluctance to alter or to criticize them must have stemmed from a widespread belief in their divine origin.[9]

Other Cretan innovations in this period influenced the Greek mainland. Thus, it may be said that the work of the Cretan Thaletas and his school contributed to the fusion of the dance with the song and metre of aristocratic choral lyric. Thaletas, born either at Elyrus or Cnossus or Gortyn, flourished in the seventh century B.C. He was said to have visited Sparta, on the advice of the Delphic oracle, to cure a plague with his music. There his musical reforms were so radical as to promote an artistic revolution. They included the elaboration of the Cretan *hyporchema*, a mimetic dance formerly associated with the cult of Cronus and the Titans, of Leto and Cretan Zeus, and, quite probably, the Cretic and Paeonic metres. The Paean itself was similar to the *hyporchema*, traditionally Cretan in origin and also connected with Thaletas. Semi-legendary but nevertheless historical, the poet and prophet Epimenides played a comparable role as a pioneer in adapting the ritual arts of an earlier Cretan religion to new forms and functions. Epimenides apparently made a visit to Athens with the purpose of introducing purificatory rites developed from Cretan cathartic practices. His legendary association with Solon effected religious reforms perhaps designed to curtail the religious rites of women in a way that is

---

[7] Cf. G 16, 26 on the very exceptional circumstances that caused the European codes to be written down.   [8] A 8, 67–71.

[9] A 8, 75.

illustrated in early Cretan legislation.[10] There was some decline of artistic activity in the sixth century B.C. in Crete itself, but Cretan artists were working abroad at this time (see pp. 230–2).

What is most impressive, considering the accidents of time and chance, is that the early Cretan alphabetic script is impressively exemplified by the fragmentary pieces of legal documents which have survived from some 10 per cent of the cities of the island in this bustling period of renaissance activity. Leaving aside the great fifth-century B.C. Code of Gortyn and other contemporary legal documents from this city, there are also fifth-century remains of legal codes from Eltyna and Lyttus. More considerable portions have survived, perhaps from the late sixth century B.C., from Eleutherna and Axus. Some pieces of still earlier legislation are available from Gortyn, Prinias, Lyttus, Cnossus and perhaps (earliest of all) from Drerus.[11] Recovery of similar precious evidence continues and the monumental corpus of *Inscriptiones Creticae* I–IV (1935–50) by Professor M. Guarducci has been most recently supplemented by the publication of novel and important texts.[12]

The Law Code of Gortyn is bound to be the principal focus of any discussion of early Cretan laws and society. It is significant that this singular document is not associated with a lawgiver, reminding us that Crete was not a colony but a centre of pilgrimage for legal inspiration. Despite the early legal fragments from various cities, ancient respect for Crete as the home of good laws did not derive from these documentary sources but from that older basis of tradition already mentioned. Plato (*Leg.* 624) tells us that the Cretans called Zeus their lawgiver and that Minos, like his brother, Rhadamanthys, was inspired by Zeus. Aristotle confirmed the reality behind this philosophic mythology when he explained that the laws of Minos were still observed among the subject population of Crete. Though exact explanation of this remark is not possible, it does indicate the possibility of some traditional strands deriving from a framework of law in Bronze Age times deeply enough entrenched in the later historical institutions to have influenced Dorian legislation and actually to have played a part in the social life of the serfs who were descended from the older populations of the island.

The Law Code of Gortyn is inscribed in twelve columns upon a circular wall which supported the structure of a theatre perhaps built in the first century B.C., although the stones of the inscription had

[10] D 162, 311–12.

[11] A 36, 310 and the comment: 'In nearly all cases the codes were inscribed on walls, either of temples or of other public buildings, and their survival is mainly due to this, since old wall-blocks were always useful for later rebuilding.'

[12] In particular see the various papers concerned with the Spensithios Decree: D 128; D 152; D 126, 47–9. Also *Kadmos* 11 (1972) 96–8; 13 (1974) 48–57; 14 (1975) 8–47; *ZPE* 9 (1972) 102–3; 13 (1974) 265–75; *Studii Clasice* 14 (1972) 7–15.

belonged to an older building which might have been a law-court. Each of the columns is about 1·5 m high and is cut upon four layers of stone; the length of the inscription is about 9 m; and each column, except the last, has from 53 to 56 lines of writing, the whole comprising a text of some 600 lines. This 'Queen of Inscriptions', though not a code in the strict sense of the word, is often described as the first European law-code; and it is the only one of its kind to have survived from ancient Greece. The document is inscribed in an archaic alphabet of eighteen letters including Ϝ (*digamma*). The non-Phoenician signs *Φ*, *X* and *Ψ* had not been introduced and *Ξ* was not used. The sounds of *φ*, *χ* were not distinguished from *π* and *κ*; *ψ* and *ξ* were represented by *πς* and *κς*. The letters *Z*, *H* and *Ω* were also not in use and were represented by *ΔΔ*, *E* and *O*. Individual letters are precisely inscribed and represent highly developed forms of the old Gortyn alphabet. See fig. 41.

The writing is *boustrophedon*, the first line of each column going from right to left. There are occasional gaps in the inscription where the engraver avoided an uneven surface of the stone, and occasional corrections of mistakes in cutting letters. Most of the inscription was apparently done by the same engraver except for the concluding portion (XI. 24ff), where there is evidence of the work of a different hand and where various supplementary provisions begin to be added. The Archaic system of paragraphing[13] which was apparently current in Crete – at Drerus, for instance – by the seventh century B.C. had ceased to be in use by the end of the following century. New sections are normally specified by means of asyndeton; emphatically new sections are also indicated by a *vacat* at so many points as to suggest a regular practice; and, although a *vacat* does occur for non-linguistic reasons, asyndeton can produce a *vacat*.[14] The Code is admirably inscribed and preserved. Its style is simple and direct, each regulation stated as a conditional sentence in the third person, the protasis containing the assumed facts, the apodosis the legal consequences or provisions.

The general state of the alphabet, forms of the letters and the *boustrophedon* style would not be inconsistent with a sixth-century B.C. dating. However, the precision and regularity of the writing seem to indicate a later date. It is also true that all our related evidence is such as to make highly speculative any effort at exact dating of Cretan inscriptions before the fifth century B.C. Only the letter forms may serve as a basis of judgement, qualified by the knowledge gained from ample fifth-century documentation that the Cretan alphabet was, like so much

---

[13] Inscriptions were written *boustrophedon*, beginning from right to left, but it was the practice to begin each new clause from right to left. If the final line of one clause ran from right to left, the first line of a new clause would also run from right to left and there would be two lines of continuous retrograde script.   [14] Further details in D 164, 4.

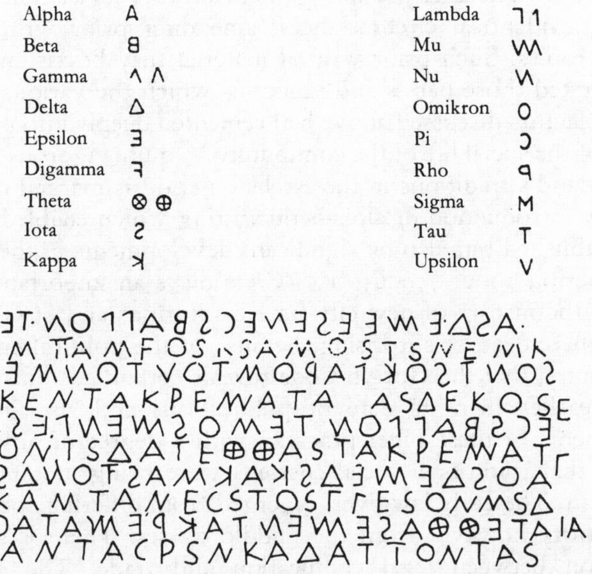
Alpha
Beta
Gamma
Delta
Epsilon
Digamma
Theta
Iota
Kappa
Lambda
Mu
Nu
Omikron
Pi
Rho
Sigma
Tau
Upsilon

ι. palmula αἰ δὲ μὲ εἶεν ἐπιβάλλοντε-
ς, τᾶς Ϝοικίας οἵτινές κ'
ἴοντι ὁ κλᾶρος, τούτονς ἔ-
κεν τὰ κρέματα. vac. αἰ δέ κ' οἱ
ἐπιβάλλοντες οἱ μὲν λεί-
οντι. δατε͂θθαι τὰ κρέματ-
α, οἱ δὲ μέ, δικάκσαι τὸν δι-
καστὰν ἐπὶ τοῖλ λείονσι δ-
ατε͂θθαι ἔ͂μεν τὰ κρέματα π-
άντα πρίν κα δάττονται. vac.

And if there should be no kinsmen, those of the household composing the *klaros* are to have the property. And if some of the next-of-kin wish to divide the property while others do not, the judge shall decree that all the property shall be in the power of those who wish to divide until they divide it.

41. The Gortyn alphabet, a passage from the Code (Column V, lines 25–34), its transcription and translation. (After D 164, 5, 43, pl. 5.)

else in Cretan manners, conservative in its retention of old forms and methods, paralleled by retention of the *boustrophedon* style through the fifth century B.C. Hence the general current agreement that the Code was a fifth-century document, with a preference by some scholars for a date not earlier than about 450 B.C., by others (perhaps rightly) for a date about 480–460 B.C.

Nevertheless, if it were possible to be more certain about the date, it would not follow that this would coincide with the first publication of a code. Though the legislation is complete in itself, the document is not a code in the common sense of that term as a systematic collection of statutes or laws so arranged as to obviate overlap or inconsistency. The Gortyn Code represents a codification, not of law, but of laws, with a significant formal arrangement common to a number of ancient codes, prompted by a need to group together statutory legislation relevant to similar or identical circumstances, amending prior written law on various topics. Such prior written material may be assumed to have incorporated those habits and sanctions which the various traditional cultural factors discussed above had cemented deeply into much earlier phases of the social life of the community. A quite vigorous renaissance of the island's traditions in the Archaic period is marked not only by the early introduction of alphabetic writing which enabled legislation to be published but also by significant developments in the Cretan art of the period about 750–650 B.C. Crete plays an important role once more in the history of new city-state institutions and of Greek art.

It is therefore not surprising, because of the political environment of the times, that the Gortyn Code reveals certain customs and habits of life earlier than its date of publication; and also incorporates amendments of these older practices with a degree of novelty which suggest that traditional social customs were being modified by state legislation. The early lawgivers emerged from differing social groups, the majority however from the middle classes. There is an obvious connexion between legal codification and trade. The commercial expansion of the period had a stimulating effect upon the aristocratic governments of Cretan cities. Although no lawgiver is associated with the Gortyn Code or other legal fragments and no merchant class developed to disturb radically the long sustained rule of land-owning aristocracies, indicating that trade was kept within limits, there is still a connexion between coinage and trade; and it may be more than a coincidence that Gortyn was among the first Cretan cities to have a coinage. For the Code enables us to gain some insight into the consequences of the introduction of a money economy, no matter how modest the scale, upon the pattern of social life in a period of change.

The Dorian communities of Crete maintained, as elsewhere, their familiar tribal organization which helped to reinforce those bonds of kinship which were of such importance generally in the social life of ancient Greece. In Crete, as in Sparta and other areas, the original populations had become tribute-paying serfs, divided out, like the land which they cultivated, and belonging inalienably to the *klaroi* or ancestral estates. Whereas in Sparta a dual monarchy persisted, in Crete there developed separate city-states with authority over modest territories; and the early monarchies had been abolished as leadership in war was transferred to aristocratic magistrates (Arist. *Pol.* 1272a14–25). The principal officials were known as *kosmoi* or collectively as the *kosmos*, drawn from certain clans (*ibid.*, confirmed by the Code v. 4–6), forming privileged hereditary groups. There was a Council of elders consisting of former magistrates and a general Assembly of citizens, which seems to have had no great authority, meeting occasionally to ratify decisions of magistrates and Council. The earliest inscriptions from Gortyn demonstrate that the personal responsibility of state officials for their state duties, which is characteristic of government in Greek antiquity, was established in Cretan cities before the sixth century B.C.[15] Early in the following century divisions of administrative responsibility are clarified by Gortynian evidence. The *ksenios kosmos* (aliens' magistrate) was concerned with foreigners, resident aliens and others, such as freedmen, not included in the tribal organizations of the free citizen class. A secretary, or recorder, to the *ksenios kosmos*, is mentioned in the Gortyn Code (XI. 14–17). In addition to specialist *kosmoi* and judges, other officials had specified duties. The *titai* (public indemnifiers) existed from the period of earliest written evidence. They could exercise supervisory duties over the *kosmoi* and could exact fines from them.[16]

The magistrates were elected according to qualifications of birth and wealth. The possibility that they may initially have governed for life cannot be readily dismissed.[17] Just as Athenian magistrates eventually governed for ten years (after an initial life-tenure), so the law on the constitution of Drerus (650–600 B.C.), perhaps the earliest surviving Greek law on stone and certainly the earliest which has survived complete, forbids a repeated tenure of the office of *kosmos* before ten years have elapsed, with severe penalties for infringement.[18] There is perhaps an implication that another clan was to have unrestricted right of tenure for a ten-year period. If that were the case, a three-year prohibition at Gortyn in the sixth century B.C. may have represented a similar kind of encroachment upon hereditary tenure, the final stage being reached with a system of annual magistracies.[19] In some Cretan cities the Council had the function of guardian of the laws.[20]

Increasing political duties of the *kosmoi* coincided with a growing complexity of legal procedure which promoted the appointment of important special officials called *dikastai*. When the *kosmoi* had assumed leadership from the tribal monarchies they may be supposed to have performed judicial duties just as they exercised the former military duties of the kings. The *kosmoi* of Gortyn (perhaps as early as seventh–sixth centuries B.C.), undertook special judicial duties. In course of time, these duties became increasingly administrative. In the Gortyn Code, for example, the *kosmoi* act directly as a judicial authority only once – when the marriage of an heiress conflicts with authorized procedure (VIII. 53–IX–1). The *ksenios kosmos* still appears in the Code as a specialist official concerned with people outside the tribal grouping of the citizen body in a way that may be compared with the Athenian polemarch's duties.

[15] D 161, 105 and n. 1.   [16] D 161, 105.
[17] D 164, 32.   [18] D 116; D 117; M–L no. 2.
[19] *Ins. Cret.* IV 14g–p 2   [20] D 161 *passim*.

The special judges called *dikastai* had appeared in Gortyn by the beginning of the fifth century B.C. These again have been compared with the *thesmothetai*, generally and insofar as they were specially appointed for judicial purposes, the outcome of a development inevitable with an expanding state apparatus and corresponding growth of litigation. Different duties were assigned to different *dikastai* according to the nature of the litigation. Thus, special *dikastai* had to do with inheritances; with *hetaireiai* (analogous to Athenian phratries), perhaps concerned with tribal law and custom, adapting these to the requirements of the state; and with pledges. In the final section of the Code *orpanodikastai* appear, especially associated with an extension of state power in the interests of property rights of males. A judge had his *mnamon* (recorder), an official attached to the court to assist the judge in procedure. We do not know how judges were appointed or paid but the Code informs us about their methods of work. In fact the Code is our only document which gives an authentic record of the processes of early Greek law. All cases are tried before a single judge and there is no sign of trial before a jury for civil cases. There is an important definition of the duties of the judge. Sometimes he has *to give judgement*, sometimes he has *to decide on oath*. As the Code states the matter: 'Whatever is written for the judge to decide according to witnesses or by oath of denial, he shall decide as is written, but in other matters he shall decide on oath according to the pleas' (XI. 26). The witnesses were not witnesses to facts, but to the proper performance of processual acts; and it was not their function to adduce evidence in the settlement of disputed facts.[21]

Within this framework of government and justice, the aristocracies adapted their ancient tribal institutions to operate within a new kind of system with marked economic, social and political inequalities. There were: (1) a minority group of free citizens; (2) the *apetairoi* (or free persons excluded from political rights); (3) the serfs; and (4) the chattel slaves. We can approximately measure the relative positions of these four classes in the Gortynian social hierarchy from the following table showing the scale of fines for offences specified in the Code (II. 2–16, 21–7).

A. For rape

(i) Against a free person	1,200 obols
(ii) Against an *apetairos*	120 obols
(iii) By a slave against a free person	2,400 obols
(iv) Against a serf by a free person	30 obols
(v) Against a serf by a serf	60 obols
(vi) Against a household slave	1, 2 or 24 obols
	depending on circumstances

---

[21] Detailed evidence in D 164, 33.

B. *For adultery*

(i) With a free woman	600–1,200 obols
(ii) With the wife of an *apetairos*	120 obols
(iii) A slave with a free woman	slave pays double
	(1,200–2,400 obols)
(iv) Slave with slave	60 obols

Amount of evidence needed for conviction was similarly dispropor-tionate between these classes. Only free men were competent witnesses in some cases (I, II, cf. III, IV; I, III, V). In explanation of the above list it should be explained that rape, seduction and adultery were treated as offences of like category, not as criminal, public wrongs but as affairs to be settled by private monetary compensation. It may be observed that fines for rape and adultery were the same with two exceptions. Adultery with a free woman incurred a full fine of 1,200 obols only if the offence occurred in her father's, brother's or husband's house; if elsewhere, it was thought to be less blameworthy and the fine was reduced by half. There is no mention of adultery between a free man and a serf's wife; and we are entitled to assume there was no legal redress in such cases. Adultery had now become a civil wrong to be punished by fines and was a concern of individuals and their families. An offender was taken prisoner by the injured family. His own family, if he was a free man, his master if he was not a free man, were told to ransom the prisoner within five days or otherwise the captors would deal with him as they thought fit. If the accused person, however, complained that he was the victim of a ruse, the affair was no longer a concern of the family and the accuser then had to swear to his testimony on oath.[22]

The tribe (*pyla*) was still politically important at the time of publication of the Gortyn Code and women were enumerated within it; and it is mentioned in other cities. So is the clan (*startos*) and, as earlier mentioned, the *kosmoi* continued to be recruited from ruling clans. The *hetaireiai* had become exclusively male corporations. It may be inferred from the Code that *hetaireiai* also were politically important in the growth of an aristocratic system, as it developed from a tribal association based firmly on kinship to an equally close-knit but privileged grouping based on narrow rights of citizenship and land tenure. It is clear from the evidence, however, that the *hetaireiai* lost this importance in later times when the state authority was established quite firmly. Gradually their function became more and more restricted to the *syssitia* (communal meals), another feature of social life with tribal roots.[23] They were institutions indigenous not only in Crete but in other parts of Greece including Sparta. Aristotle preferred the Cretan to the

---

[22] See further D 164, 28–9.   [23] D 164, 10–11.

Spartan *syssitia*, explaining that, whereas in Sparta each citizen paid a fixed contribution, failing which he was legally deprived of a share in government, the Cretan system was more communal. For, out of all the crops and the cattle produced from the public lands and the tributes paid by the serfs, one part was devoted to the worship of the gods and the upkeep of public services, and the other part to the *syssitia*, with the result that all citizens were maintained from public funds, men, women and children (Arist. *Pol.* 1272a).

A stable agrarian system explains the slowly evolved persistence of Cretan aristocracy; and the *syssitia* were basic components of the whole. When Aristotle praised the more communal Cretan organizations, directed to the maintenance of all citizens from public resources, he emphasized the contribution to these resources by the regular tributes from the serf population. Aristotle's testimony (*ap.* Ath. IV. 143A–B) can be supplemented by Dosiadas who stated that in Lyttus every man contributed a tithe of his crops to his *hetaireia*, as well as the income from the state which the magistrates divided among the households of all citizens; and each serf paid one Aiginetan stater per head.

The distribution of land and servile cultivators among a sort of tribal aristocracy must have been accompanied by modifications in the modes of inheritance among ruling groups. There was a tendency for smaller units of relationship to be fostered within the wider clan system, particularly marked by the role of the 'household' (Greek *oikos*, cf. Roman *familia*), an institution closely involved with rights of tenure of the *klaros* (lot), the family estate. The Code (IV. 24ff) provided that the father should have power over the children and the property to divide it among them; that, as long as parents lived, there was no need for division; and that, if a man or woman died, their children, or grand-children, or great-grandchildren, should have the property. Head-ship of the *oikos* and tenure of property were thus vested in the parent as long as he lived and wished to retain his proprietary rights. Nor indeed when he was dead were sons necessarily required to divide the estate among themselves; they could operate joint ownership of the single *oikos* of the dead parent. In such cases the eldest would probably take the house, fulfilling his duties to the family altars, now devolving upon him as head of the family.

When a man or woman died without children, the deceased's brothers, and brothers' children, or grandchildren, should have the property. Failing any of these, the *epiballontes* (as those heirs having the next claim were called) inherited the property. The *epiballontes* were kinsmen of any degree who, not belonging to the *oikos*, yet belonged to the same clan as members of the *oikos*.

With the increasing importance of the *oikos*, the old custom of adoption assumed fresh significance. As the clansmen's rights became more formal, so the special responsibilities of an heir to an estate increased. Until free testamentary disposition became established, the head of an *oikos* must have wished to ensure a responsible succession from within the *oikos*. So the system of adoption, through the *hetaireiai* apparatus, became a state responsibility. In the Code, adoption might be made without restriction; and a formal ceremony was held in the market-place before the assembled citizens, the adopter presenting a sacrificial victim and a quantity of wine to his *hetaireia*.[24]

The provisions of the Gortyn Code which concern an heiress are of considerable interest and importance for the social and legal historian.[25] The members of the tribe of the heiress still maintained rights of marriage to the heiress when, in certain circumstances, she did not marry the next of kin. A rule of tribal endogamy was still thus preserved, with the *epiballontes* belonging to one exogamous clan group who normally intermarried with another exogamous group, called their *kadestai*. The terms *epiballontes* and *kadestai* signify the bonds of obligation formed by kinship on the one hand, by marriage on the other. This archaic system, observed by anthropologists in various parts of the world in more recent times, depended upon the continuous intermarriage of exogamous cross-cousins, relatives being classified according as they belonged to one group or the other.

The Code defines an heiress as a daughter without a father and a brother of the same father. She could inherit her father's property but had to marry the next of kin. The immediate next of kin was the paternal uncle. If there were several of them, the oldest had prior claim. When there were several heiresses and paternal uncles, they were obliged to marry in order of age. In the absence of paternal uncles, the heiress then had to marry her paternal cousin; and, if there were several, the oldest had prior claim. Should there be several heiresses and paternal cousins, they were obliged to marry in order of age of the brothers. In this way the material interests of a patriarchal household were being protected by state legislation, now encouraging marriage between kin of the household as compared with cross-cousin marriage between clan groups. However, these newer trends were still contradicted by other stipulations deriving from older surviving matrilineal customs. Women still had significant rights to the tenure of property and land. For example, when the heiress and a male claimant were too young to marry, the heiress could have the house and half the income from the property, the other half going to the claimant. When there was no claimant, an heiress of marriageable age could hold the property and marry as she

[24] X. 33–XI. 23; D 164, 30–1.
[25] VII. 15–IX. 24; XII. 6–19; D 164, 18–27.

wished within the tribe; and if no tribesman presented himself, she was free to accept an offer from anyone else.

Marriage was allowed between a free woman and a serf (VII. 1–10). The children were free or unfree according to whether the serf lived with the free woman or vice versa. It follows that a woman who married twice might have free and unfree children. We can assume that marriages between free men and serf women were not recognized. Both husband and wife were allowed to divorce if either wished; and there were consequent rules in these cases, as also when wife or husband died, about the disposal of property (II. 45–III. 16). A father had power over children and division of property among them. A mother had power over her own property. When a father died, the houses in the town and anything in the houses (if not occupied by a serf belonging to the country estate), along with the sheep and larger animals not belonging to a serf, went to the sons. The remaining property was fairly divided, sons receiving two parts, daughter one part each. When a mother died, her property was similarly divided. Houses occupied by serfs belonged, as did the serfs, to the estate and were regarded as income-producing property in which daughters shared. Sons had clear preference over daughters in division of inheritance; but there is some evidence to indicate that women had received more generous treatment before the publication of the Code.[26]

The terminology of the Code includes titles of certain age-grades of free citizens. A boy or girl before puberty was described as *anoros* or *anebos*, after puberty as *ebion*, *ebionsa* and *orima*. An adult citizen after the age probably of about twenty was called a *dromeus* (runner), implying his right (denied to serfs) to gymnastic exercises. Conversely, an *apodromos* was a minor, not yet old enough to claim the right.[27] The youth were organized in *agelai* (herds). When they graduated from the *agelai* they were obliged to marry at the same time, apparently at a public ceremony for those of the same age-grade also belonging to groups with ties of intermarriage with other groups.[28] These customs persisted long after the publication of the Code, despite more recent developments favouring the autonomous family and property interests indicated in the Code – especially by the exception to the general rule of collective marriage made in the case of a minor allowed to marry the heiress so as to safeguard household interests. This care to ensure succession in the male line explains the right of a minor to marry an heiress as an exception to older rules; and also why she could marry at the early age of twelve (VII. 35–40; XII. 17–21).

[26] IV. 23–V. 9; D 164, 20–1.
[27] VII. 30, 35ff, 37, 54; VIII. 39, 46; XI. 19; cf. *Ins. Cret.* II V. 25A 7 (Axus).
[28] Strabo 482–4; cf. Ath. IV. 143; Nic. Dam. fr. 115; Heraclid. Pont. 3.4; D 161, 7–17.

The term *apageloi* was probably confined to adolescents just before their entry into *agelai*, which were similar to the bands of citizen novices in other states; but Cretan youths did not enter *agelai* until the end of their seventeenth year.[29]

Aristotle (*Pol.* 1264a) explains that the Cretans gave to their servile population the same rights as they had themselves, except that they were forbidden gymnastic exercises and the possession of arms. This helps us to understand why an earlier system of patriarchal slavery which we may define as 'serfdom' (in the sense that a servile peasantry was tied to the soil and paid tribute to overlords) endured for centuries after commercial chattel slavery (with slaves bought and sold like other commodities) had become a dominant form of servitude in other states. This does not mean that a transition from collective tenure of ancestral estates to narrower circles of proprietorship did not cause modifications in the serf system from time to time and perhaps from place to place; and it was no doubt affected in various ways by the simultaneous development of chattel slavery. Consequently the ancient evidence from terminology relevant to servile populations is varied, complex and by no means easy of analysis. The problem is exemplified in the Gortyn Code which has two servile terms which can be translated as 'serf' and 'slave' respectively: the *woikeus* (implying a person attached to the *oikos*); and the *dolos* (i.e. slave). The difficulty is that these two words are not used strictly to define two different conditions of servility. However, various contexts make clear that there were two different servile statuses. *Dolos* is sometimes used with the same meaning as *woikeus*, sometimes with the meaning of chattel slave. The clearest example of the latter usage occurs in a regulation about buying slaves in the market-place. Again, as we have seen, a penalty is laid down for rape against a domestic slave, so that one rule applies to a serf, another to a slave. The Code also demonstrates that a free citizen could pledge his person as security for payment of debt; he was then called a *katakeimenos*. A *nenikamenos* was a free man condemned for debt and handed over in bondage to a creditor. Although these persons lost their freedom as citizens they were not reduced to the category of chattel slaves.

The *woikeus* had access to the law-courts, though he was probably represented by his master and perhaps his rights at law were less than the rights of a free man. Serfs had other rights which distinguished their status from that of chattel slaves. They had the right of tenure of houses in which they lived and their contents. They could also possess cattle as a right. In order to pay fines assessed for various offences in the Code they must have possessed money. A serf family had a recognized social

---

[29] Hesych. *s.v.* ἀπάγελος; Sch. Eur. *Alc.* 989; D 162, 175–9, 285–6.

and legal status since a serf could marry and divorce; and a serf wife could possess her own moveable property, including livestock, which reverted to her in case of divorce. When she married, she changed masters; and when divorced she returned to her former master or his relatives.

Between the minority class of free citizens and the servile there were a number of other social groups whose exact status is difficult to define. The *apetairoi* were such a class of people who must have included, as the name implies, all those excluded from *hetaireiai* or closed corporations of male citizens, and therefore from the privileges of membership, including rights of citizenship. Within this category were perhaps members of communities subjected to a city-state but allowed a kind of autonomy. In an early fifth-century B.C. inscription from Gortyn a certain Dionysius was granted privileges including exemption from taxation, the right to sue in the same courts as citizens and a house and land in Aulon, which might have been subjected to Gortyn, with its own local government and taxes. The *apetairoi* were certainly inferior insofar as they were not full citizens, but they must have had a relatively free economic status, at least to the extent that they were neither bonded nor enslaved.

CHAPTER 39d

EUBOEA AND THE ISLANDS

W. G. G. FORREST

I. EUBOEA, 700–500 B.C.

If the end of the Lelantine War (*CAH* iii.1², 760–3) shed the light of peace on a troubled Euboea, it brought none of any kind to its history. We are left with a Chalcis still stubbornly unyielding of any archaeological truth, an abandoned Lefkandi, a prospering New Eretria and the other cities, so far as we know, much as they were before. But none of them, not even Eretria, figures more than occasionally and usually accidentally in anything that can be called the mainstream of Greek history, nor can much be said of their domestic affairs.

The aristocracies under which the war had been fought, and won or lost, were not unaffected by the challenges that faced aristocracies elsewhere and before 600 a tyrant, Tynnondas (an interestingly Boeotian name) imposed himself on the 'Euboeans' (Plut. *Sol.* 14) and others, Antileon and Phoxus, on Chalcis (Arist. *Pol.* 1304a, 1316a), but Tynnondas is remembered only for his name, Antileon and Phoxus for their departures not their presence (one was succeeded by an oligarchy, the other by a democracy). But what Aristotle, our source for both, meant by 'oligarchy' or 'democracy' is unclear. The only firm fact is that when the Athenians won a famous victory over the Chalcidians about 506 and, in effect, took over Chalcis, they settled 4,000 of their citizens on the lands of the Hippobotae, the 'Horse-breeders', a name that has a sufficiently traditional aristocratic flavour to suggest that whatever tyrannies, oligarchies or democracies had gone before did little to shake Chalcidians from their inherited ways (Hdt. v. 74–7).

Eretrian politics should have been, perhaps were, more interesting. The physical shock of the move from Lefkandi, if such it was, and be it or be it not in some way connected with defeat in the Lelantine War, together with the long-term results of colonial expansion and consequent commercial success should have done something to the fabric of Eretrian society, but there again we have only the name of one tyrant, Diagoras, who 'put down the oligarchy of the Hippeis [the 'Horsemen']', and the statement that these Hippeis were still in the

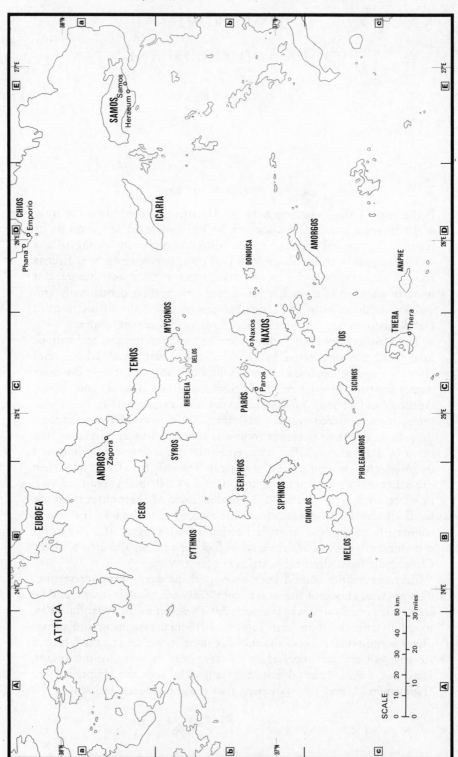

Map 14. The islands.

political saddle around 550 (Arist. *Pol.* 1306a; *Ath. Pol.* 15.2). Either Diagoras comes after 550 or he, like Antileon and Phoxus, had no lasting success. A very fragmentary shipping-law of about 525 (as well as giving us the title of the chief magistrate, the *archos*) testifies to a continuing interest in the sea as does Eretria's contribution of five ships to help the Ionians in their revolt in 499, a contribution which may have earned her a temporary, though not very plausible claim to 'thalassocracy' between 500 and 490.[1] The distribution of her pottery overseas may also owe as much to seamanship as to the talents of her potters.[2]

But the really hard fact is the building programme in the new city that begins around 700. A wall was constructed including a striking, indeed for its date unparalleled, defensive complex, the so-called West Gate (fig. 42), cutting the main road south from Chalcis, and behind it rose public buildings, sacred and profane, including a temple of Dionysus and a fine sixth-century temple to Apollo Daphnephorus, rich in sculpture (see below), while in other parts of the city remains of private houses and material from graves show continuing and growing wealth, broken only in the end by the Persian sack of 490.[3] But from whose pockets the money had come for all this, how it was extracted from them and how, precisely, it had got into them, we can only guess.

Foreign relationships are more substantial at first sight, but no more coherent. Chalcis continued to colonize in the north, adventures which ended with a joint foundation with Andros at Sane and thence produced a dispute about further expansion to Acanthus, about 655. The dispute was settled in favour of Andros when, of the arbitrators, Samos and Erythrae voted for her, and Paros for Chalcis, which shows no more than that associations of the Lelantine War period did not last more than fifty years (Plut. *Quaest. Graec.* 30). At about the same time there was further trouble in Euboea itself, in what was now Chalcis' private property, the Lelantine plain, or at least in *a* plain in which the 'famed warrior lords of Euboea' could practise their special skills against each other. Whether or not the warrior lords actually came to blows on this occasion is unknown – the poet Archilochus (below, p. 255–6) writes of it in the future tense (fr. 3 West) – but, rather later, in the first part of the sixth century, another poet, Theognis (891–4), names the plain and uses the present. 'The wine-rich plain of Lelanton is being shorn bare.' But who was shearing it and why? 'Cerinthus [a small city on the north-east coast of Euboea] is lost...good men are in exile, bad run the city. So may Zeus blast the whole clan of the Cypselidae.' The words are clear but the sense is not. We have firm geography – Cerinthus and, via the plain, Chalcis; we have the class struggle – 'good' and 'bad';

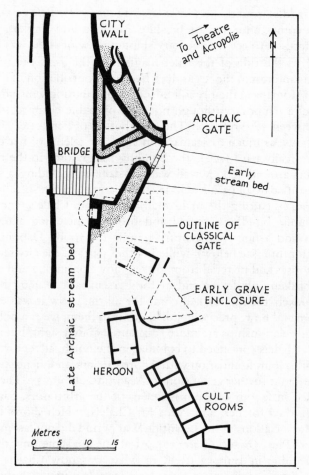

42. Eretria, the West Gate area in the sixth century B.C. (After D 6, figs. 8, 12.)

an international connexion – the Cypselids of Corinth. But even if we accept an attractive suggestion that the Cypselids might have established themselves at Cerinthus when on their way north to found Potidaea, about 600 (and a beautiful emendation in a text of Plutarch, 'Cerinthus' for 'Corinthus', which would then have these same Cypselids expelled by the Spartans in 556 or thereabouts), the roles of Chalcis and class remain dark, as dark as the reasons which later still led the Chalcidians to join with the Thebans in luckless interference with Athens about 506.[4]

This last fact serves to remind us how important Euboea always was

[4] The suggestion about Cerinthus and the Corinthians is Wade-Gery's; E 162, 75–6.

as a link between Central Greece, including Attica, and the outside
world, Thrace, Chalcidice, the Black Sea; how closely, therefore, the
island was involved in the affairs of Central Greece, and Eretria
especially in the affairs, economic and therefore political, of Tanagra,
Oropus and north-east Attica. Pausanias (IX. 22.2) mentions an early
war between Tanagra and Eretria. The tangled story of the origins of
the Athenian tyrant-slayers, the Gephyraei, involves Tanagra and Eretria
as well as Aphidna where they finally settled.[5] Later instances abound.
Thus, when an Eretrian suitor appears at the court of Cleisthenes of
Sicyon about 570 (below, p. 347), it was surely an Athenian link with
Cleisthenes, not a direct Cleisthenic interest in Eretria that brought him
there. A little later one Athenian connexion takes shape. Deeming it
prudent to flee from Athens in 556, Pisistratus found asylum in Thrace,
where Eretrian interests were strong, returned to Eretria and thence,
ten years later, mounted the expedition which won back his tyranny
(below, pp. 398f). Such things could not happen without Eretria's
official blessing and so, we may say, around the middle of the century
Eretrian politics reflected Eretrian economic ties with eastern Attica,
whence, of course, Pisistratus came. Indeed it is not impossible that the
representations of Athena and Theseus in the sculptures of the Apollo
temple later in the century owed something to this link with Attica, as
may the copious finds of fine Attic black-figure vases in Eretria.[6]

But not too much can be gleaned for the long term. An Athenian
nobleman, Chaerion, who died at Eretria about 525, may himself have
been in flight from Pisistratus (though the assumption that he was is
too readily made).[7] More solidly, in 499, when Eretria chose to fight the
Persians in Ionia, she was also choosing to fight the Pisistratids, who
had gone over to the Persians. Economic interests survive personalities,
and the presence of men like the anti-Persian Callimachus in Aphidna
or the family connexions of anti-Persian Miltiades in the Brauron area
may have seemed more seductive that the absence of old friends with
the Persians. But this is thin ice.

Euboea was like a 'scabbard lying along the flank of Central Greece'.
In the dark it is hard to appreciate the existence of a scabbard unless
it rattles. Euboea did not rattle very often after 700.

II. THE ISLANDS

Such glimpses of a political pattern in the Aegean as we can catch or
think we can catch in the late eighth century vanish with the coming
of the seventh. The apparent abandonment of the fortified settlement

[5] F 5, no. 12267.   [6] H 19, 156; H 66, 163–4.
[7] F 5, no. 600.4.

at Zagora on Andros, once an Eretrian dependency, at about the same time as the desertion of Lefkandi, invites thought, but one example of collaboration between Andrians and Chalcidians in the north would scarcely allow that thought to take the shape of Eretrian collapse and of a new Chalcidian presence in the northern Cyclades (*CAH* III.1², 768–9). In any case the collaboration was short-lived.

We are left with the basic differences of geography and race described in an earlier chapter and with the simple facts of island life. The islands were isolated communities. The Aegean lay between them, and the Aegean can be a powerful isolating factor even today. But the small ships of Archaic Greece had to face not only Poseidon but pirates. Thucydides (1. 4) is romancing when he implies that the seas were cleared in early days. The Greeks who sailed to Egypt about 660 were pirates who found respectability; Polycrates of Samos was a pirate with a state behind him; even the early campaigns of the Delian League in the 470s were against pirates as well as Persians, and some have even likened the Leaguers themselves to pirates. The best comment is a list of those whom the little coastal city of Teos decided (about 470) to include among its annual official curses: mass poisoners, dissidents, revolutionaries, traitors – and pirates (M–L no. 30). The simple truth is that the Aegean has been free of pirates only in those few periods when there was some strong naval authority to keep it free – in the days of Minos, perhaps; thereafter, in antiquity, only under Athens, under Rhodes and under Rome (after Pompey).

Nevertheless the sea was also a unifying factor. Greeks sailed as readily as they walked and, where interest led them, carried news and ideas as well as goods. It is possible to imagine a completely isolated island (not many ships will have called voluntarily on the Dolopian pirates of Scyros – though according to Plutarch (*Cim.* 8) some were foolish enough to do so), as it is possible to imagine a totally uninhabited island, but by and large, and certainly along the main sea-routes, these communities will have been as much aware of each other and of the outside world as many cities of Thessaly and much more than many cities of Arcadia. The question is how to hit a balance between these two factors; in view of the lack of evidence an unanswerable question. But, as this or that island drifts temporarily into view, we must beware of thinking that it alone was enjoying the experience, whatever it may have been. Only Paros produced an Archilochus, but there was a Simonides of Ceos, a different but no lesser poet; only Thera's drought is recorded, but even meteorologists cannot confine a drought to some 80 square kilometres; only Naxos is said to have dominated other islands, but could Tenos ever ignore Andros? Only Delos is unique – there was no anti-Pope.

1. *Paros and Archilochus*

Paros had two exports of note, its rough-grained but fine white marble and its poet, Archilochus, somewhat coarser, somewhat blacker, at least in his humour. It is the greatest of good luck for us that he lived when he did (roughly the early middle of the seventh century)[8] and was the kind of man that he was (a perfect, if somewhat extravagant, example of post-Homeric man); sad only that so little of his work survives, and that what does survive has to be treated with such caution. For, it is now very properly insisted, the words of a lyric poet must not be taken too literally, must certainly not be taken autobiographically.[9] It is no longer permitted to say 'Archilochus was an aristocrat, but a bastard aristocrat', 'Archilochus rejected the accepted code of military honour by boasting that he had thrown away his shield in battle to save his own skin', 'Archilochus loved to dance when drunk' and so on. Rather we must say that society now recognized the existence of and could sing about drunken bastard shield-throwers. That takes away a bit of the spice, but the fact remains and is important.

Archilochus (this much is certain) was the son of one Telesicles who had been the leader of Paros' greatest colonial enterprise, the founding of Thasos off the Thracian coast about 700 B.C. (above, pp. 115–17). Paros apparently kept closer ties with Thasos than did other mother cities with their colonies – a certain Aceratus (about 500 B.C.) claimed that he had held the archonship both in Paros and Thasos, and some would infer from this a not unparalleled but rare practice of double citizenship.[10] Certainly some such arrangement is needed to explain Archilochus, as much at home fighting or writing of fighting wild and woolly Thracians in the north as unneighbourly Naxians from across the strait; as happy rubbing shoulders with the Thasian general Glaucus as chasing aristocratic girls in Paros. Glaucus himself was real, as a contemporary inscription shows (M–L no. 3); I should like to believe in the girls as well. It was this mobility, of course, this new range of experiences, not only for Archilochus but for thousands of other Greeks, whether as colonists or mercenaries or as merchants (pirates?), that touched off the fresh thinking, social, political, ethical and later philosophical, of Archaic Greece. War, for example, was no longer a game, it was a business. Egyptian kings paid their mercenaries for victory, not for *arete*; Thracian barbarians, unlike Hector, did not fight according to Achilles' rules. Better, then, to throw away the shield and survive – next week's pay will buy another one. Better too than a great big fancy-pants

[8] D 53.
[9] D 35.
[10] *IG* XII. 8 suppl. no. 412; cf. C 5, 71ff and above, p. 154; A 10.

of a general 'a little knock-kneed chap, but firm on his feet and full of guts' (Fr. 114 West).

This, then, was a new world in which the individual could, was often forced to, stand on his own and Archilochus expresses the newness of it with stunning directness ('We were the scum of Greece that went to Thasos'). Not all his contemporaries will have been so frank. Fighting, drinking, loving or hating he goes for the extreme ('I have one great trick; to answer the man who wrongs me with foul abuse'), and many then as now will have been shocked. The story had it that he drove the father of one uncooperative girl-friend to suicide with his words, the father and the daughter too (Schol. Hor. *Epod.* VI. 13; cf. *Anth. Pal.* 351 et al.). One might almost believe it. But whether people liked it or not, freer-thinking was now in the air and the first practical results of it were appearing in the political revolutions of seventh-century Greece.

Not that Archilochus himself shows any bent for revolution or any great respect for the unwashed proletariat ('Ignore the railing of common folk if you want to enjoy yourself'). But at one moment he does say 'Gyges and all his wealth are no concern of mine...I've no passion for a great tyranny' (Frs. 14, 19 West). Archilochus may not want a tyranny for himself, but he knows what a tyranny is and he can envisage wanting it. It is no longer unthinkable for him, as it was for Hesiod (below, pp. 287f), that the ancestral order, the divinely-sanctioned aristocratic order, should be challenged just as Gyges had challenged the royal order of the Heraclids in Lydia. It would be nice to know whether these lines were a reflection of actual political events in Greece or merely an omen, but it matters little. If revolution had not happened, it was imminent. There were thousands of others like Archilochus who had been led or dragged not just into discontent with the conditions they knew (that was there already) but into the realization that something could be done about it, and there were a few, unlike Archilochus, who did develop 'a passion for a great tyranny'.

2. *Thera and colonization*

The problem of colonization, one of the main spurs to independence, is discussed in general elsewhere (above, ch. 37), but it is worth pausing for a moment to consider from the point of view of the colonizing power the fullest account we have of the sending out of any colony, that of Cyrene from Thera. Thera itself, tradition had it (Hdt. IV. 145ff), was occupied by trouble-makers from Sparta about the time of the establishment of the Dorian state in Laconia, that is in the late tenth century, and nothing in the remains from the island conflicts with the story (*CAH* III. 1², 770–1). Certainly Thera was a Dorian island and kept some Spartan institutions, the kingship (though not dual) and the ephorate.[11] Thera prospered but, about 640, was visited with drought. The drought, as we have said, can hardly have been local, but its effect on bare volcanic Thera must have been particularly severe, and when it had lasted seven years desperation drove the Therans to Delphi. The oracle reminded them of an earlier injunction laid upon their king, Grinnus by name, to send a colony to Libya, an injunction which the insular Therans had decided to ignore 'not daring to send a colony out into the unknown', as Herodotus puts it. Now, however, nature had made the god's voice more compelling and a colony was sent, two hundred men (probably) in two ships, led by Aristoteles son of Polymnestus, a Theran nobleman, later to be known and hence to appear in most of our sources as Battus, the Libyan word for 'King'. Nor was this a random collection of the destitute, Archilochus' 'scum'. The adventurers were carefully conscripted from all parts of Thera, only from families with more than one son, and state interest went further. A fourth-century inscription, which purports to give the terms of the original oath taken by the emigrants and in substance probably does, implies some continuing responsibility on the part of Thera at least for the first five years, provides for the admission of other Therans to Cyrene later and allows for the return of the colonists in event of failure, again for (or perhaps after) the same period. Versions of the story show substantial variations but they do not concern us. In one form or another we have here so many typical (though by no means universal) elements of the colonial movement, the noble leader (who else would lead in the seventh century?), the Delphic oracle, the concern to reproduce abroad the same social structure as had been known at home, a mother city's interest, but strictly limited interest, in the colony's future. And there is something more, common enough no doubt, but never so clearly depicted; no happy band of explorers brimful with a lust for adventure but rather two hundred reluctant Hesiods who go to sea because they have to – the penalty for refusal was death.

Just how much relief the departure of the two hundred would bring to Thera is hard to judge but the physical remains suggest no great discomfort and the bawdy jollity of her inscriptions is attractive.[12] No doubt, Apollo appeased, it rained.

3. *Delos and Naxos*

But for most of the islands Apollo was not the oracular god of Delphi or the Dorian Apollo Carneus, much in evidence at Thera. He was the

---

[11] Hdt. IV. 145ff; *IG* XII. 3, 322 etc.   [12] *IG* XII. 3, 536–7 etc.

Apollo of Delos, cult-centre of the Ionians, a rather unattractive rock in the middle of the Aegean whose inhabitants had nothing to sell except religion. This they did with startling success, a success which begins to be reflected in the adornment of the sanctuary from about the beginning of our period onwards.[13]

Delian Apollo had no doctrine to preach even in the haphazard sense that Delphic Apollo had; or at least had no oracle through which to preach it. His mission, if such it may be called, was to act as a focus for Ionian sentiment, exclusively and inclusively. We are not told of any formal ban on Dorian visitors such as there was on the Athenian Acropolis or at a sanctuary in Paros ('Entry forbidden to Dorian aliens'), but Dorians certainly do not figure, except in the shape of some Dorian pottery.[14] Again, not all Ionians were included in fact at the start, but each was welcomed as he came (did the Messenian choir of about 730 have anything to say about the Neleids of Pylus? – see *CAH* III.1², 770). By 478 Delos had become the natural centre for a national, predominantly Ionian, League of Greeks.

But religious influence invites political interest and Delos from the start engaged it. First in the field appears to have been Naxos, largest and richest of the islands, only some thirty-two kilometres to the south. Fertile, by local standards, well-endowed with a fine marble that could almost match that of her unswervingly hostile neighbour, Paros, set at a vital strategic point in mid-Aegean, Naxos prospered famously so that by 500, according to a perhaps somewhat romanticizing speaker in Herodotus (v. 30), she had an army of 8,000 men, a substantial fleet and even some sort of control over Paros, Andros and the rest of the Cyclades – 'Bright Naxos' Pindar calls her (*Pyth.* IV. 88). What kind of control or how acquired we do not know, but certainly her presence was early felt in Delos. Apart from private dedications like a late seventh-century statue dedicated by a lady called Nicandra, the Naxian state presented a mammoth statue of Apollo, some nine metres high; perhaps a sphinx atop a soaring column (though the attribution to Naxos has been doubted); a curious 'House' for some major public purpose in the centre of the sanctuary and, most impressive of all, a row of huge but amiable lions to squat alongside the main approach.[15] Such things imply an interest beyond mere devotion and something more, too, than a mere desire to advertise the produce of its quarries.

But the intricacies of Naxian politics opened the way to Delos for other powers. It is the standard story. Squabbles among the aristocrats becoming tenser as Naxian society tried to absorb its growing wealth;

[13] D 40, 276ff; D 40A.
[14] *IG* XII. 5, 225; Hdt. v. 72.
[15] D 40, 276ff; H 64, no. 1; D 7; H 61, 28; D 43, 379; D 62.

an *affaire* – an outrage against one nobleman, Telestagoras by name; tyranny with one of Telestagoras' friends as tyrant, Lygdamis. But Lygdamis was no more successful in his first attempt than the Athenian Pisistratus and the year 546 found both in exile. Lygdamis fought for Pisistratus' return to Athens; a grateful Pisistratus at once restored his friend to power in Naxos – and even trusted him with the custody of some aristocratic Athenian hostages. Lygdamis, then, in turn is said to have helped Polycrates to take over the government of Samos (Ath. 348 B, C; Hdt. I. 61; Polyaenus I. 23).

One of the spoils of victory for this tyrant cooperative was Delos, but in a cooperative profits are shared and so, from now on, Delos was open to new influences. Pisistratus 'purified' the sanctuary by digging up the corpses within sight of it and transferring them to further parts of the island, whence a century later an even more devout generation of Athenians moved them to the neighbouring island of Rheneia. When a new temple for Apollo was built around 540 it was of Attic stone. Somewhat later (about 522) Polycrates attached Rheneia to Delos and inaugurated a new festival on the island. But, for some reason or other, this autocratic bloc in the Aegean attracted the displeasure of Sparta, more interested now than she usually was in things overseas. Polycrates was attacked in 525, unsuccessfully, but he was soon murdered by a Persian; the sons of Pisistratus were chased from Attica in 510; and at some point, perhaps on the occasion of the Samian expedition, perhaps a decade later, Lygdamis was deposed in favour of those aristocrats whose power he had stolen and whose property he had confiscated to help finance, among other things, his continued, even if diluted, interest in Delos.[16] Of the aristocratic regime itself or of the 'democracy' whose installation about 500 helped to kindle the Ionian Revolt we have nothing but a tradition of success and the implication that Delos was once more under complete control. It seems a bit unfair that when the Persians crossed the Aegean in 490 they burned the city of the Naxians but heaped three hundred talents' worth of frankincense on Apollo's altar (Hdt. V. 28.1, 38.2; VI. 95–7).

4. Conclusion

In other (or even in the same) islands other things happened. The Parians who had been called in to arbitrate between Chalcis and Andros in 655 were summoned again by the Milesians in the late sixth century to sort out their political troubles (and gave a solid conservative solution). It should tell us something about Parians that they were

[16] See below, p. 403; D 40, 302–3 for the temple; below, pp. 353–6 on Sparta and the tyrants; Arist. *Oec.* II. 3.

still being called in to arbitrate in the eighteenth century A.D.[17] The Siphnians on the other hand looked only once abroad, but to very good effect. So rich had they grown on the profits of their gold and silver mines that they not only faced their public buildings with Parian marble but set up at Delphi one of its most opulent treasuries. The Pythia warned them of trouble to come but they heeded her naught – until some Samian scavengers arrived and relieved them of a hundred talents (Hdt. III. 57–8). The men of Ceos enjoyed a morality of which the severest Elder of the Kirk would have approved.[18] Seriphos achieved the blissful condition of a community that has no history.

But these are trivialities, as is most of what we know. And even the three fuller cases discussed above should serve only to remind us that in the midst of a sea of wine-darkness each island went its own way – but that their ways cannot have been wholly strange to each other.

[17] D 92, I 159.
[18] Phylarchus, *FGrH* 81 F 42 etc.

CHAPTER 40

ILLYRIS, EPIRUS AND MACEDONIA

N. G. L. HAMMOND

I. ILLYRIAN AND EPIROTIC TRIBES IN ILLYRIS AND WEST MACEDONIA

'Illyris', a geographical term which the Greeks applied to a territory neighbouring their own, covers more or less the area of northern and central Albania down to the mouth of the Aous. A description of the country has been given in *CAH* III.1², 619ff and 623.

Within Illyris the people to the north of the Shkumbi valley in Illyria were remarkably conservative in their practices during the period, *c.* 750–530 B.C., and indeed until the beginning of the Hellenistic period. In the Zadrime plain and in the Mati valley tumulus-burial was practised as in the past, and without diminution until late in the fourth century; thereafter a few tumuli only were added to the existing hundreds. Similarly the local styles of pottery persisted and the influence of Greek pottery was very slight. The tumuli were used for members of the warrior or aristocratic class. They were buried with iron weapons (spearheads up to 70 cm long, cutlasses up to 60 cm, battle-axes, knives, occasionally swords) and sometimes with bronze armour (shield, cuirass, helmet, occasionally greaves). The jewellery and fibulae of bronze in the graves were of Glasinac types, and the beads were mostly of amber.[1] In the area of Kukës on the Drin (ancient Drilon) the majority of the burials in the cemeteries of tumuli at Çinamak, Krume and Këneta were made in the seventh to fourth centuries B.C.

The same rituals were practised in Zadrime, Mati and Kukës throughout the period. There were some cremations in urns, but the main form of burial was inhumation. A scratching, breaking and scattering of pots over the upper part of the tumulus was a common feature. The offerings were traditional. We find the same ritual and offerings in Metohija–Kosovo and Glasinac, the great centre of Illyrian culture.[2] On the other hand the Scodra area has different practices, one form of urn-burial probably indicating human sacrifice, and it is

---

[1] Islami in E 37; E 36, 102ff; Jubani in E 40; E 48, 89ff; Kurti in E 46.
[2] E 48, 91f; *SA* 1971.1, 147ff; cf. E 42, 9ff.

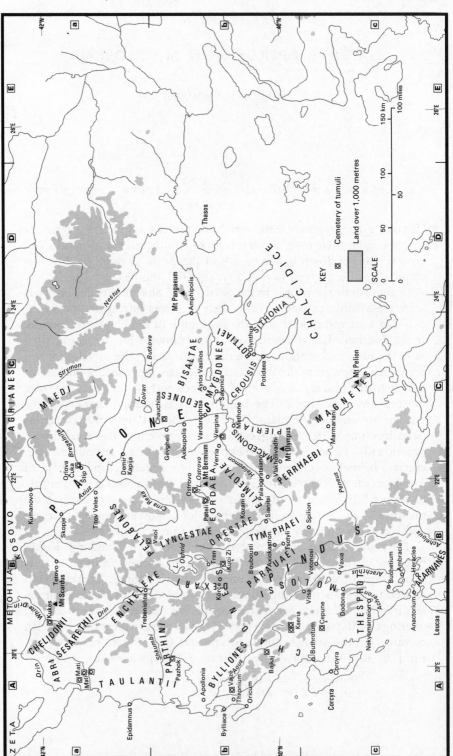

Map 15. Illyris, Epirus and Macedonia.

probable that its connexions were rather with the Zeta valley to the north-west. One interesting difference between Mati and Kukës was in the use of metals: iron for weapons and bronze for ornaments in Mati, but iron for both – e.g. pins, double pins, buckles, beads and fibulae – in Kukës; and later, towards the end of the sixth century, silver displaced iron for pins and for other articles in Kukës but not in Mati. At Pazhok in the middle Shkumbi zone the burials in the excavated tumuli ended *c.* 700 B.C.; but there are twice as many tumuli unexcavated.

In south-east Illyris events took a very different course. The Illyrian domination (see *CAH* III.1², 630) was shaken by the raids of the Cimmerians and their Thracian allies who swept through the Balkans, leaving traces of their presence in Macedonia, e.g. at Titov Veles, and penetrating perhaps via southern Illyris to Epirus, as dedications of their typical horse-trappings have been found at Dodona. In the plain of Korçë Illyrian rule ended *c.* 650 B.C., when the burials of their chieftains in Tumulus I at Kuçi Zi came to an end. The new rulers erected Tumulus II at Kuçi Zi. This eventually contained eighteen burials. Whereas the placing of cremated remains in an urn had occurred as well as the usual inhumations in Tumulus I, now there were inhumations only; there were no more bronze pendants and no more jewellery of Illyrian kinds, and one spearhead only was found. The dead were buried with bronze ear-rings, pins of bronze wire with a spiralling head (as in fig. 43, 3), double pins, single bracelets of bronze wire with overlapping ends, sometimes snake-headed, and beads of glass with coloured eyelets. Some of the old shapes persisted in the hand-made pottery; but most of the pottery was wheel-made and imitated Greek shapes such as the cothon, oenochoe and cylix. There were also some imported Greek vessels. From this tumulus there came two mouthpieces of gold foil as in fig. 43, 15; they were decorated with repoussé drops and terminated in two strings at each end, which had evidently been tied over the mouth of the dead man or woman. The tumulus went out of use in the second half of the sixth century or somewhat later.[3]

In Pelagonia, on the eastern side of the Balkan chain, there were important changes in the plain by the upper Crna Reka (ancient Erigon). In the latter part of the seventh century burials were made for the first time in large, shallow, slab-lined graves without any tumulus. In each case they were near settlements which had just formed on the rising ground at the edge of the plain. These large graves were probably for family use, and it was round them that the cemeteries of the settlements developed in the course of the sixth century. Small stelai or headstones, roughly human in shape, were found. These cemeteries seem to be those

[3] Andrea in E 4, 187f; *StH* 1972.4, 86ff with pls. XII–XIII.

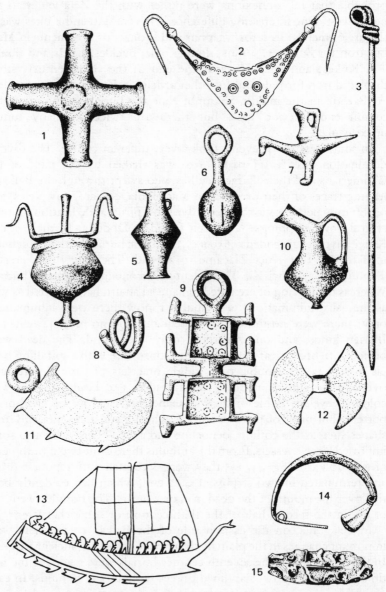

43. Seventh- and sixth-century objects from north of the Greek peninsula. 1. Cross-shaped junction, bronze in Benaki Museum; 2. Triangular plaque with two hooks, bronze from Axiokastron; 3. Pin of bronze wire with spiralling head, 9·5 cm long, from Kuçi Zi; 4. Herb-cup, bronze from Chauchitsa; 5. Biconical bronze bead with collared ends, a pendant from Vergina; 6. Slashed-sphere pendant, bronze from Chauchitsa; 7. Jug-on-bird pendant, bronze from Chauchitsa; 8. Gold hair-ring, from Marmariani; 9. Top-piece of a chain of forty-five bronze pendants, from the Mati valley; 10. Miniature bronze jug, from Pateli; 11. Bronze horse-trapping, from Kukës area, in Tirana Museum; 12. Miniature bronze double-axe, from Olynthus; 13. Galley of Illyrian type, seventh or sixth century, shown on a funerary stone stele from Novilara in Picenum; note high bowsprit and ram; 14. Two-springed fibula of bronze with triangular catch-plate, from Chauchitsa; 15. Gold mouthpiece, 8 cm long, from Chauchitsa. Various scales.

of communities of persons of more or less equal status. We can see here the beginnings of a settled life in villages or small towns. The change from a pastoral economy with hill-refuges to a settled society which practised agriculture as well as stock-raising and lived by the plain was a fundamental one. In pottery the north-west Geometric style which had been in use for centuries (see *CAH* III.1², 642) died out. Greek shapes became popular, sometimes made in a grey ware; and as in the plain of Korçë the wheel came into general use. With the dead there were some figurines of Greek types, ear-rings of bronze, single bracelets, and beads of glass with coloured eyelets. These changes may be attributed at least in part to an influx of new people *c.* 600 B.C. This is seen most notably in a large tumulus at Beranci, where the earlier burials were arranged radially to the centre (as at Visoï) but ten later burials were not so arranged and had the new features and the inventory of the first half of the sixth century.[4]

Farther north in the cemetery of Visoï tumulus-burials continued. In one cremation burial known as Visoï II offerings of gold and silver jewellery were found in a bronze crater together with silver bracelets with serpent-headed ends, a necklace of amber beads, pieces of gold inlay, and a bronze hydria. It seems that a dynasty of rulers continued in power at Visoï into the early fifth century; and its associations were rather with Trebenište near Ochrid than with the settlements in the plain of the Crna Reka.[5]

Let us turn to the literary evidence for the areas which we have described. Hecataeus, writing in the latter part of the sixth century, gave an account of the north-western tribes, which has survived only in fragments but underlies parts of Strabo's geography. The Chaones, a very powerful group of tribes in northern Epirus, extended at that time into the southern part of the lakeland; for one of their tribes, the Dexaroi, was adjacent to the Encheleae (*FGrH* 1 F 103). The name 'Dexaroi' is obviously his form of 'Dassaretai', after whom the area was called Dassaretis. The rulers then who were buried in Kuçi Zi Tumulus II were presumably Chaonian. On the other hand the Encheleae were an Illyrian group of tribes, of which the centre was north of Lake Ochrid on the upper Drin; their ruling house claimed descent from Cadmus and Harmonia (Hdt. v. 61.2; IX. 43.1; Strabo 326), and the foundation of Lychnidus (near Ochrid town) was attributed to Cadmus.

Hecataeus mentioned two tribes of another Illyrian tribal group, the Taulantii, whose homeland was in the Mati valley: the Sesarethii (F 99), living to the south of the Chelidonii (F 100, i.e. not Taulantians), and the Abri near the coast and adjacent to the Chelidonii (F 101). It is

---

[4] E 55, 142f. [5] E 54; *AI* 5 (1964) 74f.

probable that the tribes of the Kukës area were the Chelidonii (see Map 15), whatever Illyrian name lay behind the Graecized form, which meant 'swallow-men'. The tribal group of which the tumuli of Pazhok may have marked the centre was called the Parthini; and their eponymous ancestress 'Partho' figured in the genealogy of Illyrius (*CAH* III.1², 629).

On crossing the Balkan chain, we find that Hecataeus called the Orestae 'a Molossian tribe' (F 107), and Strabo (434; cf. 326) probably derived from Hecataeus his belief that the Elimeotae, Lyncestae and Pelagones, as well as the Orestae, were Epirotic or rather Molossian tribes before their incorporation by the Macedones into the Macedonian kingdom. We may conclude, then, that the archaeological division corresponded to a tribal division: the Illyrian tribes holding northern Illyris, and the Epirotic tribes, whether Chaonian or Molossian, holding the plain of Korçë and the eastern side of the Balkan chain as far north at least as Derriopus, as the plain by the Erigon was called (Strabo 327). The extension of Epirotic control was doubtless the result of much fighting, first by the Chaonian group *c.* 650 B.C. and later by the Molossian group; for their periods of power were given in that order by Strabo (323 *fin.*).[6]

II. SETTLERS ON THE COAST AND THE TRIBES IN EPIRUS

The seaboard of Illyris and Epirus was subject to a series of influences. In the ninth century the Liburnians, then the leading seapower in the inner Adriatic, expanded southwards so that by the first half of the eighth century they were established in Corcyra, the most important port of call on the route from the south either into the Adriatic or to the the heel of Italy. At this time there was considerable intercourse between Illyrian communities on both coasts of the Adriatic (see *CAH* III.1², 628). They shared a love of bronze pendants, spectacle-fibulae, and amber beads; and pottery in Apulia resembled the North-west Geometric style of Illyris in its shapes and decoration during the eighth and seventh centuries.[7] The Liburnians had developed galleys fast under oar (see fig. 43, 13), which could overtake merchantmen in most weathers. They were generally regarded as merely piratical. But they were in fact forerunners of the earliest Greek colonies in that they seized footholds on small peninsulas such as the site of Epidamnus and practised trade and piracy. In Corcyra both Liburnians and Eretrians were reported to have preceded the Corinthians; their fleets exerted a strong control over the coasting route from the Eastern Mediterranean to south Italy and Sicily.

---

[6] E 33, 443.
[7] C 159, 160f; Andrea in E 4, 200f; M. Garašanin in *Starinar* 19 (1968) 295; Ceka in E 17, 152.

The first successful challenge to Liburnian seapower came from Corinth. The Bacchiadae sent an unusually large expedition, which drove the Liburnians and the Eretrians out of Corcyra. Some of the expedition founded a colony at Palaiopolis in Corcyra, and others went on to found a colony at Syracuse.[8] This was in Thucydides' opinion the most important step in the process which made Corinth powerful. 'When Greek seafaring developed more, the Corinthians acquired their battle-fleet and put down the practice of piracy' (Thuc. I. 13.5). But the Adriatic itself was to be a *mare clausum* to the Greeks for a century more. Then about 625 B.C. the Taulantians invoked the aid of Corcyra and Corinth against the Liburnians. Again the Greeks were victorious. They planted a colony at Epidamnus, and they drove the Illyrian fleets back to the region of Scodra. Thereafter the Greeks controlled the best passage across the lower Adriatic, that from Epidamnus to Bari. In addition, the export of goods from Illyris passed through Greek hands; for the native people had no tradition of seafaring. In the foundation-legend, transmitted by Appian, *BC* II. 39, Corcyraean settlers 'were mixed in with' the local Illyrians to start the colony, and this is supported by the discovery of Corinthian funerary pottery of seventh- and sixth-century date together with Illyrian cinerary urns of local type. The city grew prosperous rapidly. The conduct of business with the Illyrians of the hinterland was conducted by a special magistrate, the *poletes* (Plut. *Mor.* 297F).

It was probably during the period of Liburnian supremacy at sea that the Taulantians and other Illyrian tribes seized the rich coastal plain between the rivers Shkumbi (ancient Genusus) and Aous. Their neighbours were Epirotic tribes inland in Dassaretis and beyond the Aous. The river itself was a natural barrier, being not fordable for most of the year, but they needed a strongpoint in the south. To meet this need they invited Corinth about 600 B.C. to join them in founding a city on the Illyrian bank of the Aous at a point up to which the river was navigable. The Corinthians sent two hundred men, and they established the city as a joint undertaking with the Illyrians. Other Greeks, including many from Corcyra, joined the settlers, and it became a predominantly Greek city with a Greek name, Gylaceia at first to commemorate the Corinthian founder and then (perhaps in 588) Apollonia in honour of the god.

Excavation has shown that the site had been open to Greek trade from earlier times. The earliest burials had Corinthian Subgeometric, Protocorinthian and seventh-century Attic pottery. From the founding of the colony and throughout its history separate cemeteries were in use for the Greek population and for the Illyrian population. The Greek

---

[8] Following Strabo 269–70, derived probably from Antiochus of Syracuse (cf. E 33, 414f).

cemetery had fine Corinthian pottery from the beginning of the colony, and the Illyrian cemetery consisted of five large tumuli. One tumulus has been excavated. It had 136 burials, of which one fifth were cremations and the rest inhumations, and it seems to have been in use from the second half of the sixth century to the early part of the second century B.C.[9] No doubt it was the burial-place of long-lived Illyrian families of the original foundation.

Apollonia was like Epidamnus in that it traded extensively with the Illyrians. But unlike Epidamnus it had rivals. Bylliace and Oricum on the Gulf of Valona were mentioned by Hecataeus in the late sixth century (*FGrH* I F 104 emending Βαιάκη to Βυλλιακή as in Strabo 316, and F 105), and inland of the Gulf there was a strong state called Thronium. Bylliace was the port of the Bylliones, an Epirotic tribe inland of Apollonia, which claimed a connexion with Neoptolemus, son of Achilles, but was regarded as Illyrian by Strabo 326. Oricum and Thronium, having been founded by Locrians and Euboeans after the sack of Troy, claimed to be Greek and not Epirotic cities. Early in the fifth century Thronium was totally destroyed by Apollonia (Paus. V. 22.2), which had become much stronger than its rivals.

The country south of the Aous mouth was called Chaonia by Hecataeus, if the emendation of Βαιάκη to Βυλλιακή is accepted in F 104 = St. Byz. *s.v.* Βαιάκη· πόλις τῆς Χαονίας,[10] and it follows that the Bylliones also were part then of Chaonia, which extended from inland of Apollonia into Dassaretis (F 103 Δέξαροι· ἔθνος Χαόνων, τοῖς Ἐγχελέαις προσεχεῖς). Some of the tribes which made up the group called the 'Chaones' had practised tumulus-burial during or at the end of the Bronze Age (see *CAH* III.1[2], 633), and continued to do so for some centuries. A tumulus at Dukat, inland of Oricum, went out of use in the eighth century.[11] The latest burials, A2 and C2, at Vajzë inland of Thronium,[12] at Bajkaj inland of Buthrotum[13] and at the cemeteries of the Kseria valley[14] can be dated to the late seventh century. This dying-out of tumulus-burial may have been due to a change of fashion rather than to a change of the ruling class. In the remote area of the Kurvelesh a tumulus with 63 burials at Çepune was used from the beginning of the Iron Age into the Hellenistic period, which suggests a continuity in the ruling family.[15]

The Corinthians and other southern Greeks who visited the coast of Epirus seem to have accepted the claims of Bylliace, Oricum and Thronium to have been founded by Greeks returning from Troy. The

---

[9] Buda in E 11; Mano in *SA* 1972.1, 107ff.

[10] See E 33, 471f.

[11] E 17.

[12] E 33, 346ff.

[13] E 13.

[14] E 33, 349ff.

[15] E 12 and *BASE* 2 (1971) 29.

Chaones claimed that their royal house was descended from Helenus, son of Priam, and Andromache, widow of Hector, and that Helenus as a refugee from Troy had founded Buthrotum on the promontory opposite to Corcyra town.[16] These claims were probably recorded by Hecataeus. Excavation at Buthrotum has yielded Protocorinthian pottery of the seventh century and then Corinthian and Attic pottery of the sixth century;[17] there are no indications there of a prehistoric settlement. The bay of Buthrotum was named 'the Ciraean Gulf', and the fertile plain inland 'the plain in Chaonian territory' by Hecataeus (F 105). The Chaonian tribes were strong enough to prevent the foundation of any colonies on their coast.

The strongest Greek state in the north-western area was Corcyra. Perhaps a mixed colony at first of Illyrian Liburni and Greeks from Eretria, it was refounded by Corinth in 733 B.C. and challenged its foundress at sea about 660. Excavation has shown that the site of the Corinthian colony, now called Palaiopolis, had late Geometric pottery of the last third of the eighth century, Corinthian Subgeometric and Protocorinthian pottery and then in the seventh century much fine Corinthian and some Attic pottery. Already about 600 B.C. a temple in Doric style was built to Hera; its stylobate was 6·46 m by 20·60 m. A century later there were small temples to Hermes and Aphrodite, and an open temenos to 'Apollo the Corcyraean'.[18] Its culture was entirely different from the cultures of the Illyrian and the Epirotic tribes, and its friends were rather the Greek colonists of Apollonia and Epidamnus. The traces of Greek trade which passed inland from Corcyra, Apollonia and Epidamnus were to be found mainly in Illyris and in the Chaonian plain. Belsh near Elbasan in central Albania for example, received some imported Greek pottery in the tenth century and then again Geometric and Early Corinthian pottery which came in part from Epidamnus; and in the sixth century Apollonia was the intermediary.[19] Similar imports have been found in tumuli at Dukat near Oricum and at Bajkaj inland of Buthrotum.

Another region associated with the heroic past was the coastal plain of the Acheron where the oracle of the dead, the 'Nekyomanteion', and the entry to Hades were located at the junction of the Acheron and the Cocytus; and this association has been supported by the discovery of a Mycenaean tomb at the sanctuary and of Mycenaean remains in the vicinity. Worship of Persephone as the goddess of the underworld is attested by some terracotta figurines for the latter part of the seventh

---

[16] Sources cited in E 33, 384ff and 412ff.
[17] Recently *Monumentet* 12 (1976) 45f.
[18] Eighth-century pottery in *Arch. Delt.* 22 (1967) *Chr.* 303ff.
[19] *Iliria* 3 (1975) 441f.

century, and the tyrant of Corinth, Periander, was said by Herodotus (v, 92η) to have consulted the Nekyomanteion[20] early in the sixth century.

Although the plain of the Acheron was exceptionally fertile, it was the Gulf of Arta which attracted the founders of colonies. The Eleans, first on the scene probably c. 700 B.C., chose an easily defended hill which one reached by sailing up the Louros river. From this colony, Buchetium, they founded two others, Elatria and Pandosia, perhaps in the mid-seventh century. The three colonies controlled a large territory which extended down to the Gulf, and they and the native Cassopaeans shared the rich promontory of Preveza, famous later for olives, pasture and fisheries. Buchetium too had its own fisheries and swampy pastures, excellent for stock-raising. But it had another advantage; it offered the most convenient port and easiest route for pilgrims going to the oracle of Zeus at Dodona. Thus we may attribute to their influence the very close connexion between Olympia and Dodona in the late eighth and early seventh century, and they probably played a part in the formation of the Dodonaean script.[21]

Farther into the Gulf recent excavations at Ambracia have revealed sherds decorated in the local North-west Geometric style (see *CAH* III.1[2], 642ff) and sherds of Corinthian Geometric pottery of the first half of the eighth century, not long after the first appearance of Corinthian pottery in Ithaca.[22] Ambracia, reachable by boat up the Arachthus, was already the natural entrepôt for the produce of central and south-east Epirus, which consisted mainly of timber, including ship-timber, floatable down the Arachthus and also available in the nearby Valtos, and cheese, skins, wool, goat-hair and livestock. As Epirus was self-supporting in food-stuffs, what it received from Corinthian merchants was evidently oil, wine and perfume in Corinthian containers, and armour, weapons and other finished goods.

Late in the tyranny of Cypselus, following a preconcerted plan, the Corinthians founded colonies at Leucas, Anactorium and Ambracia c. 625 B.C., and the sons of Cypselus added Heraclea on the Acarnanian shore. Thus they controlled both the southern side of the entry to the Gulf, the promontory of Actium soon being included in Anactorian territory, and the already established entrepôt at Ambracia. The city set in the bend of the Arachthus commanded the only entry by land from southern Greece into Epirus, and its immediate territory was exceptionally fertile; it soon surpassed Buchetium, and its influence became paramount in Central Epirus and at Dodona itself.

A great virtue of the Corinthian colonies here and on the Adriatic

[20] Dakaris in E 18.   [21] E 31; E 33, 434f.
[22] Vokotopoulou in *Arch. Delt.* 26 (1971) *Chr.* 333ff.

coast was their ability to maintain friendly relations with the native peoples whether in Epirus or Illyris. For this reason their trading contacts were exceptionally wide. For example, in the sixth century the bronze statuettes and the bronze vessels of Corinthian workshops far outdistanced the bronzework of other centres in the offerings at Dodona. Specimens of Corinthian bronzework have been found at Votonosi and Vitsa, summer centres for transhumant pastoralists; at Oricum and Apollonia and in central Albania; and at Trebenište, Tetovo and Novi Pazar in southern Yugoslavia.[23] There is no doubt that trade passed along this route into Central Europe during the sixth century to a much greater extent than up the Axius valley from the ports of the Thermaic Gulf. There was also some trade between the Adriatic and the Aegean through the lakeland. At the crossing of these two routes rich centres developed, especially at Trebenište to the north of Lake Ochrid. As the richest period there was affected by the presence of Persia in the Balkans, it will be reserved for the next volume of this history.

The influence of the Elean and Corinthian colonies on the way of life in Epirus was very small. There the unit of a primarily pastoral economy was the small tribe, often semi-nomadic through transhumance, organized as a patriarchy, and self-contained in its institutions. These tribes were only loosely associated together in three main tribal groups, known as Thesproti, Molossi and Chaones, or in smaller groups such as the Atintanes and Parauaei. All the groups were led by royal houses and the succession to the constitutional kingship was hereditary. Because each tribe was wont to move from summer pastures to winter pastures, it did not possess a continuous block of land, as a city-state did, but had access to pastures in different regions, so that it might readily transfer itself or be compelled to transfer from one tribal group to another, as we find was the case in the fourth century. Thus some tribes of the Molossian group had summer pastures on the east side of Pindus, overlooking Thessaly; one such, the Talares, although a branch of the Talares near Dodona, became absorbed into the Thessali. Vice versa, some semi-nomadic Perrhaebi, a branch of the Thessalian Perrhaebi, had pastures on the west side of Pindus (Strabo 434). Thus the whole system of tribes (*phylai*) and tribal groups (*ethne*) was entirely different from the system of city-states which had become established in most of southern Greece.

Dodona was the Mecca of this tribal society. By common consent it was the oldest shrine, and it had once been the only shrine of an oracular nature among the Greeks. Centuries of syncretism had produced a many-sided cult of wide appeal: three priestesses and three doves

[23] E.g. H 74.

perhaps originally associated with an Earth-Goddess as supreme deity; priests sleeping on the ground with unwashed feet, the eagle, the double-axe, and Zeus as supreme deity; the oak with its leaves and acorns (winter fodder for animals and men), the wild boar, the utterances of the oak and their interpretation. One example of such a fusion of ideas occurred in the most ancient hymn sung by the priestesses at Dodona:

> Zeus was, Zeus is, Zeus shall be. O mighty Zeus!
> Earth sends up the harvests, so sing of Earth as Mother.

The sacred oak was unadorned until the end of the eighth century when bronze cauldrons on tripods were placed around it. These offerings were prompted probably by current practice at Olympia; but at Dodona, itself a name for an echoing sound, the cauldrons touching one another reverberated for some mystic purpose, even as the thunder of Zeus reverberated around the peaks of his sacred Mount Tomarus. Apart from the cauldrons everything was associated with the open-air, simple life of shepherds and their flocks. The earliest description of the setting of Dodona is a fragment of the Boeotian poet, Hesiod:

There is a land Hellopie with many crops and good meadowland, wealthy in flocks and shambling cattle; therein dwell men rich in sheep and rich in cattle, men beyond number, tribes of mortal men. And there, at its edge, a city is built, Dodona; and Zeus loved it and ⟨made it⟩ to be his oracle, prized among men.

Although Hesiod used a verb which implied a city (πολίζω), the only early building remains that have been found are post-holes ringed with stones of the latest Mycenaean period. Men slept in the open or in bothies, drowsing and waking to the sound of sheep-bells in the summer night (Paus. IX. 8.1; X. 12.10; Hesiod, fr. 240).[24] The first stone buildings were of the fourth century.

As a religious centre of pastoral life, by tradition and by location Dodona appealed to pastoral groups as far afield as Mt Scardus (Šar Planina). Such offerings as Illyrian pendants and Thraco-Cimmerian horse-trappings were made by pilgrims from the north, and there were remarkable similarities between some dedications at Dodona and gifts with the dead at Trebenište, north of Lake Ochrid: for example, lions climbing on a tree in gold, pins and fibulae in silver, and portraiture on a helmet cheek-piece and on a gold death-mask. Indeed Dodona was a religious and oracular centre primarily for northern tribes, and it was only in the latter half of the seventh century that it drew the southern

[24]   E 21.

Greeks in increasing numbers.[25] Through them its fame spread to Croesus of Lydia in the following century.

III. MACEDONIA

To settled peoples mountain ranges suggest frontiers, but for transhumant pastoralists and foresters they form meeting grounds. Even today the villagers of Zagori in Epirus on the western slopes of Pindus are more closely related to the villagers of the Kastanokhoria of north-east Pindus in Macedonia than to their southern neighbours. Thus there is nothing improbable in Hecataeus describing the Orestae of north-east Pindus as 'a Molossian tribe' at a time when tribes were not static but impinged on one another in their summer pastures, even as Vlachs today come to northern Pindus from east, south and west. As Hecataeus took the tribe as the unit for description in this part of his *Periegesis*, he did not use the term 'Epirus' at all, or even 'Macedonia' in any general sense; rather he talked of territory in terms of the tribe, e.g. ἡ Χαονική (F 105), 'the land of the Chaones'.

That he covered the whole of our area is certain from the fragments.[26] It should be noted that where we should speak of 'Macedonia' Hecataeus used for the land east of the Axius the word Θράκη, because it was then occupied by the tribal group called the 'Thrakes'; so Lipaxus and Smila in Crousis were cities of 'Thrace' (F 148–9). Indeed at an earlier date the west coast of the Thermaic Gulf was also called 'Thrace', because it was then held by Thracians; thus Methone was founded in the late eighth century by Eretrians who sailed to 'Thrace' (Plut. *Quaest. Graec.* 11). Similarly when colonists from Chalcis settled on the peninsulas east of the Thermaic Gulf, the area was called Chalcidice, 'the land of the Chalcideis', and more explicitly 'in the direction of Thrace'. Hecataeus' description, which referred to the last decades of the sixth century, would have been invaluable to us, if it had survived; as it is, we can collect some scraps of information from the fragments and from authors who used his work – Herodotus, Thucydides and Strabo, whose description of Macedonia in book VII has survived unhappily only in fragments.

Let us begin with an excerpt from an epitome of that lost part of Strabo's book VII (fr. 11):

What is now Macedonia was called in earlier times Emathia. Macedonia took its name from Macedon, an early ruler. There was also a town Emathia near the sea. This territory was held by certain of the Epirotes and Illyrians, but most of it by Bottiaeans and Thracians. The Bottiaeans, they say, were from

---

[25] So under 639 B.C. Euseb. *Chron.* 96.10 (ed. Helm) *oraculo Dodonaeo primum Graecia usa est.*
[26] E 34, I 111, 146f, 310f, 415 and 432.

Crete by descent, having Botton as ruler; and of the Thracians the Pieres occupied Pieria and the area by Olympus, the Paeones that by the Axius and so called Amphaxitis, and the Edoni and the Bisaltae the rest of the land up to the Strymon.

This passage, from which the Macedones are absent, evidently described the situation or situations which existed before the Macedones entered into possession of Pieria and Emathia, and subsequently into that of other areas one by one. The tradition that Thracians occupied the area below Mt Olympus on the Pierian coast was established very early, and Orpheus was believed to lie buried there; the tradition was accepted by Thucydides who described the expulsion of the Pieres and their taking refuge near Mt Pangaeum. Graves found at Koundouriotissa in coastal Pieria may have been those of Thracians (see *CAH* iii.1², 650). The presence of 'Epirotes' in Lower Macedonia is anachronistic as a name but may be related to the expansion of the Molossian tribes which brought the Elimeotae to settle within reach of the coastal plain. The Illyrians present no problem; for the archaeological evidence is clear at Vergina and in the lower Vardar valley, that they were in control from some time in the eighth century to *c*. 650 B.C. (see *CAH* iii.1², 651f). That the Bottiaei held the plain was indicated by Thucydides' statement that the Macedones drove them out of Bottiaea into the hinterland of Chalcidice; thus the Bottiaean period of control came between that of the Illyrians and that of the Macedones. The Paeones, rated by Strabo as Thracians, held the area of which Thucydides says the Macedones took possession, being a party of 'Paeonia' (ii. 99.4). The time when the Edoni and the Bisaltae took control of their areas is not known from the literary evidence.

Our consideration of this passage from the Vatican epitome of Strabo leads us to the conclusion that the epitomizer has telescoped situations of different periods into at least the appearance of one situation, and that the description by Strabo came ultimately from a source which was used also by Thucydides or at least gave information with which Thucydides agreed. Thus, when it is sorted out, the passage commands our confidence. Two points are left. Emathia is here used as the name of the whole area from Mt Olympus to the Strymon, and this is based no doubt upon the passage in *Iliad* xiv. 226, where Hera flew from Mt Olympus and crossed Pieria and Emathia to reach 'the snowy mountains of the Thracian riders'. The name of the Macedones did not arise as possessors of that land at first, because they lived outside it – presumably by the mountain which took its name from them, τὸ Μακεδονικὸν ὄρος, situated between Pieria and the Perrhaebi (Hdt. vii. 131). Later in the fragment the Macedonian conquest is recorded but in the name not of the Macedones but of 'the so-called Argeadae'.

Before we proceed with the literary evidence, let us resume the archaeological evidence which was touched upon in *CAH* III.1², 651ff. The last Illyrian phase at Vergina, *c.* 700–650 B.C., was marked by an increasing number of iron spearheads, bronze pendants and bronze beads, and the latest group of the excavated tumuli had many offerings which were typical of the great Illyrian centre, Glasinac: e.g. biconical bronze beads as in fig. 43, 5, bronze tutuli, slashed-sphere pendants as in fig. 43, 6, sickle-shaped iron knives and whetstones. At that time, and then only, urns, sometimes standing on two feet, were used to contain the remains of (perhaps partly) cremated corpses.[27] Within the same period Illyrian groups were in occupation of Axioupolis, Gevgheli and Chauchitsa, all controlling the last defensible entries from the north into the coastal plain. The two sets of graves at Axioupolis yielded a wider range of bronze pendants than those at Vergina, and also pendants hanging on pendants (as in fig. 43, 9 from a Mati valley burial), a boss (*phalaron*) worn on a woman's belt, bronze armlets and torque, and many beads of amber (as in the Mati valley burials). Beside Grave 18 an iron spearhead was planted point upright, this being a practice of Illyrians in the fourth century according to Aristotle (*Poet.* 1461a3). The group of graves at Gevgheli contained different offerings but of the same culture: e.g. miniature bronze jugs as in fig. 43, 10, a ball-pendant, a cross-shaped junction as in fig. 43, 1 (perhaps for harness), and a large biconical bronze bead. The situation at Chauchitsa was different again, because the main group of burials was not in cist-graves or trenches, as at Axioupolis and Gevgheli, but under cairns of stones, except for the central burial which lay in the upper stones of a cairn. It is most probable that a tumulus of soil originally covered this group of burials which is on a rock outcrop, now heavily eroded, and that each cairn of stones originally covered a wooden coffin which soon rotted away.[28] The offerings spanned a longer period of time than those at Axioupolis and Gevgheli, and the warriors differed in their armament; for they had no spears, but there were swords, knives and sometimes shields in their graves. The warriors and women of Chauchitsa had the same love of pendants (as in fig. 43, 7), but little taste for amber. In addition to this main group on the rock outcrop cist-graves with similar offerings were found nearby, some being certainly of later date. At Dedeli, by the north-west corner of Lake Doiran, another set of cist-graves yielded similar objects, some contemporary with the earlier ones at Chauchitsa.

From these cemeteries we can see that the Illyrians acted as small groups, each having its own characteristics within a general framework

[27] Petsas in *Arch. Delt.* 18 *Chr.* 217f for T. LXVI–LXXI; E 34, I 396.
[28] E 34, I 348ff; E 42, 74ff.

of Illyrian tastes. This is consistent with the remark of Polybius (II. 3.2), made centuries later, that the Illyrians acted 'in groups'. Like commandos in modern war, they were not necessarily armed alike.

If the Bottiaeans came originally from Crete, we have an explanation for the appearance in this part of Macedonia of the cult of the double-axe, whether in the form of three miniatures on a pendant or of a single one, a cult which spread to Glasinac and far into Central Europe. The double-axe was not the only Minoan feature; for the importance of the priestess and the type of head-dress were Minoan too. Among those who adopted the cult were transhumant pastoralists, e.g. at Spilion and Vitsa (see *CAH* III.1, 649f). When the Bottiaei were expelled, some time after 650 or so, they sought refuge in Chalcidice and founded Iron Age Olynthus, where excavation has shown that regular occupation started not before *c.* 650 B.C.[29] Seven miniature double-axes of a specialized shape in bronze as in fig. 43, 12 and one in bone were found at Olynthus. The pottery did not resemble that at Vergina, and the great number of collared bronze beads was a feature common not to Vergina but to the Vardar valley sites. In the matter of weapons and pendants the Bottiaeans shared the tastes of the Illyrians. It would seem, then, that the Bottiaeans had not made Vergina their capital, although their influence was strong there. In their new home they showed themselves to be conservative in their ways, and in particular they showed no signs of contact with the Greek colonies in their vicinity.

As we leave the coastal area, we may turn first to the middle and upper Haliacmon valley, where Elimeotis, Tymphaea and Orestis were inhabited by Epirotic tribes, or more correctly 'Molossian' tribes if the account in Strabo was derived from Hecataeus. There Kozani in Elimeotis has yielded the most interesting remains. From a number of burials which cover our period as well as the classical period came bronze pendants, spectacle-fibulae, heavy and light armlets, biconical beads, hair-coils, and a triangular plaque with two hooks as in fig. 43, 2, which had been attached to a woman's leather belt. This last item was beautifully incised with dot-centred circles, often called 'eyes', and a larger, elaborately decorated circle in the centre. Similar pieces have been found, all also in bronze plaque, in women's graves, one at Sianitsi and two at Axiokastron (Sourdhani) which lie farther up the Haliacmon valley; one at least at Pateli in Eordaea; several pieces in museums, said to have come from Macedonia, and one reputedly from Trikkala in north-west Thessaly. It is probable that these women were priestesses; for example, the grave at Sianitsi where a woman wore this triangular plaque, contained also an anchor-shaped pendant, two long pins, a spiralling ring and beads, all of bronze, and a bit of iron plaque (as in

[29] D. Robinson, *Excavations at Olynthus* v (Baltimore, 1933) 4.

priestess burials at Vergina and Vitsa) and three vessels. On the present evidence the cult was local to the middle and upper Haliacmon valley. From graves on the west side of the Haliacmon, mainly from the district Voïon, have come spectacle-fibulae, armlets, bracelets, torques, spiralling ornaments, finger-rings – some with spiralling ends – long pins and tweezers, all in bronze; and also boar-tusks.[30] Thus this area resembles the last phase in the Korçë basin (Kuçi Zi Tumulus II) in its preference for bronze, the rareness of iron, the continued use of long bronze pins, and the habit of not putting weapons with the dead. This relationship accords with the literary evidence in that the tribes of Elimeotis, Tymphaea and Orestis were called Epirotic, whereas those of Eordaea – where Pateli was the chief cemetery – and of Vergina were of different stock.

Whereas the wheel was in general use at Tren and Kuçi Zi in the Korçe area, almost all the pottery at Pateli and Vergina was made by hand, and this was so too in western Macedonia. From the early seventh century onwards considerable amounts of wheel-made Grey Ware appeared at Palaiogratsiano near the Volustana pass from Thessaly, and several examples at Kozani and Pateli; but none at Vergina from the tumuli excavated by Andronikos. This ware was found also at Vardarophtsa and Chauchitsa east of the lower Axius, and at places in Derriopus by the Crna Reka. The best explanation of this pattern of distribution is that Greek trade was penetrating northwards via Perrhaebia and the Volustana pass into the middle Haliacmon valley, and from the ports on the eastern side of the Thermaic Gulf into the lower Axius valley. Such trade may have reached Derriopus either from the lakeland area or from the Axius valley, or from both. Sherds of Greek Geometric pottery, while common enough at Vitsa and occurring on the western side of the Pindus range, e.g. at Bajkaj and Kuçi Zi Tumulus II, were extremely rare on the eastern side: an occasional sherd at Tsotyli and Boubousti, and a number of pots and sherds at Saraj and other places in Derriopus; and a pin of Corinthian manufacture of c. 750 B.C., found at Titov Veles on the middle Axius.

A collection of bronzes was found during the making of a road near Titov Veles. Among them were two horse-trappings of Thraco-Cimmerian type as in fig. 43, 11 and a bronze pendant with a tie-on lid ('herb-cup') as in fig. 43, 4, such as has been found at Chauchitsa. A variety of bronze pendants have come from excavations at Radanja near Štip; also biconical bronze beads, and circular bronze buttons. At Orlova Čuka near Štip, where two of a cemetery of ten tumuli have been excavated, one tumulus was found to have a peribolos wall, a large central burial cist-shaped but with apsidal ends, and five other burials

[30] E 34, I 344ff.

in slab-lined cists aligned towards the central burial.[31] These arrangements have a resemblance to those at Visoï (see *CAH* iii.1², 644), and
the objects with the dead were much as at Visoï: e.g. iron sword, bronze
biconical beads, buttons, hair-coils and fibulae. It seems, then, that those
who were buried at Orlova Čuka were Illyrians, and that they lingered
on till perhaps *c.* 600 B.C., which was the date of the latest burial in the
tumulus. A collection of bronzes from Kumanovo on the Pecinj, an
eastern tributary of the Axius, is also markedly Illyrian in character:
bronze pendants, armlets, beads, buttons and a junction-piece as in fig.
43, 1. Other sites with such pendants are Demir Kapija, Fortuna–Štip,
Vučedol near Skopje, Kamen Rapeš and Zivojno.

It is probable that two sets of bronze objects which were bought from
a dealer by the British Museum came from the Vardar valley rather than
from the alleged site, Potidaea; these range from an eighth-century
fibula with a catch-plate to a variety of Illyrian-type pendants. Farther
to the east, on the route which leads from Lake Doiran to Lake Butkova
in the Strymon valley, bronze beads and buttons and a stone pot with a
loop-handle of a Glasinac type were found in a tomb at Kozlu Dere,
and a heavy bronze armlet at Houma. In the Strymon area, from the
site which became Amphipolis, a collection of bronzes, now in the
Vienna Archaeological Museum, included a miniature double-axe as at
Olynthus (fig. 43, 12), miniature jugs (as in fig. 43, 10), beads, buttons,
armlets, a spectacle-fibula and pendants of typical Illyrian kinds, all of
bronze.[32] Thus from the archaeological evidence one can visualize a
surge of Illyrian warrior-groups which not only overran the areas east
of the middle Axius and both sides of the lower Axius but also
overflowed into the Strymon basin. When their power collapsed, they
disappeared from the history of these regions, except in the middle
Strymon valley, where the Maedi[33] lived on in the fifth century; for
their eponymous ancestor, Maedus, figured as a son of Illyrius in the
genealogy of Appian, *Illyr.* 1. 2, which came from an early Greek source.

The successors to the Illyrians in the areas east of the Axius were the
Paeonians and the Edoni, who were mentioned as being both
Thracian in the fragment of the Strabo epitome (fr. 11 cited above);
but whatever their racial relationships were, it is better to keep them
separate for historical purposes. The capital of the Paeonian kings, as
we know from later writings, was at Astibus, from which Štip is derived,
but a royal cemetery of this period, *c.* 750–530 B.C., has not been found.
The lowlands through which the Pecinj and the Bregalnitsa flow
support larger populations than the high basins to the west of the Axius,

[31] E 30; R. Pasic-Vinčić in *Starinar* 21 (1970) 129 (on Orlova Čuka).
[32] E 26; E 10, 289.
[33] For the view that the Maedi were not Illyrians but Thracians see *CAH* iii.2², ch. 33*b*.

and the soil is excellent for agriculture; the Paeonians were primarily agriculturalists, as we see from the famous oxen on their early coins. Other Paeonian tribes lay to the east in the upper Strymon valley – the Agrianes and the Laeaei, for instance – and communications with them were relatively easy via Kjustendil. The group of Paeonian tribes was in control of deposits of gold, silver, copper and iron.[34] The area east of the Axius to the south of the Demir Kapija was taken over at first by Thracians, who had been allies of the Cimmerian raiders and had helped to overthrow the Illyrians.

One object which indicated the presence of Thracians was a mouthpiece of gold foil as in fig. 43, 15, usually decorated in repoussé style with circles and ridges, which had two strings at either end for tying over the mouth of a dead person. Seven of these were found at Chauchitsa in graves covering approximately the period $c.$ 650–550 B.C.; several at Zeitenlik and Kalamaria near Salonica; one at Ayios Vasilios in Mygdonia; and two at Kuçi Zi Tumulus II.[35] The example at Ayios Vasilios was in one of four slab-lined cist-graves which was intact, and the other objects were a biconical gold bead, an amber amulet, two bronze finger-rings with spiralling ends, two bronze armlets with overlapping ends, and pieces of bronze fibulae as in fig. 43, 14, and a *cothon* which has been dated $c.$ 550 B.C. Another undisturbed grave had the corpse of a man with a knife, a spearhead, and two spear-butts, all of iron, two small flat bands of gold, and the corpse of a small child. These unusual offerings and the conjunction of the warrior and the child, which may be an example of human sacrifice, are different from anything we have met hitherto in Macedonia. That Thracians raided southwards is made probable by unusual gold hair-grips (fig. 43, 8) of a shape well known in central Bulgaria, which were found in burials at Marmariani in north-east Thessaly.[36]

Next in time came the situation which is described in the fragment of the Strabo epitome, when the Paeonians had broken through the Thracian sector and reached the sea by occupying Amphaxitis, the country on either side of the lower Axius. But the areas farther east, which came to be known as Crestonia, Mygdonia, Bisaltia and the plain of the lower Strymon, were still held by the Edoni and the Bisaltae. The gold-bearing river of Crestonia was called then the Edonus, and later the Echedorus; from this we may infer that the royal tribe, the Edones, held Crestonia. The fragment went on to define the Edoni and the Bisaltae: 'the latter were called just that, Bisaltae, but of the Edoni

[34] See Map 1 in E 34, 1.
[35] *BSA* 26 (1923–5) 23; *Albania* 2 (1927) 32f and 52f; *BSA* 24 (1919–21) 21; *JHS* 41 (1921) 274. Two pieces from Kuçi Zi were on show at the Tirana Museum in 1972.
[36] See E 34, I 443.

some were called Mygdones, some Edones and some Sithones'. It is probable that the names Mygdon and (the area) Mygdonia had been handed down from the Phrygian period, together with the names of the adjacent areas Crestonia and Crousis; for Mygdon was reputed to have had two sons, Grastus and Crousis, and numerous daughters. But he was put into a new genealogy for the Thracian period, thus becoming a brother of Edonus, Biston and Odomas. The name of the Sithones was preserved in the name of the middle prong of the Chalcidic peninsula, Sithonia.

The time when the Paeones held Amphaxitis and the Edones Crestonia may be fixed approximately within two termini. Of the seven graves at Chauchitsa with gold mouthpieces the latest probably, Grave (22), had pieces of a *cothon*, and so can be dated approximately 550 B.C. As these are indicative of Thracian rulers, they give a loose *terminus post quem*. At the other end the Paeones came to dominate the whole area up to and including the Strymon basin, and they went on to attack Perinthus on the shore of the Propontis before the Persian entry into Europe (Hdt. v. 1; Strabo VII. fr. 41). Let us then suggest *c.* 525 B.C. as a *terminus ante quem* the Edoni and the Bisaltae held Crestonia, Mygdonia and Bisaltia. The positions of the various tribes are shown on Map 15.

We are left with the Macedones, for whom we have important literary evidence. Hesiod, *Eoeae* fr. 7, wrote of Deucalion's daughter as follows: 'she conceived and bare to thunder-loving Zeus twin sons, Magnes and Macedon who joys in horses, and they had their habitations by Pieria and Olympus'. In the Catalogue of Ships, referring to a very much later situation, Homer placed the descendants of Magnes by the Peneus and Mt Pelion (*Iliad* II. 756f). From this we may infer that the Magnetes had been driven out and the coast of Pieria below Mt Olympus had been occupied by the Thracian Pieres before whatever date we care to attribute to the Catalogue. The Macedones, whom Homer never mentions, evidently stayed on as inland neighbours of the Pieres. According to their own account, as reported by Herodotus, the Macedones were neighbours of the Phrygians or Briges, as they were called in Europe, when the so-called gardens of Midas lay below Mt Bermium (Hdt. VII. 73 and VII. 138.2); also, we may add, when the royal cemetery of the Briges was at Vergina on the right bank of the lower Haliacmon. Thus we may define the habitat of the Macedones, before they began to expand, as being inland of the coastal plain below Mt Olympus and situated between Mt Olympus inclusive and the river Haliacmon above Vergina, where it emerges from a long gorge, difficult to traverse. We can arrive independently at this conclusion if we study the account of the Macedones' expansion in Thucydides II. 99. For after mentioning the Elimeotae and the Lyncestae, he described the conquest of the Pieres, Bottiaei, lower Axius, Eordaea and Almopia. A glance at Map 15 shows that such conquests could have been made only from a base between the Elimeotae, the Pieres and the Bottiaei.

The homeland, then, of the Macedones for many centuries was the hilly and mountainous country bounded in the south by Kato Olympos, on the west by the Voulustana Pass and the Haliacmon river, and on the north by the spur of Mt Bermium which runs along the southern side of the great plain towards the mouth of the Haliacmon. This area contained 'the Makedonikon mountain' of Herodotus VII. 131, which lay between the coast of Pieria and the Perrhaebi; and it was less large than 'Makedonis' as Herodotus defined it in VII. 127.1.[37] This area of country had and has excellent pasture, good timber, and plenty of water; it was ideally suited for pastoralism and hunting, and had the almost unique advantage that transhumant pastoralism can be practised within its own confines, since Olympus, Titarium and the so-called Pierian Mountains afford an abundance of summer pastures. A special group of Vlachs, speaking their own dialect, held these pastures for centuries, their largest summer-village at Vlakholivadhi having had some six thousand inhabitants at its peak.[38] The Macedones must have been similar in their way of life, and their original capital, Lebaea, was probably in these hills, similar perhaps to Palaiogratsiano, where much Grey Ware has been found.

The first step in the expansion of the Macedones was associated with the adoption of a new capital, Aegeae, in place of Lebaea, and an oracle of Delphi, certainly a *vaticinium post eventum*, purported to tell the king how to act:

The noble Temenidae have royal rule over a wealth-producing land; for it is the gift of aegis-bearing Zeus. But go in haste to the Buteïd land of many flocks and wherever you see gleaming-horned, snow-white goats sunk in sleep, sacrifice to the gods and found the city of your state on the level ground of that land. (Diod. Sic. VII fr. 16)

The new capital was named Aegeae, derived in popular etymology from the goats (*aiges*), and all Macedonian kings were buried there from that time until the corpse of Alexander the Great was taken to Alexandria in Egypt. According to the tradition the new name replaced the old name, Edessa, a Phrygian word. The present writer suggested in 1968 that Aegeae was at Vergina–Palatitsa, and the suggestion has been confirmed by the excavation (still incomplete) of what are certainly royal tombs under the Great Tumulus at Vergina.[39] The capture of this

---

[37] 'Macedonia' in the same restricted sense was used once by Thucydides, at 1. 61.3.

[38] A. J. B. Wace and M. S. Thompson, *The Nomads of the Balkans* (reprint, London, 1972) 210.

[39] *Anc. Mac.* 1. 65; M. Andronikos in *AAA* 10 (1977) 1ff.

site was followed by the conquest of the area up to the Ludias river, which then flowed into the Haliacmon just before the Haliacmon entered the sea. These rivers for a time formed the line between the Macedones and the Bottiaei, as in Herodotus VII. 127.1.

This expansion of the Macedones was associated by Herodotus (VIII. 137.1) and Thucydides (II. 99.3) with a royal house, the Temenidae of Argos in the Peloponnese. Thus the Temenidae of Macedon (as in the oracle we have just cited) were a branch of the Temenidae, the royal house of Argos. Both historians were in agreement also on the number of generations which divided the first king, Perdiccas, from the reigning king. Since Thucydides numbered Archelaus (*floruit c.* 410 B.C.) the ninth of the line, we may date the *floruit* of the first king *c.* 650 on the basis of thirty years to a generation. Such a date for the arrival of Perdiccas, one incidentally which occurred in a Kings List of the Macedonians, is acceptable on other grounds; for it was then that the Temenid leader, Pheidon of Argos, fell from power, and that Illyrian rule at Vergina came to an end. At the turn of the sixth century the descent of the Macedonian royal house from the Temenidae of Argos was upheld by the Judges at Olympia when Alexander was admitted as a competitor. Interesting links between Argos and Macedon have been discovered recently. Bronze Age tumuli at Argos, it is now known, were reused for burial during the Geometric period,[40] and the users were most probably the then rulers of Argos, the Temenidae. Equally at the Macedonian capital, Aegeae (now Vergina), royal burials were under tumuli (see Justin XI. 2.1), and tumuli crowned the built-tombs at Vergina, of which one found by Rhomaios contained a marble throne and another, excavated by Andronikos, had offerings of a royal quality. Then in this last burial there was a bronze tripod, dated *c.* 460 B.C., which had been won in the games at the Argive Heraeum; and its presence is best explained by supposing that it was a family heirloom connected with the original homeland of the dynasty.

How did these members of the Temenid house win the throne of the Macedones? Herodotus must have asked that question, and he reported a part of the answer which he was given (probably by Alexander I). It was in fact a folk-tale, probably of Iranian origin (VIII. 137–8). But it contained some pointers: the chronology by generations, the flight from Argos to Illyria, the crossing-over to Upper Macedonia, the pastoral setting of horses, cattle and sheep, and the flight into 'the Gardens of Midas'. No account at all of the actual *coup d'état*! Perhaps that was discreditable, having involved the use of Illyrian troops; or perhaps it was not known.

Once in power the first Temenid king of the Macedones, Perdiccas, captured Vergina and subsequently the plain lying between Verria and

[40] E. Deilaki in *Arch. Delt.* 28 (1973) [1977] *Chr.* 95 and 98f.

the then course of the Ludias. He or his successor dispossessed the Bottiaei, driving them across the Axius, where they found a new home in the hinterland of the Chalcidic peninsula and occupied the site of Olynthus. The excavator of that site has put the occupation generally to not before 650 B.C., and it may have been a decade or two later. The expulsion of the Pieres was achieved probably before the end of the century. In both cases victory was won in battle (Thuc. II. 99.3).

The second stage was an advance inland, when the Almopes were expelled from the headwaters of the Ludias and the Eordi were killed off, except a small remnant who fled east of the Axius. Unlike the Spartans, the Macedones made no serfs; rather they occupied the good lands themselves, most of them making the transition from pastoralism to settled agriculture, which is frequently accompanied by a sharp rise in population. They now held a continuous territory which was defended on the west and north by a ring of mountains, and they made Eordaea into a bastion against the Epirotic tribes. Greater danger threatened from those Paeonians who had a footing on the west bank of the Axius, and it was in the rear of the Paeonians that the refugees from Bottiaea and Eordaea settled. But the Paeonians chose to expand eastwards and in due course clashed with the Persians.

Apart from the Greek colonies on the coast all the peoples of what we call Macedonia were organized as tribes, *ethne*, and were so called by Hecataeus, Herodotus and Thucydides – from the Orestae to the Sithones. Each *ethnos* was itself a cluster of small tribes, as we have seen was the case also among the Epirotes and the Illyrians. The Macedones were no exception to the general rule; just as there were Orestae Molossoi, Triclari Orestae, and Imphees Perrhaebi, so there were 'Argeadae Macedones' (Appian, *Syr.* 63), a tribe claiming descent from an eponymous Argeas, a son of Macedon (Steph. Byz. *s.v. Argeou* and *Argaïs*). It was this tribe which led the way in the expansion of the Macedones; for fragment 11 of the Strabo epitome continued after the mention of the Sithones. 'Of all these the so-called Argeadae became established as masters, they and the Chalcideis of Euboea.' And in fragment 20 the place Amydon (on the left bank of the lower Axius) 'was razed to the ground by the Argeadae'. It is probable that the pre-Temenid royal house (as well as the tribe) was called 'the Argeadae' and that the Temenid house took its place in the tribe; thus the Argeadae continued to be the royal tribe. But this is not to be confused with the royal house which was called the Temenidae by Herodotus, Thucydides and the oracle of Delphi.[41] Argeas belonged to the genealogy of Macedon; Temenus belonged to the genealogy of Heracles.

That the Bisaltae, Crestones and Edones generally spoke their own

[41] E 34, II 26f.

languages is clear from a remark by Thucydides (IV. 109.4), and this was true of Illyrians and Paeonians likewise. What language was spoken by the tribes of Epirus and Macedonia west of the Axius? That the oracular answers of Dodona and the Nekyomanteion from the earliest recorded times were in Greek cannot be doubted; and Herodotus must have found the Thesprotians of his day speaking Greek, as he visited Dodona in their territory and said the first priestess – a refugee from Egypt – learnt Greek among the Thesprotians (II. 56). However, to speak Greek was not to be a Greek in the sixth and fifth centuries; that was a matter of culture, not speech or race. Thus Thucydides classed the Thesprotians and indeed all Epirotic and Macedonian tribes as barbarians (I. 47.3; II. 80.5; II. 81.3 and 6; IV. 124.1). In this sense Dodona and the Dodonaei may have been an exception; for they were analogous to Delphi and the Delphians, an enclave sacred to a god, and in Dodona's case to the supreme Hellenic god, Zeus. For this reason, perhaps, Herodotus wrote of the gifts of the Hyperboreans coming from the north to 'the Dodonaeans first of the Hellenes' (IV. 33.2). That the Molossians, who were immediately adjacent to the Dodonaeans in the time of Hecataeus but engulfed them soon afterwards, spoke Illyrian or another barbaric tongue was nowhere suggested, although Aeschylus and Pindar wrote of Molossian lands. That they in fact spoke Greek was implied by Herodotus' inclusion of Molossi among the Greek colonists of Asia Minor, but it became demonstrable only when D. Evangelides published two long inscriptions of the Molossian state, set up c. 369 B.C. at Dodona, in Greek with Greek names, Greek patronymics and Greek tribal names such as Celaethi, Omphales, Tripolitae, Triphylae etc.[42] As the Molossian cluster of tribes in the time of Hecataeus included the Orestae, Pelagones, Lyncestae, Tymphaei and Elimeotae, as we have argued above, we may be confident that they too were Greek-speaking; for it is inconceivable that such a cluster included tribes speaking different languages. Inscriptional evidence of the Chaones is lacking until the Hellenistic period; but Ps.-Scylax, describing the situation of c. 380–360, put the southern limit of the Illyrians just north of the Chaones, which indicates that the Chaones did not speak Illyrian, and the acceptance of the Chaones into the Epirote Alliance in the 330s suggests strongly that they were Greek-speaking.

That the Macedones were regarded as 'barbarians' was publicized late in the sixth century when the right of Alexander, king of the Macedones, to compete in the Olympic Games was challenged. Evidently as a Macedon he would not have been admitted; he was accepted only as a Temenid of Argos (Hdt. V. 22). But this did not mean that the

[42] E 25. For a different view see *CAH* III.1², 840ff.

Macedones spoke Illyrian or Thracian. Indeed, it has become clear from
the inscribed stelai at Vergina which Andronikos has found recently,
that the fathers of Philip's Macedonians had entirely Greek names, and
we may deduce that their parents spoke Greek at the beginning of the
fourth century. What then of earlier times? Hesiod certainly thought
them to be Greek-speaking; otherwise he would not have made Magnes
and Macedon into cousins of Dorus, Xouthus and Aeolus, who were
the eponymous ancestors of the three main forms of the Greek language
(Dorian, Ionian and Aeolian). Hellanicus, writing late in the fifth
century, made Macedon a son of Aeolus; he would not have done so
unless he had supposed the Macedones to be speakers of some form
of Aeolic Greek. As the twin people, the Magnetes, did speak an Aeolic
dialect (this we know from inscriptions), there is no good reason to
deny that the Macedones spoke an Aeolic dialect, retarded indeed and
broad, because the Macedones, like the Vlachs of Vlakholivadhi, had
been a self-sufficient community on the foothills of Olympus for many
centuries.[43]

If we are correct in our conclusions, the Greek speech of the tribes
in Epirus and in Macedonia west of the Axius should not be ascribed
to the influence of the Greek colonies on their coasts. Nowhere in fact
did Greek colonies convert the peoples of a large hinterland to Greek
speech; for the differences in outlook and economy between colonists
and natives were too great. Equally so in Epirus and Macedonia. For
example, Eretria planted a colony at Methone before 700 B.C., but it
had no effect whatsoever on the culture of the people who buried their
dead at Vergina, only some fifteen miles away as the crow flies. So too
the Greek colonies in Chalcidice had no influence on the Bottiaei during
our period, as far as the archaeological evidence goes. If these tribes
of the hinterland spoke Greek, it was because they had done so before
the Dark Age. What we have seen in this chapter is the consolidation
of the Greek-speaking tribes in the north, which enabled them to fulfil
their future role of defending the frontiers of a city-state civilization and
later of leading that civilization into wider areas.

[43] See *CAH* III.1², 843ff for a different view. There is a summary of the problem in E 34, II 46ff.

CHAPTER 41

CENTRAL GREECE AND THESSALY

W. G. G. FORREST

For the period before about 700 B.C. the chief tools of the historian of Central Greece must be the spade or the map, though a few strokes of ancient pens add a welcome touch of political definition to some events of the second half of the eighth century in stories of colonization and especially of the Lelantine War (*CAH* III.1², pp. 760–3 and here ch. 39*d*) which involved not only the cities of Euboea, but southern Thessaly, Megara, Delphi and other states besides.

More importantly, it was about the same time that Boeotia produced in the poet Hesiod our only contemporary literary evidence for the social and political atmosphere of Late Geometric Greece.[1]

I. HESIOD

Hesiod's life spanned, roughly, the second half of the eighth century, spilling over, perhaps, into the seventh. His father, a trader of Aeolic Cyme, had turned his back on the dangers of the sea to settle on a farm at Ascra on the north-west slopes of Mt Helicon, a miserable village according to the poet, awful in winter and worse in summer, but not perhaps quite so bad as Hesiod's gloom would have us think – at least it was famed in antiquity for its beetroot (Ath. 4D). There Hesiod and his brother Perses were born and there, after their father's death, they fell to quarrelling over the estate, a quarrel which prompted that hard picture of the farmer's year and stern sermon on justice, the *Works and Days*, this around 700 B.C. Somewhat earlier he composed his other surviving work, the *Theogony*, an account of the genealogies of the gods of Greece attached to the myth of the succession of Cronus to Uranus and of Zeus to Cronus as Lord of the Gods, the backbone of the poem. Of other works we have only fragments.

Hesiod, like Homer, lived in the time of transition from oral to written composition. Indeed it seems likely that each was the first, or among the first, to commit to manuscript his own version of a long oral tradition. We can assess their merits as artists but not with any

[1] A 71; A 72; E 144.

286

precision their own contribution in terms of content or the stages of growth in what they inherited.

For the historian two questions pose themselves. First that of the inspiration of the *Theogony*. Primitive accounts of the origin of the world and the gods abound from Polynesia to Persia, from Germany to Japan, but the closeness of parallels with near-Eastern versions, especially with the Babylonian *Enûma Eliš*, show that the Greek was no spontaneous local creation. But when imported? Two periods of oriental contact suggest themselves, the Minoan–Mycenaean and that of the re-opening of eastern links with the founding of Al Mina, a little before 800 B.C. For the former it is argued that time would be needed for the complete absorption of eastern elements, for the latter that it offers more positive association of the east with Greece, especially with Central Greece, and that seventy-five years or so would be time enough. But even in this second context further choice is offered. That the story came via the Hittite empire to Phrygia and thence across the Aegean is unlikely if not impossible. But a route from Al Mina through Crete to Delphi (both figure in the *Theogony*) is as attractive as the more direct one to Euboea and thence Boeotia; either is a trifle more attractive than the assumption of a Mycenaean survival. If so, we have a powerful religious element to add to a possible political and a striking artistic one in the sum of Greece's debt to the east.[2] Herodotus (II. 53) may not have been too far from the truth when he said that Hesiod and Homer were the first to set down a 'theogony' for the Greeks and give the gods their appropriate functions. He need only have added a note on their sources.

Secondly we have to ask about the society in which and for which Hesiod wrote. Here the difference of his subject-matter from that of Homer justifies the assumption that what he says still applies in his own day even if much of it was inherited from the past, an assumption bolstered, for the *Works and Days*, by the autobiographical presentation. This is the origin of the gods we still revere today. This is how farmers should plan their year now, be it the way they always have or not.

The structure of Greek societies around 700 B.C. was a simple one. There was the *demos*, either the whole people or the people excluding those who in Solon's later words 'had power'. At this time it was the aristocrats who had power. There were also slaves and in a few cases, but not in Boeotia, a class somewhere 'between free and slave'. Hesiod was of the *demos* in its second sense, not perhaps so poor a member as his surly grumblings might suggest, for he speaks of farm-labourers and slaves, of mules and oxen, but what mattered in society was the line between noble and commoner, not that between richer and poorer, and Hesiod was of the commons.

[2] A 71 Introduction; E 145.

His rulers he calls *basileis*, a word which normally means 'kings' but here as elsewhere can hardly be pushed further up the social scale than 'lords'. His attitude towards them is somewhat equivocal. In the *Theogony* (esp. 80ff) they are eloquent and just, the fathers of their people, in the *Works and Days* ruthless, corrupt, oppressive.

But the contradiction is easily resolved. The *Theogony* may well have been the poem which Hesiod sang at the games in honour of the nobleman Amphidamas of Chalcis; for, therefore, an audience of noblemen. Abuse would not have won him the tripod of which he was so proud (*Works* 654ff).[3] In humbler circles he could tell the truth as he saw it, that some *basileis* were hungry for bribes, that some *basileis* behaved as the hawk had behaved to the nightingale in the fable:

> Good bird, why all this twittering?
> A stronger bird than you
> Has got you, singer though you be,
> and what he will he'll do.
>
> (*Works* 207–9; trs. H. T. Wade-Gery)

But Hesiod had one friend in court, the highest court of all, Olympian Zeus himself who through his countless agents abroad on earth was kept informed of crooked judgements and of straight ones and would deal out prosperity or disaster as appropriate.

Here, as in other things, Hesiod stood at a moment of transition, a moment of questioning between blind acceptance of aristocratic rule and revolt against it. Whether we go on to see him primarily as a private grumbler with a private grudge against individual nobles or as the precursor of Solon, Aeschylus and Euripides for whom 'the Nightingale was a real power in Greek opinion and behaviour, and the Hawk had to listen',[4] whether, that is, he was near the beginning or the end of question-time, is of little moment. What matters is that there is an element of generalization, the notion of a norm to which a *basileus* should conform, but at the same time that there is no hint that he himself could enforce conformity. There was only Zeus.

II. BOEOTIA, 700–500 B.C.

There was similar grumbling in other parts of Greece. Sooner or later than that of Hesiod, more or less coherent, we do not know. But it is to these other parts that we must look for its translation into action. In our area the spark remained unkindled.

The reason is not far to seek. The Boeotian plain was large enough and fertile enough to keep Boeotians happy with its vegetables and

---

[3] Cf. A 72 *ad loc.*; A 37, 79.   [4] E 144, 12.

grain, the fowls of Tanagra and the eels of Lake Copais, and for the
rich, to support their horses (the team of one Pagondas carried off the
prize at Olympia in 680: Paus. v. 8.7). There was not much to tempt
a Boeotian to lift his eyes above the surrounding hills and mountains
to the sea, no great urge to colonize or to exploit the new economic
opportunities that came with or after colonization elsewhere. Access to
the sea was there, to the east or south-west to the Corinthian Gulf; the
possibility of maritime adventure could occur to Hesiod, as it did later
to Epaminondas, but one ferry-trip to Euboea was enough to satisfy
the one (while brother Perses was warned against anything more
daring), and the other's naval ambitions were short-lived. Boeotia, then,
was essentially an agricultural area, and a stale agrarian economy does
not breed social, political or even much cultural excitement.

As befits a country folk, the Boeotians were not unversed in music
and song. The tradition was that the legendary founder of Thebes,
Amphion, could charm stones to move with his lyre, the gift of the
Muses; more substantially, the noted reeds of Lake Copais furnished
Boeotians with the *aulos* (a clarinet- or oboe-type instrument) and a
famous school of innovators, performers and teachers thereof, famous
and fashionable – the great Pronomus of Thebes was tutor to Alcibiades
(Ath. 184D). At the same time, a country which can produce a Hesiod,
a Pindar or a Corinna is scarcely backward.

Similarly in peasant manner, religion flourished. The gods are
everywhere in Pindar and Hesiod as they were everywhere throughout
the countryside. There were oracular sites in plenty, of Trophonius at
Lebadia, of Ismenian Apollo in Thebes, Ptoian Apollo near Acraephia,
Amphiaraus at Thebes and Oropus; cults, some brought with the
migration from Thessaly, some local, of Athena Itonia at Coronea,
Artemis at Aulis, of Heracles and the Cabiri at Thebes, and hundreds
more.[5] Around these grew sanctuaries, some substantial, respectably
rich and not unattractive to foreign dedicators or competitors (Croesus
of Lydia made gifts to Amphiaraus; Athenians and others won prizes
at the games),[6] but nothing to raise the eyebrows, nothing to suggest
any startling Boeotian artistic inspiration.

There was some not utterly disreputable sculpture and bronzework
but pottery gives the fullest picture.[7] There, alongside much imported
Corinthian ware and some Attic, exists local work in quantity. But it
is in the main derivative and dated stuff, no capturer of a foreign market.
From Geometric through orientalizing to black-figure the Boeotian
potter plodded along behind his Corinthian and Attic models and it is
hard to find studies which do not include judgements such as 'crudely

[5] A. Schachter, *The Cults of Boeotia* (1981–).
[6] Hdt. I. 52; A 36, 73, 75, 91.   [7] H 29, 1003.

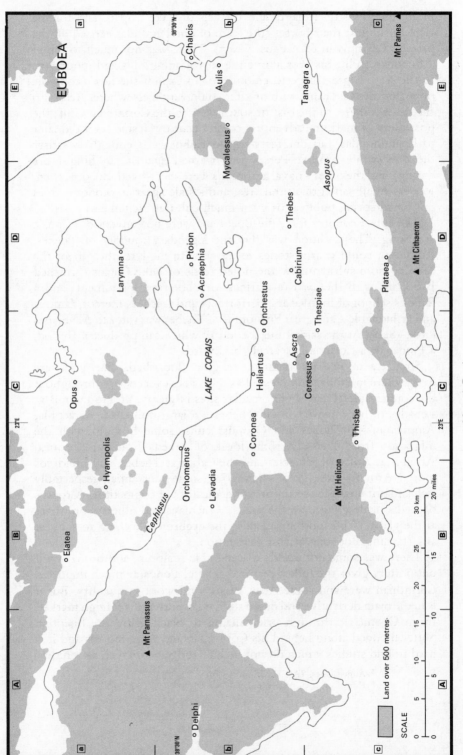

EUBOEA

Chalcis

Aulis

Tanagra

Mycalessus

Asopus

Thebes

Ptoion

Larymna

Acraephia

Cabirium

Plataea

Onchestus

Thespiae

Mt Parnes

Mt Cithaeron

Opus

LAKE COPAIS

Haliartus

Ascra

Ceressus

Hyampolis

Coronea

Thisbe

Elatea

Orchomenus

Levadia

Mt Helicon

Cephissus

Mt Parnassus

Delphi

SCALE

Land over 500 metres·

0   5   10   15   20   25   30 km

0   5   10   15   20 miles

38°30′N

23°E

Map 16. Boetia.

44. A Boeotian 'bird-cup' from Thebes. Mid
sixth century B.C. Height 23·2 cm. (Paris, Louvre
Museum A 572; after *Corpus Vasorum Antiquorum*
Louvre XVII, pl. 10.3.)

filled', 'primitive', 'humbly decorated'. There is only one original
group, the colourful and attractive 'bird-cups' (fig. 44) which roughly
span the sixth century – though even there the birds are often painted
upside-down (Boeotian taste, or painter's laziness?).

It is not that Boeotians were saving their talents for invention in other
directions. Of political development within the cities we hear very little
and that is almost certainly because there was little to record. Oligarchic
in 700 B.C., they were still oligarchic at the time of Xerxes' invasion.
One early 'law-giver' at Thebes is mentioned, Philolaus, a Bacchiad
nobleman from Corinth, whose activities, if tradition is correct, cannot
come much later than 700 (Arist. *Pol.* 1274a). But given his background,
his measures are more likely to have been regulative than revolutionary.
Only one is recorded, a law of adoption designed to maintain the
number of property-owners. More interesting is the unanswerable
question – had an oligarchy of birth moved at all towards an oligarchy
of wealth? The likely descent of Pagondas, Boeotian general in 424,[8]
from the Olympic victor of 680 argues some survival of the former,
but there was once a law in Thebes, says Aristotle (*Pol.* 1278a25), which
permitted political office only to those who had abandoned commercial
pursuits for ten years. In the absence of date or context its import cannot
be judged (e.g. whether it was permissive or restrictive), but at least
it means that by the fifth century or before some Boeotians were selling
pigs as well as breeding them – and had political ambitions besides.
Indeed Herodotus at one moment mentions an 'assembly' in Thebes.
But how constituted he does not say and in practice a '*dynasteia* of a
few men' still ruled in 480 B.C. (Hdt. v. 79; Thuc. III. 62).

[8] Thuc. IV. 91; cf. Paus. v. 8.7.

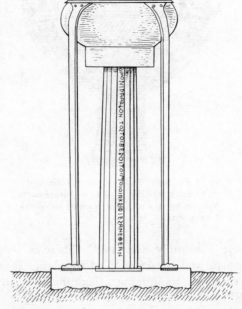

45. Reconstruction of a tripod dedication at the Ptoion
sanctuary. Late sixth century B.C. (After E 107, I, pl. 15.1;
II, 49, fig. 3; cf. A 36, 93, pl. 8, no. 13.)

More significant, however, is the political structure of Boeotia as a
whole. By the later fifth century it was a well-organized federal state,
dominated by Thebes, but unification had been slow and in our period
'Boeotia did this', 'Boeotia did not do that' are dangerous phrases to
use without thought. Geography and racial identity imposed some sense
of unity celebrated by the festival of the Pamboeotia at the sanctuary
of Athena Itonia, a festival not attested before the third century B.C.
though likely to be primitive.[9] But the unity it advertised will have been
more akin to that of the Panionia than the Panathenaea. There was no
political cohesion to back it, at least at the outset.

Homer lists no fewer than thirty-one contingents from Boeotia in the
Greek army before Troy, and though the number had been reduced by
destruction, abandonment or absorption, there were still a dozen or so
independent cities in existence around 700, among them Orchomenus
and Coronea to the west of Lake Copais, Thespiae, Haliartus, Thebes,
Acraephia to the south and east and further south again, on or near the
border with Attica, Plataea, Tanagra and Oropus. Factors encouraging
separatism were many, pride in past glory (Orchomenus had once been

[9] See n. 5.

46. Silver coin of Haliartus. Late sixth century
B.C. (London, British Museum; after *BMC
Central Greece* pl. 7.14.)

mighty and was still a serious rival to Thebes), the hostility of close
neighbours (Thespiae was only about 24 km from Thebes), religious
rivalry (Thebes coveted Acraephia's Ptoion), proximity to other states
(Larymna wavered between Boeotia and Locris, Oropus between
Eretria or Athens and Thebes, Plataea was drawn towards Athens).
There are too many variables and a sad lack of evidence.

Excavations at the Ptoion are invoked to place Theban encroachment
there early in the first half of the sixth century.[10] Two sanctuaries are
involved, one at Perdikovrysi (Apolline), one at Kastraki nearby
(belonging to the hero Ptoios), and, the argument runs, it was when
Apollo, under Theban pressure and bringing with him Theban rites,
moved in to Perdikovrysi in the late seventh century, that the locals of
Acraephia transferred the hero to Kastraki and with him the custom
of dedicating tripods in his sanctuary (fig. 45). But the chronological
and dedicatory patterns are not clear enough to impose such a simple
story. That the establishment at Kastraki was later, that there was some
shift in tripod concentration, that there was a close resemblance of the
Apollo cult with that of Ismenian Apollo at Thebes, and that Thebes
expanded northwards at some point, these are all facts, and perhaps are
best explained by some rather more haphazard version of the same
account, but a further suggestion that the fight in southern Thessaly
between (Theban) Heracles and Cycnus, retailed in the Hesiodic *Shield
of Heracles*, reflects Theban ambitions still further north at the same
period rests more on hope than evidence.[11]

Later in the century, certainly not before 550, appears the first
Boeotian coinage (fig. 46),[12] a common 'federal' type marked by a
Boeotian shield on the obverse, from Tanagra and Haliartus (identified
by their initials) and from Thebes, significantly without an initial. To
these a second issue, from about the end of the century, adds mints
at Acraephia, Coronea, Mycalessus and Pharae (near Tanagra). Meanwhile, however, Orchomenus had begun to advertise its continued

[10] E 107, 116–34 and review; E 96; E 97, 437–50; cf. in general E 120, II, III.
[11] E 109, 79–84.   [12] H 48, 108–10.

independence, real or imagined, with an issue of its own, an ear of corn in place of the shield and on the reverse an incuse following Aeginetan types (a recollection of past association?)[13] while a dedication at Olympia of the third quarter of the century celebrates an Orchomenian victory over (already federated?) Coronea.[14]

Thus it would seem that by about 500 Thebes controlled the whole of Boeotia south of Copais. Or almost. In 506 the Thebans recite the names of some loyal, local allies, the men of Thespiae, of Coronea, of Tanagra (Hdt. v. 79.2). One name is missing, that of the little city of Plataea, south-west across the Asopus river, which, possibly in 519,[15] had appealed to Athens against Theban pressure, and with Athenian (and some Corinthian) help had saved her autonomy, help which she more than repaid at Marathon and then on her own doorstep in 479. One thorn in the flank of the Boeotian pig.

III. THESSALY, 700–500 B.C.

Thessaly is little other than a bigger and better Boeotia. A still larger, even flatter plain, surrounded by yet more formidable hills and mountains which gave only one opening to the sea at the south-east corner. True, this was to the superb natural shelter of the Gulf of Pagasae through which foreign influence had spread well into the heart of the country in early centuries. But, by and large, we are dealing with another self-sufficient, stable agricultural society.

In earlier days young Jason had been able to acquire a gentleman's education at the feet of the centaur Chiron before becoming Thessaly's only great merchant-explorer, and Achilles learnt enough of the lyre to accompany his barrack-room ballads before Troy; later a much-embroidered tale may conceal a real colonial venture via Crete to Magnesia on the Maeander;[16] throughout the Dark Ages a combination of imported and local inspiration produced unpretentious but presentable Protogeometric and (less confident) Geometric pottery.[17] But, after about 700, there is little of native culture or art (beyond a line in miniature bronzes), no interest in the world abroad. Alcman sums it up:

> He was no rustic boor, nor a lubber...nor a
> Thessalian by race...(fr. 16 Page: trs. Bowra)

The *basileis* who exploited the riches of the plain and controlled its cities, Larissa and Crannon to the north-east, Pharsalus and Pherae in the south, are a little more real than those of Boeotia – at least we have

[13] See n. 12; P–W *s.v.* 'Kalaureia'.   [14] A 36, 93, no. 11.
[15] Hdt. VI. 108; Thuc. III. 68 (for the date, Gomme, *ad loc.*).
[16] E 130, nos. 378–82.   [17] H 25, 158–63.

some of their names and families, and some snippets of information about them. The Aleuadae, reputedly responsible for the first federal organization and leaders of the pro-Persian group before 480; the Scopadae, victims of collective disaster in the late sixth century (divine wrath, or the roof of their dining-hall, fell upon them), the Creondae, Echecratidae and others. Their wealth was notorious:

> Many were the serfs who drew their monthly rations
> in the halls of Antiochus and of lord
> Aleuas; many the calves that with the horned cattle
> bellowed as they were driven to the byres of the
> Scopadae; thousands of sheep were pastured across the plain
> of Crannon by their shepherds for the hospitable Creondae.

So sang Theocritus later (*Id.* XVI. 34ff). With these resources they could behave as befitted Thessalians, generously and magnificently; magnificently in their dedications to the gods (the earliest offering at Delphi known to Pausanias (x. 16.8) was made by an Echecratidas of Larissa), their banquets (more famed for their size than their savour), in their racing-stables (Thessalian horses were the first in Greece); generously in their patronage of the poets, Simonides, Anacreon and Pindar among them, though, as Simonides discovered, poetry was more appreciated for its flattery than its finesse. Indeed, when asked why Thessalians were the only people he never cheated, he replied, 'Because they are too stupid' (Plut. *Mor.* 15D).

But in the society which these men administered there were two elements unknown in Boeotia. The invading Thessalians had occupied only the plain. Of its previous population one group moved south to settle in Boeotia, some crossed the sea to establish themselves in Lesbos or the neighbouring coast of Asia Minor, others will have withdrawn to join the inhabitants of the surrounding hills, many, probably the majority, became 'Penestae', the serfs who pastured the sheep or drove the cattle and drew their rations in exchange.[18]

Naturally the central power came, though not without a struggle (Arist. *Pol.* 1269a36–8), to dominate its less well-endowed neighbours, either informally, as with the Dolopes on the eastern slopes of Mt Pindus, or formally. Three peoples in particular had some special status, the Perrhaebi along the northern border, the Magnesians on the east coast and the Phthiotic Achaeans in milder country to the south. Sometimes they are described as 'subjects', sometimes, apparently, they are included among Thessaly's 'allies', thus implying for them some ambiguous relationship similar in kind, though not necessarily in content, to that of the so-called 'subject-allies' to Athens in the

[18] E 125; E 124, 48–53.

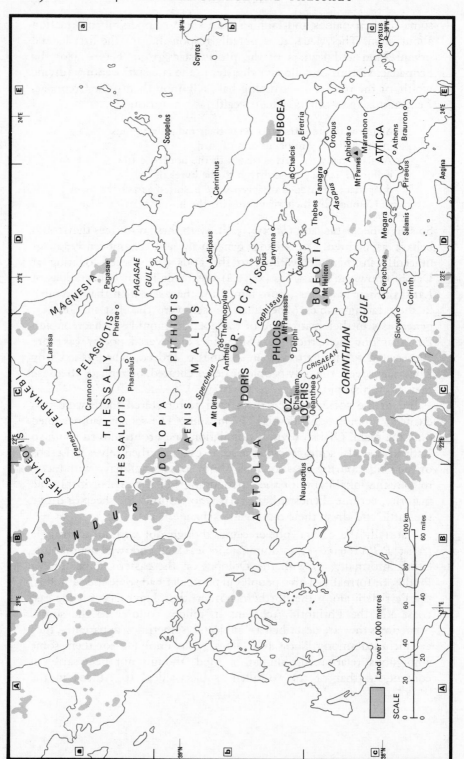

Map 17. Central Greece and Thessaly.

developed Delian League. As we shall see they were independent
enough, in the main presumably in domestic matters, for Thessaly to
claim votes for them on the Amphictionic Council; subservient enough,
presumably, to make it worth Thessaly's while to do so. Once, but only
once, they are called *perioeci*, 'dwellers-around', in a constitutional not
merely a geographical context, where two of their duties are mentioned,
to provide light-armed troops in wartime and to pay tribute, its nature
and occasion unspecified, on a scale 'laid down by Scopas', i.e. in the
sixth century or before. But that is our only clue to the mechanics of
the arrangement.[19]

The general condition of the Penestae is more readily grasped – one
of complete servitude to their Thessalian masters. But closer definition
is difficult. Much depends on numbers. Were the Thessalians nearer to
a conquering elite, as the Normans were in England, or to a new
population as the Spartans were in the Laconian plain? How far down
the scale could Thessalians be? How rich was the richest Penestes?
Theocritus gives a gloomy view of stinted rations as a reward for labour,
but a near contemporary of his, Archemachus of Euboea,[20] describes
a fairer contract, that the serf should work the land and pay a
contribution, presumably a fixed proportion of the produce, in exchange,
as did the Helot in Sparta or the Athenian *hektemoros*. He was, moreover,
given security against being sold abroad or arbitrarily killed. Some of
them, adds Archemachus, were even more prosperous than their
masters. The two pictures are not irreconcilable and other evidence is
not inconsistent with variation. References to revolts, vague but no
doubt real, or possible revolts might argue hard conditions – but there
can be discontent with inferiority of status as well as with poverty.
Penestae could be thought of as a mass fit for the lowest kind of military
duty – but one Thessalian prince in the fifth century could furnish two
or three hundred Penestae as cavalrymen from his own estate, suggesting
that Thessaly as a whole might provide some thousands.[21] Utterly
miserable yokels do not make cavalrymen.

Details, then, are obscure and other questions cannot be answered
– did the serfs belong to the state, as Helots did? Probably not. Could
a serf ever be freed, as occasionally a Helot was? Probably yes. Were
there local variations inside Thessaly as there were no doubt, in relations
with the *perioeci*? And here we must turn to the main problem – how
much of a unity was Thessaly? How did it become the federal state
which we know in the fifth and fourth centuries?

There were four regions of the plain, Hestiaeotis (north-west),
Pelasgiotis (north-east) containing most of the major cities, Thessaliotis

---

[19] E 119; A 26, 1–6.   [20] *FGrH* 424 F 1.
[21] [Dem.] XIII. 23 and Dem. XXIII. 199.

(south and west) and Phthiotis (further south and east around the city of Pharsalus), each with its villages or towns, each made up of the estates of great families, more or less powerful locally and as large as geography, economics, politics or the hand of the gods directed from time to time; now rivals, now friends in the game of dynastic intrigue. The Echecratidae seem to have been as fruitful of marriage ties as the Metelli at Rome – the name appears at Larissa, at Pharsalus and at Crannon; the Creondae and the Scopadae were distinct – but there was a Scopas, son of Creon.[22] But these links should not be assumed to be any more enduring than were those of the Metelli, nor should any one group be credited with lasting authority over the whole.

Opinions differ on the machinery through which any such authority could have been exercised. In 511 the Thessalians 'by common decision' sent a force to help the Athenian tyrants in accordance with an alliance which may date back to the 540s.[23] But that is the earliest firm evidence for a federal council or assembly and therefore, presumably, for some rudimentary kind of federal organization. A date no later is also implied by the financial arrangements introduced by a Scopas. Other references are clouded, mainly by the ambiguity of 'Thessalians' – all Thessalians or only some? Some four thousand were killed in a battle with the Phocians, too many one would think for a local levy, but that was late in the sixth century. The Thebans defeated the 'Thessalians' and their 'commander', Lattamyas, at Ceressus earlier in the same century and the rare name in the form Lattamos recurs in a late inscription from Crannon (as son of an Echecratidas!); a purely Crannonian expedition to southern Boeotia would be odd.[24] A certain Eurylochus, origin unstated (though the name recurs in Larissa in the late fifth century), led the 'Thessalian' forces in the first Sacred War c. 595–590, and the involvement of the Amphictiony in this war suggests pan-Thessalian support – but does not impose it. Before 700 Cleomachus of Pharsalus, with 'Thessalian' cavalry helped the Chalcidians to a victory in the Lelantine War, but were they Thessalians or Pharsalians (cf. CAH III.1[2], ch. 18b)?

In sum, it seems a little more likely than not that there were cases of combined action before the mid-sixth century, occasions when an ethnic consciousness, which was always there and, as in Boeotia, may already have been celebrated regularly at the sanctuary of Athena Itonia near Pharsalus, was translated into federal endeavour. In the fourth century it was asserted by the ambitious Jason of Pherae that the system on which such action was based had been created at an early but unspecified date by a certain Aleuas, nicknamed the 'Red' according

[22] D 50, 235–8.   [23] Hdt. v. 63.3; cf. below, p. 317.
[24] Below, p. 304; IG ix.2, 469.

to Aristotle who supplements (but perhaps in some measure distorts) Jason's picture.[25] Under him the four regions or 'tetrarchies' had been recognized, each further divided into *klaroi* (lots), with the duty to provide uniform contingents for the army, in all, said Jason, 6,000 horse and more than 10,000 hoplites. Regulations for the *perioeci* then followed in the time of Scopas (here it is that Aristotle may have disagreed in ascribing everything to Aleuas). In charge of the whole was a *tagos* (commander-in-chief), beneath him four tetrarchs. Aleuas, of course, was the first *tagos* – and Jason saw himself as a successor.

According to Xenophon in his account of Jason, the *tagos* was elected ('chosen' might be a better word), and, it is implied, was elected only in special circumstances, e.g. in times of war or other crisis. Some have therefore argued for a series of *ad hoc* appointments, drawing attention to the fact that other possible *tagoi* (especially those mentioned above) do appear in military contexts and to a phrase in a mid-fifth century inscription which was translated 'in periods when there was and periods in which there was not a *tagos*'. But the former could be due to accident of survival and the latter may well be a mistranslation.[26] Others feel the need of a permanent federal official. For them Jason may be recording only a fourth-century lapse in the system while the twenty-seven year 'rule of Thessaly' advertised by an inscription for a certain Daochus in the late fifth century seems to be somewhat more than temporary. But this is to tamper with Xenophon's words, and the rule of Daochus can be made, though not without difficulty, to span the twenty-seven years of the Peloponnesian War.[27]

These two views can be expanded, the latter into a story of a strong central authority established by Aleuas at an early date (*c.* 700 has been favoured, but the late sixth century has had its advocates), gradually enfeebled with the developments of cities with aspirations to independence; the former to one of spasmodic (not necessarily weak) federalism from the start. Neither rules out a real Aleuas or a real Scopas at the root of Jason's propaganda. Neither should make us overlook the fact of divisions in or between cities or regions. Nothing should tempt us to forget that behind the façade, whatever it was, lay reality – the rivalling ambitions of the great houses, of *basileis* unchallenged from below.

[25] Xen. *Hell.* VI. 1.4–4.37; Arist. frs. 497–8; cf. E 142.
[26] *IG* IX. 2, 257; E 88.
[27] *SIG*³ 274; L. Moretti, *Inscr. Agon.* 68–75, no. 29.

IV. EAST AND WEST LOCRIS, PHOCIS, MALIS, DORIS,
700–500 B.C.

The area of hills and mountains between and to the west of Boeotia
and Thessaly resolved itself after the migration period into a number
of units, some of which can be described as, some of which can only
be flattered by the name of, states; Malis in the lower, Aenis in the upper
Spercheus valley; Doris, reputedly homeland of the Dorians, by the
source of the Cephissus; Phocis around Mt Parnassus dividing Locris
into two, East (or Epicnemidian or Opuntian) Locris, the coastal strip
facing Euboea, and West (or Ozolian) Locris on the Corinthian Gulf.
Two sizeable and fertile plains at the heads of the Crisaean and Malian
Gulfs, one less fertile in the upper Cephissus valley, the rest poor upland
country or worse.

Geography, then, dictated weakness and provided powerful neighbours to exploit it. There is little history that is not tied up with the
comings and goings, failures or successes of those neighbours.

Although not formally admitted to periœcic status, the Dorians,
Aenianes and Malians were, in so far as they mattered at all, under
Thessalian control. Only of the Malians is anything domestic recorded;
that they had an urban centre at Trachis under Mt Oeta in the south,
later, in 426, to be replaced by the Spartan colony, Heraclea Trachinia;
and that their constitution once ('once' from Aristotle's standpoint)
gave political recognition to those performing or who had performed
military service, but restricted office to the former.[28]

Phocis and the Locrides are a little more substantial. The physical
division of the Locrians by the penetration of the Phocians northwards
from Parnassus towards the coast of the Gulf of Euboea produced two
communities with a strong sense of identity, some common practices
and much divergence in later development.

Each Locris enjoyed a stretch of coast-line with good harbours, the
East at Larymna and Opus, the West in the Gulf of Crisa and above
all at Naupactus, a superb strategic point at the narrows of the
Corinthian Gulf. But neither seems to have exploited them much for
its own commercial development. Presumably through lack of resources,
the East provided only seven small warships (penteconters) for the
Greek fleet in 480; the West provided none, presumably through lack
of inclination as well. In one case the wildness of the hinterland, in the
other its virtual absence meant that the harbours were there to help or
hinder passing traffic rather than as centres for the distribution of its
goods. Hindrance was the favourite game of the West Locrians. They
are lumped together with the Aetolians, Acarnanians and other wild

[28] Ath. 461E, citing Hermippus, frs. 70–1; Scythinus *FGrH* 13 F 1 et. al.; Ar. *Pol.* 1297b12–6.

men by Thucydides (I. 5) as traditionalists in the practice of piracy and brigandage, while a mid-fifth-century treaty between the cities of Oeanthea and Chaleum devotes itself entirely to the regulation (note, not suppression) of those arts. But help was available as well – at least the Corcyreans found it useful to appoint a *proxenos* in Oeanthea in the seventh century, very useful to judge from the tomb with which they honoured him in death.[29]

The same kind of distinction between coast and hinterland continued along the north shore of the Corinthian Gulf and into the Ionian sea, the 'coast' now being taken to include the offshore islands of Ithaca, Cephalonia and Leucas, but with some differences. The interior of Aetolia is even wilder than Locris immediately to the east, and affords correspondingly less evidence for life or history. There was one quasi-urban centre at Thermum at the foot of the mountains by the side of Lake Trichonis, later the religious and political centre of the Aetolian League. Some scanty traces of a primitive temple, perhaps Late Geometric, and the more substantial remains of its sixth-century successor show that Apollo Thermius was already installed to serve as focus for whatever communal purposes Aetolians pursued, but of what they were we know nothing. So too the less forbidding but still remote Acarnania had its 'capital', at Stratus on the right bank of the River Achelous, the frontier with Aetolia. A powerful enough city in the fifth century, it must have existed before but in what capacity we can only surmise. For the whole area it is enough to note that large tracts were still un-Hellenized in the late fifth century and to quote Thucydides: 'the habit of going about armed still survives [*sc.* in Locris, Aetolia, Acarnania]' (II. 68 and I. 5).

The settlements on the coast, at Calydon, Pleuron and Amphilochian Argos (inside the Ambracian Gulf) do not offer much more in the way of solid information except in small measure Calydon where late seventh- and sixth-century temples testify to the worship of Artemis Laphria and perhaps, therefore, to the existence of the later important festival which took her name. Surely, however, their concern was more with the rich ships that passed close by than with the yokels in the hills behind. But here there is a new element. Other Greek states, especially the Corinthians, established colonies on the coast or in the islands, this in itself a sign that they saw these as alien, 'barbarian' parts; the Corinthians on Ithaca, the Eretrians on Corcyra, the Corinthians later at Corcyra, Leucas, Anactorium and Ambracia. Their story belongs elewhere in this volume; we note only that their existence witnesses to the importance of the north and the west. Some went to exploit, some waited to prey on the exploiters.

[29] M–L no. 4; M. N. Tod, *Greek Historical Inscriptions* (1946) no. 34.

But to return to the Locrians. On one occasion they too indulged in a colonial adventure, to Epizephyrian Locri on the toe of Italy. Antiquity arrived at a date for this in 673 (roughly confirmed by archaeology) but could not agree on the origin, geographical or social, of the settlers. According to Aristotle and (vehemently) Polybius, they were slaves who had contaminated noble Locrian matrons during the absence of their husbands in Spartan service during the First Messenian War; according to Timaeus, free men who reproduced in Italy the free society of their homeland.[30] The discreditable version as it stands is obviously a doublet of the tale of the Spartan Partheniae at Tarentum and the link with the Messenian War is nonsensical – the Locrians would hardly wait more than forty years to act against their errant slaves. Nevertheless, the emigrants may have been some kind of unwanted 'inferior' element in Locris – such men do not necessarily forget the practices they have left behind (cf. indeed Tarentum) – nor is some link with Sparta impossible. Even if direct Spartan participation, claimed by Pausanias (at III. 3.1) is rejected, there may have been indirect contact through Tarentum, later an ally and possibly at the time an assistant in the foundation.[31] There is firmer testimony to help from Syracuse and this, with the Corcyrean link, not to mention the admission of Locrians to a site in Corinth's western 'empire', suggests Corinthian sympathy – and Corinth was still Sparta's friend in 673. The founders, then, even if surplus to domestic requirement, probably had international as well as domestic blessing for their effort.

West Locris fits more readily into this pattern than East Locris, and a West Locrian origin for the colony is further supported by similarity of alphabet.[32] On the other hand, East Locris might have found a key to the west in neighbouring Chalcis and some institutions of Italian Locri are attested for (though this does not necessarily mean that they existed only in) East Locris. Ancient authorities disagreed. We can only have doubt, even admitting the possibility of a joint interest (such as there was in Naupactus later). (See also the section on Locri Epizephyrii in ch. 38.)

Italian Locri was famed as the home of one of the earliest Greek law-codes, the work of Zaleucus who sat at the feet of Thaletas of Crete – according to others Lycurgus was his fellow-pupil (Arist. *Pol.* 1274a28–30); in either case, or neither, he may have taken with him from his homeland some love of legality, or mainland parents may have learnt from their colonial children, for there is evidence both in East and West of quite sophisticated legal procedures at a fairly early date.

---

[30] Timaeus *FGrH* 566 F 11 and 12; Polybius XII. 5–16; Aristotle's arguments are inferred from these passages (cf. Walbank *ad loc.*).   [31] Strabo 259c emended.

[32] A 36, 285.

In West Locris there are only the scantiest traces of any federal structure and the various cities managed their own affairs with little interference. The piracy law mentioned above was a private treaty between Chaleum and Oeanthea; another unidentified city passed regulations for the allotment of new land and envisaged the admission of new citizens; Naupactus appears to have negotiated independently with East Locris and Chaleum for reinforcements (all this between about 525 and 450 B.C.). But the legislation, though local, was refined. Procedures are laid down for the appointment of jurors, the imposition of fines, the conduct of cases, the lines of inheritance, taxation, relations between old and new members of the community, while in one case (at Oeanthea) there is mention of a special court for suits involving foreigners. An extract from the unknown city to give the flavour of the whole:

Unless under the pressure of war a majority of 101 men chosen from the best citizens decide to bring in at least 200 fighting-men as additional settlers, whoever proposes a division or puts it to a vote in the council of elders or in the city or in the select-men or makes civil strife... he shall be accursed... his property shall be confiscated and his house demolished just as under the law about murder.[33]

Allusions in the same inscription say something of the city's institutions. There are magistrates, *demiourgoi* and an *archos*, an aristocratic council, an assembly and what appears to be a second, presumably non-aristocratic, council. Then there are the mysterious 101 'best men'. There is no clue to the composition or the competence of the assembly. Was it open to all and frequently consulted? Or restricted and occasional? The council and the 'best men' point to the survival of aristocratic ways. A second council, the 'select-men', smacks of something different. Such bodies existed in the sixth century in Chios and in Athens and after a fashion in Sparta (in the shape of the ephors), representing something in the community other than the aristocracy, but anything similar in backward Locris can only astonish.

The Naupactus decree is our fullest evidence for the workings of East Locris, since besides controlling the status of East Locrian newcomers in Naupactian society, it lays down their rights, continuing or resumable, in their homeland. In civil and religious matters the colonist is to be treated as a foreigner, but he may return to East Locris if he wishes without payment and may inherit family property there. Similarly, next of kin in Locris may inherit a colonist's property if he presents himself in person. Allusions again help towards a wider picture. The cities of East Locris have each their own laws, but responsibility for the decree

[33] M–L nos. 13 and 20.

and for most of its administration rests with the federal government at the federal centre, Opus (from which the state took one of its names). Of this government only one magistrate is named, an *archos* as in the western city, but there is also an assembly, defined as 'The Thousand', a definition which gives no clue to its power but implies some qualification for membership – military service one would suppose since the Opuntians at Thermopylae in full force numbered just 1,000 men. Elsewhere we hear of another institution, the Hundred House-holds, basically, it seems, East Locrian, but perhaps shared with the West – certainly exported to Italy. These formed, no doubt, a traditional aristocracy like that of the Eupatridae in Athens, but we do not know that they continued to have any formal constitutional rights. In 457 the Athenians took as hostages 'the richest' Locrians – their number, 100, is suggestive (Thuc. I. 108.3). More onerous, and more certain, was their liability to provide tribute through a thousand years in expiation of the misdeeds of Locrian Ajax at Troy – two girls from their number to face death or temple-service at Ilium, at first for life, later annually. One might think that such a service merited political reward, but perhaps the honour was enough – in the third century one family volunteered to accept a monopoly.[34]

But such rites apart and when left in peace by stronger neighbours, a Locrian, be his bent for piracy, politics or litigation, could lead a fairly happy life. Aristocratic survivals there were, but they were not conspicuous, government was limited to a few, but quite a few. It was the sort of state of which Aristotle could approve.

The internal history of Phocis is obscured by one dramatic tale and one floating event. Herodotus (VIII. 27–33) describes fighting between the Phocians and the Thessalians not long before the Persian invasion. Plutarch (*Mor.* 244), in his colourful account of what may be the same campaign, adds that it was a Thessalian reprisal for a Phocian revolt in which Thessalian governors and tyrants (Thessalian nominees) had been killed. Elsewhere (*Camillus* 19.4; *Mor.* 866F) he mentions a Boeotian victory over the Thessalians at Ceressus in the extreme south-west of Boeotia, a position which could only have been approached through Phocis. In each case, then, a period of Thessalian occupation or domination, one, say, about 500, the other when? Plutarch puts Ceressus 'not long before 570'. If he was right, or nearly right, one could imagine a continuing Thessalian presence from the time of the Sacred War (below, pp. 313–18) through Ceressus to about 500. If he is wrong (and Plutarch's dates are rarely sacred) Ceressus can be absorbed into a shorter, later period of Thessalian control; Phocis before about 500 can be free.

But free or not, we know nothing of its constitution before the

[34] E 110; C 139.

liberation, and little enough thereafter. It was a federal state as is shown by the regular ascription of this or that action to 'the Phocians', not to any one of the twenty or so constituent 'cities', and by the issue of a federal coinage after about 500. But we hear more of doings in the field and at times of crisis than of every-day administration in the chief city Elatea and we cannot, therefore, readily translate the assemblies of which we hear or the structure of command into normal civilian practice. All that can be said is that there regularly seem to have been three generals, chosen by the assembly, to one of whom overall authority might be given but who still consulted the assembly on major decisions. One of these, Daiphantus of Hyampolis, did so consult before defeating the Thessalians, a man important enough (or a near enough neighbour) to earn a biography by Plutarch (*Mor.* 244B). But that biography, like so much of Phocian history, is lost.

V. DELPHI, 750–500 B.C.

So far Phocis' most important site and probably for a time its most important city have gone unmentioned – Delphi and Crisa. But, separated from the rest of Phocis by Parnassus, they had a life, and in one case a death, of their own.

Crisa, the vanished city – or rather the city that is always being found but is never there. The Classical Greek usually approached the sanctuary and oracle of Apollo at Delphi through a port on the Crisaean Gulf which he called Cirrha. But tradition told of an earlier city, Crisa, which had grown rich on its fertile plain, its links with the west (there was a story that it founded Italian Metapontum), and on traffic to Delphi. But greed bred impiety; it harassed the pilgrims and had to be crushed by a holy alliance of Thessaly, Athens and Sicyon in the First Sacred War (*c.* 590). Crisa was destroyed, its plain dedicated to Apollo to remain uncultivated for all time. Such was the story. But where and what was Crisa? Some ancient scholars noted the difference of the names, Cirrha/Crisa, and posited two sites; others the similarity and settled for one. Linguistically the latter were certainly right, but modern scholars remained divided until the archaeologists intervened. They dug first at an inland site temptingly called Chryso immediately beneath Delphi where they at once came upon a destruction level and beneath it the remains of a prosperous city – but it was Prehistoric, not Archaic. They moved to the coast, to the Classical port. Beneath it again a destruction level, beneath it a prosperous city – but again Prehistoric, not Archaic. The story of Bronze Age Crisa/Cirrha is clear; one unit, no doubt, but with a centre that moved with the times. Its impious successor, it seems, was blotted out all too thoroughly by the crusaders of 590.[35]

[35] E 121.

Nevertheless, it was in the territory of Crisa/Cirrha that Apollo first set up his sanctuary. So said the sixth-century author of the *Homeric Hymn*:

> You came to Crisa, at the
> foot of snow-capped Parnassus, a spur facing to the west.
> Rocky cliffs overhang it while a deep gulch winds below,
> a harsh valley. There Lord Phoebus Apollo resolved to build
> his temple. (282–6)

and then, when the god had found a Cretan ship at sea and brought it to the Gulf, he and the men who were to be his first priests

came to Crisa, standing out clear among its vines...and there Apollo leaped from the ship, like a star that shines at midday...entered his sanctuary and lit the flame which shone over the whole of Crisa. And the women and their daughters cried out at the shock of Phoebus. (438–47)

There had been a Mycenaean Delphi, a miserable enough place which, home though it was of some goddess, shared none of the wealth of the city in the plain below. This was destroyed by the northern invaders of about 1200 B.C., but Delphi was ignored, surviving however only to be covered soon afterwards by a fall of earth and rocks from the cliffs above. We remember the tradition that Ga, the great Earth-goddess, had been worshipped at Delphi before Apollo came – if so, she smothered her sanctuary in a shroud of her own making. Some life continued, but it was not until the eighth century that signs appear of renewed cult practices. Apollo had arrived and by 700 what must have begun as no more than a local sanctuary of Cirrha was known throughout the Greek world for its wealth (already in the *Iliad*, IX. 404–5) and its wisdom.

This is not the place to discuss the origins of Apolline worship or the nature of Greek belief in a god's power through oracles to counsel men. Suffice it that they worshipped and believed; and that no site was more fitted by nature to impose 'the shock of Phoebus'. But more is needed to explain Delphi's success and here we must pause to consider two assumptions that are often made in studies of the oracle. First, that it was all some kind of sham. Brought up outside the Olympian religion, brought up however to admire the Greeks, we are easily tempted to feel that Greeks too, being men of genius, could not have accepted that religion. And besides, how could anyone, especially the priests, be taken in by the absurdities of Delphic ritual – the frenzied ravings of Apollo's priestess, the Pythia, and all the rest? But the more extreme absurdities occur only in the anti-Delphic propaganda of the early Christian church, and, stripped of them, tradition tells us little of the real procedure. Ritual purification completed, probably at the spring of Castalia below the sanctuary, ritual sacrifice and appropriate payment made, the client was admitted to the temple to put his question. The Pythia, at first, it was said, a beautiful young local girl but, after a slight incident with an enquirer who found her as much exciting as excited, a somewhat maturer lady, became possessed of the god and gave her answer, either by casting lots or in verse, in the latter case either directly from her own lips or, very much more probably, through the agency of a priest, the *prophetes*, who was deemed capable of interpreting her inspired but unintelligible utterance. But nothing here need have been less than solemn and impressive. Besides, the Greeks, who had keen noses for corruption and imposture, smelled no more of either than was to be expected in any successful religious organization. Sparta had important officers of state, the *Pythioi*, especially charged with the preservation of Delphic oracles. Theognis, a poet not given to affected piety, could write (805–10) that the envoy to Delphi must be straighter than a die: 'Add a word [to the Pythia's answer]; where will you find a remedy? Take one away; how will you escape offending the gods?' In public and private Apollo was respected. Greeks, clients and priests alike, did believe.

But how many Greeks, how much of the time? Choice lies between 'nearly all, nearly always' and 'nearly all, but only when it suited them'. Many scholars assume that Delphi's own picture of itself as the impartial interpreter of Apollo's will, a common sanctuary which all consulted and to which all gave thanks, is correct; that the god's authority was such that he could override or ignore considerations of 'party'-politics. Others assume that such a common sanctuary cannot exist, that willingness to give advice on political matters must lead to commitment, to partiality; that no state would consult unless it had some hope of a friendly answer or would send a thank-offering to a god who had helped its enemies. That is an extreme but not distorted statement of the two positions as one example will show. About 630 B.C. an Athenian consulted Delphi with a view to making himself tyrant of Athens. He misunderstood the advice he received and failed. Comments one: 'a Greek citizen could consult the Pythia on such a subject without receiving a rebuff. He would instead receive a useful tip, if he knew how to act on it.' Comments another: 'If Delphi gave advice to Kylon, it did so because it was...hostile to the then government of Athens, because it thought Kylon would be a better man to have in power than (his opponent).'[36] The account which follows here favours the latter view. The reader must judge whether or not the pattern of consultation and dedication on which it depends is clear-cut enough to justify it.

[36] E 130, 120; E 99, 40.

The archaeological links of Mycenaean Crisa lay towards the south, across the Corinthian Gulf; the scant traces from Dark-Age Delphi point rather to the north and east, to Thessaly and Euboea, towards that Central Greek cultural unit described above. But with the sudden blossoming about 750 old ties were renewed (Corinthian pottery dominates from the start) and one new one is made, with Crete (the influence of those first Cretan priests?). But the extension was not haphazard.

It is easy, and true, to say that Delphi owed its success to the success of Greek colonization with which she was so intimately connected. No trace survives of any link with the earliest settlements, at Al Mina, at Cyme, perhaps at Sinope – not surprisingly for these were 'outside her period' – but from about 735 onwards (from the foundation of Sicilian Naxus) states turned above all to Delphi for divine sanction, divine guidance and accepted even divine initiative or divine interference in their colonial plans. But Cicero (*Div.* 1. 1.3), unwittingly, asks the important question, 'What colony did Greece send out without a prophecy from Pytho...?' What colony indeed went unblessed, or blessed by another god? Greek states at this time were divided among themselves, sufficiently divided to generate a large-scale war between two groups of allies, the so-called Lelantine War between the Euboean cities of Chalcis and Eretria in which, with varying degrees of certainty, Corinth, Samos, Erythrae, southern Thessaly and Sparta sided with the former, Megara, Miletus, Chios, Messenia and Argos with the latter. It is hardly coincidence that every colony known to have been sent out by Chalcis and her allies between 735 and about 700, some dozen or so, boasted a foundation legend in which Delphi played a part; that no colony of Eretria and her allies had such a story. Nor can it be coincidence that all but one of the Chalcidian team (the distant Samos) had some link, colonial or otherwise, with Delphi (for Thessaly, a part in the appointment of Aleuas the Red, the dedication by Echecratidas; for Sparta, what may be the earliest surviving genuine oracle; for Corinth, the archaeological evidence); that for Eretria and her friends there is nothing. Not all the tales need be true, account must be taken of accident of survival and of the nature of the evidence, but it would take a lot of special pleading to obliterate the distinction altogether.[37]

We must suppose, then, that, for some reason at which we can only guess, Eretria fell out with Chalcis as her colonists did with Chalcidians at Ischia and probably with Chalcidians and Aeolic Cymaeans at Italian Cyme, thus separating herself from the Central Greek community. Boeotia is not mentioned in the context of the war, but such straws as there are draw her towards Chalcis – Hesiod's visit, his Cymaean origin,

[37] E 100.

his mention of Delphi, possible Tanagraean presence in Italian Cyme, an early but undated war between Tanagra and Eretria, Cyme's link with Midas of Phrygia and Midas' dedication at Delphi – the earliest known by a foreign king. Through Delphi there was an easy opening to Corinth and thence (or perhaps directly through the Dorian metropolis Doris) to Sparta, through Delphi too, unimportantly but significantly, to Asine, allied with Sparta against Argos at this time, founded by a people called Dryopes who had strong ties with Delphi and with Cirrha.[38]

The overall outcome of the war is disputed (*CAH* III.1², 762). But no one can deny that Chalcis and the Thessalians won at least one memorable victory, that Sparta overran the southern Peloponnese, that Corinth and Chalcis gained the west. Not only had Delphi blessed their colonies, it had blessed their arms. Its reward was wealth (the contemporary Corinthian poet Eumelus records the dedication of a tithe of victory to Apollo) and international, though not, of course, universal glory.

To enhance this glory more startling successes were desirable, but not absolutely essential. Apollo, we must remember, was only rarely asked for an explicit forecast of the future. The standard form of question was not 'What will happen if I do *x*?' but 'Would it be a good thing if I did *x*?' Either answer, 'yes' or 'no', left the consequences of the alternative hypothetical – they might have been worse. Besides, the great bulk of enquiry, public and private, was of a simple, straightforward even trivial kind. 'Should I get married?', 'Should I go on a voyage?', 'Should we build a temple?' A little common-sense on the part of the priests, a few refusals to add verisimilitude (with unverifiable results) and general success was assured. Even failure would carry little éclat. Still, there were important enquiries, there were occasions when Apollo had to commit himself. But even here it must be remembered that a mere human being hesitates to challenge the authority of an established god. Perhaps the question had been wrongly phrased, perhaps the injunctions had been disobeyed in some particular, perhaps they had been misunderstood. And *in extremis* there remained a safety net; perhaps human priests had misrepresented the divine will. So, given the happy and lucky start of colonization where profit was unavoidable (disastrous colonies did not survive to harbour resentment) and of a war in which geography may have dictated the alliance but chance crowned it with victory, Apollo must flourish, provided only that he avoided such an error, or such a series of errors that no excuse was possible.

In fact the next crisis brought another triumph. During the next quarter-century Rhodes was introduced into the Delphic circle by Crete

---

[38] C 65, 7; Hdt. I. 14.2–3; Paus. IX. 22.2; for the Dryopians, below, n. 49.

and in 688 a joint colony was directed to Gela in Sicily; on one story a Rhodian foundation at Phaselis in southern Asia Minor was given approval at the same time.[39] In Asia Minor proper Lydia had now succeeded Phrygia as the major power of the hinterland and, a striking sign of its new-won fame, Delphi was invited to intervene in the internal affairs of a non-Greek state. In the course of a palace coup the Pythia was asked to give her judgement and her verdict came in favour of the usurper, Gyges. Six golden mixing-bowls and silver in plenty passed across the Aegean to mark Gyges' gratitude (Hdt. 1. 14.2–3). But these additions to the clientele do not affect the picture in mainland Greece. There, so far as we can see, the alignments of the late eighth century persisted. Eretria's ally Megara sent colonies to Astacus, Selymbria and Chalcedon without recorded benefit of oracle. On the other hand Delphi prompted helpful visits by the lawgiver Thaletas of Crete and the poet Terpander of Lesbos to Sparta. Much more importantly Sparta was prepared, like Lydia, to invite Apollo to take a hand in settling its constitutional problems.[40]

About 670, however, there is a dramatic change. An oracle is preserved for Megara's foundation of Byzantium (perhaps with Argive help) around 660. Pausanias (plausibly but uncontrollably) dates to 659 a war between Sparta and Arcadian Phigalea in which Delphi advised the Phigaleans; a list of the excellent things in Greece ascribed to Delphi and best dated to the aftermath of Argos' memorable victory over Sparta at Hysiae in 669 singles out the warriors of Argos (and the women of Sparta) as outstanding; finally, and most strikingly, when Cypselus staged his revolution against the Bacchiad aristocrats in Corinth in 657, he was furnished with two oracles which proclaimed him 'king' and liberator.[41] Thus old friends, Sparta and the aristocrats of Corinth, are ignored or slighted, new friends are wooed or welcomed. Something has happened.

The happening may be no more than the battle at Hysiae, for the king of Argos, Pheidon, went on after the victory to occupy Olympia and with it, presumably, to win influence in much of Arcadia. There is a case too for believing that he supported Cypselus (he was certainly on bad terms with the Bacchiads).[42] It might have seemed prudent to the Delphic priests to switch their allegiance. But a patently time-serving Delphi could no more have won admiration and influence among the Greeks than a patently bogus Delphi. There would certainly be room for some manoeuvre with an eye to future profit. But how much manoeuvre, how often? It is worth considering an alternative explanation of the apparent switch. However we account for it, however we characterize it in detail, there was a political revolution in many states

[39] E 130, no. 410.
[40] E 130, nos. 224, 223, 21 and 29.
[41] E 130, nos. 6 and 8.
[42] A 21A, 116–19.

of Greece during the seventh century. Sometimes it was peacefully achieved – a law-giver, a code, even a constitution; sometimes with violence – kings against aristocrats, aristocrats against aristocrats; in each case, however, law-giver, king or renegade aristocrat was recognizing (or exploiting) a new force in politics, a rejection of the established aristocratic order, a desire for new laws or a clearer definition of old, a new order, or just new faces. There is no doubt where Delphi stood. By giving his praise or support to Pheidon, to Cypselus, to Cylon (unsuccessfully) in Athens, Apollo was siding with the new. But there was more to its reputed association with the Spartan revolution. At one favoured date, the early eighth century, such association is out of the question – Delphi scarcely existed (but see *CAH* III. 1², 681f; cf. 736f). But at the other (the first quarter of the seventh) it would reflect perfectly that sympathy with political innovation which we have seen elsewhere. Not only that. It would inaugurate the new policy before 670, before Hysiae, and before, so far as we know, it had had success anywhere else in mainland Greece. But why then a break with Sparta after 670? Here, unfortunately, the chronological fog becomes too thick. We can only note that there were two stages in the Spartan legislation, one progressive (the 'Rhetra'), one conservative (the 'Rider'), that the former might have been too liberal for the Spartan establishment or the latter too reactionary for Delphi's taste, that there was an issue on which Sparta and Dephi may have split.

Principle, then, becomes an alternative to expediency as an explanation of the change, a principle adopted not because it had already succeeded in practice but either through extreme far-sightedness on the part of the priests – or even, dare one suggest it, through a belief that it was right. The source is not far to seek. Cretans were famous as lawgivers, Cretan cities were among the first to acquire constitutions, according to some, Crete inspired many of Sparta's institutions – and it was Cretan priests who interpreted Apollo's will at Delphi, where, it is worth adding, Crete's influence is evident in the remains throughout the seventh century (see below, p. 312).[43]

But whether as leader or as lackey, the oracle was once more on the winning side. Through the rest of the century revolution prevailed. Old allies were beset by worries, as were the Spartans in Messenia; or in exile, as were the Bacchiads (some of them appropriately in Sparta); new friends were winning, or if occasionally they lost, like unsuccessful colonies, disappeared. Once in power a dutiful Cypselus built a treasury just below Apollo's temple, perhaps the first of those elegant little store-rooms which later served to remind the passer-by on the Sacred Way of opulent beneficiaries and benefactors in the past.

But all these developments lay to the south, across the Corinthian

[43] E 106; D 144.

Gulf. North of it, immediate neighbours, Cirrha and perhaps some of the West Locrians will have shared the benefits, but did good-will spread to other Locrians or other Phocians, or even further afield? Given the total silence of our sources on all things Thessalian and Boeotian at the time, their absence from the Delphic tradition need not be significant. One can only note that entrenched aristocrats are not likely to have shown any active sympathy towards the new ideas and that when the next crisis blew up towards the end of the century Thessaly energetically and, in Boeotia, Thebes more passively, ranged themselves with those who were dissatisfied with Delphi's existing status. The crisis came about 595 when Thessaly, Sicyon and Athens charged Cirrha with interference with the oracle and declared a holy war. By 590 Cirrha had been destroyed, its plain dedicated to Apollo, never to be cultivated again, and what we have hitherto seen as its tame oracle set free. But in the sixth-century *Hymn to Apollo* the god warns his Cretan priests at the time of the foundation of future misbehaviour and future punishment – their deeds or words or pride will bring new governors to the sanctuary to rule there for all time. After about 600 Cretan contacts disappear (this is not necessarily significant – Cretan contacts everywhere seem to vanish); from about 550 at the latest, government of the oracle was in the hands of a body called the amphictiony. It must be the Sacred War that Apollo foretells and that war cannot have been quite as simple an affair as the tradition would have it.[44]

An amphictiony was an association of communities, ethnic or national, grouped around a common religious sanctuary; its purpose the administration of the sanctuary and to some extent the management of relations between its members or even of its members as a whole and outsiders. The two functions are not wholly separable and will have developed together, but it is more likely that in origin common cult led to communal arrangement than that community of interest created a religious focus. The best-known amphictiony, however, was bifocal. In classical times a dozen 'tribes' of Greece sent representatives named Pylagorae to meetings of a Council held twice-yearly, once at Delphi, once at Thermopylae. The glory of Apollo by far outshone the humbler Demeter at Anthela at the northern end of the narrow sea-shore pass between Malis and Eastern Locris, but the title of the envoys and of their meetings (Pylaea), the membership and the tradition together give Thermopylae priority. A northern cult, a northern association at some stage extended itself southwards to acquire another centre, more members and an involvement in wider areas of politics in the complexities of which details of its origins were lost. The eponymous founding hero, Amphiction had three sons whose names, Malus, Itonus and Physcus, link him with Malis, Phthiotis and Locris, a reasonable enough

[44] E 99.

beginning. Other natural accretions would be the Magnesians, the Thessalians (of Thessaliotis), the Dorians (of Doris), the Ionians (of Euboea), the Aenianes, the Phocians and the Boeotians, covering, roughly, that area of early cultural unity which we have described above and which might thus be given some religious, perhaps even some political unity as well. Less natural additions are the other Thessalian tetrads, Hestiaeotis and Pelasgiotis, less natural still the Dolopes and Perrhaebi. Surely the periœcic members at least have been added to give their Thessalian masters more weight in the Council. Delphi (as part of Phocis) was thus involved and her early archaeological history points in the right direction, but when did the Amphictiony acquire direct rights in her administration, when did informal contact become formal control? The Sacred War offers an obvious occasion for a final settlement but we cannot even guess how far the process of infiltration had advanced when war broke out. At heart the war was part of a struggle for the possession of the oracle, only in the eyes of the victors was it one for liberation, but whether it was to gain, regain or maintain possession is unclear.[45]

In one account (Athenian) it was the Athenian Solon who in the Amphictiony proposed the crusade against Cirrha. No problem here. Cirrhan-dominated Delphi's support for Cylon's attempted revolution could not have pleased the Athenian authorities at the time, especially not the archon, Megacles, who had quashed the Cylonians. It is no coincidence that the Athenian commander in the war was Megacles' son, Alcmaeon, or that his family were Solon's political friends. The case of Sicyon would be equally clear-cut, were it not for one chronological uncertainty. Signs of friendship between Cleisthenes, Sicyon's tyrant, and the new Delphi are firm, his establishment of Pythian Games at Sicyon with money from the spoils of Cirrha, his victory at the Pythian Games of 582, the building which he dedicated in the sanctuary about the same time, another dedication, by him or his successor, about 560. But are equally firm signs of hostility also with the new Delphi or with the old? In his hatred for Argos he planned to expel the Argive hero Adrastus from Sicyon – Delphi rudely rejected his proposal; after his defeat of the men of Arcadian Pellene Delphi gave them advice on the recovery of their city. But it is only economy of hypothesis, together with a story of Cypselid hostility at the start of his reign, that counts towards seeing here a parallel with Athens, a period, in this case a short period, during which Cleisthenes, at loggerheads with Corinth and Argos, found himself rebuked and his enemies succoured by the oracle, a period after 590 when a 'liberated' oracle discovered that its god was more in tune with its liberator.

For his campaign against Adrastus Cleisthenes found support in

[45] E 87.

Thebes. The Thebans allowed him to import into Sicyon the cult of a hero, Melanippus, so hated by Adrastus in life that the latter would feel bound to withdraw. But there is no evidence that they carried their sympathy further, to the point of war on Delphi. The Thessalians, on the other hand did make war, but had reasons of their own for doing so, hard though it is to tease out those reasons from the tangle of contemporary and near-contemporary propaganda, of later political argument in search of justification in the past or still later scholarship in search of a story.

The early raw material is (i) the *Hymn to Apollo* in which the god approaches Delphi through Thessaly, Euboea (the Lelantine plain and Chalcis) and thence through an apparently cooperative Boeotia (Mycalessus, Thebes, Onchestus) though with one unfortunate brush with the resident deity at Telphusium, somewhere in the west; (ii) the early-sixth century Hesiodic *Shield of Heracles* which tells how Theban Heracles once killed the brigand Cycnus near Pagasae in Phthiotis, a monster who had maltreated pilgrims on their way to Delphi;[46] and (iii) a sudden burst of interest in the story of the struggle between Heracles and Apollo for possession of the Delphic tripod, shown especially by Athenian vase-painters in the years after about 560, the years of Pisistratus who, it has been very plausibly argued, adopted Heracles as his hero.[47] A glance shows the relevance of all this to the war; the same glance shows its incoherence. Heracles, now friend of Apollo, now his enemy; Pisistratean potters apparently revelling in Pisistratean Heracles' defeat, and so on. Only the main theme stands out, dispute for possession of the oracle, with overtones of tensions inside Central Greece (Thebes and Phthiotis), inside Boeotia (? Telphusium), between new and old (Heracles against Cycnus), and of links with the wider world (Heracles and Pisistratus). Several of these are given definition or extension in the later tradition and one new element is added – trouble inside Phocis itself. Later history saw several attempts by Phocians from north of Parnassus to control Delphi and similar moves and counter-moves in our period must lie behind stories of disagreement between the two brothers, sons of Phocus, Crisus and Panopeus and of skirmishes between the Delphians and their neighbours, in the main, presumably, other Phocians.[48] In the main, but not exclusively, for room must be found for another tribe, survivors from the Dark Ages or before (the theme of new against old again). Bracketed with the Cirrhans as victims of the crusading Amphictions are the Cragallidae, another name for the Dryopes, a people who had once been centred in Trachis around

---

[46] E 109.   [47] E 129; E 85.

[48] For the impenetrable complications of the traditions see, e.g., P–W *s.vv.* 'Krisos', 'Phokis' and 'Herakles' (Suppl. III coll. 940–7).

Mt Oeta but had spread to Euboea and the islands, to Epirus, southwards to Parnassus (and thence even to Asine in the Argolid; above p. 309). Delphi figures largely in their story, so too does Heracles, as conqueror, master or patron, so their appearance in the war does not surprise, but who they were or where they were around 600 we cannot tell, a remnant of something surviving near Delphi, interested in Delphi, allied with Cirrha, and hence on the losing side.[49] Also on the losing side, by implication, were the Cypselids in Corinth and, still more distantly, Argos. Here later sources help more significantly, for Cypselus, it was said, gave one of his sons the name Pylades, scarcely to be dissociated from the heroic Pylades, Orestes' friend and member of the royal house of Cirrha, founder, on one account, of the Pylaean Amphictiony. Again, in yet another tale, Acrisius, king of Argos, after helping the Delphians in a war against their neighbours, himself founded an amphictiony at Delphi, later to absorb that of Thermopylae. Would it be rash to see here attempts by Cirrha and her southern allies to claim a voice in Thessaly's own province? Or to add the intrusion of Corinthian Sisyphus into the legends of Central Greece, or even the possible intervention of the Cypselids in Euboea?

The world of propaganda is a topsy-turvy world, and here we have little but propaganda, Greek propaganda at that, among the most ingenious and contorted known to man (Greeks rarely denied an opponent's story – they preferred to take it over and stand it on its head). But, to repeat, the main theme is clear, a struggle between Cirrha and the Amphictiony for possession of Delphi, each with its friends. Behind the Amphictiony, Thessaly, left out of the Delphic circle after 670, may merely have seen a chance to reinstate herself, but she too, like Athens and Sicyon, may have had some special grievance, may have felt some direct threat from an over-ambitious oracle. If so, the overall pattern is clear, whatever the doubts in detail. The successes of the seventh century had put Apollo's authority beyond question, but perhaps they had also turned his head a little, had prompted him to interfere, to insult, to challenge those who not only resented but had the power to make their resentment felt. Turned *his* head? Prompted *him*? No, Apollo himself was above error – it must be his priests who were to blame; new guidance was needed at the sanctuary to see that the god's true will was done.

And so indeed it was. In the developed Amphictiony each tribe had two seats on the council. This would have been a suitable moment for Athens to be granted the second 'Ionian' place (less suitable, given Cleisthenes' background, for Sicyon to become the second 'Dorian'). Athens certainly benefited in other ways, more specifically Solon, who

[49] Aeschin. III. 107; Anton. Lib. IV; E 130, no. 448; cf. E 83.

had Delphic patronage for his reforms and Delphic support in his struggle with Megara for possession of Salamis, and the family of Alcmaeon who owed to Delphi their introduction to the wealth of Lydia, who rebuilt Apollo's temple after its destruction by fire in 548 and found a grateful ally in the Pythia for their political enterprises later in the century. Meanwhile, in the 570s, their then leader, Megacles, son of Alcmaeon, had been honoured with the hand of the daughter of his father's comrade-in-arms, Cleisthenes, whose continued links with Delphi have already been mentioned. One other more general effect of his influence may be detected. Delphi before 600 was by no means an exclusively Dorian sanctuary but there is a strong Dorian flavour to it; after 600, with the advent of Ionian Athens and anti-Dorian Cleisthenes, one senses a shift of emphasis – Ionians from Naxos, Phocaea, Siphnos come as enquirers or generous dedicators, and fine objects of East Greek workmanship begin to appear.[50]

More significantly, it is only when Sparta, towards the middle of the century, gives up her traditional policy of aggressive Dorianism and begins to advertise herself as the 'Achaean' leader of a voluntary Peloponnesian alliance that she reappears on Delphi's visiting-list. Indeed it would appear that Delphi itself had a hand in persuading her to make the change, for it was on oracular advice that the Spartans decided to recover the bones of Achaean Orestes, symbol of pre-Dorian hegemony in the Peloponnese, but of hegemony to be achieved by alliance not by annexation.[51]

This is not to say that Delphi became anti-Dorian. Spartans, after all, were still, however mutedly, Dorian. So too were the Corinthians who, after the fall of the Cypselids in 582, became allies of Sparta, honoured Solonian Athens at the Isthmian Games and whom the Delphians, graciously if ungratefully, allowed to erase the name of Cypselus from his treasury. Indeed the change, such as it was, may well have been a result of an accident of politics rather than of any consciousness of race. Such consciousness existed among Greeks, but few things are harder to measure than its power to move rather than merely to irritate.

Certainly it was political accident (though perhaps with some slight racial overtones) which produced the one serious loss to the oracle's clientele after about 560. In Athens, Solon's 'party' split and Pisistratus, leader of the break-away 'left-wing', became tyrant. There was no room at Delphi both for Pisistratus and for the remaining Solonians, now led by the Alcmaeonids, and so, either by inclination or invitation, Pisistratus resigned the Delphic whip. Causes or effects? – a marriage with an Argive who had previously been the wife of a Cypselid and an association with the predominantly Ionian Apollo of Delos, an association which he shared with his friend Lygdamis of Naxos and with Lygdamis' friend, Polycrates of Samos. In the tension after Pisistratus' death his sons allowed one of their sons to offer an altar to Pythian Apollo as they offered an archonship to an Alcmaeonid, but the placatory gesture, if such it was, had no more success than the similar and contemporary overture made by Polycrates. 'Shall I call my new festival Pythian or Delian?' asked Polycrates. 'It's all the same for you', replied the Pythia, and Polycrates soon died. The Pisistratids did not survive in power much longer. Alcmaeonid intrigue, Delphic diplomacy and a Spartan army liberated Athens. In 510 (Lygdamis too had disappeared) it must have seemed a dangerous thing to displease Apollo. To flatter him, as the Alcmaeonids did by a lavish rebuilding of his temple, burnt down, false rumour had it by the Pisistratids; to obey him, as the Spartans did; to reward him as the Athenians did with their treasury at Delphi; that was the prudent course.

But to the north there was no such tidiness or harmony under the Amphictionic umbrella. Some of the confusion we have already explored, and their reasons for it, weakness of evidence, dissensions within as well as between the main units, Thessaly, Boeotia, Phocis. The simplest story would be that the Thessalians (collectively so far as we know) extended their influence southwards at the time of the Sacred War so effectively that they were able to take control of Phocis, either through puppet tyrants or by direct Thessalian government, maintaining at the same time their hold on Delphi through their majority on the Amphictionic council and their friendship with Sicyon – a Scopad of Crannon was one of the contestants for the hand of Cleisthenes' daughter in the 570s, albeit unsuccessful; that they then tried to expand further into south-west Boeotia but were pushed back with the loss, it was said, of 4,000 men from Ceressus in the territory of Thespiae, Pausanias implies by the Thespians alone, Plutarch says the 'Boeotians', a reverse which was followed, around 500, by a revolt of Phocis and the rout of a retaliatory expedition in at least two engagements, one of the Thessalian foot below Parnassus, the other of their famous cavalry at Hyampolis to the north-east.[52] The dedications received by Delphi to celebrate the Phocian success show that yet again it had chosen the profitable course, a choice virtually imposed by geography but perhaps already encouraged by Thessalian friendship with the Athenian tyrants, maintained to the end of the tyranny and even beyond when fugitive Hippias was invited to settle at Iolcus. The simplest story – and probably in outline true. But there are awkwardnesses. Thebes had also helped Pisistratus at the outset and his son, Hipparchus, dedicated at the Ptoion,[53] as, to confuse things further, did an Alcmaeonid, yet some

[52] Above, pp. 304–5.   [53] BCH 40 (1920) 237ff.

Boeotians, the Tanagraeans, felt able to consult Delphi before joining the Megarians in colonizing Heraclea in the Black Sea about the middle of the century and the Thebans themselves sought Delphic advice in their troubles around 505.[54] We must besides look for contexts for the alliance between Thebes, the Locrians and the Phocians advertised by the author of the *Shield*, and for the building across the pass at Thermopylae of a wall, the so-called 'Phocian' wall which lay in ruins when the Greek force arrived there in 480 (Hdt. VII. 176.3–4). These snags can be circumvented but not without leaving the uneasy feeling that the simplest story is not always the best.

Meanwhile, however, a new question was beginning to pose itself for Greek politicians – the cloud in the east. A matter of interest but of little concern when the Persians first appeared on the Ionian coast about 540, more pressing with their advance into Europe in 514 and then overwhelming as invasion came nearer. For states and for factions within the states this was not only a new problem, it was a new kind of problem, here reinforcing, there cutting across old friendships or enmities. For Delphi it was even more acute and even more immediate than for most. Her close ties with Gyges of Lydia may or may not have survived her switch of interest around 675. At least we hear nothing of contacts with Gyges' successors, Ardys and Sadyattes, or with the next king Alyattes until shortly before 600 when he is undergoing some change of heart in the course of war with Miletus (the figure of Periander hovers intriguingly but appropriately around the edges of the story which brings Delphic advice to Alyattes and grateful reward: Hdt. I. 19–22). But, renewed or continuing, the Lydian connexion was not broken by the events of the 590s. It was through Delphi that Alcmaeon, one of the 'liberators', made highly profitable contact with the Lydians and it was in Alyattes' son, Croesus, that Apollo found one of his most ardent admirers. The story of Croesus' association with the oracle needs no rehearsal; of his oracular 'jeux sans frontières', his lavish gifts to victorious Delphi, housed, appropriately, in the Corinthian (once Cypselid) Treasury, alliance with Sparta, surely with Delphi's support, and then the disastrous advice to cross the Halys and destroy an empire. After Croesus' defeat at the hands of Cyrus and the capture of his capital Sardis *c.* 546 'advice to cross' became a 'forecast of the result of crossing' regrettably misunderstood and indeed the whole tale of Croesus as we have it in Herodotus is cast as an apologia, but modern scholars have exaggerated the extent of contamination – Croesus' approach to the oracle shows genuine eastern traits and, above all, the richness of his gifts alone is a measure of Delphi's involvement.[55] For her, then, the Persian victory was not an alien affair. The Milesians

---

[54] E 130, no. 81.   [55] Hdt. I. 46–91; cf. E 115.

somehow contrived to make their peace with Cyrus (what were their relations with Delphi at the time?), but other Ionians suffered, among them the Phocaeans who had consulted the oracle some years before about a colony in the west. At home one close friend, Sparta, indulged in a foolish little gesture of protest, but, nearer the heart of things, Croesus himself had survived to find a place at the Persian court, and, it was said, had forgiven Apollo for any inconvenience he had caused. It did not take Delphi long to decide which friend to follow. Faced with the approach of the Persians the people of Cnidus asked for advice in the construction of a defensive canal – 'Desist' replied the Pythia, 'God would have made Cnidus an island, if he had wished it so' (Hdt. 1. 174). The theme was set for the final surrender, the theme, but not the details of its development. For to what we may call normal domestic complications, already noted, this new element was added. In Thessaly the Aleuadae medized, other noble houses did not;[56] in Athens the tyrants showed signs of medizing, but so did their enemies the Alcmaeonids; in Sparta King Cleomenes finally chose the patriotic course but his association with the oracle was murky – and in any case, when the Persians finally came he was dead and his fellow-king was at Xerxes' side; the Aeginetans, whom Delphi tried to save from an Athenian attack *c.* 504, submitted to Darius before 490 but fought bravely in 480; in Boeotia the Thebans at first fought feebly, then with most other cities collaborated with enthusiasm while Plataea and Thespiae alone stayed loyal; so too did their neighbours in Phocis – but only, Herodotus remarks (VIII. 30), because the Thessalians were on the other side. The full story of the great war will be told in a later volume. For us it is enough to note that so far as was possible in all this confusion Delphi counselled caution or submission. There was no formal presentation to the Great King of a handful of Delphic Ga or a cup of Castalian water, but the simple fact is that Apollo, together in the end with most of his amphictiony, medized.

It is no accident that thereafter Delphi ceased to be an active power in Greek politics. Still a useful moral support as she was for Sparta in the Peloponnesian War, still revered by private citizens as she was from Socrates to Plutarch, she was no longer a force, as she had been, that could make governments, promote alliances, initiate wars. It is hard not to see the glorification of the sanctuary in the years after 489 as little more than an embarrassing farce designed by the victorious Greeks to cover up the fact that their god had failed them.

Four great moments of decision. The first hardly a decision at all – in the Lelantine War Delphi had been adopted by the winning side; the second, in the political revolution of the seventh century, a triumph;

[56] E 131.

the third an error, from which she was saved by the calculated piety of the victors in the Sacred War; but the fourth an error from which she could not be saved. That a divinely-inspired oracle should produce accurate predictions of the future over a period of two hundred years and more is a belief that would tax the credulity of all but the most devout; that human priests should arrive at one original and correct answer in four would seem to be just about the right score.

CHAPTER 42

THE PELOPONNESE

N. G. L. HAMMOND

I. SOME PROBLEMS OF CHRONOLOGY

When the Pleiades, daughters of Atlas, rise, begin your harvesting; and when they are about to set, begin your ploughing. Forty days and forty nights they are in hiding, but as the year revolves they appear again, when your sickle is first being sharpened. (Hesiod, *Works and Days* 383–7)

Every shepherd and every farmer needs to know the details of the seasons and the tally of the years. Although literacy lapsed in the Dark Age, men remained numerate and counted the lunar months, each within his own small group. When these groups coalesced into a community or state, or when they engaged in a joint activity, a common standard of time-reckoning was needed. Each state created its own calendar, naming the months by a number or a deity or a festival and beginning the year wherever it pleased; occasionally a month-name, such as the Carnean month in honour of Apollo Carneus, was common to several states, but usually each state drew its names from its own sources and sometimes even had Mycenaean names. As trade and intercourse developed, the need to label the years within a community was met by naming each year after an 'eponymous' official, whether priest or magistrate, and keeping a list of the names, e.g. that of Elatus as the first eponymous ephor of Sparta in 754 B.C. (Plut. *Lyc.* 7).[1] A system which several states could share was devised at Olympia, where the festival was held once every four years and a sacred truce for its duration was observed by the participating states. The festival years were numbered consecutively and named after each winner of the foot-race (*stadion*), the first Olympiad in 776 B.C. being that of Coroebus of Elis (Paus. VIII. 26.4). Where an official held office for life, as the priestess of Hera at Argos did, the years of his or her tenure were numbered.

As these lists were compiled not for academic purposes but for practical use, it seems obvious that they were used to date actions and

[1] The year B.C. is supplied by Apollodorus, *FGrH* 244 F 335a.

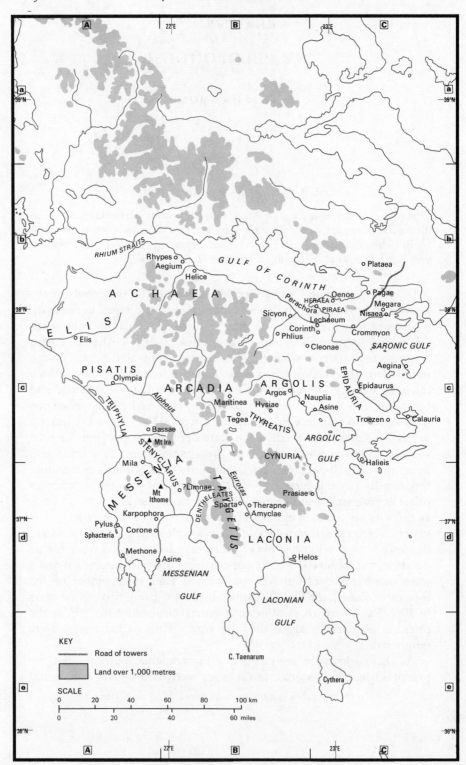

KEY

————— Road of towers

Land over 1,000 metres

SCALE

0   20   40   60   80   100 km

0   20   40   60 miles

Map 18. The Peloponnese and the Megarid.

events at the time; and it is probable that such events were noted at the appropriate place in the list. To give an example from Megara, where a memorial to one Orsippus was set up on the order of Delphi and an epitaph was composed for it, perhaps by Simonides, we learn that Orsippus was the first to win the *stadion* running naked; and the list of victors in that event having survived, we can date his victory to 720 B.C., some two centuries before the composition of the epitaph.[2] No doubt he had been recorded on the list at Olympia as the first naked runner. Or we may note an entry in the list of priestesses of Hera at Argos, which Hellanicus published late in the fifth century: 'Theocles from Chalcis together with Chalcidians and Naxians founded a city in Sicily',[3] namely Naxus *c.* 734. The probability is that Hellanicus published what he found in the list, not that he added this particular piece of information himself. In any case, once such lists were kept and years were labelled, events such as the foundation of a colony were recorded far more accurately in relation to them than to any form of genealogical reckoning. Occasionally an object of antiquarian interest supplied a dating. Thus a bronze quoit or discus at Olympia had an inscription running round it (as on a jumper's weight (fig. 47), or on the shoulder of a vase *c.* 730 B.C.),[4] which referred to the truce for the Olympic Games. Aristotle saw this quoit and read there the names of Iphitus, the reputed founder of the reconstituted games in 776, and of Lycurgus whom he equated with the reputed author of the *eunomia* at Sparta. He inferred from the inscription that they had collaborated in arranging the terms of the truce for the festival.[5] It is obvious that the truce was worthless unless it was validated by an official representative of each participating state, e.g. in Sparta's case by a King or Geron. Aristotle may in fact have been right in identifying this Lycurgus, a Geron well over sixty, with the famous legislator.[6] If he read the name of Iphitus correctly, it is the earliest inscription of which we know by report and helps to date the adoption of the alphabet.

The dating of the First Messenian War may be determined with probability in the following way. Tyrtaeus, who flourished about the middle of the seventh century, said that 'our fathers' fathers fought for nineteen years', and that in the twentieth year the enemy fled from the high mountains of Ithome. If we take seventy years as a very approximate span for the two generations (as one might in referring now to World War I), the First Messenian War ran very approximately

[2] E. L. Hicks and G. F. Hill, *GHI* no. 1 with references.
[3] *FGrH* 4 F 82.
[4] Illustrated in Ἱστορία τοῦ Ἑλληνικοῦ Ἔθνους B 198 and 483.
[5] Plut. *Lyc.* 1 and 23; Paus. v. 4.5 and 20.1; Ath. XIV. 635F.
[6] If Lycurgus carried the reform in his prime and acted at Olympia as a 'geron' over sixty, Thucydides' date of *c.* 810 B.C. is compatible with that of Aristotle.

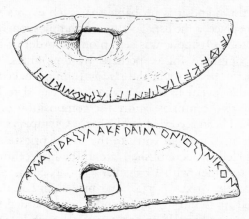

47. Stone *halter* (jumping weight) from Olympia. Inscribed Ἀκματιδας Λακεδαιμονιος νικον ανεθεκε τα πεντε
ασσκονιτει (= ακονιτει) 'Akmatidas of Sparta dedicated
this having won in the *pentathlon* with ease.' Third
quarter of the sixth century B.C. (Olympia Museum; after
Olympia-Bericht I (1937) 82–4, pl. 25; cf. A 36, 191, no. 20
for the inscription.)

from 740 to 720 B.C.[7] In the list of Olympic victors the seventh and
last Messenian victor of the century was in 736, and the first of many
Spartan victors was in 716, the combination being at least compatible
with a Messenian War of *c.* 740–720. Some Messenians who wanted to
appease Sparta at the start and were expelled by their compatriots joined
in the founding of Rhegium by Chalcidians,[8] whose activities in the west
were early and probably before 720. Some Spartans founded Taras after
the war. The archaeological evidence at Taras, including Laconian
Geometric pottery, dates the foundation within 725–700.[9] The end of
the war may then be put before 710. Finally, Asine having been
destroyed by the Argives, the refugees fled to Sparta. After the end of
the Messenian War they were settled at a new Asine in Messenia (Paus.
IV. 14.3). The excavations at Asine in the Argolid indicate that its
destruction lay within the Geometric period and not later than *c.* 720,[10]
after which the refugees were available for resettlement. In each case
there may be a margin of error, but the sum of evidence makes it most
probable that the Messenian War, the 'Twenty Year War', fell somewhere between 740 and 710 B.C.[11]

To take another example. When Pheidon re-established the traditional

[7] Tyrt. 4; E 151, 70ff.   [8] *FGrH* 555 (Antiochus) F 9 = Strabo 257.
[9] C 65, 29ff.
[10] E 197, 47ff; *Arch. Rep.* 1973, 11; H 25, 316, 363, 405; A 31, 101f.
[11] The reign of Theopompus gives a rough check in that he was king when 'the first Ephors
headed by Elatus' were elected (Plut. *Lyc.* 7), i.e. in 754 B.C., and it was he who captured Ithome.

supremacy of Argos in the Peloponnese, his most infamous act was the ousting of the Eleans and the installing of the Pisatans to conduct the Olympic festival, an event no doubt appended to the Victor List or recorded separately at Olympia. Strabo tells us that the Eleans were in charge from the 1st to the 26th Olympiad, i.e. from 776 to 676, and that a Pisatan period came when the Pisatans recovered control of their own territory; and Africanus, who used the Olympic lists, gave the 28th Olympiad as a Pisatan one, i.e. 668. Pausanias reported that the Pisatans and Pheidon conducted the games in the 8th Olympiad, which in view of what Strabo and Africanus say is likely to be a textual error or a factual error for the 28th Olympiad. That the festival records transmitted such information is clear from the reporting of a second judge being appointed in the 50th Olympiad, i.e. in 580.[12] Another event which Pausanias dated by the citation not only of an Olympiad with an Athenian victor but also of an eponymous magistrate at Athens was the battle of Hysiae in 669/8, in which Argos defeated Sparta decisively; we do not know where the event was recorded, whether at Olympia, Athens or elsewhere, but such a victory was an indispensable preliminary to Pheidon's intervention at Olympia.[13]

So far so clear, but some stories that may refer to Pheidon have chronological implications which are at variance with these dates. Thus Herodotus gave a hilarious account of a house-party at Sicyon for the suitors of Cleisthenes' daughter, which would suggest that Cleisthenes and Pheidon were contemporary in the early sixth century. At the other extreme, in a romantic story about one Actaeon of Corinth, Pheidon was represented as a contemporary of the founder of Syracuse, who flourished c. 735. Neither story offers a serious challenge to the dates drawn from the Olympic records. Indeed another version of the second story with less sensational colouring placed Pheidon's threat to Corinth just before the fall of the Bacchiad rulers of Corinth, an event normally dated c. 657.[14] A different kind of challenge was made by Ephorus and Theopompus, fourth-century historians, who used genealogies for academic purposes in order each to establish his hypothetical system of chronology: Ephorus making him a tenth-generation descendant of Temenus, and so of mid-eighth century date, and Theopompus a seventh-generation descendant and so of ninth century date. Their calculations and their differences are not worth pursuing in this context.[15] The fact is that Pheidon flourished c. 670–660 B.C., and we owe our knowledge of that fact to the records of the Olympic festival.

[12] Strabo 355; Africanus in Euseb. *Chron.* 1.196; Paus. VI. 22.2 and V. 9.4.
[13] Paus. II. 24.7; and F 2, 90.
[14] Hdt. VI. 127; Plut. *Mor.* 772C; Schol. Ap. Rhod. IV. 1212; E 182.
[15] *FGrH* 70 (Ephorus) F 115; *FGrH* 115 (Theopompus) F 393; E 151, 55ff.

II. THE PURSUIT OF POWER BY THE DORIAN STATES,
c. 750–650 B.C.

1. *Constitutional modifications at Sparta*

The men of Aegium are said to have asked Apollo of Delphi who were better than they, and to have received the answer:[16]

Best is Pelasgic Argos of all soils, best are the horses of Thrace, the women of Sparta, the men who drink the water of fair Arethusa, but better still than these are those who dwell between Tiryns and Arcadia rich in flocks, the Argives of the linen corslet, pricks of war. But you, men of Aegium, are neither third, nor fourth, nor twelfth, nor in account nor reckoning.

Question and answer epitomize the competitive spirit of the city-states. They were as whole-hearted in the race for power as their athletes were in pursuit of the olive-wreath prize at the Olympic games. In the Peloponnese Argos claimed to be the most martial not only in the eighth century to which this answer may be dated,[17] but also by tradition from the time of the Dorian invasion. In the first half of the eighth century her claim was justified by the facts; for she seems to have held Argolis, Epidauria, Thyreatis, Cynuria and Cythera at the time when she sent an expeditionary force to help the 'Achaeans' of Helos against the Dorians of Sparta in the reign of Alcamenes, father of Polydorus (Paus. III. 2.7 and 20.6–7). To break the divinely-sanctioned ties of kinship between Dorian and Dorian and to help 'Achaeans' against Dorians was a ruthless action, prompted by considerations of political expediency which seemed convincing at the time; for, if Argos could confine Sparta to the inland plain of the Eurotas valley, she had every hope of being unchallenged as the leading power in the Peloponnese.

In the mid-eighth century Argos had a fleet of warships which carried sail but were rowed into battle by single banks of oarsmen. The keel-beam of the low hull was extended in the bows so as to form a thin ram, and the side-decks served as a platform for marines. Merchantmen were broad-beamed sailing-ships with a curved hull and a deep draught by comparison; in a calm sea they were at the mercy of the warship. Sparta, on the other hand, had no ships. Thus the Argives were able to transport troops to Helos unopposed. The small towns of non-Dorian peoples at this time apparently had citadels defended by mud-brick walls, such as have been found at Halieis, and these were often held with success, as there were no siege-engines.

[16] A 50, II 1.

[17] Men of Arethusa are those of Chalcis in Euboea, the pioneer state in colonizing the west, and the linen corslet preceded the bronze armour of the hoplite. Parke would date this to the later seventh century.

Warfare was conducted normally in the open country. The best-equipped warriors, wearing defensive armour, fought each other at close quarters with spear and sword, but the majority of men with nothing more than a linen or leather jerkin for protection fought from a distance with javelins and slings and stones. Cavalrymen had a great advantage over both kinds of infantrymen, heavy-armed and light-armed as they are called, but there were very few cavalrymen in the Peloponnese. Under such conditions a war might soon degenerate into sporadic guerrilla fighting, for which the mountainous terrain was suitable, and become very protracted. But it was a destructive form of warfare in that the open country was devastated and the entire population was at risk. When a man fell in battle, he was killed and stripped, and when a town fell, its population was massacred, enslaved or evicted. Only religious prohibitions were respected: the dead were not mutilated or left un-buried, worshippers and suppliants in the precincts of the gods were inviolate, and temples of the gods were not razed as the other buildings of a captured town were. In such life-and-death struggles valour was at its highest premium. In the words of the Spartan poet Tyrtaeus: 'To die, falling in the front line, a brave man fighting for his fatherland, is honourable; but to leave one's city and its rich fields and live as a beggar is the depth of misery' (6.1–4).

When the Spartans captured Helos, they razed it to the ground and enslaved the inhabitants; but they preserved the worship of Kore, daughter of Demeter, which had been practised by the Achaeans. Confident in their conquest of Laconia, the Spartans invaded the Argolid in the reign of Nicander, father of Theopompus, gained the support of Asine and ravaged the enemy land. But later, when the king of Argos marched against Asine on the Argolic coast and laid siege to its defences, Sparta did not intervene. In the end the Asinaeans – predominantly not Dorians but Dryopes – escaped in their ships and were given sanctuary in Laconia. Their city was razed to the ground, except that the temple of Apollo was left standing (Paus. II. 36.4–5 and III. 7.4). Thus the seeds were sown of a bitter hatred between Argos and Sparta which became ineradicable.

The Spartans turned next against the Dorians of Messenia. There, as we argued in *CAH* III.1², 731, the Dorians held only the inland plains and the eastern hills in the eighth century, and Dorian 'Messene' of which Tyrtaeus wrote was probably the 'middle-land' surrounding the plain of Stenyclarus, which, like the plain of Dorian Sparta, looked inland rather than towards the sea. The border between the Dorians of Messene and the Dorians of Sparta was formed not by the spine of Taÿgetus, as later in the urban civilization of the Hellenistic period, but by the allocation of winter and summer pastures. Thus the Dorians

of Messene held the inland plains and mountains, and the Dorians of
Laconia held the whole promontory of Taenarum, including at its base
Dentheliates, the district in the north-east angle of the Messenian Gulf
in which Laconian settlements were said to have been made by King
Teleclus. The Dorians of Messene and Laconia shared a festival
attended only by Dorians at a shrine of Artemis Limnatis in northern
Dentheliates very close to the frontier of Messene. The other parts of
what was later called Messenia were still occupied by 'Achaeans' in
the sense of pre-Dorian peoples. Corone on the western shore of the
Messenian Gulf, for example, had an Olympic victor in 732 B.C., when
the Dorians were locked in combat.

When the Spartans were fighting their way to the Laconian coast, the
Dorians of Messene gained access to the coast, probably in the rich plain
at the head of the Gulf; for a contemporary poet, Eumelus of Corinth,
composed a processional hymn for 'the Messenians' who took offerings
to Apollo of Delos. War between the two groups of Dorians was said
to be justified as a means of punishing acts of sacrilege on both sides
which occurred within the precinct of Artemis Limnatis, such as the
raping of Spartan girls by Messenians and plots by Spartans to kill
Messenians there. That these alleged acts had occurred a generation
before the outbreak of war was immaterial; for the memory of the
goddess was long and the contestants hoped to win her support.
Whatever the actual bone of contention at the time, some Dorians of
Messene favoured a peaceful settlement; they were banished and found
a new home in Rhegium (see above, p. 109).

When the war was on, some Spartans questioned the rightness of
attacking 'their brothers', i.e. fellow Dorians; but the desire of the
majority was expressed in an answer attributed to the king Polydorus,
'we march against a land that is not divided into lots' (Plut. *Mor.* 231D).
It was a war of bitter fighting, entirely on Messenian soil and mainly
of a guerrilla character.[18] In the twentieth year the last fighters for
freedom fled from the great mountains of Ithome, looking back for the
last time at the rich fields of the Stenyclarus plain, and the victors, led
by their king Theopompus, occupied 'Messene spacious for dancing'
(Tyrtaeus frs. 2 and 4), reduced the survivors to serfdom as 'Helots',
and divided up the good land into lots for some 3,000 Spartiates (Plut.
Lyc. 8). The Helots were compelled to swear an oath not to revolt from
their owner, the Spartan state, the object being that if Helots broke their
oath they could not obtain religious sanctuary; to deliver half their
produce to Sparta; and themselves and their wives to attend in black

---

[18] The main source is Tyrtaeus. The detailed account in Paus. IV is worthless, being derived
from a fictional fourth-century history (see E 174); for some points of value in Paus. and Strabo
see E 166, 15ff, 75ff.

clothing and with keening the funerals of Lacedaemonian kings and senior officials (Tyrt. fr. 5; cf. Paus. iv. 14.4–5). Men, women and children lived in destitution on the land they were forced to cultivate, 'suffering like donkeys under great burdens', as Tyrtaeus said. But Tyrtaeus had less sympathy for them than Randolph had for the Tsakones (above, p. 699).

The Spartan soldiers were said to have taken an oath early in the war not to leave the field until they destroyed Messene or were destroyed themselves (Strabo 279), and this oath was connected with the tradition that men too young to have taken the oath were sent later to cohabit with Spartan girls and beget children. The sons of these unions, called Partheniae, took part in the founding of Sparta's colony, Taras, in Italy, probably in the last decade of the eighth century.[19] Another effect of the long war was that the Apella did not represent the full body of citizens and that tensions arose between the Gerousia and an unrepresentative Apella (for these bodies see *CAH* iii.1², 741). In consequence the kings Theopompus and Polydorus, son of the Alcamenes in whose reign the war started, brought from Apollo's shrine at Delphi a special injunction (called by modern scholars 'the Rider to the Rhetra'): 'but if the people declare crookedly, the Elders and Archagetae shall be adjourners'. The Gerousia proposed to append this injunction to the famous Rhetra (see *CAH* iii.1², 740), and their proposal was approved by the Apella. The sense of the thus complete document was paraphrased by Tyrtaeus in the mid-seventh century as follows:

Lord Apollo, golden-haired master of the silver bow, fulfilling his purposes from afar, has thus responded from his wealthy shrine. 'Let the beginning of counsel be with the kings, honoured by the gods, and the elders of revered age; and then let the citizens answering straightly to the proposals say what is fair and do what is right altogether, and no longer give ⟨crooked⟩ counsel to this city. And in the majority of the commons let victory and supremacy reside.' So Apollo declared concerning them in the interest of the city.[20]

This was not the last attempt in history to put together two irreconcilable political statements in one document. As a loyalist poet, Tyrtaeus underplayed the discrepancy between the original Rhetra which gave the right of discussion and decision to the commons and the Rider which enabled the Gerousia to curtail discussion and withdraw the right of decision by pronouncing an adjournment; for adjournment was evidently a euphemism for dismissal, when the Apella's view threatened to be a 'crooked' one. Thereafter the proposal became law – but only if the Gerousia was unanimous in making the

[19] Strabo 278, Arist. *Pol.* 1306b30, Polyaen. ii. 14.2.
[20] The text is doubtful and the meaning disputed. See E 160, 54–62; for other views E 172, 98f, with bibliography.

proposal and was prepared to go ahead despite popular opposition. Such
a strengthening of an inner body, whether Council, Senate or Cabinet,
is not unusual in the crisis of war; at Sparta it arose in such a crisis but
became permanent, an indication in itself that Sparta was permanently
in a state of preparedness for war. Occasions did occur later when the
Gerousia committed the state to a policy without consulting the Apella,
in the confidence that its members would be unanimous when the time
came to inform the people. But these were exceptions. In general the
tensions between king and king, or kings and elders, or among the elders
ensured that the Gerousia was not unanimous, and then there was full
discussion and the decision was made by the Apella.

Another constitutional change was attributed to King Theopompus
by Aristotle, who was illustrating his theory that monarchy lasts longest
when its powers are restricted. 'Thus the Lacedaemonian monarchy has
persisted because from the beginning it was divided into two parts and
it was modified again by Theopompus in various ways and in particular
by setting the ephors over it' (*Pol.* 1313a25). Originally concerned with
the social system, the *agoge* (see *CAH* III.1², 742), the ephors rose
to some constitutional importance when the senior ephor became the
eponymous official of the year in 754, perhaps in connexion with the
oaths made at the beginning of the year and renewed each month
between the kings and the ephors: the kings swearing to rule in
accordance with the laws of the state, and the ephors swearing on behalf
of the state to preserve the monarchy intact as long as the king kept
his oath ([Xen.] *Lac. Pol.* 15.7). The powers conferred on the ephors
vis-à-vis the kings during the First Messenian War were probably that
two ephors thenceforth accompanied the kings on a campaign as
observers and as disciplinary officers (the kings, as in Macedon, having
had absolute power of punishment during a campaign); that the ephors
took over from the kings certain judicial powers in civil cases; and that
the ephors received powers of summary arrest, and could suspend a
magistrate, including a king, from his office until he was tried. Their
status in relation to the kings was indicated by the fact that at the entry
of the kings on a ceremonial occasion everyone stood up except the
ephors, who remained seated on their official chairs.

The reforms which arose from the circumstances of the First
Messenian War brought the Spartan constitution to its classical form.[21]
It is now appropriate to describe it. The powers of the two 'Kings of
the Lacedaemonians' were indivisible. In war they made sacrifice first
at Sparta to Zeus the Leader and to his twin sons, the Dioscuri or
Tyndaridae, and then at the frontier to Zeus and Athena; they consulted
the omens, and these had to be favourable before they proceeded across

---

[21] Chief sources are Hdt. VI. 56–9; [Xen.] *Lac. Pol.*; Arist. *Pol. passim* and frs. 536–9.

the frontier or went into battle; and they exercised equal and total powers of command, any Lacedaemonian who refused to obey being laid under a curse. They rode at the head of the army, fought in person and were accompanied by the statues of the Tyndaridae. During a campaign the kings and their staff were maintained at the state's expense. At home the kings conducted state sacrifices, kept (with the Pythii) the archive of oracular responses, and took the oath first in making treaties. In justice their powers were restricted progressively, until they judged only cases of inheritance and adoption and the highway code. In policy-making they had no more say in theory than their fellow-members of the Gerousia, but in practice a king of powerful personality might wield great influence.

As intermediaries with the gods and as heads of state, the kings were treated with ceremonial respect, but their way of life was far from extravagant. Their state residence was not a palace but a tent, shared with the Pythii, and they received from the state a double portion of food in their tent, so that they could each entertain a state guest. Their own means were modest; they each had a pool of water beside their house, they kept part of the sacrificial victims and they received a pigling from every litter as a royal prerogative. They owned parcels of land in some of the Periœcic states. On the whole it was a democratic form of constitutional monarchy. But its prestige was apparent when a king died; then men and women from the families of Spartiates, Periœci and Helots were required to attend the funeral, and state business was suspended for ten days of full mourning.

The Gerousia, its life-members being twenty-eight elders and the two kings under the title of *archagetae*, had the monopoly in the initiation of policy, and the major say in the direction of policy. It tried the most important cases, including those of homicide. As a body the Gerousia was not answerable for its political and judicial decisions. The kings might be of any age, but the elders were elected at the age of sixty or more by the Apella, whenever a vacancy arose. Election was not only the highest honour but also the highest responsibility to which a Spartiate could aspire. Modern constitutions provide no parallel, and even democratically elected life-peers sitting alone in an effective House of Lords would be powerless in comparison. That the elders were supporters of the traditional establishment was inevitable in view of the social system and the nature of the Spartiate electorate; and the credit, if it is a matter of credit, for the consistent direction of Spartan policy must go primarily to them. Yet there is truth in Aristotle's criticism of the gerontocracy of Sparta, that there is an old age of the mind as well as of the body.

The five Ephors, elected annually by the Apella from Spartiates aged

between thirty and sixty, oversaw most of the daily life of the citizens.
As controllers of the *agoge* they demanded obedience and imposed
punishments and fines; on entering office they told the Spartiates to
'shave the moustache and obey the laws'; and they had powers of
summary arrest. They were in charge of internal security; they declared
war annually on the Helots, and they acted on suspicion of a plot, for
instance in the case of the Partheniae who were suspected of collaborating with the Helots. As we have seen, they could suspend a
magistrate or a king; they acted as public prosecutors against a king,
and as judges in civil cases. In the event of war they decided which
age-groups should be called up; they appointed three men who chose
300 men in their prime to serve as the royal bodyguard; and two of
them accompanied the kings in the field, where they had disciplinary
powers over the troops. As representatives of the people, they had some
religious duties. One of these was to watch the sky on a clear moonless
night, once in every nine years, and if they saw a shooting star to
suspend the kings as being out of favour with the gods and to reinstate
them only if and when the god of Delphi or Olympia expressed
willingness. In later centuries the ephors added greatly to their powers,
even summoning the Gerousia and presiding over the Apella.

'Spartiates', men over thirty who had passed through the *agoge* and
been elected to a mess (see *CAH* III.1², 741), were the only members
of the Apella. They elected all[22] their leaders – kings, elders, ephors,
minor magistrates and military commanders under the kings' general
command; they voted by acclamation, the shouts being judged by
electoral officers in a separate room. They heard, discussed and voted
for or against proposals submitted by the Gerousia; and even when their
will was frustrated by the Gerousia, their opinion was still a check on
the Gerousia. Having been trained from childhood to respect authority,
living in social units where age was respected, and being in effect
professional soldiers, the great majority of them did not resent the
authority of their leaders and the predominance of the Gerousia. At the
same time they were on an equality with one another in education,
economic status and obligation to serve the state, and that is why they
were called 'Equals' (*Homoioi*).

In the constitutional theory of ancient Greece the citizen body alone
was taken into account, so that an extreme democracy could be said to
exist in a society with a large non-citizen basis. A particular feature of
the Spartan state was noted by Aristotle (*Pol.* 1271b2): 'the whole
system of the laws is directed towards one part of excellence, military

[22] Arist. *Pol.* 1294b; cf. Pl. *Leg.* 712d. Those elected for the ephorate were probably scrutinized
by the Gerousia or/and by their predecessors in office; this would explain Aristotle's remark, that
the people played only a part in electing ephors (*ibid.* 31–2). *Contra, Historia* 29 (1980) 389f.

valour, which is of service for conquest'. Military valour, of course, included other qualities of value to a political society – a sense of honour and of obligation, discipline and unity – and it did not exclude the cultural activities for which early Sparta was particularly famous, music, dancing and poetry. The beauty and the comparative freedom of Spartan girls and women were proverbial, and although Spartiates themselves did not engage in crafts and trades the Laconian pottery of the seventh and sixth centuries was one of the finest in the Peloponnese. Aristotle classified the Spartan constitution as a mixed constitution, rightly; for it included full monarchy in military command, full oligarchy in decision-making and in judging capital charges, and full democracy in the basic equalities of citizen life and property. It is true that he had different criteria from us in some respects; for example, to him the direct election to all offices by the people was an oligarchic feature (democracy using the lot), and those thus elected and wielding power were an aristocracy (of merit in the eyes of the electors, not of course of birth). If we consider its administrative activity, Sparta had an oligarchic government. Thus Plutarch interpreted the establishment of the ephorate in the constitution first as a 'curb on the oligarchy' and second as being in fact not a relaxation but rather a strengthening of the regime; for 'it only appeared to be a popular feature and in fact intensified the *aristokratia*' (*Lyc.* 29 *fin.*).[23]

The Spartan state contained also the underprivileged: the 'Inferiors' who had failed to qualify as citizens in the *agoge* or later, and the Helots or agricultural work-force. The kings of the Lacedaemonians commanded the conscripted forces of the Periœci, who were bound by the foreign policy of Sparta and paid produce from royal estates in their territory but otherwise managed their own affairs. The Periœci engaged in crafts and trade as well as in farming. The number of Helots was more than doubled by the annexation of 'Messene', and that of the Periœci increased as the shores of the whole Messenian Gulf came into Sparta's sphere of power. Thus the economic strength and the military potential of the Lacedaemonians were greatly augmented by this acquisition of 'spear-won land'.

Excavation has added only a little to the picture.[24] At Mila near Malthi in the north of the inland plain a cult with dedications of figurines came to an end *c.* 725, evidently with the subjugation or flight of the local people. On the other hand there was continuity from Geometric to Classical times in a large tomb at Karpophora. And on the west coast by Pylus burials of the traditional kind were made in Mycenaean

[23] The Greek meanings have to be kept in mind: oligarchy being rule by the few, aristocracy rule by the best, and democracy rule by the people; in all cases direct rule is meant.
[24] E 170; E 165; *BCH* 1961, 697; see *CAH* III.1², 728f.

chamber-tombs and tholos-tombs in the Late Geometric period. There are signs of growing prosperity at Sparta in the erection of the first stone buildings in the precinct of Artemis Orthia at Limnae *c*. 725 and of a shrine soon afterwards to Menelaus and Helen at Therapne.

The poverty of what has been revealed by excavation should remind us that the Spartiates living in their messes at Sparta and their families living in the five obes of the middle valley of the Eurotas had the very simplest standard of life. They had no walls of defence and no substantial establishments. They relied on their physique and their weapons to hold the Helots to their labours and to keep their neighbours at a distance. In relation to the Perioeci and the Helots the Spartiates – perhaps 6,000 adult males *c*. 700 B.C. – were far from numerous. It was essential for the future of Sparta to maintain the birth-rate of its citizens, and practices designed for this purpose, such as polyandry and cohabitation of an old man's young wife with a man in his prime, were accepted in a society which was primitive in many ways and put the interest of family and state before the susceptibilities of the individual.[25]

2. *The other Peloponnesian states*

In the north of the Peloponnese Corinth and Megara were at loggerheads. Corinth seized the Heraea (now Perachora) and built a temple to Hera Limenia *c*. 740, and sometime later advanced into the central plain and subjugated the Megarians. One condition imposed upon the vanquished was that they must send young men and women to attend the funeral and join in the mourning at the death of one of the Corinthian ruling clan, the Bacchiadae; a similar condition to that imposed by the Spartans on the Messenians. But the Megarians revolted successfully, led by an Olympic victor of 720, Orsippus, whose epitaph included these words: 'when the enemy were cutting off much land, he freed the farthest frontier in his country's cause'. But Corinth proved the stronger. By 700 she held the Heraea and the Piraea, including Oenoe on the Corinthian Gulf and Crommyon on the Saronic Gulf (Strabo 380), and she built a temple to Poseidon of the Isthmus in thanksgiving. The gain to Corinth was very great. By advancing her northern frontier she secured her grip on the neck of the Isthmus, which had a harbour on either Gulf and a short span for portage; and her harbour by the temple of Hera Limenia was sheltered from the northerly and westerly winds to which Lechaeum was exposed. Her new territory provided timber, pasture and slopes for arboriculture. The loss to Megara was correspondingly severe, especially as the raising of sheep and the making of woollen goods were sources of her prosperity.[26]

[25] See E 151, 214ff.   [26] See E 216 and O. Broneer in *Hesp.* 7 (1938) 27.

The orbit of Corinth expanded also by sea: trading in the Gulf of Corinth as far as Ithaca early in the century, then founding strong colonies at Corcyra and Syracuse *c.* 733, and finally securing the approaches and the passage of the straits at Rhium by founding Chalcis, Macynia, Molycrium and Oeniadae *c.* 700. The aspects of her maritime activity which Thucydides[27] stressed at 1. 13.2–5 were her priority in the building of warships not only for herself but also for others – e.g. for Samos *c.* 704 – her suppression of piracy and her ability to draw revenues as a centre of exchange. To these the archaeologist today would add the change from the Geometric style to the orientalizing style and the export of Protocorinthian pottery to markets throughout the west and some in the east, where its style influenced Rhodes.

Colonial expansion and naval development went hand in hand and owed much to the leadership of the Bacchiadae. The new warships were 'triaconters' and 'pentaconters', rowed respectively by thirty oarsmen and fifty oarsmen. The hull of the pentaconter was narrow and up to 32 metres long, undecked, and with the keel-beam prolonged at the bow and sheathed with bronze, so that it could serve as a ram (fig. 48). The crew of such a warship could overhaul and master any merchantman or small piratical craft, unless there was a high wind or a tempestuous sea. It is probable that the Bacchiadae also took steps to stimulate and develop overseas trade. For example, fine pottery was produced for export not in farms and cottages but in workshops so specialized that a group of Protocorinthian pots at Thapsus in Sicily has been identified as coming from one workshop at Corinth. The same was no doubt true of ship-building with its related crafts and of metal-working in precious metals, bronze and iron. What the Bacchiadae did was to provide suitable conditions for such workshops to be set up, and then to enjoy an expanding market. Few Corinthian citizens were involved as workmen. As Herodotus remarked (II. 167.2), *all* Greeks scorned those who practised trades and crafts. This was especially true of the Lacedaemonians (he said), and the Corinthians were those who least looked down on handicraftsmen. It was only a matter of degree. The bulk of those engaged in production and trading were aliens, transient or resident, who were attracted by the facilities which Corinth provided. These facilities were partly due to her geographical position on the overland route linking Central Greece and the Peloponnese and on the isthmus between the two seas; but they were also due to the organizing ability of the Bacchiadae who 'provided exchange on both elements and so kept their city powerful through the raising of revenue'.

The Bacchiadae, a clan of some two hundred households which

---

[27] His dates here, as for the western colonies, are deliberate and not theoretical or reckoned in half-generations, as suggested, e.g. in *CQ* 19 (1969) 100. See above, pp. 89f.

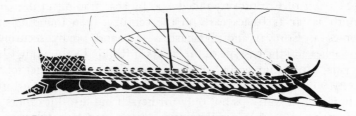

48. Penteconter, from an Athenian black-figure dinos. Late sixth century B.C.
(Paris, Louvre Museum F 62; after H 22, pl. 89; H 59, pl. 14f.)

married only among themselves, held a monopoly of offices and elected one of their number each year to serve as the leading magistrate (*prytanis* or *basileus*).[28] Men of culture and action, they included a famous epic and lyric poet, Eumelus, celebrated lawgivers and founders of colonies; their wealth at home and in the colonies was in landed property, and they served as cavalrymen and as leaders of heavy-armed infantry. The citizen society, of which they were the elite, was organized for social and religious purposes on the basis of the three Dorian tribes both in Corinthia and in the colonies. Each family owned an inalienable lot of land (*kleros*), and each colonial settler was promised a lot overseas. When population grew rapidly in Corinthia, a family might grow beyond the resources of its *kleros* and some sons might emigrate. A very early lawgiver of Corinth, Pheidon, inheriting a situation in which the original *kleroi* varied in size, tried to keep the number of households constant and control the size of the citizen body. Another Corinthian, Philolaus, a Bacchiad who flourished *c.* 730 and legislated at Thebes, tried to keep the number of *kleroi* there constant and relate the franchised population to them (Arist. *Pol.* 1265b12 and 1274a31). That these lawgivers did not solve the problems entirely may be inferred from the tradition that most of the original settlers at Syracuse came from Tenea, an agricultural area inland (Strabo 380). The land-holding family men of Corinth were certainly citizens and may have met in an assembly (*halia* in Doric); but political power remained in the hands of the Bacchiadae until *c.* 657. The first temple of Apollo, built *c.* 700, was one of their monuments.

Megara too had ports on either Gulf, Pagae and Nisaea, and controlled the routes between Central Greece and the Peloponnese. Her ability to withstand the pressures from Corinth and Athens shows how tough and well organized the Dorians of Megaris were. She compensated for loss of territory in the south by planting a colony in Sicily in 728 and a group of very strong colonies in the approaches to the Black Sea: Astacus perhaps in 711, Chalcedon in 676 and Byzantium in 668. This

[28] E 228, 295ff.

vigorous state was controlled by an aristocratic oligarchy operating through a council (*boule*) and an eponymous magistrate, the *basileus*; and the citizens owned *kleroi* which were worked by serfs (see *CAH* III.1², 724).

Achaea, a poor territory which easily became overpopulated, took part in the colonial expansion. Achaeans together with Troezenians (whom they later expelled in breach of their oath) founded Sybaris in the toe of Italy *c.* 720. Achaeans alone founded Croton in 709, Metapontum *c.* 650 and Caulonia *c.* 675–650. Their choice of sites was influenced by a desire rather for rich land than good harbourage, but they developed a portage route which avoided passage through the Straits of Messina. They planted Scione too in Chalcidice *c.* 700. It is possible that the Achaeans combined amongst themselves in founding Sybaris, since the founder was chosen from Helice, the religious centre of their loose federation; other Achaean colonies were founded from individual cities, Rhypes and Aegium. In the west they joined together in the worship of Hera on the Lacinian promontory near Croton.

The Eleans were able to satisfy their hunger for land by conquering the Pisatans and annexing the valley of the lower Alpheus in the ninth or early eighth century. In 776 they organized the Olympic festival and conducted the games, and thereby obtained a position of prestige and considerable revenues. It is probable that they planted a colony, Buchetium, on the north shore of the Gulf of Arta *c.* 700, from which a convenient route led to Dodona, a shrine similar in standing to Olympia. In the 660s, when they lost Olympia to Pheidon of Argos and the Pisatans, the Eleans planted two other colonies in the same part of Epirus, Elatria and Pandosia. Their colonies were in terrain similar to coastal Elis with swampy pastures for stock-breeding and fishponds in the lagoons.[29] The leaders of the Eleans in this period were the descendants of the great clans of the conquest and they formed a ruling oligarchy, while the people lived in a large number of very small communities.

Of Arcadia we know only that it maintained its independence against its numerous neighbours. Its hardy mountaineers were engaged mainly in pastoralism and stock-raising, and they carried their valuable ship-building timber down to the coastal towns. Tegea and Mantinea were already important as religious centres, and they offered markets to a people who were partly nomadic. Bassae in western Arcadia was also a place of worship; for votives found there included an iron statuette of a man, dating from early in the seventh century, and there were traces of iron-working to the north of the later temple-site.

The literary sources tell us little of Argos after the destruction of

[29] E 31.

Asine and the annexation of its territory. That Argos was relatively prosperous is clear from the excellent pottery which she produced in her own individual Late Geometric style and then in orientalizing style. Some of this pottery and its contents were exported, for instance to Tegea, Megara, Epidauria and Cythera. The inhabited area of Argos town was much extended at the turn of the century, and new cemeteries were made at a distance from it; a late eighth-century grave, known as the Panoply Grave, from the foot of the Larissa enables us to picture a leading warrior and his possessions in gold, bronze and iron.[30] Some Argives may have accompanied the Corinthian founders to Syracuse, as vases of Argive style were found there, but otherwise Argos was not involved in the colonizing movement. The reason was presumably that she had enough land for her citizens; in other words, while Sparta was annexing spacious Messene, Argos retained her hold on Thyreatis, Cynuria and Cythera, where indeed a little Argive and no Laconian pottery has been found. She may also have exerted pressure on the towns of the Epidaurian peninsula; for Troezen took part in founding Sybaris *c.* 720, and Halieis built a mud-brick wall of defence early in the seventh century. Then too the people of Halieis made a temple to Apollo with limestone bases for wooden columns, and these bases were spaced as in the temple of Artemis Orthia at Limnae in Laconia.[31] In the course of 700 to 650 the wall of defence was doubled and then underwent a destruction which was associated with Laconian I pottery. Perhaps Argos was punishing Halieis for an intrigue with Sparta. In the same half-century the influence of 'Daedalic sculpture' came from Crete to Argos.

The acme of Argive power was reached *c.* 670–660 under the leadership of Pheidon, a Temenid, who had been elected to the traditional office of *basileus* but exercised a despotic rule. Then Argos defeated Sparta decisively at the battle of Hysiae in Thyreatis (an area to which Sparta laid claim) and went on to support the Pisatans in expelling the Eleans from Pisatis and taking control of the Olympic festival of 668 (see above, p. 325). Pheidon was also in close touch with the ruling house of Corinth, the Bacchiadae, and his death was said to have been due to his intervention in a faction-struggle at Corinth in support of his friends. Tradition associated him with Aegina also. It seems that for a time Pheidon did 'recover the lot of Temenus', the mastery of the north-eastern Peloponnese (Strabo 358). It was then that he established for this area the use of the so-called Pheidonian measures, both dry and liquid, which facilitated the exchange of agricultural produce, Argos herself being a main producer. He was said to have dedicated 'to Hera at Argos' *obeliskoi*, spits of iron used as a medium

---

[30] E 189. *CAH* III.1², 781, fig. 86.   [31] *Arch. Delt.* 27 (1972) *Chr.* 233.

49. Stone spit-holder from the sanctuary of
Hera at Perachora. Inscribed δραχμα εγοτερα
λευ?[ο]λενε ταιδε ανακειμαι? 'I am a drachma
(dedicated to) white-armed Hera...' The
spits were fastened to the side of the upright
stele. Seventh century B.C. (Athens, National
Museum; after E 222, I, pls. 36c, 132 iii; A 36,
122–4, pl. 20, no. 17.)

of exchange; and such spits have been found in graves at Argos and
as dedications in shrines at the Argive Heraeum, Perachora (fig. 49) and
Delphi (cf. Hdt. II. 135.4). Ephorus assumed, mistakenly, that Pheidon
introduced coinage at Aegina. His measure for olive oil was commemorated by the name of a special olive oil jar, a *pheidon*.[32]

The first century of colonial expansion, *c.* 750–650, had revolutionary
effects on the artistic tastes and the economic development of many
states in the Peloponnese. The change from Geometric style to Protocorinthian style was from a sparse economy of line and a traditional
mode to a full delight in colour and bold experimentation, inspired no
doubt by contact with oriental art but indicative of a richer and more
liberated way of life. Great strides were taken in metallurgy, in the
making of weapons and the production of bronze vessels. Offerings,

[32] Hdt. VI. 127; Arist. *Pol.* 1310b16–27; frs. 480–1; *Ath. Pol.* 10; E 228, 344ff; *FGrH* 90 (Nic.
Dam.) F 35; *Etym. Mag.* 612.58.

for instance to Zeus and Hera at Olympia, now included superb bronze cauldrons mounted on tripods, beautifully made armour, and great numbers of bronze statuettes of horses and men (but not men riding horses); for these were features of aristocratic ascendancy in many parts of the Greek world. The rapid spread of the alphabet along the routes of trade helped individual men to express themselves, communicate over distances, keep records and improve methods of trading.

As mobility increased and festivals were attended by a wider clientele, higher standards were set and fine poetry and music were appreciated. The epic poems of Homer exercised an enormous influence on art and literature, but new modes were also developed, even in epic, for instance by Eumelus of Corinth who wrote of his own city's mythical past. Terpander of Lesbos and Thaletas of Gortyn in Crete won fame at Sparta as poet-musicians, the former being victorious at the 'Carnea' probably in 676 and the latter writing songs for the 'Gymnopaidiai', at which an antiphony was performed between a choir of boys and a choir of men dancing naked on a hot summer day. Terpander sang his compositions to the accompaniment of his 'seven-toned' cithara and took his libretto from well-known epic poems. One of the fragments which may be genuine praised Sparta where 'the young men's spear prospers, the Muse sings clear and wide-pathed justice is the champion of noble deeds'.[33]

In the eastern part of the Peloponnese the rising standard of life and the accumulation of some capital in propertied families and in states such as Corinth caused a change in the methods of warfare. As more and more men were able to equip themselves with iron-tipped spears, iron sword and bronze armour (shield, helmet, cuirass and greaves), they became groups of elite warriors, developed a close formation in which they helped one another, and fought against their peers in set battles.[34] The new armament was available before 700; indeed it was partly responsible for the success of colonial adventurers. But examples of developed 'hoplite warfare' (so-called from the *hoplon* or shield) occurred first in the seventh century in the Peloponnese. The battle of Hysiae between Argos and Sparta on low ground in the disputed area was an excellent example. Hoplites fought hoplites in accordance with a code which was as conventional as that of an athletic contest, and they abode by the decision. If they suffered a severe defeat, as the Spartans did at Hysiae, they might have to postpone the next engagement until a new generation of warriors was trained. This form of warfare had one advantage, that the poorer members of society and the women and children were generally not exposed to danger.

Hoplite warfare was a phenomenon of political significance. Only

[33] E 151, 281ff and E 162, 49.   [34] A 59.

50. Scene on a Corinthian alabastron from Corinth, showing a
hoplite panoply: sword, greave, thrusting and throwing (with loop)
spears, corselet, helmet. Second half of seventh century B.C. (Berlin,
Staatliche Museen inv. 3148; after H 69, pl. 33.)

the well-to-do could afford the time for training and the cost of the
equipment (fig. 50), and such warfare developed only when the
well-to-do became more numerous than they had been in pastoral
societies. What happened in states other than Sparta was a broadening
of the top layer in terms of wealth and a strengthening of its position
within society; for light-armed troops lost status by comparison, except
those who were highly trained (as archers were in Crete, for instance).
This top layer gained too in solidarity; for it was a feature of hoplite
fighting in a phalanx that neighbours had to help one another. The
people who made up the top layer were to a great extent those who
had held hereditary positions of leadership in a tribal society, but during
this century from 750 to 650 there was some infiltration by able men
who became wealthy through commercial enterprise. We are still
dealing with an aristocratic oligarchy; but a change is coming about
from the 'aristocrat' of hereditary qualifications to the 'aristocrat' of
wealth and warfare. The term 'aristoi', 'the best', was taking on a new
meaning but within a traditional society. At Sparta, as we have seen,
the situation was different. There the 'Equals' were a well-to-do group
of considerable size, strong in their own solidarity and trained as
professional soldiers. Although they lost at Hysiae, history was to show
that hoplite warfare might have been invented specifically to ensure their
success in the struggle for power.

III. THE PURSUIT OF POWER BY INDIVIDUALS, c. 650–550 B.C.

There was colonization of two kinds in this period. The colonies
themselves planted colonies and created a pattern of local power:
Syracuse, for instance, planted three colonies in south-eastern Sicily
between 663 and 598, and Megara Hyblaea planted Selinus in 628. The
mother cities themselves founded further colonies. Megara strengthened
her position in the Propontis and Black Sea by founding Selymbria in

the seventh century and Mesembria and Heraclea Pontica in the sixth century; thus her harbours, including Byzantium, Chalcedon and Astacus, were well placed to draw revenues from trade through the Bosporus. Corinth consolidated her grip on the coasting route to the west by planting further colonies: Sollium, Leucas, Anactorium, Ambracia and Apollonia Illyrica between 665 and 588. One reason for her policy was a quarrel with Corcyra which led to the first naval battle between Greek fleets *c.* 664. She planted also Potidaea in Chalcidice on the north-eastern route *c.* 600. As these colonies were independent states from the outset, it is misleading to talk of Corinth having a colonial empire; but as long as she maintained good relations with her colonies, she and they had a common interest in keeping down piracy and drawing revenues from trade which passed through their waters. The first settlers varied in number – 200 at Apollonia Illyrica and 1,000 at Leucas – but others followed to create an entirely Greek city. Thus there was every opportunity in this century for any surplus population in the Peloponnese to emigrate to the new world.

The reflex action of colonial expansion was an enormous increase in seaborne trade, accelerating after 650. The main stream flowed along the northern Mediterranean and the Black Sea, and the chief beneficiaries in old Greece were the states near the Isthmus which formed a bridge between the east and the west: Corinth, Sicyon, Megara, Aegina and as a late competitor Athens. In 650–550 Corinth held the lead in pottery and bronzework, ship-building and naval power, and after 550 it was only in pottery that Corinth was outstripped by Athens. A lesser route of trade ran from Egypt and Cyrene to Thera and Laconia or Cythera, whence one could proceed to the Argolic and Saronic Gulfs or take the direct but less safe passage westwards. Here Laconia played a leading part, and her pottery was in vogue until 550; thereafter it began to decline in popularity and in quality. It was in general, and not least in some parts of the Peloponnese, a century of remarkable prosperity.

Prosperity bred ambition, and it was the most prosperous states which provided the earliest examples of the seizure and exercise of power by one man, which the Greeks called *monarkhia* or *tyrannis*, the latter being a loan-word from Lydia, which had the overtones of oriental wealthy despotism. The link between prosperity and tyranny was observed by Thucydides (1. 13.1). 'As Greece became more powerful and made more of the acquisition of wealth than even before, then generally tyrannies were established in the states as the revenues became greater.' How is the link to be explained? Greek writers of the fourth century, such as Aristotle, tended to think that the early tyrants were 'demagogues' who reached the top with popular support in a time of faction and used mercenary troops to seize power; but it is evident that they were reading the conditions of their own time back into the seventh century.[35] Solon and Theognis, who lived so much closer to the origins of tyranny, provided a more convincing picture of the conditions which gave rise to it. In brief, desire for wealth was the root of the trouble, and it was the ruthlessness of the oligarchic leaders and the witlessness of the common people which led to tyranny. Thus Solon wrote of the faction which was almost a precondition of tyranny: 'It is the townsmen themselves who mean to corrupt the great state [Athens] in their witlessness and their pursuit of money, and it is the ruthless spirit of the leaders (*hegemones*) of the people (*demos*, not in a popular but in a total sense), who have committed great outrages and are ripe to suffer many sorrows.' Then of the sequel: 'It is from the great men that the state is corrupted, and it is through lack of understanding that the people have fallen into slavery to the one-man ruler (*monarkhos*).' Theognis of Megara, who flourished probably from 550 onwards, wrote to Cyrnus of his fear of impending tyranny as follows (41–52):

The townsmen here are still sensible, but the leaders (*hegemones*) are heading for a fall into much trouble. Good men, Cyrnus, never yet corrupted a state; but when it is the pleasure of the wicked to commit outrage, when they corrupt the people, when they give unjust judgements for the sake of their own profits and power, then... from them arise factions and killings of kindred and one-man rulers (*monarkhoi*).

If we apply these views to the conditions of the seventh century, it seems that the process was generally as follows. A traditional and more or less hereditary oligarchy remained in power within a static, agricultural, tribal society, but it was disrupted by the swing towards capitalism which Thucydides had in mind. Opportunities for personal aggrandizement arose from the new conditions, and were exploited ruthlessly by those who already had means and position. Faction grew between rival groups of oligarchs, and led to civil war and sometimes to tyranny. The common people, being without the experience of the actuality of power, showed their witlessness in trusting those who abused their trust. The struggle was initially not between the oligarchs and the people, not between the rich and the poor, but between rival leading oligarchs. Herodotus summarized the situation in words which he placed on the lips of the wise Persian King, Darius:

In an oligarchy the fact that a number of men are competing for distinction in affairs of state cannot but lead to violent personal feuds; each of them wants to get to the top and to see his own proposals carried; so they quarrel. Personal

---

[35] Writers such as Ephorus gave detailed accounts which can only be fictitious; see *FGrH* 90 (Nic. Dam.) F 57–F 61; 105 F 2; Plut. *Mor.* 553A–B; D.S. VIII. 24.

quarrels lead to open dissension and then to bloodshed; and from bloodshed the result is one-man rule (*monarkhia*). (III. 82.3)

We know more about the rise of tyranny at Corinth than at Argos, Megara and Sicyon. The closed oligarchy of the Bacchiadae, having ruled Corinth autocratically for longer than anyone could remember, was inevitably subjected to new strains by the rapid move towards capitalism during the first half of the seventh century. These strains caused faction-strife, of which a romanticized version has come down to us, but it seems that it involved Pheidon of Argos who sent help 'through friendship', presumably to one group among the Bacchiadae, and that it contributed to the fall of the Bacchiadae. The first tyrant, Cypselus, took power in 657 soon after the probable date of Pheidon's demise. He was presumably the leader of the faction which ended the rule of the Bacchiadae. As he had married into or even within the Bacchiadae, which was an endogamous group, and as he had been appointed to a magistracy, which was a monopoly of the Bacchiadae, the faction he led was within the Bacchiadae most probably.

Our best source of information is a speech by a Corinthian, which Herodotus made up in order to include the Corinthian tradition about the tyrants of Corinth. Most of it is folk-tale, but it includes two oracles issued by Delphi after the events to which they refer but still within the time of the tyranny. The first was addressed allegedly to the parents of Cypselus, then childless, and ran thus. 'Eëtion, no one honours you, right honourable though you are. Labda is pregnant, and will bring forth a rolling stone; it will fall upon one-man rulers (*monarkhoi*) and set Corinth right' (Hdt. v. 92β.2). The priest who devised this oracle wished to show hostility not towards Cypselus but towards the losers, those of the Bacchiadae who stood for autocratic rule themselves (as *monarkhoi*). The opening words may refer to Eëtion's childlessness, which was a matter of shame among Dorians and especially in a leading citizen. The second oracle was addressed allegedly to Cypselus and was supposed to have led him to seize power. 'Happy is the man who enters my house, Cypselus, Eëtion's son, king (*basileus*) of famous Corinth, himself and his sons, but no longer his sons' sons' (Hdt. v. 92ε.2). The composer of this oracle wished to flatter the tyrants as 'kings', and he worded the oracle before the time when the grandson of Cypselus did in fact succeed to the position of 'king'. We have no idea how the revolutionary *coup d'état* was achieved.[36]

It has sometimes been suggested that Cypselus, being of non-Dorian

[36] A 2, 16ff on the nature of the evidence; 43ff on tyranny at Corinth; cf. A 6, 1 14–37 and E 228, 441ff, on whose late dating of Cypselus' tyranny see M–L p. 11. Hdt. III. 52.4 represents Cypselus and his son as a *basileus*.

descent, identified himself with enmity to the Dorians and rose as champion of the non-Dorian subject peoples of Corinthia. Nothing is further from the literary tradition. There the Cypselids' claim was that they were desended through Eëtion from a famous clan of Lapiths who did battle with the Centaurs in Thessaly and through Labda from Heracles who killed some of the Centaurs; and that Eëtion's forebear, Melas of Gonousa, was a founding father of Dorian Corinth, having joined the expedition of Aletes and his Dorians, and so was an original 'Korinthios'. A scene of the troops of Melas and Aletes fraternizing, in the opinion of Pausanias (v. 18.7–8), was represented on the cedar 'Chest of Cypselus', dedicated at Olympia by Cypselus' successors in the tyranny. Thus they identified themselves with the ruling aristocracy of Dorian Corinth from its start, and their choice of themes for the chest, including Heracles' killing of the Centaurs, was as aristocratic as Pindar's choice of themes for his epinician odes.[37]

Tyranny at Megara arose from faction among the oligarchic leaders (*hegemones*), as we have seen in Theognis' verses to Cyrnus. On his way to power Theagenes won the confidence of the common people 'by slaughtering the cattle of the rich'. Since Aristotle cited this as an example of the would-be tyrant misleading the people (*Pol.* 1305a22–6), he was indicating not that Theagenes was a lover of the people but that the people failed to realize his true nature. No doubt Theagenes was a Dorian aristocrat. The origin of the tyranny at Sicyon is shrouded in the mists of folk-tale and in fourth-century historical fiction, but two details have been used to suggest a humble origin for the first tyrant Orthagoras: that his father Andreas was a cook and that his popularity with the common people led to his being elected polemarch, magistrate for war. If the facts are true, which is improbable, they do not serve this purpose; for Andreas was in charge of sacrifices on a mission to Delphi and thus was acting as a priest, and it is unlikely that anyone was elected as polemarch from the people by the people in seventh-century Dorian Sicyon. Rather priesthoods were hereditary to noble houses, and senior magistracies were the preserves of oligarchic clans.[38] As far then as the evidence goes (and it is very sketchy), we may conclude that tyranny gew out of oligarchy when the ranks of the oligarchs split and one faction-leader among the oligarchs used force to seize power; and that sometimes he enlisted the help of a part of the common people, whom he had duped into trusting him.

[37] Hdt. v. 92β.1; D.L. I. 94.1; Paus. II. 4.4; v. 18.7–8. For the cedar chest see Stuart Jones in *JHS* 14 (1894) 30, 80.
[38] D.S. VIII. 24; *FGrH* 105 F 2. Cleisthenes belonged to the tribe which was not Dorian, but the incorporation of that tribe was certainly earlier than the setting up of the tyranny. Priestly families were no doubt included in it.

In the passages which we have cited violence and bloodshed were attributed rather to the period of strife (*stasis*) which preceded tyranny than to tyranny itself; and in the collection of poems which goes under the name of Theognis the miseries of men were not tortures and killings at the hand of tyrants but the cycle of betrayal by comrades, banishment by rivals in power and penury in exile which attended *stasis*. No doubt bloodshed, banishment and expropriation were weapons in the tyrant's armoury when he first seized power. Indeed they were an integral part of the revolution he was bringing about. But they seem to have been used not indiscriminately but against rival oligarchs, such as the Bacchiadae to whom Cypselus was to be 'a rolling stone'. What the early poems did stress was not loss of life under a tyranny but loss of liberty, 'slavery'. This was probably correct; for once a tyrant had established his power, albeit by violence, his aim was not to kill but to come to terms with other aristocratic houses, pacify the state and strengthen himself against the émigrés. Within the Peloponnese the allegations of brutality and massacre which were made by later writers, such as Herodotus (v. 92η), were directed rather against the last ruler in a series of tyrants, and no doubt some of them were true.

Tyranny came to stay for three generations at Corinth (*c.* 657–583 B.C.) and for a century at Sicyon (*c.* 655–556/5). Later tyrannies, like modern ones, did not last so long. Aristotle put forward some reasons for their long life: the tyrants respected the laws, treated their subjects with moderation, forwarded the people's interests, and in the case of one man in each dynasty, Periander and Cleisthenes, were successful in war (*Pol.* 1315b13–30). We may add others. The founder of a tyranny was among the ablest of the oligarchs, and he eliminated any rivals by execution or banishment. Some of his opponents preferred compromise; then they held positions in his service. The common people were not immediately dangerous, nor in danger; they lacked weapons and experience, lived out on the land (Arist. *Pol.* 1305a18), and were satisfied if their betters gave them justice, peace and prosperity. Fortune favoured the tyrants in that the period was one of rapidly growing prosperity. They could keep their subjects prosperous and at the same time use their own wealth to cultivate friends abroad and at home, and to obtain the favour of 'the media', Delphi and Olympia. Tyrant rarely ate tyrant; for it was in their common interest to combine and keep the émigrés at arm's distance, especially since Megara, Corinth and Sicyon formed a continuous area of tyrant-land, uniquely at peace with one another for perhaps a century. There were other tyrannies of less fame and shorter duration; among them Procles at Epidaurus, Leon at Phlius, Pantaleon at Pisa, and one Hippias, perhaps at Megara but separated from Theagenes by an interval of time.

The tyrants at Corinth inherited and expanded a strong colonial system. Corcyra, held at first by the exiled Bacchiadae, was brought into the fold, and Corcyra and Corinth founded a joint colony at Epidamnus *c.* 625. Colonies were planted by Corinth alone or in conjunction with the local people at Leucas, Heraclea, Ambracia and Apollonia Illyrica within the period *c.* 625–600. Three sons of Cypselus went out as founders and probably as rulers; thus at Ambracia Gorgus was succeeded by at least two 'tyrants' of the Cypselid house. The founder of Epidamnus was a Corinthian, of a house 'descended from Heracles', specially summoned from Corinth and therefore a collaborator with the Cypselids; and the settlers were Corcyraeans in the main, but there were also some Corinthians and others of Dorian race (Thuc. 1. 24.2). As the tyrants controlled the planting of colonies, we see that their policy was pro-Dorian. Later in the rule of Periander the Corcyraeans rebelled and killed Periander's son Lycophron; and when Periander regained control of Corcyra, he sent three hundred boys, sons of leading Corcyraeans, to Alyattes, king of Lydia, to be castrated (it was said) and serve as eunuchs.

The control of the north-western area was of vital importance to the Cypselids and to Corinth; for they drew from it silver, copper, ship-building timber, hides, wool, milk-products and meat, quite apart from the profits of trade with the west. A beautiful gold bowl, dedicated at Olympia by the Cypselids as spoils from Heraclea (fig. 51), reminds us that the control even of their colonies was maintained by force of arms, for which sea power was a *sine qua non*. A son of Periander led a colony to Potidaea, which faced the Thermaic Gulf and served the Macedonian end of the trans-Balkan route via Lake Lychnitis to Epidamnus (see above, p. 133). The colonial policy of the tyrants was of the greatest benefit not only to Corinth but also to other states which profited from the resulting increase in the flow of trade.

One such beneficiary was Sicyon, famous for its bronzework. The wealth of its tyrants was displayed to the world by victories in the chariot race at Olympia by Myron in 648 and later by Cleisthenes, and at Delphi by Cleisthenes in 582, and by the treasuries which they built at these sanctuaries; that at Olympia was of bronze sheet, divided into two rooms, one in Doric style and the other in Ionic, and the bronze was said to have come from Tartessus in western Spain. Cleisthenes, tyrant *c.* 600–570, was appointed by the Amphictions of Delphi to command their forces against Crisa in the Sacred War and was given a third of the spoils (see above, p. 313). Suitors for the hand of his daughter were said to have come from as far afield as Sybaris and Epidamnus, and he held his own in a war against Argos. Never again did Sicyon stand so high. It was only rarely that the tyrants led their

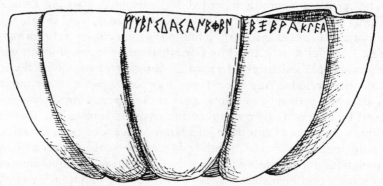

51. Gold bowl – a deep phiale – found in the bed of the River Alpheus at Olympia.
Inscribed Ρυψελιδαι ανεθεν εξ Ερακλειας 'The sons of Cypselus dedicated this (as spoils)
from Heraclea.' Late seventh or early sixth century B.C. Width 16·8 cm. Weight 836·47 g.
22·3 carat gold. (Boston, Museum of Fine Arts 21.1843; after E 234, 90, fig. 56; *ibid.* 237,
n. 348; *CAH Plates* I¹ 274; A 36, 127–8.)

hoplite armies into war. They preferred a network of alliances, of
friendly relations with foreign rulers such as Alyattes of Lydia or
Psammetichus I of Egypt, and of ties by marriage, for instance linking
Theagenes and Cylon, and Cleisthenes and Megacles. Like the kings of
Macedon, the tyrants practised polygamy to secure a dynastic succession
and promote alliances, and there may have been some substance behind
the stories of fratricide, necrophily and incest which were told by
sensation-loving writers. At one time Periander was rated one of the
Seven Wise Men of the Greek world, and he was chosen to arbitrate
between Athens and Mytilene over Sigeum (Hdt. v. 95); but every sort
of crime was of course attributed to him by later writers.

We can infer from the wording of dedications how the tyrants wished
to represent their rule. The chest within which the founder, Cypselus,
was hidden as a baby was dedicated by 'the Cypselidae' in gratitude
for his salvation by Zeus of Olympia (Paus. v. 17.5). And in the colonial
field it was 'the Cypselidae' who dedicated the golden bowl from spoils
won at Heraclea (fig. 51). Thus the change from the Bacchiadae to the
Cypselidae was a change not of principle but of family, and it seems
from the story in Herodotus III. 52.4 that the men of the tyrannical
house at Corinth and in some colonies were styled 'kings' (*basileis*). The
Sicyonian treasury at Olympia was dedicated by 'Myron and the people
(*demos*) of the Sicyonians', which implied a *basileus* in office and a
meeting of the citizen body of Sicyon.[39] In the eyes of the rulers and
most of the citizens tyranny was not so much an intermission of
constitutional government as a system of very long duration, blessed

[39] *SEG* I. 94 and E 228, 517 n. 1; Paus. VI. 19.4, whereas Paus. VI. 19.1 is a paraphrase.

52. The *diolkos* at the Corinthian Isthmus. Sixth century B.C.(After N. Verdelis, *Athenische Mitteilungen* 73 (1958) Beil. 196.)

by Delphi and Olympia, internationally recognized, and crowned with a material success which seemed to be a sign of divine favour. The origins of Cypselus were sanctified by oracular utterances and by a Moses-like myth (Hdt. v. 92), which hints of some ruler-cult at Corinth, and nobles may have regarded the ruling tyrant rather as Pindar regarded Hieron of Syracuse. Poets such as Arion, Chersias and Epigenes sang the tyrants' praises at Corinth, and Cleisthenes promoted the performance of 'tragic choruses' at Sicyon.

The tyrants beautified their cities and provided employment on public works such as the provision of water at Corinth, the aqueduct and well-house at Megara, the colonnade at Sicyon, the cutting of the Leucas canal, and the paving of the four-mile runway for hauling ships and cargoes over the Isthmus of Corinth (fig. 52).[40] They relied on harbour and market dues rather than on direct taxation, and they spent lavishly – for instance in dedicating a colossal gold statue of Zeus at Olympia and establishing new festivals at Sicyon and the Isthmus. They worshipped the orthodox gods and especially favoured the cult of Dionysus as a god of universal appeal to citizens and non-citizens alike.

[40] For the well-house see G. Gruben in *Arch. Delt.* 19 (1964) I. 37ff, and for the runway (*diolkos*) E 229, 45ff.

Of their social legislation we know only that they tried to restrict the number of slaves, check prostitution, maintain justice and keep citizens at work. They were not social revolutionaries; they seem rather to have conserved the aristocratic *status quo ante*, but their monopoly of authority was maintained by banishing or weakening other leading families. At Sicyon, which grew perhaps faster than Corinth, it is significant that Cleisthenes retained the division of citizens into four tribes unchanged. If he did re-name the three Dorian tribes 'Hogmen', 'Assmen' and 'Swinemen', as Herodotus reported (v. 68), it was as an insult to the Argives and their hero Adrastus and not to three quarters of his own citizens.

The fall of tyranny was an occasion for thanksgiving to the gods and for rejoicing in freedom. The Isthmian Games were founded in 581/80, when the last tyrant was expelled from Corinth, and a temple was built to Poseidon at the Isthmus. The Nemean Games were founded by Cleonae in 573 in honour of the Argive hero whom the tyrant Cleisthenes was disestablishing at Sicyon, and a temple was built to Zeus, in whose precinct the games were held.[41] The Isthmian and Nemean Games were celebrated every second year, whereas the Olympic and Pythian Games occurred once in four years. The establishment of the Pythian, Isthmian and Nemean Games within one decade was a remarkable phenomenon. It was a spontaneous expression of the common feelings which Greeks of every state shared, at home and overseas – gratitude to the gods, love of liberty and love of competitive athletics less for the glory of the individual than for the glory of his family and his state.

When tyranny fell, its poisonous effects within a society were revealed: the denial of liberty, the suppression of initiative, the damping down of talent, the encouragement of informers, the rewarding of collaborators and the engendering of hatred. If that society was left to itself, the next stage was *stasis*, party-strife between émigrés and collaborationists, between one aristocratic group and another, between rich and poor, and a complete distrust of one's fellows. 'Do not take a single step in reliance on these your fellow-townsmen; put no trust in their oath or their friendliness, not even if one pledges himself by Zeus Almighty, King of Gods.' 'Never befriend an exile with hope [i.e. of benefit], Cyrnus; once he gets home, he is a different man.' Theognis wrote thus with experience of *stasis* at Megara after the fall of Theagenes. Himself an aristocrat and an oligarch, he saw the peasants take power:

[41] E 213, 3ff; *Hesp.* 47 (1978) 63 and 48 (1979) 82.

Cyrnus, this city is a city still but the people are indeed different. Hitherto they had no knowledge of law or justice, but lived like deer outside this city, wearing goatskin on their backs. They're your nobles now, son of Polypaüs! The good men of old are worthless now.[42]

Others saw in this regime a very early example of democracy, radical, unbridled and short-lived (Plut. *Quaest. Graec.* 18). The swing of *stasis* brought the oligarchs into power in their turn; and in the end another tyrant arose. In this we see an early example of the disease of the city-state, which was ultimately to reduce its ability to resist foreign aggression. But in the mid-sixth century the Dorian states were not left to themselves. Sparta, exempt from tyranny herself, intervened.

IV. STRUGGLES FOR SURVIVAL AND SUPREMACY,
c. 650–530 B.C.

Defeated by Argos at Hysiae, Sparta sank to her nadir in the so-called Second Messenian War, which lasted perhaps thirty years or more. We have some contemporary evidence in the poems of Tyrtaeus; for his traditional *floruit*, 640–637 B.C., was early in the war. That the fighting was carried into Laconia and that the power of Sparta was almost broken is clear from his poems, in which the choice for the Spartan was to lose his life or lose his land:

To die, falling in the forefront of the fray, is honourable in a good soldier who fights for his fatherland. But to live a beggar's life, losing his city and fertile fields and wandering with his dear mother, aged father, little children and wedded wife, is of all things most miserable.

Take heart, for you are the stock of Heracles the invincible; Zeus has not yet turned his head away. Flinch not, fear not the masses of men, but let each bear his shield straight into the forefront, counting life his enemy and the black spirits of Death as dear as the rays of the sun.

In the crisis of the war Tyrtaeus told of 'the battle by the trench', the Spartan line being drawn up in front of it. To later generations it was the typical disposition in which, there being no way of retreat, soldiers fought to win or die perforce; and it was conjectured that there were freed Helots in the Spartan line on that occasion. That Sparta was almost overcome was due to the help which the Messenians obtained from Argos, Elis and Pisatis at the start, and it was these troops which used the hoplite tactics which Tyrtaeus described. The Arcadians, it seems, joined the Messenians later. In any case the Spartan line won

---

[42] Theognis 283–6, 333–4, 53–8; see M. L. West, *Studies in Greek Elegy* (Berlin, 1974) 41ff. Popular government ensued also at Ambracia for a time (Arist. *Pol.* 1304a31).

'the battle by the trench', and from then on Sparta slowly gained the upper hand.[43]

Memories of the last stage of the war have come down through late authors. When the Messenians were defending their last stronghold on Mt Ira in northern Messenia, the Arcadians and 'the Pylians' helped them; but Sparta obtained aid from Elis, Corinth and Samos (the last providing ships, Hdt. III. 47.1). When defeat came, some Messenians fled to Arcadia. Pylus and Methone fell probably later; and some refugees from there went to colonies in the west, such as Metapontum.[44] The Spartans left Pylus desolate but gave the site of Methone to refugees from Nauplia. During the latter part of the war Sparta inflicted defeats on Argos, which led to the people banishing the last Temenid king, Meltas, a grandson of Pheidon, and it was after this that Argos destroyed Nauplia on the ground of 'Laconizing'. Sparta entered the sixth century with the confidence of a hard-won victory, the extension of her conquests in the south-western Peloponnese, and two useful allies, Elis and Corinth. The influence of Tyrtaeus was to be as long-lasting at Sparta as that of Solon at Athens; and his poems called upon the Spartans to be loyal to the constitution in its classical form, the Eunomia including the Rider to the Rhetra.

The First Sacred War shows the military power of a widespread coalition. After its victory, in 590, the Delphic Amphictiony expanded by bringing the Dorian states of the Peloponnese into its membership, and all members took a new oath 'not to lay waste any Amphictionic city nor cut it off from running water in war or peace' (Aeschin. 2.115). That representatives of most states of mainland Greece should meet in time of peace, put a ban on some methods of war and agree to take joint action against an offender, was indeed a most remarkable development. Hitherto each state had acted as it alone pleased; now international discussion and agreement were shown to be possible. The Amphictionic oath was a reaction against total warfare and total destruction, as practised in the Peloponnese and elsewhere. Another sign of the times was arbitration to avoid war. Periander, for instance, arbitrated between Athens and Mytilene for the possession of Sigeum, and Sparta between Athens and Megara for the possession of Salamis. The Eleans, having decided to dissociate the Pisatans from the crimes

[43] For the trench Arist. *Eth. Nic.* 1116a36 with Schol.; Tyrt. fr. 10, col. 4, line 40 (ed. Prato); for Helots Paus. IV. 16.6 and Oros. I. 21.7; for allies Strabo 362, not emending the text, and Paus. VIII. 39.3–4 dating to 659 B.C. earlier clashes between Sparta and Arcadian cities. Suda *s.v. Tyrtaios* gives the date, and Plut. *Mor.* 194B puts the end *c.* 600 B.C. See *POxy* 47 no. 3316.

[44] Details are uncertain because on the liberation of the Messenians in the fourth century B.C. attempts to provide them with an early history were made by Callisthenes (*FGrH* 124 F 23) and Ephorus (*FGrH* 70 F 115), and later by Rhianus and Myron (Paus. IV. 6.1–4), and Apollodorus (*FGrH* 244 F 334). See E 166, 15ff; E 174; and E 183, 44.

committed by their tyrant Damophon, son of Pantaleon, referred all claims for compensation to the arbitration of sixteen married women, chosen one from each of the sixteen communities of Elis (Paus. v. 16.5–6). The choice of women was appropriate to a peaceful solution; no doubt Hera presided over the arbitration, as she did over the girls' races at Olympia which were conducted later by the same sixteen women. But peaceful solutions were very much the exception at the turn of the sixth century.

Spartan policy throughout the sixth century was dominated by the fear of a Messenian or Helot revolt being instigated by one or more of her neighbours: Triphylia–Pisatis, Arcadia and Argos. She needed allies who would help her to put pressure on these states. Her first ally was Elis. The Eleans were an elite body of citizens, organized in eight tribes and living in sixteen small communities (*damoi*), each of which had its own 'kings' (*basilaes*). The state was directed by a Gerousia or Council, with a small number of life-members, elected as at Sparta. The Eleans had reduced the other peoples of Elis to the status of *perioikoi*, and they were eager to expand southwards. Sparta sympathized with the oligarchic institutions of Elis and with her ambitions, and in the decade 590–580 she helped Elis to overwhelm Pisatis and reduce the people, some to serfdom, others to perioecic status. From 580 onwards two Elean umpires judged the Olympic Games. The Eleans and the Spartans were able thereafter to threaten Triphylia from either side.[45] The Arcadians were more dangerous, because they harboured Messenian émigrés and were tough fighters. Sparta tried to defeat them in war but failed in the period *c.* 600–560 B.C.

Argos was the most dangerous of all, the verdict of Hysiae not having been reversed, but she had her own problems, which included an unsuccessful war against Cleisthenes of Sicyon. When she expelled the Nauplians, she used the harbour as the base for her navy and took Nauplia's place in the Calaurian League; her ships were able to threaten the coast of Laconia from Cythera. Internal changes may have weakened her. When the last Temenid king, a grandson of Pheidon, was expelled (Diod. Sic. VII. 13.2), the title *basileus* was retained for an official but the chief executive magistrates were nine *damiorgoi*, a title which suggests that the *damos* was politically active. In the sixth century an inscription gives six *damiorgoi*. Both numbers indicate that the three Dorian tribes were equally represented in the college of *damiorgoi*. By the standard of the time Argos inclined towards democracy, just as Sparta favoured oligarchy.[46]

When the tide of tyranny ebbed, there were chances for Argos and

[45] Paus. v. 16; Arist. *Pol.* 1306a16; Paus. v. 9.4 (the most probable of the variant traditions).
[46] Strabo 368, 373; *SEG* XI. 314 and 336 with *CQ* 10 (1960) 33ff.

Sparta to intervene on opposing sides. Sparta seized them successfully. 'The Lacedaemonians put down most of the tyrants and the last (apart from those in Sicily), both at Athens and in the rest of Greece, which had been to a great extent subject to tyranny at an earlier time than Athens' (Thuc. 1. 18.1). The tyrannies in question, although listed by Plutarch (*Mor.* 859C), are not certain, because the citizens often claimed the credit for themselves; but the following cases are probable. Sparta was collaborating with the Eleans when Pyrrhus, last 'king' of the Pisatans, was overthrown *c.* 585–580. Corinth and Ambracia were in Plutarch's list, the former liberated from Cypselus II, *alias* Psammetichus, *c.* 583 and the latter from Archinus, one of 'the Cypselidae', *c.* 560. Although Ephorus attributed the liberation of Corinth to a popular rising only, the strong influence of Sparta is apparent in terms used of or at Corinth and Ambracia after the liberation. 'There [in Corinth] dwell Eunomia and her sisters, sure foundation of cities, Justice and her companion Peace...golden daughters of fair-counselling Themis' (Pind. *Ol.* 13.6); and the Ambraciotes claimed that Apollo, the Pythian Saviour, installed Eunomia, Themis and Dike in their city. The ensuing constitution at Corinth was an oligarchy, one of eight tribal groups being a strong executive (*probouloi*) and the other seven forming a Council, called the Gerousia. A papyrus fragment of the second century B.C. reads: 'Chilon the Laconian being ephor and Anaxandrides being in command put down the tyrannies among the Greeks: at Sicyon Aeschines, and Hippias...[a gap of several letters] Pisist...' The ephorate of Chilon was 556/5; Pisistratus went into exile from Athens most probably in that year; and Hippias was tyrant evidently elsewhere, probably at Megara.[47] We need not suppose that armed intervention was always necessary; the presence of a Spartan army in the vicinity or the provision of aid may have sufficed. It is significant that Pisistratus turned to Sparta's rival, Argos. Plutarch mentioned other tyrannies which were outside the Peloponnese and probably later in date.

The destruction of tyranny from without arose, according to Aristotle, *Pol.* 1312a40, when a stronger state had a constitution of the opposite kind, namely 'democracy' or 'kingship and aristocracy', this combination obtaining at Sparta which 'put down most tyrannies'. To the concept of ideology plus power Thucydides added a special reason for Sparta's success, the stability of the Spartan *politeia* (meaning way of life as well as constitution): 'it was this which gave her power and enabled her to arrange affairs in the other states' (1. 18.1). In the flux of change which was a mark of the century 650–550 Sparta stood unchanging and unshakable, and those who invoked her aid knew what

[47] *FGrH* 90 (Nic. Dam.) F 60; Arist. *Ath. Pol.* 17.4; Antonin. Liberal. 4; E 232; D. M. Leahy in *Bull. Ryl. Lib.* 38 (1956) 406ff.

they would get for the foreseeable future: support for oligarchy and troops to maintain it, if necessary. By mid-century Sparta succeeded admirably; for she exercised an indirect control over Pisatis, Elis, Sicyon, Corinth, Megara and perhaps some other states, and she kept Argos almost in isolation. The ephor Chilon, generally acclaimed as one of the Seven Wise Men of this age, may have formulated the policy. His suspicions of Argos appeared in his saying that Cythera would be better sunk beneath the waves (Hdt. VII. 235.2), and he may have initiated another system of indirect control which began in connexion with Arcadia.

A Pythian oracle explained to the Spartans their failure to win victories over the Arcadians on the ground that the Arcadians were too numerous, but went on in hexameter verse as follows:

> I shall give thee to dance in Tegea, with noisy footfall,
> and with the measuring line mete out the glorious champaign.

Sparta then attacked Tegea, bringing fetters to bind the Tegeans and rods to measure the new lands. Yet another defeat; and it was the Spartans who wore the fetters and worked the land as prisoners of war (the very fetters were later preserved in the temple of Athena Alea at Tegea). Sparta enquired again at Delphi and was told to obtain the bones of Orestes, son of Agamemnon, and become 'the protector of Tegea'. But where were the bones? The story should be read in Herodotus I. 67f. Once Sparta had the sacred relics and understood the significance of the oracle, she ceased to smite the Arcadians as all Dorians had done, and she offered herself as their protector. So Sparta and Tegea came to terms, and when the other Arcadians joined them Sparta could count on their aid against Argos, if the need should arise.

The treaty of reconciliation was inscribed by Sparta and Tegea on a stele on the bank of the Alpheus. Of its terms two were reported (not verbatim) and explained by Aristotle (fr. 592): 'to expel the Messenians from the land and not to be allowed to make ⟨men⟩ blessed' (χρηστούς, i.e. dead). The expulsion of the Messenians was the first step towards establishing a *cordon sanitaire* round Sparta's territory. As interpreted by Aristotle, who may have seen the original in full, the ban on the capital sentence was in the interest of those Tegeans who 'Laconized', i.e. who fostered the interest of Sparta; and a century later Athens was to take similar steps to protect her sympathizers in the subject states of her empire, nominally her 'allies'.[48] Sparta's offers of similar alliances to other states in the Peloponnese were widely accepted. We do not know the conditions but we can infer from later circumstances that they

[48] For the oracles see A 50, I 101f; for 'blessed' being a euphemism for 'dead' compare in modern Greek '*makarites*'; for other interpretations see E 166, 17f.

included expulsion of Messenian refugees, perhaps an undertaking to help Sparta in the event of a Helot revolt, and acceptance of Sparta's command in a joint war. This right of command (*hegemonia*) was unrestricted; thus the king or kings in command did not necessarily reveal the objective of a joint campaign. The advantages to Sparta were the indirect control of wide areas, the addition to her armed forces of a large reserve, and the buttressing of her own social system; and the advantages to an ally were peace with Sparta, defence of its territory by Sparta if it was threatened by an aggressor, and in particular defence against Argos. The cost to Sparta was negligible, because she maintained her superb army on a war footing in any case, and the cost to the ally was not definable in terms of goods or services or bases, its army being called out only against an aggressor, but consisted of the acceptance of Sparta's indirectly applied political influence in favour of a 'Laconizing' oligarchy.

After the inauguration of this policy of alliance *c.* 560 B.C., Sparta set herself up both as a liberator from tyranny and as a protector against aggression, and she brought into her fold by 550 Elis, Arcadia, Sicyon, Corinth and Megara, and perhaps Phlius and Cleonae. The resultant group of states was called literally 'The Lacedaemonians and the allies', i.e. the allies each of Sparta, not the allies of one another; and it went into action contractually in response to attack from an aggressor. 'The Spartan Alliance' is a better abbreviation for us than the current one, 'The Peloponnesian League', because it is closer to the Greek phrase and has no geographical limit. After 555 the bones of Tisamenus, son of Orestes, were brought from Helice to Sparta in an attempt to win over the Achaeans (with what result is not known), and the opprobrious names were retained at Sicyon as a continuing insult to Argos.

Sparta now felt strong enough to challenge Argos. She drove the Argives out of Cythera and the east coast of what was henceforth called Laconia (replacing Prasiae there as a member of the Calaurian League), and advanced into Thyreatis, where the Argive army stood its ground. Sparta did not call upon her allies. It was to be a battle of prestige. Three hundred champions from each side were to decide by combat who should possess Thyreatis. At nightfall, which ended the fighting, only two Argives and one Spartan were left alive; the Argives ran home and reported their victory, but the Spartan took the spoils of the Argive dead to his camp. Next day the main armies returned to see what had happened, and neither being prepared to concede defeat they set to in earnest. Both sides suffered heavy losses, but Sparta won. It was the final break through. She was now (546) acknowledged as the leading power in Greece, and the victory was celebrated in perpetuity by a special religious festival.

In the second half of the century the yardstick of Sparta's influence was the strength of the Spartan Alliance, not that of Sparta alone. Its potential on land was unrivalled. At sea Sicyon, Corinth and Megara controlled the western approaches and the Isthmus, and Sparta, having acquired Cythera and Pylus, straddled the coastal routes from the west and the south.[49] In the northern Aegean Corinth and in the Propontis Megara had naval bases in their colonies, and towards the south-east Aegina was a leading trader, with special rights at Naucratis; for Aegina seems to have transferred her friendship from Argos to Sparta sometime after 546. In view of the wide contacts of the Spartan Alliance the ancient tradition may be accepted that Sparta was responsible for the overthrow of tyrants ultimately in Phocis, Thessaly, Thasos, Naxos and Miletus, especially as the expedition which she and Corinth undertook against Polycrates of Samos *c.* 524 is well attested. Farther afield Sparta became the ally of Croesus of Lydia, the self-appointed protector of the Greeks against Cyrus of Persia and the friend of Amasis of Egypt. It was a fortunate coincidence that when Cyrus was laying the foundations of the Persian empire Sparta was creating a loosely-articulated system of power which was based on two principles, a coalition of free states and a detestation of despotism.

Within the extraordinarily mobile world of city-states any combination of political power and economic prosperity attracted talent from far afield. Thus in 650–550 Sparta became one of the leading centres of art, literature and music. The temple of Athena Poliouchus was decorated with bronze sheeting (and so known as Chalcioecus) to the design of Gitiadas, a local bronzeworker and poet; the early temple of Artemis Orthia was replaced by a temple in limestone of Doric style; the Scias, a meeting-hall for assemblies, was built by a Samian Theodorus, and the throne of Apollo at Amyclae by Bathycles and his team of craftsmen from Magnesia in Asia Minor; and a shrine in stone was erected to Helen and Menelaus at Therapne. The Laconian bronzeworkers were famous for their statuettes and vessels, which were often dedicated at Olympia or exported to distant markets, and they maintained their high standard to the end of the sixth century. Although statuettes in ivory, jewellery in gold, silver and amber, masks in clay and figurines in lead were only of moderate quality, Laconian vase-painting rivalled that of Corinth. Alcman, probably a Lydian by birth, made Sparta his home, and Stesichorus of Himera and Theognis of Megara stayed at Sparta. We see from their poems Sparta's delight in music and dancing, in the beauty of girls and boys, and in their own countryside; for example, in Alcman's *Partheneion* or these lines of Theognis (879–84):

[49] Corinth and Sparta were influential in the west (cf. Strabo 261 for Locri's appeal to Sparta), and Sparta had settlers of Laconian descent in Cyrene.

Drink the wine my vines brought me from under the peaks of Taÿgetus, vines old Theotimus, beloved of the gods, planted in the mountain glens and brought them the chill water from Platanistous. Drink thereof! You will shake off the burden of sorrows and be light of heart instead, once you put on the armour of liquor.

Alcman and Stesichorus were pioneers in choral lyric and developed the literary Doric dialect which became standard for choral performances, even in Attic tragedy later on. Choirs sang dancing or standing, as the subject demanded, and the poet composed their music and that of the accompanying instrument, using the lyre, in what was known as the Dorian mode; like the poems of Tyrtaeus, this mode was said to express courage and restraint.

At first Argos led the way in sculpture, as we see from the remarkable statues of Cleobis and Biton, and perhaps in temple architecture at the Heraeum, where a stone stylobate with widely-spaced column bases carried a wooden superstructure, and a seventh-century stoa had capitals of a very early kind; and a splendid clay mask was found at Tiryns. But as its prosperity grew Corinth overhauled Argos for intance in the development of terracotta tiles and finials, and the temple of Apollo of about 550 B.C. was a classic example of the early Doric order, built in limestone with monolithic columns (of which seven survive); it had a peristyle colonnade of 15 × 6 columns. Sanctuaries of Demeter and Kore (early seventh century) and of Aphrodite (later in the century) lay by and on the Acrocorinth, rather as meeting places for worshippers than as homes for a god or goddess. For the enlarged city the provision of water at the 'Fountain of Pirene' was achieved by a network of tunnels with manholes, nearly a mile in length. In painted pottery Corinth was pre-eminent until mid-century, after which Athens surpassed her, even in the western market. Corinth and Sicyon were foremost in the development of bronze statuettes and in the fashioning and export of bronze vessels of great beauty (fig. 53).

While Eumelus of Corinth had written processional songs (*prosodia*), Arion of Lesbos invented the dithyramb or ode in honour of Dionysus for choirs at Corinth late in the seventh century. The choral dancing and singing in the Peloponnese – at Sparta, Corinth, Sicyon, Megara and Epidaurus (Hdt. v. 83) – were part of the background from which Attic drama, both tragedy and comedy, was destined to grow. Olympia became the religious centre not just of the Peloponnese but of the whole Greek world, as we can see from the treasuries dedicated by very many states, e.g. Sicyon, Selinus, Megara and Gela. The first monumental temple on the Greek mainland was probably the temple of Hera at Olympia, completed *c.* 600. Having a peristyle colonnade of 16 × 6

53. Reconstruction of a bronze cauldron from Olympia, with nine griffin protomes, on a rod tripod decorated with lions and sphinxes, foreparts of griffins and horses. Sixth century B.C. (After E 234, 83, fig. 51.)

columns and a stylobate $50 \times 18 \cdot 76$ m, it was made of limestone, mud-brick, wood (for the original columns and superstructure) and terracotta (for roof tiles and acroteria). In this century the Dorian states of the Peloponnese and its religious centre at Olympia formed the heart of the Greek world.

CHAPTER 43

THE GROWTH OF THE ATHENIAN STATE[1]

A. ANDREWES

I. THE UNIFICATION OF ATTICA

The *Iliad* speaks of the Athenians as a single people. Homeric references to them are indeed sparse and disputable: it is anomalous that the Athenian entry in the Catalogue (II. 546–56) names only Athens itself, whereas elsewhere a king's own city is followed by a string of further place-names, the places where his warriors lived. Whatever the date when this entry was composed or the reasons for its abnormality,[2] it is further testimony to the feeling that the inhabitants of Attica were a homogeneous people with the single city of Athens as their centre. They emerged from the Dark Age with no consciousness of any internal racial difference to divide them, they spoke the same dialect, they were organized in a unitary system of tribes, and in spite of substantial local specialities they shared a common framework of rites and festivals. Of the process by which this was achieved, much necessarily remains obscure.

The Mycenaean collapse left a remnant on the Acropolis, perhaps literally beleaguered in the early stages while they still used the water supply to which access had been elaborately engineered in the thirteenth century.[3] In eastern Attica the cemetery at Perati attests a relatively prosperous twelfth-century community whose links were not with western Attica but with other Mycenaean survivors in the Aegean (*CAH* II.2[3], 666–7). This faded away, in circumstances not now discoverable,[4] and the occupation of the Acropolis also came to an end. Though the development through sub-Mycenaean to Protogeometric shows that there was no sharp cultural break but a continuous process, the Mycenaean way of life had finally ceased. We discover little of the origins or organization of those who now lived in and around the city,

---

[1] The Atthidographers are cited by their serial number in Jacoby (*FGrH*): 324 F 34 is fragment 34 of Androtion, no. 324 in the series. Such references should be taken to include reference to Jacoby's commentary. Fragments of Solon are numbered according to the edition of M. L. West, *Iambi et Elegi Graeci* II (Oxford, 1972).

[2] A 48, 145–7 with n. 72; F 9, 35; F 15, 219, esp. n. 22.

[3] F 40; H 35, 113. [4] H 35, 115–16.

but it is clear that their lives were not very secure; in the rest of Attica they avoided settlement near the sea or in isolated communities.[5]

The Ionian migration (CAH II.2^3, ch. 38) is not only important in its own right, but carries implications which may clarify our picture of Attica at the time when the movement began, in the eleventh century. The links between Attica and Ionia are such that we are bound to accept in the main the later Athenian claim to the leadership of this enterprise, though this does not exclude that participation by other Greeks which Herodotus attests (I. 146.1), whether or not they passed through Attica on their way. Evidence for an Ionian tribal system is weaker than that for the Dorian tribes, and in East Greece there may have been less uniformity, but the four old Attic tribes (below) turn up often enough to constitute a genuine link (Hdt. v. 66.2, 69.1).[6] The Apatouria, which for Herodotus (I. 147.2) was the sign of a true Ionian community, was not the only festival common to Athens and Ionia. The dialect which we call Attic–Ionic must have been effectively established before the migrants left Attica, whatever modifications it underwent subsequently in either area. If the dialect was 'due to the fusion of West Greek elements with a dialect of Mycenaean type' (CAH II.2^3, 818), possible conditions may have existed for this development in Attica by the end of the twelfth century: all we need to posit is that people whose dialects contained West Greek elements had infiltrated into a largely vacant western Attica during the troubles in which the LH IIIB period ended.[7]

The Ionian 'race', then, must have existed before about 1050 B.C., even if we have to wait till Solon (fr. 4a) for a clear expression of Athenian feeling about it. It seems now to be agreed that the settlements made by the migrants in the east Aegean were new ventures; even if they had some earlier knowledge of that region, they were not reinforcing existing settlements. These courageous ventures, and still more their general success, have rightly been claimed as a sign of Greek vitality in the eleventh century;[8] but the reverse side of this should also be noted, that they took off the most enterprising and adventurous of the eleventh-century inhabitants, a serious loss even if the numbers in each group of migrants were small.

The Athenians themselves saw these things more simply. They had always been in Attica; and if it needed change to turn them into Ionians, that was the work of Ion who came and settled among them and imposed the four tribes named after his sons. Theseus by his *synoikismos* had brought them all together and made Athens their city, and so it remained. The basic distortion is due to the fact that they were conscious of no break between the heroic period and their own times.

---

[5] H 25, 336.
[7] H 35, 252–3.

[6] A 14, I 119–20; F 9, I.
[8] H 71, 373.

They had no conception of a 'Dark Age' as we use the term; they thought at most of early disturbances and movements after the Trojan War, and even Thucydides, who makes much of these, believed that Attica had not been affected (I. 2.5–6). What he has to say of Theseus is reasonable enough, given the evidence available to him: he makes the unification the political act of a powerful king, who dissolved the separate governments of the various cities and set up a single prytaneum and council-chamber in Athens, and this is what was celebrated in the annual festival of the Synoikia (II. 15.1–2).

The festival was a reality,[9] and we cannot neglect the implications of its name and the story attached to it. The unification requires a political act at a specific time, or at least a specific conclusion to a piecemeal process. A unitary state the size of Attica is not normal in the pattern of Greek settlement, even where there was no division of race: Boeotians, Arcadians and Thessalians were conscious enough of racial unity, but did not unite in the Attic manner. The three plains of Attica are separated by barriers, easily surmounted but more marked than any in the Boeotian plain or the plain of eastern Arcadia, and they could well have supported three or more independent states, in a loose union or none at all. The king of Athens would normally have been the most influential ruler in Attica, as Thucydides presupposes, and that will have been especially true for a period when so much of the population huddled around his Acropolis. But Eleusis is eminently credible as a separate kingdom: apart from the legendary war with Erechtheus which Thucydides cites, the Homeric Hymn to Demeter tells a story with a king of Eleusis and not even an allusion to Athens. The Marathonian Tetrapolis, which in later times sent its own separate sacred embassies to Delphi and Delos,[10] is another obvious candidate; and other sites, which like these were inhabited when Protogeometric pottery was being made, might once have stood on their own.

If there was ever a unified Mycenaean kingdom of Attica (cf. *CAH* III.1², ch. 16, p. 668: the Athenian entry in the Homeric Catalogue, discussed above, cannot decide that question), it is hard to believe that this survived the collapse, and we must look to the Dark Age for the historical union of Attica. The literary evidence gives no clue to its date. It would not be safe to deduce from the Hymn to Demeter that Eleusis was still independent when it was composed, probably in the seventh century;[11] an event of this magnitude, at a date not very long before Cylon's remembered attempt to make himself tyrant, could hardly have failed to leave some trace in Athenian tradition, whereas it can easily be supposed that the traditional story of Demeter had retained its purely

---

[9] F 6, 36–8.   [10] *FGrH* 328 F 75 with commentary.
[11] F 47, 5–11.

Eleusinian colouring from an earlier age. The archaeological evidence cannot date the event either, directly, but in ch. 16 (pp. 668–9) it is argued that the prosperity apparent in Attic graves of the early ninth century resulted from the synoecism, and from the partial reclamation of Attic land for cereal culture. We cannot see the political process by which the isolated settlements in Attica were induced to join together in a unified state, only the social and economic improvement it brought, in comparison with the dark times after the Mycenaean collapse. If unification was completed around 900 the event could well have been lost to exact memory, and in consequence have been attributed to the Theseus of the heroic age, before the Trojan War.

We should think of unification in the terms of Thucydides II. 15. There was no large transfer of population, as synoecism would mean to later times, but a centralization of government. The noble families no doubt mostly found themselves a residence in or near the city, but they retained their roots elsewhere or put down such roots later. The momentum of this first advance was not maintained, either in prosperity or in reclamation of the land, and much remained to be done later.

II. THE ARISTOCRATIC STATE

The meagre stories that were told of the kings of Athens need not long detain us. Names and scenes on Attic pottery give us some idea of what was already current before the end of the sixth century, and parts of the 'history' were well enough developed before the time of Herodotus (I. 147.2, 173.3, VIII. 42, etc.). But the widespread opinion is probably right, that stemma and chronology were not systematized till Hellanicus, late in the fifth century.[12] Among his voluminous works was the first *Atthis*, a specialized history of Athens down to his own time. It was, surprisingly, some fifty years before his example was followed by a native Athenian, Cleidemus; the prominent politician Androtion wrote his more often cited *Atthis* in exile in Megara, probably in the 340s; the last, longest and greatest in this genre was the work of Philochorus, 'the first scholar among the Atthidographers', unfinished at the time of his death, probably in 263/2.[13] We know these works only from quotations, mostly by commentators on Aristophanes and the orators, and the commentators' special interests – topical allusions in their authors, or matters of Athenian cults or practices which would not be familiar to their readers – ensure that our fragments are an unrepresentative selection. Study of fragments with book-numbers shows that they devoted far more space to their own times than to early history;

---

[12] A 13, II 5–6; *FGrH* on 323a F 23.
[13] F 15; cf. *FGrH*, introductions to individual Atthidographers.

in the extreme case of Philochorus, the books dealing with his own lifetime were nearly two thirds of the whole, but they are represented by only a minute fraction of the many quotations we have. The suspicion that their contemporary political interests distorted their view of early Athens, coupled with scepticism about the possibility of their having any genuine information, has led to some excessively low estimates of their value;[14] but they knew things that we do not, and we must judge each case on its merits as best we can.

The Atthidographers faced considerable difficulties in constructing an early history for Athens. The scattered stories were not connected among themselves or with the general stock of Greek legend, and there were not names enough to furnish a king-list of adequate length. Cecrops and Erechtheus, primitive divinities not perfectly humanized, gave the list a start; but Ion, though he was the eponym of the whole race and the tribes were named after his sons, was not (or somehow could not be) brought into the royal genealogy, and came in as a military leader (so already Hdt. VIII. 44.2) for Erechtheus' war against Eleusis. Theseus' sons had somehow to be dispossessed to make room for Homer's commander of the Athenians, the shadowy Menestheus, and his father Peteos. The end-product was a dynasty of fifteen kings, from Cecrops to Thymoetes, followed by a second dynasty from Pylus headed by Melanthus and Codrus (Hdt. v. 65.3). After Codrus, reputedly father to the founders of many Ionian cities, either his son Medon or his grandson Acastus surrendered the kingship in exchange for the office of 'archon for life'; after eleven more of these, there begins a series of seven archons holding office for exactly ten years each; then the list of annual archons start with Creon, in the year 682/1.[15] The name Acastus is of interest, in that the later archons' oath referred to him (Ath. Pol. 3.3); the rest of the construction can be neglected. In effect we cannot describe or date the stages of the process by which the monarchy was dismantled.

The creation of an alternative executive officer, coexisting with the king or replacing him, seems to be a regular development in Greek constitutions; even at Sparta, where hereditary kingship survived, most of the king's functions, priestly, judicial and political, were put in commission among the aristocracy. At Athens we find a group entitled 'the nine archons'. One of them still had the official title βασιλεύς, though by now he had become an annual official; the continuity suggests that there had been no traumatic revolution. He performed many of the older rituals, and later continued to preside over the Aeropagus when it sat as a murder court. But the chief executive, by the time the historical record begins, was 'the' archon, who gave his

[14] E.g. F 9, 12–15.   [15] A 14, II 783–6.

name to the year and was in effect the head of the state. The army was commanded by a third annual official, the polemarch. The six thesmothetae, according to *Ath. Pol.* 3.4, were created much later when the other archons were already annually elected: their function, Aristotle says, was to write down and preserve 'the θέσμια (*thesmia*)' for the judgement of court cases. If so, that function should have lapsed with the publication of a written code, by Dracon or Solon, and later they appear only as presiding over lawcourts: cf. the Classical term 'Heliaea of the Thesmothetae'. But their title is hard to explain if they were never more than judges, and Aristotle may be right even if there was nothing more to go on than the etymology.[16] It is not easy to see what evidence he could have had for the date of their institution, or for his later statement (8.2) that before Solon the archons were appointed by the Areopagus.

The Council of the Areopagus was greatly venerated by later generations, who believed that it had been set up in primeval times to try legendary cases of murder; Ares' murder of Halirrhothius was reckoned as the earliest (Hellanicus, 323a F 22), and Aeschylus' version, that the court was created to deal with the case of Orestes, puts it anomalously late in the heroic age.[17] Democratic theory had it that any political powers it possessed before Ephialtes' reform of 462/1 were usurped powers, but accounts of these powers are indefinite enough: Aristotle (*Ath. Pol.* 3.6, 8.4) gives a more judicial tinge, Isocrates (VII) a moralizing one, to its supposed disciplinary role. There can hardly have been much evidence. But its title was always Council (*boulē*/βουλή), even when its role had been reduced to the trial of homicide cases, and it is inevitable that it should be seen as the descendant of the original Council of the king, whose successor presided over it when it sat as a court. Its members held office for life, an archaic feature which somehow survived into the time when it could no longer offend democratic sentiment, the Areopagus having lost its political power. We cannot be sure when the rule was established that the archons, after their year of office and passing their audit (εὔθυνα), automatically joined this Council; the 'majority' opinion reported by Plutarch (*Sol.* 19), that the Areopagus was created by Solon, is certainly a misunderstanding assisted by the Athenian tendency to ascribe all their institutions to the great lawgiver.[18] Till Solon set up the lower Council of Four Hundred, the earlier Council had no rival, and we can readily believe that its *de facto* influence was very great; its powers at this stage depended on tradition and not formal definition.

Of the administration of the early state we know hardly anything but the name of the units called *naukrariai*. There were said to be forty-eight

[16] F 22, 269–71; F 25, 174–5.   [17] *FGrH* on 323a F 1.   [18] *FGrH* on 324 F 3–4.

of them, twelve to a tribe (*Ath. Pol.* 8.3), and for their general control
of the income and expenditure of the state reference was made to laws
of Solon obsolete in the Classical period (*ibid.*, cf. Androtion, 324 F 36).
The root-word ναύκραρος probably means 'ship-captain',[19] and this may
at first have been the literal function of officers with that title. The
naucraries, which in Solon's time controlled the finances generally, may
well have begun, as ancient and modern conjectures have it,[20] as a system
for financing a fleet: Athens' early war with Aegina, and the fight for
Sigeum at the end of the seventh century (below, pp. 372, 374), show
that this would not be anachronistic for the time before Solon. The only
name we have for a naucrary, Kolias (Phot. *s.v.* Κωλιάς; Bekk. *Anecd.*
I. 175.20), suggests a local centre; if the naucraries were really
subdivisions of the kinship tribes they cannot have been simply local,
but some phratries (below) had a local base and the same could easily
be true for the tax-raising naucraries. (For Hdt. v. 71.2 see on Cylon
below; on the nature of their funds, p. 383.) Treasurers with the title
tamiai are not actually attested till Solon (*Ath. Pol.* 47.1) but were surely
earlier; officers with the odd archaic title *kolakretai* paid out money from
the naucraric funds (Androtion, 324 F 36),[21] and retained charge of
payments out of public funds till the late fifth century.

The whole population was organized in four tribes (*phylai*): Geleontes, Aigikoreis, Argades, Hopletes, supposedly named after sons of
Ion (Hdt. v. 66.2). Replaced by the ten local tribes of Cleisthenes in 507,
these older kinship tribes are shadows to us, though we may guess that,
like the three Dorian tribes of Sparta, they had formed the basis for the
regiments of the army. Each was divided into three *trittyes*, whose
purposes and function are likewise obscure: possibly it was again
military, in that a regiment embodying a quarter of the whole fighting
force of so large an area as Attica would have been unmanageably large
and have needed subdivision.[22] Four tribal kings (*phylobasileis*), chosen
from the noble Eupatridae, retained in the Classical period a vestigial
function as judges in the Prytaneum court of an inanimate object that
had caused someone's death; and a calendar of sacrifices from the end
of the fifth century includes two, described as ἐκ τῶν φυλοβασιλικῶν,
to be performed by the tribe Gleontis (*sic*), one of them jointly with
the *trittys* Leukotainiai.[23]

At a lower level the phratries survived Cleisthenes' reform and
continued as living organizations through the Classical period. Every
true-born Athenian should belong to one of these 'brotherhoods';

---

[19] A 14, I 599 n. 1, II 817–18; F 9, 67–74.   [20] Pollux VIII. 108; cf. F 9, 70–1.
[21] A 14, I 589 n. 5; II 818.
[22] Cf. F 36, II 164.
[23] J. H. Oliver, *Hesperia* 4 (1935) no. 2 (p. 21), ll. 31–50.

when citizenship was conferred on a foreigner in the fourth century it was usual to offer him membership not only in tribe and deme but also in the phratry of his choice.[24] These were certainly kinship institutions, based on the family ties that were celebrated annually at the Apatouria in the month Pyanopsion, the special feast of the phratries at which on the third day (Koureotis) sacrifices were offered for children on their introduction.[25] Though there is no direct evidence, it is likely that phratries were subdivision of the old tribes. Some certainly had a local root in a particular cult, the members still in the Classical period living mainly in this one neighbourhood,[26] and this may well be true for most of them; but it is highly unlikely that tribe, *trittys* or phratry was based on territorial division, as has been conjectured,[27] and the ancient speculation (Plut. *Sol.* 23.5) that the tribes were named for distinctive occupations is even less likely. Cleisthenes' territorial tribes were based on territorial demes, and thereafter the phratries were confined to a religious and social role; it is reasonable to suppose that before his reform, when there was no rival unit at this level, they had more extensive functions.

Quotations from the lost beginning of *Ath. Pol.* (fr. 3) ascribe to Aristotle the statement that the whole people was divided into farmers and craftsmen; and this is the preface to a strange schematic account of the four tribes and their subdivision which accords very ill with what *Ath. Pol.* has to say about *trittyes*, phratries etc. later (8.3, 21.3, 6). Plutarch (*Thes.* 25.2) ascribes to Theseus the creation of three orders, Eupatridae, farmers and craftsmen, and details some characteristically aristocratic functions of the first class but says nothing of the others. The three orders reappear briefly after Solon's reform (*Ath. Pol.* 13.2), but never thereafter. The farmers and craftsmen, and the question whether these orders ever existed, can better be left to ch. 44 (below, p. 393); nor is there space here to discuss the controversies surrounding *Ath. Pol.* fr. 3, whether Aristotle believed that the Eupatridae were created later than the other two orders, or that there had been a time when all Athenians were members of the corporations called 'clans' (genē/γένη).[28] But the Eupatridae do concern us here, an aristocracy relatively numerous for a Greek state, concentrated on Athens by the synoecism though many were associated with cults elsewhere for which they held the priesthoods. They too survived the Cleisthenic reform, and by the time for which we know any detail the clans were certainly aristocratic corporations, of which some sixty are known to us by name.[29] In the Classical period their concern was with priesthoods, ritual

[24] The earliest is M–L no. 85, l. 16, of spring 409.   [25] F 6, 232–4.

[26] A 66, 133–4; F 9, 57.   [27] A 42, II 529–30; cf. F 9, 53–5.

[28] A 66, 88–93; A 31, 105–9.   [29] F 34.

and exegesis, not a negligible basis for influence even in the developed democracy. Before Solon, it is beyond reasonable doubt that they alone were eligible for the archonship; and before Dracon the law was a matter of their expertise in traditional custom, inherited by them as a class and translated into practice in the archons' courts. Politics at this stage will have been a matter of their internal rivalries. Owing to the ambiguity of the word *genos* – 'family' in general, or one of these aristocratic corporations – it is hard to be sure whether even at the start of our record we can identify a noble clan acting as such in politics; there is certainly no sign of such action by a phratry, and it has been doubted if there was any organic connexion between clans and phratries. But there are cases in the fourth century where a particular clan appears to possess authority in the affairs of a phratry, especially over the admission of new members, and these remnants promote the suspicion that, at the time when kinship was still the basis for social and political organization, phratries were fully under the control of particular clans.[30] We shall never discover for certain the origin of the phratry, but one possibility is that it was a means of organizing the supporters of a noble clan.[31]

Besides these we hear within the phratries of groups of *orgeones*, who were mentioned in a law of Solon (Seleucus, 341 F 1) and therefore existed by his time. It has generally been held that this term covers all the non-noble members of a phratry; but the *orgeones* known to us from later inscriptions were small groups united in the worship of a hero,[32] and there is no indication that the ordinary man in the Classical period was concerned with such groups. It is perhaps more likely that these were upper-class groups of men who did not belong to the old nobility, but had achieved sufficient consequence to be accepted as privileged groups inside the phratries.[33]

III. CYLON TO SOLON

The seventh century was a period of social and political disturbance which saw the establishment of tyrannies in several states within close range of Athens (ch. 42), and it was not likely that Athens would be unaffected. We can accept from *Ath. Pol.* 2.1 that trouble between the classes, the revolutionary pressures which were manifested in Solon's time, had been building up over a long period. Nevertheless, when a young noble named Cylon attempted to make himself tyrant of Athens, popular support was given not to him but to the established authorities.

Though this may rank as the first clearly attested event in Athenian

---

[30] F 36, II 159–79; A 66, 116–34; F 39, 3–9.
[31] F 38, 137–40; F 39, 14–15; *contra* A 31, 142–4.
[32] F 43.   [33] F 39, 1–3.

history, our accounts of it diverge alarmingly. It is common ground that Cylon was an Olympic victor, and the Eusebian list dates his victory to 640. Herodotus (v. 71) very briefly says that he collected a band of his contemporaries and tried to seize the Acropolis, but he failed and sought sanctuary with the statue (of Athena); then the presidents of the *naucrari* (οἱ πρυτάνιες τῶν ναυκράρων, οἵ περ ἔνεμον τότε τὰς Ἀθήνας) persuaded them to leave on the promise that they would not be put to death, and the Alcmeonidae were charged with murdering them. This leaves much to be explained, including the reason why the Alcmeonidae were implicated. Thucydides (I. 126) is fuller. The Delphic oracle had encouraged Cylon to seize the Acropolis on the day of the greatest festival of Zeus, which he took to be the Olympic festival, not enquiring about Attic or other feasts (a parenthesis tells non-Athenian readers about the Diasia). Cylon had help from his father-in-law, Theagenes the tyrant of Megara; he succeeded in seizing the Acropolis, but a long siege followed, which the people tired of and left it to the nine archons (another parenthesis says that at that time they had control of most public affairs). Cylon and his brother escaped, but the rest, near starvation, took refuge at the altar; the archons killed them, and so the curse rested on them and their descendants. A third version in Plutarch (*Sol.* 12) appears to coincide with that of *Ath. Pol.*, of which we have only the very end, forming the first chapter of *Ath. Pol.*: here the Alcmeonid archon Megacles is named; Solon, after a considerable interval, persuaded the guilty to stand trial, and they were exiled; and the Cretan seer Epimenides purified the city.

The Eusebian date may stand; 636 or some immediately succeeding Olympiad fits well enough with the little we know of Theagenes. The contradictions of the narrative are not to be resolved; it has further been noted that Thucydides' wording suggests polemic against a version in which the attempt took place at the time of the Diasia, not the Olympia, and Herodotus' informants may perhaps have believed this.[34] Thucydides' note on the archons is no doubt in part intended to explain that they then had powers which they had not in his own time, but it is also deliberate contradiction of Herodotus, and that conflict is also beyond resolution, in spite of brave attempts, ancient (Harp. *s.v.* ναυκραρικά) and modern,[35] to show that Herodotus really meant the archons. The *naucrari* existed, but their presidents (if they existed) can hardly have competed in authority with the archons.[36]

Our difficulties arise from the sequel to this story. The Alcmeonidae were banished, perhaps after a formal trial, whether or not Solon's intervention is historical; and they returned, probably not as a result

[34] F 45, 167–72.　　　　　[35] F 50, 176–8.
[36] For attempts to find them a function, see A 44, 324–5; F 36, I 93–7.

of Solon's amnesty[37] but earlier, to play an important role in Athens' sixth-century history. The curse was invoked by Cleomenes in 508, and they were banished again and swiftly returned (Hdt. v. 70–3; Thuc. I. 126.12); and in 432 the Spartans tried to mobilize it again to discredit Pericles, whose mother was an Alcmeonid (Thuc. I. 127). On each occasion the facts must have been disputed, and not all variants have reached us: for instance, the scholiast to Aristophanes, *Eq.* 445, speaks of Cylon's sacrilege in plundering the temple of Athena, which looks like a remnant of a version which exculpated Megacles. The account being thus irremediably muddied, there is no profit in upholding Herodotus as the oldest of our authorities or invoking Thucydides' superior knowledge of Athenian tradition. An irreducible minimum remains, the attempt on the tyranny, its defeat, and the curse that weighed on the family of Megacles; the detail, already controversial before Herodotus' birth, is by now irrecoverable. The historical significance is not in doubt, that the attempt was not supported within Athens, perhaps because Megarian intervention was resented, certainly because the Athenian people was not so incensed against the aristocrats as to welcome any and every means to overthrow them.

The next certain event is the promulgation of Dracon's law-code; recent work has strengthened the case for taking 621/20 as the ancient date for this.[38] The seventh century was an age of lawgivers, whether we look to the literary tradition about Zaleucus[39] of Locri or to the earliest surviving enactment on stone, a specific constitutional provision from Drerus in Crete of the second half of the century.[40] The Drerus law does not presuppose a general codification, but it does show the city conscious of the need to have its decision on a particular point on record in a way that precluded further argument, and the more general need for certainty in the law was natural in an increasingly sophisticated community. Publication of the law was a curtailment of aristocratic privilege, in that it deprived the magistrates of their discretion to declare what the law was. Popular discontent may have played a part in promoting the change. But strife within the governing class had shown itself as a danger in the recent affair of the Cylonians, and that may well have weighed more. We have no detail about the circumstances of Dracon's appointment. He was not eponymous archon like Solon, for *Ath. Pol.* 4.1 dates his legislation to the year of Aristaechmus, and a specific personal appointment as lawgiver seems the most likely.

We know most about the law on murder, the only part of the code which Solon did not repeal. A decree of 409/8 ordered the inscription

[37] F 36, I 17 n. 24; F 15, 39–41, esp. n. 225.
[38] F 2, 92; F 15, 308 n. 58; F 48, 66–70.
[39] C 65, 68–72.   [40] M–L no. 2.

on stone of 'Dracon's law about murder',[41] and the tantalizingly incomplete text of the section on involuntary homicide, the first dozen lines, can be restored with the help of the law cited in our text of Demosthenes, XLIII. 57. The distinction between premeditated and involuntary killing was a large advance; it may sometimes have been taken into account by customary law, but that would be merely precarious, whereas here formal provision is made for establishing whether the deed was involuntary, and formal procedure is laid down for reconciling the killer and the dead man's family, if they are willing. (The decision that the act was involuntary is to be taken by 'the fifty-one, the *ephetai*'. These *ephetai* survived into the Classical period, but the origin and composition of this body is an unsolved problem, in spite of many guesses.)[42] In the rest of the text only an occasional phrase can be restored, but we may assume that the law on wilful murder likewise made the procedure more certain and defined the issues that were to come before the various courts. The republication of 409/8 and references in fourth-century orators make it clear that Dracon's law was still in force at those times, and we have no ground for thinking that it had been substantially amended.

The rest of the code, in contrast to the humanity of the law on involuntary homicide, was reputedly very harsh, as was also that of Zaleucus, but later references to it are scrappy and uncertain, so that it has been doubted if in fact Dracon legislated about anything else but murder. But the tradition of a more comprehensive code is firm enough, and the rarity of later references is accounted for by the fact that the rest of the code had been repealed; it is not easy to see where any detail about its provisions could have come from if not from a surviving text.[43] Athens and Dracon may have the credit of having reduced at least a large part of the law to writing at a relatively early date. But the code evidently did nothing to reduce the tension between rich and poor which erupted in Solon's time; and that this was due to defects in the law is implied both by the fact that Solon found it necessary to replace so much of the code, and by the wording of some of his poems (fr. 4.30–9; 36.18–20).

The constitution ascribed to Dracon in *Ath. Pol.* 4 is certainly spurious. Apart from other suspect details, the financial qualifications for eligibility to office are by themselves decisive; not only are they expressed in monetary terms, whereas Solon's classes are defined by income in kind, but the qualification for the generalship (*strategia*/ στρατηγία) is ten times that for the archonship, a relationship which fits the late fifth or the fourth century, but not the seventh when it is

[41] F 48. [42] F 9, 305–11; F 46, 48–57.
[43] F 48, 74–82.

not even certain that there was an office with the title *strategos*. This is one of those theoretical constructions by which writers hostile to the developed democracy projected into a remote past their ideas of the way in which the state ought to be run; it has been ascribed to revolutionaries of the time of the Four Hundred or the Thirty, but more probably belongs to a somewhat later period.[44] The text of the *Ath. Pol.* has been altered in places to accommodate what is evidently an intrusion into the original text, but opinion is divided on the question whether such alterations were due to the author or to later interpolation.[45]

The absence of detailed record from the seventh century, aggravated by the Athenians' tendency to introduce the figure of Solon wherever they could and to embroider stories about him, obscures much of the external history of this early period. Ships are depicted with surprising frequency on Attic Geometric vases of the mid-eighth century (*CAH* III.1², ch. 16, pp. 674–5). Most of them are warships and, whether or not the painters aimed to illustrate a story from the epic, the detail is often enough clearly contemporary; it is hard to resist the inference that Athens had a navy at this time, and for all we know the naucraries may go back to the eighth century. Its main business may have been with pirates, but we know of one war which may perhaps be dated to the early seventh century. This is Herodotus' story (v. 82–8) of the ancient quarrel between Athens and Aegina, an odd story whose purpose is in part to explain the kneeling posture of the Aeginetan statues of Damia and Auxesia, as a miraculous response to an Athenian attempt to haul them away with ropes. It seems likely that it covers up the defeat of an Athenian attack on Aegina. The details given by Herodotus do not lead us to a date, except that if he is right to place the incident soon after Aegina's liberation from primeval dependence on Epidaurus it can hardly be later than the early seventh century:[46] it has been invoked to explain a decline in Athens' overseas activities in the second half of the eighth century,[47] but it has also been seen as an incident from the wars of the early fifth century, retrojected into the remote past.[48]

Some phases of Athens' war with Megara for the possession of Salamis certainly belong to the seventh century. The position of the island, covering the bay of Eleusis and stretching out towards both Megara and the Piraeus, made it inevitable that each city would want to hold it. There was, as is usual in such matters, much argument from the heroic age, sometimes evidently spurious, as the notoriously interpolated line (*Il.* II. 558) which made the Salaminian Ajax place his ships alongside the Athenian contingent. There are few certain historical

[44] F 44, 84–101.

[45] F 49.

[46] F 41.

[47] H 25, 361.

[48] F 36, II 280–8.

facts. Theagenes' support of Cylon is clearly one, a move in a quarrel which may already have been old, but we do not know how Cylon's failure affected the position. In a famous poem, which ancient and modern critics have regarded as youthful work,[49] Solon (frs. 1–3) rebuked his countrymen as Σαλαμιναφέται (they had held and then lost Salamis? or given up the attempt to gain it?) and urged them to go against Salamis and wipe out their disgrace. Herodotus was told (1. 59.4) that Pisistratus before his tyranny had commanded the forces of Athens against Megara and had gained great glory by the capture of Nisaea and by other exploits; nothing is said here of Salamis, and *Ath. Pol.* 17.2 firmly separates Pisistratus' war (cf. 14.1) from Solon's war over Salamis. Later generations naturally assumed that Solon's crusade had been crowned with success, but the details of his capture of the island, mostly from Plutarch (*Sol.* 8–10), are unusable; and doubt is cast on the completeness of Solon's achievement by the further account in *Sol.* 10, that the war continued fiercely till it was ended by the arbitration of five named Spartans, who decided in Athens' favour.

The evidence of Plutarch and *Ath. Pol.* shows that the Atthidographers dated the Athenian capture of Salamis before Solon's archonship, but we are not sure what their grounds were, and it has been held that the capture really belongs to Pisistratus' war, and that Solon's poem (we have only eight lines to judge it by) is a work of his old age.[50] Against this is the fact that Herodotus specifically ascribes to Pisistratus the capture of Nisaea but not Salamis, and we have no positive reason to reject *Ath. Pol.* 17.2. We should then accept an early capture, but regard it as insecure in the face of continuing war until the capture of Nisaea gave Athens something to bargain with. The Spartan arbitration then closed the matter,[51] and Sparta's intervention, which might seem inappropriate at an earlier date, is less unlikely in the 560s; to relegate it to the end of the sixth century, identifying the arbitrator Cleomenes with the king of that name,[52] is extravagant. Salamis was never integrated into the territory of Athens, and the late sixth-century decree we have is generally held to refer to a cleruchy founded at that time,[53] but some arrangements must have been made earlier to safeguard it. It is to be wished that we knew more of the Athenian clan named Salaminioi, who had care of the shrine of Athena Sciras at Phalerum;[54] the cult is certainly an importation from Salamis and the clan itself probably immigrant, but the time and occasion of its arrival in Attica elude us.

It is more of a question how we should fit together the vicissitudes

---

[49] Plut. *Sol.* 8.1–2, cf. 11.1; A 13, II 217 n. 2.

[50] F 36, I 268; F 9, 113.

[51] F 51, 61.

[52] A 5, I 2.312–13.

[53] M–L no. 14 with comment.

[54] F 42.

of this local war with the activities of Megara and Athens further afield. It may be an anachronism to suppose that an offshore island in enemy hands would severely inhibit the other maritime activity of an Archaic state, but Solon's poem suggests a mood of discouragement at Athens not easily reconciled with military enterprise at Sigeum in the Troad. Yet it appears that Athens was fighting Mytilene there shortly before 600. Herodotus (v. 95), in an account of Athens' dealings with Sigeum which cannot entirely be acquitted of confusion,[55] refers to fighting in which the poet Alcaeus lost his shield, and to arbitration by Periander of Corinth which awarded Sigeum to Athens; Strabo (599–600) and Diogenes (I. 74) add the story of a famous duel in which Pittacus of Mytilene killed the Athenian Phrynon, an Olympic victor whose victory is dated to 636, while Eusebius dates the duel itself to 607/6. It was always likely that Alcaeus himself was a main source for this, and the name Phrynon has now been found in a fragmentary text (H 28.17), and a possible reference to Periander's arbitration in a fragment of commentary (x (7).15–20).[56] No ancient author gives a hint of Athens' purpose, at most a protest (Hdt. v. 94.2) that the Aeolians had no right to monopolize the Troad. 'Control' of the Hellespont could not be exercised from Sigeum,[57] if the Athenians of that time conceived of such a thing, nor could the Megarian colonies on the Bosporus be harmed or prevented from harassing Athenian shipping in the Narrows. There is more merit in a recent suggestion[58] that, in view of the difficulty at many times of year in sailing up the Hellespont at all, it was an advantage to own a port of call near the entrance and not to depend on the Mytileneans for shelter. The colonists may of course have had their own reasons for wanting to emigrate, with the concurrence of the dominant group in Athens.

The answer to the chronological problem is not to transfer the Sigeum war to a later date,[59] thereby dislocating a much wider stretch of sixth-century dates, but to admit our inability to gauge accurately the state of Athenian morale from year to year in the late seventh century: from our distance the events look very close together, but for contemporaries a short span of years could show wider changes than are required here. Solon's poem, relevant if we place it early in his career, shows how confidence could be revived, and the whole complex of events here studied shows that Athens' strength and her readiness to intervene were growing. The war should be left roughly where Greek chronological systems place it, at the end of the seventh century.

Another sign of Athenian initiative is her involvement in the Sacred

---

[55] In spite of D 75, 154–7.
[56] D 75, 159–61.
[57] A 5, I 2. 315.
[58] A 37, 89.
[59] A 5, I 2. 314–18.

War (see above, pp. 305, 313) over Delphi at the beginning of the sixth century, and here too Athenian tradition magnified the part played by Solon. The lead was taken not by him but by the Thessalians and by Cleisthenes tyrant of Sicyon, but Athens certainly took part and there is no reason to distrust the entry in the Delphian archives which according to Plutarch (*Sol.* 11.2) named as leader of the Athenian contingent not Solon but Alcmaeon. The war may well have begun just before Solon's archonship, *c.* 595, and later tradition saw it as a crusade to liberate Delphi from the oppression of Cirrha, the Phocian town in the plain below; but some lines in the Homeric Hymn to Apollo (III. 540–5), coupled with study of Delphi's alignment before and after the war, suggest that 'liberation' included a substantial change in the management of the oracle.[60] Athens' reward was one of the two Ionian seats on the Amphictiony, both of which originally belonged to the Euboeans. A generation earlier, the former Delphic regime had encouraged Cylon, and the discrediting of that regime bolstered the credit of the Alcmeonidae and damaged that of their opponents. The chronology is not certain enough to determine whether the Alcmeonidae returned to Athens before the start of the war, but however we date Alcmeon's part in the enterprise this is the beginning of the family's important sixth-century connexion with Delphi.[61] With this intervention Athens returns to the mainstream of Greek history.

IV. SOLON

With Solon we enter a different atmosphere. Enough fragments of his verse survive to show what manner of man he was, what ideals he thought it important to project, so that we know him personally as we can never, for instance, know Cleisthenes. In spite of the increase in evidence the problems remain formidable, due mainly to our ignorance of the background to his reforms, but the poems at least tell us what kinds of solution we should look for or avoid.

There can hardly have been much material for ancient writers except what Solon himself provided. Athenian tradition knew him as lawgiver and sage, the latter the more interesting topic; that is reflected in Herodotus' proportions (I. 29–33), half a sentence on the laws to four chapters of conversation with Croesus. His enrolment among the Seven Sages gave rise to much low-grade invention (Plut. *Sol.* 4–7; Diog. Laert. I. 45–67). Some detail about his life could be extracted from his verse: fr. 19 is a clear case (below, p. 389), but no other surviving fragment provides such unequivocal evidence. The political poems evidently yielded much, but not the detail of his programme or his

[60] E 99.   [61] F 5, 369–71.

achievement; the situation was familiar to those he addressed and they did not need to have the facts recited. Accordingly Aristotle and Plutarch cite them to illustrate Solon's attitude, not as evidence for what he did. A case in point is the word ἐκτήμορος (hektemoros): ancient scholars were curious about its meaning, but though it would fit easily into the metres Solon used no poem is quoted for it. Detail of that kind was to be found in his laws. Sceptical opinion has long held that the wooden *axones* on which they were inscribed must have been destroyed in the Persian sack of Athens in 480, and that the original code was so overlaid with later amendment that Solon's share in it could no longer be distinguished.[62] The case rests heavily on the usage of Attic orators in the fourth century, irresponsibly attaching the name of Solon to laws manifestly later, and brushes aside the clear evidence (Cratinus fr. 274 K, from Plut. *Sol.* 25.1; Polemon's tract against Eratosthenes, Harp. *s.v.* ἄξονι and *FGrH* 241 F 37b) that wooden *axones*, believed to contain Solon's laws, survived through the fifth century and into the third. Total certainly is impossible, but it is a reasonable working hypothesis that Solon's text was available for study by later scholars,[63] and it is not easy to see where else some of the detail can have come from, though of course some citations will be fraudulent or mistaken. The material may not always have been easy to use, not only because of the archaic wording but because a reforming law need not give a clear picture of the situation which it is intended to remedy.

At this stage the continuous text of the *Athenaion Politeia* begins, and is our most important single literary source. As one of the 158 *Constitutions* said to have been collected by Aristotle, it was composed not simply for general publication but also to serve the purposes of his school (cf. *Eth. Nic.* 1181b17), and that partly accounts for its curious proportions. In places shockingly hasty and sometimes over-compressed, it nevertheless draws on a wide range of sources, not only on the Atthidographers: of these, Androtion was the most recent and authoritative when the treatise was written, and the text has some certain points of contact with his fragments.[64] Happily the author of *Ath. Pol.* (whether Aristotle himself or one of his school) was more interested in Solon than, for example, in Pericles, and he made full use of the poems, and surely of the laws also though there is only one explicit reference (8.3). In these chapters hostile criticism of the work has been very much based on the assumption that when the author mentions a σημεῖον (8.1) or the like, that is the only ground he has for the statement for which the σημεῖον is adduced.[65] But we must not demand that in this short treatise he should validate every point with

---

[62] F 63, 278–80; F 68; F 9, 17–27, 303–5.
[64] *FGrH*, Introduction to Androtion n. 127.

[63] F 66, 1–14; A 36, 51–5; F 52.
[65] E.g. F 9, 323–4.

a full indication of his sources: though for us this is the sole survivor of fourth-century scholarship in this area, in its own time it was one book among many and by no means the fullest.[66] It was not constructed to withstand the sort of criticism it often now receives.

Solon was the son of Execestides. Aristotle (*Ath. Pol.* 5.3) and Plutarch (*Sol.* 1.2) assert that he was of high birth, but of middling wealth and station. The former is illustrated by his connexion with the family of Critias (Plato, *Tim.* 20d–e); for the latter Aristotle less convincingly cites one of the poems in which Solon sides with the poor against the rich.[67] There may have been other evidence in the poems, even evidence for the widespread view that Solon made trading voyages in the days before his archonship (Plut. *Sol.* 2.1–2), but this is an area where tradition slides easily into romance.[68] If his call for action over Salamis belongs to his earlier years, this will have forwarded his career, but otherwise we have no idea how he reached the position where both sides were prepared to trust him as mediator and lawgiver, or who his political allies were. The poems, especially the long fr. 4 but also 4a–c and 15, show him campaigning very effectively on behalf of the oppressed poor, and 36.1–2 speaks of his calling the people together and making a series of promises to them about the reforms he intended. The situation was clearly revolutionary, and the upshot was that he was appointed 'archon and mediator' for the year 594/3,[69] apparently with full powers to reform the state and its laws.

1. *Economic measures*

From the rhetoric of 36.3–17 it is clear that the most important of his promises was to remedy agrarian distress. His first witness was the land itself, which he had freed from servitude by plucking up the ὅροι (*horoi*) fixed in it in many places; then he speaks of rescuing Athenians who had been sold or had fled abroad, and of others rescued at home. His hearers knew in detail what he meant, but we have to guess, and the word *horoi* does not by itself settle the issue. Most commonly a *horos* marks a boundary, but Solon cannot be saying simply that he abolished many boundaries. From the fourth century and later we have stone *horoi* placed on land or a house that had been pledged for a stated purpose.[70] A *horos*, then, could mark an encumbrance on land, though the encumbrances of Solon's time would be very different from those familiar in the fourth century. In Solon's view these were severe enough for him to speak of the land itself as enslaved.

---

[66] F 36, I 310. [67] F 5, 322–3, 334–5. [68] F 63, 297–302.
[69] F 2, 93–9; for alternatives see A 31, 145–69; F 9, 316–21; F 5, 323–4.
[70] F 56; F 57.

Prose descriptions give us another term to explain, *hektemoros*, which was wholly obsolete in the Classical period. Aristotle (*Ath. Pol.* 2) says that there was a long struggle between the upper class and the people, that the regime was totally oligarchic, and in particular the poor were in servitude to the rich (ἐδούλευον, which in the context cannot mean literal slavery), with their children and their wives. He then gives two names for them, πελάται (*pelatai*) καὶ ἑκτήμοροι (*hektemoroi*), without making it clear whether these are two names for the same class or two separate classes. It is only the latter that he explains:

for at this rent [*sc.* the sixth part implicit in *hektemoros*] they worked the fields of the rich. The whole land was in the hands of a few (δι' ὀλίγων); and if they did not pay their rents they could be sold into slavery, themselves and their children. And all borrowing was on the security of personal liberty till Solon's time; he was the first champion of the people. The heaviest and most bitter element for the many was their servitude.

The clause on borrowing is ambiguous, in that it is not made clear whether the borrowers are a class separate from the *hektemoroi*, but Aristotle has called the obligation of the latter 'rent' as if they were tenants not borrowers, and the corresponding passage in Plutarch (*Sol.* 13.4) distinguishes between *hektemoroi* who farmed for the rich, paying them a sixth of the produce, and debtors who had borrowed on the security of their liberty. This shows how Plutarch understood Aristotle, or Aristotle's sources.

The term *hektemoros* and some clue to its meaning were almost certainly to be found in the text of Solon's law. Pollux (VII. 151) cites from Solon the word ἐπίμορτος (*epimortos*) for land worked on a share-cropping basis, and μόρτη (*mortē*) for the share paid by the cultivator. Share-cropping had given way to money rents in Classical Athens, but that change could not take place till there was more money in circulation than there was at any time in the sixth century; it is a reasonable guess that Solon found it advisable to regulate the system, and that his regulation made it clear what the system was. It is presumably from the same ultimate source that Hesychius (*s.v.* ἐπίμορτος) got the information that the word could be used not only for the land but for the man who cultivated it on a share basis; and his final note, καὶ ἑκτήμοροι οἱ τὸ ἕκτον τελοῦντες, appears to mean that *hektemoroi* were a special case of the class share-croppers, though of course a very common case since it had generated a specific name.

Hektemoroi and slavery are at the centre of Aristotle's description of the crisis, *horoi* and slavery at the centre of Solon's solution. There must be a close connexion, and the simplest answer is likely to be correct, that the *horoi* marked the fact that the cultivator was bound to pay over

a sixth of the produce to another. But the rate of payment is an obstacle
to regarding the system as oppressive, for one sixth is an improbably
low rate for share-cropping, though parallels of a kind have been found,
and though no doubt this like any system could be made oppressive
by powerful and unscrupulous men. Theories of the origin of the system
must take account of this abnormality.

The trouble has usually been understood to arise from borrowing.
With variations, the pattern that is imagined has smallholders borrowing
on the security of their land after a bad year, and then a second bad
year brought default and slavery. Solon's *horoi* can then be treated as
records of something like mortgage. This is a long way from the prose
descriptions we have, but Solon's Athens was remote from Aristotle's
and it might have been misunderstood; and Aristotle describes Solon's
remedy as cancellation, χρεῶν ἀποκοπή, which to the fourth century
would certainly mean remission of debts incurred by borrowing. That
is not decisive either: Aristotle and Plutarch make it clear that, quite
apart from the *hektemoroi*, there were debts to remit, and in any case
χρέος is a term which could cover not only debts due to borrowing but
also the payments due from the *hektemoroi*, however they arose. The low
rate of a sixth tells against borrowing, and so does the uniform rate;
it is hard enough to see why any rich man should lend to the poor for
so slight a return, and still harder to see why so many should have
adopted an identical rate that their debtors acquired this specific
designation.

These earlier theories assumed debt in coined money, and the impact
of the recent invention of coinage has been made responsible for the
whole crisis.[71] It is now agreed, with a few dissentients, that Athenian
coinage did not begin till some 50 years after Solon's archonship,[72] and
it is most unlikely that Aeginetan coinage was available in any quantity
in Solon's Athens; in any case, it was only in the fifth century that small
change was produced in enough volume to serve the transactions of
the poor. These considerations also rule out the divergent version of
Androtion (324 F 34, from Plut. *Sol.* 15.3–5), that the Seisachtheia was
not a remission of debt but a lightening of the coinage which reduced
the amount the debtor had to pay – never a plausible theory, but the
statement is useful in elucidating Solon's reform of the weight system
(below). Some other issues that were once controversial might now be
left out of account. The payment of the *hektemoroi* was one sixth, not
five sixths:[73] Aristotle and Plutarch leave no doubt on that, and the

[71] A 44, 593–4, cf. 505–12; F 51, 32–6.
[72] H 48, 58; cf. D 52, D 80; *contra* A 30, 661; H. A. Cahn, *Kleine Schriften zur Munzkunde und Archäologie* (Basel, 1975), 81–97.
[73] A 13, II 109 n. 2; F 72, 44–50.

support for five sixths that has been claimed from etymology and the lexicographers is insubstantial.[74] The view that land was then the inalienable property of the family, so that it could not be pledged by an individual, still has its supporters,[75] but much of the evidence cited tells against absolute and continuing inalienability; especially, early laws forbidding alienation imply that land was already being alienated.[76]

It seems that we have to look elsewhere for a situation that might encourage the rich to do something for the poor cultivator for which one sixth of the produce would be a reasonable return. It has been suggested that the sixths were originally dues paid by the weak to the powerful for protection in unsettled times, and resented when protection was no longer so urgently needed;[77] and this is not altogether implausible. But a less remote origin is suggested by what we now learn about the condition of Attic agriculture in the Dark Age. Settlement had been spread fairly evenly over the arable area in the Mycenaean period, but much of it was abandoned thereafter:[78] reclamation had made a significant start by the first half of the ninth century, but the process was not evenly continued or rapidly completed, if half of the rural cemeteries known from the eighth century contained no burial earlier than that time (CAH III.1², ch. 16, p. 687). The pattern of village settlement characteristic of Classical Attica was then in large measure the creation of the eighth century. We may assume that the aristocracy took the lead in this movement, as they did in the colonial ventures which in other parts of Greece took some of the surplus population overseas in this same century. The growing population could provide the needed labour. There is no knowing what kind of rights anyone may have had over the still unreclaimed land, but it is not hard to imagine that powerful and enterprising families found it possible to assign plots of land hitherto untilled to pioneers on the basis that, once established, they should pay a proportion of the crop to the noble who had assigned the plot. One sixth, implausible as interest on a loan, makes more sense if the land had previously produced no return at all.

It is likely also that the noble family would keep some of the land under its direct control. In Classical times the labour would have been provided by slaves, but before the full development of chattel slavery we should expect rather some form of dependent free labour. That might be the *pelatai* of *Ath. Pol.* 2.2 (above), if they are distinct from the *hektemoroi*. The various senses of this word found in tragedy do not fit here, but in the only other instance from Classical prose, Plato, *Euthyphro* 4c, the *pelates* is a free man in contrast with the οἰκέτης (*oiketes*) whom he was accused of murdering, and he worked as a labourer

[74] F 59.

[75] F 72, 74–87; F 56; A 31, 153–60.

[76] F 58, 153–60.

[77] F 60, 97–105.

[78] H 25, 336.

(ἐθήτευεν) with Euthyphron's family when they were farming in Naxos. Ancient commentators took *pelates* to mean one who worked for his keep, or for pay, and Plato's usage allows us to reject those lexicographers who simply equate *pelatai* with *hektemoroi*. Plato like Aristotle expected that the word would be understood, and it had vitality enough to survive as the standard translation of the Latin *cliens*. It does not look as if there were many *pelatai* in Classical Attica, but the concept was firmly rooted, suggesting that at one time, before the growth of slavery, there had been many more of them.

Like all explanations of the agrarian situation at the end of the seventh century, this is highly speculative, but it can account for the low rate of payment, and for most elements in Aristotle's description. Necessarily ignorant of the evidence modern archaeology has unearthed, Aristotle would naturally take the *morte* as a kind of rent paid to an owner, and it is then a short step to assuming that the whole land was in the hands of the few. This cannot be quite right: in his concentration on the plight of the *hektemoroi*, Aristotle has pushed out of sight Solon's class of *zeugitai* (below), whose land produced 200 measures. More important, ownership may not have been as clear-cut as it was to the fourth century. The noble had his right to the sixths, and it is likely that the *hektemoros* was bound to remain on the land and pay the sixth, but in such a system it is also probable that he could not be removed so long as he paid. Both parties thus had rights over the land, but not of ownership as Aristotle understood it.

This then was a system rather favourable than not to the cultivator, and the question is what went wrong. Solon blamed the rapacity of the rich, and after some generations they might indeed feel that they were not getting enough from land in which they had a family interest. Rapacity would do more for a man at the end of the seventh century than at its beginning. Increasing foreign trade brought increased awareness of what could be bought for silver; we cannot date precisely the stages by which Greece took to using silver as a medium of exchange, but the change certainly began well before the first introduction of coinage. Consequently there was more motive for exploiting the possibilities of oppression, which in this context means enslaving the *hektemoros*, either with a view to keeping him on the land on much harsher terms, or in order to sell him for what he would fetch. We need not assume that enslavement for default was an original feature of the scheme, but when Solon says (fr. 36.9–10) that some had been enslaved ἐκδίκως, others δικαίως, that should mean that there was some positive law on the point, and that might be one of the harsh features of Dracon's code. In any case we cannot easily set limits to what a powerful man might do at this stage of the development of the law.

Solon's remedy was cancellation, χρεῶν ἀποκοπή. As regards simple debt, that means that the creditor was merely deprived and had to be content with the fact that a threatened revolution had been averted. For the *hektemoroi*, cancellation can only mean that the payment of sixths was abolished, and Solon's boast about the *horoi* points in the same direction. That would leave the *hektemoros* on the land he cultivated, with no remaining limitation on his rights over it, rights that would easily develop into ownership in the Classical sense. It might be held that this is excluded by fr. 34, quoted by *Ath. Pol.* 12.3 to show Solon's resistance to proposals to redivide the land: οὐδὲ πιείρης χθονὸς πατρίδος κακοῖσιν ἐσθλοὺς ἰσομοιρίην ἔχειν. But there is a very great difference of tone between this and earlier poems which expressed his sympathy for the oppressed poor. The men addressed in fr. 34 did not want just release from 'slavery'; they were after plunder, ἁρπαγή, the same word that was used earlier (fr. 4.13) for the crimes of the rich, and their hope was that Solon, in spite of his mild professions, would make himself tyrant and them wealthy, as in the violent confiscation of Bacchiad property at Corinth a generation earlier (Hdt. v. 92.ε2). Solon rejected that, but there is no inconsistency in supposing that he freed the land tilled by the *hektemoroi* from the dues owed to the rich: that was not to put the base on a level with the noble.

One may wonder how Solon was able to rescue Athenians sold abroad, especially those so long away that they had lost their native dialect (fr. 36.10–12). But we may accept that he abolished slavery for debt (*Ath. Pol.* 6.1, where in contrast to 2.2 only debt is mentioned, not the fate of the *hektemoroi*), since there is no sign of it later in Athens.

It was later believed that Solon had reformed measures, weights and coinage, but *Ath. Pol.* 10, where Aristotle speaks of an 'increase' in all three, is unhappily one of his most opaque chapters;[79] and if the view taken on p. 379 is correct, Solon could not have reformed coinage, though he might have altered the units in which uncoined silver was weighed. The statement that Solon made new measures larger than the Pheidonian is relatively transparent; at least, the latter were still in use in some areas in Aristotle's lifetime, and they seem in fact to have been smaller than the Attic. The arrangement of the chapter suggests that the next clause refers to weights: 'and the mina, which previously had a weight of 70 drachmae, was filled up (ἀνεπληρώθη) with the hundred', an odd expression whatever was meant. Next, the old coin unit was the didrachm, which is true, but if 'increase' implies that Solon instituted the tetradrachm later familiar, that is false. A last sentence adds obscurely that he established weights πρὸς τὸ νόμισμα, 63 minae (instead of 60) to the talent, and the three (extra) minae were distributed over the stater and the other weights. It would be charitable to suppose that this passage was over-compressed from a fuller and clearer account.

[79] F 20; F 55; F 65.

That Athens had used Pheidonian measures before Solon is beyond
our verification, but there might have been a Solonian law abolishing
them. The next clause is more disputable. Mina and drachma belong
primarily to the system of coin weights; and the corresponding passage
in Plutarch (*Sol.* 15.3–4) is all about coinage, citing Androtion (324 F 34)
for the view that Solon reduced the weight of the drachma so that there
were 100 to the mina instead of 70. The original relation of mina and
drachma to the rest of the Athenian weight system is problematic. The
Classical stater (literally 'weigher')[80] was of 900–920 g, and there were
30 to the talent. The mina was by that time reckoned as a half-stater,
and increasingly used for material other than precious metal, but since
smaller weights were designated as fractions of the stater, not of the
mina, the latter was clearly not original to the system. The drachma,
$\frac{1}{100}$ of the mina, was used only for the weighing of precious metal, coins
or temple dedications. The term originally designated a 'handful' of
iron spits in some area where these were used for currency, as they do
not seem to have been in Attica. When silver began to be used as a
medium of currency, some state (possibly Argos)[81] took the crucial step
of fixing an official weight of silver to be taken as the equivalent of an
iron drachma. The term drachma spread widely in mainland Greece,
with surprisingly different values: in Classical times 70 to the mina in
Aegina, 150 in Corinth and Euboea, 100 at Athens.

We do not know when Athens began to use silver, but it cannot have
been as late as Solon's time, and mention of ναυκραρικὸν ἀργύριον in
his laws shows that by then the state already dealt in silver. If we could
suppose that down to 594 Athens had followed the Aeginetan system,
70 drachmae to the mina, and that Solon then decreed that in future
at Athens the mina was to be divided into 100, that would account for
what Androtion and Aristotle say. The purpose of such a change is
obscure, nor can we see why three cities so near to one another should
have adopted three different values for the drachma, but it appears not
to have been a matter of advantage in trade.[82]

The best sense that has been made of the last sentence of *Ath. Pol.*
10 (above) is that coins were issued at slightly below their nominal
weight, 63 minae of coins weighing the same as 60 minae in the regular
weight system; the state thereby gained a small mint charge.[83] This
appears to fit the facts for the Classical period, but for Solon's time the
difficulty arises that the three earliest weights we have,[84] discarded while
in good condition late in the sixth century, are some 15 per cent lighter
than their Classical counterparts. All three were official weights, so

[80] Confusingly, the word stater was also used elsewhere for coins, in Aegina for a didrachm,
in Corinth for a three-drachma coin; in Athens it was not used for any coin-weight.
[81] H 48, 314; see *CAH* IV², ch. 8*d*.   [82] G 22; *CAH* IV², ch. 8*d*.
[83] F 20.   [84] F 21.

inscribed: a stater of 795 g, and a quarter-stater and a sixth on the same standard. They were not thrown out because they had become worn, so we might deduce a change of standard at this time. Coin-weights however remained stable from the inception of Attic coinage, so the anomaly emerges that in the sixth century a mina of coins weighed more, not less, than a half-stater.[85] But we must remember that mina (an eastern term) and drachma were imports into the Athenian system. A possible solution is that in 594 they were not yet integrated into this system, but that late in the sixth century a change of standard made Attic weights heavier, producing the Classical equivalence between mina and half-stater.

It thus looks as if the Athenians were wrong to ascribe their Classical weight standard to Solon, but may have been right to suppose that he introduced a new and specifically Attic weight for the drachma. About measures there can be no certainty.

For other matters we depend on scraps from Plutarch's *Life*. Solon (24.4) restricted grants of citizenship to perpetual exiles and to those migrating to Athens with their whole families to practise a trade; Plutarch says that this was meant not so much to exclude other immigrants (though he believed these were numerous enough to be a danger, 22.1) as to encourage more solid settlers. He does not here speak of encouragement of crafts (as at 22.1 in another context), but the measure has been taken that way, and some potters from Corinthian workshops seem to have migrated to Athens. 24.1 quotes from 'the first *axon*' a law forbidding the export of any agricultural product but oil, and large but uncertain deductions have been made from this. Minor regulations, e.g. against planting olives or figs too close to a neighbour's land, show in what detail Solon was concerned with agriculture. Aristotle (*Pol.* 1266b13) adds a law laying down the maximum amount of land that one man might own, but this has left no other trace and is generally disbelieved.

2. *The constitution and the law*

Solon's main constitutional reform was as radical as his solution for the agrarian crisis: essentially, the substitution of wealth for birth as the qualification for office. There can hardly have been much evidence about the situation before Solon, but we may accept the general presumption that office was then confined to the nobility; and (in spite of *Ath. Pol.* 4.3) it is certain that Solon instituted four classes defined by income in kind, and determined which classes should be eligible for the various offices.

[85] F 54.

The first class, *pentakosiomedimnoi*, contained those with an income from their own land of 500 measures or more; *hippeis* had 300–500, *zeugitai* 200–300, those with less were *thetes*. The first name, perhaps in informal use earlier, relates directly to the classification and indicates that the base was the dry measure, *medimnos*. Wheat and barley however differed in value, and *Ath. Pol.* 7.4 says that dry and wet measures (here μέτρα) were to be taken together, a more serious disparity in that the standard wet measure (*metretes*) of oil was worth a good deal more than a *medimnos* of any produce, and a measure of wine had yet another value. A tariff of equivalents for the *medimnos* of wheat[86] is not in principle impossible, but there is no trace of any such arrangement, and Solon may have let the discrepancy stand. *Hippeis* and *zeugitai* were probably military terms in origin, cavalry and hoplites:[87] the alternative is agricultural, those who could keep a horse or a yoke of oxen, but ζευγίτης should be a passive formation and the word is used of hoplites in line (Plut. *Pelop.* 23.4). *Thetes* indeed means labourers, but we cannot press that, for in this system they need not be landless, though poorer than *zeugitai*. Probably Solon took up existing names and gave them a precise meaning defined by law. (It has been argued from *Ath. Pol.* 7.3 that no such law was extant and that Aristotle was arguing from probability,[88] but the word he uses, εὐλογώτερον, does not mean 'more probable'.) Classification by income is an Archaic feature, unparalleled in later Athens which took only capital into account. It has generally been assumed that money equivalents for the measures were instituted at some time after Solon,[89] but the evidence for this is indirect and thin, and the persistence of the classes through periods when the value of money had changed substantially (e.g. Thuc. III. 16.1; Is. VII. 39) tells against it. Land was still of basic importance in Classical Athens.

It is known that only *pentakosiomedimnoi* could be treasurers (*Ath. Pol.* 47.1), and disputed[90] whether the archonship was confined to the top class or the top two (there is no record of any change between Solon's time and 457, when *zeugitai* were admitted, *Ath. Pol.* 26.2). We do not know how the minor offices were distributed or what was open to the *zeugitai*. *Thetes* had access only to the assembly and the lawcourt (*Ath. Pol.* 7.3, cf. *Pol.* 1274a15–21).

The opening of public office to men qualified by wealth and not by birth represents a major change of principle, milder than the violent overthrow of aristocracies elsewhere but a move in the same direction. It implies that Solon was under substantial pressure from a class of men

[86] G. Thomson, *Studies...D. M. Robinson* (St Louis, 1953), 848; A 37, 93.
[87] A 44, 604–6; the name would then be later than the institution of hoplites.
[88] A 14, II 821 n. 3; F 9, 100.   [89] A 14, II 837–8 with 838 n. 1; *contra* F 62, 255–60.
[90] F 9, 101–2; A 66, 101.

who felt themselves entitled to take a hand in public affairs but had hitherto been excluded by the criterion of birth. This has left no trace in his surviving poems, except perhaps in those (frs. 32–4) which show that some people urged him to make himself tyrant. When he speaks of the troubles of Athens he inveighs against the rich and powerful, not the nobly-born, but the institution of the classes shows that the privilege of birth was a serious issue; this was perhaps a case where Solon's solution did not call for vociferous propaganda in the style of fr. 4.

Aristotle in *Pol.* 1273b40–1274a2 states firmly that the archons were appointed by direct election both before and after Solon. The contrary statement of *Ath. Pol.* 8.1, that he instituted sortition between a number of elected candidates (κλήρωσις ἐκ προκρίτων), has been widely rejected,[91] because of the superior authority accorded to the *Politics*, because sortition was later regarded as a characteristically democratic device, and because *Ath. Pol.* cites no authority. None of these is decisive. It is not only possible but likely that Aristotle had looked at the text of the relevant law since the time when the passage in the *Politics* was composed. The lot is much older than democracy, and could be seen both as leaving decision to the gods and as a means of avoiding conflict: both elements are visible in *Il.* VII. 161ff, where it is used to decide between touchy heroes who would find it easier to accept the judgement of Zeus than that of Agamemnon.[92] The opening of the archonship to non-Eupatrids was likely to cause conflict, as it did in the years following 594 (see below, pp. 392–3), and Solon may have hoped that use of the lot would make it easier to accept his new dispensation, though in fact it did not; the initial *prokrisis* of forty candidates by the tribes would exclude the really incompetent, and in the simpler world of the 590s it could be assumed that most members of the upper classes were capable of carrying out the duties of the senior magistrates. (*Ath. Pol.* 8.1 adds that Solon's system was the origin of the double sortition of his own day, when the *prokritoi* too were selected by lot. The thesis that this was Aristotle's only ground for the main statement of this section breaks down on the difficulty of providing any plausible reason[93] why he should then have attributed κλήρωσις ἐκ προκρίτων to Solon, rather than to the reform of 487, which according to *Ath. Pol.* 22.5 established this procedure for the first time since the tyranny.)

There are further controversies about council and assembly. Aristotle's account of the distribution of offices among the classes (*Ath. Pol.* 7.3) ends by saying that 'to the members of the thetic class he gave a

---

[91] F 9, 321–6.   [92] A 66, 110–15.

[93] F 9, 324 suggests the influence of Isocrates.

share (μετέδωκε) only in the assembly and the lawcourts': that is a thin
basis for concluding even that Aristotle or his source thought that Solon
gave the lower classes a vote for the first time,[94] and Plutarch (*Sol.* 18.2)
gives still less support for this view. Nor is there good ground for
thinking that a vote in the assembly was ever tied to the possession of
land, a view more often expressed than argued.[95] The real question is
when and how the 'people' showed any sign of wanting some say in
the running of affairs. Thucydides gives a hint in his version of the
Cylonian affair, when he says (1. 126.7–8, in anachronistically formal
terms) that 'the Athenians' entrusted the remainder of the siege of the
Acropolis to the archons. More important is Solon's own statement (fr.
36.1–2) that he gathered the people together and made certain promises
to them, no doubt an informal and tumultuary meeting, a stage in the
campaign which brought him to the archonship. The people had arrived
in Athenian politics, and Solon's own utterances show that he would
have seen this as a potential danger (fr. 6.37). His solution was to
formalize the procedure: whether or not he made any change in respect
of the assembly, for instance a provision for regular meetings, the
significant innovation was his new probouleutic Council of Four
Hundred, which *Ath. Pol.* 8.4 reports as a bare fact in very few words,
while Plutarch (*Sol.* 19.1) briefly gives its function, to see that nothing
came before the assembly without previous discussion. In Greek
thought a probouleutic council is always a restraint on the sovereign
assembly; Plutarch reports (19.2) that Solon thought of the two
Councils, the old Areopagus and his new Four Hundred, as two anchors
that would keep the city steady, and the passage reads as if he had found
the metaphor in Solon's verse.[96]

Solon's problem was one familiar to radical reformers. He owed his
appointment to popular discontent, which he himself had done much
to foment, and the fear was natural that some less temperate reformer
might achieve a similar position by the same means. The probouleutic
procedure could act as a check, but to use the Areopagus for this
purpose would deliver the people back into the hands of their former
oppressors, so a differently composed Council was needed. Much would
turn on its actual composition, for instance whether the *zeugitai* were
eligible, and on the mode of selection: it has been guessed from
Plutarch's wording (*Sol.* 19.1) that he picked the first Councillors
himself,[97] but ἐπιλεξάμενος could as easily mean that he caused a choice
to be made, by whatever means. It has also been guessed that these
Councillors, like the Areopagites, held office for life and that elections
were only for replacements.[98] We hear nothing of any activities of this

[94] A 14, II 847; F 9, 98.   [95] F 62, 59.   [96] A 66, 146.
[97] F 9, 92; F 51, 53.   [98] F 51, 53.

Council in the years after 594, and it did not in fact impede the rise of Pisistratus to the tyranny. Partly for this reason, and more generally because it is thought that Solon cannot have intended any large role for the popular assembly, the creation of a lower Council has been altogether denied,[99] with more heat than the issue seems to warrant; it is clear from the poems that the *demos* had become a factor to be reckoned with, so that Solon had not a free hand to determine an ideal role for the assembly.

According to *Ath. Pol.* 8.4 the Areopagus under Solon retained its existing role as the 'guardian of the laws', which is described in terms very close to those used in 3.6 for the earliest constitution, a vague and grandiose reference to its wide powers, still with the main stress on the punishment of offenders. The law cited at the end of this passage, establishing a procedure of *eisangelia* before the Areopagus to deal with conspirators against the constitution, though Aristotle has formulated it in anachronistically Classical terms, may be genuine and may form an important element in the powers that were taken from the Areopagus by Ephialtes in 462.[100]

Picking out in *Ath. Pol.* 9.1 the three reforms which most favoured the people (τὰ δημοτικώτατα), Aristotle begins with the abolition of slavery for debt, then gives two judicial measures not mentioned before and not here fully described. The right of a third party (τῷ βουλομένῳ) to take action on behalf of one who had been wronged, to which Plutarch (*Sol.* 18.6–7) gives a large significance, is seen from close examination of the classes of action to which it could apply to be confined to cases where the victim of a personal injury was for one reason or another unable to act himself;[101] even so it is a large advance, and the concept of ὁ βουλόμενος was to be developed further later. The third measure, in Aristotle's view the most portentous for the future democracy (cf. *Pol.* 1274a2ff), was the right of appeal, ἡ εἰς τὸ δικαστήριον ἔφεσις. Previously the decision of an archon had been absolute (*Ath. Pol.* 3.5);[102] ἔφεσις (*ephesis*), in other contexts a controversial term,[103] can only mean 'appeal' here; the 'court' is the ἡλιαία which we meet in Archaic laws cited by Lysias (x. 16) and Demosthenes (xxiv. 105), from which descend Heliaea as the name of the principal lawcourt of Athens[104] and the word ἡλιαστής to mean a juror. The word is cognate with ἁλία and the like, used in some other dialects to mean an assembly, and the general opinion is certainly right, that the court instituted by Solon was the whole assembly sitting in a judicial capacity.

---

[99] F 64, 60; F 9, 92–6; *contra*, e.g., F 30, 208–9.
[100] F 30, 162, 199–207.   [101] F 61, 369–82; F 67, 47–53.
[102] On these decisions, see F 71, 67–82; F 8, II 69–72.
[103] A 66, 192–5; F 8, II 72–4.   [104] A 14, II 1151 n. 3; F 33, 62–5.

The Archaic laws mentioned above give to the Heliaea more positive and independent action than the simple confirmation or reversal of an archon's verdict, and it has therefore been argued that in some way or in some circumstances it acted as a court of first instance;[105] but it is probably enough to suppose that for Solon *ephesis* included a fairly wide power of the Heliaea to vary the verdict originally given.[106] This was a very substantial reduction of the powers of the archon as against the ordinary citizen; and it is historically true that the great power exercised by the Athenian courts, as they later developed, derived originally from this institution of appeal.

It is not possible to review here Solon's much admired code of laws, which covered a wide range of human activity, often in considerable detail, but is known to us only in fragments.[107] One provision may serve as an example, that which for the first time allowed a man to dispose of his property by will. Plutarch (*Sol.* 21.3–4) gave this a wide significance, as a basic liberation for the property-owner; in fact, a man who had legitimate sons still could not leave his property away from them, and in default of sons his new liberty regularly took the form of adopting someone, usually a relative, as his son and heir. But it seems that Solon in his law used what became the standard terminology for testamentary disposition, διατίθεσθαι and διαθήκη: the provision might cover more than simple adoption.[108] This was a breach in the traditional social framework, even if a limited breach, and if we had the code complete we should be better able to estimate how revolutionary it was as a whole. We may note further that the detail of the testamentary law engaged the reforming attention of the Thirty in 404 (*Ath. Pol.* 35.2); its actual wording still mattered, an indication of the extent to which the code was still the basis of Athenian law in the late fifth century.

3. *Conclusion*

Herodotus (I. 29) and Aristotle (*Ath. Pol.* 11.1) are agreed that after his legislation Solon travelled abroad to escape those who clamoured for amendments; the wording of *Ath. Pol.* may suggest that he declared (in a poem) his intention to stay away for ten years,[109] whether or not he fulfilled this. A visit to Egypt (*Ath. Pol. loc. cit.*; Plut. *Sol.* 26.1, citing fr. 28 of Solon) is possible, though not the borrowing of a law from King Amasis (Hdt. II. 177.2) or the famous encounter with Croesus of Lydia; fr. 19 certifies his visit to King Philocyprus of Soli (Plut. *Sol.* 26.2–4) and his intention of returning from there to Athens, and the

---

[105] F 36, I 60, but see F 71, 79 n. 215; F 51, 56; F 9, 97–8; F 67, 78–82.
[106] F 53, 179.   [107] Collected by F 66.
[108] F 8, I 82–4, 149–50.   [109] F 36, I 15–16; F 63, 297–8.

visit must not be dated too early since Philocyprus' son Aristocyprus died in battle in 497 (Hdt. v. 113.2). Aristotle believed that he knew the year of Solon's death (*Ath. Pol.* 17.2), and the year is probably that given by his pupil Phanias, 560/59 (Plut. *Sol.* 32.2);[110] conceivably a genuine tradition remembered that Solon had survived the first accession of Pisistratus to the tyranny (561/60) by that much. The theme of his resistance to the rise of Pisistratus was easily embroidered: the stories (*Ath. Pol.* 14.2; Plut. *Sol.* 29–31; Diod. IX. fr. 4.20, XIX. 1.4; Diog. Laert. I. 49–54) command no confidence, and the fragments of Solon (9–11) cited by these authors as warning the Athenians against tyranny need not refer specifically to Pisistratus.[111]

There remain the poems of controversy and self-justification written after his archonship, primarily frs. 5–6, 34, 36–7 (*Ath. Pol.* 12). In contrast to the censure of the rich reported at *Ath. Pol.* 5, these mainly rebuke the *demos*, and may have been selected by Aristotle to refute the fourth-century view (cf. *Pol.* 1274a3–21) that Solon was responsible for the form contemporary democracy had taken. But the first fragment cited (5) does, as Aristotle claims, assert his impartiality. 'To the people I gave as much privilege (γέρας) as was enough for them' is regularly taken to show that Solon did not propose to give them too much, and this (like fr. 6) it does; but we must not lose sight of the fact that the *demos* had been given a great deal, according to fr. 37.1–3 things they had never even dreamt of, and the contrast with what he claims to have done for the rich and powerful is instructive. Fr. 5.3–4 ways that he took care that they suffered nothing shameful, fr. 37.4–5 that they should praise him and regard him as their friend; the best interpretation of fr. 37.7–10[112] is that he there boasts of having prevented a total disruption of the established order, and this is certainly the burden of other fragments (33a, 36.20–5). We are told that he was chosen jointly by the two sides as mediator (*Ath. Pol.* 5.2; Plut. *Sol.* 14.1–3): what did his upper-class supporters expect of him, especially in the light of his earlier poems?

A similar question arises over the proposition that he might, by attaching himself to either side, have made himself tyrant (*Ath. Pol.* 6.3, 11.2). The possibility of tyranny was real (frs. 32–3), and fr. 34 shows how tyranny could have been based on the violent dispossession of the nobles. Tyranny with upper-class support is less easy to envisage, and in the passage which comes nearest to raising such a prospect (fr. 36.22–5) Solon's claim is rather that he avoided much bloodshed: evidently there were some who wanted violent repression, but Solon's appointment shows, to the credit of the Athenian nobility, that there were enough

[110] F 5, 323–4.   [111] F 36, II 311–12; F 63, 303–7.
[112] F 69.

who preferred conciliation. Some of Solon's modern critics have regretted that he refused the tyranny,[113] on the ground that nothing else could have repressed the aristocratic feuding which troubled Athens for the next thirty years. Repression, in itself damaging, would not have prevented the faction breaking out again as soon as the restraint was removed, as it did after the Pisistratid tyranny. Solon did better: he remedied the worst grievances, and he created fresh political and judicial machinery, which did not indeed avert breakdown but did greatly affect the character of the tyranny when it came. If Pisistratus can be praised for not disturbing existing laws and institutions (Hdt. I. 59.6; Thuc. VI. 54.6), this was possible only because the laws and institutions were those of a humane sixth-century reformer and not those of the old aristocratic state.

Solon rejected tyranny on moral as well as humanitarian grounds: he would not stain his good name, but knew a better way to surpass all men. That was the painstaking and less spectacular way of comprehensive and detailed reform, inspired throughout by an undaunted sense of justice. That was Solon's essential virtue: his justice was under the protection of Zeus (fr. 13.7–32), but it was natural justice, a concern in public affairs with 'the observable consequences of human action within the social order', and with the damage that a personal injury may do to the social fabric of the city as a whole.[114] Where that called for drastic action, his reputed moderation did not hold him back from such action, but he contrived to take it without the shedding of blood. That, in the early sixth century, was a large achievement.

---

[113] F 60, 171–2; with reservations, F 51, 57–8.
[114] F 60.

CHAPTER 44

THE TYRANNY OF PISISTRATUS

A. ANDREWES

I. SOLON TO PISISTRATUS[1]

Solon's reform broke the monopoly of office enjoyed till his time by the Attic nobility. This was bound to be resented, and the following years were punctured by strife over the appointment of the archon. The bleak record in *Ath. Pol.* 13.1–2 tells of two occasions when faction prevented an appointment, and then of Damasias who, though legitimately archon, held on to office for two years and two months till he was driven out by force. The first regular celebration of the Pythian games, in 582, is dated to the year of Damasias (*Marm. Par.* ep. 38; hyp. Pind. *Pyth.*): this must be his first and legal year, which is therefore 582/1, and this enables us to sort out Aristotle's indications of interval and so to date the two earlier years of anarchy to 590/89 and 586/5.[2] We may doubt if anything certain was known beyond the fact that these two years were labelled *anarchia* in the official list, as for 404/3 when the succeeding democracy refused to recognize Pythodorus the archon of the Thirty. The case could have been similar here, not that Athens was literally without a chief magistrate in these years but that their successors did not recognize these elections as valid.[3]

Damasias' usurpation was followed, acording to *Ath. Pol.* 13.2, by a decision, 'because of the faction, to appoint ten archons, five from the Eupatridae, three from the ἄγροικοι (*agroikoi*), two from the δημιουργοί (*demiourgoi*), and these held office for the year after Damasias', that is presumably for the remaining ten months of 580/79. This unusual device does not look like mere fiction, and if there was any real evidence the most likely source is a note in the official archon-list;[4] but such a note may not have made the mechanism wholly clear. Ten archons in place of the regular nine would not make much sense, and Aristotle's emphasis here is on the importance of the chief archonship, so the compromise concerns that office:[5] either each of the ten ruled for one

---

[1] References to the Atthidographers as for ch. 43 (p. 360, n. 1).
[2] F 14, 167–72; F 2, 93–5, 102–3.
[3] F 9, 319.
[4] F 15, 174–5.
[5] A 42, II 537–41.

of the ten months remaining[6] or, less improbably, power was shared for these ten months among a commission of ten.[7] The latter is still hard to envisage in Athenian conditions, and the attractive suggestion has been made[8] that the ten were the ten candidates (πρόκριτοι) chosen by each tribe to make up the forty from whom the nine archons were then selected by lot. Such an arrangement could be prolonged beyond the single year 580/79, and that would account for the fact that after this date we hear no more about strife over the archonship; but it is a long way from what Aristotle says, and if his source was a note in the archon-list the note must have been laconic and incomplete. The mechanism of the compromise must remain questionable.

Farmers and craftsmen (the conventional translation for the latter is hard to avoid, but 'craft' must be extended to include much that we should call 'profession') figured as a primitive division of the Athenian people in *Ath. Pol.* fr. 3, and Plutarch (*Thes.* 25.2) says that Theseus separated out the three classes here named (ch. 43 above, p. 367). They have been seen as a theoretical construction retrojected into the remote past,[9] which is plausible enough for fr. 3 but does not account for their appearance in 13.2. The term *agroikos*, used here and in Dion. Hal. *Ant. Rom.* II. 8 (cf. Hesych. *s.v.* ἀγροιῶται), has elsewhere a pejorative note, 'boorish', not present in γεωργοί and γεωμόροι, the terms used by the souces of fr. 3 and others; *agroikos* is not the word a late theorist would be tempted to select, and may be a genuine survival from a time when the word was a neutral technical term. If so, the classes represent an older organization, obsolescent by the sixth century and made more so by Solon's institution of census classes; Eupatridae had a continuing function, but the other two do not reappear after 580. Eupatridae were such by inheritance, so membership of the other two classes was hereditary: that is, a non-noble made eligible for office by Solon's reform must be either *agroikos* or *demiourgos*, however far he was from being literally a small farmer or a craftsman. This then is a half-and-half compromise, five nobles to five non-nobles. An earlier Damasias had been archon in 629/8, which would make him Eupatrid, so the Damasias of 582 may have been trying to reassert Eupatrid privilege; and if we think that the majority of those eligible for the archonship under Solon's scheme were Eupatrid, the compromise is a defeat for the nobility.[10]

Thereafter silence descends on the internal politics of Athens for nearly twenty years, when it lifts on the situation in which Pisistratus made himself tyrant. Herodotus (I. 59.3) tells us briefly that the 'men

---

[6] F 73, 60.
[7] A 42, II 539–41; F 2, 103.
[8] F 4, 145–6; A 66, 103.
[9] F 81, 216–27.
[10] A 66, 102–3.

from the plain' led by Lycurgus son of Aristolaides were in conflict with
the 'coast-men' led by Megacles son of Alcmeon; then Pisistratus son
of Hippocrates, aiming at tyranny, created a third party by collecting
partisans and putting himself nominally at the head of the 'hill-men'.
There is no suggestion of any issue of principle between plain and coast,
and Herodotus no doubt saw it as a simple struggle 'about power', as
later between Isagoras and Cleisthenes (v. 66.2); nor is there any hint
what it meant to pretend to the leadership of the hill-men. *Ath. Pol.*
13.3–5 begins from political differences arising out of Solon's reforms:
some had been impoverished by the Seisachtheia, some disliked the
great changes that had been made, some were merely factious. Then
come the three parties, the coast for a 'middle' constitution, the plain
for oligarchy, while the hill-men were led by Pisistratus who seemed
most the people's champion (δημοτικώτατος). Two further components
of his party are mentioned (below), and a final note says that the parties
had their names from the districts where they farmed. A simplified
version in *Pol.* 1305a23–4 ignores the coast and assimilates Pisistratus
to the tyrants who championed the poor against the rich. Plutarch (*Sol.*
13.1–2, 29.1) follows much the same line as *Ath. Pol.*, and also assigns
the θητικὸς ὄχλος to Pisistratus.

The plain has been found the least problematic. If a single plain is
in question, that can only be the central plain round Athens, and there
are passages where τὸ πεδίον approximates to a proper name,[11] as
perhaps in Herodotus' οἱ ἐκ τοῦ πεδίου; and if Lycurgus belonged to
the clan Eteoboutadae, like his namesakes in the late fifth century and
the fourth, his land may have lain in the (later) deme Boutadae, close
to the city on the north-west. It is easy to imagine the landowners of
this plain as conservative men, even reactionaries who hoped that the
reforms of Solon could still be reversed.

For the coast, πάραλοι (*paraloi*) (Hdt. and others) and παράλιοι
(*paralioi*) (*Ath. Pol.* and others) are general terms which do not define
a specific area, any more than the Paralia of Cleisthenes' system (*CAH*
IV², ch. 6), the whole coast except that assigned to his 'City'. But
Thucydides (II. 55.1) gives us a proper name, ἡ Πάραλος γῆ καλουμένη
(the territory called Paralos) which the Peloponnesians in 430 ravaged
as far as Laurium, both the part that faced the Peloponnese and that
which was turned towards Euboea and Andros: that is, the south-eastern
promontory of Attica, the Paralia given to Pallas in the division of Attica
between the sons of King Pandion (*FGrH* 328 F 107). The case for
supposing that the main estates of the Alcmeonidae were in this area,[12]
at Anaphlystus, receives equivocal but possibly strong support from
a single ostrakon inscribed 'Megakles Anaphlystios' (*Arch. Delt.* 23

[11] F 82, 190 n. 2.   [12] F 80; cf. F 16, 143–6.

(1968) *Chr.* 29). Large numbers of ostraka survive naming Megacles son of Hippocrates from Alopece, ostracized in 486, two name Megacles son of Callisthenes, three Megacles of Acharnae:[13] it is likely that at least two men named Megacles were considered for ostracism,[14] but the suggestion is attractive that one voter was merely mistaken and thought that the son of Hippocrates was registered not in Alopece but where his land lay, in Anaphlystus.[15]

It is less easy to see the Parali as a party held together by a common economic interest, though attempts have been made[16] to take them as traders and fishermen. If the Parali took their name from Thucydides' Paralus land, we should do better to consider what kind of lead they would get from the principal landowners of the district. Solon has often been associated with the Parali and with the Alcmeonidae,[17] and when *Ath. Pol.* says that this party favoured a 'middle' constitution in opposition to the oligarchic Plain this can be understood in the sense that they wanted to maintain Solon's achievement. But if we knew more detail we should doubtless find that the Athenians of the 560s, like the contemporaries of Aristophanes, were more often concerned with current and particular problems than with the form of the constitution.

The Hill gives more trouble. Herodotus' ὑπεράκριοι (*hyperakrioi*) have been understood as 'the men from beyond the hills',[18] and the notion that Pisistratus led the disgruntled men of the periphery against two parties centred on the city has its attractions. But though most *hyper-* compounds carry the sense 'beyond', there are enough instances of 'above' or 'on top of'; and in the other occurrence of the word in Herodotus (VI. 20) τὰ ὑπεράκρια (*ta hyperakria*) must mean the hill-country behind Miletus, not the country beyond the hills.[19] The same is true for the echo in Dionysius (*Ant. Rom.* I. 13.3), and no other instance survives. While ὑπεράκριος (*hyperakrios*) is a descriptive adjective, the alternative Διάκριοι (*Diakrioi*) appears as a proper name (*Ath. Pol.*; Plut. *Sol.* 13.2, 29.1; the variant Ἐπάκριοι (*Epakrioi*) in *Mor.* 763D can be disregarded). In the division between the sons of Pandion this was the share of Lycus, described by Sophocles (fr. 24 Pearson = 872 N²) as τὸν ἀντίπλευρον κῆπον Εὐβοίας; lexicographers probably define Diacria as extending from Parnes to Brauron;[20] Pisistratus himself came from Brauron (Plato, *Hipparch.* 228b; Plut. *Sol.* 10.3). Parnes and Brauron would delimit an area of north-east Attica much of which could be called 'hill country', but this apparently coherent picture is disrupted

---

[13] R. Thomsen, *The Origin of Ostracism* (Gyldendal, 1972) 94, 104.
[14] F 5, 599.   [15] F 1, 66 n. 25, 74.
[16] A 44, 614–15; F 73, 60–1.   [17] F 36, I 17, II 65; A 44, 615; A 37, 95.
[18] J. A. R. Munro ap. F 9, 110 with n. 9; A 66, 167 n. 2.
[19] J. M. Cook, *BSA* 56 (1961) 90–2.
[20] Hesych. *s.v.* Διακρεῖς; Bekker, *Anecd.* 1.242; for the texts see F 78, 20; F 85, 24 n. 20.

by the discovery that Διακρίς was the name of the inland *trittys* of the tribe Leontis in Cleisthenes' system,[21] which according to likely but not quite certain identifications consisted of a half-circle of small demes behind Acharnae towards Parnes, plus Hecale, detached and at some distance to the east.[22] This takes us into an area which can no longer be described as 'opposite Euboea'. Perhaps the Diacria of Lycus had an unexpected extension to the west, still among the foothills of Parnes; or more than one area of Attica had a name of this derivation, as Diacrii and Diacres in Euboea appear to be distinct though not far apart.[23] Either way, this reinforces the natural impression that Diacrii etc., though we meet them only as proper names, are strongly descriptive. There does not seem to be much difference in basic meaning between *hyperakrioi* and Diacrii.

It is not easy to see any interest peculiar to the Diacrii which could have provided a basis for Pisistratus' rise to power. They were no doubt poorer than the farmers of the plain, but hardly more numerous or significantly tougher; and Diacria is inconveniently far from the city where the decisions were made. *Ath. Pol.* 13.5 adds two further groups to the party. Poverty brought in those who had been 'deprived of their debts', which would appear to mean men impoverished by the Seisachtheia (cf. 13.3): some modern critics, unable to believe in such a group, have taken them as men who had been liberated from their debts by Solon but not rescued from their poverty,[24] but ἀφῃρημένοι means 'deprived' not 'relieved' and 13.3 points the other way. Conceivably some nobles, more dependent than others on dues paid by *hektemoroi* (above, p. 382), had suffered by the Seisachtheia enough to form a distinguishable group of malcontents, but it cannot have been numerous. Secondly, those not of pure descent joined because of their fear. *Ath. Pol.* throws in the evidence of the purge of the citizen body conducted after the fall of the tyranny, when many were found to be exercising citizen rights to which they were not entitled, but as has often been pointed out[25] the tyranny itself provided a more likely opportunity for spurious citizens to creep in; it has also been surmised[26] that the nucleus of this group was formed by foreigners admitted under Solon's citizenship law (Plut. *Sol.* 24.4), but it has not been explained why these men, whose original admission was legal, should have been in special danger in the 560s. In any case these are additional groups (προσεκεκόσμηντο) which can offer no clue to the nature of the main body of Pisistratus' supporters. Lastly there is Plutarch's assertion that the party included the θητικὸς ὄχλος, the class most hostile to the rich. This has

21 F 89, esp. 94–6.
22 J. S. Traill, *Hesp.* suppl. 14 (1975) 45–7.
23 F 23, 480–1.
24 F 36, I 31; A 13, II 309; F 82, 195 with n. 73.
25 E.g. A 13, II 310 n. 2.
26 E.g. E. M. Walker in *CAH* IV[1] 145.

served as basis for a theory[27] that Pisistratus' main support came from the poor within the city, but it is unlikely that Plutarch had specific evidence unknown to other writers; rather, he reflects the general theory of tyranny based on the hostility of the poor against the rich (Arist. *Pol.* 1305a21ff, 1310b13ff, cf. *Ath. Pol.* 13.4, 14.1 δημοτικώτατος). Pisistratus, after two failures, attained the tyranny with mercenaries and foreign help, and this discourages any theory that he was swept to power by a major social upheaval.

Our sources agree that his rise to power was helped by the glory he had won in the war against Megara, and his popularity will have been all the more if his capture of Nisaea was followed by the Spartan arbitration which finally assigned Salamis to Athens (above, p. 373). This border war was presumably fought by the regular militia, and so its commander should be polemarch, as is generally supposed, but there is no evidence that Pisistratus was later supported by this militia or by a 'hoplite class'. The hoplite army of Athens had existed, and had fought together against Megara, for long enough to have acquired some sense of cohesion,[28] but if the hoplites as such ever had a grievance against aristocrats as such, for which there is no Athenian evidence, that would be in the seventh century, and so far as we can see this class was content with what Solon had done for the *zeugitai*. Further, farmers substantial enough to afford hoplite armour must have been more numerous in the plain than among the hills.

There remains the view that the parties took their names from the districts in which the leaders had their estates, which is close to what *Ath. Pol.* 13.5 says though not quite the same. The local following is then the nucleus of the party,[29] round which were gathered supporters from the city and elsewhere: Herodotus speaks explicitly (1. 62.1) of Pisistratus' supporters from the city. If we cannot discover a special interest to unite a massive party of Diacrii, we must fall back on Herodotus' statement (1. 59.3) that Pisistratus created a third party deliberately in order to make himself tyrant; the suggestion that the new party was at the start a splinter from the Coast[30] is given some colour by Isocrates' statement (XVI. 25) that the Alcmeonidae were kin to Pisistratus and on close terms with him before his usurpation, and it may be significant that the name Hippocrates is common to Pisistratus' father and to several members of the Alcmeonid family. The tyrannical ambition is credible enough in a man of his time and his standing. When Herodotus and others praise the quality of his rule, we may if we wish

---

[27] F 78, 16–17, 22–3.   [28] Cf. H 40, 151 and see further 153–4.

[29] F 85, 23.

[30] F 9, 110, but as he candidly admits (112 n. 7) the programme he attributes to the party is 'a reconstruction'.

suppose that he was conscious of his capacity to govern and had beneficent policies already thought out, more particularly that he aimed to suppress the ruinous competition for power among the aristocratic factions; but at this stage he can only be seen as one of the competitors.

II. VICISSITUDES OF PISISTRATUS

His first overt step was to drive into the agora, claiming that he had been wounded by his rivals. Herodotus and *Ath. Pol.* both say the wounds were self-inflicted, which we cannot verify, and imply that his military popularity predisposed the people to grant him a bodyguard; *Ath. Pol.* (14.1) purports to know the name of Aristion who proposed the decree. The guard was of club-bearers, which sounds more like protection against street rioting than an instrument of civil war, but with their help he seized the Acropolis. Herodotus says that he did not disturb τιμὰς τὰς ἐούσας (the existing offices) but governed well, and *Ath. Pol.* more briefly echoes this, but before his rule was well rooted the other two parties combined to drive him out. Megacles however found that he was losing the subsequent struggle with Lycurgus, so he made a pact with Pisistratus, to be sealed by the latter's marriage with Megacles' daughter. The charade by which a tall girl was dressed up as Athena, and called on the Athenians to receive Pisistratus back, is described by Herodotus though he found it hard to swallow that the clever Athenians could have been so simple-minded: modern scepticism has found various remedies,[31] but echoes of the charade can almost certainly be detected in Athenian art of the period.[32] The pact collapsed when it became clear that Pisistratus did not intend to have children by a daughter of the Alcmeonidae. This time Herodotus says that Pisistratus left the country altogether, which seems to imply that in his first 'exile' he withdrew only from Athens, not from Attica.

From Eretria he and his sons set about collecting contributions from 'the cities which were under a previous obligation to them'. Much as we should like to know what lies behind this, Herodotus (1. 61.3) does not elucidate the phrase, nor explain why Thebes gave more money than any other city, nor why there was an interval of ten years before the return was attempted. *Ath. Pol.* 15.2 does something to fill this last gap. First Pisistratus settled a place named Rhaecelus on the Thermaic Gulf (the later Aenea;[33] this implies good relations with Macedon, and Eretria with its important colonies could help him in this area). Then he went to the region of Mt Pangaeus, from which he got money to hire troops (cf. Hdt. 1. 64.1 on his later resources from the Strymon

---

[31] A 42, II 249–50; F 88, 163; the story accepted by Grote, A 25, 327 with n. 1; A 13 II 321 with n. 2.   [32] F 76, 60–3.   [33] F 23, 465.

valley). Among the mercenaries were Argives, and Lygdamis, a Naxian volunteer, also brought money and men (Hdt. I. 61.4). From Eretria they landed at Marathon, where they were joined by supporters from the city and villages, and the opposition was crushed in battle at Pallene on the road to Athens. The defeated were reassured by proclamation, hostages were taken, and the tyranny was now firmly based on mercenaries and money (Hdt. I. 64.1). *Ath. Pol.* 15.4 tells how Pisistratus disarmed the Athenians by a stratagem (also Polyaen. I. 21.2) which resembles too closely that ascribed by Thucydides (VI. 58) to Hippias in 514; its absence from Herodotus' account is suspicious and most modern critics reject it.[34]

The chronology of these events has been the subject of long controversy.[35] Herodotus says (v. 65.3) that the family ruled Athens for thirty-six years, which certainly end in 511/10, and he gives ten years to the second exile, but for the earlier stages he gives no data except that the first two tyrannies were short. That strongly suggests that his thirty-six years are for the continuous tyranny, as is now widely accepted, putting the battle of Pallene in 546 and the start of the second exile about 556. Precise dates are found in *Ath. Pol.* 14–15: seizure of power in the year of Comeas, probably 561/60;[36] five years of tyranny; eleven years of exile, starting in the year of Hegesias (not otherwise dated); six years for the second tyranny; ten for the second exile, as Herodotus. No duration is given for the third tyranny, which ended with Pisistratus' death in the year of Philoneos, probably 528/7. Aristotle's figures as transmitted leave only one year for the final tyranny in which Pisistratus grew old (17.1), and they conflict with the statement (*ibid.*) that, of thirty-three years since his first accession, he ruled for nineteen and was in exile for the rest, i.e. for fourteen years as opposed to the twenty-one provided in *Ath. Pol.* 14–15. This can be cured by a single emendation in 14.4, four years instead of eleven for the first exile,[37] and the scheme is then self-consistent except that Aristotle, following Herodotus closely for much of his narrative, has described the first two tyrannies as short. Extensive further emendations have been proposed[38] to bring Aristotle more closely into line with Herodotus; but the sources of *Ath. Pol.* may have worked on a different basis, taking Herodotus' thirty-six years as the sum of all periods of the rule of Pisistratus and his sons. *Ath. Pol.*'s figures for these periods, with the emendation given above, do add up to thirty-six; the corresponding figures in *Pol.* 1315b30–4 show a small discrepancy which is probably due to different methods of counting.[39]

---

[34] A 13, II 326 n. 1; A 44, 718; F 88, 177: *contra* A 6, 52.
[35] See F 87 for bibliography.   [36] *Marm. Par.* ep. 40; F 2, 104–9.
[37] F 36, I 23.   [38] F 15, 194–5.   [39] F 87, 222.

The Atthidographers were compelled by the pattern of their work to place each event under a specific archon, a necessity which could encourage arbitrary dates. Documentary evidence has been suggested, especially for the two archon-dates given in *Ath. Pol.* 14: for Comeas (561/60) the decree of Aristion granting Pisistratus a bodyguard, for Hegesias (556/5?) a decree exiling Pisistratus.[40] Apart from doubt whether such decrees would have been preserved, or would have carried the archons' names, it is impossible to believe that there were such documents for the whole series of dates, the more so since those given in *Ath. Pol.* do not fit well with Herodotus' account. But if we ask what sort of chronological datum is at all likely to have stuck in Athenian memory down to Herodotus' time, much the most probable of the data here offered is the total length of the continuous tyranny. 546/5 is thus acceptable for the battle of Pallene, and if we also accept ten years for the second exile, then the original usurpation may well belong somewhere around 560;[41] but there is no reason to expect that any contemporary would have recorded archon-dates for the first two tyrannies, which except in hindsight would seem no more than passing episodes.

Pisistratus' marriages and the birth-dates of his sons[42] have also been brought into the argument. The first marriage, to an Athenian of unknown name and connexions, produced two sons, Hippias and Hipparchus, who figure largely in Herodotus, and Thucydides (VI. 55.1) adds a third, Thessalus, about whom he has nothing to relate. At VI. 55 Thucydides asserts from his own superior knowledge of tradition that Hippias was the eldest son and Pisistratus' successor, and supports this with arguments that have not always been found conclusive;[43] but that is a question that must be left for Vol. IV. Pisistratus is represented as having sons who were 'youths' (νεηνίαι) at the time of his marriage to Megacles' daughter (Hdt. I. 61.1), and soon afterwards Hippias takes an active part in discussion of his father's plans in exile; he was present at the battle of Marathon, in old age (Hdt. VI. 107.3); and his son Pisistratus was archon for 522/1.[44] Unless as a son of the tyrant family he was given office abnormally young, he was born before 550, and Hippias' own birth must go back into the 570s: no chronology will make him less than 80 in 490, so we need not resist the possibility that he was still older. Secondly, Pisistratus married the daughter of an Argive named Gorgilus, Timonassa who had been married to Archinus, an Ambraciot of the Cypselid family (*Ath. Pol.* 17.4; Hdt. v. 94.1 mentions but does not name an Argive). Two sons are named, Iophon of whom

[40] F 2, 80; F 32, 46–7.
[42] F 5, 445–52.
[44] M–L no. 6c5, cf. their comment, p. 20.
[41] A 6, 544–5.
[43] A 25, 332.

nothing further is heard, and Hegesistratus who is said by *Ath. Pol.* (*ibid.*) to have 'brought' a thousand Argives to his father's help at Pallene, and by Herodotus (v. 94.1) to have been installed by Pisistratus as ruler of Sigeum. Herodotus has Argive mercenaries at Pallene, so the Argive connexion was to that extent effective, but he says nothing of Hegesistratus and the story in *Ath. Pol.* may be embroidery.[45] Since the date of the capture of Sigeum is uncertain (below), we get no help with the main chronology. According to *Ath. Pol.* 17.4 some dated the marriage with Timonassa to Pisistratus' first exile, some to his (first) period of power; it is unlikely that there was evidence either way, and (unless we adopt the improbable suggestion that he had two wives at once)[46] there is a presumption that Timonassa was dead or divorced before the marriage to Megacles' daughter, so the sons should have been born before about 557. The 'bastardy' of Hegesistratus (Hdt. *loc. cit.*) can hardly mean that the marriage was irregular, but the sons may never have been brought to Athens or introduced to an Athenian phratry.

There remains the context in which Herodotus has set the final triumph of Pisistratus. When Croesus contemplated war against the rising power of Cyrus, Delphi advised him to make the most powerful of the Greeks his allies (1. 53.3), and these he found to be the Spartans and Athenians; on this peg Herodotus hung his digressions on Athens (1. 59–64) and Sparta (65–8). The implication is that the battle of Pallene took place before the fall of Sardis to Cyrus, not necessarily long before. Though Herodotus gives regnal years for the Lydian kings from Gyges to Croesus, it does not follow that he had what we should call a 'date' for Croesus' end, for there was as yet no general framework into which such a date could be fitted.[47] Uncertain indications (Eusebius; Diog. Laert. 1. 37–8, 95, 11. 3) have suggested[48] that later Greek chronographers dated the fall of Sardis to 546/5, but if that is right it only suggests that they read out of Herodotus an exact synchronism between Pallene and Sardis which is not in his text. The Nabonidus chronicle[49] (11. 15–17) has been held to date Cyrus' conquest of Lydia to April 547, but only the first syllable of the name of the country survives and the reading of that as LU- is extremely doubtful.[50] The text says that Cyrus mustered his army in Nisan and crossed the Tigris, then next month marched to the country concerned, defeated its king, and left a garrison: whatever this is, it is not Herodotus' story of the campaign against Croesus, clearly located in an autumn (1. 77.3), and in any case Cyrus

---

[45] A 5, 1.2 298, but his chronological argument has no merit.
[46] L. Gernet, *Anthropologie de la Grèce antique* (Paris, 1968) 344–59.
[47] F 31, 133; M. E. White, *Phoenix* 23 (1969) 46.
[48] F 14, 150f, 175, 193; more briefly, on *FGrH* 244 F 332, 28, 66.
[49] B 29, Chronicle 7.   [50] B 29, 282.

could not have marched so far within the month. The same chronicle (II. 1–4) provides the clearest date for Cyrus' defeat of Astyages, 550/49; and his move against Babylon (III) belongs to 539. In Herodotus (I. 46.1) it is the fall of his brother-in-law Astyages that sets Croesus thinking of a preventive war against the Persians, which should therefore not be too long after 549, whereas the further narrative after the fall of Sardis (177–178.1) rather suggests that other campaigns intervened before Cyrus turned on Babylon;[51] that must not be pressed very hard, but it discourages any very late date for the fall of Sardis. It seems that we do not know this date, but it could come a year or two after Pallene.

III. THE TYRANNY ESTABLISHED
1. Foreign relations

Whatever the date of Pisistratus' marriage with Timonassa, his connexion with Argos and with the evidently powerful figure of Gorgilus must go back before about 560. Apart from the hired Argive troops at Pallene we see no later effects of the connexion, and after the defeat of Argos by Sparta at the time of the fall of Sardis (Hdt. I. 82) we should expect none. Herodotus (v. 63.2, 90.1) says that the Pisistratidae were close friends of Sparta, but there is no indication that this friendship went back to Pisistratus' own time; similarly, Corinthian opposition to the restoration of Hippias c. 500 (Hdt. v. 92) tells us nothing of their attitude to his father. In Central Greece the connexion with Thebes remains mysterious; the dedication of Hipparchus at the Ptoion[52] shows that it persisted but does not elucidate its basis. The support of Eretria is less surprising in view of the old links between Eretria and eastern Attica (ch. 39d above, p. 253). Further north the Thessalian connexion implied in the name of Pisistratus' son Thessalus is given some body by Thessalian support for Hippias at the end of his reign, and the Macedonian support implied in Pisistratus' settlement at Rhaecelus continued into Hippias' time (Hdt. v. 63.2, 94.1).

The maintenance of this wide network raises odd problems, what the Thebans thought of Pisistratus' defeat of Megara, or what the Thessalians thought about his close connexion with Thebes. *Ath. Pol.* 16.7 claims that Pisistratus maintained peace all round (αἰεὶ παρεσκεύαζεν εἰρήνην) and we hear of no specific mainland wars: but Thucydides (vi. 54.4) says that out of their 5 per cent tax on produce the tyrants, among other things, 'carried on Athens' wars' (τοὺς πολέμους διέφερον). The financial reference has suggested[53] that they did so with the 'many

---

[51] F 31, 137.   [52] BCH 44 (1920) 237ff; cf. M–L p. 20.
[53] A 6, 52.

mercenaries' of Herodotus I. 64.1, but this may read too much out of
the passage. The native Athenian army remained in being, if we reject
the anecdote of its disarmament (above). It had clearly been effective
earlier against Megara, and later it fought well against the Thebans (Hdt.
VI. 108), in 519 if we can trust that date (*CAH* IV). Herodotus (v. 78)
celebrates Athens' victory over the Boeotians and Chalcidians in 506
as showing the value of freedom: under the tyrants they had been no
better at war than their neighbours – though he does not tell us what
neighbours they had then fought. The army had somehow trained and
kept in practice, and the record of its wars may be incomplete; but
Aristotle may be right in supposing that Pisistratus himself worked
more by diplomacy than by arms.

His activity overseas raises questions about Athens' fleet. He sub-
dued Naxos by force and installed Lygdamis as tyrant, and this should
be immediately after Pallene since he deposited with Lygdamis the
hostages he took after the battle (Hdt. I. 64.1–2). Fifty years later
Aristagoras throught that a hundred ships were needed to deal with
Naxos (v. 31.3), but on this occasion the forces of Naxos may have
been divided. In *Pol.* 1305a37–41 Aristotle takes Lygdamis, who 'later'
became tyrant, as an instance of the danger to an oppressive oligarchy
if the people's champion is himself one of the oligarchs. The detail in
the *Constitution of Naxos* (fr. 558) sheds no further light and it is not
clear what sort of regime followed the overthrow of the oligarchy;
perhaps the money and men that Lygdamis contributed at Pallene were
from Naxos, and Pisistratus' war was only against a faction of the
Naxians. There is no clear indication that Athens had any hand in
Lygdamis' later support of Polycrates' tyranny in Samos (Polyaen.
I. 23.2), though this would make sense: Athens and Samos had a
common enemy in Mytilene (below; Hdt. III. 39.4). Herodotus explicitly
ascribes to Pisistratus the purification of Delos (I. 64.2), repeated more
thoroughly by Athens in winter 426/5 (Thuc. III. 104.1–2), a notable
assertion of Athens' primacy among the Ionian cities (cf. Solon fr. 4a).

Further afield, Herodotus never explains how Athens had lost Sigeum
since it was adjudicated to her by Periander, but he is clear that
Pisistratus had to fight for it before installing his son Hegesistratus as
governor; and a substantial naval force might be needed against the
Mytileneans. The date is quite indeterminate. The Persian conquest is
probably not relevant: Aeolis is included, rather cursorily, in Harpagus'
reduction of Ionia (Hdt. I. 141.1, 151.3, 171.1), but we need not suppose
that the Persians greatly minded whether Mytilene or Athens held
Sigeum. Calculations of Hegesistratus' age, which have played a large
part in the argument, are thus irrelevant; but his appointment, together
with Hippias' continued hold on the place at the end of the century,

suggests that Sigeum was treated as a family possession. For its value to Athens see above, p. 374.

The Thracian Chersonese is a more complex matter. Herodotus (VI. 34–41) tells how the Dolonci consulted Delphi about their war with their neighbours the Apsinthii, and were told to take as their leader the first man who offered them hospitality on their way home; and this proved to be Miltiades son of Cypselus, of a wealthy Athenian house descended from Philaeus son of Ajax, who had won a victory (unfortunately not dated) at Olympia with a four-horse chariot. Pisistratus at this time was in control, but Miltiades was powerful too (ἐδυνάστευε) and found the position irksome; so after himself consulting Delphi he took with him all the Athenians who wished to go to the Chersonese, where he was installed as 'tyrant' and built a wall from Cardia to Pactye to keep the Apsinthii out. Continually at war with Lampsacus on the other shore of the Hellespont, he was at one point taken prisoner and released only after Croesus had threatened the Lampsacenes with total destruction. Later he died childless, leaving his property and his principality to Stesagoras, the son of his half-brother Cimon. The rest of the Chersonese story concerns the tyrant's sons (*CAH* IV), but at home Pisistratus had at some time exiled Cimon, somehow formidable in spite of the simplicity which earned him the nickname κοάλεμος ('booby'); in exile he won three consecutive Olympic victories with the same team of four horses, and had the second victory in 532[54] proclaimed in Pisistratus' name, so was reconciled with him and returned to enjoy his property at Athens (Hdt. VI. 103).

There are problems of chronology again, and of relations between the tyrants of the Chersonese and those of Athens. The discovery that Cypselus was archon for 597/6 allows us to date Miltiades' birth relatively early.[55] Herodotus' wording at VI. 35.1 (εἶχε μὲν τὸ πᾶν κράτος Πεισίστρατος) and his comparative disregard of the earlier tyrannies have led some[56] to date Miltiades' departure after the final establishment of Pisistratus' power. But even if the invitation of the Dolonci came (or was arranged) very soon after Pallene, there is still much to crowd in before the fall of Sardis, after which Croesus could no longer intervene at Lampsacus; and there are reasons (above) for not dating the fall of Croesus too late. Others[57] have preferred the period of the first tyranny, which may at the time have seemed to Miltiades more permanent than it proved to be, and this would allow proper time for the development of this sequence of events.

The belief that Miltiades and Pisistratus were political allies took its

---

[54] For the date see A 66, 156–8; F 5, 300.
[55] M–L no. 6a2; F 5, 299.   [56] A 66, 166 n. 3; F 9, 328–9.
[57] A 13, II 316 n. 3; F 73, 69–70; F 74, 8.

start from the belief that they were neighbours in the Diacria:[58] the name of Miltiades' family, Philaidae, was used for the Cleisthenic deme which included Pisistratus' home. The descendants of Miltiades' heirs lived at Laciadae, outside Athens on the route which the Dolonci would have taken from Delphi, and this suits Herodotus' story better,[59] but this does not exclude a connexion with Brauron; Themistocles, from distant Phrearrhii, concerned himself with the family shrine at Phlya. It would still be rash to assume that two great houses with their centres in the same area were allies rather than rivals, and Miltiades' discontent under Pisistratus' rule, the exile of Cimon and the alleged murder of the latter by the tyrant's sons (Hdt. VI. 103.3) can all be used as arguments for hostility between these families.[60] Against this thesis are Cimon's return to his unconfiscated property, and the kindness shown by the Pisistratidae to his son the younger Miltiades (Hdt. VI. 39.1). It looks as if relations were uneasy rather than downright hostile: the Philaidae were too powerful for comfort, and Pisistratus might well prefer to have the more energetic half-brother find a tyranny of his own elsewhere.

The Chersonese venture itself must have had the tyrant's approval at all stages. Miltiades could not take colonists from Athens without Pisistratus' consent, but it is likely that by this date pressure of population had made the provision of fresh farming land welcome. Occupation of the European shore of the Hellespont greatly strengthened Athens' position there, though it would still be wrong to speak of 'control': the hostility of Lampsacus on the opposite shore was a serious matter, and Megarian colonies occupied both shores of the Bosporus. When the Pisistratidae later sent the younger Miltiades to take over the Chersonese after the death of his brother Stesagoras, the settlement was even more clearly regarded as an Athenian interest, not just a private preserve of the Philaidae.

2. *Internal affairs*

Resentment among his fellow-aristocrats must always have been a major political problem for Pisistratus, at its worst in the immediate aftermath of Pallene which Herodotus describes so bleakly (1. 64.3). He mentions explicitly (62.1) supporters who came to Pisistratus from the city and the villages, and he seems to suggest (62.2, 63.1) that the resistance was not very resolute. We are not told anything of Athens during Pisistratus' ten-year absence, but we may be sure that he chose a favourable moment to strike and we may guess that the internal situation had degenerated to such a point that many would welcome a forcible end to the factional

---

[58] F 36, II 72–4; F 9, 326–31.   [59] F 85, 25.
[60] F 74, 9–12; more cautiously F 5, 299–300.

fighting. Nevertheless some had to be exiled, and hostages taken from some families. However, the appearance of Cleisthenes as archon for 525/4 (M–L no. 6c3) shows that in time a very complete reconciliation took place even with the Alcmeonidae, and if they returned many others will have done the same. It is surely important that Cimon's property was not confiscated during his exile (VI. 103.3). It has been widely assumed[61] that Pisistratus distributed to small farmers the land of his defeated opponents, and this would have been an unsurprising retaliation for the confiscation of his own property when he went into exile (VI. 121.2), but there is no record of such confiscation and perhaps Pisistratus left their property intact as a bait to entice them back; compare the proclamation after Pallene (I. 63.2), encouraging the defeated to return to their own land and keep quiet.[62] As things settled down reconciliation would become easier. The more rosy picture which is painted in *Ath. Pol.* 16 looks at the reign as a whole, and says that he won over the upper classes by diplomacy (ταῖς ὁμιλίαις). That would include such things as the offer of a marriage connexion which Andocides (II. 26) says was made to his great-grandfather Leogoras. Further, though the series of aristocratic leaders holding the archonship in the years following Pisistratus' death (M–L no. 6c) should be interpreted as part of the process by which the succession was secured, it is unlikely that appointment to public office had not been used already by Pisistratus to shore up loyalty to the regime.

It is of basic importance that he did not disturb the existing constitution, and that that constitution was not the traditional Archaic framework but the deliberate creation of a recent, intelligent and humane reformer (ch. 43). Herodotus (I. 59.6) stresses the fact that in his first period of rule Pisistratus did not abolish existing offices or laws; Thucydides (VI. 54.6), speaking of the Pisistratid tyranny as a whole, says that the city retained its laws, except as regards appointment to office; similar statements in *Ath. Pol.* 14.3, 16.2, 8, are not cancelled by the remark in 22.1 about the disuse and lapse of Solon's laws. Our sources parade the story that Pisistratus himself once attended a summons before the Areopagus on a charge of murder, though his accuser failed to appear (*Pol.* 1315b21; *Ath. Pol.* 16.8; Plut. *Sol.* 31.3); it can be assumed that the other city lawcourts continued to function with every appearance of normality. The political process went on, and we may imagine everyday business being transacted on the Solonian system by archons, Council and Assembly; and to that extent the old governing class could continue its work. It was of some importance that the machinery should continue to revolve, but the tyrant with his bodyguard was there in the background to see that it worked as he

[61] A 13, II 328; F 88, 175; F 9, 114–15.   [62] A 30, 182–3.

wished: nobles who made their peace with the regime did not recover all that much power. Further, the institution of 'travelling judges' (below) presumably curtailed, at the least, judicial powers that the nobles had exercised locally.

Aristotle makes two main points about Pisistratus' relations with the people. He did not interfere with them, but ensured peace abroad and at home, and this was the basis of the saying that his tyranny was a golden age (ὁ ἐπὶ Κρόνου βίος, *Ath. Pol.* 16.7; cf. Plato, *Hipparch.* 229b). How much the life of ordinary men, in a time of rising prosperity, had been disrupted by aristocratic faction it is hard to say, but some disruption there must have been, and external peace was a clear gain to the farmer. Secondly, *Ath. Pol.* 16.9 says he won over the people by the material assistance he gave them, and 16.2 mentions loans to the poor to enable them to get a living as farmers (there is nothing here about distributions of land). A much repeated story told of a farmer working stony land on Hymettus, who declared that his crop was ὅσα κακὰ καὶ ὀδύναι and Pisistratus must take his tenth of them, whereupon the tyrant remitted the tax. This was solemnly quoted to instance his generosity, but one might note that it was 'pains and ills' that were remitted. More important is the reference to tours of inspection in the countryside, of which this was an incident. With this *Ath. Pol.* 16.5 joins the institution of δικασταὶ κατὰ δήμους, who lapsed with the tyranny and were reinstituted in Pericles' time. All this Aristotle takes as designed to keep the poor out of town and prevent them meddling in politics; but we are not committed to his theories of tyranny and may see Pisistratus' measures as intended to help Attic agriculture, especially the poorer farmers. The 'travelling judges' also curtailed their dependence on the local nobility, without compelling them to spend time in bringing cases to the city.

Ath. Pol. 16 speaks of 10 per cent tax on produce. Thucydides (VI. 54.5) seems to regard it as an instance of the tyrants' moderation that they exacted only 5 per cent, from which they adorned the city, fought Athens' wars (above) and sacrificed at the temples. Possibly Thucydides is speaking exclusively of Pisistratus' successors and they had reduced the rate of tax; more probably Aristotle uses δεκάτη as a generic term for a tax, and the levy was throughout 5 per cent. In the Classical period most, if not all, taxes were paid in money, but in early days when silver was not yet in common use any taxes that were collected must have been in kind, and Solon's definition of his classes by income in kind is another manifestation of this way of thinking.[63] It is improbable that nothing was taxed but agriculture, considering the

[63] D. M. Lewis, *Hesp.* 28 (1959) 244, who suggests the possibility of taxes in kind at a later date; but see L. Robert, *Hellenica* 11–12 (1960) 192ff.

part played by harbour dues and the like in state finance at other times; and Thucydides leaves out of account the resources from the Strymon and at home which according to Herodotus sustained the regime, and of which the former at least surely included silver (below). The tyranny could afford to avoid financial oppression, and the record, such as it is, suggests that Pisistratus was not personally extravagant.

No one doubts that the prosperity of Athens greatly increased during the sixth century, and many historians have been sure that Pisistratus' encouragement of trade and industry had a large share in this.[64] Their evidence is pottery, sculpture and buildings, to which it can be added that his ventures overseas stimulated trade.[65] The certain fact in all this is the spectacular development of Attic black-figure vase-painting, and the virtual obliteration of its rivals in Corinth and elsewhere, and that belongs mainly to the second quarter of the century, the process being virtually complete by the time the tyranny was firmly established. The significant point is less the distribution of vases exported from Athens than the pictorial content, which tells us much about the society for which these fine vessels were made, a society not portrayed for us in surviving contemporary literature; in general a sense of energetic expansion, in particular a growth of refinement and luxury which is an index of rising prosperity, whether the textiles, furniture, armour etc. depicted were made in Athens or imported from abroad. If we ask what Athens exported, olive oil comes naturally to mind, especially in view of Solon's prohibition of the export of any other agricultural produce, but a recent study of the 'SOS amphorae', which were primarily oil containers, suggests[66] that oil had been exported in greater quantity in the seventh century; and it has been argued, on much the same evidence, that the olive was acclimatized in Etruria by the end of the seventh century,[67] cutting off one large market. The high quality of Attic oil was still an important factor, and by the middle of the sixth century it was regularly advertised through the prizes in oil given at the Panathenaea (below). By Pisistratus' time the export trade of Athens probably depended more on the skills of her craftsmen, not only in the manufacture of fine pottery.

Athenian coinage begins around the middle of the century with the didrachms whose modern name *Wappenmünzen* ('heraldic coins') is due to the now discarded belief that the various designs of the obverse were the badges of different noble houses.[68] The date of inception, roughly fixed by archaeological parallels, suggests a connexion with Pisistratus, and the obvious historical speculation is that this coinage was intro-

---

[64] F 36, II 71; A 13, II 331ff; etc.   [65] A 44, 717.
[66] A. W. Johnston and R. E. Jones, *BSA* 73 (1978) 103–41.
[67] C 163.   [68] F 11.

duced when his power was finally established and silver was available from his Thracian mines. Analysis of the silver of the *Wappenmünzen* and of the familiar owl-coinage which succeeded them shows a higher proportion of traces of copper and gold in the former, marked enough to suggest a different origin for the silver;[69] if these results were confirmed over a larger range of coins, they would imply that the first stage of Athenian coinage depended on silver from the north, whereas silver from Athens' own mines at Laurium was not available in quantity till the second stage: the tetradrachms with Athena's head and the owl.

The types of the *Wappenmünzen* do not identify their place of origin, or relate to the tyrant family, and their variety is surprising if we compare the coinages of neighbouring Aegina and Corinth, which from their slightly earlier start continuously display an identifiable city badge, as do the Athenian owl tetradrachms. But it seems that some early East Greek coinages show a similar variety: it has proved difficult to assign to a single city each of the types of the electrum coins found in the foundation deposit of the Artemisium at Ephesus[70] and an early silver coinage on the Aeginetan standard with a similar multiplicity of types may be the product of a single mint.[71] The influence of the Cyclades and Ionia on Athenian art of the sixth century was very marked,[72] and owed much to the actual migration of particular artists. Croesus' conquest of the East Greek cities, which seemed to Herodotus to mark an epoch (I. 5.3–6), may have had some effect on this migration in the years following Pisistratus' first coup; more effect might be expected from the Persian conquest, a few years after his final establishment. He may then have taken from Ionian sources his idea of what a coinage should be, and his contacts in the Aegean are no doubt relevant.

This was a not very plentiful coinage for local use, with a quite substantial proportion of smaller denominations that might serve to pay craftsmen, but hardly enough for retail trade.[73] If Athens had for some time been accustomed to the use of silver, as suggested in ch. 43, the introduction of a specifically Athenian coinage will not have caused a major upheaval or provided a new stimulus to trade and industry. It seems then that Pisistratus' main contribution to Athenian prosperity was his care for agriculture, and the maintenance of internal and external peace. We cannot estimate what his personal encouragement may have done in various sectors, but the only material encouragement we can easily imagine would be the direct employment of craftsmen in a building programme, and that controversial matter must be left to the next section.

[69] H 48, 59 with n. 1; H 76, 25–8.
[70] H 48, 25–6, where the parallel with the *Wappenmünzen* is noted.
[71] *Ibid.* 34–5.   [72] H 66, 78–9.   [73] H 48, 58–9.

3. *Cults and buildings*

The central questions concern the cult of Athena: the Panathenaea, and
the temple or temples on the Acropolis. Not very much can be said of
the cult of Athena before the sixth century. In *Od.* IX. 79–80 Athena
goes to Marathon and Athens and enters the strong house of Erechtheus; the Athenian entry in the Catalogue (*Il.* II. 546–51) speaks of her
establishing Erechtheus in her rich temple, and of annual sacrifices;
Herodotus' version of the story of Cylon (v. 71.1) involves at least a
statue; Solon (fr. 4.3–4) asserts in solemn tones Athena's protection of
her city. The office of priestess of Athena Polias was hereditary in one
branch of the clan Eteoboutadae (Aeschin. II. 147), the priesthood of
Poseidon Erechtheus in another branch ([Plut.] 843E; Paus. I. 26.5), and
this conjunction must long antedate the sixth century.[74] The name of
the city is itself another element in the early complex which we cannot
now disentangle completely.

Pherecydes' genealogy of the Philaidae (*FGrH* 3 F 2) is quoted from
Didymus by Marcellinus (*Vit. Thuc.* 3) in a form that must be at least
in part corrupt; and to the name of Hippocleides (probably in fact a
first cousin of Miltiades the founder of the Chersonese)[75] is attached a
note, that in his archonship the Panathenaea were founded. Eusebius
dates to 566 or 565 the athletic contest of the Panathenaea. The note
need not be Pherecydes' own and entries in Eusebius are often
displaced, but this evidence points to the Panathenaic year 566/5[76] as
the first of the regular series, in which the Great Panathenaea were
celebrated every fourth year at the end of Hecatombaeon, with a minor
festival in each of the intervening years. A simpler festival may have
been held before 566, with some of the events later incorporated in the
Panathenaea, for instance the *apobates* race said to have been invented
by Erichthonius, in which a fully armed warrior dismounted from and
re-entered a chariot racing at speed.[77] Reorganization and enlargement
in the 560s fit the archaeological data: the Burgon amphora, the earliest
survivor of the prize vases with the legend 'from the games at Athens',
is dated primarily by the date of institution of the games, but its place
in the development of Attic vase-painting does not depend only on
that.[78] Again, the dedication of the officials who 'first established the
contest'[79] is dated by this reference, but the lettering suits the date.
Other athletic festivals had been founded not long before 566, the
regular Pythian series, the Isthmian and the Nemean, and it is natural

[74] F 5, 348–9; cf. A 20, I 121–2; Eur. *Erechth.* fr. 65 (Austin). 90–7.
[75] F 5, 295.   [76] F 2, 104.
[77] Jacoby on *FGrH* 334 F 4, n. 2.   [78] P. E. Corbett, *JHS* 80 (1960) 55.
[79] F 29, no. 326, the restoration partly dependent on nos. 327–8.

that Athens should follow, though her games never achieved the same prominence. The archon Hippocleides may, but need not, have been the prime mover; the proposal was surely not controversial and we may assume that all leading Athenians joined in, including the already prominent Pisistratus. Only one late source attributes the foundation to Pisistratus himself, and that probably by mere confusion.[80]

The question of the temples is no less complex. Fragments of pedimental sculpture from the sixth century survive in some quantity, as do the foundations of one pre-Classical temple (the 'Dörpfeld' temple) between the Parthenon and the Erechtheum, and partly overlaid by the latter. The foundations comprise an inner and an outer rectangle which have been dated to different periods, probably wrongly, and the internal arrangement of the two cellae, which is unique to this site, is to some extent reproduced in the later Erechtheum which is the eventual successor of the Dörpfeld temple. It has been much debated whether there was another Archaic temple on the Acropolis, later obliterated by the Parthenon; there is some archaeological argument against this, and the 'Hekatompedon inscription' (IG 1².3/4) and Herodotus' references to the pre-Classical Acropolis by their wording very strongly suggest that there was only one temple there before 490. One set of pedimental sculptures is generally agreed to belong to the 520s and to represent a reconstruction of the temple after Pisistratus' death. The remaining sculptures have been variously dated: whereas Attic pottery of this century is plentiful enough to give a fairly assured series of relative dates, this is not the case with sculpture, and in the attempt to detect an order of development these sculptures may have been spread too widely over the years.[81] An attractive recent reconstruction[82] fits many of them into the two gables of a single temple built on the outer Dörpfeld foundations. The validity of this reconstruction, and the resultant date, have yet to be settled by the archaeologists: meanwhile the historian will be tempted to guess that the same impulse which prompted the institution of the Panathenaea was also responsible for the temple, and thus to date it to the obscure period before Pisistratus' first seizure of power.

He may still have had a hand in the matter; the story of his return to Athens with Phye impersonating the goddess (above) claims for him a special relationship with Athena. It has been noted[83] that vase-painters in the middle of the century developed a fondness for scenes in which Athena escorts Heracles by chariot to his introduction among the gods, with a probable reference to the Phye scene. Heracles

[80] Jacoby on FGrH 334 F 4, n. 1.
[81] E. B. Harrison, The Athenian Agora 11; Archaic and Archaistic Sculpture (Princeton, 1965) 3–18, 31–7.   [82] F 75.   [83] F 76; F 77.

himself is disproportionately prominent at Athens in this period, suggesting that Pisistratus had a special interest in him; his neighbours at Marathon claimed (Paus. I. 15.3) to have been the first to worship Heracles as a god. We may assume that once in power he fostered the Panathenaea, though there is no direct evidence. Regulation of the recitals of Homer at the festival is better attested for Hipparchus (Plato, *Hipparch.* 228b), while the 'Pisistratean recension' of the text of Homer appears to be a late guess based on allegations that he interpolated references to Athens in the poems.[84]

No ancient evidence specifically links Pisistratus with the development of the City Dionysia, which is nevertheless one of the most important phenomena of his time. The festival 'in the city', so called in contrast with the earlier festival ἐπὶ Ληναίῳ, was held in early spring in honour of Dionysus Eleuthereus. His translation from Eleutherae to Athens was referred to a remote past (Paus. I. 38.8), but his festival betrays its relatively late origin by the fact that it was administered by the eponymous archon, not by the 'king' (*Ath. Pol.* 56.3–4). A mutilated entry in the *Marmor Parium* (ep. 43) tells us that the poet Thespis 'first' acted and produced a play in the city, with a goat as prize, at a date incompletely preserved; Suda *s.v.* Θέσπις gives the Olympiad 536–532, and a plausible guess[85] makes the precise year 534/3. It cannot be assumed that this is the date of the first institution of the festival, and it is likely that Thespis' drama was a meagre and modest beginning to the series that made the dramatic contest of the City Dionysia into one of the glories of Athens and of Greece, but a decisive step had been taken. It is hardly likely that Thespis or Pisistratus, or any contemporary, saw where it would lead; the festival was being enlarged if not created, and this inspiration was part of the process, or a by-product. It has been noted[86] that there is a marked increase at about this period in the scenes on Attic vases involving Dionysus.

Nor does any ancient evidence connect Pisistratus with the development of the Eleusinian cult, and in this case there is no specific item that can be dated to his reign. Two buildings are mainly in question: an earlier and smaller oblong structure taken to be Solonian, and the large square Telesterion usually referred to as Pisistratean, both designations little more than conventional.[87] The more important questions concern the process whereby the originally independent cult at Eleusis became a national cult and an advertisement of the benefits Athens had conferred on primeval mankind. When Eleusis was incorporated into the Athenian state, at whatever date, the bargain then struck will have included some parts of the process, e.g. the involvement

[84] F 79, 15–21.   [85] Wilamowitz, *Homerische Untersuchungen* (Berlin, 1884) 248 n. 13.
[86] F 83, 133.   [87] F 24, 67–70, 78–88; F 77, 4–5.

of the Athenian clan Ceryces in the cult. Much will be later development, e.g. the foundation of the Eleusinium at Athens or the use of the 'Lesser Mysteries' at Agrae as a preliminary to initiation at Eleusis (Plato, *Gorg.* 497c with schol.). The large square Telesterion (unlike normal Greek temples, this was built to hold a congregation) shows an expansion of interest in the sixth century. The Eleusinium at Athens, to which the *hiera* were brought on 14 Boedromion to return on the 19th in the great procession to Eleusis (*IG* II². 1078), was built early in the fifth century, but offerings on the site go back to the middle of the sixth.[88] According to Diodorus (IV. 14.3) the Lesser Mysteries were instituted by Demeter in honour of Heracles, and the story that he was initiated before he went down to Hades to fetch Cerberus was well established by the fourth century; and this has plausibly been traced to a lost poem of the middle of the sixth century on the 'Descent of Heracles',[89] a hero in whom Pisistratus had a special interest (above). These are imprecise pointers, but it is clear that the cult gained increasing attention in the sixth century,[90] and probable that Athens' share in it was developed. It would be odd if the tyrants had no part in this.

There has been controversy over the Pythium, whether there was another shrine on the north side of the Acropolis as well as the sanctuary of Apollo Pythius on the Ilissus, near which the dedication of the younger Pisistratus was found (M–L no. 11); but the alternative site is not attractive,[91] and when lexicographers attribute the Pythium without qualification to Pisistratus (Suda, Phot. *s.v.* Πύθιον; Hesych. *s.v.* ἐν Πυθίῳ χέσαι) it is likely that they mean the well-known site. The Apollo who, through his son Ion, was the ancestor of all Athenians was the Pythian Apollo (*Ath. Pol.* fr. 1, cf. Plato, *Euthydem.* 302c–d; Dem. XVIII. 141); the temple of Apollo Patrous was built in the middle of the sixth century,[92] and it has been argued that this cult was founded by Solon, whose links with Delphi were close enough.[93] It has also been held that during the tyranny Alcmeonid influence kept Delphi continuously hostile, and that Pisistratus' local shrine was meant to show respect for the Pythian Apollo while keeping distance from his Delphic priesthood.[94] The discovery that Cleisthenes was archon for 525/4 (above) alters the perspective. We do not know what the position was in the middle of the century, and our evidence of active Delphic hostility is confined to the last phase of the tyranny. In any case, the Athenian connexion with the Pythian Apollo could not simply be cut; on the contrary, the tyrants strengthened it.

[88] F 33, 150–2; F 77, 4.
[89] H. Lloyd-Jones, *Maia* 19 (1967) 206–29.
[90] F 24, 77.
[91] F 28, 19–21.
[92] F 33, 137.
[93] Jacoby, *CQ* 38 (1944) 73 = *Abh. zur gr. Geschichtschreibung* 255.
[94] F 36, II 71–2; F 88, 184; cf. ch. 41, pp. 316f.

Pausanias (I. 14.1) ascribes to Pisistratus, Thucydides (II. 15.5) more vaguely to 'the tyrants', the fountain-house called Enneacrounus which replaced the open spring Callirrhoe; concern for the water-supply was a regular feature of early Greek tyrannies, but the location of this building is an unsolved puzzle.[95] Artemis Brauronia had a precinct on the Acropolis just inside the Propylaea, no temple but an altar and a stoa, later the site of Praxiteles' statue whereas the old *xoanon* remained in Brauron (Paus. I. 23.5); there seems to be no way to date the precinct but suspicion naturally attaches to Pisistratus. That he himself lived on the Acropolis has been widely asserted,[96] but hardly demonstrated.

The creation of the agora as the civic centre of Athens was the work of the sixth century. Traces of housing disappear from the area, and wells were abandoned early in the century,[97] and the ground may to some extent have been levelled as early as 600.[98] Some of the enigmatic early buildings may have been due to Solon, but others can be dated only to the middle of the century: so the Royal Stoa[99] or the temple of Apollo Patrous (above), while several which are datable to the early fifth century must have had predecessors in the sixth. We are hampered by knowing nothing of the conditions which obtained during Pisistratus' ten-year exile, and still more by our ignorance of what went on in the twenty years before his first seizure of power, a period of considerable ferment which might have seen other initiatives besides the establishment of the Panathenaea. A probable example is the pre-Themistoclean wall of the city, whose mere existence has been denied in spite of clear indications in Herodotus and Thucydides, and various dates have been suggested for it on very general grounds. Recently it has been pointed out that the city must have had a defence wall when the Acropolis ceased to be a fortress, and the Archaic ramp which provided easy civilian access to it has now been dated: in the course of constructing it a house was destroyed, and none of the pottery found in it was later than the second quarter of the century.[100] It is natural to connect this new approach with the Panathenaea, though it need not be so early as the first celebration in 566; and by then the city had been fortified, though we cannot trace the circuit.

It is not to be supposed that Pisistratus was immune from that urge to architectural display in public building that is characteristic of the early tyrants, though we may well suppose that his sons were more active than himself. The difficulty is to determine how far there was a new building programme attributable specifically to Pisistratus, how far

[95] F 33, 197–200.   [96] A 13, II 338; A 44, 717; F 88, 177.
[97] F 33, 16.   [98] *Ibid.* 20.
[99] T. L. Shear, *Hesp.* 40 (1971) 249–50, 44 (1975) 369–70; F 33, 83–4.
[100] F 90.

he continued an activity nourished by the growing prosperity of Athens and well under way before he was established in power. His patronage was of course important to such craftsmen as were actually employed on his projects, and the buildings added to his prestige, but we should be sceptical of theories which make the employment of such craftsmen a main basis for his popularity. Rather, this was a time of hopeful expansion to which the tyrant contributed mainly by keeping the peace.

Shifts in religious practice contribute something more positive. While we may still doubt how much Pisistratus contributed in person to the beginnings of that increasing prominence of Athena as the city's goddess of which the Panathenaea are a symptom, the general tendency is certainly towards the development of public cults in which the ordinary man could take part with pride. It would be wrong to overstress the degree to which the older aristocratic cults were repressed: the Eteoboutad priestess of Athena Polias had still her part to play, but it was now enveloped in ceremonies, processions and feasts with a wider appeal, and in time the aristocratic cults would seem old-fashioned and slightly odd. To this Pisistratus surely contributed, with his special relation with Athena. Again, it is possible to overstress the view of Dionysus as the god of the common man rather than of the aristocracy,[101] but the City Dionysia, though it had rollicking and phallic features in common with the rural festivals, was in other ways a new departure not under aristocratic supervision; it is again relevant that the archon was in charge, not the king. The annexation of the Eleusinian cult by the Athenian state worked in the same direction. The spirit of the city was changing, and for the time being the change operated in favour of Pisistratus and against his rivals.

4. *Conclusion*

It is hard to see the figure of Pisistratus clearly. We first encounter him effectively in middle age, and it has been emphasized above how much we have lost by knowing nothing of his earlier career except the single fact of his military success against Megara. His activities in exile show him already then a formidable figure, to whom other Greek states felt themselves under an obligation, but we do not know how such obligations were incurred. The Athens that Pisistratus ruled was potentially a powerful state, provided it did not tear itself apart in internal feuds. The capacity or performance of its land army remains obscure, but Pisistratus evidently had a fleet by no means negligible; his activity in the Aegean, and especially his purification of Delos, point in the direction Athens was to follow in the fifth century, while the

[101] F 83, 115–22.

settlement in the Chersonese gave her a foothold on a route which would grow in importance as her dependence on wheat from South Russia increased.

In his analysis of Pisistratus (*Ath. Pol.* 16) Aristotle stresses his personal qualities: moderation, mildness, generosity and a readiness to forgive offence. Here the tyranny of Pisistratus is a golden age in comparison with the rule of his sons, while the same phrase in the possibly Platonic *Hipparchus* (299c) extends this happy period as far as the murder of Hipparchus, in 514; Thucydides ascribes to the tyrants ἀρετή and ξύνεσις (high principles and intelligence) (VI. 54.5), high praise indeed from him, and again makes the murder the turning-point (59.2); Herodotus, in general more hostile to the tyranny, to some extent concurs (V. 55, 62.2). The evidence for Pisistratus' virtues can hardly have been more than anecdotal, and we cannot check the anecdotes; the nearest we have to contemporary evidence is an obscure reference (*PMG* 607) to Simonides' comparison of Pisistratus with a Siren, possibly because of his dangerous charm.[102] The verdict of Athenian tradition was favourable to Pisistratus, at least relatively; the Athenians were ready enough to proclaim their general fear and hatred of tyranny (e.g. Ar. *Vesp.* 488, Thuc. VI. 60.1), but when they particularize it is the name of Hippias that comes up (e.g. Ar. *Vesp.* 502, *Lys.* 619).

Pisistratus' diplomatic gifts were demonstrated not only in his dealings with other Greek states, but in winning the cooperation of many of the nobles in his regime. It says much for Pisistratus that the regime could survive his death, but the tyranny was necessarily a heavy restraint on the old governing class: they might be admitted to office, but in important matters power could not be shared and the initiative in any important development would be seen to be with the tyrant. For the less politicized classes, the farmers and other workers, the tyranny was mostly gain. Their growing prosperity was protected by Pisistratus' strong government: dependent on the tyrant, they were less dependent on the local aristocracy and probably had more, not less, freedom to manage their own affairs. More positively, with the development of public cults and festivals and by other means, the city began to take up more space in men's minds than the local unit. But here, as in some other areas, there remains the large difficulty of distinguishing between the work of Pisistratus and that of his sons.

[102] G. Zuntz, *CR* 49 (1935) 6; A 9, 322-3.

CHAPTER 45a

ECONOMIC AND SOCIAL CONDITIONS IN
THE GREEK WORLD

C. G. STARR

I. INTRODUCTION

During the three centuries surveyed in this chapter (800–500 B.C.) the economic and social structure of the Greek world underwent massive alterations which set the framework for the Classic age. The general character and the tempo of development can be discerned; causes and interrelationships are often obscure. For present purposes Hesiod (*Works and Days* only), Solon, Theognis and Herodotus provide the most valuable literary testimony. The difficulties in using Homer as a historical source, suggested in *CAH* II.2³, chapter 39b, must lead one to cite the epics only with caution; Aristotle, Plato and other later authors are occasionally helpful if we keep in mind their very different intellectual milieu. Significant archaeological evidence will be noted briefly, for the second part of this chapter will survey the physical material more fully.

Economically the volume of output increased tremendously, as measured against earlier centuries, and was much diversified in types of products and in their styles. Industrial and commercial activity tended to concentrate at urban centres in the more advanced parts of Greece. After his conquest of Asia Minor the Persian king Cyrus asked about the nature of the Spartans (Hdt. I. 153), and upon receiving an answer purportedly commented, 'I have never yet been afraid of any men who have a set place in the middle of their city, where they come together to cheat each other and forswear themselves.' To this emphasis on the role of economically independent elements in Hellenic markets a modern observer would add the important fact that the accepted Greek standard of value had by Cyrus' day become coined money, even if coins themselves were not always actually used in the exchange of goods and services.

Although the focus of Greek economic activity continued to lie in the homelands bordering on the Aegean Sea, overseas trade leapt forward in the centuries under discussion. A wide interest in economic gain can be detected in the more active states, at least among their urban elements; by 500 the Greeks, though 'scattered in many regions' (Dio Chrysostom, *Or.* 36.5), were interlocked in a relatively advanced commercial system.

The social structure of this world also became more complex. The most important group continued to be the landholding descendants of the Zeus-sprung leaders of the Homeric world. During our period an aristocratic way of life and pattern of values were consciously developed and were indelibly stamped on the arts and letters of Archaic and Classical Greece. At the opposite end of the social scale slavery grew more extensive in industrial as well as home employments. Free men also populated the emergent cities and sometimes became well-to-do; it was, however, more often a level of ambitious, able rural freeholders who sought a share in political power. In these pages the term 'aristocracy' is used primarily in a social significance; the neutral phrase 'upper classes' denotes all the larger landowners regardless of ancestry or political position.

Economic and social threads will be separated here, though the division will require some repetition. Important religious, intellectual and other advances were also occurring and must be taken into account. The great social and economic progress facilitated or required alterations in other aspects of Greek life; conversely these latter areas exercised a continuing influence on the manner and degree of economic and social evolution. Aristocrats and commoners alike desired to live well and made earnest efforts to do so, by just or unjust means; but their endeavours did not lead them to concentrate so wholeheartedly on economic matters as to ignore the social, political and religious dimensions of their life.

Politically many Greek communities advanced in the eighth century to a more consciously ordered structure. Ideally the *polis* guaranteed the fundamental rights of its citizens, who might thus exercise individual initiative. Yet the elements which controlled the machinery of the *polis* were also freed by the winds of change to use that control for their own ends; the resulting tensions arose, and were eventually resolved, within the *polis* framework. The great stresses of the eighth and seventh centuries, however, are most visible in the religious evolution of the Greek world, both locally and internationally, which essentially gave confidence to those men who sailed and colonized abroad or entered upon new economic paths at home.

Modern tools and methods of economic and social investigation, as well as major economic theories, can be applied to early Greece only to suggest parameters of the possible and to raise questions of which one might not otherwise think. We cannot quantify Greek economic development in any meaningful way or even speak of gross national product or other concepts employed in modern theories of economic growth – though recent history scarcely provides as great an example of economic alterations in a world of limited resources. The many independent *poleis* of the Hellenic world varied considerably in the speed and nature of their development, and within any one state the dimensions of economic activity were minuscule. The urban centre of Attica, for instance, could scarcely have attained a population of 10,000 by the sixth century, and the largest Athenian rural estate of which we ever hear was only thirty hectares in size.

Almost all Greeks lived on a level of poverty (*penia*), as the exiled Spartan king Demaratus told Xerxes (Hdt. VII. 102). *Penia*, true, does not signify hopeless dejection but rather denotes the need to work with one's own hands in order to maintain life; only a few were *plousioi*, able to enjoy the fruits of their world without such manual labour. Even by the sixth century the Greek economic system was not modern in its scale of activity, organization, or methods, yet it had become far more supple and complex than the contemporary structure of Near Eastern monarchy.[1]

II. THE FORCES IN ECONOMIC DEVELOPMENT

Modern efforts to explain Greek economic expansion have often brought into account the rise of cities, the appearance of coinage, the concentration of political power in the hands of tyrants, the wave of colonization and the growth of trade. All of these are, logically and chronologically considered, consequences or at best attendant circumstances, though each could help to promote changes once begun.

More fundamental forces must be sought, and undoubtedly the most significant factor lay entirely outside the Aegean basin. This was the progress of the Mediterranean world in the early centuries of the first millennium B.C., and in particular the developments in the Near East which have been discussed in several chapters of this volume. Though much shaken by the invasions at the end of the Bronze Age and disruptions which had reduced Greece to a very simple level, the Near East rallied much more rapidly, and by 800 was establishing extensive cultural and economic interconnexions which were soon marked by Assyrian political mastery. The Assyrian warlords were ruthless plunderers; nonetheless they gave stability to the Near East, protected trade routes and furnished a potent source of demand for luxury goods which in turn required supplies of raw materials. To a far lesser, yet significant degree certain elements in the Aegean world were by the ninth and

[1] G 35; G 13; and for modern theory the sensitive study by J. D. Gould, *Economic Growth in History: Survey and Analysis* (London, 1972).

eighth centuries also eager for products of eastern workshops; the extent to which the Greeks could satisfy their desires depended critically on their ability to offer useful cargoes, initially of raw materials, to the more advanced eastern centres.

In the Aegean itself the Greek migrations early in the first millennium which had settled the coasts of Asia Minor had also eventually produced a cultural unification of all the shores and islands, either by settlement or by absorption; developments in any part of this Greek world were likely to reverberate in sympathetic echoes in other regions. Although Greece in the Dark Ages appears almost static when examined at any one point, there were dynamic elements which could be significant, once released. Two of these deserve special comment as being particularly relevant but not always properly appreciated: the growth in population and the intensified interest of the upper classes in the delights of wealth.

The increase in population is very commonly presented as a great jump in the eighth century, which required migration of the excess numbers of the Greek countryside. Both premise and conclusion are shaky if appraised in the light of modern demographic theory. The Greek pattern of life probably was much the same as that which has been normal in pre-industrial societies down to recent times – high infant mortality, marriage of females soon after physical maturation and a life expectancy scarcely reaching past the 30s (though hardy individuals who survived childhood could hope, with Solon fr. 10, to reach an age of seventy). In such a structure a sudden, massive increase in population is not at all likely, and we know of no marked improvement in agricultural productivity to support it.

Occupied sites became far more evident in the eighth century, and the evidence of the wells in the Athenian agora has been used to suggest that the population of this area tripled;[2] but these changes could have been largely the result of a shift from semi-nomadic life (Thuc. 1. 2). Other ingredients necessary for firm demographic analysis are equally uncertain. Skeletal material is too scanty to support the argument that fecundity increased and infant mortality declined as the Greeks passed out of the Dark Ages;[3] we have no useful information on birth rates. At the utmost it would be safe only to suggest that the population of Greece probably did recover and expand slowly after the chaos of invasions and migrations had ebbed. Colonies were small and were founded over several centuries; mercenary service drew off only limited numbers; the cities were initially tiny and even imported foreign slaves to man their workshops.

A gently increasing population, moreover, was not by itself neces- sarily a favourable factor. Hesiod's dictum (*Op.* 380) that 'more hands

[2] H 25, 360.   [3] G 2; H 72.

means more work and more increase' is not borne out by modern economic analysis, which demonstrates that growth in productivity or even in over-all production depends at least as much in improvements in techniques, skills and interest.[4] Here, at least, there is adequate evidence, to be noted later, that the leading elements in Aegean society fostered and even demanded such advances.

In the Hellenic world of the ninth and eighth centuries powerful priesthoods were lacking, and the kings were usually set aside as the machinery of the *polis* was consolidated. The galvanizing factor, accordingly, in economic growth was provided by the upper classes as a whole. Overseas contacts were stimulated by the desires of this group for foreign goods; the search for disposable wealth was much intensified. Booty gained by war and piracy continued to be an important source, but new avenues were opened. Some members of the upper classes, including the brother of Alcaeus, took service under eastern kings or local tyrants; others led colonies or engaged in long-distance trade and discovery; more turned to exploit their own countryside.

Aristocrats have at times been passive, almost parasitical elements in later western societies; the eager, ruthless drive for wealth, on the other hand, of the Greek upper classes in the Archaic era is abundantly noted in the poetry of the age from Hesiod down to Theognis. To cite only two examples Solon (fr. 11) catalogued a variety of ways of acquiring riches and concluded that those who are most wealthy 'have twice the eagerness that others have'; his contemporary Alcaeus (fr. 360, Lobel–Page) quoted an aphorism 'Wealth makes the man' and expanded it by the observation that 'No poor man is noble or held in honour'. The aphorism, incidentally, he attributed to a Spartan; the urge for luxuries affected Sparta's leading classes as much as any other down at least into the sixth century.

In sum, the factors which underlay Greek economic growth were of general Mediterranean origin. In their Aegean effects they were encouraged by a probable increase in population and still more by an energetic leading class which was freed from the trammels of ancestral patterns by the great intellectual and religious upheavals of the age. Only after the initial, decisive steps to gain contact with a wider world did cities and new economic elements emerge.

[4] J. D. Chambers, *Population, Economics and Society in Pre-Industrial England* (Oxford, 1971) 17, 30–1 (citing Habbakuk); Phyllis Deane and W. A. Cole, *British Economic Growth, 1688–1959: Trends and Structure* (2d edn; Cambridge, 1967) 98, 133–5.

III. THE AGRICULTURAL WORLD

Any detailed discussion of the changes in our period must begin in the countryside, where almost all the rural population continued to live in villages. The simple tools, household equipment and even the homes themselves did not leave a major imprint in the archaeological record, yet the agricultural world was the fundamental base for economic activity. When the concept of *chremata*, wealth or more precisely 'useful things', is defined or described in the early poets, it is specified primarily in rural terms (Solon, fr. 14 = Theognis 719ff; *Il.* v. 612–14); Solon's classification of Athenian citizens was based on their income of grain, olive oil or wine. Gold and silver, which were gained by overseas activity, also formed ingredients in the definition of *chremata*; but the main source of moveable wealth, whether for local consumption or for maritime barter, was the landscape.

The primary requirement laid upon this agricultural structure was that it support the rural population from generation to generation. In the age of expansion, however, new demands were made of it. The upper classes desired a larger variety of manufactured items; whether they were of Near Eastern origin or locally produced they had to be paid for, either in food for native commercial and industrial groups or by the transfer of olive oil, wine and other agricultural products to the Levant. Colonies required initial investments of food and seed; so too did overseas trading ventures. Pressures on the countryside were thus already mounting before cities emerged.

To meet these new demands there was no major qualitative improvement in agricultural practices, which were well adjusted to the Mediterranean climate; no new crops or animals were introduced, apart from the chicken. To some extent the growing of barley and wheat may have replaced pasturage, for historic Greeks ate much less meat than is paraded in Homeric banquets. In Attica and perhaps elsewhere olive groves and vineyards eventually were important, though the common view that this shift had gone far by the time of Solon is not well supported. Everywhere the landscape became domesticated as wild animals retreated to the mountains. Over all the amount of tilled land seems to have risen, even if this increase at times drew in areas of marginal productivity at Hesiod's Ascra or the Hymettus farm which provided rocks (*Ath. Pol.* 16.6). It is also possible that farmers worked more energetically to fill their granaries, as Hesiod insistently urged.[5]

[5] In Russia man-days per worker increased about 50 per cent from the 1920s to the 1950s (Gould (above, n. 1), 77); Marshall Sahlins, *Stone Age Economics* (London, 1974) 298ff, shows that chieftains or landlords can at times compel their subjects in simple societies to work much harder.

On the basis of probable cereal yields in a two-field system a farmer with less than two cultivable hectares could scarcely have fed a family of four. Since ancient agriculture required a great deal of hand labour, he could not have farmed more than four hectares unless he employed outsiders at critical points in the agricultural cycle. In Solonian Athens a member of the *zeugites* class, who was rich enough to afford hoplite equipment, needed a minimum of twelve hectares to produce his 200 *medimnoi* of cereal; a *pentakosiomedimnos* held thirty hectares or more. The disposable surplus available from any one hectare, over and above the food requirements of its agricultural labour, could not have been large; the one sixth which Attic debtors had to yield was a more likely range for most of Greece than the one half which Tyrtaeus (fr. 5) asserts the Messenian helots had to surrender.

The fundamental problem in the economic growth of Greece lay in the extraction of this surplus by means of significant changes in the control of the landscape. Hillsides and pastures were apparently held in common; cultivable plots were in private possession. They were 'of unequal size' at Corinth (Arist., *Pol.* 1265b) and probably generally; the degree to which they were alienable has been the subject of protracted debate.[6] Certainly in Boeotia land could be transferred by the eighth century, for Hesiod advises honour to the gods 'so that you may buy another's holding and not another yours' (*Op.* 341). Evidence for transfer occurs elsewhere, even with regard to the foundation lots of colonies (Archilochus, fr. 293 West); but concentration of rural ownership into large estates was not to be the solution. In so rurally based a world formal sale or transfer of land rights was a thing 'not done' (*Pol.* 1270a), even though it was technically possible – a family was expected to have its *kleros*. In any case land without labour was of minimal value in a cereal-growing society which did not make extensive use of machinery.

Although rural slavery existed, there is no evidence to suggest that freeholders were widely replaced by slaves in the Archaic period. Even later Aristotle (*Pol.* 1323a) observed that 'the poor man, not having slaves, is compelled to use his wife and children', and the farmer of only four hectares could scarcely have had either the capital to buy a slave or the surplus food to feed him day by day. For casual labour the landowners drew on the pool of landless *thetes*, who formed something like half the population of Attica.

The major development lay rather in the reduction of the smaller farmers to the status of peasants, i.e. no longer self-sufficient farmers but producers dependent on a secondary group which used their

[6] G 3; G 6; G 12; F 27; E. Will in G 11. 64–8 (with the dissent of A. Andrewes, *ibid.* 114–15).

surpluses on itself and other non-farming elements.[7] This evolution was the product of changes in many aspects of Hellenic society. The rise of the *polis* bound its citizens together more fully, though down to the sixth century the Greek states made only limited demands on their production. The *polis* had initially a weak structure of government, manned almost entirely by unpaid officials; from the early seventh century its army consisted of serried infantry hoplites who provided their own armour and food; only if the state tried to support a navy was any extensive financial organization required. Transfer payments existed at this time mainly in the provision of public meals and gifts to victorious athletes. Greek states relied on harbour tolls, market dues, rent of public lands and a variety of indirect taxes; landowners could resist taxation to such a degree that only under tyrants do we hear of direct levies on agricultural production.

More important changes in the countryside were occasioned by the growing expenditures for the religious structure of the *polis*. Stone temples, more numerous from about 700 onwards, required primarily labour. Still, 'cash' outlays would be made to pay sculptors and to acquire metal, timber and Corinthian rooftiles; the continuing demands of cult ceremonies and sacrifices were not inconsiderable. When urban markets appeared, they too helped to reduce the independence of nearby farmers, who exchanged crops for a growing range of manufactured wares.

The most conscious force toward changing the position of the smaller farmers was the incessant pressure of the upper classes, as they grew more eager to gain *chremata* for their own consumption and for the acquisition of foreign products. Already in Hesiod's bitter epithet 'bribe-swallowing *basileis*' (*Op.* 38) and his fable of the hawk and nightingale (202–12) the abuse of political power for private economic gain is apparent; the rise of the *polis*, dominated by the upper classes, made exploitation even easier, as Solon's comments (fr. 3) attest a century later. Another mode of extortion is suggested by Phocylides' advice (fr. 6), 'Be not the debtor of a *kakos*, or he will annoy you by asking to be paid before his time'. The mighty machine of rural debt had devastating effects, especially in Solonian Attica, as we shall see below.

Varied procedures, both public and private, could be used to reduce weaker farmers to a dependent position so that they had to yield their tiny surpluses, and the results in the many states of Greece were equally

[7] E. R. Wolf, *Peasants* (Englewood Cliffs, New Jersey, 1966) 2–4. His comment later (11) is important that it is the state 'which marks the threshold of transition between food cultivators in general and peasants. Thus, it is only when a cultivator is integrated into a society with a state – that is, when the cultivator becomes subject to the demands and sanctions of power-holders outside his rural stratum – that we can appropriately speak of peasantry.'

varied. In Thessaly, Sparta and Crete the rural population as a whole was legally bound to the soil. In remote mountain districts farmers remained independent; but the rural elements in more open and accessible districts seem commonly to have become peasants in the anthropological sense, yielding food to greater landowners, to the market, or to the religious and secular machinery of the *polis*. Even so the dynamic character of progress prevented the small farmers in the more advanced areas from being formally depressed into helotry. If many Athenians in 500 could economically be termed peasants, they still were citizens of the *polis* and could exhibit the attitudes of the chorus in Aristophanes' *Acharnians*.

The essential consequences of the changes in the countryside were the accumulation of disposable wealth, which we may term capital, under the control largely of the upper classes. This capital, consisting of food, metals and animals, could not have been a large stock, inasmuch as Greece did not produce the surpluses available in the river valleys of the Near East; but it proved adequate to fuel continuing economic growth. There was, indeed, not the need to build up large fixed capital assets which marked the industrial revolution in western Europe and America, for commerce was conducted in vessels of small capacity and industrial establishments were tiny groups of artisans with almost no machinery. Much of the surplus of society, accordingly, could remain in a few hands at the outset. The upper classes sometimes did employ their wealth in overseas trading or in leading colonies; but they did not consider themselves entrepreneurs either in improving rural yields or in supporting industrial activity. Insofar as either result was attained it was the incidental product of upper-class demands for crops and manufactured wares.

IV. THE EFFECTS OF ECONOMIC EXPANSION

The ultimate sources of Greek economic expansion lay in the agricultural world of the ninth and eighth centuries. The conduit, as we have seen, through which rural changes were funnelled was formed by its greater landowners. The effects or outward marks of economic progress, however, extended far beyond the range of the upper classes in the many tiny *poleis*, who unleashed strengths in Greek society which they could not fully control. These effects may be summed up first as the rise of trade and industry, with specialized, independent manpower, and then eventually the appearance of urban centres and the spread of coinage.

Objects such as obsidian had been transported about the Aegean since at least the Mesolithic period; in the Mycenaean age interchanges of luxury items, metals and pottery had been extensive. During the Dark

Ages, on the other hand, foreign material in any area was extremely limited until Attic Protogeometric pottery – both actual examples and also its attractive style – began to spread abroad in the tenth century. Beads of faience, blue frit and glass have been found in two tombs of this century at Lefkandi in Euboea. Ninth-century evidence includes a bronze bowl, now considered Phoenician, in the Ceramicus cemetery at Athens and ivory, glass beads and gold in an Agora grave and in Euboea. By the eighth century ivories, Near Eastern objects and artistic impulses from Phoenicia appear abundantly in Crete, and by this time Geometric styles interacted throughout the Aegean and exerted an influence as far west as the earliest levels of Carthage.

All too often this marked increase in overseas contacts has been treated simply as a search for profit through deliberate trade, an interpretation which ignores several fundamental problems.[8] The historian must, that is, explain not only how desirable objects or raw materials could be found in the Near East and in the western Mediterranean, but also the manner in which conscious, effective demand arose in the Aegean world. How, too, did a specialized type of trader emerge who had the capital to acquire a stock of items? or again how could he secure protection both in and outside his homeland? Modern studies of simple societies suggest that this range of problems is a difficult one, and that exchange is often masked or even thought of in terms of reciprocal gifts by adventurous leaders who do not call themselves traders.

For the early Greek world these questions must be given a balanced answer. Movement of physical goods in the Aegean was expanding by 800 and spread farther thereafter. At least by the time of *Odyssey* VIII. 159–64, where Odysseus is accused of being 'one who, faring to and fro with his benched ship, is a captain of sailors who are merchantmen, one who is mindful of his freight, and has charge of a homeborne cargo, and the gains of his greed', the concept of making gains by seaborne exchange was consciously understood. The seafarers, too, who set up a trading post at Al Mina in Syria by the end of the ninth century, frequented it continuously. Yet in the first stages of Greek economic advance 'trade' must not be overemphasized. Commercial motives were not a primary force either in the settlement of Asia Minor or in western colonization; above all the rise of specialized industrial and commercial classes is at times dated much too early, and their significance exaggerated.

Once under way, however, commerce expanded remarkably. Very commonly in recent studies the view of Bücher and Hasebroek that Greek commerce was a traffic purely in luxuries has been accepted, and

[8] So John Hicks, *A Theory of Economic History* (Oxford, 1969). Sahlins' study is a useful corrective. Also G 27.

certainly the upper classes were in general the element which had the funds to buy. The range of wares and the systematic organization of trading activity were also more limited than in the modern world; but it yet remains certain that raw materials as well as manufactured products were moved back and forth through the Mediterranean.

To judge from early modern commercial patterns textiles may have been a very important item in Archaic Greek trade. Richly designed robes are visible on female statues and in vase-paintings, and were often mentioned in poetry; Xenophanes (fr. 3) scornfully described the purple-clad lords of Colophon, 'haughty, adorned with well-dressed hair, steeped in the scent of skilfully-prepared unguents'. Miletus had a textile trade with Sybaris in Italy which was so important that the Milesians went into mourning on the news of the destruction of its commercial partner (Hdt. VI. 21). If most woven goods were probably luxuries, the wool being loaded onto a ship at Cyrene in the famous Arcesilas cup (Paris BN 4899) must be accounted a bulk item.

Like textiles, timber does not survive well in archaeological contexts, but it had often to be imported for buildings and ships. Metals were also vital, for Greece had only limited deposits of copper, iron and silver, with which to meet the needs of its workshops for armour, tools, statues and other purposes, both for home consumption and for export. Grain imports, on the other hand, were minor until almost 500, when some cities expanded enough to require more food than could be transported to them by land.[9] The slave trade, which grew across the Archaic period, involved both skilled courtesans like the famous Rhodopis and unskilled personnel destined to provide labour in the ports and shops of the Greek cities.

The most visible surviving evidence of trade is pottery, which was used to contain perfumes and ointments, for olive oil and wine, and for many other purposes. Far too much discussion of Greek commerce has been based on its distribution and volume, a hazardous procedure in view of the other items which may have entered into seaborne exchange as well as the accidents of archaeological investigation; but in the most general way ceramic evidence may suggest that trade abroad underwent a great jump in the seventh century (Protocorinthian and Corinthian ware) and again in the sixth century, when Athenian black-figure and red-figure vases swept the market from France and Italy to Russia and the Near East.

By this latter point a host of colonies and trading posts supported

---

[9] B 89, 35, notes the lack of evidence for the export of Egyptian grain until the fifth century but like most scholars still connects the foundation of Naucratis with such a trade; C 225; Heichelheim, P–W (Suppl. VI) s.v. 'Sitos', admits large-scale grain movements only in the fifth century. In the sixteenth century scarcely 1 per cent of Mediterranean cereal consumption was provided by maritime trade in a marginal, spasmodic fashion (F. Braudel, *Capitalism and Material Life 1400–1800* (New York, 1973) 84–6).

a continuous and fairly large trade network centring on such Aegean states as Miletus, Corinth, Aegina and eventually Athens. In its initial stages the network was begun and at least for a century or more supported by adventurous men from the upper classes. Sappho's brother traded to Egypt, as did Solon. Colaeus of Samos, who opened up the Spanish route, and Sostratus of Aegina, who may have been the dedicant of an anchor at the Etruscan port of Pyrgi, were also probably of similar origins. By the sixth century, however, trade had apparently fallen into the hands of independent shipowners who beat about the Mediterranean as opportunities warranted; certain types of Athenian vases at this time were clearly designed for sale in Etruria. Sailing vessels, which normally ran from seventy or eighty tons upwards to a few hundred tons, experienced much less technological improvement than did war galleys; even so, better knowledge and organization of markets could have brought a considerable increase in shipping efficiency.[10]

Important though this overseas network became, the decisive advances in trade and industry occurred in the home waters of Greece. Only a small part even of the urban population ever cared to commit itself to maritime dangers – 'the land can be trusted, but not the sea' (Pittacus 10, Snell) – and the main source of demand was internal. The fierce sense of independence of each *polis*, however, and the costs of land transport led to the rise of many small economic centres along the Aegean coasts.

By the sixth century these points had groups of resident traders operating on their own account, and also independent industrial sectors, but their origins are murky. The scanty evidence in Homer and Hesiod does not support the well-known theory that artisans were originally contained within aristocratic households (*Hauswirtschaft*); the smithy mentioned in the *Works and Days* appears to have been autonomous. Fundamental needs for daily life were always satisfied largely within the home, but the creation of effective demand for locally produced wares such as armour and the great Dipylon vases entailed the patronage of more than one upper-class household. Recent excavations at Sardis even demonstrate that in this Lydian capital some gold refiners and jewellers worked not in the palace but near the commercial centre. Although craftsmen were dependent on noble tastes both generally and more specifically in the case of commissioned statues and other objects, they plied their trades in their own shops and at their own risk.

Industrial activity had never totally ceased in the Dark Ages. Before

[10] J. F. Shepherd and G. M. Walton, *Shipping, Maritime Trade and the Economic Development of Colonial North America* (Cambridge, 1972), illustrate such improvements in an era when the average size of vessels was less than one hundred tons.

900 a silver refinery existed at Argos, and a bronze foundry at Lefkandi; potters, woodworkers and smiths continued to exist everywhere. From the ninth century onwards, nonetheless, there was tremendous technological progress in Greek industries, and specialization of crafts developed to some degree. By the beginning of the Classic era the Greek world had acquired the stock of skills and methods which it, and the Romans thereafter, normally relied upon for the rest of ancient history.

This advance was almost entirely the result of borrowing from Near Eastern sources; the technique of gold granulation used in the jewellery found in ninth-century Athens (see Plates Vol.) thus came from the Levant before 800. In areas such as stone-working the Greeks did develop new tools and distinctive ways of handling their materials; but if Aegean workers in metal, stone, clay and probably wood gained mastery abroad and also in home markets their success was due mainly to other factors. One was the encouragement which they received from their society to experiment and to evolve artistic styles: 'Whatever the Greeks borrow from the barbarians they improve upon in the end' ([Plato], *Epinomis* 987d). The other major impetus was the independent and relatively competitive spirit nurtured in Greek markets. In an initial stage Hesiod (*Op.* 25–6) had already observed how 'neighbour vies with his neighbour as he hurries after wealth...potter is angry with potter, and craftsman with craftsman'; by the sixth century artistic pride could lead to the taunt which the painter Euthymides placed on an amphora (Munich 2307), 'As never Euphronius'.

The centres in which artisans and traders lived were by the sixth century true cities, no longer villages almost exclusively agricultural in character. The history of Greek urban development is unfortunately studded by semantic confusion as well as chronological error. The major Greek communities shifted from the loose structure of the *ethnos* to the far more tightly integrated *polis* system before 700, but a *polis* was not in itself a city, even if the concentration of all significant activity at one point was an important encouragement to urbanization. Athens, for example, did not change from a group of villages into an urban agglomeration with its focus in the agora until the last part of the seventh century; embellishment of its public and religious centres came only under the Pisistratids. The provision of fountain houses and aqueducts, a mark of increasing concentration of population, can be dated firmly to the late seventh and early sixth centuries, and by this time most of the significant cities of later centuries can be said to have appeared.

In the definition of a city the presence of specialized economic sectors is essential along with the physical patterns of its public architecture, yet social, political and religious requirements were the primary causes for the emergence of cities in Greece. The major buildings of an early city were its temples; economic functions did not affect the planning of urban centres until the fifth century.[11]

In the cities the upper and lower classes of the *poleis* played their political, religious and cultural roles; but cities also provided important sources of demand and gave protection, legal and physical, to the expanding commercial and industrial groups. From the surrounding countryside the cities needed food, water and people, and these requirements had some effect in turning at least near-by farmers into peasants dependent on markets. Aristotle (fr. 510) reports friction at Naxos between city dwellers and villages over the low price the former would offer for fish; yet cities compensated at least indirectly for their exploitation of the rural world by quickening its economic and social changes.

Artisans and traders moved about the Greek world and even farther, and they could settle in foreign states as resident aliens (metics); a recent calculation suggests that at least half the potters and vase-painters known at Athens during black-figure and early red-figure production had foreign names, even though they all worked fully within the Athenian artistic tradition.[12] The prominence of metics especially later at Athens, however, must not mislead us; in most cities down to 500 local citizens and slaves provided the necessary manpower for the newer pursuits.

These groups were not large. In the Athenian potteries of the sixth century probably few more than one hundred persons were active at any one time; an urban population which exceeded several thousand was rare and required the import of grain by sea. Cities and countryside were not sundered. Where city walls existed, they were more often draped about the urban core than independent in shape; in the Cleisthenic reorganization of Attica the city of Athens itself was given no special place. Yet the vitality of cities does not depend wholly on their size; cultural and artistic forces in Greek civilization had now an urban framework.

At about the same time as cities became visible geographical centres of economic life coinage appeared as a tangible economic force.[13] Trade was conducted mainly in oral terms and largely via exchange of goods, accounting was scarcely necessary for private purposes in a society where agency and credit were limited, but supple economic activity came to require a standard measure and medium of value. As Herodotus (1. 94) reports the tradition, coinage began in Lydia. Although it is difficult to draw practical distinctions between earlier lumps of precious

---

[11] H 56; H 81.   [12] H 18A, 9–10; H 20.
[13] On coinage see *CAH* IV[2], ch. 8*d*. On its purposes G 22; G 8.

metal and the Lydian electrum pellets of the late seventh century, arranged on fixed relationships of weight (stater, $\frac{1}{3}$, $\frac{1}{6}$, $\frac{1}{12}$...on to $\frac{1}{96}$), numismatic evolution was certainly continuous thereafter. Soon the pellets were stamped with recognizable designs of animals and other devices, and at least by the middle of the sixth century Aegina had begun an extensive coinage of silver staters marked by a sea turtle. In the western Mediterranean Himera and Selinus started coining, perhaps from Spanish silver, soon thereafter; and by 500 most – though not all – the major states of the Greek world had mints which operated at least occasionally.

The swiftness with which the invention was adopted in an era of tiny economic and political units suggests that it met significant needs. Coinage was issued by states for public objectives as for building navies or paying the mercenaries of tyrants, for fines and tolls on commercial activity (evidence for which begins in the mid-sixth century), perhaps for expenses in the construction of temples, and even no doubt to advertise the growing pride and power of the minting *poleis*. Private purposes, especially in relation to commerce and the payment of dowries, were served by coinage only incidentally. The electrum issues of Asia Minor were struck in small enough fractions to be economically useful, but the mints of Greece itself produced very limited amounts of smaller denominations in silver until the fifth century. Then copper coinage also began to appear, particularly in the west, for market needs.

Yet money did provide a mode of translating immoveable assets into reckoning assets, and those who could acquire a surplus over their needs came to place that surplus in coinage. The tendency, inevitably, was to hoard and so to immobilize coins; but surviving hoards which had been buried down to 500 are extremely few. For this lack two reasons may be suggested: the upper classes came only slowly to consider coinage a prime vehicle for their wealth; and also most men had too little surplus to be able to freeze it as permanently as did Persian monarchs. Coinage, in sum, was not in itself a potent economic force until well after 600, and its appearance cannot be taken as a cause for the rise of tyrants or for other manifestations of social and economic unrest. Still, once society had grown sufficiently mobile for the concept of coinage to take hold Greek economic life became wedded to the new invention.

V. ECONOMIC TENSIONS

Wherever we can see to any depth into the turbulence of the centuries from 800 to 500, the causes were mainly aristocratic contentions and interstate rivalries. Modern historians are often inclined to seek economic roots for political and social unrest; as far as one can do so in early Greece, the explanation must be in rural terms. The forces which led men to venture on overseas colonization have been discussed in chapter 37; above all the colonists wanted their own plots of land. At home contention arose over rural debts and enslavement or exploitation of the weaker farming elements; there was also strife between the aristocrats proper and ambitious men who stood just below them. Since political rights in the *polis* were tied primarily to land ownership or free use of land, these problems were the more critical.

Precision on many aspects of these issues can be attained only by framing arbitrary hypotheses. The existence of modern debate over the possibility of legal transfer of land ownership has already been noted; even less clear is the process by which one farmer fell into lasting debt to a neighbour. The vagaries of agricultural disaster which can strike one plot and not another are usually compensated in a simple world by temporary loans, as Hesiod envisaged (*Op.* 349–51, 477–8). Larger and more permanent debts are commonly the product of an entrance into a market system where rewards and losses are outside the farmer's control. Hesiod, again, does not speak of interest (*tokos*), though this price of borrowing was well known in Classical times. Nor can we specify clearly the nature of either debtors or creditors. Solon attests that some Athenians had been sold into slavery; presumably these had been very small farmers who quickly exhausted their margin of security. Other Athenian debtors were still tied to their land but had to yield a full sixth of their crops; these were quite possibly middling but unsuccessful farmers who would be grouped in Solon's class reform as *zeugites*. Since men of this level normally fleshed out the ranks of the phalanx, their independence was a matter of importance to the state.

The lenders were necessarily men possessing *chremata*. These would in the first instance have been the aristocratic landowners, but middling farmers could rise as well as fall; other men, too, might gain wealth, as Solon fr. 11 suggests, by overseas ventures (or mercenary service). The rise of such *kakoi* was a theme which Theognis reiterated in criticizing the society of the late sixth century, and in contemptuously calling them men who had once worn goatskins (54–5) he reveals their rural origins. Even clearer testimony to the existence of ambitious rural elements which were not aristocratic is provided by Hesiod's *Works and Days*, for the usual description of this work as a peasant poem totally misconstrues its picture of independent farmers, distinct from the *basileis*. These men, true, could be oppressed by those who held political power; yet they bought slaves, filled their granaries by 'work with work upon work' (382), and in the heat of summer sat in the shade and drank wine from Byblos (589) – this at a time when any imported object was a great luxury. It should be recalled, too, that in the late eighth century

Hesiod envisaged his successful auditor as launching his own ship and selling excess crops by sea.

All in all, the rural situation must have been a complicated one in many parts of Greece. In some areas the farming populations sank into legal dependence; at Samos, Miletus, and elsewhere there was civil strife. Only at Athens, however, do we gain a brief, but bright illumination of problems and remedies as shown in the work of Solon, archon in 594.

His activity has been discussed in detail in chapter 43. Here one may note that Solon's elevation to the position of reformer and reconciler was not solely a reaction to rural problems of debt. Athens was suffering from bitter aristocratic factionalism, which had been evident in Cylon's abortive effort at tyranny and was to appear later in the rise of Pisistratus; and also from discontent over Athenian failure in a war with Megara. In Solon's own verse (fr. 10.3) there is stress on the fact that 'a city is destroyed of great men'. The breadth and vision of Solon's reforms also deserve emphasis; though he placed remedies for rural debt and enslavement first, he encouraged the settlement of metics and promoted the training of sons in their fathers' skills. Yet he must not be interpreted as a modern economic wizard, who engaged, for example, in conscious inflation through reform of weights, measures and coinage. The Argive king Pheidon traditionally took similar action; but for Pheidon it is certain that his activity consisted only of defining measures of grain and wine. Solon's ill-reported steps were probably no more than minor modifications of measures and perhaps of weights in connexion with his definition of classes in terms of rural income. Coinage, after all, was not yet struck at Athens, or by Pheidon.[14]

Solon's reforms did not fully remove the manifold sources of trouble in sixth-century Athens, which soon experienced the rule of the tyrant Pisistratus and his sons. Pisistratus supported farmers by extending state loans – perhaps a necessary step once Solon had banned loans secured by the body of the debtor – as well as burdening the rural population with a direct 10 per cent tax on production. More important for the future tranquillity of the Athenian state was his encouragement of civic patriotism by his religious, political and architectural actions and by the damping of the vehemence of aristocratic contentions. Most other tyrants of early Greece followed very similar policies; though their role in initiating economic development is often overemphasized, their strengthening of the *polis* structure and their patronage of arts and letters indirectly encouraged continuing economic growth.

If Athens and the other states of Hellas came safely through the upheavals of the age of expansion, the causes were many. In the rise

---

[14] Kraay, F 19, a study which has been unsuccessfully attacked by H. Cahn and others. E 202.

of the *polis* the aristocrats were leaders and often were the element which profited most directly, yet it is apparent that even their political dominance came under attack by self-assertive *kakoi*, i.e. middling farmers who energetically seized opportunities. In the fundamental concepts of the *polis*, moreover, all free citizens had rights as well as duties. Hesiod's *Works and Days* contains extended arguments, both practical and ethical, against injustice; later leaders such as Solon of Athens and Pittacus of Mitylene could appeal to a general public consciousness; if aristocrats became too self-seeking a *polis* often accepted, if only temporarily, a tyrant whose actions were usually directed first at repressing his fellow aristocrats. Nor is there any reason to introduce modern concepts of class warfare and picture all aristocrats as ruthless exploiters for personal profit. The poets of the period (Mimnermus, fr. 2; Alcaeus, fr. 360; Solon, frr. 1, 24; et al.) make it clear that poverty (*penia*) was one of the worst evils which could afflict their aristocratic audience, and preceding pages have sufficiently illuminated the desire for gain which attended Greek expansion; yet aristocrats vied at least as much for honour and cultural eminence as for wealth (Phocylides, fr. 9; Sappho, fr. 148; Hdt. 1. 30). The economic tensions of the age were a reflection of growth, not of decline; and the great enlargement of the Greek world, both overseas and in the local rise of cities, also helped to diminish the intensity of conflict.

In the relations of the Greek *poleis* during these centuries modern scholars have often sought to discover economic motives. The earliest known war, the struggle between Chalcis and Eretria over the Lelantine plain in the late eighth century, has thus been treated as rivalry of two trade leagues; and colonization has at times been explained as efforts to secure trading advantages. Very little of this line of argument has any merit. The colony at Ischia was sited with some eye to Etruscan metal sources, but most Greek settlements overseas were always agriculturally based. Their continuing demand for Greek products was satisfied by private, not public, commercial ventures. Even if Athenian vases drove Corinthian ware out of overseas markets in the sixth century, we do not know who the shippers of either type of pottery were; the occasional trademarks on the foot of Athenian vases are mainly Ionic.[15] Greek colonies were fundamentally new *poleis*, not subject areas of the early modern type which had to engage in subterfuge to escape Spanish or Portuguese trading monopolies.

This does not mean that Greek states were uninterested in commerce and industry. When Phocaean refugees from Persian rule tried to settle islands near Chios, the Chians refused to permit it (Hdt. 1. 165), 'fearing

[15] G 21; G 21 A.

lest the Phocaeans should establish a market there, and exclude their merchants from the commerce of those seas'. All states tapped commercial gains through market and harbour dues, which were a major source of actual cash revenues for public treasuries. The *polis* provided at least partial compensation for this exploitation, if not always intentionally, by standardization of weights and measures, issue of coinage, better water supplies and harbour works; Corinth even built a causeway across its isthmus to facilitate the passage of ships.

The development of the Hellenic states down to 500, however, provides no place for a powerful urban bourgeoisie. Assemblies and upper classes alike were rurally based, and could even look askance at the rise of commercial and industrial sectors in cities and ports; an enduring ideal of the *polis* was self-sufficiency (*autarkeia*). These elements, moreover, were a small part of the population of any state, with almost no formal organization; and in any case the political machinery of the *polis* was too limited to go far beyond guaranteeing local order and justice in its markets. The effort of the Pisistratids to gain control of the Hellespont was an unusual foreign step which may not have had the commercial motive often assigned to it.

If we look at the economic growth of Greece as a whole over the period 800–500, it is impossible to define that expansion in statistical terms; the numbers of stone temples built in the era and the volume of surviving statues, vases and other objects may subjectively support the suggestion that economic quickening began to be visible in the eighth century, grew in the seventh century, but attained major proportions only in the sixth century. What is certain is that by ever more skilful exploitation of native resources and a geographical position between the developed Near East and the barbarian farther shores of the Mediterranean the population of Greece covered its needs, expanded its numbers to some degree and even produced a modest surplus. On that surplus, local and international, rested the development of such great shrines as Olympia and Delphi and also the architectural and sculptural embellishment of the *poleis*; so too philosophers, poets and others could be given the leisure necessary for their magnificent achievements.

This economic activity, it should be recalled, was essentially carried on by free men. In a few areas farmers sank into bondage, slavery became more prevalent in the workshops of Greece, but even peasants remained citizens of the *polis*. Economic progress led to very different results in the ancient Near East and in early modern Europe; the roots of the difference lie in the tiny scale of Greek political organization and its inheritance of a sense of general communal unity. By 500 the more advanced Hellenic centres had developed an interwoven structure, differentiated in economic elements but focused on 'a set place in the middle of their city, where men come together to cheat each other and forswear themselves'. The last clause in Cyrus' observation also deserves stress; by 500 B.C. important parts of the Greek world had developed a conscious economic drive. Even though a work-ethic of modern type never became master and 'profit' was a simply felt concept, the spirit of Greek market places was summed up on a black-figure vase showing the sale of oil (Vatican 413) and inscribed, 'Oh father Zeus may I get rich'.[16]

VI. SOCIAL DEVELOPMENTS

From the Dark Ages the Greeks inherited an intricate social pattern and code of behaviour in sexual and other relationships. Above the family (*oikos*), which included the physical possessions necessary for survival, there were territorial units ranging from village to *ethnos*, religious groupings about local shrines, brotherhoods, ties between aristocrats and their followers, and many others.

Any single Greek, male or female, adult or child, was thus linked to his fellows by many bonds of different sorts, which he usually accepted both in their limitations and in their support of his existence. We lack reliable ancient evidence to explore in depth these social patterns, important though they were; it is equally impossible to speak firmly about alterations unless we import recent anthropological and sociological theory. Much attention, for instance, has been given in modern studies to the *genos* or clan as a focus for aristocratic activity, yet the *genos* does not appear in Homer and its presence even in Attica shrinks primarily to priestly families if the evidence is closely inspected.[17] In general one may surmise that the rise of the *polis* slowly gave an overarching unity to its population and that territorial units gained strength at the expense of other groupings; but even a statement such as this applies primarily to Athens.

More can be said about the evolution of classes during the great changes of Greek life, which acted as a centrifuge to spin apart and to differentiate elements in the population. On the top of the spectrum was the small group of leading families which became an aristocracy, i.e. a class stamped by shared values and way of life differing markedly from other elements in society and accepted by those others as 'the best' (*aristoi*). Archaeologically a distinction in grave goods begins to be perceptible by the ninth century; in Archaic poetry an aristocratic outlook is clearly manifest from Archilochus onwards. The eighth

[16] H 18, fig. 212.   [17] G 5.

century, thus, appears to have been the critical stage in the conscious evolution of Greek aristocracy.

In any one *polis* truly aristocratic families were numbered only in the range of the one hundred noble 'houses' of Locri Epizephyrii (Polyb. XII. 516). Below the major landowners proud of their lineage stood masses of middling farmers, who reinforced the ranks of the infantry phalanx as it became the dominant tactical formation on the battlefields in the seventh century. This level could be praised by the poets, as in Phocylides' assertion (fr. 12), 'Midmost in a *polis* would I be'; it did not, however, form a distinct class, and even the concept of an independent political force termed 'the hoplite class' can be misleading. Aristotle, true, refers to constitutions based on membership in the infantry phalanx as against aristocracies on horseback (esp. *Pol.* 1288a, 1297b, 1321a); but his views of early Greek history are seriously distorted by the political conditions of the fourth century. Aristocrats stood beside the middling farmers in the phalanx, and politically as well as economically there is no evidence that *kakoi* worked as a group rather than for individual advantage. Socially, in particular, successful men of this stamp sought to acquire the aristocratic pattern of life, an effort well attested in the poetry of Theognis. The poorest landowners and the landless *thetes* were, on the other hand, quite distinct as the lowest rung of the agricultural world.

When cities came into existence, they supported industrial and merchant groups. Historians especially in the earlier years of the twentieth century tended to magnify the role of these elements as if they had formed a bourgeoisie; yet they cannot be completely dismissed in their invigorating influence on Greek life. The disdain for physical labour and economic gain which stamps the work of Plato and Aristotle (e.g. *Pol.* 1277b) was a philosophical construct never fully applicable to Greek economic life. Even if Herodotus (II. 167) makes the observation that in his day traders and artisans had little repute except in Corinth, there is adequate information that they had pride in their callings and could attain wealth; two potters at Athens dedicated a bronze statue to Athena.[18]

Slavery was a different matter. Greece had known household slavery in the Dark Ages, and the figure of Eumaeus in the *Odyssey* as well as Hesiod's references attests scattered rural slavery; but in the expansion of Greek economic life the workshops came to need more manpower of dependent character than could be drawn from the countryside, even though women were also active to some degree in industry and trade. The consequence was a growth in industrial slavery. Chios is reported as the first state thus to use slaves acquired from non-Greek sources

[18] F 29, no. 178.

(Theopompus, *FGrH* 115 F 122); Solon's poetry shows that Athenians themselves could be sold into slavery in other Greek states, from which he somehow ransomed them.

Marxist and Christian thinkers agree in the vehemence of their denunciations of slavery. Without denying the evil effects of the institution it must be observed that down to 500 industrial slavery in Greece was of very restricted scope.[19] Its appearance suggests first that the workshops of the more advanced Greek states had a steady enough demand to warrant the purchase of slaves and also that their owners had sufficient capital to acquire such forced labour. True rural slavery, as already noted, remained limited as against the spread of helotry. Indeed, Greek states had as many variations in bondage, whether for debt or by purchase, as they did in citizen classifications.

VII. ARISTOCRATIC LIFE

The most important force in social evolution during our period was the crystallization of aristocratic standards and a way of life generally accepted by a community or even officially enforced by rules and officials in the Cretan states and in Sparta. As the term aristocracy is used in the present chapter, its pattern existed only in embryo in Homeric *arete*;[20] and in view of the extensive modern hostility to elites it should also be noted that Greek aristocratic patterns were essentially a refinement and clarification of general Hellenic views of life. Hesiod, who cannot be termed an aristocrat, illustrates aspects of ethical and social attitudes which were later part and parcel of aristocratic thought.

By the time of Sappho and Alcaeus, in the late seventh century, the pattern had become conscious and articulated. All poets of the Archaic period expressed its values and thus helped to spread it as a common Hellenic heritage; even more important for its transmission were the frequent intermarriages of aristocrats from different *poleis* and also their rivalries and meetings at the international athletic festivals of Olympia, Delphi and elsewhere, the rise of which was in many ways a mark of aristocratic consolidation. The same verse is attributed both to Solon (fr. 23) and to Theognis (1253–4): 'Happy he who has dear children, whole-hooved steeds, hunting hounds and a friend in foreign parts.'

Since there were no hereditary titles in ancient Greece, aristocrats could identify themselves only on the basis of lineage; but landed wealth was also an important requirement. Seventh-century archons at Athens were chosen 'on birth and wealth' (*Ath. Pol.* 3); when Simonides was

---

[19] The standard view may be found in G 13, ch. III, with abundant references; a very different one in G 30, which received a Marxist critique in G 23.

[20] G 32; G 7; A 63, 302–11. A very different view in G 1, 34.

asked who were well-born, his reply ran, 'Those rich from of old' (Stobaeus, *Anthologium* IV. 29). The possession of wealth became, if anything, more important as Greece developed, for Theognis attacks those parvenus who might win away his beloved Cyrnus in bitter tones which suggest some social mobility by the close of the sixth century.

An evident characteristic of the developed aristocratic way of life was its male orientation. Men associated together in the agora, gymnasium and symposia, to a degree unusual in the aristocratic societies of modern Europe. Homosexuality was accepted, on this level, by the sixth century, when nudity was normal in athletic sports. Women perhaps sank correspondingly in position. Hesiod engages in terse depreciations of the female sex; Semonides of Amorgos went much farther in his vitriolic differentiation of women as such evil types as sows, vixens or bitches. Yet it is at least interesting that in the fragments of Sappho there is not one surviving word to reveal deep bitterness on the relation of the sexes. If the most richly appointed graves of our period were normally of women, does that fact attest only the ostentation of their husbands?

Another ingredient in the aristocratic ethos was its emphasis on military valour and athletics; both eventually attained prominence at Sparta, thanks to local conditions, but were significant at Athens and elsewhere. Aristocrats vied in athletic contests, local and panhellenic; they hunted in peacetime; and above all they showed their magnificence in owning horses and even chariots, a prime example of what Thorstein Veblen called 'conspicuous consumption' inasmuch as horses were difficult to maintain in the Greek landscape and of no economic utility. Still, horses and chariots appear abundantly in archaeological contexts, both as figurines and as subjects of vase-paintings; and names compounded with Hippo- were common on the aristocratic level. Unlike Homeric heroes, however, who tended sheep and drove ploughs in peacetime, historic Greek aristocrats did not demonstrate physical prowess by actually labouring on the land; they were *plousioi*.

In athletics as in the political and social life of the *polis* the bitter contentiousness or agonistic spirit of the developed aristocratic pattern is present. After the kings disappeared there was no one power which could check this factionalism for honour, and also for profit; the history of Athens in the earlier sixth century illustrates how far aristocratic rivalry could divide a state. Aristocratic ethics did not emphasize the telling of truth (as in contemporary Persia) or charity and brotherly love; its tone was far franker, as in the advice of Theognis (363–4), 'Speak your enemy fair, but when you have him in your power be avenged without pretext'. Vicious verbal attacks on the ancestry or personal life of opponents were standard from Archilochus and Alcaeus on to Athenian politicians of the fourth century; assassinations to avenge outraged honour or the exile of defeated opponents were common. Aristocrats did have a moral code, which was in most respects summed up in Aristotle's ethical treatises; but it was not of a high order. The statement 'Nothing too much' was its most famous precept from Hesiod onward.

Outward display of wealth was a requisite for that 'proper greatness of spirit' which Aristotle (*Eth. Nic.* 1123b) considered an aristocratic virtue. The upper classes of the tiny *poleis* could not afford the pomp of Assyrian and Persian monarchs; instead of gold and silver vessels Greek aristocrats had to make do with elaborately painted vases, but they came to the agora distinguished by purple robes at Colophon or by golden cicadas in their hair at Athens. The recently discovered statue of Phrasikleia shows an aristocratic female with earrings, necklace, bracelet, elaborate hair crowned by a *stephane* and a robe elegantly woven and decorated. In boasting that he ate 'not what is nicely prepared but demands common things like the rabble', Alcman (fr. 33) attests distinction even in diet; elegance in furniture and aristocratic leisure are shown in the symposia scenes on vases.

In modern eyes this uneconomic ostentation is reprehensible, but before entirely condemning the Greek aristocratic way of life we must put into the scales a truly great fruit of the Archaic era. The aristocrats, that is to say, supported with remarkable openness of mind the cultural expansion of their age, which underlay Classical achievements. Very generally the aristocrats lived in the urban centres of artistic and intellectual fervour; Sappho dismisses some unfortunate girl as 'a farm-girl in farm-girl finery... even ignorant of the way to lift her gown over her ankles' (fr. 57). By their commissions and purchases the aristocrats supported the swift developments of the arts; into intellectual progress they entered more directly. Thales, the first philosopher and counsellor of the Ionian Greeks, was of aristocratic lineage as were most later philosophers. Except for Aesop the writers in poetry and prose were of aristocratic origin. Greek thought in the Archaic era is marked by its freedom of speculation and invention, by a sense of personal worth and even individual independence (though the poets lamented human *amechania* or helplessness before divine power), by a lack of trammels imposed either by superstition or social convention. These qualities were given more scope both by the expansiveness of contemporary social and economic structures and also by the character of the leading classes.

As the Greek world developed toward 500, its aristocracies very often lost their political pre-eminence and had to share power in the various *poleis* with other elements, either the whole citizen body as at Athens or the broad group of rural freeholders of phalanx standing as at Sparta. Their economic strength was thereby attenuated; their leading social position and their influence on Greek culture were not weakened. Aristocrats had placed their stamp on that civilization during the centuries in which its fundamental characteristics, already evident in the Homeric epics and in Dipylon pottery, were made conscious, were elaborated, and were refined. In later centuries Greek culture never lost this imprint but passed it on via the Romans to modern western civilization.

THE MATERIAL CULTURE OF ARCHAIC GREECE

JOHN BOARDMAN

It would be heartening to believe that our knowledge of the material conditions of life in ancient Greece improves as attention shifts from the earlier periods to the later. In many respects it becomes the poorer and it is for the earliest settlements and their comparatively simple trappings that we have the fullest evidence. Continuous occupation of the major sites has rendered it difficult to do more than sample the evidence for any given period and it is possible, for instance, still to be unsure whether even Athens had a city wall in the sixth century B.C.: evidence for it is allusive only, in texts, and on the ground there is nothing. Criteria other than acreage have to be applied to determine population numbers and in the Archaic period none inspire confidence. Even relative growth and decline, which might be gauged from the sizes of cemeteries, must depend upon more complete survival and excavation that it has generally proved possible to achieve. While the increasing sophistication of life greatly diversifies the archaeological record it has also meant that the range of possibly relevant evidence has widened to include important classes of objects which have survived irregularly (metalwork) or not at all (parchment, papyri, textiles). True, the figure arts of Greece tell more through detailed depiction of life. This has meant, for instance, that we learn about eighth-century weapons mainly from excavated objects, sixth-century ones from pictures of them or allusions in poetry, and it is not easy to say which period is the more reliably and completely served. The greater diversity of artefacts does at least mean that greater precision is possible in definition of date and origin, and this proves, as other chapters have shown, a vital source of conventional historical information, especially about trade and about the origins of Greeks far from home.

Our knowledge of the mainland cities is poorer than that of new colonial foundations or of the comparatively recent foundations on the eastern shores of the Aegean. In the older cities of Greece where an acropolis had been a central fortified feature, as in Athens, occupation had long before outgrown it and, as in Athens, we may be left uncertain whether the lower town was fortified. It is likely that Pisistratus

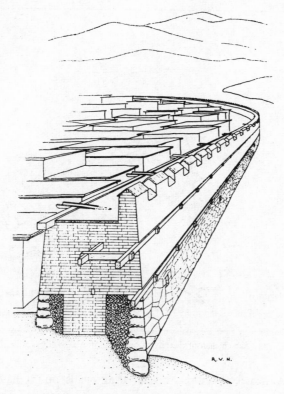

54. The late seventh-century wall at Smyrna, reconstructed by R. V. Nicholls. See also p. 202, fig. 31. (After D 24, 112, fig. 34; D 25, 73, fig. 20.)

provided some sort of perimeter, though the ease of access by his own men (returning) and later by Spartans and Persians, suggests that our difficulties in locating it on the ground reflect its light and impermanent character.[1] Athens was quick to devote its acropolis to the gods and to lay out its administrative area round the agora (see below, and Plates Vol.) but of the rest of the town all we can judge is that although occupation may have been dense in the agora area before it was cleared (by Solon?) it could still accommodate minor cemeteries and industry – a potter's yard. Athens seems to have remained a shapeless, ill-defined settlement, muddled by its past until lawgivers and a tyrant family take it in hand.

In other cities, like Corinth, Argos, Eretria, the acropolis was more of a fortified refuge for the settlement on the lower slopes. The possibilities of defence for the lower town were naturally taken more

[1] H 79, 61–4; F 90; F 84.

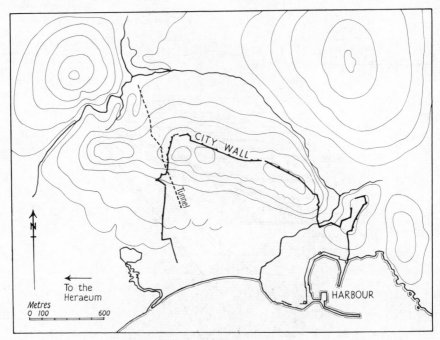

55. Sketch plan of the city of Samos. (After D 97, figs. 21, 24.)

seriously. At Eretria it seems that long walls might have run from acropolis to harbour already in the seventh century. This has been thought less likely at Corinth but there is evidence for at least local fortification in the area of the potters' quarter on the lower slopes of Acrocorinth.[2]

For architectural show and elaboration of town plans and fortifications we have to look elsewhere. Excavation and the accidents of history have ensured for us a clear record of the great walls of Smyrna (fig. 54) down to its fall in the early sixth century.[3] It cannot have been unique but a site which relied, as Smyrna did, on the isolation of a peninsula presents different problems from one dependent on an inland acropolis, like the homeland cities mentioned in the last paragraph or, for instance, Samos, where the walls embracing the heights, harbour and a stretch of coastline were most probably built under Polycrates (fig. 55). Here too we find an early example of the sophistication of towers and ditch, and Herodotus' brief account of the Spartan siege suggests that they were a stout obstacle. In a town like this the whole walled area (a triangle with roughly 1·5 km sides) was not built up and the wall line

[2] Corinth – H 79, 64; E 224. Eretria – H 79, 61; D 6, 130ff; D 14, 89–94.
[3] See *CAH* II.2², 798–800, and above, pp. 197, 202–3; D 73.

was dictated by natural features and the need to protect the water supply.[4] At Smyrna nature, in the form of the size of the peninsula, determined what could be walled and there was a big extramural suburb.

Serious urban planning could only be attempted on a new site or on an old one destroyed by a natural disaster. So Smyrna had a grid plan on major axes for its houses already in the seventh century after a disaster of around 700, and that such admittedly elementary planning was familiar already in the late eighth century is suggested by the fact that Megara Hyblaea in Sicily also seems to have been laid out on axes. Moreover, it may be that a regular area here was allotted as an agora.[5] This need not have any deep political implications – an assembly place was an obvious need for commercial and military purposes if nothing else. Megara could not have been unique but elsewhere it is only at sites like Paestum (Posidonia) that traces of the early layout are easily discerned, and they are more readily determined for sixth-century towns, notably in secondary western colonies, than in the seventh century.

For the town and country houses themselves our evidence is even scantier than in the previous period, but, to judge from the comparative simplicity of the later Classical houses, we need assume no dramatic advances on the simple one-roomed structures, usually with an open porch. Smyrna probably gives the pattern for the richest Greek town houses of the seventh century (fig. 56), some probably two-storied, flat-roofed with brick walls on stone socles, their blocks carefully faced.[6] The large, irregularly shaped house at the south-west corner of the Athenian agora,[7] which some have taken for the Pisistratan town house, has rooms opening on to a central court and it may be that this common Classical plan was already in use in the sixth century. It implies far greater complexity of the living unit and commensurate wealth. We find no tyrant palaces in Greece but the court and open verandah (*pastas*) are features of major domestic buildings on the eastern fringes of the Greek world, at 'Larisa' in Aeolis (fig. 57) and Vouni in Cyprus, and they contribute to the design of the Classical house.[8] We would expect no architectural elaboration on Archaic houses in the form of columns in the newly devised orders, but clay tiling and the painted or relief decoration which goes with it were probably not long reserved for sanctuary architecture alone.

The agricultural and technological developments of the Archaic period have been touched upon in the preceding section, and the former at least had a profound effect on the development of Greek society and

[4] H 79, 108–10, 295; Hdt. III. 54–5; D 89.
[5] C 169; C 170; H 79, 28–9. Above, p. 108, fig. 19.
[6] D 25, 70–4; D 24, 14ff.
[7] F 33, 27–8.
[8] H 52, 339–40; H 49.

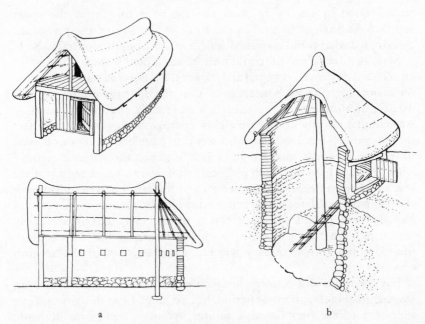

56. Reconstruction of a seventh-century house and granary at Smyrna, by R. V. Nicholls. (After E. Akurgal, *Die Kunst Anatoliens* (1961) 301, figs. 2, 5.)

institutions. The changes were mainly a matter of shift in emphasis, however, towards specialist crop production with an eye to export and barter in some states, but not, so far as we can judge, involving new crops or radically new techniques. State concern in such matters may be judged from Solon's legislation against the casual cutting down of olive trees and regulations about the distances from boundaries at which they should be planted.[9] The introduction of the domestic hen to Greece from the east at the end of the eighth century must have made a perceptible but not very important contribution to variety of diet.

Technological change was also more a matter of volume than significantly innovatory, except perhaps for some luxury crafts where Greek studios belatedly learned, or re-learned, techniques of granulation and filigree with gold, the cutting of hard semi-precious stones with the bow drill (a familiar implement to the carpenter, of course) and cutting wheel, the manufacture of faience and glass.[10] The expanding economy and population created a demand for more metal goods answered by the metal-seeking trade and the establishment of emporia which had begun by the end of the ninth century in the east, and in

[9] F 66, F 60a, b and cf. 90.
[10] A 7, 56–8, 76, 126–9; H 16, 139–40, 379–81; H 78; H 41.

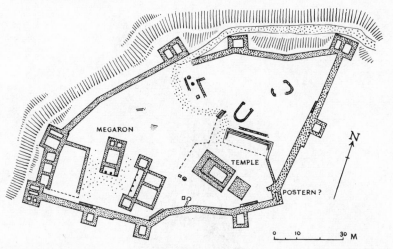

57. Plan of the acropolis and 'palace' at Buruncuk ('Larisa'). Late sixth century B.C. (After H 52, 239, fig. 134.)

the eighth in the west, as we have seen. The main users of domestic agricultural or military equipment, enjoyed improved versions of gear already familiar in the eighth. We might imagine that the dramatic advances in marble sculpture and monumental architecture from the end of the seventh century on implied notable technological progress, but this is probably not true. The marble sculpture was in part inspired by Egypt, but in Greece iron tools far more effective than any implements in the hands of Egyptian sculptors were already in general use.[11] Monumental architecture was imposing and it involved the handling of heavy loads but the methods used relied more on manpower than engineering skills, and the early temples (even most of the Classical ones) show little understanding of building loads and stresses.[12] The architects played safe in their construction methods and the sources of the labour force at their disposal give us more to think about than their qualifications as engineers. Rule of thumb dominates even the most ambitious projects. There were no 'nationally' recognized standards of measurement such as obtained through large areas of the Near East and Egypt, and although a standard would have been used for a single project, another might apply for its neighbour and there are many irregularities of measurement.[13] Standard weights were clearly not in general use in Greece until the end of the Archaic period. They never appear on the scale pans in vase scenes where like is always weighed against like, and consider the non-commensurability of early coin standards. Perhaps it was only when coinage began to play a role as

[11] H 19, 19.   [12] H 33, ch. 2.   [13] H 31.

58. Reconstruction of an orientalizing
bronze cauldron and stand from Olympia.
Early seventh century B.C. Height about
1·5 m. (After E 234, 82, fig. 49.)

bullion that accurate weighing against agreed standards became
essential, and observation of Egyptian masons could have taught the
merit of accurate linear measurement. In some ways, however, it is the
application of Greek flair and subtlety rather than the predetermined
layouts and grids of the Egyptian craftsmen and sculptors that guaranteed the Greek artist that freedom of expression which could lead to
radically new rendering even of traditional subjects. That they could
rise to major engineering projects too, however, is shown by Eupalinus'
tunnel at Samos, cut for a kilometre through the hillside.[14]

If observed changes were so much of degree rather than substance,
how do we explain the surely radical difference in the quality and
appearance of everyday life, at least in cities, between the eighth and
the sixth centuries? The opening phase of this period is what
archaeologists have come to call the orientalizing, and it is likely that
we should look overseas for the sources of this new, if only superficially
new, life-style. The metal-seeking which established emporia in the east
at Al Mina, in the west on Ischia, was the signal for important new
developments which were profoundly to affect the culture of homeland

[14] D 55.

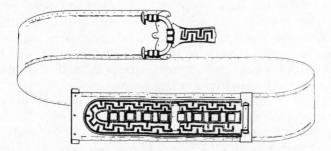

59. An Ionian bronze belt of Phrygian pattern, from Emporio,
Chios. Seventh century B.C. (After D 22, 215, fig. 140.)

Greece. In the west the way was open for land-seeking, for the
colonization of south Italy and Sicily which relieved the pressure at
home and was soon to create new and rich markets for Greek wares.
And from the east began a flow not merely of metals but also of finished
goods, and we may be sure, craftsmen, which between them determined
the new orientalizing styles.

Of the technological gifts from the east we have remarked those of
luxury crafts, the handling of gold and hard stones, to which we should
add the carving of ivory. Crete and Attica had experience of these
innovations even earlier[15] but it is only in the seventh century that we
can see Greek studios in command of the new techniques and producing
wares which we could regard as wholly Hellenic in character. In
bronzework the great tripod cauldrons which had been the pride of the
Geometric sanctuaries are slowly replaced by the new eastern cauldron
(fig. 58), on conical or rod stands, with their exotic animal-head (lions
and griffins) and siren attachments which Greek craftsmen soon copy
and adapt to their own idioms.[16] The new cauldron type with incurving
rim is going to be dominant in both domestic and dedicatory matters,
but the change is again really superficial and the most striking novelty
the finer specimens presented was the cast or traced figure decoration
that many of them carried. Ionian ladies learn to wear and have made
for them bronze belts of Phrygian pattern (fig. 59)[17] and by the end of
the seventh century they have invented their own version of the flowing
eastern sleeved garments, adapted to the demands of the Greeks' rather
primitive skills in dress-making, so that the *chiton* required no tailoring
but simply the folding, buttoning and belting of a rectangular piece of
cloth. The older *peplos*, a heavier garment and with a longer history in
Greece, was still worn and is even simpler in make. The only other

[15] See *CAH* III.1², 783; A 7, 56ff.   [16] E 233.
[17] D 22, 214ff; D 21; D 54, 49–53.

significant changes in dress may be the embroidery and woven patterns learned from the east and some of the more extravagant forms of jewellery, notably earrings. The Greeks, however, were not so easily won over by eastern example to the extravagant displays of jewellery and dress as the Etruscans, who were being exposed to similar influences by both easterners and Greeks at that time.

This mêlée of orientalia introduced into or adapted by the Greek world owned a variety of sources. The metalwork displays elements of Urartian, Assyrian, Syrian and Cypriot derivation and the products are well distributed through Greek lands. Apart from Phrygian influence on the still rather provincial Ionians and the odd phenomenon of the apparent eastern immigrants in central Crete discussed on p. 225, we can discern no particular period or place dominated by any one eastern source: there was no sudden and wholly Neo-Hittite or Assyrian or Babylonian period of fashion in Corinth or Athens, just a gradual infiltration and acceptance of the new forms.

The effect on what are called the monumental arts may have been more profound yet the results differ so markedly from their putative models that here too we may regard eastern and Egyptian example as hardly more than a catalyst, determining and shaping Greek intentions. The east introduced the mould for clay high-relief figurines to the Greek world and with it what has become rather misleadingly called the Daedalic style.[18] This informed the minor arts of much of Greece in the seventh century but it introduced a stereotype and was essentially decorative rather than monumental. Knowledge of Egyptian art after the mid century led to Greek exploitation of the harder stone, their white island marble, for the first time, and the creation of figures at life size or more. We know these best – the *kouroi* and *korai* – as dedications and grave markers, but a prime use for monumental statuary must have been as cult images and it is at about this time that the temple-houses, *oikoi*, for these images begin to receive a monumental form and, again probably through inspiration from Egypt, are decorated with architectural orders: first the Doric in homeland Greece, then the orientalizing Ionic in the East Greek world.[19] The temples are the only major works of architecture of this period and must have dominated the towns in which they stood. They were a physical expression of the presence of the patron deity but also a demonstration of the wealth and labour-command of the ruling class, generally aristocratic, which commissioned them. Their appearance probably represents the major physical change in the appearance of towns in the Archaic period, since the houses remained humble and imposing fortifications were, as we have seen, exceptional.

[18] H 19, 13–15; H 2.   [19] H 52, chs. 10, 12.

The main contribution of the east to the material appearance of life in Greece must be the impetus given to the figurative arts. In the eighth century many artefacts were decorated with abstract Geometric or orientalizing patterns. In the sixth century the majority of clay vases, serving many more purposes than such do today, carried figure decoration. Virtually every other class of artefact in any material could be similarly decorated, from the bronze strips fastening the handles inside shields[20] to wood or ivory boxes; from patterned dress (Athena's *peplos* carried scenes of the gigantomachy) to finger-rings. All major buildings carried figure decoration in the round, relief or painted, and we cannot easily make adequate allowance for much else perishable, in wood or fabric, which might have been adorned in the same manner. The sixth-century Greek lived in a world of icons, scenes of mythology, of the gods, of heroic encounters. Some of them were inscribed with the names of the participants – many clay vases, for example, or the ivory Chest of Cypselus at Olympia as described by Pausanias (v. 17–19), or the relief decoration of the Sicyonian and Siphnian treasuries at Delphi.[21] The rich mythology of the land had long been explored and rehearsed by the poets, but the most immediate source for the average Greek would not have been the formal literary, but the tale told at mother's knee (there can be as many oral traditions as there are mouths to expound them) and the multitude of images around him and on almost everything he handled.[22]

The contrast with Geometric Greece is dramatic but the change was gradual and the easy art-historical explanation is to attribute it to the example of the east, or to say that the Greeks took from the east what they recognized would serve them to express their interest in narrative. The truth is subtly different. The east may have inspired Greece to develop her figurative arts in the eighth century but the idiom adopted, the Geometric, owed nothing to the east. When eastern styles do take effect and encourage, for instance, the detailed drawing of black-figure vases or the outline drawing styles or the Daedalic reliefs, they carry with them images of no narrative content whatever, only the animal friezes which are the banal surface-fillers of most seventh-century art and merely replace the Geometric meanders and zigzags, or static Daedalic frontality. The Geometric artist had managed better, and the narrative aspirations of Greek artists were best served where oriental influence was slightest, as on the painted and relief vases of Athens and the islands. Not until the sixth century were these orientalizing trappings fully shaken off and the artists were able to exploit for their narrative the slightly greater freedom offered by techniques which had

---

[20] H 50.   [21] H 19, 157–60.
[22] H 18, ch. 13; H 42; H 50; H 19.

60. Symposium, from an Athenian black-figure cup by the Heidelberg Painter. About 560 B.C. (Taranto Museum 110339; after *Arch. Rep.* 1960/1, 39; H 10, 27, no. 13bis.)

been suggested by the east. These too were not long to satisfy them. With the sixth century the artist-craftsman presents us with as varied a view of Greek story-telling as do the poets, and closer, perhaps, because less ambitious or consciously innovating, to the underlying narrative with its origins in the Dark Ages or before. Greek rulers were great propagandists, they used myth and religion to serve political ends, and they were served by poets and artists. Whatever the degree of literacy in Archaic Greece, which we may regard as considerable only by contrast with what went before, and however assiduous attenders the Greeks may have been of public performances, the more lasting and influential messages would have been conveyed visually, and there is more to learn from Greek narrative art than illustration of extant texts. (On narrative art see Plates Vol.)

Art is also an increasingly important source of information about contemporary life. Although genre scenes only become at all popular in the later Archaic period[23] it was customary for the actors of myth in art to be equipped in modern dress. We learn a great deal about behaviour and even about regalia in this way. To take an example from a subject inevitably popular on vases designed to serve a feast, from about 600 B.C. scenes show symposia, at first in a mythological setting, at which the guests recline on *klinai*. The practice seems to have been originally an eastern nomadic one but there is one exceptional example of it for an Assyrian king, and for some reason the Greeks adopted the practice enthusiastically. The layout of the symposium with couches round a room, three-legged side tables and the other gear for eating and drinking, become familiar from vases (fig. 60) long before

[23] H 18, ch. 12.

we are able to recognize the excavated plans of dining rooms.[24] The *klinai* themselves are depicted in detail and we distinguish a luxury variety with plank-like legs and a lighter one with turned legs, more like a high bed. Other exotic furniture is introduced at about this time – the folding stool (*diphros okladias*) from the east or Egypt, and later in the sixth century Sparta seems to have taken to Egyptian thrones with legs fashioned as whole lion legs rather than just with the lion-paw feet in the older eastern manner.[25]

It was the east, almost certainly, that introduced the use of perfumed oils. By the later sixth century the young man's oil bottle, strigil and sponge become as natural a part of his personal gear as in later days his pipe, spectacles and pocket book. The practice of oiling and scraping the skin is of uncertain antiquity. It is not a Homeric way of taking a bath or self-cleansing, nor is it eastern, and the strigil in its specially shaped bronze form is not met until the mid-sixth century. Earlier it might have been of reed (as reported at Sparta) or even like a sickle knife.[26] There had been small containers for oil in the Dark Ages, even, but at the end of the eighth century the smaller Protocorinthian *aryballoi* are the first of a long series of oil flasks, mainly for male use, and the oiling–scraping practice is likely to go back at least as far. The iris-scented oil of Corinth was known to Pliny (*HN* XIII. 2.1) and *hirinon* is painted on the rim of a late Archaic Athenian flask. Knowledge of other foreign oils and perfumes is implied by the copies of Lydian vessels (the so-called *lydia*) designed, we imagine, for Lydian *bakkaris*, and the clay copies of Egyptian *alabastra* (the Corinthian clay 'alabastron' has a different ancestry), both introduced in the sixth century.[27]

The production of the elegantly decorated aryballoi for perfumed oil was an important factor in the prosperity of Corinth's potters' quarter, though we can hardly say that they were necessarily a significant factor in that city's trade. But this sort of specialist production in the potters' quarter can be a useful indicator of trade in the wares themselves, in the materials they contained, and perhaps in other more important materials which they accompanied.[28] There were many other specialist workshops to serve the luxury market at home and abroad but the only products which we can trace with any success apart from the ubiquitous clay pottery are bronze vessels. Sparta and Corinth are prominent here but other studios can and will be recognized. The success they enjoyed may be gauged both from the dedications at the Greek sanctuaries and from the more remarkable pieces which travelled far beyond Greek lands – the famous Vix crater from the grave of a Celtic princess near

[24] H 39; H 34.
[26] H 17; H 6.
[28] G 10; G 34.

[25] H 63, 43–6, 15–18.
[27] G 4A; Semonides fr. 16 West.

Paris is the best known example,[29] or the many craters from Illyrian tombs. There was a brisk trade with the barbarian too, up the Adriatic into the Balkans and from the head of the Adriatic into Switzerland and central Europe.

The bronze vessel types which were exported are Greek in design and it is an accident of survival that the biggest and best are found outside Greece. The Greeks could think big for themselves too – Cypselus' big beaten gold statue of Zeus at Olympia (Strabo 378); the Samian six-talent crater with griffin protomes and seven-cubit bronze kneelers as support (Hdt. IV. 152); the silver crater with its iron base made by Glaucus of Chios for Alyattes to dedicate at Delphi (Hdt. I. 25); the life-size silver bull recovered by the French from beneath the Sacred Way at the same site.[30] The exotic and colossal were not for export only. The potters, however, sought their markets more deliberately. The lively production of column craters at Corinth must have been their response to an appreciative market in Etruria, but it was the Athenians who started to produce deliberate export models like the Tyrrhenian amphorae of the second quarter of the sixth century, while in the second half of the century some pottery owners, notably Nicosthenes, copied Etruscan shapes to decorate in the Athenian black-figure style for the Etruscan market. The Nicosthenic amphora had such a special appeal that virtually all examples went to Cerveteri. Other Etruscan shapes taken up for export were the *kyathos* (dipper), one-handled *kantharos* and deep one-handled cups.[31] Athens and Corinth are the prime exporters of painted pottery in the Archaic period, yet they were by no means the only, or even always the leading artistic centres of Greece. Other cities which were either more self-sufficient in food and materials, or which were engaged in handling rather than producing goods for trade (like Aegina, Chios) may have felt less need to develop an industry for the export of manufactured goods.

Of the ships in which trade was conducted we know all too little, and that from representations on vases or deductions about performance from remarks in texts. The warship powered by oar and, at need, by sail, is more familiar. Of the bireme, with two levels of oarsmen, there are no unequivocal representations until the sixth century. Then too we see the occasional merchantman, heavier, full-bodied vessels with and without oarsmen.[32] One seems threatened by a pirate bireme on an Attic cup (fig. 61).[33]

The trappings of war are better documented from pictures (fig. 62) and dedications at sanctuaries.[34] The regular hoplite panoply was

[29] C 94; A 7, 220–1.   [30] E 81.

[31] H 18, 36–7, 64–5.   [32] H 59; H 22, 53–5.

[33] H 21; H 22, 65–8; H 18, fig. 180.   [34] H 69; H 70, ch. 3; H 5.

61. A merchantman and a bireme, from an Athenian black-figure cup. About 520 B.C. (London, British Museum B 436; cf. H 21, pl. 5; C. T. Torr, *Ancient Ships* (1894) pl. 4.)

62. A hoplite, with Corinthian helmet, linen/leather corselet, greaves, hoplite shield and spear, from an Athenian black-figure vase by the Amasis Painter. About 540 B.C. (Kings Point, Schimmel Collection; after H 68, pl. 71 below; H 10, 67.)

devised by the mid-seventh century although many elements of it were in use far earlier. The phalanx depended for its efficiency on its discipline, and the hoplites depended for their safety more on their armour than their agility or even, often, their spearsmanship.[35] The Corinthian helmet best covered face and neck but was also hot and soundproof, which could prove a disadvantage, and there were other varieties developed in Greece – the miscalled Chalcidian, the more primitive Illyrian with open face, the Cretan which may be one of the earliest types and which was short in the neck and fairly open at front, and the East Greek with its strange peak. The Attic was lighter and less protective but had a neck-guard and often hinged cheek-pieces. Metallurgically even the earliest Corinthian one-piece helmets attest considerable technical skill. Most had short horsehair crests. Corselets were sheet metal, two-piece and calling them 'bell-corselets' describes well enough their shape which seems to have been inspired by central European armour.[36] After the mid-sixth century the linen corselet begins to appear, with shoulder pieces tied across the chest and flaps (*pteryges*) below the waist but it does not entirely replace the bell-corselet, which is itself adapted to carry flaps, until the fifth century, when other varieties too appear.

Greaves are clipped on to shins and there were other clip-on pieces for the upper arm, thighs and ankles though these must seldom have been worn and are very seldom shown on vases. The circular shield was clamped to the left forearm by a central armgrip (*porpax*) and a handgrip by the rim (*antilabe*); it was usually made of wood with bronze attachments and perhaps also covered with hide. The main offensive weapon was the thrusting spear, at its best equipped also with a pointed butt (*sauroter*) which could be used for the *coup de grâce* on a fallen foe. The long sword of Geometric type was slowly replaced by the shorter stabbing sword, and the slashing *kopis* or *machaira* is seen by the end of the Archaic period, but the sword was a decidedly secondary weapon for a hoplite and its prominence in art may be prompted by the heroic occasions on which it is shown in use. In the seventh century the hoplite may be shown carrying a second spear also, probably for throwing. From all this it can be seen that the equipping of a hoplite was a complicated and expensive matter and there can be little doubt that many a phalanx must have advanced with several underequipped members. The provision of the necessary metal by the state (in Classical Athens the city provided the basic shield and spear for veterans' orphans: *Ath. Pol.* 42.4) or acquisition of it by the individual presented a special economic problem, met and recognized in various ways, and perhaps hardly less significant than the social implications of reliance

[35] A 59.   [36] H 73.

in the field on a well-equipped or disciplined citizen army instead of aristocrat champions with rabble support.

Slingers, bowmen, cavalry and light-armed spearsmen were of course used, but irregularly, and it seems from the vases that a hoplite might ride to assembly point with a squire. Whether a chariot could be used in a similar manner is not known and it has become unfashionable to believe that chariots were ever used for serious matters in Archaic Greece, but only for racing and processions.[37] The introduction of Thracian riding dress and equipment (the light *pelta* shield) and of Scythian bowman's rig (the patterned track-suit, pointed cap and bow-case *gorytos*) to Athens in the second half of the sixth century can plausibly be explained by Pisistratus' north Greek interests, but they make no lasting contribution to the military scene.[38]

Almost all this we learn from pictures. At Olympia there is a good series of arms dedications and the Cretan armour has been discussed on pp. 226–7, but we are sadly short of material evidence for corselets and swords and, of course, bows. Fortunately some artists took pains with such details. The heroic duels which are the commonest subjects on vases left little occasion for studies of the phalanx itself, although Corinth provides one or two examples on vases of the mid-seventh century. (See Plates Vol. for these and other documents on warfare.) We turn to the poets[39] for a more personal view of fighting as a hoplite, from Archilochus' abandonment of his hoplite shield, always an encumbrance when being pursued, to Tyrtaeus' clarion call to engage the enemy standing 'foot to foot, shield to shield, crest to crest, helmet to helmet, chest to chest, grasping your sword or long spear' and remarking the wisdom for safety's sake of advancing shoulder to shoulder.

We seem to know much more of the religious life of the Greeks in the Archaic period through their literature but in fact much of our evidence even for newly inagurated festivals like the Great Panathenaea is late, and we do well to insist on the contemporary physical evidence for cult, and to remember what physical demands their gods made upon them. In most towns the only building larger than a one- or occasionally two-storied house would have been the temple and these were already reaching a formidable size in the seventh century, especially in the East Greek world, while the sixth century has Ionian tyrants planning and building some of the largest temples ever to be seen in Greece. The command of cheap labour implied by these structures is of considerable social importance, as has been remarked in the preceding section of this chapter, and there must have been times when construction work

[37] H 40.   [38] H 13; H 75.
[39] H 69, ch. 8.

occupied the attention if not the hands of the majority of a city population. Such ostentatious piety was not confined to home, however, and national sanctuaries such as Delphi and Olympia attracted dedications of Treasuries, small temple-like buildings given by cities as thankofferings. These appear first in the first half of the sixth century, Delphi enjoying homeland dedications, Olympia ones especially from the western Greeks who must have been influenced by the publicity value of the sanctuary. These small buildings are architecturally lavish, and often more finely decorated with sculpture than the larger *oikoi* for the gods, yet they seem to have served no practical purpose except as repositories for offerings, not always of the dedicating state.[40]

Popular minor dedications of the Geometric period had been clay or bronze figures of animals, a type of offering found more often now in smaller sanctuaries. The aristocratic offerings of tripods at Olympia and Delphi continue through the period of the tyrants, but the dedications are often now more explicit in their form – spoil from a victory – or in the inscriptions which now normally accompany major works and which record victories over fellow Greeks, or a tithe from a lucky deal, or simply thanks for services rendered. In a rather different category are the marble youths and maidens, *kouroi* and *korai*, which represent more permanent service to the deity than flesh and blood.[41] These are works for the local rather than national sanctuaries, and we have seen them to be as vital an expression of the new monumental arts of Greece as the new stone temples with their architectural orders had been.

A rather different opportunity for personal ostentation in a public setting was offered by burial monuments.[42] The great funerals depicted on the Geometric grave vases, with massed mourners and processions, seem to have given place to more modest ceremonial but the tendency to extravagance needed constantly to be curbed by legislation, in Athens from the time of Solon on. The actual disposal of the dead, by inhumation or burning, remained comparatively modest, as did the accompanying offerings, and there are few exceptions, even in the richest sixth-century burials of Athens, where jewellery or elaborate furniture is also interred. It was a different matter above ground. Over the rich Geometric graves of Athens there had been large painted vases and the practice did not entirely die out, but generally the markers for early Greek graves were no more than rough stone slabs. During the seventh century some of these may carry relief figures representing the dead, but the evidence for this is not totally convincing, and when Athens' cemeteries start sporting well-cut stelai around 600 they are austerely decorated. By then, however, the *kouros* was being used as a

[40] H 38; E 116; E 234, 97–104.   [41] H 62; H 64.
[42] H 51, chs. 5, 9, 12.

grave marker in the islands and in the sixth century this practice becomes general, with *korai* less commonly serving graves of women, while the stelai of Athens and some other parts of Greece carry relief figures representing the dead in an idealized youthfulness, only later differentiated by attributes of an athlete, or warrior, or an older man with his stick and dog.[43] The Athens stelai, and a few elsewhere, were also topped by sphinxes and may carry painted or relief subsidiary panels. They are expensive sculptural masterpieces, and the pride in them felt by the living is attested by several epitaphs which name the sponsor of the monument, as well as the dead and his near kin. Artists barely lag behind in seizing the opportunity for proud advertisement on the commemorative monuments, be they dedicatory or funereal, and the inscribed bases are our prime source for names in a period still poorly served by the records of later writers on art.[44]

The hard ware for the good life may have been mainly inspired by foreign arts, as we have seen, but behaviour was not. Here again vase scenes come to our aid.[45] The sixth century saw the beginnings of formal dramatic presentations developing from the choruses and dithyrambs of earlier years. This is no place for considering the early history of the Greek theatre – not even its physical setting for which at the best we may assume earth slopes and wooden stands – but humbler levels of entertainment are as well or better attested even than the simpler cult practices, and there are points at which the informal secular touch the more formal religious. In Corinth, then Athens, and to a lesser degree other cities in the first half of the sixth century, the vases present popular entertainers whom we call komasts, usually dressed in a close-fitting and possibly padded tunic, but sometimes naked and sometimes dancing with women, dressed or naked, in what was clearly a jolly bottom-slapping display (fig. 63). In the mid century their behaviour and appearance come closer to those of satyrs, Dionysus' familiars, who in their usual form are also inventions of the early sixth century. The occasion may be a simple, rowdy enactment of the Dionysiac rout accompanying drunken Hephaestus back to Olympus, but we are witnessing a popular form of the play-acting of divine occasions which will soon establish in a more formal manner the satyr plays and the dramatic performances which attend Dionysiac festivals. Here perhaps we are after all considering the beginnings of the Greek theatre more directly than in traditions about Arion and others.

It is only really with the late Archaic period that the finds and representations combine to offer a very full account of many aspects of private life. The townscape in which a people lives can both determine

[43] F 30A; H 19, ch. 8. [44] F 16.
[45] A 68, part 1; E 226.

63. Komast dancer from a Corinthian black-figure plate, from Corinth. About 580–570 B.C. (Copenhagen, National Museum 1631; *Corpus Vasorum Antiquorum* Copenhagen II pl. 90. 4b; E 226, n. 38.)

and reveal much of its way of life and the Athens of Pisistratus was beginning to take a form which was to be the pattern of all Classical cities. Other places may have been similarly developed – Corinth, the colonial cities – but we hear and see far less about them, and the intended layout of Smyrna which had been thwarted by Alyattes at the start of the sixth century shows what an Ionian city may have looked like even fifty years earlier. In Athens the acropolis had become devoted to the service of the gods, though temporarily occupied by a tyrant and his family, and carried one major Doric temple, as lavishly decorated with architectural sculpture as any in mainland Greece, as well as smaller, equally decorative cult buildings. There was a small columned *propylon* but the walls were still probably just the Mycenaean, reinforced. Dedications of statuary by private citizens begin to cluster along the paths on the rock.[46] In the lower town an area in the agora had been cleared of houses and reserved for the Assembly, theatrical displays and public business, and was taking shape as an administrative area flanked by public buildings on the west – a probable Council House for the Solonian 400, the pre-prytaneum town house, a temple of Apollo Patrous.[47] Beyond lay the potters' quarter, on the way to the Dipylon Gate and the line of Athens' probable walls. New fountain houses adorned and served the city and its citizens, businessmen whose affairs led to the furthermost corners of the Mediterranean, artists who were

[46] F 26.   [47] F 33.

already setting standards for Greece to follow, poets and politicians who were to shape the culture of the Classical world.

Much of this, in Athens and elsewhere, is directly attributable to the patronage of an aristocratic family or a tyrant, sustained by cheap or slave labour. On the other hand, where the labour was cheap but the inspiration lacking it hardly required constitutional restraint to ensure an austere life style, although even Sparta seems, in material detail, not so very pallid a version of other Archaic Greek towns.[48] But in the Athens of less than 200 years before only whispers of such cosmopolitan activity disturbed the quiet tenor of the county-town of Attica, and even mid-sixth-century Athens was by no means a dominant power, politically or militarily, in Archaic Greece. Progress had been sudden, exciting, and held promise of the ability to face greater challenges, to compass new achievements.[49]

[48] E 161; E 176A.
[49] Several topics in this section are further discussed, and illustrated, in the Plates Volume.

CHRONOLOGICAL CHART

This chart has been compiled by the editors with the help of the authors and of Dr N. J. Richardson (Literature).

A full alphabetical list of Greek colonies with their foundation dates appears at the end of chapter 37.

464

GREECE

MAINLAND EXCEPT ATHENS

c. 740–720 1st Messenian War
736 last Messenian victor at Olympia
720 Orsippus (Megarian) victor at Olympia
716 first Spartan victor at Olympia [Lelantine War]

ATHENS AND EAST GREECE
682/1 first annual archon, Athens

676 Eleans still in charge of Ol. Games
669/8 Argos defeats Sparta at Hysiae
668 Pheidon in charge of Ol. Games
c. 664 first naval battle; Corinth v. Corcyra
657 Cypselus seizes power at Corinth
c. 655 Orthagoras seizes power at Sicyon
c. 650 first Temenid king of Macedones

648 Myron of Sicyon wins chariot race at Olympia

c. 650–620 2nd Messenian War

c. 636–632 Cylon
c. 625 Periander succeeds at Corinth
621/20 Dracon
Athenian war with Mytilene

c. 600 Cleisthenes succeeds at Sicyon

EGYPT

747–716 Py (Piankhy)

c. 720–715 Bocchoris

c. 715–702 Shabako

c. 702–690 Shebitku

690–664 Taharqa

664–656 Tantamani (Upper Egypt)

DYNASTY XXVI
664–610 Psammetichus I

Greeks established at Naucratis

610–594 Necho II

THE EAST

ASSYRIAN EMPIRE
744–27 Tiglath-Pileser III

726–722 Shalmaneser
722 Samaria destroyed by the Assyrians
720 Hamath destroyed by Assyrians
721–705 Sargon II
715 Revolt in Cilicia quelled
712 Yamani at Ashdod
709 Record of Cypriot tribute to Sargon II
704–681 Sennacherib
c. 700 break in occupation at Al Mina

ANATOLIA

696 Revolt in Cilicia quelled; Tarsus destroyed
696/5 Destruction of Gordium by Cimmerians; death of Midas
680–669 Esarhaddon c. 680–640 Gyges
673/2 Esarhaddon's prism

668–626 Ashurbanipal
664 fall of Egyptian Thebes to Ashurbanipal

648 fall of Babylon to Ashurbanipal

BABYLONIAN EMPIRE
612 fall of Nineveh to Babylon
c. 610–560 Alyattes

605–562 Nebuchadrezzar
605 Nebuchadrezzar defeats Necho II at Carchemish

750

700

650

600

COLONIES	ARCHITECTURE AND ART	LITERATURE	
		[The Homeric poems]	750
c. 750 Pithecusa founded			
734 Naxos (Sicily) founded			
733 Syracuse founded		730 Eumelus fl.	
	c. 725 first stone temple of Artemis Orthia, Sparta		
c. 720 Sybaris founded	720–690 Early Protocorinthian		
706 Taras founded	Drerus bronze figures		
Chalcis and Eretria begin colonization of Chalcidice			
Colonization in Hellespont and Propontis begins			
Pontus known to Greeks			
	c. 700 first stone temple of Apollo, Corinth	700 Hesiod fl.	700
	700–600 'Daedalic' style of sculpture		
	700–675 Early Protoattic		
688 Gela founded	690–670 Middle Protocorinthian I		
679 Locri Epizephyrii founded	675–650 Middle Protoattic	675–640 Archilochus fl.	
668 (or 659) Byzantium founded	670–650 Middle Protocorinthian II		
657 Istrus founded			
	650–640 Late Protocorinthian	650 Terpander fl.	650
c. 650 Thasos founded	640–625 Transitional Corinthian	650 Callinus fl.	
Intensive colonization of Pontus begins	650–620 Late Protoattic	650 Semonides fl.	
647 Olbia founded		640 Tyrtaeus fl.	
Colonization by Corinth in N.W. Greece and Illyris			
c. 640 Colaeus' voyage to Tartessus	Start of Athenian black-figure		
632 Cyrene founded	625–595 Early Corinthian	630–625 Mimnermus fl.	
	First marble kouroi	Alcman fl.	
	First coinage in Lydia		
c. 600 Massalia founded	c. 600 temple of Hera, Olympia		600
c. 600 Panticapaeum founded			

	THE EAST	EGYPT	GREECE
600	586 fall of Jerusalem to Babylon	594–589 Psammetichus II 592 Nubian expedition 589–570 Apries	c. 600 Smyrna destroyed 595–590 1st Sacred War 594/3 Solon archon and legislator c. 585 death of Periander c. 583 end of tyranny at Corinth 582/80 Damasias archon 582 Cleisthenes wins chariot race at Olympia 581/80 Isthmian Games founded 580 Elis appoints second judge at Ol. Games 573 Nemean Games founded 566/5 reorganization of Panathenaea
550	556–539 Nabonidus c. 560–546 Croesus PERSIAN EMPIRE 559–530 Cyrus 546 Persians take Cyprus c. 545 Persians take Sardis 539 Persians take Babylon	570–526 Amasis	c. 560 alliance Sparta–Tegea c. 560 first tyranny of Pisistratus 556/5 Chilon eponymous ephor, Sparta 556/5 end of tyranny at Sicyon development of Boeotian League 546 Sparta defeats Argos 546/5 battle of Pallene and establishment of tyranny in Athens
	530–522 Cambyses 522–486 Darius	525 Persians take Egypt	528/7 death of Pisistratus 525/4 Cleisthenes archon 525 or 515 Lygdamis of Naxos deposed 524/3 death of Polycrates
500			510 Hippias expelled from Athens c. 506 Athens defeats Chalcis and Boeotians

600   550   500

COLONIES

c. 600–550 Siris destroyed

c. 580 Pentathlus fails at Lilybaeum
580 Acragas founded
571–555 Phalaris of Acragas

Athenian colonization in Hellespontine region
c. 550 Camarina revolt against Syracuse

c. 540 battle of Alalia

c. 514–512 Dorieus fails at R. Cinyps
510 Sybaris destroyed by Croton
c. 510 Dorieus fails at Heraclea

ARCHITECTURE AND ART

595–575 Middle Corinthian

c. 580 temple of Artemis, Corcyra
c. 580–570 first major Athena temple, Athens Acropolis

Komast cups, Sophilos
c. 570 François Vase
575–550 Late Corinthian
c. 565 first coinage in Aegina ('turtles')
c. 560 first coinage in Athens, Corinth
c. 560 Sicyonian Treasury, Delphi
c. 560 first dipteron, Samos

Little Master cups
c. 550 temple of Artemis, Ephesus, begun
Amasis Painter
c. 550 first coinage in western colonies
548 temple of Apollo, Delphi, destroyed
Exekias
c. 540 second temple of Apollo, Corinth
c. 540 first dipteron, Samos, destroyed
Invention of red-figure

Vix crater

525 Siphnian Treasury, Delphi
c. 520 'Pisistratid' temple of Athena, Athens
'Alcmaeonid' temple of Apollo, Delphi
c. 520 Athens 'owl' coinage begins
temple of Apollo, Eretria
temple of Aphaea, Aegina

LITERATURE

610–575 Sappho fl.
610–575 Alcaeus fl.
600–575 Solon fl.
585 Thales fl.

Stesichorus fl.
570–550 Anaximander fl.

550–530 Theognis fl.

545 Anaximenes fl.
540 Hipponax fl.
540–520 Ibycus fl.
534/3 first tragedy in Athens City Dionysia (Thespis)

575–490 Anacreon
556–468 Simonides
570–475 Xenophanes
525–500 Pythagoras fl.

500 Hecataeus fl.
500 Heraclitus fl.

BIBLIOGRAPHY

ABBREVIATIONS

AJA   *American Journal of Archaeology*
AJP   *American Journal of Philology*
Anal. Or.   Analecta Orientalia
Anat. Stud.   *Anatolian Studies*
Anc. Macedonia I   *Ancient Macedonia* I: Papers read at the first International Symposium held in Thessaloniki 26–29 August 1968. Institute for Balkan Studies. Thessalonica, 1970
Anc. Macedonia II   *Ancient Macedonia* II: Papers read at the second International Symposium held in Thessaloniki 19–24 August 1973. Institute for Balkan Studies. Thessalonica, 1977
Annales du Service   *Annales du Service des Antiquités de l'Egypte*
Annali Ist. Ital. Num.   *Annali dell' Istituto italiano di numismatica*
Ann. Arch. Arabes Syr.   *Annales archéologiques arabes de Syrie*
Ant. Class.   *Antiquité Classique*
Arch. Anz.   *Archäologischer Anzeiger*
Arch. Class.   *Archeologia Classica*
Arch. Delt.   ᾽Αρχαιολογικὸν Δελτίον
ARW   *Archiv für Religionswissenschaft*, Freiburg
Ath. Mitt.   *Athenische Mitteilungen. Mitteilungen des deutschen archäologischen Instituts, Athenische Abteilung*
Atti e Mem. Soc. Magna Grecia   *Atti e Memorie della Società Magna Grecia*

Bul. Ark.   *Buletin Arkeologjik*, Tirana
BAR   *British Archaeological Reports*
BCH   *Bulletin de correspondance hellénique*
BICS   *Bulletin of the Institute of Classical Studies of the University of London*
Boll. d'Arte   *Bollettino d'Arte*
BSA   *Annual of the British School of Archaeology at Athens*
BASOR   *Bulletin of the American Schools of Oriental Research*
Bull. Arch. Maroc.   *Bulletin d'archéologie marocaine*
Bull. Inst. fr. Caire   *Bulletin de l'Institut français d'archéologie orientale, Le Caire*
BUSS   *Buletin për shkencat shoqërore*, Tirana
BUST   *Buletin i Universitetit Shtetëror të Tiranës*, Seria shkencat shoqërore, Tirana

CAH   *The Cambridge Ancient History*
Calif. Stud. Class. Ant.   *California Studies in Classical Antiquity*
Cl. Phil.   *Classical Philology*
CQ   *Classical Quarterly*
CR   *Classical Review*
CRAI   *Comptes-rendues de l'Académie des inscriptions et belles-lettres*

Dial. di Arch.   *Dialoghi di Archeologia*

Eph. Arch.   Ἐφημερὶς Ἀρχαιολογική
Ep. Chron.   Ἠπειρωτικὰ Χρονικά

Harv. Theol. Rev.   *Harvard Theological Review*
Hist. Zeitschr.   *Historische Zeitschrift*

IEJ   *Israel Exploration Journal*

JDAI   *Jahrbuch des deutschen archäologischen Instituts*
JEA   *Journal of Egyptian Archaeology*
JHS   *Journal of Hellenic Studies*
JNES   *Journal of Near Eastern Studies*
Journ. of Philol.   *Journal of Philology*

Kr. Chr.   Κρητικὰ Χρονικά

MAG   *Mitteilungen der Anthropologischen Gesellschaft in Wien*
Marb. W. Pr.   *Marburger Winckelmannsprogram*
Mat. po Arch. Rossy   *Materialy po Arkheologii Rossy*
Mél. d'arch. et d'hist.   *Mélanges d'archéologie et d'histoire*
Mél Ecole franç. Rome   *Mélanges de l'Ecole française de Rome*
Mém Acad. Roy. Belg.   *Mémoires de l'Académie royale de Belgique*
Mon. Ant.   *Monumenti Antichi*

Num. Chron.   *Numismatic Chronicle*
Not. Scav.   *Notizie degli scavi di antichità*

Op. Arch.   *Opuscula Archaeologica*
Opusc. Ath.   *Opuscula Atheniensia*

PAE   Πρακτικὰ τῆς Ἀρχαιολογικῆς Ἑταιρείας
Phil. Trans. Royal Soc., London   *Philosophical Transactions of the Royal Society, London*
Präh. Zeit.   *Prähistorische Zeitschrift*
Proc. Amer. Philos. Soc.   *Proceedings of the American Philosophical Society*
P–W   Pauly–Wissowa–Kroll–Mittelhaus, *Real-Encyclopädie der classischen Altertumswissenschaft*

RDAC   *Report of the Department of Antiquities, Cyprus*
REA   *Revue des Etudes Anciennes*
REG   *Revue des Etudes Grecques*
Rend. Accad. Lincei   *Rendiconti della Accademia nazionale dei Lincei*

Rev. Arch. Revue Archéologique
Rev. Phil. Revue de philologie, de littérature et d'histoire anciennes
Riv. Stor. dell'Ant. Rivista storica dell'antichità
Riv. Stor. Ital. Rivista storica Italiana
Riv. Stud. Liguri Rivista di studi liguri
Röm Mitt. Römische Mitteilungen. Mitteilungen des Deutschen archäologischen Instituts, Römische Abteilung

SA Studia Albanica
SIMA Studies in Mediterranean Archaeology

TAPA Transactions and Proceedings of the American Philological Association

ZÄS Zeitschrift für Ägyptische Sprache
Zeit. Pap. Epigr. Zeitschrift für Papyrologie und Epigraphik
Zeitschr. deutsch. Morgenländische Gesellschaft Zeitschrift der deutschen morgenländischen Gesellschaft

BIBLIOGRAPHY

A. GENERAL

1. Anderson, J. K. *Ancient Greek Horsemanship.* Berkeley–Los Angeles, 1961
2. Andrewes, A. *The Greek Tyrants.* London, 1956
3. Aymard, A. 'Mercenariat et histoire grecque', *Annales de l'Est* 22 (1959) 16–27
4. Bechtel, F. *Die griechischen Dialekte* I. Berlin, 1921; reprint 1963
5. Beloch, K. J. *Griechische Geschichte.* 2nd edn. Strassburg–Berlin, 1912–27
6. Berve, H. *Die Tyrannis bei den Griechen* I–II. Munich, 1967. With full bibliography
7. Boardman, J. *The Greeks Overseas.* London, 1980
8. Bonner, R. J. and Smith, G. *The Administration of Justice from Homer to Aristotle.* Chicago, 1930–8
9. Bowra, C. M. *Greek Lyric Poetry.* 2nd edn. Oxford, 1961
10. Brunt, P. A. 'Athenian settlements abroad', *Ancient Society and Institutions. Studies presented to V. Ehrenberg*, 71–92. Oxford, 1966
11. Burn, A. R. *The Lyric Age of Greece.* London, 1960
12. Bury, J. B. and Meiggs, R. *A History of Greece.* 4th edn. London, 1975
13. Busolt, G. *Griechische Geschichte.* 2nd edn. Gotha, 1893–1904
14. Busolt, G. and Swoboda, H. *Griechische Staatskunde* I–II. Munich, 1920–6
15. Collitz, H. and Bechtel, F. *Sammlung der griechischen Dialekt-Inschriften* I–IV. Göttingen, 1884–1915
16. Diller, A. *The Tradition of the minor Greek Geographers.* Lancaster, Pennsylvania, 1952
17. Diller, A. 'The authors named Pausanias', *TAPA* 86 (1955) 268–78
18. Drews, R. 'The first tyrants in Greece', *Historia* 21 (1972) 129–44
19. Dunbabin, T. J. *The Greeks and their Eastern Neighbours.* London, 1957
20. Farnell, L. R. *Cults of the Greek States.* Oxford, 1909

21. Forrest, W. G. 'Two chronographic notes', *CQ* 63 (1969) 95–110
21A. Forrest, W. G. *The Emergence of Greek Democracy.* New York–Toronto, 1966
22. Frazer, J. G. 'The prytaneum, the temple of Vesta, the Vestals, perpetual fire', *Journ. of Philol.* 14 (1885) 145–72
23. Friedländer, P. and Hoffleit, H. B. *Epigrammata.* Berkeley, 1948
23A. Frisk, H. *Griechisches etymologisches Wörterbuch* I–II. Heidelberg, 1953–70
24. Gomme, A. W., Andrewes, A. and Dover, K. J. *A Historical Commentary on Thucydides* IV. Oxford, 1970
25. Grote, G. *History of Greece* III. London, 1888
26. Gschnitzer, F. *Abhängige Orte in Griechischen Altertum.* Munich, 1958
27. Guarducci, M. *Epigrafia Greca* I. Rome, 1967
28. Güngerich, R. *Dionysius Byzantinus.* Berlin, 1927
29. Halliday, W. R. *The Greek Questions of Plutarch.* Oxford, 1928
30. Hammond, N. G. L. *A History of Greece.* 2nd edn. Oxford, 1967
31. Hammond, N. G. L. *Studies in Greek History.* Oxford, 1973
32. Hammond, N. G. L. *Migrations and Invasions in Greece and adjacent Areas.* New Jersey, 1976
33. Helm, R. *Die Chronik des Hieronymus. (Die griech. Schriftsteller der ersten drei Jahrh., Eusebius* 7). Berlin, 1956
34. Hoffmann, O. *Die griechischen Dialekte* I, 35–99. Göttingen, 1891
35. How, W. W. and Wells, J. *A Commentary on Herodotus.* Oxford, 1912
35A. Jeffery, L. H. 'Comments on some archaic Greek inscriptions', *JHS* 69 (1949) 25–38
36. Jeffery, L. H. *The Local Scripts of Archaic Greece.* Oxford, 1961
37. Jeffery, L. H. *Archaic Greece, the City-States c. 700–500 B.C.* London, 1976
38. Kirsten, E. *Die griechische Polis als historischesgeographisches Problem des Mittelmeerraumes.* Bonn, 1956
39. Kirsten, E. and Kraiker, W. *Griechenlandkunde.* 5th edn. Heidelberg, 1967
39A. Hooker, J. T. *Mycenaean Greece.* London, Henley and Boston, 1977
40. Larsen, J. A. O. *Greek federal States.* Oxford, 1968
41. Matthews, V. J. *Panyassis of Halicarnassus.* Leiden, 1974
42. Meyer, Ed. *Forschungen zur alten Geschichte* I–II. Halle, 1892–9
43. Meyer, Ed. *Theopomps Hellenika.* Halle, 1909
44. Meyer, Ed. *Geschichte des Altertums* III. 2nd edn, ed. H. E. Stier. Stuttgart, 1937
45. Moretti, L. *Richerche sulle leghe greche.* Rome, 1962
46. Murray, O. *Early Greece.* London, 1980
47. Nilsson, M. P. *Homer and Mycenae.* London, 1933
48. Page D. L. *History and the Homeric Iliad.* Berkeley, 1959
49. Parke, H. W. *The Oracles of Zeus.* Oxford, 1967
50. Parke, H. W. and Wormell, D. E. W. *The Delphic Oracle* I–II. Oxford, 1956
51. Parry, A. (ed.) *The Making of Homeric Verse: The Collected Papers of Milman Parry.* London, 1971
52. Pfeiffer, R. *Callimachus* I (1949), II (1953). Oxford
53. Philippson, A. and Kirsten, E. *Die griechischen Landschaften* I–III. Frankfurt am Main, 1950–9

54. *Princeton Encyclopaedia of Classical Sites*, ed. R. Stilwell. Princeton, 1976
55. Pritchett, W. K. *Ancient Greek Military Practices* Part 1 (University of California Publications in Classical Studies 7). Berkeley, 1971 (Reissued in 1974 as *The Greek State at War* Part 1)
56. Schoene, A. *Eusebi chronichorum libri duo. Edidit A. Schoene.* 1875-6
57. Schmitt, R. *Einführung in die griechischen Dialekte.* Darmstadt, 1977
58. Schwyzer, E. *Dialectorum Graecarum exempla epigraphica potiora.* Leipzig, 1923, reprint 1960
59. Snodgrass, A. M. 'The hoplite reform and history', *JHS* 85 (1965) 110-22
60. Snodgrass, A. M. 'An historical Homeric society?', *JHS* 94 (1974) 114-25
61. Snodgrass, A. M. *Archaic Greece.* London, 1980
62. Starr, C. G. 'The early Greek city-state', *Parola del Passato* 12 (1957) 97-108
63. Starr, C. G. *The Origins of Greek Civilization 1100-650 B.C.* New York, 1961
64. Thumb, A. and Scherer, A. *Handbuch der griechischen Dialekte* II. Heidelberg, 1959
65. Ventris, M. and Chadwick, J. *Documents in Mycenaean Greek.* 1st edn. Cambridge, 1956 (2nd edn. by J. Chadwick, Cambridge, 1973)
66. Wade-Gery, H. T. *Essays in Greek History.* Oxford, 1958
67. Wallace, M. B. 'Early Greek proxenoi', *The Phoenix* 24 (1970) 189-208
68. Webster, T. B. L. *The Greek Chorus.* London, 1970
69. Wehrli, F. *Die Schule des Aristoteles.* 2nd edn. Basel–Stuttgart, 1969
70. West, M. L. *Early Greek Philosophy and the Orient.* Oxford, 1971
71. West, M. L. *Hesiod: Theogony.* Oxford, 1971
72. West, M. L. *Hesiod: Works and Days.* Oxford, 1978

B. THE EAST, EGYPT AND CYPRUS

I. THE EAST

1. Aharoni, Y. 'Hebrew inscriptions from Arad', *Yediot* 30 (1966) 32-8
2. Aistleitner, J. *Wörterbuch der ugaritischen Sprache.* Berlin, 1963
3. Astour, M. C. *Hellenosemitica, an Ethnic and Cultural Study in West Semitic Impact on Mycenaean Greece.* Leiden, 1965
4. Barnett, R. D. 'Karatepe, the key to Hittite hieroglyphs', *Anat. Stud.* 3 (1953) 53-95
5. Barnett, R. D. 'Mopsos', *JHS* 73 (1953) 141-3
6. Bean, G. E. *Turkey's Southern Shore.* London, 1968
7. Bean, G. E. *Lycian Turkey.* London, 1978
8. Bikai, P. M. 'Tyre: Report of an excavation', Ph.D. dissertation, Berkeley, California, 1976
9. Bing, J. D. 'Tarsus: a forgotten colony of Lindos', *JNES* 30 (1971) 99-109
10. Birmingham, J. 'Surface finds from various sites (in Anatolia)', *Anat. Stud.* 14 (1964) 29-33
11. Blumenthal, E. *Die altgriechische Siedlungskolonisation im Mittelmeerraum unter besondere Berücksichtigung der Südküste Kleinasiens.* Tübingen, 1963

12. Boardman, J. 'Tarsus, Al Mina and Greek chronology', *JHS* 85 (1965) 5–15

13. Boardman, J. Review of Ploug, *Sūkās* II, *Gnomon* 47 (1975) 427–8

14. Borger, R. *Die Inschriften Asarhaddons Königs von Assyrien*. Graz, 1956

15. Coldstream, J. N. Review of Riis, *Sūkās* I and Ploug, *Sūkās* II, *AJA* 79 (1975) 155–6

16. Cross, F. M. 'An interpretation of the Nora stone', *BASOR* 208 (1972) 13–19

17. Donner, H. and Röllig, W. *Kanaanäische und aramäische Inschriften* I–III. Wiesbaden, 1962–4

18. Downey, G. *A history of Antioch*. Princeton, 1961

19. Dussaud, R. *Topographie historique de la Syrie antique et médiévale*. Paris, 1927

20. Edwards, G. P. and R. B. 'Red letters and Phoenician writing', *Kadmos* 13 (1974) 48–57

21. Forrer, E. *Die Provinzeinteilung des assyrischen Reiches*. Leipzig, 1920

22. Frankfort, H. *The Art and Architecture of the Ancient Orient*. Harmondsworth, 1954

23. Gadd, C. J. 'Inscribed prisms of Sargon II from Nimrud', *Iraq* 16 (1954) 173–201

24. Gadd, C. J. 'The Harran inscriptions of Nabonidus', *Anat. Stud.* 8 (1958) 35–92

25. Garbini, G. 'Tarso e Gen.10.4', *Bibbia e Oriente* (Genoa, 1965), 13–19

26. Gjerstad, Einar 'The stratification of Al Mina (Syria) and its chronological evidence', *Acta Archaeologica* 45 (1974) 107–23

27. Goldman, H. *Excavations at Gözlü küle, Tarsus* III: *The Iron Age*. Princeton, 1963

28. Gomme, A. W. 'The legend of Cadmus and the logographoi', *JHS* 33 (1913) 53–72, 223–45

29. Grayson, A. K. *Assyrian and Babylonian Chronicles*. Locust Valley, New York, 1975

30. Harper, R. F. *Assyrian and Babylonian Letters belonging to the Kouyunjik Collections of the British Museum*. Chicago, 1892–1914

31. Heidel, A. 'The octagonal Sennacherib prism in the Iraq Museum', *Sumer* 9 (1953) 117–88

32. Hereward, D. 'Inscriptions from Pamphylia and Isauria', *JHS* 78 (1958) 56–77

33. Hoepfner, W. 'Topographische Forschungen', *Ergänzungsband zu den Tituli Asiae Minoris* 5. Öst. Akad. Wiss. Phil. Hist. Klasse, Denkschriften 106, Vienna, 1972

34. Jean, Ch.-F. and Hoftijzer, J. *Dictionnaire des inscriptions sémitiques de l'ouest*. Leiden, 1965

35. Johns, C. H. W. *Assyrian Doomsday Book*. Leipzig, 1901

36. Karst, J. (ed.) *Eusebius, Armenische Chronik*. Leipzig, 1911

37. Keil, J. 'Das Problem der ältesten griechischen Kolonisation Kilikiens', *Mitt. des Vereines Klassischer Philologen in Wien* 3 (1926) 9–18

38. Kent, R. G. *Old Persian Grammar*. 2nd edn. New Haven, 1953

39. Kohler, J. and Ungnad, A. *Assyrische Rechtsurkunden*. Leipzig, 1913

40. Kruse, G. 'Mopsos', P–W s.v.
41. Langdon, S. and Zehnpfund, R. *Die neubabylonischen Königsinschriften.* Leipzig, 1912
42. Lie, A. G. *The inscriptions of Sargon II, king of Assyria.* I. *The Annals.* Paris, 1929
43. Luckenbill, D. D. *The Annals of Sennacherib.* Chicago, 1924
44. Luckenbill, D. D. *Ancient Records of Assyria and Babylonia* I–II. Chicago, 1926–7
45. Lyon, D. G. *Keilschrifttexte Sargons Königs von Assyrien.* Leipzig, 1883
46. Magie, D. *Roman Rule in Asia Minor.* Princeton, 1950
47. Maluquer de Motes, J. 'Nuevas orientaciones en el problema de Tartessos', *Primer symposium de Preistoria peninsular*, 273–301. Pamplona, 1960
48. Masson, E. *Recherches sur les plus anciens emprunts sémitiques en grec.* Paris, 1967
49. Mazzarino, S. *Fra oriente e occidente.* Florence, 1947
50. Naveh, J. 'A Hebrew letter from the seventh century B.C.', *IEJ* 10 (1960) 129–39
51. Naveh, J. 'More Hebrew inscriptions from Meṣad Ḥashavyahu', *IEJ* 12 (1962) 27–32
52. Naveh, J. 'The excavations at Meṣad Ḥashavyahu – preliminary report', *IEJ* 12 (1962) 89–113
53. Nylander, C. *Ionians in Pasargadae.* Acta Universitatis Upsaliensis, Boreas 1. Uppsala, 1970
54. Olmstead, A. T. 'The text of Sargon's Annals', *American Journal of Semitic Languages and Literature* 47 (1930) 259–80
55. Parpola, S. *Neo-Assyrian toponyms.* Kevelaer, 1970.
56. Peckham, J. B. 'The Nora inscription', *Orientalia* 41 (1972) 457–68
57. Piepkorn, A. C. *Historical Prism Inscriptions of Ashurbanipal* 1. Chicago, 1953
58. Ploug, G. *Sūkās* II. Copenhagen, 1973
59. Pritchard, J. B. (ed.) *Ancient Near Eastern Texts relating to the Old Testament* 3rd edn. Princeton, 1969
60. Ras el Basit: Reports on the excavations: P. Courbin, *Rev. Arch.* 1974, 174–8; *Ann. Arch. Arabes Syr.* 22 (1972) 45–61; 23 (1973), 25–38; 25 (1975), 59–71; *Archéologia* 116 (1978) 48–62
61. Reinhold, M. *History of purple as a status symbol in antiquity* (= *Latomus* Coll. 116). Brussels, 1970
62. Renan, E. 'Notice sur huit fragments de patères de bronze portant des inscriptions phéniciennes très-anciennes', *Journal des Savants* 1877, 487–94
63. Riis, P. J. *Sūkās* I. Copenhagen, 1970
64. Saggs, H. W. 'The Nimrud Letters, 1952 – Part VI', *Iraq* 25 (1963) 70–80
65. Schneider, K. 'purpura' P–W s.v.
66. Smith, S. *Babylonian historical Texts relating to the Capture and Downfall of Babylon.* London, 1924
67. von Soden, W. *Grundriss der akkadischen Grammatik* (Anal. Or. 33; Rome, 1952).

68. Stamm, J. J. *Die akkadische Namengebung* (= Mitt. der vorderas.-aegypt. Gesellschaft 44, 1939)

68A. Streck, M. *Assurbanipal und die letzten assyrischen Könige bis zum Untergange Ninevehs* I–III. Leipzig, 1916

69. Sznycer, M. 'L'inscription phénicienne de Tekke, près de Cnossos', *Kadmos* 18 (1979) 89–93.

70. Tadmor, H. 'The campaigns of Sargon II of Assur', *Journal of Cuneiform Studies* 12 (1958) 22–42, 77–100

71. Tadmor, H. 'Fragments of an Assyrian stele of Sargon II' *Atiqot*, English series 9–10 (1971) 192–7

72. Taylor, J. du Plat. 'The Cypriot and Syrian pottery from Al Mina, Syria', *Iraq* 21 (1959) 62–92

73. Thomas, D. W. *Documents from Old Testament Times*. London, 1958

74. Touloupa, E. 'Bericht über die neuen Ausgrabungen in Theben', *Kadmos* 3 (1964) 25–7

75. Walser, G. *Die Völkerlisten auf den Reliefs von Persepolis*. Berlin, 1966

76. Waterman, L. *Royal Correspondence of the Assyrian empire*. Ann Arbor, 1930–6

77. Weidner, E. F. 'Jojachin, König von Juda, in babylonischen Keilschrifttexten', *Mélanges offerts à René Dussaud* II, 923–45. Paris, 1939

78. Weissbach, F. *Die Keilinschriften der Achämeniden*. Leipzig, 1911

79. Weissbach, F. H. 'Zu den Inschriften der Säle im Palaste Sargon's II von Assyrien', *Zeitschr. deutsch. Morgenländische Gesellschaft* 72 (1918) 161–85

80. Winckler, H. and Abel, L. *Die Keilschrifttexte Sargons*. Leipzig, 1889

81. Winckler, H. 'Griechen und Assyrer', *Altorientalischer Forschungen* 1 (1893) 356–70

82. Wiseman, D. J. *Chronicles of Chaldaean Kings (626–556 B.C.) in the British Museum*. London, 1961

83. Woolley, L. 'Excavations near Antioch in 1936', *Antiquaries Journal* 17 (1937) 1–15

84. Woolley, L. 'Excavations at Al Mina, Sueidia', *JHS* 58 (1938) 1–30, 133–70

85. Woolley, L. 'The date of Al Mina', *JHS* 68 (1948) 148

86. Woolley, L. *A Forgotten Kingdom*. Harmondsworth, 1963

87. Young, R. S. 'Gordion on the royal road', *Proc. Amer. Philos. Soc.* 107 (1963) 348–64

88. Zgusta, L. *Kleinasiatische Personennamen*. Prague, 1964

II. EGYPT

89. Austin, M. M. *Greece and Egypt in the Archaic Age*. Cambridge, 1970

90. Basch, L. 'Phoenician oared ships', *The Mariners' Mirror* 55 (1969) 139–62, 227–45

91. Basch, L. 'Trières grecques, phéniciennes et égyptiennes', *JHS* 97 (1977) 1–10

92. Bernand, A. *Le Delta égyptien d'après les textes grecs* I. *Les confins libyques*. Cairo, 1970

93. Breasted, J. H. *Ancient Records of Egypt* IV. Chicago, 1906
93A. Burkert, W. 'Das hunderttorige Theben und die Datierung der Ilias', *Wiener Studien* 10 (1976) 5–21
94. Caminos, R. A. 'The Nitocris adoption stele', *JEA* 50 (1964) 71–101
95. Cook, R. M. 'Amasis and the Greeks in Egypt', *JHS* 57 (1937) 227–37
96. Dohan, E. H. *Italic Tomb Groups*. Philadelphia, 1942
97. Erman, A. and Wilcken, U. 'Die Naukratisstele', *ZÄS* 38 (1900) 127–35
98. Fakhry, A. *Siwa Oasis*. Cairo, 1944
99. Fakhry, A. *The Oasis of Siwa*. Cairo, 1950
100. Gardner, E. A. *Naukratis* II, 1885–6. London, 1888
101. Gunn, B. 'Notes on the Naukratis stele', *JEA* 29 (1943) 55–9
102. Hogarth, D. G. 'Excavations at Naukratis', *BSA* 5 (1898–9) 26–97
103. Hogarth, D. G. 'Naukratis, 1903', *JHS* 25 (1905) 105–36
104. Hopfner, T. 'Orient und griechische philosophie', *Beihefte zum alten Orient* 4 (1925)
105. Jonckheere, F. *Les médecins de l'Égypte pharaonique*. Brussels, 1958
106. Junker, H. 'Die Stele des Hofarztes 'Irj', *ZÄS* 63 (1928) 53–70
107. Kienitz, F. K. *Die politische Geschichte Aegyptens vom 7 bis zum 4 Jahrhundert vor der Zeitwende*. Berlin, 1953
108. Lefebvre, G. *Essai sur la médecine égyptienne de l'époque pharaonique*. Paris, 1956
108B. Lloyd, A. B. 'Perseus and Chemmis', *JHS* 89 (1969) 79–86
109. Lloyd, A. B. 'Triremes in the Saite navy', *JEA* 58 (1972) 268–79
110. Lloyd, A. B. *Herodotus Book II. Introduction*. Leiden, 1975
111. Lloyd, A. B. 'Were Necho's triremes Phoenician?', *JHS* 95 (1975) 45–61
112. Lloyd, A. B. *Herodotus Book II. Commentary*. Leiden, 1976–
113. Lloyd, A. B. 'Necho and the Red Sea, some considerations', *JEA* 63 (1977) 142–55
113A. Masson, O., Martin, G. T., Nicholls, R. V. *Carian Inscriptions from North Saqqâra and Buhen*. London, 1978
113B. Masson, O. and Yoyotte, J. *Objets pharaoniques à inscription carienne*. Cairo, 1956
114. Morenz, S. *Die Begegnung Europas mit Aegypten*. Berlin, 1968
115. Petrie, W. M. F. *Tanis* II. London, 1888
116. Petrie, W. M. F. *Naukratis* I, 1884–5. London, 1898
117. Petrie, W. M. F. *Hyksos and Israelite Cities*. London, 1906
118. Petrie, W. M. F. *Seventy Years in Archaeology*. London, 1932
119. Posener, G. 'Les douanes de la méditerranée dans l'Égypte Saïte', *Rev. Phil.* 21 (1947) 117–31
120. Prinz, H. *Funde aus Naukratis des VII und VI Jahrhunderts v. Chr*. Leipzig, 1906
121. Ratré, S. 'Un "chouabti" du général Potasimto au musée d'Annecy', *Bull. Inst. fr. Caire* 61 (1962) 45–53
122. Roebuck, C. 'The grain trade between Greece and Egypt', *Cl. Phil.* 45.4 (1950) 236–47
123. Rowe, A. 'New light on objects belonging to the generals Potasimto and Amasis in the Egyptian Museum', *Annales du Service* 38 (1938) 157–95

124. Sauneron, S. and Yoyotte, J. 'La campagne nubienne de Psammétique II et sa signification historique', *Bull. Inst. fr. Caire* 50 (1952) 157–207

125. Smallwood, E. M. *Documents illustrating the principates of Nerva, Trajan and Hadrian.* Cambridge, 1966

126. Spalinger, A. 'The year 712 B.C. and its implications for Egyptian history', *Journ. of the American Research Center in Egypt* 10 (1973) 95–101

127. Vandier, J. 'L'intronisation de Nitocris', *ZÄS* 99 (1973) 29–33

128. Vercoutter, J. 'Les Haou-Nebout', *Bull. Inst. fr. Caire* 46 (1947) 125–8; 48 (1949), 107–209

129. Wilcken, U. *Grundzüge und Chrestomathie der Papyruskunde.* Leipzig, 1912

130. Yoyotte, J. 'Potasimto de Pharbaithos et le titre "grand combattant – maître du triomphe"', *Chronique d'Égypte* 28 (1953) 101–6

III. CYPRUS

131. Amadasi, M. G. Guzzo and Karageorghis, V. *Excavations at Kition* III. *Inscriptions Phéniciennes.* Nicosia, 1977

132. Clerc, G., Karageorghis, K., Lagarce, E. and Leclant, J. *Fouilles de Kition* II. *Objets Egyptiens et Egyptisants.* Nicosia, 1976

133. Gjerstad, E. 'Decorated metal bowls from Cyprus', *Op. Arch.* 4 (1946) 1–18

134. Gjerstad, E. *The Cypro-Geometric, Cypro-Archaic and Cypro-Classical Periods* (The Swedish Cyprus Expedition, IV. 2). Stockholm, 1948

135. Gjerstad, E. 'The Phoenician colonization and expansion in Cyprus', *RDAC* 1979, 230–54

136. Gjerstad, E. and others. *Greek Geometric and Archaic Pottery found in Cyprus.* Stockholm, 1977

137. Hill, Sir George F. *A History of Cyprus* I. Cambridge, 1940

138. Karageorghis, V. *Excavations in the Necropolis of Salamis* I, II and III. Nicosia, 1967, 1970, 1973

139. Karageorghis, V. *Salamis in Cyprus, Homeric, Hellenistic and Roman.* London, 1969

140. Karageorghis, V. *Kition, Mycenaean and Phoenician Discoveries in Cyprus.* London, 1975

141. Karageorghis, V. 'A *favissa* at Kakopetria', *RDAC* 1977, 178–201

142. Karageorghis, V. *Two Cypriote Sanctuaries of the end of the Cypro-Archaic Period.* Rome, 1977

143. Karageorghis, V. 'Pikes or oboloi from Cyprus and Crete', *Antichità Cretesi. Studi in onore di Doro Levi* II, 168–72. Catania, 1978

144. Karageorghis, V. 'The relations between the tomb architecture of Anatolia and Cyprus in the Archaic period', *Proc. of the Xth Int. Congress of Classical Archaeology*, 361–8. Ankara, 1978

145. Karageorghis, V. and Des Gagniers, J. *La céramique chypriote de style figuré. Age du Fer (1050–500 av. J.-C.).* Rome, 1974–5

146. Lewe, B. *Studien zur archaïschen kyprischen Plastik.* Diss. Dortmund, 1975

147. Masson, O. and Sznycer, M. *Recherches sur les Phéniciens à Chypre.* Paris, 1972

148. Sjöqvist, E. 'Die Kultgeschichte eines Cyprischen Temenos', *ARW* 30 (1932) 308–59

IV. CYPRIOT SCRIPT

149. Karageorghis, V. 'Fouilles à l'Ancienne-Paphos de Chypre: les premiers colons grecs', *CRAI* 1980, 122–36 (with contributions by E. and O. Masson, 134–6)
150. Masson, E. *Étude de vingt-six boules d'argile inscrites trouvées à Enkomi et Hala Sultan Tekke (Chypre)*. Göteborg, 1971 (= SIMA XXXI: 1)
151. Masson, E. *Cyprominoica. Répertoires, documents de Ras Shamra, essais d'interprétation*. Göteborg, 1974 (= SIMA XXXI: 2)
152. Masson, E. 'Les écritures chypro-minoennes. Etat présent des re-cherches', *Annali Scuola Normale di Pisa* 1978, 805–16
153. Masson, E. 'Le chypro-minoen 1 ...', *Colloquium Mycenaeum, Actes du 6ème colloque international sur les textes mycéniens et égéens...1975* 397–409. Neuchâtel–Genève, 1979
154. Masson, O. *Les inscriptions chypriotes syllabiques*. Paris, 1961
155. Masson, O. 'Kypriaka', *BCH* 92 (1968) 380–6
156. Masson, O. 'Bronze de Delphes à inscription chypriote', *BSC* 95 (1971) 302–4
157. Masson, O. 'Les inscriptions chypriotes syllabiques de 1961 à 1975', *Colloquium Mycenaeum* 361–71
158. Masson, O. 'Le syllabaire chypriote classique: remarques sur les signes des séries en X, Y, Z', *Annali Scuola Normale di Pisa* 1978, 817–32
159. Masson, O. 'Une nouvelle inscription de Paphos concernant le roi Nikoklès', *Kadmos* 19 (1980) 65–80
160. Masson, O. *La Chapelle d'Achoris à Karnak*. (forthcoming)
161. Mitford, T. B. 'Kafizin and the Cypriot Syllabary', *CQ* 44 (1950) 97–106
162. Mitford, T. B. *Studies in the Signaries of South-Western Cyprus* = Univ. of London, Inst. of Class. Studies, Bulletin Suppl. No. 10 (1961)
163. Mitford, T. B. *The Inscriptions of Kourion*. Philadelphia, 1971
164. Mitford, T. B. 'The Cypro-Minoan inscriptions of Old Paphos', *Kadmos* 10 (1971) 87–96
165. Mitford, T. B. *The Nymphaeum of Kafizin. The Inscribed Pottery*. Berlin, 1980
166. Mitford, T. B. and Masson, O. *Silbeninschriften von Rantidi – Paphos = Ausgrabungen in Alt-Paphos auf Cypern*, Heft 2
167. Mitford, T. B. and Masson, O. *Silbeninschriften von Kouklia – Paphos = Ausgrabungen in Alt-Paphos auf Cypern* (in preparation)
168. Neumann, G. 'Zur Deutung der kyprischen "Bulwer-Tafel"', *Kadmos* 2 (1963) 53–67
169. Neumann, G. 'Beiträge zum Kyprischen', *Kamdos* 14 (1975) 167–73
170. Tell Keisan, report on excavations, *Revue Biblique* 83 (1976) 90

C. COLONIZATION
(For Anatolia and Eastern Approaches see B)

I. GENERAL

1. Bérard, J. *L'expansion et la colonisation grecques jusqu'aux guerres médiques.* Paris, 1960
2. Bilabel, F. *Die ionische Kolonisation.* Leipzig, 1920
3. Desborough, V. 'The background to Euboean participation in early Greek maritime enterprise', *Tribute to an Antiquary. Essays presented to Marc Fitch*, 25–40. London, 1976
4. Forrest, W. G. 'Colonization and the rise of Delphi', *Historia* 6 (1957) 160–75
5. Graham, A. J. *Colony and Mother City in ancient Greece.* Manchester, 1971
6. Graham, A. J. 'Patterns in early Greek colonization', *JHS* 91 (1971) 35–47
7. Gwynn, A. 'The character of Greek colonization', *JHS* 38 (1918) 88–123
8. Lampros, S. *De conditorum coloniarum graecarum indole, praemiisque et honoribus.* Leipzig, 1873
9. Langlotz, E. *Die kulturelle und künstlerische Hellenisierung der Küsten des Mittelmeers durch die Stadt Phokaia.* Cologne, 1966
10. Roebuck, C. *Ionian Trade and Colonization.* New York, 1959
11. Rougé, J. 'La colonisation grecque et les femmes', *Cahiers d'histoire* 15 (1970) 307–17
12. Salmon, E. T. *Roman Colonization under the Republic.* London, 1969
13. Schaefer, H. 'Eigenart und Wesenszüge der griechischen Kolonisation', *Heidelberger Jahrbücher* 4 (1960) 77–93
14. Schmid, P. B. *Studien zu griechischen Ktisissagen.* Freiburg i. d. Schweiz, 1947

II. THE WEST

15. Adamesteanu, D. 'Nouvelles fouilles à Gela et dans l'arrière-pays', *Rev. Arch.* 49 (1957) 20–40, 147–80
16. Adamesteanu, D. 'Le suddivisioni di terra nel Metapontino', *Problèmes de la terre en Grèce ancienne*, ed. M. I. Finley (Ecole pratique des hautes études. Civilisations et Sociétés 33) 49–61. Paris, 1973
17. Adamesteanu, D. *La Basilicata antica – storia e monumenti.* Di Mauro, Italy, 1974
18. Adamesteanu, D. 'Indigeni e Greci in Basilicata', *Atti del convegno di studio su le genti della Lucania antica e le loro relazioni con i Greci dell'Italia, Potenza-Matera 18–20 Ottobre 1971*, 27–45. Rome 1974
19. Adamesteanu, D. 'Serra di Vaglio e il problema della penetrazione greca in Lucania', *Godišnjak* 13. Centar za Balkanološka Ispitivanja, Knjiga 11 (Akad. Nauk. i umjetnosti Bosne i Hercegovine), 213–19. Sarajevo, 1976
20. Adriani, A. and others. *Himera* I. *Campagne di scavo 1963–5.* Rome, 1970
21. d'Agostino, B. 'La civiltà del Ferro nell'Italia meridionale e nella Sicilia', *Popoli e civiltà dell'Italia antica* II, 11–94. Rome, 1974
22. d'Agostino, B. 'Tombe "principesche" dell'orientalizzante antico da Pontecagnano', *Mon. Ant.* 49 (1977) 1–110

23. d'Agostino, B. 'Grecs et "indigènes" sur la côte tyrrhénienne au VIIe siècle: la transmission des idéologies entre élites sociales', *Annales: Économies, Sociétés, Civilisations* 32 (1977) 3–20

24. Albore-Livadie, C. 'L'épave etrusque du Cap d'Antibes', *Riv. Stud. Liguri* 33 (= *Hommage Benoit* I, 1967), 300–26

25. Albore-Livadie, C. 'Remarques sur un groupe de tombes de Cumes', *Cahiers du Centre Jean Bérard* 2 (Naples, 1975) 53–8

26. Allegro, N. and others. *Himera* II. *Campagne di scavo 1966–73*. Rome, 1976

27. Almagro, M. *Ampurias. A History of the City and Guide to the Excavations*. Barcelona, 1956

28. Anamali, S. 'Les villes de Dyrrhachion et d'Apollonie et leurs rapports avec les Illyriens', *Studime Historike* 30.2, 125–35. Tirana, Univ. de l'état, 1971

29. Arias, P. 'Medma', *Enciclopedia dell'arte antica* 4 (1961)

30. *Vacat*

31. Asheri, D. 'Osservazioni sulle origini dell'urbanistica Ippodamea', *Riv. Stor. Ital.* 87 (1975) 5–16

32. Bakhuizen, S. C. 'Iron and Chalcidian colonization in Italy', *Mededelingen van het Nederlands Instituut te Rome* 37 (1975) 1–12

33. Beaumont, R. L. 'Greek influence in the Adriatic Sea before the fourth century', *JHS* 56 (1936) 159–204

34. Bérard, J. *La colonisation grecque de l'Italie méridionale et de la Sicile dans l'antiquité*. Paris, 1957

35. Berchem, D. van 'Sanctuaires d'Hercule-Melqart. Contribution à l'étude de l'expansion phénicienne en Méditerranée', *Syria* 44 (1967) 73–109, 307–36

36. Bernabò Brea, L. *Akrai*. Catania, 1956

37. Bernabò Brea, L. *Sicily before the Greeks*. London, 1957

38. Bernabò Brea, L. Contribution to debate in *Taranto nella civiltà della Magna Grecia. Atti del decimo convegno di studi sulla Magna Grecia*, 391ff. Naples, 1971

39. Bernabò Brea, L. and Cavalier, M. *Mylai*. Novara, 1959

40. Bernabò Brea, L. and Cavalier, M. *Meligunis-Lipara* II. *La necropoli greca e romana nella contrada Diana*. Palermo, 1965

41. Bevilacqua, F. and others. *Mozia* VII (Centro di studio per la civiltà fenicia e punica). Rome, 1972

41A. Bicknell, Peter J. 'The date of the battle of the Sagra river', *Phoenix* 20 (1966) 294–301

41B. Bicknell, Peter J. 'The date of the fall of Siris', *Parola del Passato* 23 (1968) 401–8

42. Blakeway, A. A. 'Prolegomena to the study of Greek commerce with Italy, Sicily and France in the eighth and seventh centuries B.C.', *BSA* 33 (1932–3) 170–208

43. Blazquez, J. M. *Tartessos y los origines de la colonizacion fenicia en occidente*. Salamanca, 1975

44. Braccesi, L. *Grecità adriatica: un capitolo della colonizzazione greca in occidente*. 2nd edn. Bologna, 1977

45. Buchner, G. 'Nota preliminare sulle ricerche preistoriche nell'isola d'Ischia', *Bull. di Paletnologia Italiana*, n.s. 1 (1936–7) 65–93

46. Buchner, G. Discussion in *Metropoli e Colonie di Magna Grecia*, 263–74. Naples, 1964

47. Buchner, G. 'Pithekoussai, oldest Greek colony in the west', *Expedition* 8 (1966) 4–12

48. Buchner, G. 'Recent work at Pithekoussai', *Arch. Rep. for 1970–71*, 63–7

49. Buchner, G. 'Pithecusa: scavi e scoperte 1966–71', *Le genti non greche della Magna Grecia. Atti del undicesimo convegno di studi sulla Magna Grecia*, 361–74. Naples, 1972

50. Buchner, G. 'Nuovi aspetti e problemi posti degli scavi di Pithecusa con particolari considerazioni sulle orificiere di stile orientalizzante antico', *Cahiers du centre Jean Bérard* 2 (Naples, 1975) 59–86

51. Buchner, G. 'Testimonianze epigrafiche semitiche del viii secolo a.C. a Pithekoussai', *Parola del Passato* 33 (1978) 130–42

52. Buchner, G. and Boardman, J. 'Seals from Ischia and the lyre-player group', *JDAI* 81 (1966) 1–62

53. Buchner, G. and Russo, C. F. 'La coppa di Nestore e un'iscrizione metrica da Pitecusa dell viii secolo av. Cr.', *Rend. Acad. Lincei* 10 (1955) 215–34

54. Cantarella, R. "*Η ΜΕΓΑΛΗ ᾽ΕΛΛΑΣ*", *La città e il suo territorio. Atti del settimo convegno di studi sulla Magna Grecia*, 11–25. Naples, 1968

55. Cary, M. 'A Euboean colony in Corcyra', *CR* 40 (1926) 148–9

56. Castagnoli, F. 'Topografia e urbanistica', *Atti e Mem. Soc. Magna Grecia* 13–14 (1972–3) 47–55

56A. Cazzaniga, I. 'L'estensione alla Sicilia della espressione Magna Graecia in Strabone (vi.1.2)', *Parola del Passato* 26 (1971) 26–31

57. Cebeillac-Gervasoni, M. 'Les nécropoles de Mégara Hyblaea', *Kokalos* 21 (1975) 3–36

58. *Les Céramiques de la Grèce de l'Est et leur Diffusion en Occident*. Paris–Naples, Centre Jean Bérard, 1978

59. Compernolle, R. van 'Ségeste et l'hellénisme', *Phoibos* 5 (1950–1) 183–228

60. Compernolle, R. van 'La date de la fondation d'Apollonie d'Illyrie', *Ant. Class.* 22 (1953) 50–64

61. Compernolle, R. van *Étude de chronologie et d'historiographie siciliotes*. Brussels, 1960

62. Cook, R. M. 'Reasons for the foundation of Ischia and Cumae', *Historia* 9 (1962) 113–14

63. Dakaris, S. I. "*Ἐκ τοῦ ἀρχαίου νεκροταφείου τοῦ ᾽Ανακτορίου*', *Eph. Arch.* 1953–4 (Part 3) 77–88

64. Drögemüller, H.-P. 'Untersuchungen zur Anlage und zur Entwicklung der Städte "Grossgriechenlands"', *Gymnasium* 72 (1965) 27–62

64A. Drögemüller, H.-P. *Syrakus. Zur Topographie und Geschichte einer griechischen Stadt (Gymnasium* Beiheft 6). Heidelberg, 1969

65. Dunbabin, T. J. *The Western Greeks*. Oxford, 1948

66. Foti, G., Zancani Montuoro, P., Stoop, M. W. and Pugliese Carratelli, G. 'Scavi a Francavilla Marittima', *Atti e Mem. Soc. Magna Grecia* 6–7 (1965–6) 7–21

67. Foti, G. 'La documentazione archeologica in Calabria', *Economia e società nella Magna Grecia. Atti del dodicesimo convegno di studi sulla Magna Grecia,* 341-52. Naples, 1973

68. Foti, G. 'La ricerca del sito di Sibari', *Atti e Mem. Soc. Magna Grecia* n.s. 13-14 (1972-3) 9-15

69. Franciscis, A. de '*ΜΕΤΑΥΡΟΣ*', *Atti e Mem. Soc. Magna Grecia* 3 (1960) 21-67

70. Frederiksen, M. W. 'Archaeology in south Italy and Sicily 1973-6', *Arch. Rep. for 1976-7,* 43-76

71. Gabrici, E. 'Cuma', *Mon. Ant.* 22 (1913)

72. Garbini, G. 'Un iscrizione aramaica a Ischia', *Parola del Passato* 33 (1978) 143-50

73. Genière, J. de la 'Alla ricercà di abitati antichi in Lucania', *Atti e Mem. Soc. Magna Grecia* 5 (1964) 129-38

74. Genière, J. de la 'Note sur la chronologie des nécropoles de Torre Galli et Canale-Janchina', *Mél. d'arch. et d'hist.* 76 (1964) 7-23

75. Genière, J. de la 'Contribution a l'étude des relations entre Grecs et indigènes sur la mer ionienne', *Mél. Ecole Franç. Rome* 82 (1970) 621-36

76. Genière, J. de la 'Aspetti e problemi dell'archeologia del mondo indigeno', *Le genti non greche della Magna Grecia. Atti del undicesimo convegno di studi sulla Magna Grecia,* 225-272. Naples, 1972

77. Genière, J. de la 'C'è un "modello" Amendolara?', *Annali della scuola normale superiore di Pisa (classe di lettere e filosofia),* serie 3, 8·2 (1978) 335-54

78. Genière, J. de la 'Ségeste et l'hellénisme', *Mél. Ecole Franç. Rome* 90 (1978) 33-48

79. Genière, J. de la and Nickels, A. 'Amendolara (Cosenza): Scavi 1969-1973 a S. Nicola', *Not. Scav.* 29 (1975) 483-98

80. Greco, E. 'In margine a Strabone vi.l.2', *Parola del Passato* 25 (1970) 416-20

81. Greco, E. 'Il *ΤΕΙΧΟΣ* dei Sibariti e le origini di Poseidonia', *Dial. di Arch.* 8 (1974-5) 104-15

81A. Guarducci, M. 'Iscrizione arcaica della regione di Siri', *Atti e Mem. Soc. Magna Grecia,* n.s. 2 (1958) 51-61

81B. Guarducci, M. 'Sirie Pyxunte', *Arch. Class.* 15 (1963) 238-45

82. Guzzo, P. G. 'Napoli', *Enciclopedia dell'arte antica* 5 (1963)

83. Guzzo, P. G. 'Scavi a Sibari', *Parola del Passato* 28 (1973) 278-314

84. Halliday, W. R. 'The Eretrians in Corcyra', *CR* 40 (1926) 63-4

85. Hänsel, B. 'Scavi eseguiti nell'area dell'acropoli di Eraclea negli anni 1965-1967', *Not. Scav.* 27 (1973) 400-507

86. Hencken, H. 'Syracuse, Etruria and the north', *AJA* 62 (1958) 259-72

87. Heurgon, J. *Trois études sur le "ver sacrum"* (Coll. Latomus, 26). Brussels, 1957

88. Hind, J. G. F. 'Pyrene and the date of the "Massaliot sailing manual"', *Riv. Stor. Dell' Ant.* 2 (1972) 39-52

89. Humphreys, S. C. 'Il commercio in quanto motivo della colonizzazione greca dell'Italia e della Sicilia', *Riv. Stor. Ital.* 77 (1965) 421-33

90. Hüttl, W. *Verfassungsgeschichte von Syrakus.* Prague, 1929

91. Isserlin, B. S. J., Coldstream, J. N. and Snodgrass, A. 'Motya (Trapani): Rapporto preliminare sugli scavi degli anni 1961–1965', *Not. Scav.* 24 (1970) 560–83

92. Isserlin, B. S. J. and Taylor, J. du Plat *Motya* 1. Leiden, 1974

93. Jodin, A. *Mogador, comptoir phénicien.* (Et. et trav. Arch. Maroc. 2, 1966). Tangiers, 1966

94. Joffroy, R. *Le trésor de Vix.* Paris, 1954

95. Johannowsky, W. Contribution to debate in *Dial. di Arch.* 3 (1969) 149–51

96. Johannowsky, W. 'Problemi relativi a Cuma arcaica', *Cahiers du centre Jean Bérard* 2 (Naples, 1975) 98–105

97. Kesteman, J. P. 'Les ancêtres de Gélon', *Ant. Class.* 39 (1970) 395–413

98. Klein, J. 'A Greek metalworking quarter – eighth-century excavations on Ischia', *Expedition* 14 no. 4 (1972) 34–9

99. Koch, H. 'Studien zu den campanischen Dachterrakotten', *Röm. Mitt.* 30 (1915) 1ff.

100. Koldewey, R. and Puchstein, O. *Die griechischen Tempel in Unteritalien und Sicilien.* Berlin, 1899

101. Lacroix, L. *Monnaies et colonisation dans l'occident grec.* (*Mém. Acad. Roy. Belg.* 58, 2). Brussels, 1965

102. Langlotz, E. *The Art of Magna Graecia. Greek Art in Southern Italy and Sicily.* London, 1965

103. La Rocca, E. 'Due tombe dell'Esquilino. Alcune novità sul commercio euboico in Italia Centrale nell'VIII secolo a.C.', *Dial. di Arch.* 8 (1974–5) 86–103

104. Lepore, E. 'Osservazioni sul rapporto tra fatti economici e fatti di colonizzazione in Occidente', *Dial. di Arch.* 3 (1969) 175–212

105. Lo Porto, F. G. 'Satyrion (Taranto). Scavi e ricerche nel luogo del piu antico insediamento laconico in Puglia', *Not. Scav.* 89 (1964) 177–279

106. Lo Porto, F. G. 'Gli scavi sull' acropoli di Satyrion', *Boll. d'Arte* 49 (1964) 67–80

107. Lo Porto, F. G. 'Metaponto. Scavi e ricerche archeologiche', *Not. Scav.* 20 (1966) 136–231

108. Lo Porto, F. G. 'L'attività archeologica in Puglia', *La Magna Grecia nel mondo ellenistico. Atti del nono convegno di studi sulla Magna Grecia,* 245–64. Naples, 1970

109. Lo Porto, F. G. 'Topografia antica di Taranto', *Taranto nella civiltà della Magna Grecia. Atti del decimo convegno di studi sulla Magna Grecia,* 343–85. Naples, 1971

110. Lo Porto, F. G. 'Civiltà indigena e penetrazione greca nella Lucania orientale', *Mon. Ant.* 48 (1973) 149–250

111. Lo Porto, F. G. 'Vasi cretesi e pseudocretesi in Italia', *Antichità Cretesi. Studi in onore di Doro Levi* 11, 173–88. Catania, 1978

112. Maggiani, A. and Settis, S. 'Nuove note medmee', *Klearchos* 53–6 (1972) 29–75

113. Martin, R. 'Histoire de Sélinonte d'après les fouilles récentes', *CRAI* 1977, 50–63

114. Mattingly, H. B. 'Athens and the western Greeks: *c.* 500–413 B.C.', *Atti*

del I convegno del centro internazionale di studi numismatici (Supplemento al *Annali Ist. Ital. Num.*, 12–14). Rome, 1969

115. Merante, V. 'Sulla cronologia di Dorieo e su alcuni problemi connessi', *Historia* 19 (1970) 272–94

116. Miller, M. *Studies in chronography 1. The Sicilian colony dates.* New York, 1970

117. Miro, E. de 'La fondazione de Agrigento e l'ellenizzazione del territorio fra il Salso e il Platani', *Kokalos* 8 (1962) 122–52

118. Morel, J.-P. 'Les Phocéens en occident: certitudes et hypothèses', *Parola del Passato* 107 (1966) 378–420

119. Morel, J.-P. 'L'expansion phocéen en occident: dix années de recherches (1966–1975)', *BCH* 99 (1975) 853–96

120. Napoli, M. 'La ricerca archeologica di Velia', *Parola del Passato* 21 (1966) 191–226

121. Napoli, M. *Il museo di Paestum.* Naples, 1969

122. Neutsch, B. and others. *Herakleiastudien. Arch. Forsch. in Lukanien* II. (*Röm. Mitt.* Ergänzungsheft 11, 1967)

122A. Niemeyer, H.-G. 'Auf der Suche nach Mainake: Der Konflikt zwischen literarischer und archäologischer Überlieferung', *Historia* 29 (1980) 165–89

123. Orlandini, P. 'Storia e topografia di Gela dal 404–282 a.C. alle luce delle nuove scoperte archeologiche', *Kokalos* 2 (1956) 158–76

124. Orlandini, P. 'Lo scavo del Thesmophorion di Bitalemi e il culto delle divinità ctonie a Gela', *Kokalos* 12 (1966) 8–39

125. Orlandini P. and Adamesteanu, D. 'L'acropoli di Gela', *Not. Scav.* 16 (1962) 340–408

126. Orsi, P. 'Thapsos', *Mon. Ant.* 6 (1895) 89–150

127. Orsi, P. 'Gli scavi intorno a l'Athenaion di Siracusa degli anni 1912–17', *Mon. Ant.* 25 (1918) 383–752

128. Page, D. L. 'Stesichorus: the Geryoneïs', *JHS* 93 (1973) 138–54

129. Paget, R. F. 'The ancient ports of Cumae', *JRS* 58 (1968) 152–69

130. Pearson, L. Review of van Compernolle, *Etude de chronologie et d'historiographie siciliotes*, *Gnomon* 34 (1962) 579–83

131. Pelagatti, P. 'Naxos – Relazione preliminare delle campagne di scavo 1961–4', *Boll. d'Arte* 49 (1964) 149–65

132. Pelagatti, P. Contribution to debate in *Kokalos* 10–11 (1964–5) 245–52

133. Pelagatti, P. 'L'attività della Soprintendenza alle Antichità della Sicilia Orientale fra il 1965 e il 1968', *Kokalos* 14–15 (1968–9) 344–57

134. Pelagatti, P. Contribution to debate in *Dial. di Arch.* 3 (1969) 141–4

135. Pelagatti, P. 'Naxos II – Ricerche topografiche e scavi 1965–70', *Boll. d'Arte* 57 (1972) 211–19

136. Pelagatti, P. 'Camarina e il territorio Camarinense', *Kokalos* 18–19 (1972–3) 182–4

137. Pelagatti, P. and Voza, G. *Archeologia nella Sicilia sudorientale.* Naples (Centre Jean Bérard), 1973

138. Pelagatti, P. and Voza, G. *Archeologia nella Sicilia sudorientale. Addenda al catalogo.* Turin, 1974

139. Pembroke, S. 'Locres et Tarente', *Annales, Économies, sociétés, civilisations* 25 (1970) 1240–70

140. Peroni, R. Contribution to debate in *Dial. di Arch.* 3 (1969) 159–62

141. Piraino, M. T. 'Iscrizione inedita di Poggioreale', *Kokalos* 5 (1959) 159–73

142. Pruvot, G. 'Un navire "Etrusco-Punique" au Cap d'Antibes', *Archéologie* 48 (July 1972) 16–19

143. Quilici, L. *Siris-Heraclea (Forma Italiae* III.1). Rome, 1967

144. Quilici, L. 'Carta archeologica della piana di Sibari', *Atti e Mem. Soc. Magna Grecia* 9–10 (1968–9) 91–155

145. Rainey, F. G. 'The location of archaic Greek Sybaris', *AJA* 73 (1969) 261–73

146. Ridgway, D. 'Coppe cicladiche da Veio', *Studi Etruschi* 35 (1967) 311–21

147. Ridgway, D. 'The first western Greeks: Campanian coasts and southern Etruria', *Greeks, Celts and Romans*, ed. Christopher and Sonia Hawkes, 5–38. London, 1973

148. Ridgway, D. and Dickinson, O. T. P. K. 'Pendent semicircles at Veii: a glimpse', *BSA* 68 (1973) 191–2

149. Rizza, G. 'Leontini: Scavi e ricerche degli anni 1954–1955', *Boll. d'Arte* 42 (1957) 63–73

150. Rizza, G. 'Siculi e Greci sui colli di Leontini', *Cronache di arch. e di storia dell'arte* 1 (1962) 3–27

151. Sanctis, G. de 'Callimaco e Messina', *Atti Acad. Torino* 63 (1927–8) 112–17

152. Schmiedt, G. 'Antichi porti d'Italia', *L'Universo* 47 (1967) 2–44

153. Sjöqvist, E. *Sicily and the Greeks. Studies in the interrelationship between the indigenous populations and the Greek colonists.* Ann Arbor, 1973

154. Strøm, I. *Problems concerning the origin and early development of the Etruscan orientalizing style.* Odense, 1971

155. Tomasello, E. 'Monasterace Marina: Scavi presso il tempio dorico di Punta Stilo', *Not. Scav.* 26 (1972) 561–643

156. Torelli, M. 'Il santuario di Hera a Gravieca', *Parola del Passato* 26 (1971) 44–67

157. Tränkle, H. 'Cato in der vierten und fünften Dekade des Livius', *Mainz. Akad. Wiss. u. Lit. Abhand. d. Geistes- und Sozialwissenschaftlichen Klasse*, 1971 no. 4, 109–37

158. Trendall, A. D. 'Archaeology in S. Italy and Sicily 1967–9', *Arch. Rep. for 1969–70*, 32–51

159. Trump, D. *Central and Southern Italy before Rome.* London, 1966

160. Tusa, V. 'L'attività archeologica della Soprintendenza alle antichità della Sicilia Occidentale nel quadriennio 1968–71', *Kokalos* 19 (1973) 392–436

161. Vallet, G. *Rhégion et Zancle.* Paris, 1958

162. Vallet, G. 'La colonisation Chalcidienne et l'hellénisation de la Sicile orientale', *Kokalos* 8 (1962) 30–51

163. Vallet, G. 'L'introduction de l'olivier en Italie centrale d'après les données de la céramique', *Hommages à Albert Grenier* III, 1554–63. Brussels, 1962

164. Vallet, G. 'La cité et son territoire dans les colonies grecques d'occident',

La città e il suo territorio. Atti del settimo convegno di studi sulla Magna Grecia, 67–142. Naples, 1968

165. Vallet, G. 'Espace privé et espace public dans une cité coloniale d'occident, Mégara Hyblaea', *Problèmes de la terre en Grèce ancienne*, ed. M. I. Finley (Ecole pratique des hautes études. Civilisations et societiés 33), 83–94. Paris, 1973

166. Vallet, G. and Villard, F. 'Les dates de la fondation de Mégara Hyblaea et de Syracuse', *BCH* 76 (1952) 289–346

167. Vallet, G. and Villard, F. *Mégara Hyblaea* II. *Céramique archaïque*. Paris, 1964

168. Vallet, G. and Villard, F. 'Les Phocéens en Mediterranée occidentale à l'époque archaïque et la fondation de Hyélè', *Parola del Passato* 107 (1966) 166–90

169. Vallet, G. and Villard, F. 'Les problèmes de l'Agora et de la cité archaïque', *Mélanges d'archéologie et d'histoire* 81 (1969) 7–35

170. Vallet, G., Villard, F. and Auberson, P. *Mégara Hyblaea* I. *Le quartier de l'agora archaïque*. Rome, 1976

171. Villard, F. *La céramique grecque de Marseille*. Paris, 1960

172. Vita A. di 'La penetrazione siracusana nella Sicilia sudorientale alla luce delle piu recenti scoperte archeologiche', *Kokalos* 2 (1956) 177–205

173. Vita, A. di 'Breve rassegna degli scavi archeologici condotti in provincia di Ragusa nel quadriennio 1955–1959', *Boll. d'Arte* 44 (1959) 347–363

174. Voza, G. 'La topografia di Paestum alla luce di alcune recente indagini', *Arch. Class.* 15 (1963) 223–32

175. Waele, J. A. de *Acragas Graeca* (Archaeologische studien van het Nederlands Historisch Instituut te Rome, Deel III). The Hague, 1971

176. Wells, P. S. 'Late Hallstatt interactions with the Mediterranean', *Ancient Europe and the Mediterranean*, ed. V. Markotic, 189–96. Warminster, 1977

177. Wells, P. S. 'West central Europe and the Mediterranean', *Expedition* 21 no. 4 (1979) 18–24

178. Westlake, H. D. Review of van Compernolle, *Etude de chronologie et d'historiographie siciliotes*, *CR* 76 (1962) 266–8

179. Wever, J. de 'La χώρα massaliote d'après les fouilles récentes', *Ant. Class.* 35 (1966) 71–117

180. Whitaker, J. I. S. *Motya*. London, 1921

181. Woodhead, A. G. *The Greeks in the West*. London, 1962

182. Wuilleumier, P. *Tarente des origines à la conquête romaine*. Paris, 1939

183. Zancani Montuoro, P. Contribution to debate in *La città e il suo territorio. Atti del settimo convegno di studi sulla Magna Grecia*, 170–8. Naples, 1968

184. Zancani Montuoro, P. Contribution to debate in *La Magna Grecia e Roma nell' età arcaica. Atti del ottavo convegno di studi sulla Magna Grecia*, 219–26. Naples, 1969

III. NORTH AEGEAN

185. Bakalakis, G. *Proanaskaphikes ereunes sti Thraki*. Salonica, 1958
186. Bonfante, G. 'A note on the Samothracian language', *Hesperia* 24 (1955) 101–9
187. Bradeen, D. W. 'The Chalcidians in Thrace', *AJP* 73 (1952) 356–80
188. Coincy, H. de 'L'île de Thasos', *La Géographie* 38 (1922) 405–26
189. Daux, G. and others. *Guide de Thasos*. Paris, 1968
190. Dusenberg, E. B. 'A Samothracian necropolis', *Archaeology* 12 (1959) 163–70
191. Dusenberg, E. B. 'The south necropolis of Samothrace', *Archaeology* 17 (1964) 185–92
192. Dusenberg, E. B. 'Samothrace, the south necropolis', *Archaeology* 20 (1967) 116–22
193. Fraser, P. M. *Samothrace* 11.1. *The inscriptions on stone* (ed. Karl Lehmann). New York, 1960
194. Graham, A. J. 'The foundation of Thasos', *BSA* 73 (1978) 61–101
195. Harrison, E. 'Chalkidike', *CQ* 6 (1912) 93–103, 165–78
196. Lazarides, D. *Thasos and its Peraia*. Athens, Center of Ekistics, 1971
197. Lazarides, D. Σαμοθράκη καὶ ἡ περαία τῆς. Athens, Center of Ekistics, 1971
198. Lehmann, K. *Samothrace* 11.2. *The inscriptions on ceramics*. New York, 1960
199. Lehmann, K. *Guide to Samothrace*. 4th edn. New York, 1975
200. Picard, C. 'L'Héraklès Thasios, son sanctuaire, son culte' (review of Launey, M. *Études Thasiennes* 1. Paris, 1944), *Journal des Savants* 1949, 111–33
201. Pouilloux, J. *Recherches sur l'histoire et les cultes de Thasos* 1–11. Paris, 1954–8
202. Salviat, F. 'Une nouvelle loi thasienne: institutions judiciaires et fêtes religieuses à la fin du IVe siècle av. J.C.', *BCH* 82 (1958) 193–267
202A. Zahrnt, M. *Olynth und die Chalkidier*. Munich, 1971

IV. THE BLACK SEA AND APPROACHES

203. Akurgal, E. 'Recherches faites à Cyzique et à Ergili', *Anatolia* 1 (1956) 15–24
204. Akurgal, E. and Budde, L. *Vorläufiger Bericht über die Ausgrabungen in Sinope*. Ankara, 1956
205. Alexandrescu, P. 'Les rapports entre indigènes et Grecs à la lumière des fouilles de la nécropole d'Histria', *VIIIe Congrès international d'archéologie classique*, 336–9. Paris, 1965
206. Alexandrescu, P. 'Les importations grecques dans les bassins du Dniepr et du Boug', *Rev. Arch.* 1975, 63–72
206A. Asheri, D. *Über die Frühgeschichte von Herakleia Pontike*, Ergänzungsband zu den *Tituli Asiae Minoris* 5. Öst. Akad. Wiss. Phil. Hist. Klasse, Denkschriften 106. Vienna, 1972
207. Belin de Ballu, E. *Olbia*. Leiden, 1972
208. Blavatsky, V. D. 'An underwater expedition to the Azov and Black Seas', *Archaeology* 16 (1963) 93–8

209. Bravo, B. 'Une lettre de plomb de Berezan', *Dialogues d'histoire ancienne* 1 (1974) 111–87

210. Buiskikh, S. B. and Ostroverkhov, A. S. 'Raboty na Yagorlytskom poseleny', *Arkheologicheskie Otkrytiya* (1977) 304–5

211. Burstein, S. M. *Outpost of Hellenism: The Emergence of Heraclea on the Black Sea* (Univ. of California publications. Classical Studies). Berkeley, Los Angeles, London, 1976

211A. Burstein, S. M. 'Heraclea Pontica: the city and subjects', *The Ancient World* 2 (1979) 25–8

212. Condurachi, E. (ed.) *Histria* II. Bucharest, 1966

213. Dimitriu, S. and Alexandrescu, P. 'L'importation de la céramique attique dans les colonies du Pont-Euxin avant les guerres médiques', *Rev. Arch.* 1973, 23–38

214. Drews, R. 'The earliest Greek settlements on the Black Sea', *JHS* 96 (1976) 18–31

215. Farmakovsky, B. V. 'Archäologische Funde im Jahre 1909', *Arch. Anz.* 1910, 195–244

216. Farmakovsky, B. V. 'Archaichesky period v Rossy', *Mat. po Arch. Rossy* 34 (1914) 15–78

216A. Firatli, N. and Robert, L. *Les stèles funéraires de Byzance gréco-romaine* (Bibliothèque archéologique et historique de l'Institut Français d'Istanbul 15). Paris, 1964

217. Graham, A. J. 'The date of the Greek penetration of the Black Sea', *BICS* 5 (1958) 25–42

218. Graham, A. J. '*OIKHIOI ΠΕΡΙΝΘΙΟΙ*', *JHS* 84 (1964) 73–5

219. Hind, J. G. F. 'The Greek colonization of the Black Sea area in the archaic and classical period' (unpublished Ph.D. thesis). Cambridge, 1969

220. Hoepfner, W. *Herakleia Pontike – Eregli. Eine baugeschichtliche Untersuchung*, Ergänzungsband zu den *Tituli Asiae Minoris* 2.1. Öst. Akad. Wiss. Phil. Hist. Klasse, Denkschriften 89. Vienna, 1966

221. Kocybala, A. 'Greek colonization on the north shore of the Black Sea in the archaic period' (unpublished Ph.D. thesis). University of Pennsylvania, 1978

222. Labaree, B. W. 'How the Greeks sailed into the Black Sea', *AJA* 61 (1957) 29–33

223. Minns, E. H. *Scythians and Greeks*. Cambridge, 1913

224. Minns, E. H. 'Thirty years of work at Olbia', *JHS* 65 (1945) 109–12

225. Noonan, T. S. 'The grain trade of the northern Black Sea in antiquity', *AJP* 94 (1973) 231–42

226. Noonan, T. S. 'The origins of the Greek colony of Panticapaeum', *AJA* 77 (1973) 77–81

227. Onaiko, N. A. *Antichny import v Pridneprov'e i Pobuzh'e v VII–V vekach do n.e.* Moscow, 1966

228. Rostovtzeff, M. *Iranians and Greeks in S. Russia*. Oxford, 1922

229. Sokolov, G. *Antichnoe Prichernomor'e*. Leningrad, 1973

230. Wąsowicz, A. *Olbia pontique et son territoire. L'aménagement de l'espace*. Paris, 1975

V. NORTH AFRICA

231. Boardman, J. 'Evidence for the dating of Greek setlements in Cyrenaica', *BSA* 61 (1966) 149–56

232. Boardman, J. and Hayes, J. *Excavations at Tocra 1963–65; the Archaic Deposits* I. London, 1966

233. Boardman, J. and Hayes, J. *Excavations at Tocra 1963–65; the Archaic Deposits* II *and later deposits*. London, 1973

234. Carter, T. H. 'Reconnaissance in Cyrenaica', *Expedition* 5 no. 3 (1963) 18–27

235. Chamoux, F. *Cyrène sous la monarchie des Battiades*. Paris, 1953

236. Dušanić, S. 'The ὅρκιον τῶν οἰκιστήρων and fourth-century Cyrene', *Chiron* 8 (1978) 55–76

237. Goodchild, R. G. *Cyrene and Apollonia, an historical guide*. 2nd edn. United Kingdom of Libya, 1963

238. Graham, A. J. 'The authenticity of the ὅρκιον τῶν οἰκιστήρων of Cyrene', *JHS* 80 (1960) 94–111

239. Rowe, A. 'The round, rectangular, stepped and rock-cut tombs at Cyrene', *Cyrenaican Expedition of the University of Manchester 1952*, 4–26. Manchester, 1956

240. Stucchi, S. *L'Agora di Cirene*. Rome, 1965

241. Stucchi, S. *Cirene 1957–66. Un decennio di attività della missione archeologica Italiana a Cirene*. Tripoli, 1967

242. Treidler, H. 'Eine alte ionische Kolonisation in numidischen Afrika', *Historia* 8 (1959) 257–83

243. Vickers, M. and Reynolds, J. M. 'Cyrenaica 1962–72', *Arch. Rep. for 1971–2*, 27–47

244. Villard, F. 'Céramique grecque de Maroc', *Bull. Arch. Maroc.* 4 (1960) 1–26

245. White, D. 'Archaic Cyrene and the cult of Demeter and Persephone', *Expedition* 17 no. 4 (1975) 2–15

D. THE GREEK ISLANDS AND EAST GREECE

I. ISLANDS AND EAST GREECE

1. Åkerström, Å. 'A horseman from Asia Minor', *Medelhavsmuseet Bulletin* 4 (1964) 49–53

2. Akurgal, E. 'Les fouilles de Phocée', *Anatolia* I (1956) 4–11

3. Akurgal, E. *Die Kunst Anatoliens von Homer bis Alexander*. Berlin, 1961

4. Akurgal, E. *Ancient Civilizations and Ruins of Turkey*. Ankara, 1973

5. Auberson, P. 'Chalcis, Lefkandi, Erétrie au VIIIe siècle', *Cahiers du centre Jean Bérard* 2 (Naples, 1975) 9–14

6. Auberson, P. and Schefold, K. *Führer durch Eretria*. Berne, 1972

7. Bakalakis, G. 'Notes Cycladiques', *BCH* 88 (1964) 539–58

8. Bakhuizen, S. C. *Chalcis-in-Euboea, Iron and Chalcidians Abroad*. Leiden, 1976

9. Barron, J. P. 'The sixth-century tyranny at Samos', *CQ* 14.2 (1964) 210–29

10. Bean, G. E. *Aegean Turkey*. London, 1966

11. Bean, G. E. *Turkey beyond the Maeander*. London, 1971

12. Bent, W. *The Cyclades*. London, 1885

13. Bérard, C. *L'Hérôon à la porte de l'ouest. Eretria, Fouilles et Recherches* III. Berne, 1970

14. Bérard, C. *Topographie et urbanisme de l'Erétrie archaïque: l'Hérôon. Eretria, Fouilles et Recherches* VI, 89–94. Berne, 1978

15. Betancourt, P. *The Aeolic Style in Architecture*. Princeton, 1977

16. Blinkenberg, C. *Lindos, Fouilles et recherches* II.1. Copenhagen, 1941

17. Boardman, J. 'Chian and Naucratite', *BSA* 51 (1956) 55–62

18. Boardman, J. 'Early Euboean pottery and history', *BSA* 52 (1957) 1–29

19. Boardman, J. 'A Greek vase from Egypt', *JHS* 78 (1958) 4–12

20. Boardman, J. 'Chian and early Ionic architecture', *Antiquaries Journal* 39 (1959) 170–218

21. Boardman, J. 'An Anatolian Greek belt handle', *Anatolia* 16 (1966) 193–4

22. Boardman, J. *Excavations in Chios 1952–1955. Greek Emporio*. London, 1967

23. Buschor, E. *Altsamische Standbilder* I–V. Berlin, 1934–61

24. Cook, J. M. 'Old Smyrna, 1948–1951', *BSA* 53/4 (1958/9) 1–34

25. Cook, J. M. *The Greeks in Ionia and the East*. London, 1962

26. Cook, J. M. 'Old Smyrna: Ionic Black Figure and other sixth-century figured vases', *BSA* 60 (1965) 114–42

27. Cook, J. M. *The Troad*. Oxford, 1973

28. Cook, R. M. 'Fikellura pottery', *BSA* 34 (1933–4) 1–98

29. Cook, R. M. 'Ionia and Greece in the eighth and seventh centuries B.C.', *JHS* 66 (1946), 67–98

30. Cook, R. M. 'The distribution of Chiot pottery', *BSA* 44 (1949) 154–61

31. Cook, R. M. 'A list of Clazomenian pottery', *BSA* 47 (1952) 123–52

32. Cook, R. M. *Corpus Vasorum Antiquorum, British Museum* VIII. London, 1954

33. Cook, R. M. *Clazomenian Sarcophagi (Kerameus* III). Mainz, 1981

34. Cook, R. M. and Hemelrijk, J. M. 'A hydria of the Campana Group in Bonn', *Jahrbuch Berliner Museen* 5 (1963) 107–20

34A. Coldstream, J. N. 'The Phoenicians of Ialysos', *BICS* 16 (1969) 1–8

34B. Craik, E. M. *The Dorian Aegean*. London, Henley and Boston, 1980

35. Dover, K. J. 'The poetry of Archilochos', *Archiloque: Entretien Hardt* X (1964), ch. 5, 181–212

36. Ebner, P. 'Il mercato dei metalli preziosi nel secolo d'oro dei Focei', *Parola del Passato* 21 (1966) 111–27

36A. Emlyn-Jones, C. J. *The Ionians and Hellenism*. London, Henley and Boston, 1980

37. Fehr, B. 'Zur Geschichte des Apollonheiligtums von Didyma', *Marb. W. Pr.* 1971–2, 14–59

38. Freyer-Schauenburg, B. *Elfenbeine aus dem samischen Heraion*. Hamburg, 1966

39. Freyer-Schauenburg, B. *Samos* XI. *Bildwerke der archaïschen Zeit und des strengen Stils*. Bonn, 1974

40. Gallet de Santerre, H. *Délos primitive et archaïque*. Paris, 1958

41. Greifenhagen, A. 'Ein ostgriechisches Elfenbein', *Jahrbuch Berliner Museen* 7 (1965) 125–56

42. Gruben, G. 'Das archaïsche Didymaion', *JDAI* 78 (1963) 78–182

43. Gruben, G. 'Naxos und Paros', *Arch. Anz.* 1972, 319–79

44. Guarducci, M. 'Un'antica offerta alla Era di Samo', *Studi in onore di Aristide Calderini e Roberto Paribeni* I, 23–7. Milan, 1956

45. Guarducci, A. 'L'epigrafe arcaica dell'Apollo dei Nassii a Delo', *Annuario* 21–2 (1959/60) 243–7

46. Hanfmann, G. M. A. 'Ionia, leader or follower?', *Harvard Studies in Classical Philology* 61 (1953) 1–26

47. Hanfmann, G. M. A. 'Archaeology and the origins of Greek culture', *The Antioch Review* 25.1 (1965) 41–59

48. Hogarth, D. G. 'Lydia and Ionia', *CAH* III[1], 501–26. Cambridge, 1925

49. Huxley, G. L. *The Early Ionians*. London, 1966

50. Huxley, G. L. 'Simonides and his world', *Proc. Royal Irish Acad.* 78 (1978) 231–47

51. Isler, H. P. *Samos* IV. *Das archaïsche Nordtor und seine Umgebung im Heraion von Samos*. Bonn, 1978

52. Jacobsthal, P. 'The date of the Ephesian foundation-deposit', *JHS* 71 (1951) 85–95

53. Jacoby, F. 'The date of Archilochos', *CQ* 35 (1941) 97–109

54. Jantzen, U. *Samos* VIII. *Ägyptische und orientalische Bronzen aus dem Heraion von Samos*. Bonn, 1972

55. Jantzen, U. and others. 'Die Wasserleitung des Eupalinos', *Arch. Anz.* 1973, 72ff. and 401ff.; 1975, 19ff.

56. Jeffery, L. H. 'The courts of justice in Archaic Chios', *BSA* 51 (1956) 157–67

57. Kardara, C. *Rhodiake Aggeiographia*. Athens, 1963

58. Kastenbein, W. 'Untersuchungen am Stollen des Eupalinos auf Samos', *Arch. Anz.* 1960, 178–98

59. Kienast, H. J. *Samos* XV. *Die Stadtmauer von Samos*. Bonn, 1978

60. Kinch, K. F. *Fouilles de Vroulia*. Berlin, 1914

61. Kleiner, G. *Alt-Milet*. Wiesbaden, 1966

62. Kontoleon, N. M. '*ΠΑΡΙΑ ΙΩΝΙΚΑ ΚΙΟΝΟΚΡΑΝΑ*', *AAA* 1 (1968) 178–81

63. Krause, C. *Das Westtor. Eretria, Fouilles et Recherches* IV. Berne, 1972

64. Labarbe, J. 'Un décalage de 40 ans dans la chronologie de Polycrate', *Ant. Class.* 31 (1962) 153–88

65. Langlotz, E. *Studien zur nordostgriechischen Kunst*. Mainz, 1975

66. Laumonier, A. *Les cultes indigènes en Carie*. Paris, 1958

67. Mellaart, J. 'Iron Age pottery from southern Anatolia', *Belleten* 19, no. 74 (1955) 115–36

68. Mellink, M. J. 'Local, Phrygian and Greek traits in northern Lycia', *Rev. Arch.* 1976, 21–34

69. Merkelbach, R. and West, M. L. 'Ein Archilochos-papyrus', *Zeit. Pap. Epigr.* 14 (1974) 97–113
70. Metzger, H. 'Perspectives nouvelles', *Rev. Arch.* 1967, 344–61
71. Metzger, H. *Anatolia* II. *First Millennium B.C. to the End of the Roman period.* London, 1969
72. Mitchell, B. 'Herodotus and Samos', *JHS* 95 (1975) 75–91
73. Nicholls, R. V. 'Old Smyrna; the Iron Age fortifications and associated remains on the city perimeter', *BSA* 53/54 (1958/9) 35–137
74. Oliver, J. H. 'Text of the so-called Constitution of Chios', *AJP* 80 (1959) 296–301
75. Page, D. L. *Sappho and Alcaeus.* Oxford, 1955
76. Pedley, J. G. *Greek Sculpture of the Archaic Period: the Island Workshops.* Mainz, 1976
77. Petrakos, B. 'Dédicace des 'Αειναῦται', *BCH* 87 (1963) 545–7
78. Popham, M. R. and Sackett, L. H. *Lefkandi* I. London, 1979–80
79. Rankin, H. D. 'Archilochos' chronology and some possible events of his life', *Eos* 65 (1977) 5–15
80. Robinson, E. S. G. 'The coins from the Ephesian Artemision reconsidered', *JHS* 71 (1951) 156–67
81. Roebuck, C. 'The economic development of Ionia', *Cl. Phil.* 48.1 (1953) 9–16
81A. Roebuck, C. *Ionian Trade and Colonization.* New York, 1959
82. Roebuck, C. 'Tribal organisation in Ionia', *TAPA* 92 (1961) 495–507
83. Rubensohn, O. 'Paros', P–W s.v.
84. Sakellariou, M. B. 'Συμβολὴ στὴν ἱστορία τοῦ φυλετικοῦ συστήματος τῆς Ἐφέσου', *Ellenika* 15 (1957) 220–31
85. Schmidt, G. *Samos* VII. *Kyprische Bildwerke aus dem Heraion von Samos.* Bonn, 1968
86. Schmidt, G. 'Eine Brychon-Weihung und ihre Fundlage', *Ath. Mitt.* 87 (1972) 165–85
87. Tarditi, G. *Archilochus.* Rome, 1968
88. Thomas, N. 'Recent acquisitions by Birmingham City Museum', *Arch. Rep.* 1964–5, 64–70
89. Tölle-Kastenbein, R. *Samos* XIV. *Das Kastro Tigani: die Bauten und Funde griechischer, römischer und byzantinischer Zeit.* Bonn, 1974
90. Tölle-Kastenbein, R. 'Miszellen zur Topographie der Stadt Samos', *AM* 90 (1975) 189–214
91. Tölle-Kastenbein, R. *Herodot und Samos.* Bochum, 1976
92. de Tournefort, J. Pitton *Voyage into the Levant.* London, 1741
93. Treu, M. *Archilochos.* Munich, 1959
94. Tuchelt, K. *Die archaïschen Skulpturen von Didyma.* Berlin, 1970
95. Walter, H. *Samos, das griechische Heraion von Samos.* Munich, 1965
96. Walter, H. *Samos* V. *Frühe samische Gefässe.* Bonn, 1968
97. Walter, H. *Das Heraion von Samos.* Munich – Zurich, 1976
98. Walter-Karydi, E. 'Aeolische Kunst', *Antike Kunst*, Beiheft 7 (1970) 3–18
99. Walter-Karydi, E. *Samos* VI.1. *Samische Gefässe des 6. Jahrhunderts v. Chr.* Bonn, 1973
100. White, M. 'The duration of the Samian tyranny', *JHS* 74 (1954) 36–43

II. CRETE

101. Alexiou, S. 'Tête archaïque en poros du Musée de Candie', *BCH* 76 (1952) 1–17
102. Alexiou, S. Reports on excavations at Tsoutsouros, *Arch. Delt.* 18 (1963) *Chr.* 310–11; 19 (1964) *Chr.* 444
103. Benton, S. 'Herakles and Eurystheus at Knossos', *JHS* 57 (1937) 38–43
104. Boardman, J. 'Early Iron Age tombs at Knossos', *BSA* 56 (1961) 68–80
104A. Boardman, J. *The Cretan Collection in Oxford.* Oxford, 1961
105. Boardman, J. 'Archaic finds at Knossos', *BSA* 57 (1962) 28–34
106. Boardman, J. 'Daedalus and monumental sculpture', *Pepragmena tou Δ' Diethnous Kretologikou Synedriou*
107. Bosanquet, R. C. 'Excavations at Praesos, I', *BSA* 8 (1901/2) 231–70
107A. Branigan, K. *The Foundations of Palatial Crete.* London, 1970
108. Brock, J. K. *Fortetsa.* Cambridge, 1956
109. Coldstream, J. N. *Knossos: the Sanctuary of Demeter.* London, 1973
110. Coldstream, J. N. 'Knossos 1951–61: Orientalising and Archaic pottery from the town', *BSA* 68 (1973) 33–63
111. *Dädalische Kunst auf Kreta im 7. Jahrhundert.* Hamburg, Museum für Kunst und Gewerbe, 1970
112. Davaras, C. *Die Statue aus Astritsi.* Berne, 1972
112A. Davaras, C. *Guide to Cretan Antiquities.* New Jersey, 1976
113. Demargne, P. *La Crète Dédalique.* Paris, 1947. Review by Dunbabin, T. J. in *Gnomon* 24 (1952) 191–7
114. Demargne, P. 'La Crète archaïque d'après des publications récentes', *Rev. Arch.* 1974, 301–6
115. Demargne, P. and Van Effenterre, H. 'À propos du Serment des Drériens', *BCH* 61 (1937) 327–32
116. Demargne, P. and Van Effenterre, H. 'Recherches à Dréros', *BCH* 61 (1937) 5–32, 333–48
117. Demargne, P. and Van Effenterre, H. 'Recherches à Dréros. II. Les inscriptions archaïques', *BCH* 62 (1938) 194–5
118. Deshayes, J. Reports on excavations at Itanos, *BCH* 75 (1951) 201–9
119. Ducrey, P. and Picard, O. 'Recherches à Lato', *BCH* 93 (1969) 792–822
120. Ducrey, P. and Picard, O. 'À propos de l'histoire de Lato', *Antichità Cretesi. Studi in onore di Doro Levi* II, 75–80. Catania, 1978
121. Dussaud, R. 'Itanos', *Syria* 26 (1949) 394–5
122. Forster, E. S. 'Praesos; the terracottas', *BSA* 8 (1901/2) 271–81
123. Guarducci, M. 'Ancora sull'inno cretese a Zeus Dicteo', *Antichità Cretesi. Studi in onore di Doro Levi* II, 32–8. Catania, 1978
124. Hampe, R. *Kretische Löwenschale des siebten Jahrhunderts.* Heidelberg, 1969
125. Headlam, J. W. 'The procedure of the Gortynian inscription', *JHS* 13 (1892/3) 48–69
126. Hoffmann, H. *Early Cretan Armorers.* Mainz, 1972
126A. Hood, M. S. F. and Smyth, D. *Archaeological Survey of the Knossos Area.* London, 1980
127. Hutchinson, R. W. and others. 'Unpublished objects from Palaikastro and Praisos, II', *BSA* 40 (1939/40) 40ff

128. Jeffery, L. H. and Morpurgo Davies, A. 'Ποινικαστας and ποινικαζεν', *Kadmos* 9 (1970) 118–54

129. Johannowsky, W. 'Frammenti di un dinos di Sophilos da Gortina', *Annuario* 27/28 (1955/56) 45–51

130. Kirsten, E. 'Amnisos', 'Dreros', 'Lato' and Lyttos', P–W Suppl. 7 (1940) 129–49, 342–65, 427–35

131. Kirsten, E. *Das dorische Kreta* 1. Würzburg, 1942

132. Kontoleon, N. M. 'Παρατηρήσεις εἰς τὴν δαιδαλικὴν τέχνην τῆς Κρήτης', *Pepragmena tou Γ΄ Diethnous Kretologikou Synedriou* 1 (1973) 134–53

133. Kunze, E. *Kretische Bronzereliefs*. Stuttgart, 1931

134. La Rosa, V. 'Capitello arcaico da Festos', *Antichità Cretesi. Studi in onore di Doro Levi* 11, 136–48. Catania, 1978

135. Lebessi, A. 'The Fortetsa gold rings', *BSA* 70 (1975) 169–76

136. Lebessi, A. Report on excavations at Gouves, *AAA* 4 (1971) 384–92

137. Lebessi, A. Report on excavations at Lyttos, *Arch. Delt.* 26 (1971) *Chr.* 493–9

138. Lebessi, A. Reports on excavations at Kato Syme, *PAE* 1972, 193–203; 1973, 188–99; 1974, 222–7; 1975, 322–9; *Ergon* 1974, 118–20; 1975, 171–5; 1976, 179–84; 1977, 175–81

139. Lebessi, A. 'Δύο ἐπιτύμβιες ὑστεροαρχαϊκὲς Κρητικὲς Στῆλες', *Antike Plastik* 12 (1973) 7–14

139A. Lebessi, A. *ΟΙ ΣΤΗΛΕΣ ΤΟΥ ΠΡΙΝΙΑ*. Athens, 1976

140. Le Rider, G. *Monnaies crétoises du Ve. au Ire. siècle av. J.-C.* (Études crétoises 15). Paris, 1966

141. Levi, D. 'Arkades, una città cretese all'alba della civiltà ellenica', *Annuario* 10/12 (1927–9 (1931))

142. Levi, D. 'I Bronzi di Axos', *Annuario* 13/14 (1930/31) 43–146

143. Levi, D. 'Gli scavi di 1954 sull'acropoli di Gortina', *Annuario* 33/34 (1957) 207–88

144. Marcadé, J. 'Un casque crétois', *BCH* 73 (1949) 421–36

145. Marinatos, S. Reports on excavations at Amnisos, *PAE* 1933, 93–100; 1936, 81–6; 1938, 130–8

146. Marinatos, S. 'Le temple géometrique de Dréros', *BCH* 60 (1936) 214–85

147. Michaud, J.-P. Reports on excavations at Prinias, *BCH* 95 (1971) 1055–6; 98 (1974), 715ff

148. Pendlebury, J. D. S. *The Archaeology of Crete*. London, 1939

149. Platon, N. Report on excavations at Praisos, *Kr. Chr.* 1953, 485–6

150. Platon, N. Reports on excavations at Onythe Goulediana, *PAE* 1954, 377–82; 1955, 298–303; 1956, 226–8

151. Platon, N. Reports on excavations at Lyttos, *Kr. Chr.* 1955, 567; 1957, 336

152. Raubitschek, A. E. 'The Cretan inscription BM 1969. 4–2.1; a supplementary note', *Kadmos* 9 (1970) 155–6

153. Rizza, G. and Scrinari, V. S. M. *Il santuario sull'acropoli di Gortina* 1. Rome, 1968

153A. Rizza, G. 'Le terrecotte di Axòs', *Annuario* 45/6 (1969) 211–302

154. Snodgrass, A. M. 'Cretans in Arcadia', *Antichità Cretesi. Studi in onore di Doro Levi* 11, 196–201. Catania, 1978

155. Spyridakis, S. 'Salamis and the Cretans', *Parola del Passato* 31 (1976) 345–55
156. Tiré, C. and Van Effenterre, H. *Guide des fouilles françaises en Crète*. Paris, 1966
157. Tzedakis, G. Report on excavations at Phalasarna, *Arch Delt.* 24 (1969) *Chr.* 433–4
158. Van Effenterre, H. *La Crète et le monde grec de Platon à Polybe*. Paris, 1948
158A. Van Effenterre, H. *Le Palais de Mallia et la Cité Minoenne* I–II. Rome, 1980
159. Welter, G. and Jantzen, U. 'Das Diktynnaion', *Forschungen auf Kreta, 1942* (ed. F. Matz, Berlin, 1951), 106–17
160. West, M. L. 'The Dictaean Hymn to the Kouros', *JHS* 85 (1965) 149–59
161. Willetts, R. F. *Aristocratic Society in Ancient Crete*. London, 1955 and Westport, Connecticut, 1980
162. Willetts, R. F. *Cretan Cults and Festivals*. London and New York, 1962 and Westport, Connecticut, 1980
163. Willetts, R. F. *Ancient Crete, a Social History*. London and Toronto, 1965 and 1974
164. Willetts, R. F. *The Law Code of Gortyn*. Berlin, 1967
165. Willetts, R. F. 'The Cretan Koinon: epigraphy and tradition', *Kadmos* 14 (1975) 143–8
166. Willetts, R. F. *The Civilization of Ancient Crete*. London, 1977
167. Willetts, R. F. 'Cretan law and early Greek society', *Antichità Cretesi. Studi in onore di Doro Levi* II, 22–31. Catania, 1978

E. THE GREEK MAINLAND

I. ILLYRIS, EPIRUS AND MACEDONIA

1. Alexander, J. 'The spectacle fibulae', *AJA* 69 (1965) 7ff
2. *Ancient Macedonia: papers read at the first international Symposium, 1968.* Thessaloniki, 1970
3. Andrea, Zh. Report on excavations at Kuçi Zi, *Bul. Ark.* 1969, 27ff
4. Andrea, Zh. 'La civilisation des tumuli du bassin de Korçë', *SA* 1972.2, 187ff
5. Andrea, Zh. 'La civilisation des tumuli du bassin de Korçe et sa place dans les Balkans du sud-est', *Iliria* 4 (1976) 133ff
5A. Andrea, Zh. 'Tumat e Kuçit të Zi', *Iliria* 6 (1976) 163ff
6. Andronikos, M. *Vergina* I: *the cemetery of the tumuli*. Athens, 1969
7. Bailey, D. M. 'Some grave groups from Chauchitza', *Opusc. Ath.* 9 (1969) 21ff
8. Bouzek, J. 'The beginning of the Protogeometric pottery and the "Dorian Ware"', *Opusc. Ath.* 9 (1969) 41ff
9. Bouzek, J. *Graeco-Macedonian Bronzes: analysis and chronology*. Prague, 1973
10. Bouzek, J. 'Macedonian bronzes', *Památky archeologické* 65 (1974) 278ff
11. Buda, A. Report on excavations at Apollonia, *BUST* 1969.2, 238ff
12. Budina, D. Report on excavations at Çepunë, *Bul. Ark.* 1969, 49ff
13. Budina, D. Report on excavations at Bajkaj, *Bul. Ark.* 1971, 57ff
14. Carapanos, C. *Dodone et ses ruines*. Paris, 1878

15. Casson, S. 'Excavations in Macedonia', *BSA* 24 (1919–21) 1ff and 26 (1923–25) 1ff
16. Casson, S. *Macedonia, Thrace and Illyria*. Oxford, 1926
17. Ceka, N. Report on excavations at Dukat, *Iliria* 3 (1975) 139ff
18. Dakaris, S. I. 'Das Taubenorakel von Dodona und das Totenorakel bei Ephyra', *Antike Kunst* 1963, 1 Beiheft, 35ff
19. Dakaris, S. I. οἱ γενεαλογικοὶ μῦθοι τῶν Μολοσσῶν. Athens, 1964
20. Dakaris, S. I. *Cassopaia and the Elean colonies*. Athens, 1971
21. Dakaris, S. I. *Dodona*. Ioannina, 1971
22. Dakaris. S. I. Θεσπρωτία. Athens, 1972
23. Edson, C. F. 'Early Macedonia', *Anc. Macedonia* I, 17ff
24. Evangelides, D. ''Ηπειρωτικαὶ 'Ερευναί', *Ep. Chron.* 10 (1935) 192ff
25. Evangelides, D. 'Ψήφισμα τοῦ Βασιλέως Νεοπτολέμου ἐκ Δωδώνης', *Arch. Eph.* 1956, 1ff
26. Foltiny, S. 'Eisenzeitliche Funde aus Amphipolis', *MAG* 93/94 (1964) 90ff
27. Franke, P. R. *Alt-Epirus und das Königtum der Molosser*. Erlangen, 1954
28. Garašanin, M. 'Contribution à la chronologie de l'âge du fer en Macédoine', *Ziva Antika* 10 (1960) 173ff
29. Garašanin, M. *La préhistoire sur le territoire de la République Socialiste de Serbie* II. Belgrade, 1973
30. Garašanin, M. and D. 'Report on excavations at Radanja', *Zbornik Štip* 1 (1958/59) 9ff
31. Hammond, N. G. L. 'The colonies of Elis in Cassopaea', 'Αφιέρωμα εἰς τὴν "Ηπειρον, εἰς μνήμην Χριστοῦ Σούλη. Athens, 1956
32. Hammond, N. G. L. 'The kingdoms of Illyria *circa* 400–167 B.C.', *BSA* 61 (1966) 241ff
33. Hammond, N. G. L. *Epirus*. Oxford, 1967
34. Hammond, N. G. L. *A History of Macedonia* I (1972) and II (1978). Oxford
35. Hammond, N. G. L. 'The archaeological background to the Macedonian kingdom', *Anc. Macedonia* I, 53ff
36. Islami, S. and Ceka, H. 'Nouvelles données sur l'antiquité illyrienne en Albanie', *SA* 1964.1, 91ff
37. Islami, S., Ceka, H., Prendi, F. and Anamali, S. Report on excavations at Mati, *BUSS* 1955.1, 110ff
38. Jubani, B. Report on excavations at Çinamak, *Bul. Ark.* 1969, 37ff; 1971, 41ff; and 1974, 42ff
39. Jubani, B. 'Traits communs dans les rites d'inhumation', *Les Illyriens et la genèse des Albanais*. Tirana, 1971
40. Jubani, B. 'Aperçu de la civilisation tumulaire de l'Albanie du nord-est', *SA* 1972.2, 203ff
40A. Karaiskaj, G. 'Fortifikimet prehistorike në Shqipëri', *Monumentet* 14 (1977) 19ff
41. Kilian, K. 'Zur eisenzeitlichen Transhumanz in Nordgriechenland', *Archäologisches Korrespondenzblatt* 4 (1973) 431ff
42. Kilian, K. 'Trachtzubehör der Eisenzeit zwischen Ägäis und Adria', *Prähistorische Zeitschr.* 50 (1975) 9ff
43. Korkuti, M. *Shqiperia Arkeologjike*. Tirana, 1971

44. Kouleïmani, I. Report on excavations at Vitsa in *Arch. Delt.* 21 (1966) *Chr.* 289ff

45. Kurti, D. 'Vestiges de civilisation illyrienne dans la vallée du Mati', *Les Illyriens et la genèse des Albanais* 147ff. Tirana, 1971

46. Kurti, D. 'Nouveaux éléments sur la civilisation illyrienne des tumuli de Mati', *Iliria* 4 (1976) 237f

47. Lepore, E. *Ricerche sull'antico Epiro.* Naples, 1962

48. Luka, Kolë. *Les Illyriens et la genèse des Albanais.* Tirana, 1971

49. Mačkić, P., Simaska, D. and Trbuhović, V. Report on excavations at Saraj in *Starinar* 11 (1960) 199ff

50. Makridis, Th. Χαλκὰ Μακεδονικὰ τοῦ μουσείου Μπενάκη, *Arch. Eph.* 1937.2, 512ff

51. Mano, A. Reports on excavations at Apollonia in *SA* 1972.1, 107ff and *Iliria* 1 (1971) 202ff

52. May, J. M. F. *The coinage of Damastion.* London, 1939

53. Mikulčić, I. Report on excavations at Orlova Čuka near Karaorman, *Zbornik Štip* 2 (1960–61) 47ff

54. Mikulčić, I. *Pelagonija.* Skopje, 1966

55. Novak, G. and others. *Époque préhistorique et protohistorique en Yougoslavie – Recherches et résultats.* Belgrade, 1971 (with bibliography for individual sites)

56. Papazoglu, F. 'Les origines et la destinée de l'état Illyrien: *Illyrii proprie dicti', Historia* 14 (1965) 143f

57. Papazoglu, F. *The Central Balkan tribes in pre-Roman times.* Amsterdam, 1978

58. Petsas, Ph. Reports on excavations at Vergina in *Arch. Delt.* 17 (1961–62) 218ff and *Chr.* 230ff; 18 (1963) *Chr.* 217ff; and *Makedonika* 7 (1967) 324ff

59. Pingel, V. 'Eisenzeitliche Gräber von Dedeli und Marvinca in Jugoslawisch-Makedonien', *Marb. W. Pr.* 1970, 7ff

60. Popov, R. 'Hallstattzeitliche Gräberfunde aus Gewgelia in Südwest-mazedonien', *Präh. Zeit.* 9 (1917) 66ff

61. Prendi, F. Report on excavations at Vodhinë, *BUSS* 1956.1, 180ff

62. Prendi, F. Report on excavations at Vajzë, *BUSS* 1957.2, 78ff

63. Prendi, F. Report on excavations at Kakavi and Bodrishtë, *BUSS* 1959.2, 190ff

64. Prendi, F. 'Un aperçu sur la civilisation de la première période du fer en Albanie', *Iliria* 3 (1975) 109ff

65. Prendi, F. and Budina, D. 'La civilisation illyrienne de la vallée du Drino', *SA* 1970.2, 61ff

65A. Report on excavations 1974–75. *Iliria* 6 (1976) 331ff

66. Rey, L. 'Bohemica', *Albania* 4 (1932) 40ff

67. Robinson, D. *Excavations at Olynthus*, x: *Metal and minor finds.* Baltimore, 1941

68. Romiopoulou, K. Report on excavations at Spilion, *AAA* 4 (1971) 1, 37ff

69. Romiopoulou, K. 'Some pottery of the Early Iron Age from Western Macedonia', *BSA* 66 (1971) 353ff

70. Romiopoulou, K. ῾Ταφαὶ πρωῖμου ἐποχῆς τοῦ σιδήρου εἰς ἀνατολικὴν Πίνδον᾽, AAA 4 (1971) 1, 37ff

71. Shqiperia Arkeologjike. Tirana, 1971

72. Toçi, V. 'La population illyrienne de Dyrrhachion à la lumière des données historiques et archéologiques', Iliria 4 (1976) 301ff

73. Ugolini, L. M. Albania Antica I (1927), II (1932), III (1942). Rome.

74. Vickers, M. 'Some Early Iron Age bronzes from Macedonia', Anc. Macedonia II, 17ff

75. Vokotopoulou, I. P. Reports on excavations at Vitsa in Arch. Delt. 22 (1967) Chr. 348ff; 23, 287ff; 24, 249f; 25, 305ff; 26, 333ff

II. THESSALY AND CENTRAL GREECE

76. Amandry, P. 'Vases, bronzes et terres cuites de Delphes', BCH 62 (1938) 307-31

77. Amandry, P. 'Rapport préliminaire sur les statues chryséléphantines de Delphes', BCH 63 (1939) 86-119

78. Amandry, P. La mantique apollinienne à Delphes. Paris, 1951

79. Amandry, P. Review of Defradas, J. (E93). Rev. Phil. 30 (1956) 268-82

80. Amandry, P. 'Oracles, littérature et politique', REA 61 (1959) 400-13

81. Amandry, P. 'Statue de Taureau en argent', Études Delphiques (BCH Suppl. IV, 1977) 273-93

82. Axenidhis, Th. D. ῾Η Πελάσγις, Λάρισα καὶ ἡ ἀρχαία Θεσσαλία. Athens, 1947-9

83. Barrett, W. S. 'Bacchylides, Asine and Apollo Pythaeus', Hermes 82 (1954) 421-44

84. Bequignon, Y. La vallée du Spercheios. Paris, 1937

85. Boardman, J. 'Herakles, Delphi and Kleisthenes of Sikyon', Rev. Arch. 1978, 227-34

86. Buck, R. J. 'The formation of the Boiotian League', Cl. Phil. 67 (1972) 94-101

87. Cauer, F. 'Amphiktione', P-W s.v. (1894)

88. Chadwick, J. ῾ΤΑΓΑ and ΑΤΑΓΙΑ᾽, Studi linguistici in onore di V. Pisani I (1969) 231-4

89. Cloché, P. Thèbes de Béotie. Namur, 1952

90. Crahay, R. La littérature oraculaire chez Hérodote. Paris, 1956

91. Daux, G. 'Le Trésor de Sicyone à Delphes et ses fondations', CRAI 1922, 68-9

92. Daux, G. Pausanias à Delphes. Paris, 1936

93. Defradas, J. Thèmes de la propagande delphique. Paris, 1954. See E 79

94. Delcourt, M. L'Oracle de Delphes. Paris, 1955

95. Dovateur, A. 'Un fragment de la constitution de Delphes d'Aristote', REG 46 (1933) 214-23

96. Ducat, J. 'Le Ptoion et l'histoire de Béotie', REG 77 (1964) 283-90

97. Ducat, J. Les kouroi du Ptoion. Paris, 1971

98. Ducat, J. 'La confédération béotienne', BCH 97 (1973) 59-73

98A. Dyggve, E. and Poulsen, F. Das Laphrion. Copenhagen, 1948

99. Forrest, W. G. 'The First Sacred War', *BCH* 80 (1956) 33–52
100. Forrest, W. G. 'Colonisation and the rise of Delphi', *Historia* 6 (1957) 160–75
101. *Fouilles de Delphes*. Paris, 1902–
102. Fowler, B. 'Thebes and the Tanagran federal issues', *The Phoenix* 11 (1957) 164–70
103. von Gaertringen, H., Lippold, G. and Staehlin, F. 'Thessalia', P–W s.v. (1936)
104. Gschnitzer, F. 'Namen und Wesen der thessalischen Tetrarchen', *Hermes* 82 (1954) 451–64
105. Gschnitzer, F. 'Zum Tagos der Thessaler', *Anz. Altertumsw. Öst. human. Gesellschaft* 7 (1954) 191–2
106. Guarducci, M. 'Creta e Delfi', *Stud. e Materiali di Storia delle Religioni* 19/20 (1943–6) 85–114
107. Guillon, P. *Les trépieds du Ptoion*. Paris, 1943. Reviewed by Feyel, M. in *REG* 56 (1943) 348–66
108. Guillon, P. *Le Béotie antique*. Paris, 1948
109. Guillon, P. *Le bouclier d'Héraclès*. Aix-en-Provence, 1963
110. Huxley, G. L. 'Troy VIII and the Lokrian Maidens', *Ancient Society and Institutions* (Studies presented to V. Ehrenberg), 147–64. Oxford, 1966
111. Keramopoullos, A. D. 'ΘΗΒΑΙΚΑ', *Arch. Delt.* 3 (1917) 1–503
112. Kip, G. *Thessalische Studien*. Diss. Hal., 1910
113. Kirchberg, J. *Die Funktion der Orakel im Werke Herodots*. Hypomnemata 11 (1965)
114. Kirsten, E. 'Plataiai', P–W s.v. (1950)
115. Klees, H. *Die Eigenart des griechischen Glaubens an Orakel und Seher*. Stuttgart, 1965
116. La Coste-Messelière, P. de *Au Musée de Delphes*. Paris, 1936
117. Larsen, J. A. O. 'Orchomenos and the foundation of the Boeotian confederation', *Cl. Phil.* 55 (1960) 9–18
118. Larsen, J. A. O. 'A new interpretation of the Thessalian confederation', *Cl. Phil.* 55 (1960) 229–48
119. Larsen, J. A. O. 'Perioikoi', P–W s.v. (1937)
120. Lauffer, S. 'Ptoion', P–W s.v. (1959)
121. Lerat, L. 'Krisa', *Rev. Arch.* 32 (1948) 621–32 (*Mélanges C. Picard*)
122. Lerat, L. *Les Locriens de l'ouest*. Paris, 1952
123. Lerat, L. 'Fouilles à Delphes à l'est du grand sanctuaire', *BCH* 85 (1961) 316–66
124. Lotze, D. *ΜΕΤΑΞΥ ΕΛΕΥΘΕΡΩΝ ΚΑΙ ΔΟΥΛΩΝ*. Berlin, 1959
125. Miltner, F. 'Penestai'. P–W s.v. (1937)
126. Momigliano, A. 'Tagia e tetrarchia in Tessaglia', *Athenaeum* 10 (1932) 47–53
127. Morrison, J. 'Meno of Pharsalus, Polycrates and Ismenias', *CQ* 36 (1942) 57–78
128. Oldfather, W. 'Lokris', P–W s.v. (1926)
129. Parke, H. W. and Boardman, J. 'The struggle for the tripod', *JHS* 77 (1957) 276–82

130. Parke, H. W. and Wormell, D. E. W. *The Delphic Oracle* I–II. Oxford, 1956; cf. review by Forrest, W. G., *CR* 72 (1958) 67–70

130A. Poulsen, F. *Thermos*. Copenhagen, 1934

131. Robertson, N. 'The Thessalian expedition of 480 B.C.', *JHS* 96 (1976) 100–20

132. Rossch, P. *Thespies et la confédération béotienne*. Paris, 1965

133. Roux, G. *Delphes*. Paris, 1970

134. Schmidt, J. 'Philolaos 3', P–W s.v. (1938)

135. Schober, F. 'Phokis', P–W s.v. (1941)

136. Sordi, M. 'La guerra tessalo-focese del V secolo', *Rivista di Filologia* 31 (1953) 235–58

137. Sordi, M. 'La prima guerra sacra', *Rivista di Filologia* 31 (1953) 320–46

138. Sordi, M. *La lega tessala*. Rome, 1958

139. Sourvinou-Inwood, C. 'The myth of the first temples at Delphi', *CQ* 29 (1979) 231–51

140. Staehlin, F. *Das hellenische Thessalien*. Stuttgart, 1924

141. Threpsiades, I. Reports on excavations at Aulis, *PAE* 1956–61 (cf. Chronique des Fouilles, *BCH* 86 (1962) 776–9)

142. Wade-Gery, H. T. 'Jason of Pherae and Aleuas the Red', *JHS* 44 (1924) 55–64

143. Wade-Gery, H. T. 'Kynaithos', *Greek Poetry and Life* (Oxford, 1936) 56–78 (= *Essays in Greek History* (Oxford, 1958) 17–36)

144. Wade-Gery, H. T. 'Hesiod', *The Phoenix* 3 (1949) 81–93 (= *Essays in Greek History* (Oxford, 1958) 1–16)

145. Walcot, P. *Hesiod and the Near East*. Cardiff, 1966

146. Westlake, H. D. *Thessaly in the fourth century B.C.* London, 1935

147. Westlake, H. D. 'The medism of Thessaly', *JHS* 56 (1936) 12–24

148. Wolters, P. and Bruns, G. *Das Kabirenheiligtum*. Berlin, 1940

148A. Woodhouse, W. J. *Aetolia*. Oxford, 1897

III. LACONIA AND MESSENIA

149. Andrewes, A. 'The government of classical Sparta', *Ancient Society and Institutions: Studies Presented to Victor Ehrenberg*. Oxford, 1966

150. Boardman, J. 'Artemis Orthia and chronology', *BSA* 58 (1963) 1ff

151. den Boer, W. *Laconian Studies*. Amsterdam, 1954

152. Butler, D. 'The competence of the Demos in the Spartan Rhetra', *Historia* 11 (1962) 385ff

153. Cartledge, P. *Sparta and Lakonia; a regional history 1300–362 B.C.* London, 1979

153A. Cartledge, P. 'The peculiar position of Sparta in the development of the Greek city-state', *Proceedings of the Royal Irish Academy* 80c (1980) 91ff

154. Chrimes, K. M. T. *Ancient Sparta*. Manchester, 1952

155. Coldstream, J. N. and Huxley, G. L. (eds.) *Kythera*. London, 1972

156. Dawkins, R. M. and others. *The Sanctuary of Artemis Orthia at Sparta*. London, 1929

157. Dickins, G. 'The growth of Spartan policy', *JHS* 32 (1912) 1ff

158. Ehrenberg, V. 'Der Damos im archaïschen Sparta', *Hermes* 68 (1933) 288ff

159. Forrest, W. G. *A History of Sparta 950–192 B.C.* London, 1968

160. Hammond, N. G. L. 'The creation of classical Sparta', *Studies in Greek History*. Oxford, 1973

161. Holladay, A. J. 'Spartan austerity', *CQ* 27 (1977) 111–26

161A. Hooker, J. T. *The Ancient Spartans*. London, 1980

162. Huxley, G. L. *Early Sparta*. London, 1962 (with full references to ancient sources)

163. Jones, A. H. M. *Sparta*. Oxford, 1967

164. Kahrstedt, U. *Griechisches Staatsrecht* I. *Sparta und seine Symmachie*. Göttingen, 1922

165. Karpophora. Reports on excavations, in *AAA* 1 (1968) 205f and *Arch. Eph.* 1973, 25ff

166. Kiechle, F. *Messenische Studien*. Kallmünz, 1959

167. Kiechle, F. *Lakonien und Sparta, Vestigia*. Berlin, 1963

168. Kroymann, J. *Sparta und Messenien*. Berlin, 1937

169. Michell, H. *Sparta*. Cambridge, 1952

170. Mila. Report on excavations, in *Arch. Delt.* 27 (1972) *Chr.* 259f

171. Nichoria. Reports on excavations, in *BCH* 84, 700; 85, 697f; *Arch. Delt.* 27 (1972) *Chr.* 266ff

172. Oliva, P. *Sparta and her social problems*. Prague, 1971

173. Page, D. L. *Alcman. The Partheneion*. Oxford, 1951

174. Pearson, L. 'The pseudo-history of Messenia and its authors', *Historia* 11 (1962) 397ff

175. Roussel, P. *Sparte*. Paris, 1939

176. Starr, C. G. 'The credibility of early Spartan history', *Historia* 14 (1965) 257ff

176A. Stibbe, C. M. *Lakonische Vasenmaler des 6. Jdts v. Chr.* Amsterdam, 1972

177. Tod, M. N. and Wace, A. J. B. *Catalogue of the Sparta Museum*. Oxford, 1906

178. Toynbee, A. J. *Some Problems of Greek History*. London, 1969 (with bibliography)

179. Wade-Gery, H. T. 'The Rhianus-Hypothesis', *Ancient Society and Institutions: Studies Presented to Victor Ehrenberg*, 289ff. Oxford, 1966

180. Wide, S. *Lakonische Kulte*. Leipzig, 1893

IV. THE ARGOLIC PENINSULA

181. Alexandri, O. *Ἄργος, Arch. Delt.* 16 (1960) *Chr.* 93; 18 (1963) *Chr.* 57ff

182. Andrewes, A. 'The Corinthian Actaeon and Pheidon of Argos', *CQ* 43 (1949) 70ff

183. Andrewes, A. 'Ephorus Book I and the kings of Argos', *CQ* 1 (1951) 39ff

184. Blegen, C. W. 'Excavations at the Argive Heraeum 1925', *AJA* 29 (1925) 413ff

185. Bommelaer, J. F. and others. 'Argos', *BCH* 94 (1970) 765ff; 95 (1971) 736ff; and 96 (1972) 155ff

186. Charitonidis, S. I. 'Excavations at Argos and Nauplia', *BCH* 78 (1954) 410ff; *PAE* 1952, 413ff; 1953, 191ff; 1954, 232ff; 1955, 233ff; and *Arch. Delt.* 21 (1966) *Chr.* 125ff

187. Cook, J. M. 'The Cult of Agamemnon at Mycenae', *Geras A. Keramopoullou*, 112ff. Athens, 1953

188. Courbin, P. 'Argos', *BCH* 77 (1953) 258ff; 78, 175ff; 79, 312ff; 80, 183ff and 366ff; 81, 322ff and 665ff; and *Fasti Archaeologici* 10 (1955) 135ff

189. Courbin, P. 'Une tombe géométrique d'Argos', *BCH* 81 (1957) 322–86

190. Courbin, P. *La céramique géométrique de l'Argolide*. Paris, 1966

191. Courbin, P. *Tombes géométriques d'Argos* i. Paris, 1974

192. Deïlaki, E. and Kritsos, Ch. Report on excavations at Argos, *Arch. Delt.* 28 (1973) *Chr.* 94ff

193. Deshayes, J. *Argos. Les fouilles de la Deiras*. Paris, 1966

194. Frödin, O. and Persson, A. W. *Asine. Results of the Swedish Excavations, 1922–30*. Stockholm, 1938

195. Hägg, I. and R. 'Asine', *Arch. Delt.* 27 (1972) *Chr.* 231ff; 28 (1973) *Chr.* 155ff

196. Hägg, I. and R. (eds.) *Excavations in the Barbouna area at Asine* i. Uppsala, 1973

197. Hägg, R. *Die Gräber der Argolis: i, Lage und Form der Gräber*. Uppsala, 1974. (With full bibliography, pp. 164–9)

198. Hammond, N. G. L. 'An early inscription at Argos', *CQ* 10 (1960) 33ff

199. Jameson, M. H. 'Excavations at Porto Cheli and vicinity, Preliminary Report. 1: Halieis 1962–68', *Hesperia* 38 (1969) 311ff. Also in *Arch. Delt.* 27 (1972) *Chr.* 233ff

200. Kallipolitis, V. G. and Petrakos, V. Ch. 'Troezen', *Arch. Delt.* 18 (1963) *Chr.* 52

201. Kelly, T. 'A history of Argos ca. 1100 to 546 B.C.' Ph.D. Diss. Univ. of Illinois, 1964

202. Kelly, T. *The Early History of Argos*. Minneapolis, Minnesota, 1976

203. Papachristodoulou, I. C. 'Excavations at Argos', *Arch. Delt.* 23 (1968) *Chr.* 127ff; *AAA* 2 (1969) 159ff; *Arch. Delt.* 24 (1969) *Chr.* 106ff

204. Protonotariou-Deilaki, E. 'Excavations at Argos and Tiryns, and in the Argolid', *AAA* 3 (1970) 180ff; *Arch. Delt.* 19 (1964) *Chr.* 122ff; 24 (1969) *Chr.* 104; 25 (1970) *Chr.* 154ff

205. Säflund, G. *Excavations at Berbati, 1936–1937*. Stockholm, 1965

206. Styrenius, C.-G. and Vidén, A. 'New excavations at Asine', *AAA* 4 (1971) 147ff

207. Tomlinson, R. A. *Argos and the Argolid from the end of the Bronze Age to the Roman occupation*. London and Ithaca, N.Y., 1972

208. Verdelis, N. M. Excavations at Argos in *Arch. Delt.* 17 (1961/2) *Chr.* 55ff; 18 (1963) *Chr.* 63; at Tiryns in *Arch. Delt.* 17 (1961/2) *Chr.* 54ff; *Ath. Mitt.* 78 (1963) 1ff; at Mycenae in *PAE* 1962, 67ff; 1963, 107ff

209. Vollgraff, C. W. 'Fouilles d'Argos', *BCH* 28 (1904) 364ff and 31 (1907) 139ff

210. Vollgraff, C. W. *Le Sanctuaire d'Apollon Pythéen à Argos*. Paris, 1956

211. Waldstein, C. and others. *The Argive Heraeum* i–ii. Boston and New York, 1902–5

V. CORINTHIA AND MEGARA

212. Bowra, C. M. 'Two lines of Eumelus', *CQ* 13 (1963) 145ff
213. Broneer, O. *Isthmia* 1. *Temple of Poseidon*. Princeton, 1971
214. *Corinth, Results of Excavations conducted by the American School of Classical Studies at Athens* (1929–1957) in 16 volumes. See also reports in *Hesperia* 1965–
215. Dunbabin, T. J. 'The early history of Corinth', *JHS* 68 (1948) 59ff
216. Hammond, N. G. L. 'The Heraeum at Perachora and Corinthian encroachment', *BSA* 49 (1954) 93ff
217. Hammond, N. G. L. 'The main road from Boeotia to the Peloponnese', *Studies in Greek History*. Oxford, 1973
218. Hanell, K. *Megarische Studien*. Lund, 1934
219. Oost, S. I. 'Cypselus the Bacchiad', *Cl. Phil.* 67 (1972) 10ff
220. Oost, S. I. 'The Megara of Theagenes and Theognis', *Cl. Phil.* 68 (1973) 186ff
221. Payne, H. G. G. *Necrocorinthia*. Oxford, 1931
222. Payne, H. G. G. and Dunbabin, T. J. *Perachora* I–II. Oxford, 1940, 1962
223. Robinson, H. S. *The urban development of ancient Corinth*. Athens, 1965
224. Roebuck, C. 'Some aspects of urbanization at Corinth', *Hesperia* 41 (1972) 96–127
225. Salmon, J. 'The Heraeum at Perachora and the early history of Corinth and Megara', *BSA* 67 (1972) 159ff
226. Seeberg, A. *Corinthian Komos Vases* (University of London, Institute of Classical Studies, Bull. Suppl. 27). London, 1971
227. Servais, J. 'Hérodote et la chronologie des Cypselides', *Ant. Class.* 38 (1969) 28ff
228. Will, E. *Korinthiaka*. Paris, 1955
229. Wiseman, J. *The Land of the Ancient Corinthians* (Studies in Mediterranean Archaeology). Göteborg, 1978

VI. THE REST OF THE PELOPONNESE

230. Anderson, J. K. 'A topographical and historical study of Achaea', *BSA* 49 (1954) 72ff
231. Dugas, C. and others. *Le Sanctuaire d'Aléa Athéna à Tégée au IVe siècle*. Paris, 1924
232. Hammond, N. G. L. 'The family of Orthagoras', *CQ* 6 (1956) 45ff
233. Herrmann, H. V. *Die Kessel der orientalisierenden Zeit* (Olympische Forschungen VI). Berlin, 1966
234. Herrmann, H. V. *Olympia, Heiligtum und Wettkampfstätte*. Munich, 1972
235. Kunze, E. *Dritter Bericht über die Ausgrabungen in Olympia, 1938–9*. Berlin, 1941
236. Leahy, D. M. 'The dating of the Orthagorid dynasty', *Historia* 17 (1968) 1ff
237. Miller, S. G. Reports on excavations at Nemea. In *Hesperia* 44 (1975) 144ff; 45 (1976) 174ff; 46 (1977) 1ff; 47 (1978) 58ff; 48 (1979) 73ff

238. Oost, S. I. 'Two notes on the Orthagorids of Sicyon', *Cl. Phil.* 69 (1974) 118ff
239. Rudolph, H. 'Die ältere Tyrannis in Sikyon', *Chiron* 1 (1971) 75ff

F. ATHENS AND ATTICA

I. GENERAL

1. Bicknell, P. J. *Studies in Athenian Politics and Genealogy* (*Historia*, Einzelschr. 19). Wiesbaden, 1972
2. Cadoux, T. J. 'The Athenian Archons from Kreon to Hypsichides', *JHS* 68 (1948) 70–123
3. Cataudella, M. R. *Atene fra il VII e il VI secolo: aspetti economici e sociali dell'Attica arcaica*. Catania, 1966
4. Cavaignac, E. 'La désignation des archontes athéniens jusqu'en 487', *Rev. Phil.* 2.48 (1924) 144–8
5. Davies, J. K. *Athenian Propertied Families 600–300 B.C.* Oxford, 1971
6. Deubner, L. *Attische Feste*. Berlin, 1932
7. French, A. *The Growth of the Athenian Economy*. London, 1964
8. Harrison, A. R. W. *The Law of Athens* I–II. Oxford, 1968–71
9. Hignett, C. *A History of the Athenian Constitution*. Oxford, 1952
10. Hill, I. T. *The Ancient City of Athens*. London, 1953
11. Hopper, R. J. 'Observations on the *Wappenmünzen*', *Essays...Stanley Robinson*, 16–39. Oxford, 1968
12. Hopper, R. J. *The Acropolis*. London, 1971
13. Jackson, D. A. *East Greek Influence on Attic Vases*. London, 1976
14. Jacoby, F. *Apollodors Chronik*. Berlin, 1902
15. Jacoby, F. *Atthis*. Oxford, 1949
16. Jeffery, L. H. 'The inscribed gravestones of Archaic Attica', *BSA* 57 (1962) 115–53
17. Johansen, K. E. *Attic grave reliefs*. Copenhagen, 1951
18. Johnston, A. W. and Jones, R. E. 'The "SOS" amphora', *BSA* 73 (1978) 103–41
19. Kraay, C. M. 'The archaic owls of Athens', *Num. Chron.* 6, ser. 16 (1956) 43–68
20. Kraay, C. M. 'An interpretation of Ath. Pol. ch. 10', *Essays...Stanley Robinson*, 1–9. Oxford, 1968
21. Lang, M. and Crosby, M. *Weights, Measures and Tokens* (*The Athenian Agora* x). Princeton, 1964
22. Ledl, A. *Studien zur älteren athenischen Verfassungsgeschichte*. Heidelberg, 1914
23. Meritt, B. D., Wade-Gery, H. T. and McGregor, M. F. *The Athenian Tribute Lists* I. Cambridge, Mass., 1939
24. Mylonas, G. E. *Eleusis and the Eleusinian Mysteries*. Princeton, 1961
25. Ostwald, M. *Nomos and the Beginnings of the Athenian Democracy*. Oxford, 1969
26. Payne, H. and Young, G. M. *Archaic Marble Sculpture from the Acropolis*. London, 1936

27. Pečirka, J. 'Land tenure and the development of the Athenian polis', *Geras* (Prague, 1963) 183–201

28. Pickard-Cambridge, A. *The Dramatic Festivals of Athens.* 2nd edn., ed. J. Gould and D. M. Lewis. Oxford, 1968

29. Raubitschek, A. E. *Dedications from the Athenian Acropolis.* Cambridge, Mass., 1948

30. Rhodes, P. J. *The Athenian Boule.* Oxford, 1972

30A. Richter, G. M. A. *The Archaic Gravestones of Attica.* London, 1961

31. Strasburger, H. 'Herodots Zeitrechnung', *Historia* 5 (1956) 129–61

32. Sumner, G. V. 'Notes on chronological problems in the Aristotelian *Ἀθηναίων Πολιτεία*', *CQ* n.s. 11 (1961) 31–54

33. Thompson, H. A. and Wycherley, R. E. *The Athenian Agora* XIV: *The Agora of Athens.* Princeton, 1972

34. Toepffer, J. *Attische Genealogie.* Berlin, 1889

35. Traill, J. S. *The political organisation of Attica: a study of the demes, trittyes and phylai and their representation on the Athenian council* (*Hesperia*, suppl. XIV). Princeton, 1975

36. Wilamowitz-Moellendorff, U. von *Aristoteles und Athen* I–II. Berlin, 1893

37. Wycherley, R. E. *The Athenian Agora* III. *Literary and epigraphical testimonia.* Princeton, 1957

II. THE EARLY PERIOD

38. Andrewes, A. 'Phratries in Homer', *Hermes* 89 (1961) 129–40

39. Andrewes, A. 'Philochoros on Phratries', *JHS* 81 (1961) 1–15

40. Broneer, O. 'A Mycenaean fountain on the Athenian Acropolis', *Hesperia* 8 (1939) 317–433

41. Dunbabin, T. J. '*Ἔχθρη παλαιή*', *BSA* 37 (1936/7) 83–91

42. Ferguson, W. S. 'The Salaminioi of Heptaphylai and Sounion', *Hesperia* 7 (1938) 1–74

43. Ferguson, W. S. 'The Attic Orgeones', *Harv. Theol. Rev.* 37 (1944) 61–140

44. Fuks, A. *The Ancestral Constitution.* London, 1953

45. Jameson, M. H. 'Notes on the sacrificial calendar from Erchia', *BCH* 89 (1965) 154–72

46. MacDowell, D. M. *Athenian Homicide Law.* Manchester, 1963

47. Richardson, N. J. *The Homeric Hymn to Demeter.* Oxford, 1974

48. Stroud, R. S. *Drakon's Law on Homicide.* Berkeley, 1968

49. Wilcken, U. 'Zur drakontischen Verfassung', *Apophoreton*, 85–98. Berlin, 1903

50. Wüst, F. R. 'Zu den πρυτάνιες τῶν ναυκράρων und zu den alten attischen Trittyen', *Historia* 6 (1957) 176–91

III. SOLON

51. Adcock, F. E. 'The reform of the Athenian state', *CAH* IV[1], 26–58. Cambridge, 1926

52. Andrewes, A. 'The survival of Solon's *Axones*', *ΦΟΡΟΣ: Tribute to Benjamin Dean Meritt*, 21–8. New York, 1974

53. Bonner, R. J. and Smith, G. *The Administration of Justice from Homer to Aristotle* i. Chicago, 1930

54. Chambers, M. H. 'Aristotle on Solon's reform of coinage and weights', *Calif. Stud. Class. Ant.* 6 (1973) 1–16

55. Crawford, M. H. 'Solon's alleged reform of weights and measures', *Eirene* 10 (1972) 5–8

56. Fine, J. V. A. *Horoi (Hesperia* Suppl. 9). Princeton, 1951

57. Finley, M. I. *Land and Credit in Ancient Athens.* New Brunswick, 1952

58. Finley, M. I. *The Use and Abuse of History.* London, 1975

59. Fritz, K. von 'The meaning of *ΕΚΤΗΜΟΡΟΣ*', *AJP* 61 (1940) 54–61

60. Gilliard, C. *Quelques réformes de Solon.* Lausanne, 1907

61. Glotz, G. *La solidarité de la famille dans le droit criminel en Grèce.* Paris, 1904

62. Kahrstedt, U. *Staatsgebiet und Staatsangehörige in Athen.* Stuttgart–Berlin, 1934

63. Linforth, I. M. *Solon the Athenian.* Berkeley, 1919

64. Niese, B. 'Über Aristoteles' Geschichte der athenischen Verfassung', *Hist. Zeitschr.* 33 (1892) 38–68

65. Rhodes, P. J. 'Solon and the numismatists', *Num. Chron.* 7.15 (1975) 1–11

66. Ruschenbusch, E. *ΣΟΛΩΝΟΣ ΝΟΜΟΙ (Historia,* Einzelschr. 9). Wiesbaden, 1966

67. Ruschenbusch, E. *Untersuchungen zur Geschichte des athenischen Strafrechts.* Cologne, 1968

68. Schreiner, J. *De corpore iuris Atheniensium.* Diss. Bonn, 1913

69. Stinton, T. C. W. 'Solon, Fragment 25', *JHS* 96 (1976) 159–62

69A. Stroud, R. S. *The axones and kyrbeis of Drakon and Solon* (University of California Publications in Classical Studies 19). Berkeley, 1979

70. Vlastos, G. 'Solonian Justice', *Cl. Phil.* 41 (1946) 65–83

71. Wolff, H. J. 'The origin of judicial litigation among the Greeks', *Traditio* 4 (1946) 31–87

72. Woodhouse, W. J. *Solon the Liberator.* Oxford, 1938

IV. PISISTRATUS

73. Adcock, F. E. 'Athens under the Tyrants', *CAH* iv¹, 59–71. Cambridge, 1926

74. Berve, H. *Miltiades (Hermes* Einzelschr. 2). Wiesbaden, 1937

75. Beyer, I. 'Die Datierung der grossen Reliefgiebel des alten Athenatempels der Akropolis', *Arch. Anz.* 1977, 44–74

76. Boardman, J. 'Herakles, Peisistratos and sons', *Rev. Arch.* (1972) 57–72

77. Boardman, J. 'Herakles, Peisistratos and Eleusis', *JHS* 95 (1975) 1–12

78. Cornelius, F. *Die Tyrannis in Athen.* Munich, 1929

79. Davison, J. A. 'Peisistratus and Homer', *TAPA* 86 (1955) 1–21

80. Eliot, C. W. J. 'Where did the Alkmaionidai live?', *Historia* 16 (1967) 279–86

81. Gernet, L. 'Les dix archontes de 581', *Rev. Phil.* 3.12 (1948) 216–27

82. Hopper, R. J. '"Plain", "Shore", and "Hill" in early Athens', *BSA* 56 (1961) 189–219

83. Kolb, F. 'Die Bau-, Religions- und Kulturpolitik der Peisistratiden', *JDAI* 92 (1977) 99–138

84. Lauter-Bufé, H. and Lauter, H. 'Die vorthemistokleische Stadtmauer Athens nach philologischen und archäologischen Quellen', *Arch. Anz.* 1975, 1–9

85. Lewis, D. M. 'Cleisthenes and Attica', *Historia* 12 (1963) 22–40

86. Raubitschek, A. E. *Dedications from the Athenian Akropolis.* Cambridge, Mass., 1949

87. Rhodes, P. J. 'Pisistratid chronology again', *Phoenix* 30 (1976) 219–33

88. Schachermeyr, F. 'Peisistratos 3', P–W 19, 156–91. 1938

89. Traill, J. S. 'Diakris, the inland trittys of Leontis', *Hesperia* 47 (1978) 89–109

90. Vanderpool, E. 'The date of the pre-Persian city-wall of Athens', *ΦΟΡΟΣ: Tribute to Benjamin Dean Meritt*, 156–60. New York, 1974

91. Wade-Gery, H. T. 'Miltiades', *JHS* 71 (1951) 212–21 (= *Essays in Greek History* (Oxford, 1958) 155–70)

G. ECONOMIC AND SOCIAL CONDITIONS

The following entries may also be consulted: B 89, 122; C 10, 42, 58, 62, 89, 104, 163–5, 209, 225; D 29, 36, 81–2, 161, 163–4; E 223–4; F 5, 7, 21, 27, 35, 38–9, 46, 48–9, 54–7, 59–61, 65, 67–8, 71.

1. Adkins, A. W. H. *Merit and Responsibility.* Oxford, 1960

2. Angel, J. L. 'Ecology and population in the eastern Mediterranean', *World Archaeology* 4 (1972) 88–105

3. Asheri, D. 'Laws of inheritance, distribution of land, and political constitutions in ancient Greece', *Historia* 12 (1963) 1–21

4. Asheri, D. *Distribuzioni di terre nell'antica Grecia.* Memorie dell'Accademie delle scienze di Torino, classe di scienze morali, storiche e filologiche, 4a ser. 10 (1966)

4A. Boardman, J. 'The olive in the Mediterranean: its culture and its use', *Phil. Trans. Royal Soc., London* B.275 (1976) 187–96

5. Bourriot, F. 'Recherches sur la nature du genos: étude d'histoire sociale athénienne, periodes archaïque et classique', Sorbonne thesis, 1975

6. Cassola, F. 'Sull'alienabilità del suolo nel mondo greco', *Labeo* 11 (1965) 206–19

7. Calhoun, G. M. 'Classes and masses in Homer', *Cl. Phil.* 29 (1934) 192–208

8. Christ, K. 'Die Griechen und das Geld', *Saeculum* 15 (1964) 214–29

9. Cook, R. M. 'Speculations on the origin of coinage', *Historia* 7 (1958) 259–62

10. Cook, R. M. 'Die Bedeutung der bemalten Keramik für den griechischen Handel', *JDAI* 74 (1959) 114–23

11. Finley, M. I. (ed.) *Trade and Politics in the Ancient World.* Proceedings of the Second International Conference of Economic History, Aix-en-Provence, 1962. Paris, 1965

12. Finley, M. I. 'The alienability of land in Ancient Greece', *Eirene* 7 (1968) 25–32

13. Finley, M. I. *The Ancient Economy*. Berkeley, 1973

14. Gauthier, P. *Symbola: les étrangers et la justice dans les cités grecques*, *Annales de l'Est*, no. 42, 1972

15. Gerlach, J. *Aner Agathos*. Diss. Munich, 1932

16. Grierson, P. *The Origins of Money*. London, 1977

17. Hasebroek, J. *Staat und Handel im alten Griechenland*. Tübingen, 1928. (= *Trade and Politics in Ancient Greece*. London, 1933)

18. Hasebroek, J. *Griechische Wirtschafts- und Gesellschaftsgeschichte bis zur Perserzeit*. Tübingen, 1931

19. Hasebroek, J. *Trade and politics in ancient Greece*. London, 1933

20. Heichelheim, F. M. *An Ancient Economic History* I–II. Leiden, 1958–64

21. Johnston, A. W. 'Trademarks on Greek vases', *Greece & Rome* 2 ser. 21 (1974) 138–52

21A. Johnston, A. W. *Trademarks on Greek Vases*. Warminster, 1979

22. Kraay, C. M. 'Hoards, small change, and the origins of coinage', *JHS* 84 (1964) 76–91

23. Lencman, J. A. *Die Sklaverei im Mykenischen und Homerischen Griechenland*. Wiesbaden, 1966

24. Pečirka, J. 'Homestead farms in classical and hellenistic Hellas', *Problèmes de la terre en Grèce ancienne*, ed. M. I. Finley (Ecole pratique des hautes études. Civilisations et sociétés 33), 113–47. Paris, 1973

25. Pleket, H. W. 'Technology in the Greco-Roman world', *Talanta* 5 (1973) 6–47

26. Pleket, H. W. 'Zur Soziologie des antiken Sports', *Mededelingen van het Nederlands Instituut te Rome* 36 (1974) 57–87

27. Polanyi, K., Arensberg, C. and Pearson, H. (eds.) *Trade and Market in the Early Empires*. Glencoe, Illinois, 1957

28. Ridley, R. T. 'The economic activities of the perioikoi', *Mnemosyne* 27 (1974) 281–92

29. Roebuck, C. A. *Ionian Trade and Colonization*. New York, 1959

30. Starr, C. G. 'An overdose of slavery', *JEH* 18 (1958) 17–32

31. Starr, C. G. *The Economic and Social Growth of Early Greece 800–500 B.C.* New York, 1977

32. Strasburger, H. 'Der soziologische Aspekt der homerischen Epen', *Gymnasium* 60 (1953) 97–114

33. Strasburger, H. 'Der Einzelne und die Gemeinschaft im Denken der Griechen', *Hist. Zeitschr.* 177 (1954) 227–48

33A. Sutherland, C. H. V. 'Corn and coin', *AJP* 64 (1943) 129–47

34. Vallet, G. and Villard, F. 'Céramique grecque et histoire économique', *Études Archéologiques*, ed. P. Courbin, 205–12. Paris, 1973

35. Will, E. 'Trois quarts de siècle de recherches sur l'économie grecque antique', *Annales* 9 (1954) 7–22

36. Will, E. 'Limites, possibilités et tâches de l'histoire économique et sociale du monde grec antique', *Études Archéologiques*, ed. P. Courbin, 153–66. Paris, 1963

H. MATERIAL CULTURE AND ART

The following entries may also be consulted – excluding purely local studies and excavation reports: A 1, 7, 19, 39, 59, 61; B 12, 26, 53, 89–91, 95–6, 109, 111; C 52–3, 58, 65, 98–100, 102, 111, 153–4, 159, 223, 228; D 1, 8, 15, 17–21, 23, 28–34, 40–1, 52, 57, 65, 76, 98, 104A–6, 111–13, 126, 129, 133, 148; E 1, 8, 85, 116, 129, 221, 226, 233–4; F 13, 17–18, 30A, 76–7.

1. Adam, S. *The Technique of Greek Sculpture in the Archaic and Classical Period.* London, 1966
2. Adams, L. *Orientalizing Sculpture in soft limestone (BAR Suppl. 42).* Oxford, 1978
3. Åkerström, Å. *Die architektonische Terrakotten Kleinasiens.* Lund, 1966
4. Akurgal, E. *The Birth of Greek Art.* London, 1968
5. Anderson, J. K. *Military Theory and Practice in the age of Xenophon.* Berkeley–Los Angeles, 1970
6. Anderson, J. K. 'Sickle and *xyele*', *JHS* 94 (1974) 166
7. Bakalakis, G. *Hellenica Amphiglypha.* Salonica, 1946
8. Beazley, J. D. *Attic Black-Figure Vase-Painters.* Oxford, 1956
9. Beazley, J. D. *Attic Red-Figure Vase-Painters.* Oxford, 1963
10. Beazley, J. D. *Paralipomena.* Oxford, 1971
11. Berve, H. and Gruben, G. *Griechische Tempel und Heiligtümer.* Munich, 1961
12. Berve, H. and Gruben, G. *Greek Temples, Theatres and Shrines.* London, 1963
13. Best, J. G. P. *Thracian Peltasts and their influence in Greek Warfare.* Groningen, 1969
14. Blümel, C. *Die archaisch-griechische Skulpturen der staatlichen Museen zu Berlin.* Berlin, 1964
15. Boardman, J. *Archaic Greek Gems.* London, 1968
16. Boardman, J. *Greek Gems and Finger Rings.* London, 1970
17. Boardman, J. 'Sickles and strigils', *JHS* 91 (1971) 136–7
18. Boardman, J. *Athenian Black Figure Vases.* London, 1974
18A. Boardman, J. *Athenian Red Figure Vases; the Archaic Period.* London, 1975
19. Boardman, J. *Greek Sculpture; the Archaic period.* London, 1978
20. Burford, Alison *Craftsmen in Greek and Roman Life.* Ithaca, New York, 1972
21. Casson, L. 'Hemiolia and triemiolia', *JHS* 78 (1958) 14–18
22. Casson, L. *Ships and Seamanship in the Ancient World.* Princeton, 1971
23. Castagnoli, F. *Orthogonal town planning in antiquity.* Cambridge, Mass., 1971
24. Clairmont, C. *Gravestone and Epigram.* Mainz, 1970
25. Coldstream, J. N. *Greek Geometric Pottery.* London, 1968
26. Coldstream, J. N. 'Hero-cults in the age of Homer', *JHS* 96 (1976) 8ff
27. Coldstream, J. N. *Geometric Greece.* London, 1977
28. Cook, R. M. 'A note on the absolute chronology of the eighth and seventh centuries B.C.', *BSA* 64 (1969) 13–15
29. Cook, R. M. *Greek painted pottery.* 2nd edn. London, 1972

30. Coulton, J. J. 'Lifting in early Greek architecture', *JHS* 94 (1974) 1–19
31. Coulton, J. J. 'Towards understanding Greek temple design; general considerations', *BSA* 70 (1975) 59–99
32. Coulton, J. J. *The Architectural Development of the Greek Stoa*. Oxford, 1976
33. Coulton, J. J. *Greek Architects at Work*. London, 1977
34. Dentzer, J. M. 'Aux origines de l'iconographie du banquet couché', *Rev. Arch.* 1971, 215–58
35. Desborough, V. R. d'A. *The Last Mycenaeans and their Successors*. Oxford, 1964
36. Drerup, H. 'Griechische Architektur zur Zeit Homers', *Arch. Anz.* 1964, 180–219
37. Drerup, H. *Griechische Baukunst in geometrischer Zeit* (*Archaeologia Homerica* II, part O). Göttingen, 1969
38. Dyer, L. 'Olympian treasuries and treasuries in general', *JHS* 25 (1905) 294–319
39. Fehr, B. *Orientalische und griechische Gelage*. Bonn, 1971
40. Greenhalgh, P. A. L. *Early Greek Warfare*. Cambridge, 1973
41. Harden, D. B. 'Ancient Glass, 1: Pre-Roman', *Arch. Journal* 125 (1969) 46–72
42. Henle, J. *Greek Myths: a vase-painter's notebook*. Bloomington–London, 1973
43. Jacobsthal, P. *Greek pins and their connexions with Europe and Asia*. Oxford, 1956
44. Jantzen, U. *Griechische Greifenkessel*. Berlin, 1955
45. Jantzen, U. 'Greifenprotomen von Samos, ein Nachtrag', *Ath. Mitt.* 73 (1958) 26–49
46. Jeffery, L. H. *The Local Scripts of Archaic Greece*. Oxford, 1961
46A. Jeffery, L. H. '*ΑΡΧΑΙΑ ΓΡΑΜΜΑΤΑ*; some ancient Greek views', *Studien zur Geschichte und Epigraphik der frühen Aegaeis, Festschrift für Ernst Grumach*, ed. W. C. Brice, 152–66. Berlin, 1967
47. Jenkins, R. J. H. *Dedalica*. Cambridge, 1936
47A. Kraay, C. M. *Greek Coins in History*. London, 1969
48. Kraay, C. M. *Archaic and Classical Greek Coins*. London, 1976
49. Krause, C. 'Grundformen des griechischen Pastashauses', *Arch. Anz.* 1977, 164–79
50. Kunze, E. *Archaische Schildbänder* (Olympische Forschungen II). Berlin, 1950
51. Kurtz, D. C. and Boardman, J. *Greek Burial Customs*. London, 1971
52. Lawrence, A. W. *Greek Architecture*. Harmondsworth, 1957
53. Lawrence, A. W. *Greek Aims in Fortification*. Oxford, 1979
54. Lorimer, H. L. *Homer and the monuments*. London, 1950
55. Maier, F. G. *Griechische Mauerbauinschriften*. Heidelberg, 1959
56. Martin, R. *L'Urbanisme dans la Grèce antique*. 2nd edn. Paris, 1974
57. Mellink, M. J. 'Notes on Anatolian wall painting', *Mélanges Mansel* (1974) 537–47
58. Möbius, H. Review of Bakalakis, *Hellenica Amphiglypha*, *Gnomon* 24 (1952) 366–8 (= *Studia Varia* (Wiesbaden, 1967) 207–8)

59. Morrison, J. S. and Williams, R. T. *Greek Oared Ships*. Cambridge, 1968
60. Overbeck, J. *Die antike Schriftquellen zur Geschichte der bildenden Künste bei den Griechen*. Leipzig, 1868; reprinted 1971
61. Richter, G. M. A. *Archaic Greek Art*. New York, 1949
62. Richter, G. M. A. *Kouroi, Archaic Greek Youths*. London–New York, 1960
63. Richter, G. M. A. *The Furniture of the Greeks, Etruscans and Romans*. London, 1966
64. Richter, G. M. A. *Korai, Archaic Greek Maidens*. London, 1968
65. Ridgway, B. S. *The Archaic Style in Greek Sculpture*. Princeton, 1977
66. Robertson, C. M. *A History of Greek Art* I–II. Cambridge, 1975
67. Schäfer, J. *Studien zu den griechischen Reliefpithoi des 8.–6. Jahrhunderts v. Chr*. Kallmünz, 1957
68. Simon, E. and Hirmer, M. & A. *Die griechischen Vasen*. Munich, 1976
69. Snodgrass, A. M. *Early Greek Armour and Weapons*. Edinburgh, 1964
70. Snodgrass, A. M. *Arms and Armour of the Greeks*. London, 1967
71. Snodgrass, A. M. *The Dark Age of Greece*. Edinburgh, 1971
72. Snodgrass, A. M. *Archaeology and the Rise of the Greek State*. Cambridge, 1977
73. Snodgrass, A. M. 'The first European body-armour', *The European Community in Later Prehistory* (Studies in Honour of C. F. C. Hawkes; ed. J. Boardman, M. A. Brown and T. G. E. Powell; London, 1971) 31–50
73A. Thompson, M., Mørkholm, O and Kraay, C. M. *An Inventory of Greek Coin Hoards*. New York, 1973
74. Vokotopoulou, I. Χαλκαὶ Κορινθιουργεῖς πρόχοι. Athens, 1975
75. Vos, S. *Scythian Archers and Archaic Attic Vase Painting*. Groningen, 1963
76. Wallace, W. P. 'The early coinages of Athens and Euboia', *Num. Chron.* 7.2 (1962) 23–42
77. Ward-Perkins, J. B. *Cities of Ancient Greece and Italy*. London, 1974
78. Webb, V. *Archaic Greek Faience*. Warminster, 1978
79. Winter, F. E. *Greek Fortifications*. London, 1971
80. Wokalek, A. *Griechische Stadtbefestigungen*. Bonn, 1973
81. Wycherley, R. E. *How the Greeks Built Cities*. London, 1967 reprint

INDEX

Numbers in italic type refer to maps; bold type indicates major discussions.

hoplites, 340–1, 437, 454–7; *see also zeugites*

horoi, 377–84 *passim*

Houma, bronze armlet from, 278

household *see oikos*

housing, **455**; in colonies, **150**, (Syracuse) 106, (Megara Hyblaea) 107–8, (Berezan) 126; on Crete, 227, 228; in East Greece, 202–3

Huelva, tombs of, 63

'Hundred Houses', 190, 304, 437

hunting, 158, 439

Hyampolis, *16 Ba*, 317

Hybla Heraea (Ragusa (?)), *10 Dc*, 177

Hyblon, king of Sicels, 197

Hyele *see* Elea

Hymn to Apollo, 314, 375

Hypanis (Bug), *liman* of, 124–6, 129

hyperakrioi see 'hill-men'

Hysiae, *18 Bc*; battle of, 310, 325, 338, 340, 353, 464

Ialysus, *12 Bd*, 6

Iasus, *12 Bd*, 203

Ibycus of Rhegium, 219

Ida, Mt *13 Cb*; sanctuary at, 223, 225–6, 232

Idalium, *4 Cb*, 8, 59, 61; Common Syllabary at, 71, 72, 76, 78, 80–2

Illubru, 18

Illyrians, *6 Bb*; language of, 284; in Lower Macedonia, 274, 275–6, 278

Illyris, **261–6**, 465; colonies in, 131–3

Imbros, *9 Cb*, 161

immigration, at Athens, 384

Inarōs, 37–8

Inatus (Tsoutsouros (?)), *13 Dc*, 229

Incoronata, *1 Bb*, 175, 184

Indigetae, *5 Bb*, 142

industry, 192, 215, 425, **428–9**, 438; *see also* pottery; technology; trade

inheritance: at Athens, 389; at Gortyn, 244–6; at Naupactus, 155, 303

intermarriage, 43, 48, 147–8, 155–7, 179, 199

Io, rape of, 6–7

Iolcus, 317

Ion, 364

Ionia, Ionians, *12*, **361**; colonizing activity of, 147, 172–5, 186, 211–13 (Egypt), 213 (North Africa), 213 (in North East), 213–14 (West); conquered by Lydia, 197, 199, 218; cult centre of, 258; culture of, 202–10, 220, 440; deported to Babylon, 22–3; influence of, in Cyprus, 69–70; league of, 217; as mercenaries and traders in Egypt, 43–4, 212–13; as name for Greeks, 1–3; as race, 361; revolt of, 251, 259; *see also* Eastern Greeks

Ionic order, 56, 204–5, 450

Ira, Mt, *18 Ac*, 352

Irasa, battle of, 137

iron, 103, 261, 263

Ischia *see* Pithecusa

isopolity (dual citizenship), 154–5; *see also* citizen rights

Istanbul *see* Byzantium

Isthmian Games *see* Games

Isthmus of Corinth, *diolkos* at, 349, 350

Istria *see* Istrus

Istrus (Istria, Histia), *7 Ab*, 123, 124, 150–1, 161, 465

Italy, S.: colonies in, 94–7, 97–103, 109–13, 163, 169–75, 180–6; contact with Greece in Bronze Age, 95; internal developments of states, 189–95; pre-colonization trade in, 95–7; *see also entries for individual states*

Itanus, *13 Eb*, 232–3

Ithaca, 301

Ithome, Mt, *18 Ad*, 328

ivories, 208–9, 226, 449

Jagorlik, 129

Jason of Pherae, 298–9

Jauchina, *11 Bd*; cemeteries of, 171

jewellery, 450; Cretan, 226; Illyrian, 261–5 *passim*; Macedonian, 275–9 *passim*; Near Eastern influence on, 13, 429; S. Italian, 147–8; *see also* bronzework

Jews, 22, 29, 44, 51

Kafizin, *4 Cb*; signaries of, 72, **80–2**

Kakopetria, *4 Bb*, 61

Kalamaria, find from, 279

Kamen Rapeš, finds from, 278

Karomemphitai, 44–5

Karpophora, *18 Ad*, 333

Karteros (Amnisus), *13 Db*

Kastraki, sanctuary of, 293

Kastri, Thracian settlement at, 117

Kato Syme, *13 Dc*, 222–3, 229, 231, 232

Kavalla *see* Neapolis in Greece

Kavousi, *13 Eb*, 62, 222

Kēneta, cemetery of, 261

Kerch *see* Panticapaeum

Khargeh Oasis, *2 Ab*, 48

Khilakku, 18–19

Khorsabad, Sargon's 'Display Inscription' from, 57

kingship, monarchy: at Athens, 362, 263–4; on Crete, 240; at Cyprus, 60–70 *passim*; in Ionian cities, 199–200; at Sparta, 330–3, 364; *see also* tyranny

Kittim (Citium), 3, 22

Körce, *15 Bb*, 263–5, 277

Korčula *see* Black Corcyra

Koundouriotissa, graves from, 274

Kouretes, 232

kouroi, 450, 458–9; *see also* sculpture